Commerce

For UGC-NET/SLET and Other Competitive Examinations

Objective Type Questions

Atlantic Research Division

ATLANTIC

PUBLISHERS & DISTRIBUTORS (P) LTD

Published by

ATLANTIC

PUBLISHERS & DISTRIBUTORS (P) LTD

7/22, Ansari Road, Darya Ganj,
New Delhi-110002
Phones : +91-11-40775252, 23273880, 23275880, 23280451
Fax : +91-11-23285873
Web : www.atlanticbooks.com
E-mail : orders@atlanticbooks.com

Branch Office
5, Nallathambi Street, Wallajah Road,
Chennai-600002
Phones : +91-44-64611085, 32413319
E-mail : chennai@atlanticbooks.com

Disclaimer:

The author and the publisher have taken every effort to the maximum of their skill, expertise and knowledge to provide correct answers to questions in the book. Even then if some mistakes persist in the content of the book the publisher does not take responsibility for the same. The publisher shall have no liability to any person or entity with respect to any loss or damage caused, or alleged to have been caused directly or indirectly, by the information contained in this book. Hence, the book should be taken as a general guide only.

The publisher has fully tried to follow the copyright law. However, if any work is found to be similar, it is unintentional and the same should not be used as defamatory or to file legal suit against the author/publisher.

If the readers find any mistake we shall be grateful to them to point those to us so that these can be corrected in the next edition.

All disputes are subject to the jurisdiction of Delhi court only.

Printed in India at Nice Printing Press, A-33/3A, Site-IV,
Industrial Area, Sahibabad, Ghaziabad, U.P.

General Information

About the NET

The National Educational Testing Bureau of University Grants Commission (UGC) conducts National Eligibility Test (NET) to determine eligibility for lectureship and for award of Junior Research Fellowship (JRF) for Indian nationals in order to ensure minimum standards for the entrants in the teaching profession and research. The Test is conducted in Humanities (including languages), Social Sciences, Forensic Science, Environmental Sciences, Computer Science and Applications and Electronic Science.

The Council of Scientific and Industrial Research (CSIR) conducts the UGC-CSIR NET for other Science subjects, namely, Life Sciences, Physical Sciences, Chemical Sciences, Mathematical Sciences and Earth Atmospheric Ocean & Planetary Sciences jointly with the UGC. The tests are conducted twice in a year generally in the months of June and December. For candidates who desire to pursue research, the Junior Research Fellowship (JRF) is available for five years subject to fulfillment of certain conditions. UGC has allocated a number of fellowships to the universities for the candidates who qualify the test for JRF. The JRFs are awarded to the meritorious candidates from among the candidates qualifying for eligibility for lectureship in the NET. JRFs are available only to the candidates who opt for it in their application forms.

The test for Junior Research Fellowship is being conducted since 1984. The Government of India, through its notification dated 22nd July, 1988 entrusted the task of conducting the eligibility test for lectureship to UGC. Consequently, UGC conducted the first National Eligibility Test, common to both eligibility for Lectureship and Junior Research Fellowship in two parts, that is, in December 1989 and in March, 1990.

NET Schedule

UGC conducts NET twice a year, i.e., in the months of June and December. The notifications announcing the June and December examinations are published in the months of March and September respectively in the weekly journal of nation-wide circulation, viz, Employment News.

NET Results Declaration Schedule

The result of June, UGC-NET is declared generally in the month of October. Similarly December, UGC-NET result is usually declared in the month of April. The UGC-NET results published in the Employment News are also available on UGC website.

UGC-NET in Objective Mode from June, 2012 Onwards

1. The UGC-NET will be conducted in objective mode from June 2012 onwards. The Test will consist of three papers. All the three papers will consist of only objective type questions and will be held on the day of Examination in two separate sessions as under:

Session	Paper	Number of Questions	Marks	Duration
First	I	60 out of which 50 questions are to be attempted	50 × 2 = 100	1¼ Hours (09.30 a.m. to 10.45 a.m.)
First	II	50 questions all of which are compulsory	50 × 2 = 100	1¼ Hours (10.45 a.m. to 12.00 Noon.)
Second	III	75 questions all of which are compulsory	75 × 2 = 150	2½ Hours (01.30 p.m. to 04.00 p.m.)

2. The candidates are required to obtain minimum marks separately in Paper-I, Paper-II and Paper-III as given below:

Category	Minimum marks (%) to be obtained		
	Paper-I	Paper-II	Paper-III
General	40 (40%)	40 (40%)	75 (50%)
OBC	35 (35%)	35 (35%)	67.5 (45%) rounded off to 68
PH/VH/SC/ST	35 (35%)	35 (35%)	60 (40%)

Only such candidates who obtain the minimum required marks in each Paper, separately, as mentioned above, will be considered for final preparation of result.

However, the final qualifying criteria for Junior Research Fellowship (JRF) and eligibility for Lectureship shall be decided by UGC before declaration of result.

3. The syllabus of Paper-I, Paper-II and Paper-III will remain the same.

4. The candidates will be allowed to carry the carbon printout of OMR Response Sheets with them on conclusion of the examination.

5. There will be no negative marking.

Preface

The book has been designed for those appearing in UGC-NET/SLET in the subject of Commerce. It would also be useful for candidates preparing for competitive exams like IAS, IPS, IFS, PCS, etc. The book is very comprehensive and covers almost all possible objective type questions for these exams. The questions set in UGC-NET/SLET and various other competitive examinations in the previous years have also been used for preparing this book.

In spite of our best efforts to cover all possible questions, the paper may contain some questions which are not covered in this book and can be answered only if the candidate has a thorough knowledge of the topics covered in the syllabus. For a thorough and elaborate knowledge of the subject, candidates are advised to read the following books published by Atlantic Publishers and Distributors (P) Ltd.: (i) *Fundamentals of Cost Accounting: Theory, Problems and Solutions* by I. Narsis; (ii) *Introduction to Commerce* by Amit Vikram; (iii) *Corporate Tax Planning* (6th Edition) by Kaushal Kumar Agrawal; (iv) *Dictionary of Commerce and Management* by S.N. Chand; (v) *Dictionary of Commerce and Management* by K.C.S. Ranganayakulu; (vi) *Company Law* by Madhu Tyagi and Arun Kumar; (vii) *Economics of Taxation* by Sayed Afzal Peerzade; (viii) *ERP: The Future of Business Automation* by Zubair H. Shaikh; (ix) *Human Dimensions for Total Quality Management* by Nayantara Padhi and Sasmita Palo; and (x) *India's Transforming Financial Sector* by Manoranjan Sharma.

Atlantic Research Division

Contents

1

Business Environment

1. The factors included in the total environment of business are
   (a) Economic (b) Political-legal
   (c) Social culture (d) All of the above

2. A stable and dynamic political environment is indispensable for
   (a) enhance the export.
   (b) business growth.
   (c) Both (a) and (b).
   (d) None of the above.

3. In the following which internal factor influence the strategy and other decisions of the business?
   (a) Mission and objective
   (b) Management structure and nature
   (c) Value system
   (d) All of the above

4. Which of the following is not the financial factor?
   (a) Brand equity
   (b) Financial policies
   (c) Capital structure
   (d) Financial position

5. The micro forces need affect all the firm in a particular industry in the same way.
   (a) Partially (b) Necessarily
   (c) Not necessarily (d) None of these

6. Those who supply the inputs like raw materials and components to the company are known as
   (a) consumers (b) competitors
   (c) suppliers (d) customers

7. The competition which satisfy a particular category of desire is called
   (a) generic competition.
   (b) brand competition.
   (c) product form competition.
   (d) None of the above.

8. The consumer encounters the
   (a) product form competition.
   (b) brand competition.
   (c) desire competition.
   (d) generic competition.

9. Any group that has an actual potential interest in or impact on organisation's ability to achieve its interests is known as
   (a) Wholesaler
   (b) Marketing intermediaries
   (c) Consumers
   (d) Public

10. The low income may be the reason for the very few demand for a product
    (a) in a developed country.
    (b) in a developing country.
    (c) Both (a) and (b).
    (d) None of the above.

11. The new economic policy has components
    (a) Privatisation (b) Globalisation
    (c) Liberalisation (d) All of the above

12. A mixed economy is necessarily a economy
    (a) Organised
    (b) Controlled
    (c) Planned
    (d) None of the above
13. Every sector of the economy employs natural, human and material resources and contributes to the aggregate flow of goods and services during a time period. This aggregate flow of goods and services represents the total income earned by factors of production employed during the year and is popularly called
    (a) Per head income.
    (b) Per capita income.
    (c) National income.
    (d) None of the above
14. The basic objectives of the companies act are
    (a) a check on their transactions where there was a possibility of conflict of duty and interest.
    (b) a ceiling on the share of profit payable to managements as remuneration for services rendered.
    (c) a minimum standard of good behaviour and business honesty in company promotion and management.
    (d) All of the above.
15. The Restrictive Trade Practices (RTPs) are described in
    (a) Section 33(3) (b) Section 33(1)
    (c) Section 33(2) (d) None of these
16. In the following which measures the government has taken to protect consumer interest?
    (a) Development and expansion of the public sector
    (b) Statutory regulation
    (c) Both (a) and (b)
    (d) None of the above
17. The role of consumerism has
    (a) liaison with government and with producers.
    (b) consumer education.
    (c) product rating.
    (d) All of the above.
18. The process whereby activities or enterprises that were once performed or operated by the government and its employees are now performed, managed or owned by private business and individuals is known as
    (a) Globalisation (b) Privatisation
    (c) Localisation (d) None of these
19. Distributes vouchers across the population and attempts to allocate assets approximately evenly among voucher holders. This process is known as
    (a) equal-access voucher privatisation.
    (b) sale to outsiders.
    (c) management-employee buy-out.
    (d) spontaneous privatisation.
20. The characteristics of a global company is/are
    (a) the units respond to some common strategy.
    (b) it is a conglomerate of multiple units but all linked by common ownership.
    (c) multiple units drawn on a common pool of resources such as money, credit, information, patents, trade names.
    (d) All of the above.
21. The feature of the industrial policy is
    (a) liberalisation of foreign investment and technological participation.
    (b) delicensing with certain exceptions.
    (c) Both (a) and (b).
    (d) None of the above.
22. In the three and a half decades of industrialisation, the gross domestic product increased

(a) Near about 15 per cent
(b) 10 per cent
(c) 20 per cent exact
(d) 18 per cent

23. Industrial development would be possible with the increment of
(a) employee
(b) technology skill
(c) managerial skill
(d) Both (b) and (c)

24. What is the first factor of industrial development?
(a) Surplus of technical skill
(b) Design
(c) Motivation
(d) Planning.

25. What are the salient features of industrial development?
(a) Special assistance for the development of small industries.
(b) Encouragement to the cooperative sector.
(c) Achievement of self-reliance.
(d) All of the above.

26. What is the full form of IRDA?
(a) Indian Regulation Development Authority
(b) Industrial Regulation and Development Authority
(c) Insurance Regulatory and Development Authority
(d) None of the above

27. What are the laws that gave the government enormous control over the management ?
(a) Company Act (b) Industrial Act
(c) MRTP (d) Both (a) and (b)

28. Which one of the following laws controlled over merger, amalgamations, takeovers, etc.?
(a) NASDOC (b) IRDA
(c) DR (d) MRTP

29. The "heavy industry" strategy of the Mahalanobis model was initiated in
(a) Fourth Plan (b) First Plan
(c) Second Plan (d) Third Plan

30. Which sector produced non-importable commodity?
(a) Roadways (b) Railway
(c) Electricity (d) Both (a) and (b).

31. The expanded production of fertilizers, textiles and buildings require some
(a) economical growth.
(b) power production.
(c) domestic production of the necessary capital goods.
(d) None of the above.

32. The most promising source of saving to finance development is
(a) profits of railway.
(c) the profits of organised sector.
(c) only the profit of private sector.
(d) profits of government sector.

33. In which year the family planning programme was changed to family welfare programme?
(a) In 1977 (b) In 1969
(c) In 1966 (d) In 1968

34. What are the weaknesses of earlier approach to industrial development?
(a) It did not have the wider support of adequate agricultural development.
(b) It was not fully planned.
(c) It was not efficiency implemented.
(d) All of the above.

35. In how many industries the State was to play an active role?
(a) 15 industries
(b) 13 important industries
(c) 16 firm
(d) 12 industries

36. With the industrial policy resolution of 1956, the future development of key industries became the exclusive responsibility of the State,
(a) 16 (b) 15
(c) 18 (d) 17

37. Central Government investment in industrial enterprises increased substantially in
(a) one decade (b) four decades
(c) two decades (d) three decades

38. Why the public sector took over a number of sick units from the private sector?
(a) Due to the deficiency of managerial planning.
(b) Due to the social obligations of protecting employment.
(c) Due to low manufacturing.
(d) None of the above.

39. In which type of industries, the public sector units play a dominant role?
(a) Steel industries
(b) Petrochemical
(c) Fertilizers
(d) All of the above

40. What is the full form of NTC?
(a) Non-textile Corporation
(b) National Thermal Corporation
(c) National Textile Corporation
(d) None of the above

41. In which industry, units in the co-operative sector account for over half of the total production?
(a) Petrochemical industry
(b) Steel industry
(c) Sugar industry
(d) None of the above

42. Choose the correct statement.
(a) The public sector will have responsibility for meeting social need.
(b) The public sector would play useful in augmenting basic resources of country like land, forest and water.
(c) Both (a) and (b).
(d) Public sector would not play a useful role in population controls.

43. One of the criticisms levelled against the development strategy in India is that ____ should have been given greater importance than industry
(a) public sector
(b) agricultural sector
(c) hilly sector
(d) private sector

44. In which duration considerable import substitution has taken place in many important areas in capital goods, organic chemicals?
(a) Four decades (last)
(b) Two decades
(c) Five decades
(d) Three decades

45. In the Indian context, the emphasis on import substitution often run counter to
(a) the objective of sports development.
(b) the objective of managerial development.
(c) the objective of technological development.
(d) the objective of skill development.

46. Which law emphasised the importance of continuous development and expansion of export-oriented production?
(a) Company Act
(b) Export Policy Resolution of 1970
(c) MRTP
(d) IRDA

47. What was the growth rate of the industrial output in the last four decades?
(a) 6% per annum
(b) 5.5% per annum

(c) 4.5% per annum
(d) 5% per annum

48. What was the industrial production growth rate during 1951-65?
(a) 6% per annum
(b) 7.2% per annum
(c) 7% per annum
(d) 8% per annum

49. What was the industrial growth rate during Seventh Plan?
(a) 9% per annum
(b) 10% per annum
(c) 8.5% per annum
(d) 8% per annum

50. In the initial years of planning, industrial development was largely based on
(a) import substitution.
(b) transportation.
(c) export substitution.
(d) None of the above.

51. What was the rate of growth of industrial production during the Sixth Plan?
(a) 4.5% (b) 7%
(c) 5.5% (d) 6%

52. By whom the rehabilitation packages suggested?
(a) MRTP
(b) Policy Resolution of 1970
(c) BIFR
(d) IRDA

53. What is the full form of BIFR?
(a) Board for Industrial and Financial Reconstruction
(b) Board of Industry and Foreign Regulation
(c) Board of Investigator for Rural Industry
(d) None of the above

54. Growth is a _______ for achieving social justice.
(a) prerequisite
(b) requisite
(c) important feature
(d) None of the above

55. What is the full form of SWOT?
(a) Single optimization technique
(b) Strengths, weaknesses, opportunities and threats
(c) Software warehousing of threats
(d) None of the above

56. Micro environment consists of
(a) Marketing.
(b) Competitors.
(c) Suppliers.
(d) All of the above.

57. Macro environment consists of
(a) demographic forces.
(b) cultural forces.
(c) technological forces.
(d) All of the above.

58. What are the factors which contribute to the business success?
(a) Physical assets
(b) Financial factors
(c) Marketing resources
(d) All of the above.

59. Competitors, customers and public are the part of
(a) business necessities.
(b) macro environment.
(c) micro environment.
(d) None of the above.

60. What is the work of HRM in a particular firm?
(a) To check the production quality.
(b) Generate quality, morale and commitment in work.
(c) To increase production.
(d) None of the above.

61. What are the important external factors that constitute the economic environment of business?
(a) Economic system
(b) Economic condition
(c) Economic policy
(d) All of the above.

62. During 1985-90, the GDP grew at an average rate of
(a) 8% (b) 7%
(c) 5.7% (d) 6%

63. What is/are the main objective/es of the policy initiatives?
(a) Reduction of the current account deficit in the balance of payments.
(b) Raising GDP growth to around 6% by mid-1990.
(c) Reducing the government deficity to 6.5% of GDP in 1991-92.
(d) All of the above.

64. The SAP has been forced on the economy because of several reasons. They are
(a) growing inefficiency in the use of resources.
(b) excess of consumption and expenditure over the revenue.
(c) over protection.
(d) All of the above.

65. In the late 1960s and 1970s, any manufacturer who had to import capital goods and components had to satisfy
(a) IRDA (b) MRTP
(c) DGTD (d) None of these

66. What are the main points for the critical assessment of new economic policy?
(a) What are the achievements and failures of the policy?
(b) Is the policy unavoidable?
(c) Only (b)
(d) Both (a) and (b)

67. When was the First Five-Year Plan launched?
(a) 1951 (b) 1953
(c) 1950 (d) 1952

68. What are the main objectives of Five Year Plan?
(a) Setup a socialist society based on equality.
(b) Achieve full employment.
(c) Reduce inequalities of income and wealth.
(d) All of the above.

69. In which year the government began to believe that mini-plants constituted appropriate technology, notwithstanding strong evidence to the contrary?
(a) In 1961
(b) During 1960
(c) In the 1970s
(d) None of the above.

70. What do you mean by DGTD?
(a) Director General of Total Development
(b) Director General of Trade Development
(c) Director General of Technical Development
(d) None of the above

71. When the population policy in India received a new impetus?
(a) In April 1976 (b) In May 1976
(c) In May 1977 (d) In June 1977

72. Which Plan introduced the time and target approach to family planning?
(a) Eight Plan (b) Fourth Plan
(c) Sixth Plan (d) None of these

73. Environment is synonymous with
(a) relations
(b) people
(c) situational variables
(d) task

74. "Focus on social environment" is related to
(a) human relations
(b) unity of direction
(c) unity of command
(d) All of the above

75. A statutory meeting requires a notice of at least
(a) 21 days (b) 30 days
(c) 7 days (d) 14 days

76. Quorum for a board meeting
(a) 1/2 of total no. of directors or three directors, whichever is higher.
(b) 1/2 of total no. of directors or three directors, whichever is lower.
(c) 1/3 of total no. of directors or two directors, whichever is higher.
(d) None of the above.

77. Auditors of a joint stock company are appointed by
(a) election at the annual general meeting.
(b) directors of the company.
(c) annual general meeting.
(d) None of the above.

78. Internal check helps in
(a) continuous audit.
(b) preventing frauds and errors.
(c) detecting frauds and errors.
(d) None of the above.

79. Duties of a company auditor are defined by
(a) Companies Act, 1956.
(b) Memorandum of Association.
(c) Agreement between company and the auditor.
(d) Articles of Association.

80. A company auditor can be removed by
(a) any director
(b) general meeting
(c) board of directors
(d) managing director

81. A vacancy caused by resignation of an auditor is filled by
(a) general meeting
(b) board of directors
(c) managing director
(d) None of the above

82. A government company is one in which not less than _____ of the paid up capital is held by government.
(a) 100% (b) 50%
(c) 52% (d) 51%

83. A public corporation is created by
(a) Ministry of Industry
(b) Special act of Parliament
(c) Ministry of Finance
(d) All of the above

84. Chamber of Commerce is a form of
(a) Consolidation
(b) Trade association
(c) Federation
(d) Merger

85. Minutes of a meeting must be signed by
(a) chairman and the secretary.
(b) secretary of the company.
(c) chairman of the meeting.
(d) managing director of the company.

86. Which of the following is a public corporation?
(a) ONGC (b) DCM
(c) TISCO (d) TELCO

87. 'Fishing culture' is classified in
(a) genetic industry
(b) construction industry
(c) extractive industry
(d) None of the above

88. Non-registration of a patnership does not affect
(a) the right of the firm to sue third parties.
(b) the right of the third party to proceed against the firm or its partners.

(c) the right of a partner to sue the firm.
(d) Any of the above.

89. Which one of the following is not the distinctive feature of the co-operative form of business organisation?
(a) One-share one-vote system
(b) Service before self
(c) Democratic management
(d) Corporate status

90. In addition to consumer forums which one of the following looks after the interests of consumers?
(a) Company Law Board
(b) High Courts
(c) Bureau of industrial costs and prices
(d) MRTP

91. Membership of the Institute of Company Secretaries of India is a qualification which a person shall possess in order to be eligible for appointment as a secretary in the case of
(a) all public sector undertakings.
(b) a company having a paid-up capital of ₹ 20 lakhs or less.
(c) companies in which public are substantially interested.
(d) a company having a paid-up share capital of ₹ 25 lakhs or more.

92. The secretaty of a company has
(a) no duty to deduct income tax unless requested by the employee.
(b) a statutory duty to deduct income tax at source.
(c) no duty to deduct income tax unless both the employee and the I.T.O. make such arequest.
(d) no duty to deduct income tax unless a notice has been received from the I.T.O.

93. Keeping the company's register of charges and making it available for inspection is a
(a) general duty of the secretary.
(b) contractual duty of the secretary.
(c) duty delegated to the secretary by the Board.
(d) statutory duty of the secretary.

94. The maximum period for which the register of members can be closed at a time after giving seven days previous notice is
(a) 30 days (b) 45 days
(c) 7 days (d) 15 days

95. The minutes of the board meetings
(a) are open to inspection by members on payment of the prescribed fee.
(b) must be kept open for inspection by the members.
(c) must be circulated or advertised.
(d) are not open to inspection by members.

96. The Company Secretary may be held liable for not holding the statutory meeting
(a) on the resolution of the board of directors.
(b) on the resolution of the general body.
(c) on the petition of the creditors.
(d) under Section 165 of the Companies Act.

97. The minutes book containing the procceedings of general body meeting shall, at the registered office of the company
(a) be kept for inspection for one day.
(b) be kept for inspection for two hours perday.
(c) not be kept for inspection.
(d) be kept for inspection for 10 days.

98. Which one of the following practices is permissible under the Code of Ethics to be followed by an auditor?
(a) Understatement of the facts only for tax planning purposes.

(b) An auditor who gives an export opinion on a client company may be and under writer of the same.
(c) Engaging in a business can jointly with the client.
(d) Prescribing a fee contingent upon the tax liabilities/saving effected.

99. For granting subsidy to the sick units. The audit required would be
(a) Internal audit
(b) Financial audit
(c) Statutory audit
(d) Management audit

100. When a company engages a Chartered Accountant as its internal auditor, the external auditor
(a) should ignore the existence of internal audit.
(b) need not check the areas covered by internal audit.
(c) should examine the system and efficiency of internal audit and devise a suitable audit programme.
(d) should incorporate the internal auditor's report with his own.

101. A Chartered Accountant is not disqualified to be an auditor of a company if he is
(a) the managing director of that company.
(b) an employee of the company.
(c) a shareholder in that company.
(d) indebted to the company for ₹ 1000.

102. A partnership firm, when not registered is
(a) allowed to carry on business subject to certain disabilities.
(b) allowed to carry on business only with the special permission of the registrar of firms.
(c) allowed to carry on business subject of payment of penalty.
(d) deemed to be illegal association and is disallowed to carry on business.

103. Partnership is a form of business organisation in which business debts can be recovered from
(a) the firm and all the partners.
(b) the firm and the managers.
(c) all the managers and partners.
(d) the managing partners.

104. Of the following organisations, the easiest to wind up is the
(a) multinational corporation.
(b) public limited company.
(c) partnership firm.
(d) private limited company.

105. Most of the public sector enterprises in India are joint stock companies because this enables the
(a) government to exercise greater control.
(b) company to earn high profits.
(c) management to work with high operational autonomy.
(d) government to enter any business.

106. The contacts signed by the promoters of a company
(a) continue to be the personal liability of the promoters.
(b) cease to be the personal liability of the promotors after the company is formed.
(c) are legally binding upon the company after it is formed.
(d) can be ratified by the company after its incorporation.

107. Which one of the following types of registered companies will be the most appropriate for the promotion of science, culture, religion, etc.?
(a) Government company.
(b) Company limited by share.
(c) Company limited by guarantee.
(d) Unlimited company.

108. A joint stock company's letterhead must, by law, have the address of the
(a) Registered office
(b) Head office
(c) Managing director
(d) Factory

109. Who among the following has no right to speak at the AGM?
(a) Proxy holder
(b) Chairman of the company
(c) Whole-time director of the company
(d) As everybody has a right to speak at the AGM.

110. Which one of the following is the correct sequence of steps in the formation and commencement of business of a public limited company?
(a) Memorandum, Filing of Prospectus, Issue of Prospectus, Minimum Subscription
(b) Memorandum, Issue of Prospectus, Filing of Prospectus, Minimum Subscription
(c) Memorandum, Minimum Subscription, Filing of Prospectus, Issue of Prospectus
(d) None of the above.

111. Clause in the Articles of Association can be altered by
(a) an ordinary resolution in the general meeting.
(b) a special resolution of the board of directors.
(c) obtaining permission from the Central Government.
(d) a special resolution in the general meeting.

112. Under the Companies Act, 1956, the 'financial year' of a company
(a) may be more or less than a calendar year, but it shall not exceed 20 months.
(b) may be more or less than a calendar year, but it shall not exceed 20 months.
(c) must be exactly 12 months.
(d) must not be less than 12 months.

113. 'Doctrine of Constructive Notice' is the notice
(a) to outsiders dealing with the company as to the contents of the Memorandum and Articles of Association.
(b) of alteration of 'Objects' clause to the Registrar of Companies.
(c) of change of name to the members of the company.
(d) to the public as to the issue of prospectus.

114. A 'blue chip' security is one which
(a) almost every investor is willing to buy.
(b) gives assured high returns.
(c) is issued by the reputed and profit making companies.
(d) offers the highest liquidity and sells always much above par.

115. A meeting of the Board of directors must be held at least once every
(a) four months and at least three such meetings must be held every year.
(b) three months and at least four such meetings must be held every year.
(c) six months.
(d) two months.

116. The power to make calls on shares can be exercised by the
(a) company secretary on his own.
(b) shareholders of the company in general meeting.
(c) managing director of the company.
(d) Board of directors of the company.

117. One of the important powers that must be exercised by the Board of directors at

the meetings of the Board of directors and cannot be delegated to a committee or any of the managerial personnel is the power to
(a) take decisions on investment of company funds.
(b) make loans.
(c) declare dividends.
(d) issue debentures.

118. The annual general meeting can be called by the
(a) non-executive director of the company
(b) company secretary
(c) Board of directors
(d) managing director

119. Internal auditor is appointed by the
(a) statutory auditor
(b) shareholders of the company
(c) Board of directors of the company
(d) Institute of Internal Auditors of India

120. Which one of the following is true of the position of an auditor regarding the system of internal check in the organisation?
(a) He should monitor and supervise the system of internal check.
(b) He should acquaint himself with the system of internal check.
(c) He has nothing to do with the system of internal check.
(d) He himself should lay down the system of internal check.

121. The auditor has a right to ask for information and explanation from the
(a) directors of the company.
(b) past auditors of the company.
(c) internal auditors of the company.
(d) officers of the company.

122. In the case of audit of statutory report, an auditor is expected to give his report on the
(a) authorised capital, subscribed capital and paid up capital.
(b) number of shares allotted, amount received in cash and summarised receipts and payments account.
(c) directors' qualification shares, calls in arrears and calls in advance.
(d) profit and loss account, balance sheet and directors' report.

123. Working papers which contain a record of the audit work are the property of the
(a) Auditor
(b) Company
(c) Government of India
(d) Registrar of Companies

124. Sampling is used in the case of
(a) test checks by the auditor.
(b) collection of debts by the accountant.
(c) checking pass book entries by the accountant.
(d) supervision by the works manager.

125. A continuous audit is not suitable where
(a) there is no urgency to finalise the accounts on a particular date.
(b) transactions are few but complicated.
(c) system of internal check in operation is not satisfactory.
(d) internal audit work is being carried on in a satisfactory manner.

126. The first auditors of a company are appointed by the
(a) shareholders of the company.
(b) registrar of company.
(c) board of directors of the company.
(d) promoters of the company.

127. Social obligation of accounting refers to
(a) servicing the needs of various stakeholders.
(b) the completion of journal entries.
(c) the preparation of final accounts.
(d) cost recording.

128. Which one of the following is not an advantage of the incorporation of a company?
   (a) Capital contibutions forming part of the joint stock of the company
   (b) Perpetual succession
   (c) Freedom to do any business
   (d) Limited liability of members

129. According to the latest guidelines, a company cannot issue
   (a) irredeemable preference shares.
   (b) both equity and preference shares simultaneously.
   (c) partially convertible debentures.
   (d) non-convertible debentures.

130. To enable a company to pay dividends, a special authority is
   (a) needed only in the Memorandum.
   (b) not needed either in the Memorandum or in the Articles.
   (c) needed only in the Articles.
   (d) needed either in the Memorandum or in the Articles.

131. A company can invest money in another company only if it is so authorised by its
   (a) Auditors
   (b) Memorandum of Association
   (c) Company Secretary
   (d) Articles of Association

132. Which one of the following is not a feature of a private company as per Indian Companies Act?
   (a) Ban on floating of debentures
   (b) Prohibition of any invitation to the public
   (c) Limitation on the number of its members
   (d) Restriciton on the right to transfer its shares

133. According to the Companies Act, which one of the following companies can commence allotment of shares even before the minimum subscription is subscribed or paid?
   (a) Private company
   (b) Chartered company
   (c) Public limited company
   (d) Government company

134. Which one of the following types of companies deals with only its shareholders for their benefit?
   (a) Chit-fund company
   (b) Banking company
   (c) Private limited company
   (d) Nidhi company

135. Those companies which can register themselves without the word "limited" under licence granted by the Central Government are
   (a) Public companies
   (b) Private companies
   (c) Charitable companines
   (d) None of the above

136. Which one of the following reports is to be placed before the Parliament by a government company?
   (a) Annual report
   (b) Statutory report
   (c) Director's report
   (d) Income report

137. Which one of the following is a joint stock company as per Companies Act, 1956?
   (a) A partnership firm with fixed capital
   (b) A society with fixed reserve fund
   (c) A charitable trust
   (d) None of the above

138. Which one of the following documents is known as Doctrine of Constructive Notice?
   (a) List of working directors
   (b) The prospectus of the company

(c) The certificate of commencement of business
(d) The memorandum and the Article of Association

139. Under the Companies Act, which one of the following powers can be exercised by the board of directors?
(a) Power to borrow money in excess of the paidup capital.
(b) Power to sell any of the company's undertakings.
(c) Power to reappoint on auditor.
(d) Power to make call.

140. The statutory meeting of the company must be held within six months
(a) of obtaining the certificate of commencement of business.
(b) from filing of statement in lieu of prospectus.
(c) from the date when the first board of directors meeting was held.
(d) of obtaining the certificate of incorporation.

141. A public limited company can offer preemptive rights only to the
(a) short-term creditors of the company.
(b) debenture holders.
(c) existing equity shareholders.
(d) directors of the company.

142. Under the law, the inspector who does the inspection of the company's account has to submit his report to the
(a) shareholders of the company.
(b) company's board of directors.
(c) secretary to the company.
(d) Central Government.

143. Audit report along with annual accounts is given by
(a) Internal auditor
(b) Stautory auditor
(c) Secretariat auditor
(d) Government auditor

144. Management audit is ordered by the
(a) Board of directors
(b) Securities Exchange Board of India
(c) Government
(d) Workers of a company

145. When an auditor detects material weaknesses in the internal checks and control system of the company under audit, it should report his finding as per
(a) ICWAI orders
(b) ICAI orders
(c) SEBI orders
(d) MAOCARO orders

146. The remuneration of an auditor of a partnership firm is fixed by
(a) the government.
(b) the Partnership Act.
(c) the Companies Act.
(d) None of the above.

147. Insofar as a company is concerned, which one of the following pairs is not correctly matched?
(a) Stautory audit — Mandatory
(b) Internal audit — Obligatory
(c) Management audit — Volutary
(d) Continuous audit — Optional

148. Where the auditor places a high degree of reliance on an internal control procedure, the acceptable risk of over-reliance would be
(a) Moderate (b) Low
(c) High (d) Nil

149. Minimum Alternative Tax (MAT) is applicable to the
(a) Co-operative society
(b) Joint stock company
(c) Sole proprietory concern
(d) Partnership firm

150. A qualified company secretary is needed to be appointed as secretary to a company only on the basis of the

(a) paid-up capital of the company.
(b) business of the company.
(c) listing of the company on any stock exchange.
(d) location of the company.

151. Doctrine of Indoor Management is reflected in
(a) *Daimler Ltd.* vs. *Continental Tyre and Rubber Co. Ltd.*
(b) *Kingston Cotton Mill's case.*
(c) *Royal British Bank* vs. *Turquand's case.*
(d) *Solomon* vs. *Solomon Ltd.*

152. The board of directors has to call the general body meeting giving a constructive notice of X days to all members entitled to attend the meeting. Here X stands for
(a) 14 (b) 21
(c) 7 (d) 11

153. The doctrine by which an outsider is presumed to have a prior knowledge of the contents of Memoradum and Articles of Association of a company is technically known as
(a) doctrine of retrospective notice.
(b) doctrine to constructive notice.
(c) ignorantia legis haud excusat.
(d) doctrine of indoor management.

154. Any causal vacancy in the office of a stautory auditor caused by the resignation of the auditor shall be filled by the company
(a) at the annual general meeting.
(b) at the board meeting.
(c) at the statutory meeting.
(d) by means of a circular resulution.

155. In verification of assets, the duty of the auditor is
(a) to satisfy himself that they are properly valued.
(b) to satisfy himself with regard to the existence, ownership and value of the assets.
(c) to ensure that assets have actually been acquired.
(d) to ensure that they are clearly stated in the balance sheet.

156. Who among the following is the 'Officer who is in default' within the definition given under Section 5 of the Companies Act, 1956?
(a) Secretary
(b) Contractor who has been assigned to complete certain work within stipulated time
(c) Supplier of raw material
(d) All employees

157. In vouching, an auditor verifies
(a) both the authority and authenticity of transactions.
(b) the authenticity of transactions only.
(c) the authority of transactions only.
(d) the arithmatical accuracy of the transactions only.

158. A file which contains rules governing the organisation under audit is known as
(a) Routine file (b) Precedence file
(c) Current file (d) Permanent file

159. Consider the following statement.
A company can be compared with a river which retains its identity through the parts which compose it, are constantly changing.
Which one of the following characteristic of a company is implied from the above statement?
(a) Artificial legal person
(b) Limited liability
(c) Separate property
(d) Perpetual succession

160. Which one of the following describes the correct effect when a registered partnership firm is dissolved?
(a) The partners cannot start any other business within one year of dissolution.
(b) One or two of the old partners can continue the business of the firm with a new name.
(c) The partners will not be entitled to any personal loans from banks.
(d) All the partners will be relieved from the debt obligations of the firm.

161. Which one of the following is correct regarding management audit?
It is a method
(a) to evaluate the efficiency of accounts departments throughout the organisation from the highest to lower levels.
(b) to evaluate the efficiency of management at all levels throughout the organisation from the highest to lower levels.
(c) to determine the compliance with accounting standards by the management.
(d) to determine the efficiency of Management Information System (MIS).

162. Which one of the following documents is not required for permanent file in audit of a non-corporate enterprise?
(a) Copy of the registration certificate of the enterprise
(b) Copy of the constitution of the enterprise
(c) Copy of the financial statements of the enterprise
(d) Copy of the appointment letter of an auditor

163. Change of the registered office of a company from one place to another in the same city required which one of the following resolution?
(a) Special resolution with government approval
(b) Board resolution
(c) Ordinary resolution
(d) Special resolution

164. Which of the following is an important advantage of vertical combination?
(a) It helps in coordinating the sequential operations.
(b) It helps in avoiding competition.
(c) It helps in capturing the market.
(d) It helps in controlling quality.

165. When a statement in lieu of prospectus is to be filed with the Registrar of Companies, it must be drafted in accordance with the particulars set out in which of the following?
(a) Schedule III (b) Rule 4-CCCA
(c) Table E (d) Schedule II

166. First auditors of a company are appointed by board of directors
(a) after commencement of the production.
(b) within gestation period.
(c) within six months of the date of registration of the company.
(d) within one month of the date of registration of the company.

167. Section 161(1) of the Companies Act requires the annual report of the companies to be signed by which of the following?
(a) Chairman and Company Secretary
(b) Auditor and Company Secretary
(c) General Manager and Company Secretary
(d) Managing Director and Company Secretary

168. Which one of the following is not an advantage of interim audit?
   (a) The final audit can be completed soon.
   (b) Audit staff will prepare notes when they finish the interim audit.
   (c) There is moral check on the staff.
   (d) It is good where publication of figures is necessary.

169. Which one of the following is applicable to vouching and post audit?
   (a) Important items from the balance sheet are taken.
   (b) Procedural tests are applied.
   (c) Investigation into the items of non-recurring nature.
   (d) Examination of profit and loss account, and balance sheet for present and past years.

170. To whom, is the auditor's report pursuant to a special audit of a company furnished?
   (a) Board of directors of the company
   (b) Shareholders of the company
   (c) Concerned State Government(s)
   (d) Central Government

171. Which one of the following is not a specific duty of an internal auditor?
   (a) Assessment of plans and targets
   (b) Examination of organisational structure
   (c) Carrying out investigations, *suo moto*
   (d) Testing the adequacy of internal control system

172. What do testing and test checking in relation to auditing mean?
   (a) To select and examine total universe from a large number of similar items.
   (b) To select and examine a representative sample from a large number of similar items.
   (c) To select and examine a representative small item from among a small universe.
   (d) To select and examine a representative sample even when discrepancies are found.

173. Working papers should not record
   (a) the nature, timing and extent of audit procedures performed.
   (b) the audit plan.
   (c) the audit programmes.
   (d) the conclusions drawn from the evidence obtained.

174. Which one of the following is not the primary purpose of audit working papers?
   (a) Record of the evidence accumulated and results of the tests.
   (b) Basis for planning an audit.
   (c) Data for determining the proper type of audit report.
   (d) Basis for preparing tax-return and filings with SEBI.

175. Audit notebook is a
   (a) record of mistakes and errors detected during the course of auditing accounts books.
   (b) record of important points and enquiries which an auditor has to refer to his clients.
   (c) record of work performed by an auditor.
   (d) personal notebook of an auditor.

176. Quorum for shareholders meeting of a private company is
   (a) 4 (b) 5
   (c) 2 (d) 3

177. A company is holding company of another if it holds ____ capital of another company.
   (a) 40% (b) 25%
   (c) 51% (d) 30%

178. A laissez-faire economy is found under the economic system of
(a) Communism (b) Capitalism
(c) Socialism (d) None of these

179. An extra-ordinary meeting may be called by
(a) Directors of the company.
(b) Shareholders of the company.
(c) Company law board.
(d) Any of the above.

180. Auditor of a company is appointed for a period of
(a) from one annual general meeting to the next annual general meeting.
(b) five years.
(c) one year.
(d) two years.

181. Internal check is a part of the whole system of
(a) Final audit (b) Interim audit
(c) Internal control (d) Internal audit

182. A company issues prospectus within
(a) 120 days of its registration.
(b) 90 days of its registration.
(c) 60 days of it's registration.
(d) 30 days of its registration.

183. A partner who has retired continues to be liable for obligations incurred after his retirement, if
(a) he left the firm without two months.
(b) he has not been paid his share in the capital and profit.
(c) he does not give public notice.
(d) None of the above.

184. One of the consequences of non-registration of a partnership firm is that
(a) the partner of such a firm cannot sue third parties.
(b) a partner cannot sue the other partner to enforce a right arising from a contract.
(c) the official assignee or receiver will have no power on the property of the dissolved firm.
(d) third parties cannot sue the firm for claims exceeding ₹ 100.

185. Which one of the following is an example of a company incorporated by a special Act of Parliament?
(a) State Trading Corporation Limited
(b) Bharat Heavy Electrical Limited
(c) Life Insurance Corporation of India
(d) Indian Oil Corporation

186. Integration of various units of similar character producing similar products or engaged in the same sphere of business activity under a single form of management and control is called
(a) circular of mixed combination.
(b) lateral or allied combination.
(c) vertical combination.
(d) horizontal combination.

187. Which of the following is not a speculator on the stock exchange?
(a) Stag (b) Broker
(c) Bull (d) Bear

188. Contango charges are paid by
(a) Bear to stag
(b) Bull to stag
(c) Bull to the bear speculator
(d) Bear to the bull speculator

189. Renumeration of auditor is fixed by
(a) Directors
(b) Shareholders
(c) The appointing authority
(d) Memorandum of Association

190. The minimum number of directors in a public limited company is
(a) 3 (b) 5
(c) 7 (d) 50

191. Partnership can be dissolved by giving notice when

(a) partnership is at will.
(b) partnership is for a fixed period.
(c) partnership is for a special purpose.
(d) None of the above.

192. A private company may start its business on the receipt of
(a) certificate of commencement of business.
(b) minimum subscription.
(c) certificate of incorporation.
(d) None of the above.

193. Holding company which does not carry on its own business but manages the business of subsidiary companies.
(a) Pure holding company
(b) Primary holding company
(c) Parent holding company
(d) None of the above

194. The exception to the doctrine of constructive notice is provided in
(a) Doctrine of indoor management.
(b) Lifting the corporate veil.
(c) Doctrine of ultra vires.
(d) All of the above.

195. In which form of combination, the combining firms keep their separate identity?
(a) Complete consideration
(b) Federation
(c) Partial consolidation
(d) All of the above

196. The extra-ordinary general meeting requires a notice of
(a) 21 days (b) 35 days
(c) 7 days (d) 14 days

197. When at an annual general meeting of a company no auditor is appointed or reappointed. In that case
(a) The board of directors appoints a person to fill the vacancy.
(b) The managing director of the company appoints a person to fill that vacancy.
(c) The Central Government appoints a person to fill the vacancy.
(d) None of the above can appoint a person to fill that vacancy.

198. 'Audit in depth' means
(a) intensive audit of each and every.
(b) audit of each and every item.
(c) audit of a few selected items.
(d) intensive audit of a few items.

199. Fishing has been classified as
(a) Genetic industry
(b) Manufacturing industry
(c) Extractive industry
(d) None of the above

200. If a partnership firm is not registered with the registrar of firms
(a) the members can enforce their rights among themselves.
(b) it has to pay penalty for non-registration.
(c) the members can file suit against the third party.
(d) None of the above.

201. A company is called an artifical person because
(a) it exists only in contemplation of law.
(b) it is invisible and intangible.
(c) it cannot be sued in the court of law.
(d) it does not have the shape of a normal man.

202. The first directors of a public company are appointed by the
(a) Promoters (b) Government
(c) Public (d) Shareholders

203. Under the Companies Act, a company must have
(a) Manager
(b) Board of directors

(c) Management director
(d) All of the above

204. A person is disqualified from being appointed as a director of a company if
(a) he is an undischarged insolved.
(b) he has applied to be adjudged insolved.
(c) he is of unsound mind.
(d) All of the above.

205. The most important clause in the Memorandum of Association of a company is
(a) Liability clause.
(b) Objects clause.
(c) Registered office clause.
(d) Name clause.

206. "A person dealing with a company has a right to assume that internal requirements prescribed have been observed." This rule is laid in
(a) doctrine of indoor management.
(b) doctrine of ultra virus.
(c) doctrine of constructive notice.
(d) None of the above.

207. When four cotton textile mills form a business combination, it is called
(a) Lateral combination
(b) Vertical combination
(c) Horizontal combination
(d) All of the above

208. Internal audit helps in
(a) Audit in depth (b) Internal check
(c) Internal control (d) Statutory audit

209. Which of the following is a statutory audit?
(a) Cost Audit
(b) Management Audit
(c) Financial Audit
(d) All of the above

210. Audit of company accounts is
(a) Unnecessary (b) Compulsory
(c) Advisable (d) All of the above

211. Internal auditor of a company must be a
(a) need not possess any professional qualification.
(b) chartered or cost accountant.
(c) charted accountant.
(d) cost accountant.

212. Company X Ltd. is the holding company of Y Ltd. Company Z Ltd. is the subsidiary of Y Ltd. What is the relation of X Ltd. and Z Ltd.?
(a) Z Ltd. is the holding company of X Ltd.
(b) There is no relation between X Ltd. and Z Ltd.
(c) X Ltd. is the holding company of Z Ltd.
(d) None of the above.

213. A copy of annual return should be filed with the Registrar of Companies within ______ days of annual general meeting.
(a) 45 (b) 60
(c) 30 (d) 42

214. "The environment of business consists of all those external things to which it is exposed and by which it may be influenced, directly or indirectly." This statement said by
(a) Wleer and Torch
(b) Copen
(c) Reinecke and Shcoell
(d) None of the above

215. *Introduction to Business* wrote by
(a) Schoell (b) Reincke
(c) Copen (d) Both (a) and (b)

216. "In environment, there are external factors, which constantly spin out opportunities and threats to the business firm." Who said this statement?
(a) Richman
(b) Torch
(c) Copen
(d) William Gluck and Jouch

217. "There are lot of pressures and controls which are mostly outside the control of individual firm and its managers." Who said this state ment?
(a) Copen (b) Richman
(c) Both (a) and (b) (d) Tery

218. "A good environment is good business", who said?
(a) Dr. R. Rajan
(b) Dr. M.S. Swaminathan
(c) Dr. S.S. Rao
(d) Dr. M. Singh

219. Which one of the following cannot be included under the nature of relationship between business and environment?
(a) Dynamic
(b) Interdependence
(c) Fixed
(d) Social change

220. Which of the following is not a components of environment?
(a) Political factors
(b) Economical factors
(c) Geographical factors
(d) None of the above

221. External environment of business is
(a) Economic (b) Physical
(c) Demographic (d) All of the above

222. Physical environment includes
(a) Climate
(b) Water
(c) Natural resources
(d) All of the above

223. Natural environment includes
(a) Air (b) Water
(c) Earth (d) All of the above

224. The economic environment of a business includes
(a) Economic policies
(b) Economic conditions
(c) Economic system
(d) All of the above

225. Which of the following is not an essential feature of social environment?
(a) Bailment
(b) Competitiveness
(c) Respect for the individual
(d) Better quality of life

226. Which of the following is not an essential feature of social environment?
(a) Insurance
(b) Importance of change and experimentation
(c) Social status
(d) Love for knowledge and education

227. The New Economic Policy of India is a precious gift of
(a) Mr. Venkateshwar Ray
(b) Dr. Manmohan Singh
(c) Mr. Jaswant Singh
(d) Dr. K.S. Rao

228. The New Economic Policy, 1991 was announced in
(a) July 1992 (b) June 1991
(c) July 1991 (d) June 1992

229. Which of the following statement is true?
(a) The scheme of globalisation means acceptance of an outward looking policy of economic development in place of inward-looking one.
(b) The new economic policy means an adoption of such type of policies which aim at reduction of fiscal deficits, wiping out of the current account.
(c) The fundamental objective of this policy is to bring about a qualitative and sustained innovation in the standard of living of the people of India.
(d) All of the above.

230. Which one of the following is not a recommendation of the Chakravarty Committee, 1985 in respect of financial system in India?
(a) Death Fund
(b) Pension Funds
(c) Plan to set up a National Stock Exchange
(d) Setting up of SEBI

231. Regulatory environment contains
(a) policies related to imports and exports.
(b) policies related to distribution and pricing.
(c) Both (a) and (b).
(d) cost of human resources.

232. Administrative control contains
(a) GDP
(b) GNP
(c) Economic planning
(d) Industrial policy

233. The supplier environment consists of factors related to the
(a) Reliability of product
(b) Cost
(c) Both (a) and (b)
(d) Technology

234. The supplier environment consists of factors related to the
(a) Life cycle (b) R&D
(c) Spare parts (d) Price

235. Which kinds of aspects should be considered at the time of investment planning?
(a) Telecommunication
(b) Transportation
(c) Power
(d) All of the above

236. Which functions performs by the Indian economy?
(a) Consumption (b) Growth
(c) Production (d) All of the above

237. Which of the feature are responsible for underdevelopment of Indian economy?
(a) Inequitable distribution of wealth and income
(b) Heavy population pressure
(c) Low per capita income
(d) All of the above

238. The GDP is the money value of all the final goods and services produced in the _____ territory of a country in an year's time.
(a) political
(b) foreign
(c) domestic
(d) neither foreign nor the domestic

239. GDP consists of
(a) Service
(b) Per unit market price
(c) Gross output of goods
(d) All of the above

240. Gross domestic product at market prices includes _______ taxes.
(a) all corporate (b) all direct
(c) all indirect (d) None of these

241. NFIA means
(a) no factor income from abroad
(b) net financial income from aims
(c) net factor income from abroad
(d) None of the above

242. NDP + NFIA = ?
(a) GNP (b) PPG
(c) NNP (d) GDP

243. DFI means
(a) donation factor income
(b) domestic factor income
(c) domestic financial income
(d) All of the above

244. DFI + NFIA = ?
(a) GDP (b) NNP
(c) LPG (d) GNP

245. New Direct Tax Code is an outcome of
(a) Central Budget 2008-09
(b) Central Budget 2006-07
(c) Central Budget 2009-10
(d) Railway Budget 2009-10

246. Indian Planning Commission was constituted in
(a) 1950 (b) 1951
(c) 1948 (d) 1949

247. Which of the following controls the working for sharemarket in India?
(a) BIFR (b) SEBI
(c) MRTP (d) FERA

248. Which tax is collected by Panchayat?
(a) Custom Duty
(b) Sales Tax
(c) Tax on local fairs
(d) Land Revenue

249. Madhya Pradesh has the highest production of ______ in India.
(a) Bajra (b) Soyabean
(c) Jawar (d) Ragi

250. Consumer movement got its conspicuous beginning and development in which country?
(a) Japan
(b) India
(c) Russia
(d) United States of America

251. Corporate Tax is
(a) Service Tax (b) Direct Tax
(c) Indirect Tax (d) Gift Tax

252. Where located the Consumer Education and Research Centre?
(a) Ahmedabad (b) Delhi
(c) Jaipur (d) Pune

253. CGSI means
(a) The Corporate Guidance Society of India
(b) The Co-operation Goodwill Society of India
(c) The Consumer Guidance Society of India
(d) None of the above

254. Where located the Consumer Guidance Society of India?
(a) Pune (b) Kolkata
(c) Mumbai (d) Delhi

255. The consumer movement is growing, ____ in India at present.
(a) slow but fast (b) fast but slow
(c) fastly (d) slowly

256. Which one of the following cannot be included under the consumer responsibilities?
(a) Proof.
(b) To understand the viewpoint of the seller before making a complaint.
(c) Don't understand the viewpoint of the seller before making a complaint.
(d) Complaints.

257. Which one of the following is not the objective of MRTP Act, 1961?
(a) Checking restrictive trade practices
(b) Checking unfair trade practices
(c) Promoting competition
(d) Checking monopoly

258. Which one of the following services is not covered under Consumer Protection Act?
(a) The services of a lawyer
(b) The services of a teacher
(c) The services of a banker
(d) The services of a doctor

259. Which one of the following cannot be included under the consumer rights?
(a) Right to choose the worst from a variety of offers.
(b) Right to get the genuine grievances redressed.

(c) Right to be heard if there is any grievance or suggestions.
(d) Right against exploitation by unfair trade practices.

260. The Consumer Protection Act, 1986 has listed the _____ rights it seeks to protect in India.
(a) banker (b) consumer
(c) producer (d) seller

261. Which of the following is not the responsibilities of the consumers?
(a) The consumers, in asserting their rights, should not inconvenience or hurt other sections of the public.
(b) The consumers should, as a rule, complain against a system and not attack individuals who are incumbents of post.
(c) The consumers should make vague complaints.
(d) The consumers should make a specific complaint, with supporting evidence.

262. Which one of the following aspects of consumer protection is not cover under the consumer education and information programmes?
(a) Creation of food-borne diseases
(b) Product labelling
(c) Product hazards
(d) Health

263. The Consumer Protection Act, 1986 came into force on
(a) 1 June 1986 (b) 1 June 1987
(c) 1 July 1987 (d) 1 July 1986

264. The Consumer Protection Act, 1986 extends to the whole of India except the State of
(a) Pondicherry
(b) Rajasthan
(c) Jammu and Kashmir
(d) Chandigarh

265. The Consumer Protection Act, 1986 applies to all goods and
(a) Coins
(b) Services
(c) All immovable property
(d) Indian Rupees

266. Goods means
(a) all immovable property
(b) all movable property
(c) decree
(d) auctionable claims

267. Goods includes
(a) Grass
(b) Crops with land
(c) Rare coins
(d) All of the above

268. A Central Consumer Protection Council establishment by the
(a) Central Government
(b) State Government
(c) President of India
(d) Parliament

269. A State Consumer Protection Council establishment by the ______ government in each State.
(a) Prime Minister
(b) Respective State
(c) Home Minister
(d) Only the President of India

270. Which one of the is not included under the objective of Consumer Protection Councils?
(a) The right to be informed about the ownership of goods.
(b) The right to be protected against marketing of goods and services which are hazardous to life and property.
(c) The right to be assured, wherever possible, access to a variety of goods at comparative prices.
(d) The right to consumer education.

271. The district forum shall consist of
(a) a lady social worker.
(b) a person who is qualified to be a District Judge who shall be its President.
(c) a person of eminence in the field of education, trade or commerce, who shall be a member.
(d) All of the above.

272. The First Industrial Policy of India announced by the Dr. Shyama Prasad Mukherjee on
(a) 6-4-1951 (b) 6-4-1955
(c) 6-4-1948 (d) 6-4-1950

273. The Industrial Policy, 1990 was announced by the
(a) Shri Manmohan Singh
(b) Shri Ajeet Singh
(c) Shri T.R. Dhir
(d) Shri Jaswant Singh

274. The New Industrial Policy announced on
(a) 20-6-1992 (b) 20-7-2011
(c) 24-7-1991 (d) 20-7-1991

275. Which one of the following statement is not true?
(a) Separation power is an important feature of Indian Constitution.
(b) The Industrial Policy, 1991 reforms have reduced the industrial licensing requirement.
(c) Exchange rate policy and the policy in respect of cross-border movement of capital are not important for business.
(d) The trade policy can significantly affect the fortunes of firms.

276. Which one of the following is not included under the object of New Industrial Policy, 1991?
(a) To attain International Competitiveness
(b) To abolish on the gains already made
(c) To correct the distortions or weakness that may have crept in
(d) To maintain a sustained growth in productivity and gainful employment

277. Who are the drivers of globalisation?
(a) Financial Flows
(b) Communications
(c) International Trade
(d) All of the above

278. The world economy has been emerging as a ______ economy.
(a) traditional (b) global
(a) domestic (d) Both (a) and (b)

279. Who counted—"All institutions have to make global competitiveness a strategic goal"?
(a) A.D. Honga (b) Terry
(c) Peter Drucker (d) Guleek

280. Forms of mixed economy consist of
(a) Co-operative sector
(b) Public sector
(c) Private sector
(d) All of the above

281. Which one of the following is not the characteristics of mixed economy?
(a) Joint sector
(b) Public control
(c) Economy independency
(d) Public interest

282. Which one of the following is not the characteristics of mixed economy?
(a) Economic freedom
(b) Economic planning
(c) Importance to the individual enterprises
(d) Private control

283. Economic infrastructure includes
(a) Communication (b) Water
(c) Transport (d) All of the above

284. Which one of the following is not means of Water Transport in India?
(a) Coastal transport
(b) Inland water transport
(c) Railway
(d) Oceanic transport

285. A separate Industrial Policy for Small Units was declared for the first time on
(a) 4 April 2008 (b) 6 August 1991
(c) 4 April 2010 (d) 3 April 2001

286. The strategies of marketing adopted by firm to achieve growth for
(a) Expand markets
(b) Add more products
(c) Add more markets
(d) All of the above

287. Which is the corporate citizen?
(a) Panchayat
(b) Reliance Industries Ltd.
(c) Ram
(d) None of the above

288. Which one of the following is not feature of business environment?
(a) In position to change environment
(b) Symbiotic relationship
(c) Dynamic
(d) All of the above

289. Which of the following is not feature of linkage between environmental scanning and strategic management?
(a) Strategy implementation
(b) Environmental scanning
(c) Strategy formulation
(d) All of the above

290. The advantages of environmental study are
(a) development of action plans to deal with technological advancements.
(b) analysis of competition strategies and formulation of effective counter-measures.
(c) development of broad strategies and long-term policies of the firm.
(d) All of the above.

291. Technological environment involves
(a) System complexity
(b) R & D
(c) Problem of techno-structure
(d) All of the above

292. Which of the following is component of economic environment?
(a) Industry (b) Transport
(c) Agriculture (d) All of the above

293. Economic environment consists of
(a) Population
(b) Per capita income
(c) New economic policy
(d) All of the above

294. Which of the following points covered by dconomic environment?
(a) Money market
(b) Economic system
(c) Infrastructure
(d) All of the above

295. Political environment consists of
(a) Role of executive
(b) Role of judiciary
(c) Role of legislature
(d) All of the above

296. Which one of the features is not covered under political environment?
(a) Political boundaries
(b) Constitution of India
(c) Caste system
(d) Direction of the government

297. Social cultural environment involves
(a) Scientific spirit (b) Social audit
(c) Culture creates (d) All of the above

298. Which of the following points is/are covered by socio-cultural environment?

(a) Ethics in business
(b) Education
(c) Social responsibility
(d) All of the above

299. Which of the following is component of Socio-cultural environment?
(a) Agriculture (b) R & D
(c) Education (d) Population

300. Which points deciding markets to enter?
(a) Number of countries to market in
(b) The type of countries to enter
(c) Volume of foreign sales
(d) All of the above

301. Rama Co. Ltd. has decided to go global, it must decide on the best mode of entry. The usual entry strategies are
(a) Franchising (b) Licensing
(c) Exporting (d) All of the above

302. Which one of the following is not indicator of market potential on the basis of demographic characteristics?
(a) Dominant values
(b) Population density
(c) Rate of population growth
(d) Size of population

303. Which of the following is not indicator of market potential on the basis of economic factors?
(a) Income distribution
(b) GNP per capital
(c) Climatic conditions
(d) Rate of growth of GNP

304. Which of the following factor affecting to organisational structure?
(a) Man-power
(b) Size of market
(c) Corporate objective
(d) All of the above

305. Which one of the following is not limitation of Indian Industrial Policy 1991?
(a) The policy is silent about tackling the growing industrial sickness.
(b) The liberalisation of the rules relating to direct foreign investment, permitting 51 per cent equity in a wide range of industries.
(c) The policy is drafted at the behest of IMF which means virtual surrender of economic sovereignty of the country to a foreign agency.
(d) Virtual scrapping of licensing means absence of a mechanism to determine priorities and to develop backward areas.

306. A mixed economy is ______ a planned economy.
(a) statutory (b) compulsory
(c) necessarily (d) voluntary

307. India has completed ____ Five Year Plans.
(a) ten (b) eight
(c) nine (d) None of these

308. Which of the following is not an objective of Economic Planning?
(a) Achieve full employment.
(b) Increase production to the maximum possible extent so as to achieve a higher level of national and per capita income.
(c) Set up a capitalist society.
(d) Reduce inequalities of income and wealth.

309. When introduced Indian Contract Act in India?
(a) 1 July 1872 (b) 1 Sep. 1872
(c) 1 July 1980 (d) 1 Sep. 1875

310. The Indian Contract Act, 1872 applies upon
(a) Delhi (b) Mumbai
(c) Jaipur (d) All of these

311. Economic role of government is
(a) Promotional role
(b) Entrepreneurial role

(c) Regulatory role
(d) All of the above

312. Which one of the following is not the economic role of government?
(a) Social welfare
(b) Planning role
(c) Transportation system
(d) All the work related to opposed to public policy

313. Which one of the following is not the elements of economic system?
(a) Reward (b) People
(c) Resource (d) All of the above

314. Economic system consists of
(a) Land (b) Management
(c) Regulation (d) All of the above

315. Which of the following is component of economic system?
(a) Customer (b) Employee
(c) Creditors (d) All of the above

316. Economic system considered ____ because they play very important role in economic development.
(a) capital (b) investor
(c) market (d) All of the above

317. Which of the following consists by economic system?
(a) Suppliers (b) Labour
(c) Owner (d) All of the above

318. According to A.F. Mcgann and Jack C. Roustom, "Types of Economic Systems" may be
(a) market-directed economic system.
(b) tradition-directed economic system.
(c) command-directed economic system.
(d) All of the above.

319. "The system in which the material instruments of production are owned or hired by private persons and are operated at their order with a view to selling at a profit the goods and services that help to produce." Who said this statement?
(a) Dr. Sampurnanand in *Socialism* vs. *Capitalism*
(b) Dr. P.K. Gole in *Socialism* vs. *Capitalism*
(c) A.C. Pigou in *Socialism* vs. *Capitalism*
(d) None of the above

320. Capital economic system consists of
(a) existence of competition.
(b) right to own private property.
(c) profit motive.
(d) All of the above.

321. Which of the following point covered by capitalist economic system?
(a) Price mechanism
(b) Unplanned economy
(c) Economic freedom
(d) All of the above

322. Capitalist economic system consists of
(a) labour power as a commodity.
(b) individualism.
(c) commodity economy.
(d) All of the above.

323. Which one of the following is not characteristic of capitalist economic system?
(a) Consumer sovereignty
(b) Occupational freedom
(c) Interdependence
(d) Central economic planning

324. Which one of the following is not the merit of capitalism?
(a) Benefits of perfect competition
(b) Individual incentive
(c) Economic instability
(d) Flexible and dynamic economy

325. Which one of the following is not the advantage of capitalism?
(a) Adaptability
(b) Monopolistic profit

(c) Capital formation
(d) Economic inequalities

326. Which one of the following is not the demerit of capitalism?
(a) Inefficient production
(b) Class conflict
(c) Neglecting national interests
(d) Social interest

327. Which one of the following is not the limitation of capitalism?
(a) Exploitation
(b) Monopoly
(c) Capital formation
(d) Unemployment

328. Socialist economic system consists of
(a) central planning.
(b) role of State.
(c) social ownership of the means of production.
(d) All of the above.

329. Which of the following point covered by the socialist economic system?
(a) Freedom of consumption and production
(b) Labour as trustee and employees
(c) Economic and social equality
(d) All of the above

330. Which one of the following is not the characteristic of socialist economic system?
(a) Goal of social welfare
(b) Market mechanism
(c) Restriction on production
(d) Collectivist economy

331. Socialism came into force for social development, but it has one limitation which is
(a) bureaucratic tendency.
(b) maximum use of national resources.
(c) full employment.
(d) production planning.

332. Which one of the following is not the merit of socialism?
(a) Accumulation and possibilities of growth
(b) Eradication of exploitation
(c) State capitalism
(d) No cyclical fluctuations

333. Which of the following is/are not the advantages of socialism?
(a) Eradication of parasites
(b) Increase in government powers
(c) Lack of rational calculation of cost
(d) Both (b) and (c)

334. The present Companies Act, 1956 came into force on ______ 1956.
(a) 1 December (b) 1 July
(c) 1 April (d) 1 June

335. The basic objectives of Indian Companies Act, 1956 is/are
(a) Due recognition of the legitimate interest of shareholders and creditors and of the duty of management not to prejudice to jeoparadise those interests.
(b) A minimum standard of good behaviour and business honesty in company promotion and management.
(c) Proper standard of accounting and auditing.
(d) All of the above.

336. Which of the following is not objective of Indian Companies Act, 1956?
(a) Provisions for greater and effective control over and voice in the management for shareholders.
(b) A check on their transactions where there was a possibility of conflict of duty and interest.
(c) A ceiling on the share of profits payable to management as remuneration for services rendered.
(d) All of the above.

337. Which of the following is not true with regard to Memorandum of Association?
(a) The Memorandum of a company limited by shares or by guarantee shall also state the liability of its member is limited.
(b) The name of the company with 'limited' as the last word or the name in the case of Public Limited Company, and with Private Limited as the last words of the name in the case of private limited company.
(c) The state in India in which the operated office of the company is to be situated.
(d) In the case of a company having a share capital no subscriber of the Memorandum shall take less than one share.

338. The quorum of general meeting in case of a public limited company is
(a) Four members (b) Five members
(c) Two members (d) Eight members

339. It is a statutory duty of a company secretary to
(a) borrow money in the name of the company.
(b) observe all legal formalities without being specifically authorised by the BoD.
(c) register transfer of shares of the company without being specifically authorised by the directors.
(d) make allotment of shares without the consent of director.

340. The minute books of company's meeting can be examined by
(a) debentureholders on payment of fee.
(b) shareholders without paying any fee.
(c) any person on payment of fee.
(d) All of the above.

341. Minutes of the meeting of the members of the company are to be confirmed by
(a) as per Articles of the Association.
(b) chairman of the BoD.
(c) chairman of the immediate next meeting.
(d) chairman of the same meeting.

342. Which one of the following is not most important documents of the company?
(a) Prospectus
(b) Bin card
(c) Articles of Association
(d) Memorandum of Association

343. Memorandum of Association of any company consists of
(a) Place clause (b) Objective clause
(c) Name clause (d) All of the above

344. Which one of the following is not the subject-matter of Articles of Association of a company?
(a) Alteration of share capital
(b) Dividends
(c) Issue of share capital
(d) Name of the company

345. Articles of Association of a company is fundamental documents and it plays very important role in regulating of company because it consists of
(a) registered place.
(b) how to inform shareholders.
(c) borrowing powers of the company.
(d) underwriting of shares.

346. Which of the following statement is true?
(a) Fair competition is the hallmark of a free enterprise economy.
(b) The economic liberalization has increased the relevance of competition policy.
(c) In 1980 at least 40 countries had competition laws.
(d) All of the above.

347. Which of the following is restrictive business practices selected by competitive law?
   (a) Market allocation
   (b) Price fixing
   (c) Restraint of output
   (d) All of the above

348. Competitive law has been made for controlling monopolistic trade practices. Which of the following is restrictive business practices selected by competitive law?
   (a) Collusive tendering
   (b) Exclusive dealing
   (c) Exclusionary practices
   (d) All of the above

349. Which of the following point covered by the competitive law?
   (a) Conscious parallelism
   (b) Reciprocal exclusivity
   (c) Refusal to deal
   (d) All of the above

350. Which one of the recommendations is not centered by the competition law committee in India?
   (a) Mergers
   (b) Agreement among enterprises
   (c) Abuse of dominance
   (d) None of the above

351. The Competition Act enacted in _____ in India.
   (a) July 2002 (b) Dec. 2001
   (c) Dec. 2002 (d) Dec. 2003

352. Which of the following statement is correct?
   (a) This Act, which extends to the whole of India except the state of Jammu and Kashmir.
   (b) The Act deals mainly with anti-competitive agreements.
   (c) With the coming into effect of the Competition Act, 2002, the MRTP Act, 1969 was repealed and the MRTP commission was dissolved.
   (d) All of the above.

353. Which of the following is the function of the Competition Commission of India?
   (a) Eliminate practices having adverse effect on competition.
   (b) Promote and sustain competition.
   (c) Protect the interest of consumers.
   (d) All of the above.

354. Which factors must be considered by the Competition Commission in determining dominant position?
   (a) Size and resources of the enterprise
   (b) Size and importance of competitors
   (c) Market share of the enterprise
   (d) All of the above

355. Which of the following point must be considered by the Competition Commission at the time of determining dominant position?
   (a) Market structure
   (b) Size of market
   (c) Countervailing buying power
   (d) All of the above

356. The Competition Act, 2002 set up a Competition Commission for control competition and above objects. So which factors must be considered by the Competition Commission at the time determining dominant position?
   (a) Social cost
   (b) Size of the competitors
   (c) Social obligation
   (d) All of the above

357. Which factors must be considered by the Competition Commission at the time determining adverse effect of an agreement?

(a) Accrual of benefits to consumers
(b) Creation of barriers to new entrants in the market
(c) Driving existing competitors out of the market
(d) All of the above

358. MRTP Act, 1969 consists of
(a) based on the size as a factor.
(b) competition offences implicit or not defined.
(c) based on the pre-reforms scenario.
(d) All of the above.

359. The Competition Act, 2002 consists of
(a) no combination regulation.
(b) no penalties for offences.
(c) complex in arrangement and language.
(d) All of the above.

360. The competitive commission covers which points?
(a) No competition advocate rate for the CCI
(b) Registration of agreement compulsory
(c) Unfair trade practices covered
(d) All of the above

361. Indian Competition Law 2002 consists of
(a) based on the post reforms scenario.
(b) based on structure as a factor.
(c) penalties for offences.
(d) All of the above.

362. The Consumer Protection Act, 1986 consists of
(a) Complaints (b) Services
(c) Goods (d) All of the above

363. The redressal forum of consumer consists of
(a) State Consumer Forum
(b) District Consumer Forum
(c) National Consumer Forum
(d) All of the above

364. Which of the following includes under characteristics of Business?
(a) Diversification
(b) Globalisation
(c) Competition
(d) All of the above

365. Product proliferation represents introducing different brands in the same
(a) Product price (b) Product design
(c) Product line (d) Product quality

366. Mission is a statement which defines the role that an organisation plays in a
(a) Capital (b) Shop
(c) Society (d) Market

367. Business goals consist of
(a) Power
(b) Quality of Product
(c) Challenging
(d) All of the above

368. The Indian Institute of Management, Ahmedabad (IIMA) was set up in ____ to pioneer professional management education in the country.
(a) 1982 (b) 1942
(c) 1952 (d) 1962

369. The strategies adopted to achieve growth are
(a) add more markets.
(b) diversify into a new areas.
(c) increase market share.
(d) All of the above.

370. Which of the following is limitation environmental analysis?
(a) Environmental analysis in and of itself is not a sufficient guarantor of organisational effectiveness.
(b) Environmental analysis offers one basis for organisational learning.
(c) Environmental analysis does not foretell the future, nor does it

eliminate uncertainty for any organisation.
(d) All of the above.

371. Hutch Essar was acquired by
(a) Reliance (b) Tata Mobile
(c) Bharti Airtel (d) Vodafone

372. Privatisation is the result of
(a) Domestic Compulsion
(b) Global Compulsion
(c) Economic Compulsion
(d) Market Compulsion

373. Which of the following statement is true?
(a) Government responsibilities to business are much greater than the obligations of business to government.
(b) Government establishes and enforces laws and regulations under which the business functions.
(c) The Directive Principles of State policy are a unique feature of our Constitution.
(d) All of the above.

374. Which are main reasons for Rural Poverty?
(a) Joint family system
(b) Rapid population growth
(c) Illiteracy
(d) All of the above

375. The fundamental rights are in the nature of ______ requiring the state not to do certain acts and are prohibitive in character.
(a) exploitation (b) infringement
(c) injustice (d) injunctions

376. Indian Mercantile Law is based on
(a) English Mercantile Law
(b) American Law
(c) European Law
(d) Japani Law

377. Indian Contract Act was passed in
(a) 1876 (b) 1878
(c) 1872 (d) 1879

378. An agreement enforceable by law is called
(a) Illegal Agreement
(b) Valid Contract
(c) Void Agreement
(d) Voidable Contract

379. An agreement created by words spoken or written is called
(a) Voidable Contract
(b) Express Agreement
(c) Implied Agreement
(d) Quasi Contract

380. An implied agreement is created by
(a) Automatically (b) Conduct
(c) Orally (d) Registration

381. A void agreement is an agreement which is
(a) enforceable at the option of one of the parties.
(b) restricted by government.
(c) enforceable at law.
(d) not enforceable at law.

382. An agency can be terminated by
(a) revocation by the principal.
(b) agreement.
(c) revocation by the agent.
(d) on insolvency of the principal.

383. Which of the following is a mercantile agent?
(a) Auctioneer (b) Husband
(c) Guardian (d) Servant

384. The Sale of Goods Act came into force from
(a) July 1, 1935 (b) July 1, 1932
(c) July 1, 1942 (d) July 1, 1930

385. Which of the following are specified goods?
(a) Goods which will be a manufactured.
(b) Goods available for sale and which can be identified.

(c) Goods which will be procured by the seller.
(d) Goods which is held for resale.

386. The Partnership Act came into force from
(a) 1956 (b) 1970
(c) 1932 (d) 1972

387. A minor
(a) can be admitted to the loss of partnership as a partner.
(b) can become a partner of firm.
(c) cannot be partner of firm.
(d) can be admitted to the benefits of partnership.

388. Whether the liability of a partner is
(a) Joint
(b) Limited
(c) Unlimited, Joint and Several
(d) Unlimited

389. What is the minimum age to become a partner?
(a) 18 years (b) 15 years
(c) 20 years (d) 21 years

390. In which cases a firm can be dissolved by the Court?
(a) Misconduct
(b) Insanity of a partner
(c) Transfer of interest
(d) All of the above

391. The Negotiable Instrument Act came into force from
(a) 1890 (b) 1891
(c) 1881 (d) 1818

392. The Negotiable Instrument Act is applicable to the whole of Indian including the State of
(a) Port Blair
(b) Jammu and Kashmir
(c) Nepal
(d) None of the above

393. The Negotiable Instrument Act, 1881 specially deals with
(a) Cheque
(b) Promissory Notes
(c) Hundi
(d) All of the above

394. Characteristic(s) of a negotiable instrument is/are
(a) transferee can sue in his own name.
(b) easy transferability.
(c) transferee's title free from all defects.
(d) All of the above.

395. Income Tax Act came into force from
(a) 1961 (b) 1960
(c) 1965 (d) 1962

396. The term 'Person' includes (in case of Income Tax, Act 1961)
(a) a Firm.
(b) a Company.
(c) a Hindu Undivided Family.
(d) All of the above.

397. Which is 'Tax Assessment Period'?
(a) 5 April to 31 March
(b) 1 April to 31 March
(c) 1 January to 31 December
(d) 1 June to 31 May

398. Company under Section 2(7), the expression 'Company' is defined to mean the following.
(a) Any institution, association or a body, whether incorporated or not and whether Indian or non-Indian, which is declared by general or special order of the central Board of Direct Taxes to be a company.
(b) Any body corporate incorporated under the laws of foreign country.
(c) Any institution, association or a body which is assessed or was assessable/assessed as a company for any

assessment year commencing on or before April 1, 1970.
(d) All of the above.

399. The Finance Act, 2009 gives income tax rates for which assessment year?
(a) 2009-10 (b) 2002-03
(c) 2010-11 (d) 2000-01

400. Income of previous year chargeable to tax in the
(a) immediately succeeding assessment year.
(b) immediately preceding assessment year.
(c) current year.
(d) same previous year.

401. Which part of the first schedule to a Finance Act gives advance tax rates for different assessees?
(a) Part I of the first schedule
(b) Part II of the first schedule
(c) Part III of the first schedule
(d) All of the above

402. Residential status of an assessee can be
(a) different for current years.
(b) different for different previous years in the same assessment year.
(c) different for previous years.
(d) different for different assessment years.

403. To which state Nano car product has been shifted from West Bengal?
(a) Gujarat (b) Haryana
(c) Andhra Pradesh (d) Karnataka

404. Tax incident is highest in the case of
(a) resident but not ordinarily resident.
(b) resident and ordinarily resident.
(c) non-resident.
(d) None of the above.

405. Allowances received by Indian nationals outside India from the Government of India are
(a) depend upon fact and circumstances of the case.
(b) chargeable to tax in India.
(c) exempt from tax in India.
(d) None of the above.

406. Income earned from a manufacturing business in Delhi, which is controlled from Nepal, is chargeable to tax in case of
(a) resident but not ordinarily resident.
(b) resident and ordinarily resident.
(c) non-resident.
(d) All of the above.

407. Share of profit received by a partner from a partnership firm assessed as such is
(a) chargeable depending upon facts and circumstances of the case.
(b) exempt from tax in the hands of the partner.
(c) chargeable to tax in the hands of the partners.
(d) None of the above.

408. Income of a religious trust is chargeable to tax as income of
(a) a body of individuals.
(b) individual.
(c) an association of persons.
(d) None of the above.

409. The tax rate applicable in case of domestic company is
(a) 22 per cent (b) 48 per cent
(c) 35 per cent (d) 38.5 per cent

410. As per the provisions of Section 115(7)A, in case of a company having total income less than 30 per cent of book profit, the total income of the shall be deemed to be
(a) 40 per cent of book profit.
(b) 30 per cent of book profit.
(c) 30 per cent of net profit as per Profit and Loss A/c.
(d) None of the above.

411. Seller under Section 206(C) means
(a) any company
(b) Central/State Government
(c) local authority
(d) All of the above

412. Professional Services under Section 194(7) include
(a) Advertising
(b) Legal Services
(c) Medical Services
(d) All of the above

413. Deduction of tax under Section 194(EE) is applicable in case of
(a) National Saving Scheme, 1987 and 1992.
(b) National Savings Scheme, 1987 only.
(c) National Savings Scheme, 1992 only.
(d) None of the above.

414. Section 194(C) is applicable in case of a contract between a resident contractor and
(a) any co-operative society.
(b) any company.
(c) any trust.
(d) All of the above.

415. The relevant form in which declaration is to be furnished in the case of interest other than interest on securities is
(a) Form No. 15
(b) Form No. 15H
(c) Form No. 13
(d) Form No. 15F

416. Mrs. Prem Koli wins a lottery on December 11, 2010 for ₹ 250,000. The Tax deducted at sources shall be
(a) ₹ 100,000 (b) ₹ 90,000
(c) ₹ 110,000 (d) ₹ 120,000

417. Refreshment provided by an employer to all employees during working hours in office premises is
(a) exempt from tax up to ₹ 35 per day.
(b) exempt from tax.
(c) chargeable to tax.
(d) None of the above.

418. Interest Rate Policy is a part of
(a) Monetary policy
(b) Fiscal policy
(c) Industrial policy
(d) None of the above

419. Issue Schedule of Companies Act, 1956 consists of
(a) date of earliest closing of the issue.
(b) date of opening of the issue.
(c) date of closing of the issue.
(d) All of the above.

420. Credit rating means—(under SEBI guide lines, 2000)
(a) if the rating has been obtained from one credit rating agencies, disclosure shall be made of all ratings including unaccepted rating.
(b) all the credit ratings obtained during the previous three years before filling of the offer document for any of its listed debt—Securities at the time of accessing the market through a rated debt—Security shall be disclosed.
(c) the credit rating obtained from a credit rating agency for the proposed issue of debt security including convertible instruments.
(d) All of the above.

421. Which of the following are characteristics of a company?
(a) Artificial person
(b) Incorporated association
(c) Legal entity distinct from its member
(d) All of the above

422. Common seal of company includes
(a) the seal should have the company's name engraven in legible characters.

It may consist of the words 'corporate seal', the place of the company and the date of its incorporation.
(b) the seal should be made of some metal.
(c) the purpose of seal is to furnish evidence regarding authenticity of a document.
(d) All of the above.

423. Conversion of a private company into a public company may be grouped under
(a) conversion by operation of law
(b) conversion by choice
(c) conversion by default
(d) All of the above

424. The Memorandum of a limited company consists of
(a) the name of the state, in which the registered office of the company is to be situated.
(b) the object of the company.
(c) the name of the company with 'Limited' or 'Private Limited' as the last word(s) of the name in the case of a Public Company or a Private Company as the case may be.
(d) All of the above.

425. Which of the following statement is correct?
(a) The Memorandum of Association of a company contains the fundamental conditions upon which alone the 937 company has been incorporated.
(b) According to Section 2(28) of the Companies Act, 1956, 'Memorandum' means "Memorandum of Association of a company as originally framed or altered time to time in pursuance of any previous companies law or of this Act".
(c) In the formation of a company is to prepare a document called the Memorandum of Association.
(d) All of the above.

426. Alteration of capital clause includes
(a) to sub-divide its shares, or any of them, into shares of smaller amount than fixed by the Memorandum, but the proportion of paid and unpaid on each share must remain the same.
(b) to increase its authorised share capital by such amount as it thinks expedient by issuing fresh shares.
(c) to consolidate and divide all the or any of its share capital into shares of larger amount than its existing shares.
(d) All of the above.

427. Minimum issued equity capital of a company should be ₹
(a) Two crores (b) Five crores
(c) Six crores (d) Ten thousands

428. The appointment of a banker is necessary as it has to receive the share application along with
(a) Allotment Money
(b) Application Money
(c) Second Call
(d) First Call

429. The amount of authorised nominal capital of a company limited by share and its division into shares of a fixed amount are given in the which is prepared before the certificate of incorporation is obtained by a company.
(a) Articles of Association
(b) Register of Members
(c) Agreement
(d) Memorandum of Association

430. Prospectus includes
(a) Expenses of the issue
(b) Minimum subscription
(c) Brokerage and previous issue for cash
(d) All of the above

431. _____ are advised to read the risk factors carefully before taking a investment decision in this offering.

(a) Purchaser (b) Seller
(c) Investor (d) Manager

432. The offer document shall also contain the information and statement specified in chapter VI of
(a) SEBI guideline - 2000
(b) SEBI guideline - 2001
(c) SEBI guideline - 2002
(d) SEBI guideline - 2003

433. Under the provisions of Companies Act, 1956 a company, can issue
(a) Only Deferred Shares
(b) Preference Shares, Equity Shares and Sweat Shares
(c) Only Preference Shares
(d) Only Equity Shares

434. Preference shareholders are
(a) Customers of the company
(b) Creditors of the company
(c) Employee of the company
(d) Owners of the company

435. Part of capital, which can called up at the time of winding of company, is called
(a) Reserve capital
(b) Uncalled capital
(c) Issued capital
(d) Authorised capital

436. When shares are forfeited, the share capital account is defeated by
(a) Calls in arrears
(b) Paid up amount
(c) Nominal value of such shares
(d) Called up amount

437. After the reissue of forfeited share, balance of forfeited share account is transferred to the following
(a) Profit and loss account
(b) Capital reserve account
(c) General reserve account
(d) Capital A/c

438. Security Premium account can be used for
(a) Payment of tax
(b) Writing off preliminary expenses
(c) Redemption of debentures
(d) Payment of liabilities

439. Which of the following is not essential elements of valid contract?
(a) Free consent
(b) Two person
(c) Voidable
(d) Lawful consideration

440. Which of the following may be considered in sound mind person?
(a) Cow
(b) Drunker
(c) Lunatic
(d) A person who takes rational judgment

441. A company can issue its shares at premium under the provisions of following section of Companies Act
(a) 78 (b) 79
(c) 80 (d) 76

442. According to Table 'A' of the Companies Act, 1956 a company can pay interest on calls in advance at the rate of
(a) 9% (b) 12%
(c) 6% (d) 7%

443. Right shares mean the shares which are
(a) issued to tax authorities.
(b) issued to employee.
(c) issued to promoters.
(d) issued to existing shareholders.

444. What is percentage maintained by Marine Insurance Companies for Reserve for unexpired risk?
(a) 60% of net premium
(b) 100% of net premium
(c) 50% of net premium
(d) 70% of net premium

445. When were General Insurance Companies Nationalised?
(a) 1956 (b) 1971
(c) 1972 (d) 1973

446. Who is the chairman of the 13th Finance Commission?
(a) B.K. Chaturvedi (b) D.S. Sharma
(c) C.R. Rao (d) Vijay Kelkar

447. Which of the following is kinds of insurance?
(a) Social Insurance
(b) General Insurance
(c) Life Insurance
(d) All of the above

448. The characteristics of general insurance are
(a) Insurable Interest
(b) All essentials of valid contract
(c) Indemnity
(d) All of the above

449. Doctrine of subrogation is related with
(a) General Insurance Act, 1971
(b) Indian Contract Act, 1872
(c) Indian Partnership Act, 1932
(d) Indian Companies Act, 1956

450. Kinds of general insurance are
(a) Fire Insurance
(b) Marine Insurance
(c) Life Insurance
(d) All of the above

451. General insurance covered
(a) Re-insurance
(b) Premium
(c) Ceding company
(d) None of the above

452. When were Life Insurance Companies Nationalised?
(a) 15 June, 1980 (b) 30 Dec., 1970
(c) 19 Jan., 1956 (d) 17 July, 1956

453. Indian Banking Act is known as
(a) Indian Research and Development Bank Act, 1970
(b) Banking Companies (Acquisition and Transfer of Undertakings) Act
(c) Banking Regulation Act, 1949
(d) Indian Banking Companies Act, 1972

454. Indian Banking Business is controlled by
(a) Indian Banking Act, 1880
(b) Banking Act, 1870
(c) The Property and Tax Authority Act, 1930
(d) Indian Companies Act, 1956

455. Banking Companies Act was passed on
(a) 1 July, 1985
(b) 1 July, 1970
(c) 17 Feb., 1949
(d) 20 Nov., 1949

456. When was Banking Co. Regulation Act implemented?
(a) 1947 (b) 1950
(c) 1949 (d) 1960

457. How many schedules are there in the amended form of final accounts of Banking Co.?
(a) 8 (b) 16
(c) 19 (d) 17

458. What is the rate of statutory reserve to be maintained under Section 17 of Banking Companies Act?
(a) 15% of Net Profit
(b) 35% of Net Profit
(c) 10% of Net Profit
(d) 20% of Net Profit

459. In which year 15 Banks were nationalised?
(a) 1960 (b) 1976
(c) 1969 (d) 1973

460. A General Insurance Company carrying on more than one type of insurance business prepares

(a) a separate profit and loss account for each type of business.
(b) a separate revenue account and a combined Profit and Loss A/c.
(c) a separate revenue account for each type of business.
(d) All of the above.

461. A non-banking asset is
(a) money at call and short notice.
(b) any asset acquired from the debtors in satisfaction of claim.
(c) building and furniture purchased from foreign market.
(d) All of the above.

462. Bank show the provision for income tax
(a) under real liabilities and tax authorities.
(b) under the head other liabilities and provisions.
(c) under the head of unexpired assets.
(d) under the head borrowings.

463. Performing assets means
(a) bank balance with RBI.
(b) cash balance with RBI.
(c) those loans and advance which generate income.
(d) money at call and short notice.

464. The Environment Protection Act came into force from
(a) 1996 (b) 1991
(c) 1986 (d) 1987

465. The Negotiable Instrument Act includes
(a) Cheque
(b) Promissory Note
(c) Both (a) and (b)
(d) Money

466. Goods includes (in case of Sale of Goods Act, 1930)
(a) Biscuit (b) Bread
(c) Pencil (d) All of the above

467. The Sale of Goods Act, 1930 covered
(a) Guarantee (b) Condition
(c) Goods (d) All of the above

468. Contract of indemnity deals
(a) General Insurance Contract Act, 1971
(b) Indian Companies Act, 1956
(c) The Indian Partnership Act, 1932
(d) Indian Contract Act, 1872

469. Types of contracts are
(a) Voidable Contract
(b) Void Contract
(c) Illegal Contract
(d) All of the above

470. The Environment (Protection) Act, 1986 covers
(a) Noise Pollution (b) Solid Wastage
(c) Water Pollution (d) All of the above

471. The Environment Audit started in India from
(a) 1995 (b) 1982
(c) 2011 (d) 1992

472. What is surcharge rate on corporate tax under Corporate Tax Assessment year 2011-12
(a) 9% (b) 10%
(c) 7.5% (d) 5%

473. In Union Budget 2011-12 the surcharge of 7-5% on domestic companies has been reduced to
(a) 2% (b) 4%
(c) 5% (d) 3%

474. For the year 2011-12, dividend received by an Indian Company from its foreign subsidiary will be taxed at a
(a) 15% (c) 45%
(b) 25% (d) 35%

475. In Union Budget 2011-12, the lower rate of central excise duty hss been increased from 4% to ______.
(a) 5% (b) 7%
(c) 9% (d) 13%

476. In Union Budget 2011-12, standard rate of service tax retained at ____.
(a) 7% (b) 9%
(c) 10% (d) 30%

477. MODVAT is known as
(a) CAT (b) DET
(c) CENVAT (d) MAT

478. Development Corporation is
(a) RHCO (b) UBI
(c) RBI (d) EBI

479. Decree issued by
(a) Governor
(b) Court
(c) President of India
(d) Prime Minister

480. Public Trust is
(a) Bombay
(b) Kandla Port Trust
(c) Calcutta
(d) All of these

481. 'CENVAT' related with
(a) Transport
(b) Special Excise Duty
(c) Money
(d) Foreign Currency

482. Code of Criminal Procedure started from
(a) 1975 (b) 1976
(c) 1973 (d) 1974

483. National Stock Exchange of India certified by
(a) SEBI
(b) Finance Ministry
(c) RBI
(d) Companies Act

484. SEBI has reduced the process duration time limit of Right Issue from 109 days to
(a) 62 days (b) 43 days
(c) 89 days (d) 72 days

485. Industry (Development and Regulation) Act introduced from
(a) 1952 (b) 1951
(c) 1954 (d) 1953

486. Which of the following is component of social cultural environment?
(a) Population (b) R and D
(c) Education (d) Agriculture

487. How much constitute has India in respect overseas shipping in the world?
(a) 3% (b) 8%
(c) 1% (d) 2%

488. 'CENVAT' introduced from
(a) 1-4-2004 (b) 1-4-2003
(c) 1-4-2000 (d) 1-4-2001

489. An agreement created by words spoken or written is called?
(a) Express Agreement
(b) Void Agreement
(c) Implied Agreement
(d) Voidable contract

490. An implied agreement is created by
(a) Conduct (b) Registration
(c) Orally (d) Writing

491. An agency can be terminated by
(a) Revocation by the principal
(b) By Notice
(c) On insolvency of the principal
(d) Agreement

492. Is consumerism well developed in India?
(a) Yes (b) Can't say
(c) No (d) None of these

Directions: Questions 493 to 504 are of multiple statement type. Choose the correct answers from the codes given below.

493. The auditor is generally expected to carry out the following in a particular seriatim
1. Verification of assets and liabilities.
2. Vouching of transactions.
3. Checking of valuation of assets and liabilities.

Codes:

(a) 2, 1, 3 (b) 3, 1, 2
(c) 1, 3, 2 (d) 3, 2, 1

494. Read the following statements and choose the correct answer from the given codes:
1. Political environment refers to all forces which have an economic impact on business.
2. Economic environment refers to all forces which have an economic impact on business.
3. Technological environment exercise not considerable influence on business.
4. Social and cultural environment refers to the influence exercised by certain factors.

Codes:

(a) only 1 and 2 statements are true
(b) all the above statements are true
(c) 1, 2 and 4 are true
(d) all the statements are false.

495. Which is the correct combination about targets of 11th plan (2007-2012)?
1. Growth Rate (Annual) original = 9.0%
2. Agriculture Growth Rate = 4% p.a.
3. Growth Rates in Industry and Services = 9 to 11%
4. Saving Rate = 34.8% of GDP
5. Investment Rate = 36.7% of GDP

Codes:

(a) 2, 3 and 4 (b) 3 and 5
(c) 1, 2, 3, 4 and 5 (d) 3 only

496. What is/are the effect(s) of non-registration of a partnership firm?
1. The partners cannot sue outsiders.
2. Outsiders cannot sue the firm.
3. A partner cannot sue for the dissolution of the firm.
4. A partner cannot sue the firm or any other partner of the firm.

Codes:

(a) 4 only (b) 1 and 2
(c) 2, 3 and 4 (d) 3 and 4

497. The books of accounts and other books and papers of every company shall be open to inspection during business hours by the following.
1. The Registrar of Companies
2. Such officers of the government as may be authorised by the Central-Government in this behalf.
3. Such officers of the Securities and Exchange Board of India as may be authorised by it.

Which of the above is/are correct when such inspection is made without giving any previous notice to the company?

Codes:

(a) 2 and 3 (b) 1, 2 and 3
(c) 1 only (d) 1 and 2

498. The National Advisory Committee on Accounting Standards shall consist of
1. One member each to be nominated by ICAI, ICWAI and ICSI.
2. One representative each of the Central Government. RBI and Comptroller and Auditor General of India.
3. A professor of Accountancy, Finance or Business Management from university or a deemed university.

Codes:

(a) 1, 2 and 3 (b) 2 and 3
(c) 1 only (d) 1 and 2

499. Which of the following are stated in the objects clause of the Memorandum of Association of a public limited company?
1. General and Specific objects
2. Main objects
3. Secondary objects
4. Objects incidental to main objects
5. Other objects.

Codes:

(a) 2, 3 and 4 (b) 1, 2 and 4
(c) 2, 4 and 5 (d) 1, 3 and 5

500. Which of the following statements are correct?
1. A minor is not competent to become a member of a company.
2. A firm cannot be treated as a member of a company.
3. A foreigner may become a member of a company.
4. A partnership firm cannot hod shares in a company in the individual names of partners as joint holders.

Codes:

(a) 1, 3 and 4 (b) 1, 2 and 3
(c) 1 and 2 (d) 2, 3 and 4

501. Which of the following statements are correct?
1. Compare the lists of debtors and creditors.
2. Check the total of cash book.
3. Ensure that no entry remained unposted.
4. Check the trial balance.

What is the correct balance of these functions to be performed by an auditor to locate errors?

Codes:

(a) 4, 3, 1, 2 (b) 1, 2, 4, 3
(c) 4, 2, 1, 3 (d) 1, 3, 4, 2

502. Which of the following statements are correct?
1. Cover performance audit
2. Protect the interests of the shareholders
3. Cover proprietory audit
4. Refer to audit of work done by the management accountant.

Codes:

(a) 1 and 3 are correct.
(b) 1 and 2 are correct.
(c) 2 and 4 are correct.
(d) 3 and 4 are correct.

503. Which of the following statements regarding a private company are correct?
1. A private company can proceed to allot shares without having to wait for minimum subscription.
2. There are restrictions on the powers of Board of Directors of a private company as to the selling of whole or part of the undertaking.
3. A private company can keep its affairs secret.
4. Right of pre-emption does not apply to a private company.

Codes:

(a) 2 and 3 (b) 1, 2 and 4
(c) 1, 2, 3 and 4 (d) 1, 3 and 4

504. Consider the following statements related to non-corporate audit.
1. The auditor is to ascertain the nature of revenue expense.
2. The auditor is to ascertain the weakness of internal control system.
3. The auditor is not to ascertain the Type of internal control system applicable for sensitive items in organisation.
4. The auditor is not to ascertain the appropriateness of books of account.

Which of the statements given above are correct?

Codes:

(a) 3 and 4 (b) 1, 2 and 4
(c) 1 and 2 (d) 1, 2 and 3

Directions: Questions 505 to 534 are of matching type. Match List I with List II and select the correct answer using the codes given below the list.

505. **List I**
A. Reinecke and School
B. William Glueck and Jauche
C. Richman and Coupan
D. Shri Joel Dean

List II

1. "The environment of business consists of all those external things to which it is exposed and by which it may be influenced directly or indirectly."
2. "In environment, there are external factors, which constantly spin out opportunities and threats to the business firm."
3. "There are lot of pressures and controls which are mostly outside the control of individual firm and its managers."
4. Managerial Economics.

Codes:	A	B	C	D
(a)	1	2	3	4
(b)	1	3	2	4
(c)	2	4	3	1
(d)	4	3	2	1

506. **List I (Act)**

A. Indian Contract Act
B. Indian Partnership Act
C. Environment Protection Act
D. The Sale of Goods Act

List II (Formation — Year)

1. 1872 2. 1932
3. 1986 4. 1930

Codes:	A	B	C	D
(a)	3	4	2	1
(b)	1	2	3	4
(c)	4	3	2	1
(d)	1	4	3	2

507. **List I (Items/Subject Matter)**

A. Tax Assessment year
B. Agreement
C. Promissory note or cheque
D. Goods

List II (Related Business Act)

1. Income Tax Act, 1961
2. Indian Contract Act, 1872
3. Negotiable Instrument Act, 1880
4. The sale of Goods Act, 1930

Codes:	A	B	C	D
(a)	2	4	3	1
(b)	3	1	4	2
(c)	3	2	4	1
(d)	1	2	3	4

508. **List I (Authors)**

A. Lord Justice Lindley
B. Chief Justice Marshall
C. Prof. Haney
D. Justice Joeshph

List II (Definition of a Company)

1. "A company is an association of many persons who contribute money or monies worth to a common stock and employed in some trade or business and who share the profit and loss arising therefrom. The common stock so contributed is denoted in money and is the capital of the company. The persons who contribute to it or to whom it pertains are members. 228. The proportion of capital to which each member is entitled is his share. The shares are always transferable although the right to transfer is often more or less restricted."
2. "A corporation is an artificial being, invisible intangible, existing only in contemplation of the law. Being a mere creation of law, it possesses only the properties which the charter of its creation confers upon it, either expressly or as incidental to its very existence."
3. "A company is n artificial person created by law, having separate entity, with a perpetual succession and common seal."
4. A Joint Stock company to which the Companies Act applies comes into existence only when it is registered under the Act.

Codes:	A	B	C	D
(a)	2	3	4	1
(b)	1	4	2	3
(c)	1	2	3	4
(d)	4	3	2	1

509. **List I (Section of Companies Act, 1956)**

A. 43A B. 108
C. 149 (2A) D. 165

List II (Subject Matter)

1. Private company to become deemed public company in certain cases
2. Transfer of shares or debentures not to be registered except on production of instrument of transfer
3. Restriction on commencement of business in respect of ancillary objects
4. Statutory meeting and statutory report

Codes:	A	B	C	D
(a)	4	3	2	1
(b)	3	4	2	1
(c)	1	3	4	2
(d)	1	2	3	4

510. **List I (Section of Companies Act, 1956)**

A. 187C B. 187D
C. 198 D. 295A

List II (Subject Matter)

1. Declaration by person not holding beneficial interest in any share
2. Investigation of beneficial ownership of shares in certain cases
3. Overall maximum managerial remuneration and managerial remuneration in case of absence of or inadequacy of profits
4. Unpaid dividend to be transferred to special dividend account

Codes:	A	B	C	D
(a)	4	1	2	3
(b)	1	2	3	4
(c)	4	3	2	1
(d)	4	2	3	1

511. **List I (Basic Principles of Income Tax)**

A. An Individual
B. Trustee
C. A Hindu Undivided Family
D. Firm

List II (Their Provisions)

1. Under the Income Tax Act 1961, a natural person, i.e., a human being. Deities and Statutory Corporations are assessable as 'Judicial Person'. 'Individual' includes a minor or a person of unsound mind.
2. Under a discretionary trust have to be assessed in the status of 'individual' and not in the status of association of persons.
3. Those which consist of all persons lineally descended from a common ancestor and includes their wives and unmarried daughters. Profits made by a Joint Hindu Family are chargeable to tax as income of the Hindu undivided family as a distinct entity or unit of assessment. Once a family is assessed as a Hindu undivided family, it will continue to be assessed as such till a finding of partition is given by the Assessing Officer under section 171.
4. "Relationship between persons who have agreed to share the profits of business carried on by all or any of them acting for all." Persons who have entered into partnership with one another are called individually partners and collectively a firm and the name under which their business is carried on is called the firm name.

Codes:	A	B	C	D
(a)	1	3	2	4
(b)	4	3	2	1
(c)	1	2	3	4
(d)	1	4	2	3

512. List I (Management Thinkers)

A. Musselman and Hughes
B. R.S. Buskirk, D.J. Green and W.C. Rodgers
C. Keith and Gubellini
D. Arthur M. Weimer

List II (Their Statements)

1. Business represents the organised efforts of enterprises to supply consumers with goods and services.
2. Business "is a system created to satisfy society's needs and desires."
3. A Business "is nothing more than a person or group of persons property organised to produce or distribute goods or services."
4. Business is that "complex field of commerce and industry in which goods and services are created and distributed — in the hope of profit within a framework of laws and regulations."

Codes:	A	B	C	D
(a)	4	3	1	2
(b)	1	2	3	4
(c)	1	2	4	3
(d)	4	3	2	1

513. List I (Products)

A. Maruti B. Ispat
C. Vizag steel D. ModiLuft

List II (Mission Statements)

1. "Building Trust World-wide"
2. "Success in Different Moulds"
3. "Infrastructuring India"
4. "Miles and Smiles"

Codes:	A	B	C	D
(a)	3	4	2	1
(b)	4	3	1	2
(c)	1	2	4	3
(d)	1	2	3	4

514. List I

A. Regulatory Role
B. Promotional Role
C. Entrepreneurial Role
D. Planning Role

List II

1. SEBI
2. Transportation System
3. Formation of Enterprises
4. Development of Economic Structure

Codes:	A	B	C	D
(a)	4	3	2	1
(b)	4	1	3	2
(c)	1	2	3	4
(d)	4	2	3	1

515. List I

A. National Association of Manufacturers
B. Halm
C. Loucks and Hoots
D. George Halm

List II

1. "From the point of view of public welfare, competition serves as a regulator and reducer of prices, as an incentive to improved production efficiency, as a guarantor that we shall get what we want and as a protector of the freedom of production."
2. "Without competition, the capitalist economy would become stagnant, unproductive and exploitative."
3. "It has possessed a flexibility and adaptability and a resiliency which have permitted it to would its forms and process into conformity with innumerable changes in its environmental setting."
4. "Monopolistic policies are the outgrowth of the consistent application of the profit motive which is the main driving force of the unplanned private enterprise system."

Codes:	A	B	C	D
(a)	1	3	4	2
(b)	3	1	4	2
(c)	3	1	2	4
(d)	1	2	3	4

516. **List I (Economic system)**

A. Capitalism B. Socialism
C. Communism D. Mixed

List II (Features)

1. Managers are selected on the basis of ability
2. Profits recognised
3. No depreciation permitted
4. Public and private sector

Codes:	A	B	C	D
(a)	4	3	2	1
(b)	1	2	3	4
(c)	3	4	2	1
(d)	2	1	3	4

517. **List I (Gross Capital Formations Rate as % of GDP)**

A. 37-7 B. 34-9
C. 34-5 D. 36-5

List II (Year)

1. 2006-07 2. 2007-08
3. 2008-09 4. 2009-10

Codes:	A	B	C	D
(a)	3	2	1	4
(b)	1	2	4	3
(c)	4	3	2	1
(d)	1	2	3	4

518. **List I (Foreign Exchange Reserve as on Dec, 31, 2010)**

A. Foreign Currency Assets
B. Gold
C. Reserve Tranche with IMF
D. SDR

List II (Value in billion dollar)

1. 267.814 2. 22.470
3. 1.972 4. 5.078

Codes:	A	B	C	D
(a)	4	3	1	2
(b)	2	1	3	4
(c)	3	1	2	4
(d)	1	2	3	4

519. **List I**

A. Economic Policy
B. Economic System
C. Socialism System
D. Mixed Economic System

List II

1. Capitalist Economic System
2. Licensing
3. Control Planning
4. Govt. Control and Ownership

Codes:	A	B	C	D
(a)	1	2	3	4
(b)	2	4	3	1
(c)	4	2	3	1
(d)	4	3	2	1

520. **List I (Year)** / **List II (Anual Rate of Growth of GDP)**

A. 2007-08 1. 9-3%
B. 2008-09 2. 6-8%
C. 2009-10 3. 8-0%
D. 2010-11 4. 8-6%

Codes:	A	B	C	D
(a)	4	3	2	1
(b)	1	2	3	4
(c)	3	2	4	1
(d)	4	1	3	2

521. **List I (Environmental factors)**

A. Economic environment
B. Political environment
C. Socio-cultural environment
D. Natural environment

List II (Their features)

1. Growth strategy
2. Role of judiciary
3. Culture creates people
4. Transport-depend on geographical factors

Codes:	A	B	C	D
(a)	1	3	2	4
(b)	1	3	4	2
(c)	4	3	2	1
(d)	1	2	3	4

522. **List I (Industrial Policy)**

A. First Industrial Policy
B. Second Industrial Policy
C. Third Industrial Policy
D. Fourth Industrial Policy

List II (Announced Date)

1. 6-4-1948
2. 30-4-1956
3. 25-12-1977
4. 23-7-1980

Codes:	A	B	C	D
(a)	2	3	4	1
(b)	1	2	4	3
(c)	4	3	2	1
(d)	1	2	3	4

523. **List I (Components of Business Environment)**

A. Social Environment
B. Political Environment
C. Economic Environment
D. Regulator Environment

List II (Factors of Components)

1. Awarness and work ethics
2. Packaging
3. Balance of Payment
4. MRTP

Codes:	A	B	C	D
(a)	1	2	4	3
(b)	1	2	3	4
(c)	3	2	1	4
(d)	4	3	2	1

524. **List I**

A. Focus on social environment
B. Focus on physical environment
C. One person one superior
D. One head one plan

List II

1. Traditional theorist
2. Human Relationists
3. Unity Direction
4. Unity of command

Codes:	A	B	C	D
(a)	2	1	4	3
(b)	1	2	3	4
(c)	4	3	2	1
(d)	3	2	1	4

525. **List I**

A. Partners and Firm
B. Sole Properietorship
C. Public Limited Company
D. Nominal Partnership

List II

1. Agent and principle relationship
2. Prospect us
3. Personal Supervision
4. Firm image

Codes:	A	B	C	D
(a)	4	2	3	1
(b)	1	2	4	3
(c)	1	3	2	4
(d)	2	3	1	4

526. **List I**

A. Statutory functions of a Secretary
B. Advice to the Board of Directors
C. Filing tax returns
D. Image of organisation

List II

1. Non-statutory function
2. Executive function
3. Functions imposed by law
4. Public Relations Officer

Codes:	A	B	C	D
(a)	3	2	1	4
(b)	1	2	3	4
(c)	3	4	1	2
(d)	4	3	2	1

527. **List I**
A. Continuous audit
B. Internal audit
C. Occasional audit
D. Periodical audit

List II
1. Continuous review of the operations and records of the business by special staff.
2. Audit which is non statutory.
3. Audit convenient and useful specially in the case of small concerns.
4. Audit work carried on almost simultaneously with the recording of transactions.

Codes:	**A**	**B**	**C**	**D**
(a)	4	3	2	1
(b)	2	1	4	3
(c)	4	1	2	3
(d)	2	3	4	1

528. **List I (Organisation)**
A. Joint Stock Company
B. Co-operative Society
C. Statutory Corporation
D. Partnership

List II (Associated with)
1. Memorandum of Association (MoA)
2. Special Act
3. Mutual contract
4. Bye-laws

Codes:	**A**	**B**	**C**	**D**
(a)	1	3	4	2
(b)	1	2	3	4
(c)	1	4	2	3
(d)	2	3	1	4

529. **List I (Type of audit)**
A. Management audit
B. Statutory audit
C. Audit of non-corporate enterprise
D. Internal control and audit

List II (Function)
1. Report to the shareholders
2. A future oriented, independent and systematic evaluation of activities at all levels
3. Both accounting and operational controls
4. Voluntary
5. Report to company law board

Codes:	**A**	**B**	**C**	**D**
(a)	2	1	4	3
(b)	2	3	4	1
(c)	4	3	5	1
(d)	4	1	5	3

530.

List I (Records)	**List II (Examples)**
A. Accounting Records	1. Casual leave report
B. Legal Records	2. Invoice
C. Correspondence Records	3. Minutes
D. Personnel Records	4. Copy of letter sending product details and rates

Codes:	**A**	**B**	**C**	**D**
(a)	1	3	4	2
(b)	2	4	3	1
(c)	1	4	3	2
(d)	2	3	4	1

531. **List I (Matter for audit examinations)**
A. Cash payments
B. Plant and machinery
C. Bank O.D. balance
D. Disagreement between the bank balance shown by cash book and bank pass book

List II (Audit technique adopted)
1. Direct confirmation
2. Physical verification
3. Vouching
4. Reconciliation review
5. Test checking

Codes:	A	B	C	D
(a)	4	2	1	5
(b)	3	1	2	4
(c)	4	1	2	5
(d)	3	2	1	4

532. **List I (Committees)**

A. Standing Committee
B. Ad-hoc Committee
C. Executive Committee
D. Advisory Committee

List II (Explanations)

1. Authority to take and exectue decisions
2. Exists continuously for an indefinite period of time
3. Authority only to make recommen dations
4. Constituted temporarily for specific purpose

Codes:	A	B	C	D
(a)	2	4	3	1
(b)	4	2	1	3
(c)	2	4	1	3
(d)	4	2	3	1

533. **List I (Type of combinations)**

A. Association
B. Federation
C. Partial consolidation
D. Complete consolidation

List II (Illustrations)

1. Cartel
2. Chamber of commerce and industry
3. Holding company
4. Amalgamation

Codes:	A	B	C	D
(a)	1	2	4	3
(b)	2	1	4	3
(c)	1	2	3	4
(d)	2	1	3	4

534. **List I**

A. Contract of Uberrimae Fidei
B. Right of Eminent Domain
C. Statement in lieu of prospectus
D. System of one man one vote

List II

1. Public utility concern
2. Co-operative society
3. Partnership
4. Sole trading concern
5. Public limited company

Codes:	A	B	C	D
(a)	3	2	1	4
(b)	1	2	5	2
(c)	1	3	5	4
(d)	3	1	5	3

Directions: Questions 535 to 546 consist of two statements, one labelled as 'Assertion (A)' and the other as 'Reason (R)'. You have to examine these two statements carefuly and decide if the Assertion A and the Reason R are individually true and if so, whether the Reason is a correct explanation of the Assertion. Select your answer to these items using the codes given below.

(a) Both A and R are true and R is the correct explanation of A.
(b) Both A and R are true but R is not the correct explanaton of A.
(c) A is true but R is false.
(d) A is false but R is true.

535. **Assertion (A):** Audit is conducted to find out the financial position of a concern.

Reason (R): The objects of audit are the detection and prevention of errors and frauds.

536. **Assertion (A):** Internal audit must be carried out by a qualified chartered accountant.

Reason (R): It is a management tool.

537. **Assertion (A):** If the directors of a company commit any irregular act but within the provisions of the Companies Act or Memorandum of Articles such acts will be binding on the company. But, in turn, the company may claim damages from the directors for such acts.

Reason (R): The directors have to conduct the affairs of the business in a manner which is not deteremental to the interests of the company.

538. **Assertion (A):** Nowadays, it is obligatory on the part of companies to disclose in their annual reports, work done for benefit of the society.

Reason (R): Annual reports are used by members of the society in one capacity or another.

539. **Assertion (A):** Internal check is a system of organising accounting function whereby duties of different clerks are arranged in such a way that work of one person is automatically checked by another.

Reason (R): Fraud is not possible without collusion between two or more persons, and at the same time possibilities of errors are reduced to a minimum by internal check.

540. **Assertion (A):** Vouching is an inspection by auditor of documentary evidence supporting and substantiating transactions in the books of accounts.

Reason (R): A thorough vouching system reduces the need for verification of assets and liabilities.

541. **Assertion (A):** Accounting information refers to only those events which are concerned with entity.

Reason (R): Accounting information is presented in the form of financial statements.

542. **Assertion (A):** Nowadays, it is obligatory on the part of companies to disclose in their annual reports, work done for the benefit of the society.

Reason (R): Annual reports are used by members of the society in one capacity or another.

543. **Assertion (A):** The auditor of a proprietary firm need not be bound by professional properiety.

Reason (R): Proprietary auditor is responsible only to the person(s) who appoint(s) him.

544. **Assertion (A):** The main purpose of auditing is to verify that the accounts have been prepared according to the principles of accounting and to see whether the financial statements so prepared reflect a true and fair view of the state of affairs of a business.

Reason (R): Auditing starts after the completion of recording of transactions in the books of account.

545. **Assertion (A):** The auditor should visit the particular concern at intervals and check the book of accounts.

Reason (R): Some precaution is required to be taken by the auditor to avoid weaknesses of continuous audit.

546. **Assertion (A):** Once incorporated, the name of a public limited company cannot be changed.

Reason (R): The name of a public limited company must be distinct and should not mislead or resemble that of any other company.

ANSWERS

1. (d)	2. (b)	3. (d)	4. (a)	5. (c)	6. (c)
7. (a)	8. (b)	9. (d)	10. (b)	11. (d)	12. (c)
13. (c)	14. (d)	15. (b)	16. (c)	17. (d)	18. (b)
19. (a)	20. (d)	21. (c)	22. (a)	23. (d)	24. (d)
25. (d)	26. (c)	27. (d)	28. (a)	29. (c)	30. (d)
31. (c)	32. (c)	33. (a)	34. (d)	35. (d)	36. (d)
37. (b)	38. (b)	39. (d)	40. (c)	41. (c)	42. (c)
43. (b)	44. (a)	45. (c)	46. (b)	47. (b)	48. (b)
49. (c)	50. (a)	51. (c)	52. (c)	53. (a)	54. (a)
55. (b)	56. (d)	57. (d)	58. (d)	59. (c)	60. (b)
61. (d)	62. (c)	63. (d)	64. (d)	65. (c)	66. (d)
67. (a)	68. (d)	69. (c)	70. (c)	71. (a)	72. (b)
73. (c)	74. (a)	75. (a)	76. (c)	77. (b)	78. (c)
79. (a)	80. (b)	81. (a)	82. (d)	83. (b)	84. (b)
85. (a)	86. (a)	87. (a)	88. (b)	89. (a)	90. (d)
91. (b)	92. (b)	93. (d)	94. (a)	95. (a)	96. (d)
97. (b)	98. (b)	99. (b)	100. (c)	101. (c)	102. (b)
103. (a)	104. (c)	105. (a)	106. (a)	107. (c)	108. (a)
109. (a)	110. (c)	111. (d)	112. (a)	113. (a)	114. (c)
115. (b)	116. (d)	117. (c)	118. (c)	119. (c)	120. (a)
121. (d)	122. (b)	123. (a)	124. (a)	125. (d)	126. (c)
127. (a)	128. (c)	129. (a)	130. (b)	131. (d)	132. (a)
133. (a)	134. (d)	135. (c)	136. (a)	137. (d)	138. (d)
139. (d)	140. (a)	141. (c)	142. (d)	143. (b)	144. (a)
145. (d)	146. (a)	147. (b)	148. (c)	149. (b)	150. (a)
151. (a)	152. (b)	153. (b)	154. (a)	155. (b)	156. (a)
157. (a)	158. (d)	159. (d)	160. (b)	161. (b)	162. (a)
163. (b)	164. (a)	165. (a)	166. (d)	167. (d)	168. (c)
169. (b)	170. (d)	171. (b)	172. (b)	173. (b)	174. (d)
175. (b)	176. (c)	177. (c)	178. (b)	179. (d)	180. (a)
181. (c)	182. (b)	183. (c)	184. (a)	185. (c)	186. (d)
187. (b)	188. (c)	189. (c)	190. (a)	191. (a)	192. (c)

193. (a)	194. (a)	195. (b)	196. (a)	197. (c)	198. (d)
199. (c)	200. (d)	201. (a)	202. (a)	203. (b)	204. (d)
205. (b)	206. (a)	207. (c)	208. (c)	209. (c)	210. (b)
211. (a)	212. (c)	213. (b)	214. (c)	215. (d)	216. (d)
217. (c)	218. (b)	219. (c)	220. (d)	221. (d)	222. (d)
223. (d)	224. (d)	225. (a)	226. (a)	227. (b)	228. (b)
229. (d)	230. (a)	231. (c)	232. (d)	233. (c)	234. (c)
235. (d)	236. (d)	237. (d)	238. (c)	239. (d)	240. (c)
241. (c)	242. (c)	243. (b)	244. (b)	245. (c)	246. (a)
247. (b)	248. (c)	249. (b)	250. (d)	251. (b)	252. (a)
253. (c)	254. (c)	255. (d)	256. (c)	257. (c)	258. (b)
259. (a)	260. (b)	261. (c)	262. (a)	263. (c)	264. (c)
265. (b)	266. (b)	267. (d)	268. (a)	269. (b)	270. (a)
271. (d)	272. (c)	273. (b)	274. (c)	275. (c)	276. (b)
277. (d)	278. (d)	279. (c)	280. (d)	281. (c)	282. (d)
283. (d)	284. (c)	285. (b)	286. (d)	287. (b)	288. (d)
289. (d)	290. (d)	291. (d)	292. (d)	293. (d)	294. (d)
295. (d)	296. (c)	297. (d)	298. (d)	299. (c)	300. (d)
301. (d)	302. (c)	303. (c)	304. (d)	305. (c)	306. (c)
307. (a)	308. (c)	309. (b)	310. (a)	311. (d)	312. (d)
313. (d)	314. (d)	315. (d)	316. (d)	317. (d)	318. (d)
319. (c)	320. (d)	321. (d)	322. (d)	323. (d)	324. (c)
325. (d)	326. (d)	327. (c)	328. (d)	329. (d)	330. (c)
331. (a)	332. (c)	333. (d)	334. (c)	335. (d)	336. (d)
337. (c)	338. (b)	339. (b)	340. (b)	341. (d)	342. (b)
343. (d)	344. (d)	345. (a)	346. (d)	347. (d)	348. (d)
349. (d)	350. (d)	351. (c)	352. (d)	353. (d)	354. (d)
355. (d)	356. (d)	357. (d)	358. (d)	359. (d)	360. (d)
361. (d)	362. (d)	363. (d)	364. (d)	365. (c)	366. (c)
367. (d)	368. (c)	369. (d)	370. (d)	371. (d)	372. (a)
373. (d)	374. (d)	375. (d)	376. (a)	377. (c)	378. (b)
379. (b)	380. (b)	381. (d)	382. (d)	383. (a)	384. (d)
385. (b)	386. (c)	387. (d)	388. (c)	389. (a)	390. (d)
391. (d)	392. (b)	393. (d)	394. (d)	395. (a)	396. (d)

397. (b)	398. (d)	399. (a)	400. (a)	401. (a)	402. (d)
403. (a)	404. (b)	405. (c)	406. (d)	407. (b)	408. (c)
409. (d)	410. (b)	411. (d)	412. (d)	413. (b)	414. (d)
415. (d)	416. (c)	417. (b)	418. (a)	419. (d)	420. (d)
421. (d)	422. (d)	423. (d)	424. (d)	425. (d)	426. (d)
427. (b)	428. (b)	429. (d)	430. (d)	431. (c)	432. (a)
433. (a)	434. (d)	435. (b)	436. (d)	437. (b)	438. (b)
439. (c)	440. (d)	441. (a)	442. (c)	443. (d)	444. (b)
445. (b)	446. (d)	447. (d)	448. (d)	449. (a)	450. (d)
451. (d)	452. (c)	453. (b)	454. (a)	455. (c)	456. (c)
457. (b)	458. (d)	459. (c)	460. (b)	461. (d)	462. (b)
463. (c)	464. (c)	465. (c)	466. (d)	467. (d)	468. (a)
469. (d)	470. (d)	471. (d)	472. (c)	473. (c)	474. (d)
475. (a)	476. (c)	477. (c)	478. (a)	479. (b)	480. (d)
481. (b)	482. (c)	483. (b)	484. (b)	485. (b)	486. (c)
487. (c)	488. (c)	489. (a)	490. (a)	491. (c)	492. (d)
493. (a)	494. (c)	495. (c)	496. (a)	497. (b)	498. (a)
499. (c)	500. (c)	501. (a)	502. (b)	503. (b)	504. (c)
505. (a)	506. (b)	507. (d)	508. (c)	509. (d)	510. (b)
511. (c)	512. (b)	513. (d)	514. (c)	515. (d)	516. (b)
517. (d)	518. (d)	519. (a)	520. (b)	521. (d)	522. (d)
523. (b)	524. (a)	525. (c)	526. (a)	527. (c)	528. (c)
529. (a)	530. (d)	531. (d)	532. (c)	533. (c)	534. (d)
535. (c)	536. (d)	537. (a)	538. (d)	539. (b)	540. (c)
541. (b)	542. (c)	543. (c)	544. (a)	545. (d)	546. (d)

2

Financial and Management Accounting

1. Which English alphabet is similar to the shape of an account?
   (a) H (b) I
   (c) T (d) None
2. How many sides does an account have?
   (a) One (b) Two
   (c) Three (d) None
3. Where are all the transactions of a particular account recorded?
   (a) Under more than two accounts
   (b) Under the particular account
   (c) Under any account
   (d) None of the above
4. Ledger contains various _____ in it.
   (a) entries (b) accounts
   (c) transactions (d) None of these
5. The ______ in a ledger helps in locating the accounts contained in it.
   (a) pages (b) serial number
   (c) folio (d) None of these
6. The process of transfer of entries from day book to ledgers is called
   (a) Transaction
   (b) Simple posting
   (c) Ledger posting
   (d) Journal posting
7. Ledger is also called
   (a) Cash books
   (b) Subsidiary book
   (c) Principal book of accounts
   (d) None of the above
8. The pages of ledger are consecutively
   (a) Colored (b) Numbered
   (c) Printed (d) None of these
9. The book which all accounts of the firm are maintained is known as
   (a) Journal (b) Daybook
   (c) Cash book (d) Ledger
10. Which of the following is not the basic objective of preparing ledger?
    (a) To know financial position of the business.
    (b) To known debtors and creditors of the business.
    (c) To know whether proprietor has sold his house.
    (d) To know effect of common transactions of the business.
11. Overcasting of purchases journal would affect
    (a) Supplier's account and purchase account
    (b) Sales account
    (c) Purchase account
    (d) None of the above
12. Sales to Benson ₹ 500 posted to his account as ₹ 50 would affect
    (a) Benson's account
    (b) Cash account
    (c) Sales account
    (d) None of the above
13. Sales to Mr. Gill recorded in purchase journal would affect

(a) Sales account
(b) Purchases account and Mr. Gill's account
(c) Sales account, Purchases account and Mr. Gill's account
(d) None of the above

14. Purchases made on credit not recorded at all would affect
(a) Supplier's account
(b) Purchases account and supplier's account
(c) Purchases account
(d) None of the above

15. Amount paid to Gagan posted to the credit side of his account would affect
(a) Cash account and Gagan's account
(b) Gagan's account
(c) Cash account
(d) None of the above

16. Amount received from Sita Ram posted to the credit of Mela Ram would affect
(a) Mela Ram's account
(b) Sita Ram's account and Mela Ram's account
(c) Sita Ram's account
(d) None of the above

17. A separate journal is kept for
(a) all type of transactions.
(b) each type of transactions which are repetitive in nature and sufficiently large in number.
(c) each transaction.
(d) None of the above.

18. Any donation received for a specific purpose is a
(a) Assets (b) Liability
(c) Capital receipts (d) Revenue receipts

19. Cash book contains
(a) all receipts only.
(b) all payments only.
(c) all receipts and payments of cash.
(d) All of the above.

20. Journal proper is meant for recording
(a) return of goods.
(b) all such transactions for which no special journal has been kept by the business.
(c) credit purchase of fixed assets.
(d) None of the above.

21. Purchase journal is kept to record
(a) all credit purchases.
(b) all purchases of goods.
(c) all credit purchases of goods.
(d) None of the above.

22. Sales journal is used to record
(a) credit sales of assets.
(b) credit sales of goods.
(c) cash sales.
(d) None of the above.

23. Expenditure incurred by a publisher for acquiring copyrights is a
(a) Reserve expenditure
(b) Deferred reserve expenditure
(c) Capital expenditure
(d) None of the above

24. Which one of the following should be considered a revenue expenditure?
(a) Loss of ₹ 10,000 incurred in increasing the sitting accomodation of a hotel.
(b) ₹ 1000 paid for the execution of a new plant.
(c) Repair to machinery purchased, second hand.
(d) Damage paid on account of breach of a contract to supply certain goods.

25. Which one of the following is a capital expenditure?
(a) Royalty paid in instalments for the purchase of rights to manufacture and sell patient medicines.

(b) Compensation paid to Directors on termination of their services.
(c) Expenditure incurred in connection with the renewal of a Trade Mark.
(d) Gratuities paid to Directors on termination of their services.

26. Amount spent on an advertisement campaign, the benefit of which is likely to last for three years is a
(a) Revenue expenditure
(b) Capital revenue expenditure
(c) Contingent expenditure
(d) Deferred revenue expenditure

27. Which one of the following is capital expenditure?
(a) Purchase of raw material
(b) Purchase of a delivery van
(c) Cost of advertisement
(d) Purchase of machine oil

28. Which one of the following will be treated as revenue expenditure?
(a) Interest paid on loan during the construction of works.
(b) Cost incurred for a new exit as required under the local bodies by laws.
(c) A dealer in purchasing sewing machines and spends some money on the repair of ten machines damaged while in transit.
(d) Cost of pulling down an old building as also the payment made to the architect for the plan of a new building.

29. Revenue is generally recognised as being earned at that point of time when
(a) production is completed
(b) debts are collected
(c) sale is effected
(d) cash is received

30. Expenditure incurred on research is an example of
(a) revenue expenditure.
(b) deferred revenue expenditure.
(c) partly capital expenditure are partly revenue expenditure.
(d) capital expenditure.

31. Payment of compensation to a worker who has been dicharged from service is a
(a) revenue expenditure.
(b) capital expenditure.
(c) non-business expenditure.
(d) referred revenue expenditure.

32. Goods sold for cash is an example of
(a) Revenue (b) Expenses
(c) Loss (d) Liability

33. Salaries paid is an example of
(a) Assets (b) Loss
(c) Expenses (d) Revenue

34. Income is the excess of _____ over.
(a) expenses/revenue
(b) revenue/expenses
(c) profit/less
(d) assets/liabilities

35. Goods sold on credit ₹ 50,000 is the example of
(a) Loss (b) Expenses
(c) Profit (d) Revenue

36. Current assets include
(a) Machinery (b) Furniture
(c) Bills receivable (d) Bills payable

37. Which of the following is a non-current liability?
(a) Loan
(b) Debtors
(c) Prepaid insurance
(d) Stock

38. Cash received from debtors would be deemed as of funds.

(a) Uses (b) Gain
(c) No flow (d) Sources

39. If net profit is ₹ 90,000 after writing off preliminary expenses of ₹ 10,000, then the funds from operation will be
(a) ₹ 10,000 (b) ₹ 100,000
(c) ₹ 90,000 (d) ₹ 80,000

40. If net profit is ₹ 20,000 after writing off goodwill ₹ 2000 and loss on sale of plant ₹ 4000, funds from operation will be
(a) ₹ 24,000 (b) ₹ 26,000
(c) ₹ 20,000 (d) ₹ 22,000

41. If net profit is ₹ 30,000 after writing off goodwill ₹ 6000 and depreciation on furniture ₹ 2000, fund from operation will be
(a) ₹ 32,000 (b) ₹ 36,000
(c) ₹ 38,000 (d) ₹ 26,000

42. Purchase of typewriter would result in ______ of fund.
(a) service (b) no flow
(c) change (d) application

43. Generally the term fund is used to mean the difference between
(a) Profit and loss A/C and Balance sheet
(b) Current assets and current liabilities
(c) Current liabilities and non-current liabilities
(d) Current assets and non-current liabilities

44. If the change, because of a business transaction results in the increase of fund then the transactions responsible for such a change is said to be
(a) schedule of change in working capital
(b) uses of fund
(c) funds flow statements
(d) source of fund

45. If the total of services of fund equals ₹ 50,000 and total of applications of funds equals ₹ 30,000 then the net increase in working capital will be to the extent of
(a) ₹ 80,000 (b) ₹ 20,000
(c) ₹ 30,000 (d) ₹ 50,000

46. If a particular current asset in the current year is more than what was in the previous year, then the change in the current assets results in ______ of working capital.
(a) increase (b) zero
(c) decrease (d) None of these

47. If the gross profit is ₹ 30,000 and the expenses resulting in the application of funds are ₹ 7000 then fund from operation will be
(a) ₹ 30,000 (b) ₹ 7000
(c) ₹ 23,000 (d) ₹ 37,000

48. Any gain on the sale of non-current assets should be from the net profit and the loss must be to the net profit in determining fund from operation
(a) deducted, deducted
(b) added, reduced
(c) added, added
(d) deducted, added

49. Given Net profit during the year ₹ 25000: debtors in the beginning ₹ 75000 and debtors of the end ₹ 10,000? What would be the amount of cash from operation?
(a) ₹ 22,500 (b) ₹ 32.500
(c) ₹ 25.000 (d) ₹ 34,000

50. C and D are equal partners. Their capital balances on dissolution of the firm are ₹ 25,000 and ₹ 15,000 respectively. Total cash available is ₹ –30,000
How should this cash be distributed between C and D?
(a) ₹ 20,000 to C and ₹ 10,000 to D
(b) ₹ 18,750 to C and ₹ 11,250 to C
(c) ₹ 15,000 each
(d) All of the above

51. A and B are partners in the ratio of 2 : 1. They admit C for 1/4 share who contributes for ₹ 3000 for his share of goodwill. The total value of goodwill of the firm is
(a) ₹ 1200 (b) ₹ 15,000
(c) ₹ 3000 (d) ₹ 9000

52. Goodwill of a firm of A and B is valued at ₹ 30,000. It is appearing in the books at ₹ 12,000. C is admitted for 1/4 share, what amount he is supposed to bring for goodwill?
(a) ₹ 7,500 (b) ₹ 10,500
(c) ₹ 3,000 (d) ₹ 4,500

53. A and B are partners sharing profit and losses in the ratio of 2 : 5. They admit C on the condition that he will bring goodwill in cash which is distributed between A and B. C's share in future profit or loss is to be one fourth. The new profit sharing ratio of A, B and C will be
(a) 7 : 6 : 15 (b) 6 : 7 : 15
(c) 6 : 15 : 7 (d) 15 : 6 : 7

54. A, B and C are the partners in a business firm sharing their profits in the ratio of 4 : 3 : 2. A new partner D enters the firm. The new profit sharing ratio of A, B, C and D is 5 : 4 : 2 : 1. D contributes a goodwill of ₹ 36,000. This goodwill is to be allocated among A, B and C. Which one of the following will be the correct allocation?

	A (₹)	B (₹)	C (₹)
(a)	16,000	12,000	8,000
(b)	12,000	8,000	16,000
(c)	12,000	NIL	24,000
(d)	24,000	NIL	12,000

55. X and Y are sharing profits in the ratio of 4 : 3, Z joins and the new ratios are 7 : 4 : 3 what is sacrificing ratio?
(a) 1 : 3 (b) 3 : 9
(c) 1 : 2 (d) 2 : 6

56. One of the consequences of non-registration of partnership firm is that
(a) The partner of such a firm cannot sue third parties.
(b) A partner cannot sue the other partner to enforce a right arising from a contract.
(c) The official assignee or receiver will have no power on the property of the dissolved firm.
(d) Third parties cannot sue the firm for claims exceeding ₹ 100.

57. A, B and C were partners sharing profits and losses in the ratio of 2 : 2 : 1. A retires, B and C purchase share of A by paying ₹ 30,000 and ₹ 40,000. What is new profit sharing ratio
(a) 3 : 4 (b) 1 : 2
(c) 4 : 3 (d) 2 : 1

58. A, B and C were partners sharing profits in the ratio of 3 : 5 : 7. C retires and his share were taken up by A and B in the ratio of 3 : 2. What is new ratio?
(a) 6 : 7 (b) 7 : 6
(c) 13 : 12 (d) 2 : 13

59. A and B are partners. A's capital is ₹ 10,000 and B's capital is ₹ 6,000. Interest is payable @6% p.a. B is entitled to a salary of ₹ 300 per month. Profit for the current year before interest and salary to B is ₹ 8000. Divide the profit between A and B.
(a) ₹ 1270 and ₹ 1270
(b) ₹ 1720 and ₹ 1720
(c) ₹ 4150 and ₹ 4150
(d) ₹ 8000 and ₹ 8000

60. A and B are partners sharing profits in proportion of 3:2 with capitals of ₹ 40,000 and ₹ 30,000 respectively. Interest on capital is agreed at 5% p.a. B is to be allowed an annual salary of ₹ 3,000 which has not been withdrawn.

During 1999, the profits for the year prior to calculation of interest on Capital but after charging B's salary amounted to ₹ 12,000. A provision of 5% of this amount is to be made in respect of commission to the manager.

What is the amount of manager's commission?

(a) ₹ 800 (b) ₹ 900
(c) ₹ 600 (d) ₹ 700

61. A partnership firm earned net profit during the last three years as follows

Year	Net Profit ₹
1983	17,000
1984	20,000
1985	23,000

The capital invested in the firm throughout the above mentioned period has been ₹ 80,000. Having regard to the risk involved, 15% is considered to be a fair return on the Capital.

What is the value of goodwill on the basis of 2 year's purchase of average super profits earned during the above mentioned three years?

(a) ₹ 16,000 (b) ₹ 15,000
(c) ₹ 14,000 (d) ₹ 13,000

62. A firm earns a profit of ₹ 15,000 per year. In the same business a 10% return is generally expected. The total assets of the firm are ₹ 1,70,000. The value of other liabilities is ₹ 60,000. What is the value of goodwill?

(a) ₹ 40,000 (b) ₹ 50,000
(c) ₹ 20,000 (d) ₹ 30,000

63. The equation for the debit equity ratio is

(a) Current Assets/Current Liability
(b) Long term Debit/Equity Capital
(c) Liquid Assets/Current Liability
(d) Net Profit/Net Sales

64. Which one of the following is correct about margin of safety ratio?

(a) Operating Profit/Contribution
(b) Contribution/Sales of BEP
(c) Capital Employ/Net Worth
(d) Contribution/Sales Value

65. Modern Leasing Co. Ltd. has debt equity ratio 8:1. It has decided to issue bonus shares in the ratio of 1:1. The debt equity ratio after the issue would be

(a) 1:8 (b) 1:4
(c) 8:1 (d) 4:1

66. Which one of the following ratio is the indicator of the long term solvency of the firm?

(a) Time interest earned ratio
(b) Acid test ratio
(c) Debt equity ratio
(d) None of the above

67. To test the liquidity of a firm concern which of the following ratios are useful?

(a) Inventory turnover ratio
(b) Bad Debit to sales ratio
(c) Capital turnover ratio
(d) Acid turnover ratio

68. If earning per share of X Limited is ₹ 15 and the price earnings ratio of other similar companies is ₹ 10, then the market value of the share of ₹ X Ltd. will be

(a) ₹ 75 (b) ₹ 25
(c) ₹ 300 (d) ₹ 150

69. Which one in the following is least suited for measuring return on investment?

(a) Operating income ratio, Total assets turnover.
(b) Net income after interest but before taxes, average total shareholders equity.
(c) Income.
(d) Net operating income before interest and taxes, average total assets.

70. Given in the following table is data for various companies in the same industry

	A	B	C	D
Current Assets	150	140	100	120
A/C Receivable	60	50	50	70
A/C Receivable	65	50	55	50
Current Liabilities	100	120	80	130

The two firms which appear to be having better liquidity position are

(a) A and C (b) B and D
(c) A and B (d) B and C

71. Consider the following financial information in respect of two companies namely 'M' Co. and 'Z' Co.

Items of Assets and Liabilities	'M' Co. (₹)	'Z' Co. (₹)
Current Assets	7,50,000	7,50,000
Closing Inventory	3,00,000	2,50,000
Goodwill	5,00,000	3,50,000
Current Liabilities	3,00,000	5,00,000

Based on the above data, acid test ratio of 'M' Co. in comparison to 'Z' Co. is

(a) Equal (b) Lower
(c) Indeterminate (d) Higher

72. Redeemable preference shares is
(a) Current assets
(b) Non-current assets
(c) Current liability
(d) Non-current liability

73. For the purpose of calculating ROI capital employed means
(a) Current Assets – Current Liabilities
(b) Net Fixed Assets
(c) Fixed Assets + Current Assets – Current Liabilities
(d) Gross Block

74. Given that the net profit for a certain year of Company 'X' Ltd. is ₹ 1,23,000, equity-share capital for the same period is ₹ 10,00,000 and reserve and surplus is ₹ 2,30,000, the rate of return on owner fund would be
(a) 10%
(b) 9.98%
(c) 12.3%
(d) None of the above

75. Consider the following data.

Fixed Costs = ₹ 40,000
Variable Costs = ₹ 30,000
Rate of Income Tax = 30%
Return on Capital Employed = 10%

Based on the above data the sales volume required to increase the return on capital employed to 18% would be

(a) ₹ 8,000 (b) ₹ 8.500
(c) ₹ 5,000 (d) ₹ 7,500

76. If the rate of gross profit is 20% on cost of goods sold and the sales are ₹ 150,000 then the total gross profit would be

(a) ₹ 37,500 (b) ₹ 25,000
(c) ₹ 30,000 (d) None of these

77. Given that

Current Ratio = 2.5
Acid Test Ratio = 1.5
Net Working Capital = 60,000

The Value of Current Liabilities will be

(a) ₹ 60,000 (b) ₹ 100,000
(c) ₹ 15,000 (d) ₹ 40,000

78. Interest Coverage Ratio is given by
(a) Debt Capital/Interest on Debt
(b) Net Profit/Interest on Debt
(c) Profit before Tax/Interest on Debt
(d) Earning before Interest and Tax/Interest on Debit

79. Given that

Sales = ₹ 50,000
Variable Cost = ₹ 20,000
Fixed Cost = ₹ 10,000
Capital = ₹ 200,000

The profit value ratio will be
(a) 20% (b) 25%
(c) 60% (d) 10%

80. EBIT/Total Assets Ratio is
(a) Profitability Ratio
(b) Liquidity Ratio
(c) Turnover Ratio
(d) Solvency Ratio

81. A particular firm provided the following data for 1994
Current Ratio = 25:1
Liquid Ratio = 1.5:1
Net Working Capital = ₹ 300,000
Current Assets and Current Liabilities of this firm are respectively
(a) ₹ 300000 and ₹ 100000
(b) ₹ 500000 and ₹ 100000
(c) ₹ 500000 and ₹ 200000
(d) ₹ 300000 and ₹ 150000

82. Project Engineering Ltd. has an adverse current ratio which one of the following would improve this ratio?
(a) Collection of some of the current accounts receivables.
(b) Sale of fixed assets for cash.
(c) Collection from sundry debtors.
(d) Use of cash to pay off some long term debts.

83. Given that the current ratio is 2:1 if the net working capital is ₹ 60,600, then the amount of current liabilities would be
(a) ₹ 121,200 (b) ₹ 90,900
(c) ₹ 30,300 (d) ₹ 60,600

84. Given that

Fixed Assets	₹ 10,00,000
Current Assets	₹ 600,000
Total Net Profit	₹ 2,60,000
Current Liabilities	₹ 300,000

Which one of the following will be the correct ROI?
(a) 0% (b) 35%
(c) 23% (d) 14.5%

85. If the stock turnover ratio is 4 times and the collection period is 30 days the operating cycle would be
(a) 90 days (b) 120 days
(c) 30 days (d) 60 days

86. Given that

Closing Stock	₹ 30,000
Opening Stock	₹ 20,000
Sales	₹ 100,000
Administrative and Selling Expenses	₹ 20,000
Purchases	₹ 70,000

The operating ratio is
(a) 75% (b) 80%
(c) 50% (d) 65%

87. When sales is ₹ 4,80,000, gross loss is 25% on cost, purchases is ₹ 3,50,000 and closing stock is ₹ 60,000, the stock in the begining would be
(a) ₹ 1,34,000 (b) ₹ 350,000
(c) ₹ 70,000 (d) ₹ 94,000

88. Which one of the following statements is not correct? A high gross profit margin ratio is the result of
(a) an increase in the proportionate volume of higher margin items.
(b) higher sales prices, cost of goods sold remaining constant.
(c) income in the sales return, cost of goods sold remaining the same.
(d) lower cost of goods sold, sales price remaining constant.

89. Collection of debtors would
(a) decrease current ratio
(b) increase current ratio
(c) increase debtors turnover
(d) no effect on current ratio

90. The stock turnover ratio may be calculated as

(a) $\dfrac{\text{Turnover at cost}}{\text{stock at cost}}$

(b) $\dfrac{\text{Turnover at selling price}}{\text{stock at selling price}}$

(c) $\dfrac{\text{Cost of goods sold}}{\text{Average stock}}$

(d) Any of the above

91. Credit sales of a company during the year are ₹ 1,20,000, debtors ₹ 20,000 and bills receivable ₹ 10,000. The average collection period is
(a) 5 months (b) 6 months
(c) 3 months (d) 4 months

92. The ratios which measure relative contribution of financing by owners and financing provided by outsiders are called
(a) Leverage Ratio
(b) Liquidity Ratio
(c) Profitability Ratio
(d) Activity Ratio

93. Financial indicators of four companies are as follows:

Company	Current Ratio	Debt Equity Ratio	Rate of return on invest	Fixed Assets Turnover
P	2.0:1	215:1	10%	5
Q	2.5:1	3.0:1	25%	4
R	1.5:1	4.0:1	20%	3
S	1.0:1	3.5:1	15%	2

In general which of the above companies would fall in the highest risk class?
(a) R and S (b) P and S
(c) P and Q (d) Q and R

94. Identify the formula that is used to calculate the test capital turnover ratio
(a) Credit Sales/Net Worth
(b) Credit Sales/Capital Employed
(c) Net Sales/Capital Employed
(d) Net Sales/Average Accounts Payable

95. Identify the item that is not taken into account in computing the current ratio.
(a) Bank (b) Cash
(c) Bank overdraft (d) Stock

96. The stock turnover ratio is
(a) Activity ratio
(b) Financial ratio
(c) Profitability ratio
(d) Solvency ratio

97. The operating ratio is obtained by dividing cost of goods sold plus operating expenses by
(a) Current Assets (b) Fixed Assets
(c) Net Sales (d) Net Purchases

98. The return on equity, capital ratio is obtained by dividing net profit (after tax) less preference dividend by
(a) Total Capital
(b) Equity Capital
(c) Current Liabilities
(d) Current Assets

99. The net profit ratio is the ratio of net profit to
(a) Net credit sales
(b) Net cash sales
(c) Capital employed
(d) Net total sales

100. The gross profit ratio is the ratio of gross profit to
(a) Closing stock (b) Net total sales
(c) Net cash sales (d) Net credit sales

101. If the current ratio stands at 2:1 an equal increase in current assets and current liabilities would _____ the current ratio.
(a) cause fluctuations in
(b) not change
(c) increase
(d) decrease

102. Identify the formula that is used to calculate the return on equity capital ratio

(a) $\dfrac{\text{Net profit after taxes + Interest}}{\text{Capital employed}}$

(b) $\dfrac{\text{Net profit after taxes + preference dividend}}{\text{Equity shareholders funds}}$

(c) $\dfrac{\text{Divident per share}}{\text{Earning per share}}$

(d) $\dfrac{\text{Net profit}}{\text{Capital employed}}$

103. Which of the following is the test of the long term liquidity of a business?
(a) Stock turnover ratio
(b) Interest coverage ratio
(c) Current ratio
(d) Operating ratio

104. The sale of inventory on account will cause the quick ratio to
(a) Not change (b) Become zero
(c) Decrease (d) Increase

105. In the computation of the debtors turnover ratio accounts receivable includes
(a) Creditors and B/P
(b) Debtors and B/R
(c) Debtors and creditors
(d) Bank overdraft and loan

106. In the debt equity ratio, equity referes to
(a) only equity capital
(b) both preference equality capitals plus all reserves
(c) only preference capital
(d) only reserves

107. What does the return total assets take into account?
(a) Shareholder's fund
(b) Income before tax and interest on fixed liability
(c) Total outside liability
(d) Income after taxation

108. What does the ROI take into account?
(a) Shareholder's investment
(b) Net fixed assets
(c) Operating expenses
(d) Net worth

109. The collection period of the ratio between
(a) 365/Debtors turnover
(b) 240/Debtors turnover
(c) 120/Debtors turnover
(d) 90/Debtors turnover

110. In case of a limited company, the term financial statements includes
(a) Balance sheet
(b) Profit and loss and balance sheet
(c) Profit and loss account, profit and loss appropriation account and balance sheet
(d) None of the above

111. The assets of a business can be classified as
(a) Only current assets
(b) Fixed and current assets
(c) Only fixed assets
(d) None of the above

112. The term fixed assets includes
(a) Cash
(b) Payment in advances
(c) Furniture
(d) Stock in trade

113. The term current assets includes
(a) temporary investments
(b) cash surrender value of life insurance
(c) long term investments
(d) None of the above

114. The term current assets does not include
(a) bill receivable
(b) long term depressed changes
(c) payment in advance
(d) None of the above

115. Price-earning ratio is equal to market price per equity share divided by

(a) liquid assets
(b) earning per share
(c) current assets
(d) current liabilities

116. Dividing the net profit by the paid up amount equity sharecapital yields
(a) earning per share
(b) rate of return on equity share capital
(c) temporary investment
(d) None of the above

117. Return on total assets ratio is equal to divided by total assets is
(a) net income before preference dividend and interest paid
(b) current liabilities
(c) earning per share
(d) current assets

118. Acid test ratio is equal to quick current assets divided by
(a) total liabilities
(b) total assets
(c) current liabilities
(d) current assets

119. Acid test ratio should normally be
(a) 1:1 (b) 2:1
(c) 2:2 (d) 1:2

120. If cost of goods sold is ₹ 100,000, other; operating expenses are ₹ 20,000 and total net sales are ₹ 150,000 the operating ratio will be equal to
(a) 70% (b) 100%
(c) 70% (d) 80%

121. If income after taxation is ₹ 6 lakhs, the amount of taxation being ₹ 1 lakh and the total of shareholders fund being ₹ 18 lakhs, the return on shareholders fund is equal to
(a) 75% (b) 100%
(c) 33% (d) 50%

122. Given that fixed assets are at ₹ 600,000 current assets ₹ 400,000 share capital ₹ 500,000, fixed liabilities ₹ 2,50,000, current liabilities ₹ 2,50,000, the solvency ratio will be
(a) 40% (b) 50%
(c) 20% (d) 30%

123. Given that current liabilities are at ₹ 300,000, current ratio is 3:1 and quick ratio is 1:1, the value of stock will be
(a) ₹ 900,000 (b) ₹ 12,00,000
(c) ₹ 300,000 (d) ₹ 1,600,000

124. The issue of equity capital in exchange of plant and machinery will cause the return on equity capital to
(a) Decrease
(b) Fluctuate
(c) Remain unchanged
(d) Increase

125. In the calculation of return on shareholders investments the referred investment deals with
(a) preference and equity capital only
(b) all appropriations
(c) all reserves
(d) All of the above

126. Gross profit is a ____ ratio.
(a) liquid (b) solvency
(c) activity (d) profitability

127. The return on investment (ROI) may be calculated as

(a) $\dfrac{\text{Net profit} - \text{preference divident}}{\text{No. of equity shares}}$

(b) $\dfrac{\text{Return on Investment}}{\text{Net profit ratio}}$

(c) $\dfrac{\text{Net profit before interest, tax and dividend}}{\text{Capital employed}}$

(d) $\dfrac{\text{Net profit after interest, tax and dividend}}{\text{Shareholder's fund}}$

128. The satisfactory ratio between internal and external equity is
(a) 3 : 1 (b) 4 : 1
(c) 1 : 1 (d) 2 : 1

129. The satisfactory ratio between share holder's funds and long terms loan is
(a) 3 : 1 (b) 4 : 1
(c) 1 : 1 (d) 2 : 1

130. The ideal ratio between total long term funds and total long terms loan is
(a) 2 : 1 (b) 1 : 1
(c) 4 : 1 (d) 3 : 1

131. The net income of the company should ideally be ______ times of the fixed internal charges.
(a) 5 or 6 (b) 6 or 7
(c) 3 or 4 (d) 4 or 5

132. In the debt equity ratio,external equity refers to
(a) debentures and current liability
(b) only debentures
(c) reserve
(d) only current liabilities

133. What does creditors turnover ratio take into account?
(a) Total credit purchase
(b) Total credit sales
(c) Total cash purchases
(d) Total cash sales

Given: Average stock ₹ 20,000, closing stock ₹ 2000 more than the opening stock.

134. What is the amount of opening stock?
(a) ₹ 21,000 (b) ₹ 22,000
(c) ₹ 19,000 (d) ₹ 20,000

135. What is the amount of closing stock?
(a) ₹ 20,000 (b) ₹ 21,000
(c) ₹ 18,000 (d) ₹ 19,000

136. Identify the formula that is used to calculate the reserve to capital ratio
(a) Reserve/Capital
(b) Capital/Loan
(c) Debts/Equity
(d) Debenture/Capital

For Q. 137-141, use the following information

Trading and Profit and Loss Account

	₹		₹
To opening stock	43,500	By sale	–2,25,00
To purchases	1,83,000	By closing stock	–46,500
To gross profit c/d	45,000		
	2,71,500		2,71,500
To standing expenses	–24,000	By gross profit b/d	
To net profit	–24,000		
	45,000		45,000

Balance Sheet

Liabilities	₹	Assets	₹
Equity share capital	21,10,000	Fixed assets	1,65,000
Current reserve	15,000	Current assets	
Profit + loss A/C	21,000	Stock	46,500
Bills payable	10,500	Sundry debtors	24,000
Creditors	45,000	Bank	66,000
	3,01,500		3,01,500

137. What is gross profit ratio?
(a) 30% (b) 40%
(c) 10% (d) 20%

138. What is proprietary ratio?
(a) .100 times (b) .102 times
(c) .92 times (d) .82 times

139. What is debtors turnover ratio?
(a) 8.38 times (b) 9.38 times
(c) 6.38 times (d) 7.38 times

140. What is current ratio?
(a) 4.46 times (b) 5.46 times
(c) 2.46 times (d) 3.46 times

141. What is stock turnover ratio?
(a) 5 times (b) 6 times
(c) 3 times (d) 4 times

142. Identify the item which is not an operating expenses.
(a) General management salaries
(b) Advertising expenses
(c) Loss on sale of motor car
(d) Depreciation of office equipment

143. Identify the item that is not taken into account in computing the current ratio.
(a) Bank (b) Cas
(c) Bills recoverable (d) Land

144. What does the 'net worth' of a business signify?
(a) Current – total liabilities
(b) Total assets
(c) Total assets – total liabilities
(d) Fixed assets – current assets

Given: Total credit sales – 7,30,000
Debtors – 100,000
Bills – 72,000

145. What is average daily credit sales?
(a) 4000 (b) 5000
(c) 2000 (d) 3000

146. What is average collection period?
(a) 112 days (b) 180 days
(c) 86 days (d) 96 days

147. The firm is said to be more geared, if equity capital is more than the debentures and
(a) Reserve
(b) Preference share capital
(c) Total assets
(d) Loan

148. Proprietary ratio indicates the relationship between proprietor's funds and
(a) Share capital (b) Debentures
(c) Reserve (d) Total assets

149. If the rate of gross profit is 25% on cost by goods sold and the sales are ₹ 200,000, the amount of profit will be
(a) ₹ 45,000 (b) ₹ 50,000
(c) ₹ 40,000 (d) None of these

150. Payment of interim dividend is a
(a) No flow of fund
(b) Service of fund
(c) Application of fund
(d) All of the above

151. The fund as used in funds flow statement means
(a) current assets
(b) current liabilities
(c) current assets minus current liabilities
(d) cash

152. If the profit is 25% of the cost price then it is
(a) 33% of the sale price.
(b) 20% of the sale price.
(c) 125% of the sale price.
(d) 30% of the sale price.

153. Payment of a liability result in
(a) decrease in total assets.
(b) no change in total assets.
(c) increase in total assets.
(d) None of the above.

154. Which of the following are current assets?
(a) Account receivable
(b) Bank loan for three years
(c) Debenture sinking fund investments
(d) Long-term investment

155. Which one in the following statements is correct?
(a) An increase in current liabilities causes a decrease in the working capital.
(b) A decrease in current liabilities causes an increase in the working capital.
(c) An increase in the current assets cause a decrease in the working capital.
(d) A decrease in the current assets an increase in the working capital.

156. For the purpose of analysing changes in financial position, enterprises prepare
   (a) cash flow statement and fund flow statement.
   (b) balance sheet and profit and loss A/C.
   (c) statement of changes in working capital and statement of cash from operations.
   (d) statement of cash from operation and balance sheet.

157. Which one of the following pairs is not correctly matched?
   (a) Increase in current liability: Service of fund
   (b) Increase in working capital: Application of fund
   (c) Issues of bonus share: Service of fund
   (d) Issues of share: Service of fund

158. Wages paid on the erection of a new machinery should be debited to
   (a) Profit and Loss account
   (b) Wages account
   (c) Cash account
   (d) Machinery account

159. While making an adjusting entry in respect of closing stock we debit
   (a) Trading account
   (b) Closing stock
   (c) Profit or loss account
   (d) Purchases account

160. Prepaid expenses appearing in trial balance will appear in
   (a) Depreciation account
   (b) Balance sheet
   (c) Profit and Loss account
   (d) Trading account

161. An estimate of future bad debts is known as a
   (a) Bad receivable
   (b) Doubtful Debts
   (c) Reserve/provision for doubtful/bad receivable
   (d) Debtors

162. Whilemaking theadjusting entry in respect of depreciation _____ account is credited.
   (a) asset (b) stock
   (c) liabilities (d) None of these

163. Expenses which remain unpaid at the end of the according period are termed as _____ expenses.
   (a) recoverable (b) reserve
   (c) outstanding (d) None of these

164. Expenses which have been paid in the accounting year for non accounting period are termed as _____ expenses.
   (a) prepaid (b) reserve
   (c) postpaid (d) asset

165. Cost of goods sold = purchases + stock _____ + direct expenses – stock _____.
   (a) closing, valued
   (b) opening, closing
   (c) closing opening
   (d) opening, valued

166. How would you classify 'cash'?
   (a) Fixed liability
   (b) Fixed assets
   (c) Current liability
   (d) Current assets

167. Into what kind of asset should goodwill be classified?
   (a) Current (b) Floating
   (c) Intangible (d) Liquid

168. Which of the following transactions results in increase of assets and increase in owner's equity?
   (a) A dividend is decreased
   (b) Bonus shares issued
   (c) Shares issued for cash
   (d) All of the above

169. If a business had liability totalling ₹ 25,000 and owner's equity to ₹ 10,000 the assets will be
(a) ₹ 15,000 (b) ₹ 40,000
(c) ₹ 25,000 (d) None of these

170. Which is the adjustment entry for interest on capital?
(a) Capital A/C Dr.
To interest A/C
(b) InterestA/C Dr.
To capital A/C
(c) Capital A/C Dr.
To interest on capital
(d) Interest on capital A/C Dr.
To capital A/C

171. How would the date of balance sheet be properly worked?
(a) As on Dec. 31,1999
(b) Fortheyearended Dec. 31,1999
(c) Dec. 31,1999
(d) None of the above

172. Purchase of office items like table and chair would result in
(a) increase in assets.
(b) increase in capital.
(c) decrease in capital.
(d) decrease in liabilities.

173. _____ is a normal account which aims at determining the cost of production of finished goods manufactured during particular period of time.
(a) Manufacturing account
(b) Trading account
(c) Balance sheet
(d) Profit or loss account

174. _____ is the excess of cost of goods sold over sale price of goods.
(a) Net profit (b) Net loss
(c) Gross loss (d) Gross profit

175. _______ is the excess of selling price over the cost price of goods sold plus direct expenses.
(a) Net profit (b) Gross profit
(c) Gross loss (d) Net loss

176. The balance of the petty cash is
(a) An asset (b) A liability
(c) An expense (d) An income

177. Fixed assets are
(a) meant for resale.
(b) kept in the business for use over a long period of time for earning income.
(c) liabilities + current assets.
(d) meant for conversion into cash as quickly as possible.

178. Stock is
(a) intangible.
(b) included in the category of fixed assets.
(c) tangible.
(d) part of current assets.

179. Closing stock is valued at
(a) market value
(b) cost or market price whichever is lower
(c) cost
(d) None of the above

180. A balance sheet is
(a) loss of assets and liabilities.
(b) statement sharing the distribution of profit.
(c) trading account.
(d) trial balance.

181. The balance sheet is a _____ of the assets, liabilities and capital of a concern as on particular date.
(a) picture (b) balance
(c) statement (d) document

182. A gross profit is transferred to the _____ side of the profit and loss account.
(a) current (b) debit
(c) credits (d) None of these

183. Capital is the excess of _____ over _____
(a) liabilities, assets to outsider
(b) liabilities, assets
(c) revenue, expenses
(d) assets, liabilities to outsider

184. Net assets of a business on January 1 and January 31 are ₹ 10,000 and ₹ 12,000 respectively. If the owner had invested ₹ 1,000 during January, find the net income for January.
(a) ₹ 1,000 (b) ₹ 2,000
(c) ₹ 3,000 (d) None of these

185. Purchase of a car priced at ₹ 300,000 at term ₹ 30,000 cash and the balance in 12 equal monthly instalments results in
(a) decrease in total assets
(b) increase in total assets
(c) creation of fictitious assets
(d) no change in total assets

186. Which of the following statement is correct?
(a) The work of book-keeping is usually entrusted to junior employees.
(b) Function of the book-keeping is performed by the book-keeper.
(c) Book-keeping is very old.
(d) All of the above.

187. "Accounting is the art of recording, classifying and summarising in a significant manner and in terms of money, transactions and events which are of a financial character and interpreting the results thereof." This definition is
(a) J. Betty
(b) Gestonburg
(c) American Institute of Certified Public Accountants
(d) None of the above

188. Accounting principles are divided into two types. These are
(a) Accounting Concepts
(b) Accounting Conventions
(c) Both (a) and (b)
(d) Accounting Standard

189. Accounting is the language of
(a) Accountant
(b) Business
(c) Books of Accounts
(d) None of the above

190. Which of the following is not included under Accounting Concepts?
(a) Business Entity Concept
(b) Continuity Concept
(c) Money Measurement Concept
(d) None of the above

191. Which of the following errors will not affect the trial balance?
(a) Purchase returns book for December was overcast by ₹ 200.
(b) Sales book c/f ₹ 2200 instead of ₹ 2000.
(c) Goods for ₹ 300 purchased on cash, expenses account was debited instead of purchase account.
(d) None of the above.

192. Which of the following items is not taken in to account while computing current ratio?
(a) Sundry debtors (b) Overdraft
(c) Sundry creditors (d) Furniture

193. Which of the following is not related with money measurement concept?
(a) Business is treated as separate from the proprietor.
(b) All business transaction should be expressed only in money.
(c) The transactions which cannot be expressed in money, will not be recorded in accounting books.
(d) Only (c).

194. Which of the following is not an example of money measurement concept?
(a) Labour management relation
(b) Sales promotion policy

(c) Labour unrest
(d) All of these

195. Which of the following equation is related with dual aspect concept?
(a) Capital = Total Assets – Outsider's Liabilities
(b) Total Assets = Total Liabilities
(c) Total Assets = Capital + Outsider's Liabilities
(d) All of the above

196. Which expenses is a capital nature?
(a) Salary (b) Stationary
(c) Depreciation (d) Wages

197. Depreciation is a charge against
(a) Company (b) Books of A/c
(c) Profit (d) Assets

198. General reserve created from
(a) revenue profit (b) capital profit
(c) only profit (d) by sale of assets

199. Profit from sale of assets is example for
(a) capital profit (b) revenue profit
(c) loss (d) None of these

200. Dividend can be declared from
(a) secret reserve (b) revenue profit
(c) capital profit (d) All of the above

201. "Fixed assets are valued according to cost, if you have to settle their worth, is it more? Is it less? We leave you to guess. If you can, can you value the earth?"
(a) Anthony (b) T.G. Tokhey
(c) Anonymous (d) G. Betty

202. The term current assets does not include
(a) B/R (b) Debtors
(c) Goodwill (d) Stock

203. The term fixed assets does not include
(a) Furniture
(b) Plant
(c) Land and Building
(d) Prepaid expenses

204. If the total assets of a company amount to ₹ 1,50,000 and owner's equity is ₹ 70,000, the amount of liabilities will be
(a) ₹ 90,000 (b) ₹ 1,00,000
(c) ₹ 70,000 (d) ₹ 80,000

205. Balance is a statement of
(a) Capital (b) Assets
(c) Liabilities (d) All of these

206. Amount receivable by a company against credit sales are usually called
(a) Creditors (b) B/P
(c) Sundry Debtors (d) B/R

207. Owner's equity could be understood as comprising _____ and _____.
(a) retained earnings
(b) contributed capital
(c) Both (a) and (b)
(d) liabilities

208. In case of joint stock company, financial statements refer to
(a) trial balance and P & L A/c.
(b) balance sheet.
(c) balance sheet, P & L A/c and P & L appropriation A/c.
(d) profit and loss A/c.

209. Cost of sales in the case of trading company is equal to
(a) Sales – Gross Profit
(b) Opening Stock + Purchases + Incidental Expenses – Closing Stock
(c) Both (a) and (b)
(d) Sales – Closing Stock

210. Which of the following statement are true?
(a) The statement showing the result is known as Profit and Loss Account.
(b) The statement disclosing status of investment is known as Balance Sheet.

(c) The Balance Sheet comprises of a list of assets, liabilities and capital as given date.
(d) The preparation of the financial statements is the responsibility of top management.

211. Which of the following importance is provided by Balance Sheet?
(a) It is a measure of the firm's liquidity
(b) It is a measure of the firm's solvency
(c) It gives a concise summary of the concern's resources and liabilities and owner's equity
(d) All of the above

212. Which one of the following is not an example of intangible assets?
(a) Sologan
(b) Patents and Trade Marks
(c) Land
(d) Copyright

213. Cost of intangible fixed assets are _____ over their useful lives.
(a) amortised (b) depreciated
(c) allocated (d) charged

214. Which one of the equation is a correct?
(a) Total Assets = Total Liabilities + Owner's equity
(b) Total Assets = Current Liabilities
(c) Total Assets = Long-term Liabilities
(d) Total Asset = Fixed Assets

215. Which one of the following formula would be apply for the calculation of Interest on Drawings?
(a) $\frac{\text{Amount of the drawings} \times \text{Rate of interest}}{100}$
(b) $\frac{\text{Rate of interest}}{100 \times \text{Amount of drawing}}$
(c) $\frac{\text{Total of product} \times \text{Rate of interest}}{100 \times 12}$
(d) None of the above

216. Ravi and Prem are partners in a firm. They agree to make drawings from the firm on the first day of each month as: Ravi ₹ 2,000 p.m. and from ₹ 2,500 p.m. The Interest on Drawings is charged @ 10% P.Q. The books of the firm are closed on 31st December, 2008. Calculate the interest on drawings.
(a) For Ravi ₹ 1,300
(b) For Prem ₹ 1,625
(c) Both (a) and (b)
(d) For Both ₹ 1,600 each

217. The minimum number of partner must be for partnership firm
(a) 2 (b) 1
(c) 4 (d) 3

218. Which one of the following is not part of partnership firm's goodwill?
(a) Personal Goodwill
(b) Institutional Goodwill
(c) Implied Goodwill
(d) Goodwill related to Casual event

219. Amit and Sumit are partner sharing profit and losses in ratio of 3 : 2. They admit Mukul into partnership who bring ₹ 25,000 at this capital and ₹ 15,000 as goodwill for 1/5 share of profit. No goodwill exists in the book's, what will be enteries in the books of A/c?
(a) Goodwill A/c Dr. 15,000
To Amit Capital A/c 9,000
To Sumit Capital A/c 6,000
(b) Cash A/c Dr. 40,000
To Mukul Capital A/c 25,000
To Goodwill A/c 15,000
(c) Both (a) and (b)
(d) Cash A/c Dr. 40,000
To Amit Capital A/c 20,000
To Sumit Capital A/c 20,000

220. Unrecorded liability, when paid by a firm on its dissolution is debited to

(a) partner's capital account
(b) realisation account
(c) unrecorded liability account
(d) None of the above

221. A and B are partners sharing profits in the firm in the ratio of 2 : 3. Goodwill appears in the books of firm at ₹ 10,000. C joins the firm for 1/5 share of profits. His share of goodwill is estimated to be ₹ 15,000. The old partners account will be credited with goodwill by
(a) ₹ 75,000 (b) ₹ 65,000
(c) ₹ 50,000 (d) ₹ 40,000

222. Mohan and Sohan are partner sharing profits in the ratio of 7 : 3. They admit Mukul for 1 of share of profit in the firm. No goodwill account appears in the books of the firm but it is valued at ₹ 25,000. It is now agreed that no goodwill account is to remain in the books. What will be journal entries in the firm's books of A/c?

(a) Goodwill A/c Dr. 25,000
To Mohan Capital A/c 17,500
To Sumit Capital A/c 7,500

(b) Mohan Capital A/c Dr. 13,125
Sohan Capital A/c Dr. 5,625
Mukul Capital A/c Dr. 6,250
To Goodwill A/c 25,000

(c) Both (a) and (b)

(d) Mohan Capital A/cDr. 12,500
Sohan Capital A/c Dr. 12,500
To Mukul Capital A/c 25,000

223. Which of the formula use for determine the gain ratio?
(a) Gain = Old Ratio – Sacrifice Ratio
(b) $\text{Gain Ratio} = \frac{\text{Old Ratio} - \text{Total of New Ratio}}{2}$
(c) Gain Ratio = New Profit Sharing Ratio – Old Profit Sharing Ratio
(d) None of the above

224. The profit ratio of A, B, C, who are partners in a firm is 4 : 3 : 2. After D is admitted. Their sacrificing ratio will be
(a) 3 : 2 : 1 (b) 5 : 3 : 2
(c) Equal (d) 4 : 3 : 2

225. Which of the following statements about the admission of a new partner to a firm is true?
(a) All accumulated profits and reserves are to be transferred to the profit and loss adjustment account on admission of a new partner.
(b) In case memorandum account is opened, the assets and liabilities appear in the new balance sheet at their revised values.
(c) In case the newly admitted partner pays cash for his share of goodwill. It will be credited to old partners capital account in their sacrificing ratio.
(d) None of the above.

226. When any partner retires and the remaining partners carry on the business with the firm's property without any final settlement of accounts the outgoing partner is entitled to
(a) interest at mutually agreed rate.
(b) interest @ 6% per annum of the amount due to him.
(c) such share of the profits as may be proportionate to his share of the firm's property.
(d) None of the above.

227. When interest is to be allowed on the capitals of the partners, it is generally calculated on the
(a) capital in the end of the year.
(b) average Capital.
(c) capital in the beginning of the year.
(d) None of the above.

228. A firm had a capital balance of ₹ 1,00,000 at the beginning of a year. At the end of

the year, the firm has total assets of ₹ 1,50,000 and total liabilities of ₹ 1,50,000 and total liabilities of ₹ 70,000. If the total with drawals during the period were ₹ 30,000. What was the amount of net profit/net loss for the year?

(a) ₹ 10,000 loss
(b) ₹ 50,000 loss
(c) ₹ 20,000 loss
(d) ₹ 10,000 profit

229. A and B invest ₹ 2,00,000 and ₹ 1,00,000 respectively in a partnership, and agree to divide profit/loss equally after providing for interest @ 10% per annum on original capital, and salaries of ₹ 24,000 and ₹ 48,000 respectively. How much amount A would get if the period's net income (before interest and salaries) is ₹ 90,000

(a) ₹ 38,000 (b) ₹ 90,000
(c) ₹ 45,000 (d) ₹ 89,000

230. A and B are equal partners. When partnership was dissolved their capitals are ₹ 30,000 and ₹ 40,000 respectively. After all assets are sold and liabilities paid, there is cash balance of ₹ 60,000. The amount of profit loss on realisation is

(a) Loss of ₹ 10,000
(b) Profit of ₹ 10,000
(c) Profit of ₹ 20,000
(d) Profit of ₹ 30,000

231. A company can purchase its own

(a) Debentures
(b) Equity shares
(c) Preference shares
(d) All of the above

232. The minimum amount that should be called by a company with application for its shares is the following per cent of face value of shares

(a) 15% (b) 10%
(c) 5% (d) 2%

233. After reissue of forfeited shares the balances of share forfeited account will be transferred to

(a) capital reserve account
(b) share capital account
(c) general reserve account
(d) shareholder's account

234. The rate of commission payable on the issue of shares should not be more than the following

(a) 4% (b) 5%
(c) 2% (d) 3%

235. A company can not issue

(a) redeemable preference shares
(b) redeemable debentures
(c) redeemable equity shares
(d) None of the above

236. Premium received on the issue of shares is shown in

(a) assets side of the balance sheet
(b) liabilities side of the balance sheet
(c) debit side of profit and loss account
(d) credit side of profit and loss account

237. M. Ltd. forfeited 50 shares of ₹ 100 each issued do X (₹ 80 called up) on which the allotment money of ₹ 30 and the first call money of ₹ 20 have not been received. The company reissued these shares @ ₹ 90 per share as fully paid up. The amount to be trasferred to capital reserve account would be

(a) ₹ 1,500 (b) ₹ 2,000
(c) ₹ 500 (d) ₹ 1,000

238. The Share Capital, General Reserve and Profit and Loss Account (Cr.) of B Ltd. stood at ₹ 6,00,000 (dividend into 60,000 shares of ₹ 10 each), ₹ 1,20,000 and ₹ 1,80,000 respectively. A majority of 40,000 shares had been acquired by A Ltd. and at the time of acquisition undistributed profit and general reserve

amounted to ₹ 1,00,000. The present value of the minority interest would be

(a) ₹ 2,66,667 (b) ₹ 3,00,000
(c) ₹ 2,00,000 (d) ₹ 2,60,000

239. In case the shares are forfeited, the capital account is debited by

(a) called up amount on shares
(b) nominal value of shares
(c) uncalled up amount on shares
(d) paid up amount on shares

240. A company issued 1,00,000 equity shares of the face value of ₹ 100 each at ₹ 100 per share. So far ₹ 75 per share has been called up including ₹ 25 on allotment and ₹ 25 on first call X to whom 200 shares were issued failed to pay the first call. His shares were forfeited and re-issued to Y at ₹ 70 per shares as fully paid up. The amount to be transferred to capital reserve A/c would be

(a) ₹ 8,000 (b) ₹ 10,000
(c) ₹ 4,000 (d) ₹ 6,000

241. What shall be the amount of shareholders fund, if equity share capital is ₹ 16,00,000 8% preference share capital is Profit and loss A/c balance (Cr.) ₹ 41,000, preliminary expenses ₹ 20,000, and short term liabilities ₹ 30,000?

(a) ₹ 19,14,000 (b) ₹ 19,34,000
(c) ₹ 15,00,000 (d) ₹ 18,94,000

242. X Ltd. forfeited 30 shares of ₹ 10 each fully called up for non-payment of allotment money of ₹ 3 per share and call money of ₹ 4 per share. These shares were re-issued for ₹ 8 per share fully paid. What is the amount to be transferred to capital reserve A/c?

(a) ₹ 30 (b) ₹ 90
(c) ₹ 300 (d) ₹ 60

243. Redeemable preference share of ₹ 1,00,000 are redeemed at a premium of 5% for which fresh equity shares of ₹ 40,000 are issued at par. What amount should be transferred to capital redemption reserve account?

(a) ₹ 40,000 (b) ₹ 1,05,000
(c) ₹ 60,000 (d) Nil

244. A company issued debentures of ₹ 60,000 at discount of ₹ 3,000 on Apirl 1, 2009. They are repayable in equal instalments each on March 31, every year. The financial year of the company ends on 31st December every year. The financial year of the company ends on 31st December every year. How much discount will be written off in the second year?

(a) ₹ 1,500 (b) ₹ 1,125
(c) ₹ 1,000 (d) ₹ 625

245. Which of the following is not include in calculation of purchase consideration?

(a) payment method
(b) lump sum method
(c) net assets method
(d) None of the above

246. Which one of the following is not correct equation?

(a) Goodwill = Purchases Consideration – Net Tangible Assets
(b) Capital Reserve = Net Tangible Assets – Purchases Consideration
(c) Capital Reserve = Goodwill + Total Assets
(d) Purchase Consideration = Agreed Value of Assets taken over – Agreed estimated value of liabilities taken over

247. What entry will be pass on the due of interest on purchase consideration?

(a) Vendor's A/c Dr.
To Interest A/c
(b) Interest A/c Dr.
To Vendor' A/c
(c) Cash A/c Dr.
To Interest A/c
(d) Interest A/c Dr.
To Cash A/c

248. What entry will be made at the time purchase of business?
(a) Business Purchases A/c Dr.
To Assets A/c
(b) Business Purchases A/c Dr.
To Cash A/c
(c) Business Purchases A/c Dr.
To Vendors A/c
(d) None of these

249. X, Y and Z are partners in XYZ Co. They are sharing profits and losses in the ratio of 2 : 2:1. Following is their Balance Sheet as on 31st March, 2010.

Balance Sheet

Creditors	30,000	Plant and Machinery	38,000
B/P	6,000	Goodwill	8,000
Capital			
X	40,000	Debtors	38,000
Y	40,000	Cash	12,000
Z	20,000	Stock	40,000
	1,36,000		1,36,000

It was decided to sell the business to ABC Ltd. which agreed to allot 12,000 Fully paid equity shares of ₹ 10 each at 5% premium in full satisfaction of the purchases consideration. The company assumed the liabilities except the Bills Payable and took over all the assets except Cash Balance. Find out Amount of Purchases Consideration.
(a) 1,30,000 (b) 1,40,000
(c) 1,26,000 (d) 1,20,000

250. The fair value of share is the average of
(a) par value and yield value
(b) intrinsic value and yield value
(c) intrinsic value and par value
(d) par value and market value

251. In holding companies dividends received out of profits of the subsidiary companies must be
(a) credited to revenue account
(b) debited to investment account
(c) credited to investment account
(d) debited to revenue account

252. Ram of Allahabad filed a petition in the court for adjudication as insolvent. At that time one month's salary due to five clerks amounted to ₹ 2,000, one month's wages due to ten workers amounted to ₹ 1,500, rent and rates due amounted to ₹ 500. Income Tax due amounted to ₹ 1,200 and one month's rent due amounted to ₹ 1,000. The amount of preferential creditors would be
(a) ₹ 4,200 (b) ₹ 6,200
(c) ₹ 2,000 (d) ₹ 3,200

253. If Earningprice (E.P.) ratio is 0.5 and earning per share (EPS) is ₹ 8, the market price of the share will be
(a) ₹ 160 (b) ₹ 0.40
(c) ₹ 40 (d) ₹ 100

254. A company issued 50,000 equity shares of ₹ 10 each. ₹ 8 paid up and 50,000. 8% preference shares of ₹ 100 each. Expected profits are ₹ 10,00,000. Normal rate of dividend on equity shares is 16%. Provision for taxation 60% and 10% of the profits is transferred to reserves. The value of equity share will be
(a) ₹ 50 (b) ₹ 40
(c) ₹ 45 (d) None of these

255. Accounting Standard -14 is related with
(a) Depreciation Accounting
(b) Amalgamation
(c) Valuation of Assets
(d) Valuation of stock

256. Accounting Standard -14 is a nature of
(a) Compulsory (b) Injunction
(c) Mandatory (d) All of these

257. Machoo Ltd. takes over Bagoo Ltd. the capital of Bagoo Ltd. 1,00,000 equity shares of ₹ 10 each. The intrinsic values were Machoo Ltd. ₹ 40 (per share) and Bagoo Ltd. ₹ 25 (per share). Fractional shares are 500. The market value of shares of Machoo Ltd. was ₹ 60 (per share). Calculate purchase consideration.
(a) ₹ 25,20,000 (b) ₹ 25,40,500
(c) ₹ 25,00,000 (d) ₹ 25,10,000

258. X Ltd. and Y Ltd. engaged in the same type of business, decided to amalgamation and for the purchase of their business. Z Ltd. was formed on 31st March, 2011. Their Balance Sheets were as follows

Balance Sheet

Liabilities	X Ltd.	Y Ltd.
Share Capital fully paid of shares of ₹ 10 each	2,00,000	1,60,000
Reserve Fund	12,000	6,000
P&L A/c	8,000	14,000
Creditors	30,000	66,000
	2,50,000	2,46,000

Assets	X Ltd.	Y Ltd.
Building	1,40,000	1,10,000
Machinery	50,000	56,000
Debtors	16,000	30,000
Stock	26,000	24,000
Cash	18,000	26,000
	2,50,000	2,46,000

Calculate purchase consideration.
(a) For X 2,00,000 and Y 1,20,000
(b) For X 2,20,000 and Y 1,80,000
(c) For X 1,20,000 and Y 1,20,000
(d) None of these

259. What entry will be made at cancellation of lost capital?
(a) Share Capital A/c Dr.
To Company A/c
(b) Share Capital A/c Dr.
To Capital Reduction A/c
(c) Capital Reduction A/c Dr.
To P & L A/c
To Goodwill A/c
(d) Share Capital A/c Dr.
To Bank A/c

260. Which one of the not way of internal reconstruction?
(a) By Reduction in Share Capital.
(b) By Agreement with Companies Creditors.
(c) By Sale of Assets.
(d) By Alteration in Share Capital of Company.

261. Mohan Ltd. goes into voluntary liquidation due to financial difficulties. Its assets and liabilities are
Assets: Fixed Assets ₹ 3,60,000 Current Assets ₹ 40,000.
Liabilities: Creditors ₹ 40,000 and B/P ₹ 40,000. Its paid up capital is ₹ 4,00,000. The assets are sold to a new company (Sohan Ltd.) for ₹ 2,88,000 which will be satisfied by the issue of 25,000 shares of ₹ 10 each. ₹ 8 paid up and the balance in cash. Liabilities were paid and liquidation expenses were ₹ 8,000. What will be purchase price payable?
(a) ₹ 2,20,000 (b) ₹ 1,20,000
(c) ₹ 2,88,000 (d) ₹ 2,30,000

262. The basic purpose of funds flow statement is to indicate
(a) increase or decrease in working capital.
(b) increase or decrease in liabilities.
(c) increase or decrease in assets.
(d) financial position.

263. Which one of the following is liverage ratio?

(a) Current Ratio
(b) Debt Equity Ratio
(c) Inventory Ratio
(d) Operating Ratio

264. Which of the following statement is correct?
(a) R.O.I. measures overall profitability
(b) Low gearing is prefearable to high gearing
(c) Debt equity ratio is solvency ratio
(d) All of the above

For Q. 265-268, use following Balance Sheet

Balance Sheet
as on 31st Dec., 2010

Equity Share Capital	15,00,000	Fixed Assets	14,00,000
Reserve and Surplus	1,00,000	Stock	5,00,000
6% Debentures	3,00,000	Debtors	2,00,000
Overdraft	1,00,000	Cash	1,00,000
Creditors	2,00,000		
	22,00,000		22,00,000

265. Liquid ratio will be
(a) 1 : 5 : 0.5 (b) 1 : 5
(c) 1.5 : 1 (d) 1 : 2 : 1

266. Debt equity ratio is
(a) 40% (b) 37%
(c) 37.5% (d) 60.70%

267. Solvency ratio will be
(a) 10% (b) 70%
(c) 72% (d) 72.72%

268. Stock working capital ratio is
(a) 130% (b) 120%
(c) 110% (d) 100%

269. Long term solvency is indicated by
(a) Liquid ratio
(b) Rate of return
(c) Capital gearing ratio
(d) Debt equity ratio

270. R.O.I. ratio is calculated to measure
(a) the relationship between goods sold and inventory level.
(b) short term liquidity position of blong term solvency of business.
(c) long term solvency of business.
(d) earning power of net assets of business.

271. If the cost of goods sold is ₹ 1 lakh, the value of Opening and Closing stock is ₹ 20,000 and ₹ 30,000 respectively, the stock turnover ratio will be
(a) 4 times (b) 3.3 times
(c) 5.5 times (d) 5 times

272. Average payment period 2 to 4 months hence creditors turnover will be
(a) 3 months (b) 5 months
(c) 6 months (d) 7 months

273. Which one of the following items represent a potential use of working capital?
(a) Declaration of share dividend
(b) Goodwill amortisation
(c) Sale of fixed assets at loss
(d) Net loss from operations

274. Which of the following is not normally paid from the working capital?
(a) Redemption of debentures
(b) Payment of wages
(c) Purchase of raw materials
(d) Payment to creditors

275. Which of the following will result in flow of funds?
(a) Depreciation of assets
(b) Appreciation in value of buildings
(c) Writing off goodwill
(d) Purchase of furniture

276. Which of the following is not a sources of 'funds'?
(a) Issue of share capital
(b) Purchase of machinery

(c) Long term loan raised
(d) Profit earned during the year

277. Cash from operation is equal to
(a) Net profit + Non cash expenses + decrease in current assets
(b) Net profit + increase in current assets
(c) Net profit + decrease in current liabilities
(d) Net profit after tax

278. Sales for the year ₹ 40,000, Purchase ₹ 30,000, Expenses ₹ 5,000, Creditors at the start ₹ 10,000, Creditors at the end ₹ 15,000, Cash from operation will be
(a) ₹ 5,000 (b) ₹ 20,000
(c) ₹ 15,000 (d) ₹ 10,000

279. Net profit for the year ₹ 13,000. Interest received in advance on 1-1-2010 ₹ 1,000 and 31-12-2010 ₹ 2,000. Cash from operation will be
(a) ₹ 8,000 (b) ₹ 12,000
(c) ₹ 10,000 (d) ₹ 14,000

280. Net Profit ₹ 70,000, Opening Balance of Income received in advance ₹ 30,000, Closing balance of Income received in advance ₹ 40,000. Find out cash from operation
(a) ₹ 75,000 (b) ₹ 72,000
(c) ₹ 70,000 (d) ₹ 80,000

281. Net Profit ₹ 50,000, Opening Creditors ₹ 10,000, Closing Creditors ₹ 15,000. Find out cash from operation
(a) ₹ 45,000 (b) ₹ 40,000
(c) ₹ 55,000 (d) ₹ 50,000

282. Contribution is
(a) Sales–Fixed Cost
(b) Sales–Total Cost
(c) Sales–Variable Cost
(d) None of the above

283. Profit will be the same under absorption costing and marginal costing only when
(a) there is only closing stocks.
(b) there is no opening or closing stocks.
(c) opening stocks are lower than closing stocks.
(d) there is only opening stocks.

XY Co. sold in two successive years 7,000 and 9,000 units and incurred a loss of ₹ 10,000 and earned ₹ 10,000 as profit respectively. The selling price per unit is ₹ 100. Find out answer of the following questions. (Q. 284 to 286)

284. The amount of fixed cost
(a) ₹ 75,000 (b) ₹ 72,000
(c) ₹ 80,000 (d) ₹ 70,000

285. The number of units to break even
(a) 7,500 units (b) 17,000 units
(c) 8,000 units (d) 7,000 units

286. The number of units to earn a profit of ₹ 50,000
(a) 13,500 units (b) 15,000 units
(c) 14,000 units (d) 13,000 units

287. Which one of the following statement is incorrect?
(a) Absorption costing is more suitable for decision taking than marginal costing.
(b) Fixed costs are not included in the valuation of stock under marginal costing.
(c) The technique of marginal costing is also known as variable costing.
(d) Contribution is also known as marginal income.

288. Which one of the following statement is incorrect?
(a) Marginal costing technique is used by the management for decision making.
(b) Marginal costing is a method of ascertaining cost.
(c) Sales above break even point indicate profits.
(d) In marginal costing, cost are classified into variable and fixed cost.

The sales turn over and profit during the two years were as below:

Year	Sales	Profit
2009	₹ 2 lakh	₹ 20,000
2010	₹ 3 lakh	₹ 40,000

Find out answer of the following questions (Q. 289 to 291).

289. What will be P/V Ratio?
(a) 25% (b) 40%
(c) 20% (d) 30%

290. What is amount of fixed cost?
(a) ₹ 30,000 (b) ₹ 40,000
(c) ₹ 20,000 (d) ₹ 25,000

291. What will be BEP (in ₹)?
(a) 1,00,000 (b) 1,40,000
(c) 1,20,000 (d) 1,30,000

292. Which one of the following statement is incorrect?
(a) Sales below break-even point means profit.
(b) Margin of safety indicate profit.
(c) Contribution Margin = Sales × P/V ratio.
(d) P/V ratio indicates profitability.

293. Material cost variance is due to
(a) change in quantity used
(b) change in material mix
(c) change in price of material
(d) All of the above

294. Variance is the difference between
(a) standard and actual level of activity
(b) budgeted and actual level of activity
(c) actual and fixed level of activity
(d) Both (a) and (b)

295. Labour rate variance is due to
(a) defective materials
(b) overtime allowance
(c) poor working conditions
(d) None of the above

296. When the actual cost incurred is more than the, there is variance, known as
(a) Favourable
(b) Standard Cost
(c) Standard Cost and Favourable
(d) Unfavourable

297. Standard cost is a tool of cost control and cost
(a) Planning (b) Co-ordination
(c) Reduction (d) Management

298. A budget is a detailed plan of operations for specific _____ period.
(a) past (b) future
(c) present (d) None of these

299. Which of the following component is not part of budgetary control?
(a) Compare actual with budgets
(b) Targets
(c) Action
(d) None of the above

Consider the following data and give the answer of the following questions (Q. 300 to 302).

Raw Material	Standard	Actual
X	40 units @ ₹ 50 per unit	50 units @ ₹ 50 per unit
Y	60 units @ ₹ 40 per unit	60 units @ ₹ 45 per unit

300. What is MPV?
(a) ₹ 320 (F) (b) ₹ 400 (A)
(c) ₹ 300 (A) (d) ₹ 350 (A)

301. What is MUV?
(a) ₹ 520 (A) (b) ₹ 560 (F)
(c) ₹ 500 (A) (d) ₹ 450 (F)

302. What will be MMV?
(a) ₹ 70 (A) (b) ₹ 70 (B)
(c) ₹ 60 (A) (d) ₹ 60 (F)

303. Which of the following is characteristics of the budgetary control?

(a) Continuous comparison
(b) Establishment
(c) Co-ordination
(d) None of the above

304. Which one of the ratio is not included under the budgetary control ratio?
(a) Capacity ratio
(b) Activity ratio
(c) Cash ratio
(d) Productivity ratio

305. Master budget is prepared by the
(a) Employee (b) Committee
(c) Manager (d) None of these

306. Which one of the following statement is not correct?
(a) A manager is frequently required to make decision which involve alternative choices.
(b) All cost concepts are not relevant in decision-making.
(c) All cost are relevant in decision-making.
(d) Decision-making is a future oriented activity.

307. Which of the formula is related for computing studdown sales?

(a) $\dfrac{\text{Variable Cost} - \text{Avoidable Costs on shut down}}{\text{P / V Ratio}}$

(b) $\dfrac{\text{Fixed Cost} - \text{Avoidable Costs on shut down}}{\text{Contribution Ratio}}$

(c) $\dfrac{\text{Fixed Cost} - \text{Avoidable Costs on shut down}}{\text{Variable Ratio}}$

(d) None of the above

308. Which of the cost is related with decision making?
(a) Marginal cost (b) Full cost
(c) Fixed cost (d) None of these

309. Which one of the factor is not influencing pricing decision?
(a) Trade customs
(b) Management's pricing strategy
(c) Market force
(d) Orders

310. The net profits will be maximised when contribution is
(a) Minimised (b) Equal
(c) Maximised (d) None of these

311. Responsibility accounting seeks to establish a relationship between planning and controlling by
(a) controlling cost and performance.
(b) establishing a system of collective responsibility.
(c) fixing organisational responsibilities for profit planning and control.
(d) dividing standards of work performance.

312. Responsibility accounting is a system of _____ where responsibility is assigned for the control cost.
(a) reduce (b) control
(c) management (d) All of these

313. Which one of the centre is not part of responsibility centre?
(a) Stock centre
(b) Profit centre
(c) Revenue centre
(d) Expense centre

314. Each responsibility centre is put under the charge of a responsible
(a) Accountant (b) Employee
(c) Manager (d) All of the above

315. Which one of the following is not kinds of Partnership?
(a) Constructive partnership
(b) Fixed term and non-fixed term partnership

(c) Partnership at will and particular partnership
(d) Limited and unlimited partnership

316. Which one of the following is not essential for a sound system of budgetary control?
(a) Budget centre (b) Flexibility
(c) Chart (d) Budget

317. Which statement is/are true?
(a) Since the life of the business is assumed to be indefinite, the financial statement of the business should be prepared only when it goes into liquidation.
(b) In accounting all business transactions are recorded as having a dual aspect.
(c) It is on the basis of going concern concept that the assets are always valued at market price.
(d) All of the above.

318. The system of recording transactions based on dual aspect concept is called
(a) Double entry system
(b) Single entry system
(c) Double account system
(d) None of the above

319. According to money measurement concept, the following will be recorded in the books of accounts of the business
(a) Value of furniture
(b) Quality of company's product
(c) Health of the manager of the company
(d) None of the above

320. Which one of the item is not capital nature?
(a) Expenditure incurred on issue of equity shares.
(b) Money raised by issue of equity shares.
(c) Carriage paid on goods purchased.
(d) Cost of formation of a new company.

321. ₹ 10,000 spent on replacement of worn out part of the machine will be charged as
(a) Revenue expenditure
(b) Deferred revenue expenditure
(c) Capital expenditure
(d) All of the above

322. Discount allowed on issue of shares is an example of
(a) Deferred revenue expenditure
(b) Capital expenditure
(c) Revenue expenditure
(d) All of the above

323. Depreciation of fixed assets is an example of
(a) Deferred revenue expenditure
(b) Revenue expenditure
(c) Capital expenditure
(d) All of the above

324. Which one of the following items should be taken as of a capital nature?
(a) ₹ 2,000 paid for erection of a new machine.
(b) A sum of ₹ 5,000 was expended on dismantling, removing and reinstalling plant, machinery and furniture.
(c) ₹ 2,000 spent on dismantling, removing and reinstalling plant and machinery to more convenient site.
(d) ₹ 800 paid for removal of stock to a new site.

325. Which of the following items should be taken as of a revenue nature?
(a) Damage paid on account of the breach of a contract to supply a certain goods.
(b) Legal expenses incurred in defending a suit for breach of contract to supply goods.
(c) A sum of ₹ 2,000 was spent on painting the new godown.
(d) All of the above.

326. Which of the following statement is correct?

(a) Stock at the end, if appears in the trial balance, is taken only to the balance sheet.
(b) Salary paid in advance' is not an expense because it neither reduces assets not increases liabilities.
(c) Creating reserve for discount on creditors is not strictly according to principle of conservation.
(d) All of the above.

327. Which of the following statement is incorrect?
(a) The term 'Current Assets' and 'Liquid Assets' have synonymous meanings.
(b) All current assets are fictitious assets.
(c) The 'Current Liabilities' is used to denote those liabilities which are payable after a year.
(d) All of the above.

328. Income Tax paid by a sole proprietor on his business income should be
(a) deducted from the capital A/c in the balance sheet
(b) deducted to the trading account
(c) debited to the profit and loss account
(d) All of the above.

329. Which of the following statement is true?
(a) All accumulated profits and reserve are not be transferred to profit and loss adjustment account on admission of a new partner.
(b) In case the newly admitted partner pays cash for his share of goodwill, it will be credited to the old partners in their sacrificing ratio.
(c) When goodwill account is raised on admission of a partner the amount is credited to the old partners in their old profit.
(d) All of the above.

330. A and B are partners sharing profit in the ratio of 3 : 2. They admit a new partner R with 1/5 share in the profit which he takes equally from A and B. The new profit sharing ratio between the partners will be
(a) 5 : 3 : 2 (b) 8 : 12 : 5
(c) 2 : 2 : 1 (d) None of these

331. Depreciation fund at the time of admission of a new partner is transferred to
(a) P and L A/c
(b) Trading A/c
(c) Revaluation A/c
(d) None of the above

X, Y and Z were partners sharing profit and losses in the ratio of 3 : 2 : 1. Calculate the new and gaining ratio in each of the following cases (Q. 332 to 334).

332. When X retires

	New Ratio	Gaining Ratio
(a)	2 : 2	2 : 3
(b)	2 : 1	2 : 1
(c)	2 : 1	1 : 2
(d)	2 : 2	2 : 2

333. When Y retires

	New Ratio	Gaining Ratio
(a)	1 : 3	3 : 2
(b)	3 : 2	2 : 3
(c)	2 : 3	1 : 3
(d)	3 : 1	3 : 1

334. When Z retires

	New Ratio	Gaining Ratio
(a)	2 : 3	2 : 3
(b)	3 : 2	3 : 2
(c)	1 : 4	4 : 1
(d)	3 : 1	3 : 1

335. A, B and C are partners in a firm sharing profit in the ratio of 2 : 2 : 1. C dies on 1 April 2010. The profit for the accounting year ending on 31st December, 2010 amounts to ₹ 16,000. What will be share

of the deceased partner in the profits of the firm?

(a) ₹ 5,000 (b) ₹ 4,000
(c) ₹ 800 (d) None of these

336. X, Y and Z are sharing profits in the ratio of 2 : 2 : 1. Z dies on 1 April, 2010. Sales for the year 2010 amount to ₹ 3,00,000 out of which sales of ₹ 1,00,000 amounted between the period from 1 January, 2010 to 1 April, 2010. The profit for the year amounted to ₹ 30,000. What will be deceased partner's share in the profits of the firm?

(a) ₹ 2,500 (b) ₹ 3,000
(c) ₹ 2,000 (d) None of these

337. Which of the following statement is true?

(a) The amount due to the retiring partner on account of goodwill is debited to the continuing partners in their gaining ratio.
(b) The retiring partner may claim a share in the profit of the firm even after his retirement if his account is not settled.
(c) The amount due to the retiring partner is transferred to his loan account in case it is not paid immediately.
(d) All of the above.

338. X, Y and Z are partners sharing profit in the ratio of 2 : 2 : 1. Z retired. The new profit sharing ratio between X and Y will be

(a) 1 : 1 (b) 3 : 2
(c) 2 : 1 (d) None of these

339. In the event of death of a partner, the accumulated profit and losses are shared by the partners

(a) New profit sharing ratio
(b) Capital ratio
(c) Old profit sharing ratio
(d) None of the above

340. In the event of dissolution of firm, the partner's assets are first used for payment of the

(a) Firm's liabilities
(b) External liabilities
(c) Personal liabilities
(d) None of the above

341. The absence of any contract to the contrary, capital profit on dissolution of a partnership firm is credited to the partners.

(a) In profit sharing ratio
(b) In capital ratio
(c) In gaining ratio
(d) Equally

342. Which of the following statement is correct?

(a) Any amount realised from the sale of an unrecorded asset is credited to the realisation A/c.
(b) Partner's wife loan is treated at par with other liabilities of the partnership firm.
(c) Dissolution of a firm automatically results in dissolution of a partnership.
(d) All of the above.

343. A company has issued shares of ₹ 100 each on which ₹ 80 has been paid up and the company declares a dividend of 25%. The amount of dividend per share comes to ₹ 20. On the basis of a normal rate of return of 10%, the market value of the share will be

(a) ₹ 250 (b) ₹ 200
(c) ₹ 100 (d) ₹ 150

344. Consolidate the existing shares of smaller amounts into shares of larger amounts. For example, the existing 1,00,000 shares of ₹ 1 each may be consolidated into 10,000 shares of ₹ 10 each. The entry in the books of company will be

(a) Share Capital A/c Dr. 1,00,000
(₹ 10 each)
To Share Capital A/c 1,00,000
(₹ 1 each)

(b) Share Capital A/c Dr. 1,00,000
(₹ 1 each)
To Share Capital A/c 1,00,000
(₹ 10 each)

(c) Share Capital A/c Dr. 1,00,000
(₹ 10 each)
To Share Capital A/c 1,00,000
(₹ 10 each)

(d) Share Capital A/c Dr. 1,00,000
(₹ 1 each)
To Share Capital A/c 1,00,000
(₹ 1 each)

345. The liquidation can take place in any of
(a) by voluntary winding up.
(b) by compulsory winding up by the court.
(c) winding up subject to supervision of the court.
(d) All of the above.

346. X Company has 10,000 shares of ₹ 10 each, ₹ 8 paid up and the company decides not to call the remaining ₹ 2 per share. In such a case, the shareholder's liability gets reduced and the partly paid-up (Shares of ₹ 10 each, ₹ 8 paid up) become shares of ₹ 8 each fully paid up share capital remaining of the same. The entry will be
(a) Share capital A/c Dr. 20,000
(₹ 2 each)
To Share Capital A/c 20,000
(b) Share Capital A/c Dr. 80,000
(₹ 10 each)
To Share Capital A/c 00
(₹ 8 each)
(c) Share Capital A/c Dr. 80,000
(₹ 8 each)
To Share Capital A/c 80,000
(₹ 10 each)
(d) None of the above

347. Which of the following is the reason of compulsory winding up of the company?
(a) If default is made in filling statutory reports or in holding statutory meetings.
(b) If the company is unable to pay its debts.
(c) If the courts is of the opinion that it is just and equitable that the company be wound up.
(d) All of the above.

348. Which of the following statement is correct?
(a) A firm earn no profit or incurs no loss at BEP.
(b) Marginal costing technique is used by management for election making.
(c) In Marginal costing, cost are classified into variable and fixed cost.
(d) All of the above.

349. Which of the following statement is correct?
(a) Contribution margin = Sales × P/V ratio.
(b) BEP is the point at which total revenue is equal to total cost.
(c) BEP is the point at which total revenue is equal to total cost.
(d) All of the above.

350. Which of the following statement is false?
(a) Contribution is always equal to fixed cost.
(b) Marginal costing is a method of ascertaining cost.

(c) A firm incurs a loss when contribution is equal to fixed cost.
(d) All of the above.

351. Which of the following statement is true?
(a) MOS indicates profit.
(b) Profit volume ratio indicates profitability.
(c) In marginal costing, managerial decisions are guided by contribution rather than by profit.
(d) All of the above.

352. Which of the following statement is false?
(a) MOS implies BEP.
(b) If the margin of safety is high, actual sales are very near to the break even sales.
(c) A firm earn profit when contribution is equal to fixed cost under variable cost.
(d) All of the above.

353. Which of the following statement is incorrect?
(a) In marginal costing stock is valued at fixed cost.
(b) Sales below break even point means profit.
(c) MOS = Break even sales – Variable cost.
(d) All of the above.

354. A company having 10,000 shares of ₹ 10 each, fully paid up, decides to pay back ₹ 2 per share. The entry will be
(a) Share Capital A/c Dr. 20,000
To Sundry shareholders A/c 20,000
(b) Sundry shareholders A/c Dr. 20,000
To Bank A/c 20,000
(c) Both (a) and (b)
(d) Share Capital A/c Dr. 20,000
To Bank A/c 20,000

355. Given Balance Sheet of X Ltd. as on March 31, 2011 Y Ltd. acquired 40,000 shares of X Ltd. on October 1, 2010 at ₹ 7,80,000. H Ltd. valued the machinery at ₹ 2,50,000 and current assets at ₹ 2,75,000. What will be minority interest?
(a) ₹ 1,70,000 (b) ₹ 85,000
(c) ₹ 1,85,000 (d) ₹ 1,80,000

356. In question no. 355 given above the capital profit will be
(a) ₹ 2,50,000 (b) ₹ 1,50,000
(c) ₹ 4,00,000 (d) ₹ 3,00,000

357. In question no. 355 given above the cost of control will be
(a) ₹ 50,000 (b) ₹ 15,000
(c) ₹ 60,000 (d) ₹ 75,000

			₹
Share Capital: 50,000 shares@ ₹ 10 each	5,00,000	Land and Building	5,00,000
		Machinery	3,00,000
General Reserve as on January 1,2006	2,00,000	Current Assets	2,00,000
Profit and Loss A/c 1,50,000			
Add: Profit for 2003 50,000	2,00,000		
Creditors	1,00,000		
	10,00,000		10,00,000

Balance Sheet
as at 31-12-2010

	H Ltd. (₹)	S Ltd. (₹)
Share Capital, Shares of ₹ 100 each	5,00,000	2,00,000
General Reserve	1,00,000	—
Profit and Loss A/c	80,000	—
6% Debentures	—	1,00,000
Trade Creditors	75,000	45,000
	7,55,000	3,45,000

Fixed Assets	3,50,000	1,50,000
Stock	90,000	40,000
Debtors	60,000	30,000
6% Debentures in S Ltd. (acquired at par)	60,000	—
Shares in S Ltd. 1500 @ ₹ 80	1,20,000	—
Bank	75,000	25,000
Profit and Loss A/c	—	1,00,000
	7,55,000	3,45,000

H Ltd. acquired the shares on May 1, 2010. 188. The Profit and Loss A/c of S Ltd. showed a debit balance of ₹ 1,50,000 on January 1, 2010. During March, 2009 goods costing ₹ 6,000 were destroyed by fire and the insurance paid only ₹ 2000.

Trade creditors of S Ltd. include ₹ 20,000 for goods supplied by H Ltd. on which the later company made a profit of ₹ 2000. Half of the 189 goods were still in stock. Find out the answer of the following questions (Q. 358 to 361).

358. Minority interest will be
(a) ₹ 19,000 (b) ₹ 20,000
(c) ₹ 25,000 (d) ₹ 40,000

359. Cost of control is
(a) ₹ 75,000 (b) ₹ 35,000
(c) ₹ 72,000 (d) ₹ 70,000

360. Stock reserve will be
(a) ₹ 2,000 (b) ₹ 1,000
(c) ₹ 500 (d) ₹ 3,000

361. Capital loss will be
(a) ₹ 1,50,000 (b) ₹ 1,20,000
(c) ₹ 1,36,000 (d) ₹ 1,30,000

362. Which of the following statement is correct?
(a) Angle of incidence if the angle formed by the sales line and the total cost line at the BEP.
(b) Marginal cost is same as variable cost.
(c) Break even chart is the graphic representation of cost volume profit relationship.
(d) All of the above.

363. Given, Fixed cost = ₹ 2,00,000, Variable cost = ₹ 5, Sales price = ₹ 10 per unit. Find out BEP (In Units).
(a) 30,000 (b) 45,000
(c) 40,000 (d) 60,000

364. Given, Fixed cost = ₹ 2,00,000, Variable cost = ₹ 5, Sales price = ₹ 10 per unit. If selling price is reduced by 10%. The new BEP will be
(a) 75,000 (b) 49,000
(c) 50,000 (d) 40,000

365. The P/V ratio on X Co. Ltd. is 40% and its MOS is 50%. Find out the net profit, if sales volume is ₹ 8,00,000
(a) ₹ 1,80,000 (b) ₹ 1,70,000
(c) ₹ 1,60,000 (d) ₹ 1,40,000

366. The P/V Ratio of X Ltd. is 40% and its MOS is 50%. Find out BEP, if sales volume is ₹ 8,00,000
(a) ₹ 4,50,000 (b) ₹ 1,20,000
(c) ₹ 4,00,000 (d) ₹ 30,000

367. A company earned a profit of ₹ 30,000 during the year 2010-11. If the Marginal cost and selling price of a product are ₹ 8 and ₹ 10 per unit respectively, find out P/V ratio
(a) 10% (b) 30%
(c) 20% (d) 25%

368. A company earned a profit of ₹ 30,000 during the year 2010-11. If the marginal cost and selling price of a product are ₹ 8 and ₹ 10 per unit respectively.

The MOS will be
(a) ₹ 1,40,000 (b) ₹ 1,20,000
(c) ₹ 1,50,000 (d) ₹ 1,30,000

369. A Ltd. has earned contribution of ₹ 2,00,000 and net profit of ₹ 1,50,000 on sales ₹ 8,00,000. Calculate MOS.
(a) ₹ 5,50,000 (b) ₹ 6,00,000
(c) ₹ 4,20,000 (d) ₹ 4,00,000

370. Financial statement involves
(a) The income statement.
(b) The statement of appropriation of profit.
(c) The statement of changing financial position.
(d) All of the above.

371. Which of the following statement is not false?
(a) Financial statement concept are also known as generally accepted accounting principles.
(b) The balance sheet shows a stock positions of the financial status of the firms.
(c) Financial statement are the end product of financial accounting process.
(d) All of the above.

372. Which of the following statement is true?
(a) Budget help in planning, communicating, coordinating, motivating the employee, controlling the evaluating the performance of manager.
(b) Budget is a short run financial plan which acts as a guide to achieve the predefined targets.
(c) Budget is a detailed plan of operations for a specific period.
(d) All of the above.

373. Which of the following statement is true?
(a) There are different steps in setting a budget system in a firm.
(b) Budget is different from a forecast.
(c) Budget may be classified according to type of activity, nature of activity, flexibility of business cycle.
(d) None of the above.

374. GLT Ltd. for standard production of 10,000 kg. of Chemical X, the overheads are charged at ₹ 6 (i.e. 3 hours × ₹ 2 per hour) i.e. total ₹ 60,000. As the actual product is only 9,000 kg the standard overheads charged is only ₹ 54,000 i.e., 9,000 × ₹ 6). The actual overheads incurred are however ₹ 52,000. The variable overhead variance is
(a) ₹ 3,000 (A) (b) ₹ 2,000 (F)
(c) ₹ 2,000 (A) (d) ₹ 3.000 (F)

375. The budgeted monthly production of X Ltd. is 10,000 kg resulting in annual budgeted production of 1,20,000 kg. The annual budgeted fixed overheads are ₹ 14,40,000 (₹ 1,20,000 × 12). The fixed overhead rate for X Ltd. is
(a) ₹ 15 per kg. (b) ₹ 16 per kg.
(c) ₹ 12 per kg. (d) ₹ 13 per kg.

376. The total annual budgeted hours of X Ltd. are ₹ 3,60,000 and Budgeted fixed overheads are ₹ 14,40,000. What will be fixed overhead Rate?
(a) ₹ 3 per hour (b) ₹ 4 per hour
(c) ₹ 2 per hour (d) None of these

377. There is a fixed overhead ₹ 1,20,000 of X Ltd. per month and output is 10,000 kg giving a fixed cost per unit of ₹ 12. The total cost per unit is ₹ 20 + ₹ 12 (i.e. 32). The standard contribution per unit, therefore is ₹ 8 (i.e. ₹ 40-32). The actual contribution for firm is ₹ 10 (i.e. ₹ 42-32). The sales margin variance will be
(a) 20,000 (F) (b) 20,000 (A)
(c) 10,000 (F) (d) 10,000 (A)

378. Which of the following statement is true?
(a) Total material variance can be subdivided into material price and material usage variance.
(b) Total labour variance may be divided into labour rate and labour efficiency variance.

(c) Variable overhead variance is consisting of overhead efficiency variance and overhead expenditure variance.
(d) All of the above.

379. Which of the following statement is true?
(a) There are different method of fixing transfer pricing.
(b) Responsibility that each member of organisation who has control over cost or revenue, should be a separate responsibility centre.
(c) Difference responsibility centres can be grouped into cost centres; profit centres or investment centres.
(d) All of the above.

380. Which of the following statement is true?
(a) A profit is one which a manager has control over costs as well as revenue.
(b) Transfer price is the rate at which goods or services are transferred by one division to another in the same organisation.
(c) Cost centre is one in which a manager is held responsible for the costs incurred in the respective decision.
(d) All of the above.

381. Considering the highest and lowest production from given figure.

Month	Production (Units)	Semi variable (₹)	Fixed (₹)	Variable (₹)
June	15,000	66,000	45,000	21,000
July	50,000	1,15,000	40,000	75,000
Difference	35,000	49,000		

Variable element per unit will be
(a) ₹ 1-70 (b) ₹ 2-40
(c) ₹ 1-40 (d) ₹ 1-20

382. Compute the amount of fixed cost from the information given below

Sales ₹ 80,000
Variable cost ₹ 40,000
Profit ₹ 20,000
(a) ₹ 35,000 (b) ₹ 45,000
(c) ₹ 20,000 (d) ₹ 30,000

383. Given—Total sales revenue is ₹ 50,000. Variable cost is ₹ 20,000 and sale in terms of funds is ₹ 1,000 then contribution will be
(a) ₹ 45,000 (b) ₹ 60,000
(c) ₹ 30,000 (d) ₹ 40,000

384. Given—Sales ₹ 50,000, Profit ₹ 5,000, VC = 80%. Find out P/V ratio
(a) 30% (b) 50%
(c) 20% (d) 40%

385. Taking above figure (q. 384) find out the fixed cost
(a) ₹ 7,000 (b) ₹ 9,000
(c) ₹ 5,000 (d) ₹ 6,000

386. Taking above figure find out the sales volume to earn a profit of ₹ 5,000
(a) ₹ 60,000 (b) ₹ 70,000
(c) ₹ 50,000 (d) ₹ 40,000

387. A Co. Ltd. manufacturing printing machine has the capacity to produce 600 machine per annum. The Marginal cost of each machine is ₹ 300 and each machine is sold for ₹ 375. Fixed overheads are ₹ 30,000 per annum. BEP will be (in ₹) (in unit)
(a) 1,50,000 units, 400 (₹)
(b) ₹ 1,60,000 (unit), 300 (₹)
(c) ₹ 1,50,000,400 (units)
(d) All of the above

388. Given—Sales = ₹ 1,50,000, VC = ₹ 1,20,000, FC = ₹ 15,000, BEP will be
(a) ₹ 74,000 (b) ₹ 15,000
(c) ₹ 75,000 (d) ₹ 60,000

389. A Co. Ltd. purchased a business for ₹ 2,20,000. The purchase price was paid

by 6% debenture. 6% debenture of ₹ 2,00,000 were issued at 10% premium for the purpose of this purchase. Which of the entry will be in the book of A Ltd.?

(a) Business purchase A/c Dr. 2,20,000
    To Vendor A/c 2,20,000
(b) Vendor's A/c Dr. 2,20,000
    To 6% Deb. A/c 2,00,000
    To Premium on Issue of 6% Deb. A/c 20,000
(c) Both (a) and (b)
(d) None of the above

390. Which of the following entry would be passed at the time purchases of business?

(a) Business Purchase A/c Dr.
    To Vendor's A/c
(b) Various Assets A/c Dr.
    Goodwill A/c Dr.
    To Various Liabilities A/c
    To Vendors A/c
(c) Various Assets A/c Dr.
    Goodwill A/c Dr.
    To Various Liabilities A/c
    To Business Purchase A/c
(d) All of the above

391. Which of the following is merits of amalgamation of the companies?

(a) Competition is over
(b) Easy in distribution of product
(c) More capital
(d) All of the above

392. Which of the following entry will be passed in the books of Vendor's company at the time purchasing of business?

(a) Purchasing Company A/c Dr.
    To Realisation A/c
(b) Realisation A/c Dr.
    To Assets A/c
(c) Liabilities A/c Dr.
    To Realisation A/c
(d) All of the above

393. Which of the following expenses will be allocated on time basis?

(a) Interest (b) Salary
(c) Wages (d) All of these

394. Which one of the following is term of AS-14?

(a) Transferee company
(b) Amalgamation
(c) Transferor company
(d) All of the above

395. Which one of the following is not merits of amalgamation?

(a) Control on business
(b) Control over market
(c) Over capitalisation
(d) Economic

396. Given the Balance Sheet of X Ltd. compute the value of the Company's shares by assets method.

Balance Sheet
as on 31st December 2010

Liabilities	₹	Assets	₹
20,000 Equity shares of ₹ 10 each	2,00,000	Fixed Assets	2,50,000
General Reserve	45,000	Current Assets	1,00,000
Profit and Loss A/c	10,000	Goodwill	20,000
5% Debentures	50,000		
Current Liabilities	65,000		
	3,70,000		3,70,000

On 31st December 2010 the fixed assets were valued at ₹ 1,75,000 and the goodwill of ₹ 25,000.

(a) ₹ 9.15 (b) ₹ 9.10
(c) ₹ 9.25 (d) ₹ 9.19

397. Which of the following statement are true?

(a) External reconstruction is recorded by purchase method of accounting information.
(b) Reconstruction Account is opened for the purpose of internal reconstruction.

(c) There is no need to liquidate a company in case of internal reconstruction.
(d) All of the above.

398. Pre-incorporation profit is credited to which account?
(a) General Reserve
(b) Profit and Loss A/c
(c) Capital Reserve
(d) P & L Appropriation A/c

399. The types of capital of a company are
(a) Subscribed capital
(b) Authorised capital
(c) Uncalled capital
(d) All of the above

400. Conservatism concept represents.
(a) An auditor is not valuer.
(b) Anticipate no profit and provide for all losses.
(c) Stock should be valued at cost price and market price whichever is less.
(d) For every debit, there is a credit.

401. The dual aspect concept of accounting says.
(a) Depreciation should be charged on cost price.
(b) For every debit, there is a credit.
(c) Depreciation is a charge against profit.
(d) No vouching without any voucher, no voucher without its vouching.

402. "An item should be regarded as material if there is reason to believe that knowledge of it would influence the decision of informed investor." This statement is referred by
(a) ICAI (b) ICWAI
(c) AICPA (d) IDBI

403. Fictitious assets known as
(a) Closing assets
(b) Current assets
(c) Floating assets
(d) Deferred expenditure

404. Fictitious assets consists
(a) training and development expenditure
(b) preliminary expenses
(c) debit balance of profit and loss account
(d) All of the above

405. Which of the following is not concept of accounting?
(a) Entity concept
(b) Cost concept
(c) Matching concept
(d) Stock valuation

406. The prescribed title of the Balance Sheet is
(a) Balance Sheet of ... (Name of Trader)
As at .... (Date of Balance Sheet)
Liabilities ₹ Assets ₹
(b) Balance Sheet of... (Name of Trader)
For the Year Ended
Liabilities ₹ Assets ₹
(c) As at .....(Date of Balance Sheet)
Balance Sheet of...
Liabilities ₹ Assets ₹
(d) Balance Sheet of ...
Year ....
Liabilities ₹ Assets ₹

407. Which of the following is classification of assets?
(a) Contingent assets
(b) Current assets
(c) Fixed assets
(d) All of the above

408. Long term liabilities
(a) Long term public deposits
(b) Loan on mortgage
(c) Long term loans from financial institutions
(d) All of the above

409. Forms of income statement are
(a) Trading accounting
(b) Manufacturing account

(c) Profit and Loss account
(d) All of the above

410. Methods of analysis and iterpretation of financial statement are
(a) Average analysis
(b) Preparation of comparative statements
(c) Ratio analysis
(d) All of the above

411. Which of the following items to be deducted from net profit?
(a) Appreciation in fixed assets
(b) Dividends or interest on investment
(c) Retransfer of excess provision
(d) All of the above

412. Which of the following is non-trading charges?
(a) Discount on issue written off
(b) Provision for taxation
(c) Loss on sale of non-current assets
(d) All of the above

413. Average age of inventory calculated as
(a) Average age of inventory
$$= \frac{365}{\text{Inventory}} \times 100$$
(b) Average age of inventory
$$= \frac{365}{\text{Inventory Turnover}}$$
(c) Average age of inventory
$$= \frac{\text{Inventory Turnover}}{100} \times 365$$
(d) Average age of inventory
$$= \frac{\text{Inventory}}{\text{Turnover}} \times \frac{365 \times 100}{2}$$

414. Stock velocity (in months) calculated as
(a) Stock velocity (in months)
$$= \frac{\text{Average Stock}}{\text{Cost of Goods Sold}} \times \frac{365}{12}$$
(b) Stock velocity (in months)
$$= \frac{\text{Cost of Goods Sold}}{\text{Average Stock}} \times \text{No. of year}$$
(c) Stock velocity (in months)
$$= \frac{\text{Average Stock}}{\text{Cost of Goods Sold}} \times \text{No. of months in a year}$$
(d) Stock velocity (in months)
$$= \frac{\text{Cost of Goods Sold}}{365} \times 12$$

415. Average disbursement period can be find out as
(a) $\frac{\text{Accounts Payable}}{\text{Net Credit Purchases}} \times \text{No. of working days}$
(b) $\frac{\text{Net Credit Purchases}}{\text{Accounts Payable}} \times \text{No. of working days}$
(c) $\frac{\text{Net Credit} + \text{Purchases}}{\text{No. of working days}} \times \text{Accounts Payable}$
(d) $\frac{\text{Net Credit Purchases}}{\text{Opening Balance of Accounts}} \times 365$

416. Net worth can be calculated as
(a) $\text{Net Worth} = \frac{\text{Total Assets}}{\text{Total Equity}} \times \text{Proprietary Fund}$
(b) $\text{Net Worth} = \frac{\text{Total Assets}}{\text{Shareholder's Equity}}$
(c) $\text{Net Worth} = \frac{\text{Shareholder's fund}}{\text{Total Assets}}$
(d) $\text{Net Worth} = \frac{\text{Total Assets}}{\text{Total Resources}} \times \text{Shareholder's Fund}$

417. What is the formula for calculating ratio of Total Assets to Liabilities?

(a) $\frac{\text{Total Assets}}{\text{Fixed Liabilities}} \times 100$

(b) $\frac{\text{Total Assets}}{\text{Total Liabilities}}$

(c) $\frac{\text{Fixed Liabilities}}{100} \times \text{Total Assets}$

(d) $\frac{\text{Total Liabilities}}{\text{Total Property}} \times 100$

418. Financial stability refers tothe capacity of an undertaking to meet its financial obligation, both ______ and ______.
(a) bills receivables and bills payables
(b) current and fixed assets
(c) financial position and solvency position
(d) short-term and long term

419. AS-3 is related with
(a) Accounting Systems
(b) Cash Flow Statement
(c) Depreciation Accounting
(d) Fund Flow Statement

420. Revised AS-3 issued by
(a) Company
(b) The Institute of Chartered Accountant of India
(c) The Institute of Company Secretories of India
(d) The President of India

421. Given.

Provision for Taxation Account

Particulars	Amount	Particulars	Amount
To Bank A/c (Tax paid)	–	By Balance b/d	–
		By ..... ?	–
To Balanced c/d	–		

What will be in place of interrogation remark?
(a) By Interim Dividend
(b) By Profit and Loss A/c
(c) By Machinery Account
(d) Proposed Dividend

422. Given.

Adjusted Profit and Loss Account

Particulars	Amount	Particulars	Amount
To Depreciation	9,900	By Balance b/d	68,000
To Drawings	20,000	By .... (Balancing Figure)	—
To Provision for Taxation	8,000		
To Balance c/d	71,000		
	1,08,900		1,08,900

the balance figure represents
(a) Loss from bank
(b) Loss from operations
(c) Funds from bank
(d) Funds from operations

423. Which of the following is not items of application of funds?
(a) Sale of fixed assets
(b) Increase in working capital
(c) Payment of cash dividend
(d) Purchase of fixed assets

424. Given.

Statement of Fund Flow

Sources	Amount	Application	Amount
Funds from Operations	40,900	Fixed Assets Purchased	4,400
Capital		Drawing	20,000
Introduced	10,000	Tax-paid	4,000
		Balance Figure	22,500
	50,900		50,900

What will be in place of balance figure?
(a) Accumulated depreciation
(b) Decrease in working capital
(c) Funds from operations
(d) Increase in working capital

425. Cash flow from operating activities includes
(a) Cash receipts from customers
(b) Cash payments for overheads
(c) Cash paid to employees
(d) All of the above

426. Budgetary control consists
(a) Recording (b) Control
(c) Planning (d) All of the above

427. Budget centre is a section of the organisation of an undertaking defined for the purpose of
(a) Responsibility centre
(b) Budgetary control
(c) Budget responsibility
(d) Budget requirements

428. The limitation of budgeting is/are
(a) Time effect.
(b) Budgeting is not a substitute of management.
(c) Danger of rigidity.
(d) All of the above.

429. Fixed budget is a budget which is designed to remain unchanged irrespective of the actually attained
(a) Budget allowance
(b) Dynamic
(c) Level of responsibility
(d) Level of activity

430. Given.

Flexible Budget
(Year ending 31st Dec., 2010)

Element of Cost	Level of Activity				
	50%	60%	75%	90%	100%
Variable Expenses:	₹	₹	₹	₹	₹
Materials	24.00	28.80	36.00	43.20	—
Labour	25.60	30.72	38.40	46.08	—
Other Expenses	3.80	4.56	5.70	6.84	

Which of the following figure will be at 100% level of activity?
(a) 49.00, 50.30 and 27.60
(b) 48.00, 51.20 and 7.60
(c) 49.00, 51.20 and 30.70
(d) 48.00, 49.20 and 7.60

431. "Functional budget is a budget of income or expenditure appropriate to, or the responsibility of a particular function." It is said by
(a) SBI (b) ICAI
(c) ICMA (d) RBI

432. "The cash budget is an estimate of cash receipts and disbursements for a future period of time." This statement is said by
(a) Malchman and Salvin
(b) J.R. Betty
(c) R. Anthony
(d) Harry G. Guthmann and H.E. Dougall

433. Present value method includes
(a) Present value index method
(b) Net present value method
(c) Terminal value method
(d) All of the above

434. Cost of preference share capital can be calculated as

(a) $C_p = \dfrac{\text{After Tax Cost}}{1 - \text{Tax Rate}}$

(b) $C_p\,(\text{before tax}) = \dfrac{\text{After Tax Cost}}{1 - \text{Tax Rate}}$

(c) $C_p = \dfrac{1 - \text{Tax Rate}}{\text{Dividend per Share}}$

(d) $C_p = \dfrac{\text{Dividend per Share}}{1 - \text{Tax Rate}}$

435. Cost of Debenture (after tax) calculated as

(a) $C_d\,(\text{after Tax}) = \left(\dfrac{i}{NP} \times 100\right)$

(b) $C_d\,(\text{after Tax}) = \left(\frac{NP}{i} \times 100\right)(\text{Tax} - 1)$

(c) $C_d\,(\text{after Tax}) = \left(\frac{i}{NP} \times 100\right)(1 - \text{Tax})$

(d) $C_d\,(\text{after Tax}) = \frac{EPS}{MP} \times 100$

436. Standard hour is a hypothetical hour which represents the amount of work which should be performed in one hour under
(a) Standard conditions
(b) Standard time
(c) Standard hour
(d) Standard profit

437. Revised standard quantity can be find out by

(a) $RSQ = \frac{\text{Standard Qty. for each Material}}{\text{Total of Standard Qty. of all types of Materials}} \times \text{Actual Mix Total}$

(b) $RSQ = \frac{\text{Standard Qty. for each Material}}{\text{Actual Mix Total}} \times 100$

(c) $RSQ = \frac{\text{Total Standard Qty.}}{\text{Standard Qty. for each Material}} \times \text{Total Actual Mix}$

(d) $RSQ = \frac{\text{Standard Cost} - \text{Actual Cost}}{\text{Total Standard Qty.}} \times \text{Total Actual Mix}$

438. Standard Cost – Actual Cost = ?
(a) Labour cost price variance
(b) Material cost price variance
(c) Material cost variance
(d) Standard mix

439. Actual Output × Standard Rate per Unit of Output = ?
(a) Labour cost variance
(b) Standard material cost variance
(c) Labour efficiency variance
(d) Labour price variance

440. Material yield variance will be calculated when
(a) Rate of material presented there
(b) Rate of yield presented there
(c) Yield variance
(d) Standard Rate presented there

441. Standard rate calculated as

(a) $SR = \frac{\text{Standard Price}}{\text{Standard Output}}$

(b) $SR = \frac{\text{Standard Cost of Standard Output}}{\text{Standard Total Mix}}$

(c) $SR = \frac{\text{Standard Total Mix}}{\text{Actual Mix Total}}$

(d) $SR = \frac{\text{Standard Cost of Standard Output}}{\text{Standard Output}}$

442. Given.
Sales Price Variance = Actual Qty. (Budged Price – Actual Price)
? = 5000 (₹ 3 – ₹ 3.00)
The sales price variance will be
(a) SPV = 9 (b) SPV = 15000
(c) SPV = 45000 (d) SPV = 0

443. The rate of interest depends on the risk of
(a) Investment decisions and capital costs
(b) Capital project
(c) Investment
(d) Capital expenditure planning

444. Decrease in cost as a result of reduced volume of sales happens
(a) Fixed overhead variance
(b) Cost volume variance

(c) Sales volume variance
(d) Sales price variance

445. B.E.P. as a percentage of full capacity calculated as

(a) $\frac{\text{Total Variable Costs}}{\text{Total Sales Volume}} \times \text{Total Output}$

(b) $\frac{\text{B.E. Sales Volume}}{\text{Full Capacity Sales Volume}} \times 100$

(c) $\frac{\text{Full Capacity Sales Volume}}{\text{B.E. Sales Volume}} \times \frac{365}{100}$

(d) $\frac{\text{Fixed Costs}}{\text{Total Sales Revenue}}$

446. Cash B.E.P. can be find out as

(a) Cash B.E.P. $= \frac{\text{Constribution per Unit}}{\text{Profit and Loss} \times \text{E.E.P}} \times \text{Cash Received from Bank}$

(b) Cash B.E.P. $= \frac{\text{Constribution per Unit}}{\text{Cash Fixed Costs} + \text{Loan Received from Bank}}$

(c) Cash B.E.P. $= \frac{\text{Cash Fixed Costs} + \text{Loan Instalment}}{\text{Contribution per Unit}}$

(d) $\text{Cash B.E.P.} = \frac{\text{Profit}}{\text{B.E.P.}} \times \text{P / V Ratio}$

477. Which of the following statement is true?

(a) Responsibility reporting requires grouping and defining responsibility within an organisation structure, determining and assigning costs to appropriate levels and activities and placing a strong emphasis on cost controllability.
(b) Responsibility reporting is the crucial phase of responsibility accounting.
(c) Responsibility accounting is based on the notion that a responsibility centre manager should be held accountable for controllable costs.
(d) All of the above.

448. If there is no risk, the rate of interest called

(a) Risk rate
(b) Risk free rate
(c) Investment project
(d) Safe property

449. The excess of actual or budgeted sales over the break even sales is known as the

(a) Profit margin of safety
(b) Margin of safety
(c) Fixed cost
(d) Loss

450. Margin of safety ratio calculated as

(a) $\text{MOS} = \frac{\text{Budgeted Sales} - \text{Break even Sales}}{100} \times \text{Budgeted Sales}$

(b) $\text{MOS} = \frac{\text{Budgeted Sales} - \text{Break even Sales}}{\text{Budget Sales}}$

(c) $\text{MOS} = \frac{\text{Budgeted Sales} - \text{Break even Analysis}}{\text{Budget Sales}} \times \text{Profit Goal}$

(d) $\text{MOS} = \frac{\text{Budgeted Sales} - \text{Budgeted Profit}}{\text{Fixed Cost}} \times 100$

451. The internal rate of return can be defined as that rate which equates the present value of cash inflows with the present value of cash outflows of an

(a) Present value
(b) Marginal efficiency
(c) Inflow of cash
(d) Investment

452. Which of the following is type of Investment decisions?
(a) Expansion of new business
(b) Replacement and modernisation
(c) Introducing a new line
(d) Expansion of existing business

453. Given.

Balance Sheet
As at 31st December....... 2010

Liabilities	₹	Assets	₹
Share Capital:		Bank	1,20,000
Authorised Capital:			
20,000 Equity Shares @ ₹ 10 each	2,00,000		
Issued, Subscribed, Called-up and Paid-up Capital:			
	1,20,000		1,20,000

Issued, Subscribed, Called up and Paid up capital will be
(a) ₹ 1,30,000 (b) ₹ 1,40,000
(c) ₹ 1,10,000 (d) ₹ 1,20,000

454. Given.

Bank A/c	Dr.	4600
Forfeited Share A/c	Dr.	?
To Share Capital A/c		

(Being amount received in reissue of shares to 60@ ₹ 100 shares and balance is taken from forfeiture A/c)

The Forfeited Share A/c will be passed by
(a) ₹ 10,600 (b) ₹ 1,400
(c) ₹ 4,600 (d) ₹ 2,000

455. Given.

5% Debenture Account

Date 2010	Particulars	Amount ₹
Dec. 31	To cum. Debentures A/c	1,00,000
Dec. 31	....	7,00,000
		8,00,000

Date 2011	Particulars	Amount ₹
Jan. 1	By Balance b/d	8,00,000
		8,00,000

What entry will be passed for ₹ 7,00,000?
(a) Sinking fund A/c
(b) Opening balance c/d
(c) Debentureholders A/c
(d) Bank A/c

456. Commission on amount paid to shareholders calculated by

(a) $\dfrac{\text{Percentage of Commission} \times \text{Balance of Amount}}{\text{Percentage of Commission}} \times 100$

(b) $\dfrac{\text{Percentage of Commission} \times \text{Balance of Amount}}{100 + \text{Percentage of Commission}}$

(c) $\dfrac{\text{Percentage of Commission}}{\text{Percentage of Commission} \times \text{Balance of Amount}}$

(d) $\dfrac{\text{Percentage of Commission} \times \text{Balance of Amount}}{100 + \text{Percentage of Commission}}$

457. Which accounts to opened in vendor company's?

(a) Purchasing company's account
(b) Realisation account
(c) Shareholder's account
(d) All of the above

458. Which of the following errors will not affect the trial balance?
(a) Purchase returns book for December was overcast by ₹ 200.
(b) Sales book c/f ₹ 2200 instead of ₹ 2000.
(c) Goods for ₹ 300 purchased on cash, expenses account was debited instead of purchase account.
(d) None of the above.

459. Which of the following items is not taken into account while computing current ratio?
(a) Sundry Debtors
(b) Overdraft
(c) Sundry Creditors
(d) Furniture

460. When shares are forfeited, capital account debited by
(a) Forfeited amount of shares
(b) Called up amount of shares
(c) Paid-up amount of shares
(d) Nominal value of shares

461. The basic purpose of funds flow statement is to indicate the
(a) increase or decrease in assets.
(b) financial position.
(c) increase or decrease in working capital.
(d) increase or decrease in liabilities.

462. Accounting rules, procedures and methods should be observed alike and should not be changed from year to year. This is called accounting convention of
(a) Conservatism (b) Going concern
(c) Consistency (d) Full disclosure

463. The liability of a partner in respect of the firm's debt is limited up to the amount of
(a) his guarantee to
(b) his capital in the firm
(c) no limit
(d) his capital and loan given to the firm

464. A and B are partners sharing profits in the ratio of 7 : 3. C is admitted for 3/7 share in the profits. The new profit sharing ratio of the partners will be
(a) 7 : 3 : 3 (b) 5 : 3 : 3
(c) 14 : 6 : 15 (d) 7 : 6 : 7

465. In the event of dissolution of a partnership firm, the provision of doubtful debt is transferred to
(a) Profit and Loss A/c
(b) Sundry debtor's A/c
(c) Partner's capital A/c
(d) Realisation A/c

466. Liability of partners for firm's debt is
(a) Separate
(b) Joint
(c) Joint and separate
(d) None of the above

467. The current ratio of a firm is 2 : 1 which one would improve the ratio
(a) to borrow money for a short period.
(b) to pay a current liability.
(c) to give an interest bearing promissory note to a creditor in payment of the full amount due to him.
(d) to purchase goods for cash.

468. Which one of the following is not the object of preparing funds flow statement?
(a) To show, how general expansion on business has been financed.
(b) To show the earnings of the business over a period of time.
(c) To illustrate the relationship between profits from operations on the one

hand and raising of new capital or contracting term loan on the other.
(d) To show the results of current financial management.

469. Net working capital is equal to
(a) Difference between current assets and current liabilities
(b) Owners + creditor capital
(c) Value of all current assets
(d) Value of all assets

470. Liquid assets are equal to
(a) Current assets less inventories and prepaid Exp.
(b) Value of all current assets
(c) Sum of cash and bank balances
(d) None of the above

471. A and B were sharing profit of a business in the ratio of 3 : 2. They admit C into partnership, who gets 1/3 of the share of profit from A, 1/2 of the share of profit from B. What will be the new profit sharing ratio?
(a) 3 : 2 : 1 (b) 3 : 2 : 2
(c) 3 : 2 : 5 (d) 2 : 1 : 2

472. Assets of the business mean
(a) Cash + Capital
(b) Liabilities – Capital
(c) Capital + Drawings
(d) Liabilities + Capital

473. Amount set aside out of divisible profit and invested outside is known as
(a) Fund (b) Reserve
(c) Secret reserve (d) Capital reserve

474. Which one of the following is not correctly matched?
(a) Rights share — Issued to new
(b) Secured debentures — Mortgage deed
(c) Redeemable — Preference shares
(d) Convertible — Debentures

475. If Earnings Price (EP) ratio is 0.05 and Earnings per share is ₹ 8, the market price of share
(a) ₹ 160 (b) ₹ 0.40
(c) ₹ 40 (d) ₹ 100

476. If current ratio is 2.5, quick ratio is 1.5, and the net working capital is ₹ 15000, the value of inventory will be
(a) ₹ 37,500 (b) ₹ 52,500
(c) ₹ 10,000 (d) ₹ 15,000

477. A firm has total current assets of ₹ 10,000 (including inventory of ₹ 4000) and total current liabilities of ₹ 3000. What will be the amount of short term bank borrowings to make the quick ratio 1.5?
(a) ₹ 3,000 (b) ₹ 1,000
(c) ₹ 11,000 (d) ₹ 5,000

478. While preparing funds flow statement an increase in working capital is regarded as
(a) neither application nor source.
(b) application of funds.
(c) both application as well as source.
(d) source of funds.

479. For assessing the firm's efficiency of operation, we need to analyse the combined effect of the following pair of ratios.
(a) Earnings per share and coverage ratio.
(b) The net profit margin and the net operating profit rate of return.
(c) Debt to net worth and interest coverage ratio.
(d) The current ratio and the inventory turnover ratio.

480. Liquidity ratios are used
(a) to evaluate the performance of the firm over a period of time.
(b) to assess the financial position of the firm at a point of time.

(c) to assess the present and expected earnings of the firm.
(d) to judge a firm's ability to meet short term obligations.

481. What will be the Return on Investment (ROI) if total assets, (including investment in corporate securities of ₹ 20,000) are ₹ 1,00,000, net profit margin 10% and gross profit margin is ₹ 10,000 (or 20% of sales)
(a) 20% (b) 25%
(c) 5% (d) 10%

482. Which of the following is not source of funds?
(a) Issue of shares for consideration other than cash.
(b) Issue of share capital.
(c) Sale of fixed assets.
(d) Issue of bonus shares.

483. The debt equity ratio of a company for three consecutive years was as follows
2004—399 : 28
2005—493 : 34.
2006—624 : 42
The above ratios show
(a) That the long term liquidity of the company is improving from year to year.
(b) That the interests of creditors are not safe in the company.
(c) That the company's financial structure is sound.
(d) That the company is capable meeting its short term liabilities.

484. If average collection period is 15 days and average accounts receivable is ₹ 45,000, what will be the total annual credit sales?
(a) ₹ 6,75,000 (b) ₹ 1,87,500
(c) ₹ 10,80,000 (d) ₹ 16,20,000

485. A company has profit before tax (PBT) of ₹ 2,00,000. If time interest earned is 5, what is the total interest charge?
(a) ₹ 40,000 (b) ₹ 50,000
(c) ₹ 20,000 (d) ₹ 33,333

486. Gearing ratio means the following ratio:
(a) Long term debt/equity capital.
(b) Long term debt + preference capital/ Net worth.
(c) Long term debt/equity capital + preference capital.
(d) Long term debt/preference capital.

487. If trade creditors are ₹ 10,000, unpaid expenses 10% of creditors; current ratio is 2 : 1 and stock is ₹ 7,000, then quick assets will be
(a) ₹ 14,000 (b) ₹ 15,000
(c) ₹ 10,000 (d) ₹ 12,000

488. The profit on the reissue of forfeited shares are transferred to
(a) General reserve
(b) Profit and Loss A/c
(c) Capital reserve
(d) Capital A/c

489. The accounting convention of matching means
(a) Expenses of a period to be matched with the revenue of the same period.
(b) Profit for the sales to be matched with the sales revenue.
(c) Partners must get equal share in profit.
(d) Profit for the period to be matched with the investment.

490. Debtors ₹ 8,400; Reserve for bad debts - ₹ 400; cost of sales ₹ 36,000; Profit 40% of sales debt collect period is
(a) 75 days (b) 86 days
(c) 45 days (d) 49 days

491. According to the money measurement concept the following will be recorded in the books of accounts

(a) Commission payable to salesman
(b) Directors and managers discussion
(c) Quality control in business
(d) None of the above

492. Revenue is generally recognised as being earned at the point of time, when
(a) Cash is received
(b) Sale is effected
(c) In financial year
(d) Production is complete

493. The current ratio of a firm is 5 : 3. Its net working capital is ₹ 20,000. The value of its current assets will be
(a) ₹ 20,000 (b) ₹ 60,000
(c) ₹ 30,000 (d) ₹ 50,000

494. The convention of conservatism implies that
(a) revenue must not be recognised unless it is accrued.
(b) Expected future losses must be provided for.
(c) Both of the above.
(d) None of the above.

495. Unless written off, the loss on issue of debentures is shown
(a) on the debit side of P and L A/c
(b) on the asset side of the balance-Sheet
(c) Both (a) and (b)
(d) None of the above

496. The cost of goods sold is ₹ 50,000. The value of opening and closing stock is ₹ 15,000 and ₹ 25,000 respectively. The stock turnover ratio will be
(a) 3.3 times (b) 1.25 times
(c) 2 times (d) 2.5 times

497. In case of admission of a new partner, the amount of goodwill brought in by him in the firm is shared by the old partners
(a) in the ratio of their capital
(b) in their old profit sharing ratio
(c) in the new ratio
(d) in their sacrificing ratio

498. In order to test the liquidity of the business which of the following ratio is used
(a) Acid test ratio
(b) Debt equity ratio
(c) Proprietary ratio
(d) Inventory turnover ratio

499. When all partners are insolvent the loss is borne by
(a) Creditors (b) Government
(c) Employers (d) Partners

500. Teeming and lading relates to
(a) Bribery of cash for some benefits.
(b) Frauds relating to the receipt of money from debtors.
(c) Misappropriation of cash.
(d) Pilferage of stock.

501. The owner of the business is treated as a creditor for the money invested by him is
(a) Money measurement concept.
(b) Lost concept.
(c) Business entity concept.
(d) Realisation concept.

502. Break Even, means
(a) Revenues are more than cost.
(b) Costs are more than the revenue.
(c) Revenues and cost are equal.
(d) None of the above.

503. In Garner Vs. Murray, the deficiency of the insolvent partners are borne by the solvent partners in the
(a) Capital ratio
(b) Profit sharing ratio
(c) Equal ratio
(d) None of the above

504. Copyright is a
(a) Real account
(b) Nominal account
(c) Personal account
(d) None of the above

505. Which of the following ratio is a ratio of solvency?

(a) Gross profit ratio
(b) Current ratio
(c) Return on capital employed
(d) Net profit ratio

506. Which of the following is a current liability?
(a) Bank overdraft (b) Debenture
(c) Share premium (d) Long term loan

507. In absence of partnership deed, the Interest on capital will be provided at _____ p.a.
(a) 6%
(b) 10%
(c) 5%
(d) Will not be provided

508. 'Garner Vs. Murray' relates to
(a) Hire purchase (b) Contract
(c) Deficiency A/c (d) Insolvency

509. Current account is prepared under
(a) Fluctuating capital
(b) Fixed capital
(c) Both fluctuating and fixed
(d) None of the above

510. On retirement of a partner which account is not prepared
(a) Adjustment A/c
(b) Revaluation A/c
(c) Distribution A/c
(d) Realisation

511. When a goodwill account is raised at the time of admission of a new partner then credit is given to the old partners in their
(a) New ratio
(b) Capital ratio
(c) Sacrificing ratio
(d) Old profit sharing ratio

512. The application money payable on a share should not be less than ____% of face value of share.
(a) 25% (b) 15%
(c) 5% (d) 10%

513. In which of the following way share application money can not be used
(a) repayment of application money.
(b) repayment of money on failure to get listed in a stock exchange.
(c) some fixed asset may be acquired.
(d) adjustment of excess money against allotment of shares is permitted to be dealt with, in stock exchange.

514. Given. Stock turnover 6 times
Total sales ₹ 3,00,000
Gross profit ratio 20%
Closing stock ₹ 4000 more than opening stock
The opening stock is
(a) ₹ 40,000 (b) ₹ 42,000
(c) ₹ 36,000 (d) ₹ 38,000

515. Going concern assumption of accounting is also known as
(a) Monetary unit assumption
(b) Accounting period assumption
(c) Continuity assumption
(d) None of the above

516. When we buy furniture on cash, we debit
(a) Furniture account
(b) Purchase account
(c) Cash account
(d) None of the above

517. The relationship between the consignor and the consignee is that of a
(a) Principal and agent
(b) Principal and distributor
(c) An agent and principal
(d) None of the above

518. In case of an unregistered firm a partner can not
(a) get interest on his capital
(b) get a share in profit
(c) get interest on loan
(d) file a suit against another partner

519. The Balance Sheet is only
(a) A statement (b) An account
(c) A summary (d) None of these

520. Intangible assets usually fall in the category of
(a) Fixed assets
(b) Semi fixed assets
(c) Current assets
(d) None of the above

521. Which one of the following is shown first when the assets are arranged in the order of their liquidity ?
(a) B/R (b) Cash in hand
(c) Debtors (d) Investment

522. Which one of the following is shown last, when the liabilities are arranged in the order of their performance?
(a) Bank overdraft
(b) Income received in advance
(c) B/P
(d) Outstanding expenses

523. When the amount of 'Calls in advance' is received, the accounting entry will be made as
(a) Bank A/c Dr.
To Call in advance A/c
(b) Call in advance A/c Dr.
To Relevant Call A/c
(c) Calls in advance A/c Dr.
To Bank A/c
(d) None of the above

524. When two or more existing companies go into liquidation and a new company is formed to take over their business, this activity is known as
(a) Amalgamation
(b) External reconstruction
(c) Internal reconstruction
(d) Absorption

525. Accounting standard (AS) 14 issued by ICAI on 'Accounting for Amalgamations' came into effect in respect of accounting period commencing on or after
(a) 1st April, 1995 (b) 1st April, 1994
(c) 1st April, 1997 (d) 1st April, 1996

526. If a new company Chandrika (New) Ltd. is formed to take over the business of an existing company Charu Ltd., it is a case of
(a) Amalgamation
(b) Absorption
(c) Internal reconstruction
(d) External reconstruction

527. Which of the following term is used when two or more existing companies go into liquidation and a new company is formed to take over their business?
(a) Absorption
(b) External reconstruction
(c) Internal reconstruction
(d) Amalgamation

528. The term 'Internal Reconstruction' includes
(a) Alternation of share capital
(b) Reduction of share capital
(c) Variation of shareholder's rights
(d) All of the above

529. Sonu Ltd. having 10,000 equity shares of ₹ 10 each decides to convert the share capital into equity stock. The accounting entry will be made as
(a) Equity Share Capital (₹ 10) A/c Dr. ₹ 100 000
To Equity Stock A/c ₹ 100 000
(b) Equity Stock A/cDr. ₹ 100 000
To Equity Share Capital (₹ 10) ₹ 100 000
(c) Both (a) and (b)
(d) None of the above

530. If current assets ₹ 2,00000, Stock ₹ 1,00,000 and working capital ₹ 1,20,000, then the current ratio will be

(a) 2.75 : 1 (b) 1.5 : 1
(c) 2.5 : 1 (d) 1.25 : 1

531. If total assets ₹ 2,60,000, total Debt ₹ 1,80,000, current liabilities ₹ 20,000, then the debt equity ratio will be
(a) 2 : 1 (b) 1 : 1
(c) 4 : 1 (d) 3 : 1

532. The 'Interest Coverage Ratio' is calculated by the following formula

(a) $\frac{\text{Net Profit after interest and taxes}}{\text{Interest on Long term debt}}$

(b) $\frac{\text{Interest on Long term debt}}{\text{Net Profit before interest and taxes}}$

(c) $\frac{\text{Interest on Long term debt}}{\text{Net Profit after interest and taxes}}$

(d) $\frac{\text{Net Profit before interest and taxes}}{\text{Interest on Long term debt}}$

533. Which of the following is not a limitation of ratio analysis?
(a) Accuracy of accounts are considered.
(b) Reality behind the statements are not considered.
(c) Not free from bias.
(d) Only quantitative factors are considered.

534. Out of the following, which statement is false in the context of responsibility accounting?
(a) Responsibility reporting is an accounting and management reporting system directed towards controlling costs according to responsibility centres.
(b) For successful implementation of the system the manager incharge of responsibility centre must know what is expected of him to achieve.
(c) Corrective actions should be taken but not communicated to the individual responsible centre.
(d) Managers or functional departments (Production/personnel) may be treated as cost centres.

535. Procedure for forfeiture and their reissue of shares is given in
(a) Articles of Association
(b) Prospectus
(c) Memorandum of Association
(d) None of the above

536. Current ratio is increased when
(a) cash is received from debtors
(b) debentures are converted into
(c) wages are paid
(d) old furniture is sold for cash

537. Income and expenditure account has a/an
(a) no opening balance
(b) opening debit balance
(c) opening credit balance
(d) None of the above

538. A public company having a share capital
(a) cannot file a statement in lieu of prospectus.
(b) may file a statement in lieu of prospectus.
(c) Must issue a prospectus.
(d) All of the above.

539. What is irredeemable preference shares?
(a) Which are repayable after a specified period.
(b) Which are not repayable during the life of the company.
(c) Which become equity shares after a specified period.
(d) None of the above.

540. Short sales in a stock exchange means
(a) selling shares and then buying the same shares.
(b) signing transfer deed without filling in the name of the transferee.

(c) selling those shares which one does not have.
(d) None of the above.

541. Capital gearing is the ratio between
(a) Equity capital and preference capital.
(b) Equity capital and fixed interest securities.
(c) Equity capital and debentures.
(d) None of the above.

542. Liablities in a company are ₹ 80,000 and owner's equity is ₹ 70,000. What is the amount of total equity?
(a) ₹ 10,000 (b) ₹ 1,50,000
(c) ₹ 80,000 (d) ₹ 70,000

543. The minimum subscription is to be received in
(a) 160 days (b) 130 days
(c) 120 days (d) 45 days

544. Bills receivable endorsed are debited to
(a) Creditors account
(b) B/R account
(c) Debtors account
(d) All of the above

545. Interest receivable on investments by a charitable institution will be shown on
(a) dr. side of income and expenditure A/c.
(b) assets side of balance sheet.
(c) liability side of the balance sheet.
(d) None of the above.

546. Receipts and payment account is a summary of
(a) dr. and cr. balances of ledger accounts.
(b) income and expenses.
(c) cash receipts and payments.
(d) None of the above.

547. On the admission of a partner, decrease in the value of machinery is debited to
(a) machinery a/c
(b) old partner's capital a/c
(c) P and L Adj. a/c
(d) None of the above

548. In partnership, who among the following can step out easily?
(a) Retiring partner (b) Infant
(c) Widow (d) None of these

549. Contingent liability is shown in the balance sheet due to
(a) convention of conservation
(b) convention of full disclosure
(c) going concern concept
(d) convention of materiality

550. Unclaimed dividends is shown in the balance sheet of company under the head
(a) current assets
(b) current liabilities
(c) reserves and surplus
(d) provisions

551. Increase in share premium account results in a
(a) Neither source nor use of fund
(b) Source of fund
(c) Use of fund
(d) None of the above

552. Purchases account always has a
(a) credit balance
(b) either debit or credit balance
(c) debit balance
(d) All of the above

553. If the rate of gross profit is 10% of the cost and the sales amount to ₹ 30,000 the cost of goods sold will be equal to
(a) 27,272 (b) 12,672
(c) 27,000 (d) 26,667

554. X and Y are partners in the ratio of 7 : 3. Z is admitted for 2/7 share. What is the new ratio?
(a) 7 : 4 : 5 (b) 7 : 3 : 4
(c) 7 : 2 : 2 (d) 7 : 3 : 2

555. X and Y are partners in the ratio of 3 : 2. Z is admitted and the new ratio is 4 : 3 : 2. What is the sacrificing ratio?
(a) 7 : 3 (b) 1 : 2
(c) 3 : 2 (d) 4 : 3

556. On admission of a new partner, good is raised for ₹ 20,000. This amount is debited to
(a) cash account
(b) goodwill account
(c) partner's account
(d) None of the above

557. Suspense account is required when
(a) errors are not quickly located and final accounts are to be prepared without delay.
(b) there are errors.
(c) debit side of trial balance is short.
(d) credit side of trial balance is short.

558. An expense of ₹ 500 paid as cartage of a new machine purchased should be debited to
(a) Machine A/c (b) Cash A/c
(c) Cartage A/c (d) All of the above

559. What is the adjustment entry for closing stock?
(a) Stock A/c Dr.
To Trading A/c
(b) Opening Stock A/c Dr.
To Closing Stock
(c) Trading A/c Dr.
To Stock A/c
(d) None of the above

560. Which of the following is an accounting equation?
(a) Assets = Liabilities – Equity
(b) Assets = Equities
(c) Assets = Equities + Liabilities
(d) None of the above

561. Receipts and payments A/c is a
(a) Nominal A/c (b) Personal A/c
(c) Real A/c (d) None of these

562. Which of the following statements does not apply to receipts and payment A/c?
(a) Balance at the end represents cash balance.
(b) It is similar to profit and loss A/c.
(c) It is summary of cash transactions.
(d) It shows both capital as well as revenue itemss.

563. Income and expenditure A/c begins with
(a) credit balance (b) debit balance
(c) no balance (d) None of these

564. Sales + Closing Stock – Purchases – Gross Profit is equal to
(a) Purchases returns
(b) Cost of goods sold
(c) Wages
(d) Opening stock

565. Capital redemption reserve is created out of
(a) General reserve
(b) Share premium A/c
(c) Sinking fund
(d) Share forfeiture A/c

566. When shares are issued to promoters, what is the accounting entry?
(a) Promotion expenses Dr.
To Share Capital A/c
(b) Goodwill A/c Dr.
To Share Capital A/c
(c) Promoters' personal A/c Dr.
To Share Capital A/c
(d) Bank A/c Dr.
To Share Capital A/c

567. 'Higher the ratio, the lower profitability', is applicable to
(a) Debtor's turnover ratio
(b) Current ratio

(c) Operating ratio
(d) Return on investment

568. Wages paid is
(a) not a flow of fund
(b) a source of fund
(c) an application of fund
(d) None of the above

569. Assets of business = ₹ 20,000
Liablities = ₹ 3,600
What is the owner's equity?
(a) ₹ 20,000 (b) ₹ 3,600
(c) ₹ 23,600 (d) ₹ 16,400

570. Cost of goods sold = ₹ 2,00,000
Gross Loss = 25% of sales
What is the amount of sales?
(a) ₹ 2,40,000 (b) ₹ 2,50,000
(c) ₹ 2,00,000 (d) ₹ 1,60,000

571. Goodwill is a
(a) intangible asset (b) current asset
(c) liquid asset (d) fictitious asset

572. When dividend is declare, it must be paid within
(a) 45 days (b) 60 days
(c) 30 days (d) 42 days

573. Cash A/c shown in the trial balance shows
(a) cash balance on the date of trial balance.
(b) cash receipts during the year.
(c) cash payments during the year.
(d) None of the above.

574. Which of the following accounts will usually have a credit balance?
(a) Bills payable
(b) Bills receivable
(c) Misc. expenditure
(d) Sales return

575. Net worth of a business means
(a) only equity capital
(b) total assets of the business
(c) total assets less liabilities
(d) total share capital

576. The credit balance of a bank account shows
(a) bank overdraft
(b) balance in bank account
(c) Both (a) and (b)
(c) None of the above

577. The most rigorous test of liquidity is
(a) stock turnover ratio
(b) current ratio
(c) debtors turnover ratio
(d) acid test ratio

578. The effect of irregular allotment is that it is
(a) Voidable (at the option of the shareholder)
(b) Legal
(c) Illegal
(d) Void

579. Double entry principle means
(a) maintaining the double account for all business transactions.
(b) writing two times the same entry.
(c) having debit for every credit, and similarly, credit for each debit.
(d) writing all the entries twice in the book.

580. A sale of goods to Vaibhav Deep for cash should be debited to
(a) Sale of goods A/c
(b) Vaibhav's A/c
(c) Cash A/c
(d) None of the above

581. A withdrawal of cash from business by the proprietor of the firm should be credited to
(a) Proprietors' account
(b) Drawing account
(c) Capital
(d) Cash account

582. The preparation of a trial balance helps in
(a) locating errors of omission.
(b) locating clerical errors.
(c) locating compensatory errors.
(d) locating errors of principle.

583. A cheque received and deposited in the bank on the same day is recorded in the
(a) credited in the cash book.
(b) cash column of the cash book.
(c) debited in the cash book.
(d) baitk column of the cash book.

584. A reserve is charge against
(a) Profit and loss appropriation account
(b) Trading account
(c) Profit and loss account
(d) None of the above

585. Which of the following is created by debiting the profit and loss account?
(a) Dividend equalisation fund
(b) Provisions
(c) Sinking fund for redemption of debentures
(d) All of the above

586. Any reserve which is not apparent on the face of the balance sheet is known as
(a) Inner reserve
(b) Secret reserve
(c) Hidden reserve
(d) Any of the above

587. Expenditure incurred by a publisher for acquiring copyrights is a
(a) revenue expenditure
(b) deferred revenue expenditure
(c) capital expenditure
(d) None of the above

588. Immediately after purchasing a new truck ₹ 1000 is paid to have the name of the company and other advertising material painted on the truck. This ₹ 1000 is a
(a) revenue expenditure
(b) capital expenditure
(c) deferred revenue expenditure
(d) None of the above

589. A return inwards book is kept to record
(a) returns of goods purchased.
(b) returns of goods sold.
(c) returns of anything sold.
(d) returns of anything purchased.

590. Bills receivable book is a part of the
(a) Journal
(b) Ledger
(c) Profit and Loss account
(d) Balance sheet

591. A sale of ₹ 2000 wrongly entered in the purchase book
(a) increases the gross profit by ₹ 4000
(b) decreases the gross profit by ₹ 2000
(c) increases the gross profit by ₹ 2000
(d) None of the above

592. Which of the following is an operating expenses?
(a) Expired insurance
(b) Depreciation of plant
(c) None of the above
(d) All of the above

593. Which of the following are current assets?
(a) Account receivable
(b) Bank loan for three years
(c) Debentures sinking fund investments
(d) Long term investments

594. Insurance unexpired accounts is a
(a) nominal account
(b) real account
(c) personal account
(d) None of the above

595. Goodwill account is a
(a) real account
(b) personal account
(c) nominal account
(d) None of the above

596. Bank overdraft account of a
(a) real account
(b) nominal account
(c) personal account
(d) All of the above

597. Contingent liability is shown due to
(a) convention of materiality
(b) dual aspect concept
(c) convention of conservatism
(d) convention of full disclosure

598. Which item is shown on the debit side of a trial balance?
(a) Over expenses by the firm
(b) Purchases returns
(c) Prepaid expenses
(d) Rent outstanding

599. Sales on account is recorded in
(a) sales book (b) general journal
(c) cash book (d) journal

600. The credit balance in the bank account is
(a) an asset (b) an expenses
(c) a capital (d) a liability

601. Cash sales are recorded in
(a) journal (b) purchase book
(c) cash book (d) sales book

602. Error of commission do not permit
(a) correct the total of balance sheet.
(b) correct totalling of trial balance.
(c) the trial balance to agree.
(d) None of the above.

603. An item of ₹ 72 has been debited to a personal account as ₹ 27 is an error of
(a) Omission
(b) Principle
(c) Commission
(d) None of the above

604. Sales to Shyam of ₹ 500 not recorded in the books would affect
(a) Cash account
(b) Shyam's account
(c) Sales account
(d) Sales account and Shyam's account

605. Which of the following accounts is increased by credit entries?
(a) Sales return account
(b) Bank overdraft
(c) Purchases account
(d) Goodwill account

606. A bill of exchange is drawn by a
(a) Debenture holder
(b) Share holder
(c) Debtor
(d) Creditor

607. If a share of ₹ 10 issued at a premium of ₹ 1, on which ₹ 9 (including premium) have been called and ₹ 7 (including premium) paid is forfeited the capital account should be debited by
(a) ₹ 7 (b) ₹ 6
(c) ₹ 8 (d) ₹ 9

608. If vendors are issued fully paid shares of ₹ 1,00,000 in consideration of net assets of ₹ 1,20,000 the balance of ₹ 20000 will be credited to
(a) aapital reserve account
(b) goodwill account
(c) vendor's account
(d) profit and loss account

609. Partner's salaries to be debited to
(a) profit and loss account
(b) trading account
(c) profit and loss appropriation account
(d) None of the above

610. In the absence of any partnership deed, interest on partner's loan will be allowed at the rate of
(a) 9% (b) 12%
(c) 5% (d) 6%

611. On the admission of a new partner the decrease in the value of assets is debited to

(a) old partner's capital account
(b) revaluation account
(c) assets account
(d) new partner's capital account

612. Goodwill of a firm of A and B is valued at ₹ 30000. It is appealing in the books at ₹ 12000. C is admitted for 1/4 share. What amount he is supposed to bring for goodwill?
(a) ₹ 7500 (b) ₹ 10500
(c) ₹ 3000 (d) ₹ 4500

613. A and B are partners in the ratio of 2 : 1. They admit C for 1/4 share who contributes for ₹ 3000 for his share of goodwill. The total value of goodwill of the firm is
(a) ₹ 9000 (b) ₹ 15000
(c) ₹ 3000 (d) ₹ 12000

614. When a firm is dissolved, profit or loss on realisation is shared by the partners
(a) in the ratio of their capital balances.
(b) in the ratio laid down in Garner V. Murray.
(c) equal.
(d) in the profit sharing ratio.

615. C and D are equal partners. Their trial capital balances on dissolution of the firm are C ₹ 25000 and D ₹ 15000. Total cash available is ₹ 30000. How should this cash be distribute between C and D?
(a) ₹ 18750 to C and ₹ 11250 to D
(b) According to decision in Garner V. Murray
(c) ₹ 15000 each
(d) ₹ 20000 to C and ₹ 10000 to D

616. At the time of dissolution an unrecorded asset taken by Mr. X a partner should be debited to
(a) Assets A/c
(b) Mr. X's Capital A/c
(c) Realisation A/c
(d) None of the above

617. A second hand machinery was purchased for ₹ 1,00,000 five years ago and was overhauled by carrying out some current repairs at a cost of ₹ 10,000. It has also an accumulated depreciation of ₹ 50,000. It has been disposed of in the beginning of the sixth year for ₹ 60,000. profit or loss on such disposal shall be
(a) no profit, no loss
(b) loss of ₹ 40,000
(c) profit of ₹ 10,000
(d) loss of ₹ 50,000

618. Concept of conservatism refers to taking into account
(a) only cash profit.
(b) only profit realised.
(c) profit realised and all possible losses.
(d) all profit.

619. Which one of the following accounting standards is not mandatory in India?
(a) Inventory and depreciation accounting.
(b) Fixed assets accounting and revenue recognition.
(c) Monetary assets and depreciation accounting.
(d) Non-monetary assets and fixed assets.

620. Payment of compensation to a worker, who has been discharged from service, is a
(a) deferred-revenue expenditure.
(b) capital expenditure.
(c) revenue expenditure.
(d) non-business expenditure.

621. Expenditure incurred on research is an example of
(a) deferred-revenue expenditrue.
(b) capital expenditure.
(c) party capital expenditure and partly revenue expenditrue.
(d) revenue expenditrue.

622. ₹ 19,500 debited to building repairs on 31st December 1993 included ₹ 9,500 as the cost of building a small room for the watchman. A bill of ₹ 800 for colour wash of the whole building during the year was not received till December 1993. The amount to be debited to profit and loss account would be
(a) ₹ 10,800 (b) ₹ 9,500
(c) ₹ 20,300 (d) ₹ 19,500

623. Account books for how many proceeding years should be preserved in good condition?
(a) 10 (b) 13
(c) 5 (d) 8

624. In the event of dissolution of a firm,the partners' personal assets are first applied for payment of
(a) the firm's liabilities.
(b) the personal liabilities.
(c) the preferential and tax liabilities.
(d) Both the personal and firm's liabilities.

625. A, B, C, D are partners sharing profits and losses in the raito 3 : 3 : 2 : 1. The partnership is dissolved and D becomes insolvent. C brings only his share of loss shows his inability to contribute anything towards D's deficiency. According to Garner vs. Murray ruling D's deficiency in the total will be shared by
(a) A, B and C in their profit sharing ratio.
(b) A and B in their capital ratio.
(c) A, B and C equally.
(d) A, B andC in their captial ratio.

626. According to Companies Act, a "reserve capita" is created
(a) for issue to the existing shareholders as rights of shares.
(b) for a specific purpose at any time during its working life.
(c) for conversion of FCDS into equity shares.
(d) as the uncalled portion of share capital of a limited company to be called only in the event of winding up.

627. Amount set apart to meet probable losses on account of bad debts is a
(a) provision
(b) liability
(c) contingent liability
(d) reserve

628. Consider the following income statement

Credit side.	
By Gross income	1,00,000
By profit on sale of investment	5,000
	1,05,000
Debit side.	
To Salaries	8,000
Add: Outstanding	2,000
	10,000
To Stationery	2,000
To Rent	3,000
To provision for depreciation	10,000
To Bad debts	2,000
To Loss on sale of machinery	3,000
To Provision for taxation	10,000
To Net income	65,000
	1,05,000

Which one of the following will be the correct 'Fund from operation'?
(a) ₹ 75,000 (b) ₹ 73,000
(c) ₹ 92,000 (d) ₹ 83,000

629. It is given that the cost of the stock is ₹ 100. However its current market price is ₹ 95 (buying)and ₹ 90 (selling). If the market price is interpreted in the sense of

replacement cost, the stock should be valued at

(a) ₹ 90 (b) ₹ 93
(c) ₹ 95 (d) ₹ 100

630. When sale is ₹ 4,80,000, gross loss is 25% on cost, purchase is ₹ 3,50,000 and closing stock is ₹ 60,000, the stock in the beginning would be

(a) ₹ 1,34,000 (b) ₹ 3,50,000
(c) ₹ 70,000 (d) ₹ 94,000

631. Which one of the following is not a current liability?

(a) Loan instalment payable in the current year.
(b) Temporary bank overdraft.
(c) Arrears of preference dividend.
(d) Acceptances.

632. Given that

Closing stock	₹ 30,000
Opening stock	₹ 20,000
Sales	₹ 1,00,000
Administrative and Selling expenses	₹ 20,000
Purchases	₹ 70,000

The operating ratio is

(a) 75% (b) 80%
(c) 65% (d) 50%

633. If a minor choose to continue as a partner on attaining the age of majority, he will be liable to the debts of the firm from the date of his

(a) choosing to become a partner at a subsequent date.
(b) attaining majority.
(c) guardian giving the option.
(d) admissjon to profits of the firm.

634. The liability of the Karta in a joint Hindu family is

(a) unlimited.
(b) limited to his interest in the joint family.
(c) limited to the private properties of all the members.
(d) limited to the entire property of the family.

635. The proprietor of a business is treated as a creditor for capital introduced by him according to

(a) cost concept
(b) business entity concept
(c) dual aspect concept
(d) money measurement concept

636. Which one of the following statements is correct?

(a) Real accounts relate to assets of a business.
(b) Capital of a firm is reduced by borrowing.
(c) When there is no change is proprietor's capital it is an indication of loss in business.
(d) Nominal accounts refer to false transactions.

637. Trade discount allowed on sales is

(a) credited to customer's account
(b) debited to profit and loss account
(c) debited to customer's account
(d) None of the above

638. Accounting principle represent

(a) inviolable laws fixed by the legal boards.
(b) a consensus at a particular time to the recording of accounting transactions.
(c) laws fixed by the respective governments.
(d) laws fixed by accounting experts.

639. How does an overcosting of purchase day book affect the cost of sales and profit?

(a) Cost of sales is increased while profit is decreased.
(b) Cost of sales is decreased while profit is increased.

(c) Cost of sales is increased, gross profit is decreased.
(d) Both cost of sales and profit are increased.

640. Consistency with reference to application of accounting principles refers to the fact that
(a) income and assets have not been overstand.
(b) companies in the same industry use identical accounting procedures and method, and are consistent.
(c) all methods and procedures have been utilised.
(d) accounting methods and procedures used have been consistently applied from year to year.

641. The following are the figures relating to a trader.

Opening stock	₹ 10,000
Closing stock	₹ 11, 000
Purchases	₹ 70,000

The goods are sold at a profit of 30% on cost. The amount of sales will be
(a) ₹ 89,700 (b) ₹ 21,000
(c) ₹ 1,04,000 (d) ₹ 91,000

642. When a goodwill account is raised at the time of admission of a new partner, credit is given to old partners in their
(a) capital ratio
(b) new profit sharing ratio
(c) old profit sharing ratio
(d) ratio of sacrifice

643. A and B were equal partners in a firm on 1-1-1982, they admitted C on the following conditions
C should bring ₹ 10,000 as capital, and ₹ 5,000 as goodwill, in future A, B and C would share profits and losses in the ratio of 2 : 1 : 2. A and B will share the goodwill in the ratio of
(a) 1 : 3 (b) 2 : 1
(c) 1 : 1 (d) 3 : 1

644. On 31st December, 1982 the assets and liabilities of a firm were ₹ 40,000 and ₹ 30,000 respectively. The firm was dissolved and a sum of 60 paise in a rupee was paid to the creditors. What was the loss on realisation?
(a) ₹ 18,000 (b) ₹ 22,000
(c) ₹ 10.000 (d) ₹ 12,000

645. When an incoming partner purchases his share from one of the existing partners
(a) the assets of the firm will be augmented to the extent of the payment received from the new partner.
(b) the total assets of the firm do not change.
(c) the change in the total assets of the firm will depend upon the structure of the assets.
(d) the total assets of the firm will be reduced if the existing partner withdraws the share surrendered.

646. Subscription amounting to ₹ 7,500 appear on the credit side of Income and Expenditure Account after adusting subscriptions outstanding ₹ 600 and subscription received in advance ₹ 450. The amount of subscription to be shown in the Receipts and Payments Account for the same year will be
(a) ₹ 7,350 (b) ₹ 6,450
(c) ₹ 8,550 (d) ₹ 7,650

647. While preparing the final accounts from incomplete records, the capital is to be taken as equal to the
(a) total assets.
(b) value of fixed assets.
(c) net assets.
(d) difference between the current assets and current liability.

648. If sales are ₹ 60,000 gross profit is 1/3 on cost; purchases are ₹ 49,000 and the closing stock is ₹ 9,000 the opening stock will be

(a) ₹ 20,000 (b) ₹ 49,000
(c) Nil (d) ₹ 5,00

649. Debentures redeemed but not claimed by the debenture holders appear in the balance sheet as 'Debentures redeemed but not paid' under the heading

(a) unsecured loans
(b) secured loans
(c) contingent liabilities
(d) current liabilities

650. Profit on re-issue of forfeited shares is transferred to

(a) Capital reserve A/c
(b) General reserve A/c
(c) Profit and Loss A/c
(d) Share capital A/c

651. Consider the following items which appear under "Reserves and Surpluses" of balance sheet of a company

(a) Share premium
(b) Profit and Loss account
(c) Capital reserve
(d) Capital redemption reserve

652. If earnings per share of X Limited is ₹ 15 and the price earnings ratio of other similiar companies is ₹ 10, then the market value of the share of X Ltd. will be

(a) ₹ 75 (b) ₹ 25
(c) ₹300 (d) ₹ 150

653. Given in the following table is data for various companies in the same industry:

	A	B	C	D
Current Assets	150	140	100	120
A/C Receivable	60	50	50	70
Turnover Ratio	6.5	5.0	5.5	5.0
Current Liabilities	100	120	80	130

The two firm which appear to be having better liquidity position are

(a) A and C (b) A and B
(c) B and D (d) B and C

654. Profits can be fraudulently inflated by

(a) treating capital expenditure as revenue.
(b) suppression of sales returns.
(c) omission of prepaid expenses.
(d) overestimation of liabilities.

655. The trial balance of a manufacturing concern at the close of its financial year showed the following revenue balance.

	₹
Raw material and Stores consumed	2,00,000
Salaries and wages	50,000
Other manufacturing expenses	1,00,000
Sales	3,00,000

The closing stock at selling rates amounted to ₹ 80,000. The management wants to change the basic of valuation of closing stock from selling rates to cost or market price, whichever is lower. Besides the figures given above, no other data are available.

The closing stock value is

(a) ₹ 73,684.22 (b) ₹ 64,385.40
(c) ₹ 83,674.30 (d) ₹ 75,933.50

656. Teeming and Lading refers to

(a) bribery for securing orders.
(b) frauds related to the receipt of cash fromdebtors.
(c) misappropriation of cash by showing fictious purchases.
(d) pilferage of stock.

657. Which one of the following pairs is correctly matched?

	Item	Voucher to be checked
(a)	Bank with drawals	pay-in-slip
(b)	Returns outward	Credit note issued by the supplier

(c)	Del Credere Commission	B/R Book
(d)	Returns inward	Debit note issued by the firm

658. Qualification share is a requirement prescribed for
   (a) auditors of the company
   (b) directors of the company
   (c) officers of the company
   (d) creditors of the company

659. What is the correct sequence in which the capital of a company is raised?
   (a) Nominal, Issued, Called-up, Subscribed
   (b) Issued, Subscribed, Called-up Nominal
   (c) Issued, Nominal, Subscribed, Called-up
   (d) Issued, Nominal, Called-up, Subscribed

660. Allotment of shares can be taken up only after
   (a) directors have taken up qualification shares.
   (b) it is approved by the shareholders in the general body meeting.
   (c) clearance is obtained from the controller of capital issues.
   (d) minimum subscribed is recevied.

661. Those preference shares which do not enjoy the right to share additional profits come under the category of
   (a) non-participating preference shares.
   (b) irredeemable preference shares.
   (c) participating preference shares.
   (d) non-cumulative preference shares.

662. Under the Companies Act, 1956, the balance sheet and profit and loss account of a company are required to be signed by the manager or the secretary of the company and by how many directors including the managing director?
   (a) Three (b) Two
   (c) One (d) All of the above

663. Rights issue refers to the shares issued to
   (a) existing directors
   (b) employees
   (c) public
   (d) None of the above

664. Bonus shares can be issued by a company
   (a) out of share premium not collected in cash.
   (b) out of the reseves created by revaluation of fixed assets.
   (c) out of free reserves built out of genuine profits.
   (d) without any provision for it in the Articles of Association of the company.

665. Which one of the following types of companies deals with only its shareholders for their benefit?
   (a) Authorised capital
   (b) Paid up capital
   (c) Reserve capital
   (d) Uncalled capital

666. Share premium received by issuing shares can be used for
   (a) issue of bonus shares.
   (b) remuneration to management.
   (c) payment of dividend.
   (d) any business purpose.

667. Financial disintermediation results in larger
   (a) securities-related income.
   (b) access to financial institutions.
   (c) participation of foreign financial institutions.
   (d) fee-based income.

668. Consistency with reference to application of accounting principles refer to the fact that
   (a) accounting methods and procedures used have been consistently applied from year to year.

(b) companies in the same industry use identical accounting procedures and methods.
(c) income and assets have not been over stated.
(d) All the methods and procedures have been utilized.

669. Making the provision for bad and doubtful debts in anticipation of actual bad debts is on the basis of
(a) convention of consistency.
(b) conventions of disclosure and consistency.
(c) convention of disclosure.
(d) convention of conservatism.

670. Following data appear in the books of XY and Co. as on 31.03.13.

Capital Account	₹ 13,00,000
Drawing Account	₹ 12,000
Land and Building Account	₹ 10,00,000
Goodwill Account	₹ 3,50,000
Suspense Account (Dr)	₹ 50,000
Loss by theft Account	₹ 20,000
Business loss	₹ 50,000
Loan given to AB and Co.	₹ 60,000

What will be the amount of sundry creditors?
(a) ₹ 3,42,000 (b) ₹ 2,42,000
(c) ₹ 2,30,000 (d) ₹ 1,72,000

671. Under the accrual concept, which one of the following will be shown as an asset/ liability in the balance sheet of an entity?
(a) Interest paid but not due
(b) Interest due but not paid
(c) Interest due but not received
(d) Interest due and paid

672. When shares are forfeited, the share capital account is debited by
(a) called-up amount
(b) paid-up amount
(c) market value of the shares
(d) nominal value of the shares

673. A company can pay dividend out of
(a) undistributed profits of the previous financial years.
(b) money provided by the Central and State Governments for the payment of dividends in pursuance of their guarantees.
(c) profits of the company for the year for which dividends are to be paid.
(d) All of the above.

674. The following figures are taken from a Balance Sheet.

	₹
Equity share capital	1,10,000
6% Preference share capital	30,000
General reserve	50,000
Reserve for contingencies	20,000
6% Mortage debentures	50,000
Sundry creditors	20,000
Preliminary expenses	5,000
Prepaid expenses	4,000

In this case, the debt equity ratio is
(a) 24 : 1 (b) 1 : 2
(c) 2 : 1 (d) None of these

675. Which one of the following statements is correct? Civil liability of an auditor implies liability for
(a) misappropriation of goods
(b) misappropriation of cash
(c) misfeasance
(d) fraud

676. Following are the information pertaining to X Company Ltd.
Right to buy one share @ ₹ 17 per share for every five shares of ₹ 10 each held in

the company. Market value of the shares on the date of such offer is ₹ 35 per share. Which one of the following is the value of the right?

(a) ₹ 3.00 (b) ₹ 8.67
(c) ₹ 13.00 (d) ₹ 4.50

677. Which one of the following statements regarding forfeiture of shares is not correct?

(a) Board may consider the request from the defaulting ex-shareholder for the cancellation of forfeiture before the disposal of forfeited shares.
(b) Return of allotment of re-issue of forfeited shares is filed with the Registrar of Companies.
(c) The title of the new purchaser is not affected by any irregularity in the forfeiture or sale of the shares.
(d) Forfeited shares may be re-issued at a discount or at a premium.

678. Which one of the following is correct for cooperative organisations?

(a) There is a cap on the dividend payment.
(b) There is a cap on the maximum number of members.
(c) There is a ceiling on the salaries paid to employees of cooperative organisations.
(d) There are restrictions on their business growth.

679. When does a retiring partner of a partnership firm continue to be liable for obligations incurred after his retirement?

(a) When he had left the firm within 3 months of joining it.
(b) When he does not give public notice.
(c) When unpaid amount is not transfered to him.
(d) All of the above.

680. Liability of shareholders of a limited company or of a company limited by guarantee can be made unlimited only it is expressly agreed to by which of the following?

(a) The Registrar of joint stock companies
(b) Each and every member concerned
(c) A majority of shareholders
(d) A qualified majority

681. M/s. ABC Ltd. forfeited 20 shares of ₹ 10 each, ₹ 8 called up, on which X had paid application and allotment money of ₹ 2 and ₹ 3 respectively. These shares were re issued to Y at ₹ 6 each fully paid. What was the balance in share forfeiture account before the shares were re-issued?

(a) ₹ 100 (b) ₹ 160
(c) ₹ 40 (d) ₹ 60

682. A sum of ₹ 50,000 was spent by a factory in overhauling its existing plant and machinery, and it enhanced its working life by five years. The aforesaid expenditure is

(a) deferred revenue expenditure.
(b) revenue expenditure.
(c) partly capital and partly revenue expenditure.
(d) capital expenditure.

683. If a radio seller-proprietor buys a radio for his personal use from out of business funds, the amount paid for the radio will be treated as 'drawings' of the proprietor because of the

(a) going concern concept
(b) dual aspect concept
(c) matching concept
(d) business entity concept

684. What would be the amount of sales when opening stock is ₹ 50,000; purchases ₹ 1,50,000; wages ₹ 20,000; closing stock ₹ 40,000 and gross profit is 1/7th of sales?

(a) ₹ 1,86,669 (b) ₹ 2,00,000
(c) ₹ 2,10,000 (d) ₹ 1,80,000

685. How is a speculator, who buys the shares of a new company with a view to selling them at a premium to genuine investors before allotment, known?
(a) As a Bull (b) As a Bear
(c) As a Stag (d) As a Lame Duck

686. Which one of the following is not indicated by an increase in the gross profit ratio as compared to that for the previous period?
(a) Invoices for purchases omitted from the account.
(b) An increase in the sale price of the goods sold without corresponding increase in costs.
(c) Stock in trade at the beginning valued at a figure lower than it should have been.
(d) Stock omitted from the inventory at the end of the period.

687. XYZ Ltd. provides the following information:

Net Profit	₹ 1,600
Profit on sale of investments	₹ 480
Depreciation	₹ 5,200
Loss on sale of machinery	₹ 200
Increase in stock	₹ 1,000
Increase in creditors	₹ 1,000

What is the amount of funds from operations of the company?
(a) ₹ 8520 (b) ₹ 6520
(c) ₹ 7000 (d) ₹ 7520

688. While auditing, the auditor finds a balance of ₹ 10,000 in goodwill account and ascertains that the amount has not been written off for a long period. What may be the course of action for the auditor?
(a) He may recommend the concern to write off goodwill over a period of 5 years.
(b) He may allow goodwill to appear forever.
(c) He may advise the concern to write off the goodwill.
(d) He may insist the concern to write off the goodwill in the same year.

689. The following information is available regarding subscription from the members of X Club during the year 2003-04.

Subscription Income	:	₹ 28,000
Outstanding subscription at the end of the year	:	₹ 1,160
Outstanding subscription at the beginning of the year	:	₹ 360
Subscription received in advance	:	₹ 640

What is the amount of receipt of the club from subscription during the year 2003-04?
(a) ₹ 27,840 (b) ₹ 29,520
(c) ₹ 28,160 (d) ₹ 29,000

690. A steel fabrication firm receives an income for service rendered by its design engineer to a friendly party. How should this be treated in the profit and loss account of the firm?
(a) Should be shown as non-operating income.
(b) Should be shown as sales income.
(c) Should be shown as miscellaneous income.
(d) Not an income of the firm.

691. Which of the following assets does not depreciate?
(a) Patents
(b) Plant and Machinery
(c) Furniture
(d) Land

692. Balance in a petty cash book is
(a) a profit (b) an asset
(c) an expense (d) None of these

693. Sales book is part of
(a) Balance Sheet (b) Journal
(c) Ledger (d) None of these

694. In the purchase book, the record is in respect of
(a) credit purchases of goods dealt in
(b) cash purchase of book
(c) all purchase of goods dealt in
(d) None of the above

695. Purchases of office furniture ₹ 2,500 has been debited to general expense account. It is
(a) a clerical error
(b) an error of omission
(c) a compensating error
(d) an error of principle

696. Manufacturing account is prepared to
(a) ascertain the cost of the goods manufactured.
(b) show the sale proceeds from the goods manufactured during the year.
(c) ascertain the profit or loss on the goods produced.
(d) None of the above.

697. Outstanding rent is a
(a) Real account
(b) Nominal account
(c) Personal account
(d) None of the above

698. Outstanding interest income is
(a) an expense (b) an asset
(c) a liability (d) None of these

699. The general manager is entitled to a commission of 5% on profit before deducting such commission. What is the amount of commission if profit is ₹ 10,500?
(a) ₹ 525 (b) ₹ 552.65
(c) ₹ 500 (d) None of these

700. A firm sells goods at a gross margin of 25% on sales. Opening stock was ₹ 40,000 and closing stock was ₹ 30,000. Purchases during the period were ₹ 1,10,000. What is the amount of salary?
(a) ₹ 2,00,000 (b) ₹ 1,50,000
(c) ₹ 1.60,000 (d) ₹ 1,20.000

701. On the admission of a partner, goodwill is raised for ₹ 45,000. This amount is debited to
(a) Goodwill account
(b) Cash account
(c) Capital accounts of partners
(d) None of the above

702. R and K are partners sharing profits in the ratio of 4 : 3. S joins and the new ratio of R, K and S is 7 : 4 : 3 What is the sacrificing ratio?
(a) Equal (b) 4 : 3
(c) 1 : 2 (d) 2 : 1

703. X and Y are partners sharing profits and losses in the ratio 3:2; X's son Z is admitted as a partner. X makes a gift of ₹ 1/5 share out of his profits to Z. Goodwill of the firm is valued at ₹ 40,000. Z will pay
(a) ₹ 8,000 to X and ₹ 8,000 to Y
(b) ₹ 8,000 to X
(c) ₹ 4,000 to X and ₹ 4,000 to Y
(d) Nothing at all

704. Profits on revaluation of assets and liabilities at the time of retirement of a partner will be credited to
(a) remaining partners in their gaining ratio.
(b) all the partners in their old ratio.
(c) all partners in their profit sharing ratio.
(d) remaining partners in their profit sharing ratio.

705. Realisation account is a
(a) Nominal account
(b) Personal account

(c) Real account
(d) None of the above

706. Subscription income of See Too Club for the year 1987 is ₹ 4,500. Subscription received in advance during 1987 is ₹ 360, and subscription outstanding on 31st December, 1987 is ₹ 140. What amount on account of subscriptions will be entered in the receipts and payments accounts for the year ending 31st December, 1987?
(a) ₹ 4,720 (b) ₹ 4,280
(c) ₹ 4,500 (d) ₹ 5,000

707. Which of the following accounts open with an opening balance?
(a) Trading account
(b) Income and expenditure account
(c) Receipts and payment account
(d) None of the above

708. Sale of growing grass in the case of a sports club is
(a) a revenue receipt
(b) a capital receipt
(c) an asset
(d) None of the above

709. Which of the following items results in flow of funds?
(a) Transfer of profit to general reserve
(b) Goodwill written off
(c) Issue of bonus shares
(d) Building sold on credit

710. In order to save income tax, which method should be followed when prices are showing a rising trend?
(a) LIFO
(b) FIFO
(c) Weighted average method
(d) None of the above

711. The term depletion is used in relation to
(a) Fictitious asset (b) Wasting asset
(c) Current asset (d) Fixed asset

712. A company usually can not issue shares at a discount of more than
(a) 15%
(b) 20%
(c) 10%
(d) can not issue shares at a discount

713. In the Balance Sheet of a company, 'loose tools' is shown under
(a) Current liabilities (b) Fixed assets
(c) Current assets (d) None of these

714. The best time to raise capital by a company is during
(a) Boom (b) Recovery
(c) Depression (d) Recession

715. A company can trade on equity when it has issued
(a) debentures and preference and equity capital.
(b) only equity capital.
(c) only preference capital.
(d) All of the above.

716. Total of sales book of a company indicates
(a) total credit purchases for the period.
(b) total sales of the period.
(c) total cash purchases for the period.
(d) None of the above.

717. A company has credited sinking fund for redemption of debentures. When the investments in S.F. are sold, at a profit, the accounting entry is
(a) S.F. A/(c) Dr.
To S.F. Investments A/(c)
(b) To S.F. Investments A/(c) Dr.
To Debentures
(c) To S.F. Investments A/(c) Dr.
To S.F. A/(c)
(d) None of the above

718. Over capitalisation refers to
(a) raising more capital than is warranted by its earning power.
(b) over-estimating the rate of capitalisation.

(c) excess of capital.
(d) excessive rate of dividend on equity shares.

719. Rights issued implies that
(a) equity shares are issued at a discount.
(b) the new shares of a company are issued to the existing shareholders.
(c) equity shares are issued at a premium.
(d) All of the above.

720. A purchase of ₹ 1,250 was entered in the purchase book as ₹ 2,150. It is an error of
(a) Commission
(b) Principle
(c) Compensating error
(d) Ommission

721. Assets in the balance sheet of a company are arranged in the order of
(a) Book value (b) Permanence
(c) Liquidity (d) Market value

722. A firm is dissolved
(a) when all the partners except one die or retire.
(b) when a partner retires.
(c) when a partner dies.
(d) All of the above.

723. On a ten rupee share, ₹ 8 has been called up, on forfeiture the amount to be debited to the share capital account will be
(a) ₹ 8 (b) ₹ 5
(c) ₹ 10 (d) None of these

724. A, B and C are partners in the ratio of 5 : 3 : 2, B retires the new ratio of A and C is
(a) Equal (b) 5 : 2
(c) 3 : 2 (d) 5 : 3

725. X, Y and Z are partners in the ratio of 1/2, 1/3 and 1/6. Z dies, the gaining ratio of X and Y will be
(a) 2 : 3 (b) Equal
(c) 3 : 2 (d) None of these

726. Given Cost of goods sold ₹ 60,000 Sales ₹ 82,000 Sales returns ₹ 2,000.
The operating ratio is
(a) 75% (b) 80%
(c) 20% (d) 5%

727. In the above question, the gross profit ratio is
(a) 25% (b) 80%
(c) 5% (d) 20%

728. Which of the following is an application of fund
(a) issue of share capital.
(b) sale of fixed asset.
(c) purchase of fixed asset.
(d) None of the above.

729. When closing stock is shown in the trial balance it appears
(a) Only in Balance sheet
(b) Only in Trading A/c
(c) Both in Trading A/c and Balance sheet
(d) All of the above

730. Which of the following is an accounting equation?
(a) Assets = Liabilities – Capital
(b) Assets = Capital
(c) Capital = Assets + Liabilities
(d) Assets = Capital + Liabilities

731. An ordinary resolution at a general meeting of the shareholders is required for
(a) issue of share capital at a discount
(b) reduction of share capital
(c) creation of reserve capital
(d) reduction of share capital

732. Which formula is used for calculating inventory turnover ratio?
(a) Sales/Average inventory at sales value.
(b) Sales/Average inventory at cost.
(c) Cost of goods sold/Average inventory at cost.
(d) All of the above.

733. Partners current accounts are opened when their capitals are
(a) Fluctuating
(b) Fixed
(c) Fixed or fluctuating
(d) None of the above

734. If the operating expenses exceed gross profit, the excess is referred to as
(a) operating loss.
(b) operating income.
(c) non-operating income.
(d) non-operating expenses.

735. Accounting is
(a) a systematic and regular record of events affecting a firm with a view to obtaining a clear financial picture.
(b) preparation of various financial statements over a period of time of a firm to measure its performance in monetary terms.
(c) the art of recording, classifying and summarising in a significant manner and in terms of money, transactions and events which are, in part at best financial in character, and interpreting thereof.
(d) nothing but book-keeping.

736. Aush started business on 1st April, 1995 with a capital of ₹ 25,000 and a loan of ₹ 12,500. Total assets and liabilities at the end of 31st March, 1996 amounted to ₹ 75,000 and ₹ 12,500 respectively. He invested a further capital of ₹ 12,500 during the year and withdrew ₹ 7,500 during the erelevant financial period. His closing capital and profits would be respectively.
(a) ₹ 70,000 and ₹ 47,500
(b) ₹ 62,500 and ₹ 32,500
(c) ₹ 55,000 and ₹ 42,500
(d) ₹ 50,000 and ₹ 40,000

737. A person started business with a cash of ₹ 22,000 and stock of ₹ 3,000 on 1st January, 1996. During the year he made a profit of ₹ 6,000. His creditors were paid ₹ 4,500 for the office furniture supplied. He took goods worth ₹ 3,500 for his daughter's wedding on 30th June, 1996. The gross assets of his business on 31st December, 1996 was
(a) ₹ 23,500 (b) ₹ 20,500
(c) ₹ 27,500 (d) ₹ 26,500

738. In stock valuation, application of the principle "at cost price or market price whichever is lower" will result in the valuation of stock sometimes at cost price and at other times at market price. This is an application of the principle of
(a) Conservatism (b) Disclosure
(c) Consistency (d) Materiality

739. Amount spent on an advertisement campaign, the benefit of which is likely to last for three years is a
(a) revenue expenditure
(b) capital expenditure
(c) contingent expenditure
(d) deferred revenue expenditure

740. In the case of a sole proprietorship, assets in Balance Sheet items are conveniently shown in
(a) order of liquidity
(b) order of fixity
(c) order of dates of acquisition
(d) alphabetical order

741. Revenue is generally recognised as being earned at that point of time when
(a) production is completed.
(b) debts are collected.
(c) sale is effected.
(d) cash is received.

742. Which one of the following statements is correct?

(a) If the cost of machinery is more than the book value, than depreciation need not be provided.
(b) Depreciation is not the process of valuation of asset it is a process of allocation of cost of asset to the period of its economic life.
(c) In the absence of any legal provisions, if the auditor finds that provision made for depreciation is inadequate, then he is not required to refer to it in his report.
(d) When the plant and machinery maintained in good condition, through repairs and renewals, depreciation need not be provided.

743. Which one of the following will be related as revenue expenditure?
(a) A dealer in sewing machines, purchases sewing machines and spends some money on the repair of ten machines damaged while in transit.
(b) Cost incurred for a new exit as required under the local bodies' buy laws.
(c) Interest paid on loan during the construction of works.
(d) Cost of pulling down on old building as also the payment made to the architect for the plan of a new building.

744. The following figures (all in ₹) relate to non-trading concern.

1st January, 1995 stock of medicines	5,000
1st January, 1995 outstanding creditors for medicines	3,000
Amount paid for medicines during the years	15,000
Value of medicines spoiled during the year	400
Stock of medicines on 31st December, 1995	3,500

The amount to be debited to Income and Expenditure account would be
(a) ₹ 18,000 (b) ₹ 13,500
(c) ₹ 15,000 (d) ₹ 18,500

745. A cultural club discloses that subscriptions received during a particular accounting period as per Receipts and Payments account amount to ₹ 57,360. Subscription outstanding (opening and closing) was ₹ 4,800 and ₹ 6,000 respectively. Subscription received in advance (opening balance and closing balance) amounted to ₹ 3,600 and ₹ 2,160 respectively. The amount to be posted to Income and Expenditure account would be
(a) ₹ 60,000 (b) ₹ 63,360
(c) ₹ 57,360 (d) ₹ 54,000

746. Owner's equity stands for
(a) Current Assets minus Fixed Liabilities.
(b) Fixed Assets minus Fixed Liabilities.
(c) Total Assets minus Total Liabilities.
(d) Fixed Assets minus Current Liabilities.

747. Which one of the following is an intangible asset?
(a) Patent Right
(b) Furniture
(c) Losse tools
(d) Investment in shares

748. That portion of the share capital which can be called up only on the windingup of the company is the
(a) reserve capital.
(b) subscribed capital.
(c) issued capital.
(d) authorised capital.

749. If vendors are issued fully paid shares of ₹ 80,000 in consideration of net assets of ₹ 60,000, then the balance of ₹ 20,000 will be
(a) credited to capital reserve account.
(b) credited to share premium account.

(c) debited to profit and loss account.
(d) debited to goodwill account.

750. Sales ₹ 4,00,000, Stock turnover 10, Gross Profit 25%. What is the amount of average stock?
(a) ₹ 32,000 (b) ₹ 25,000
(c) ₹ 40,000 (d) ₹ 30,000

751. Payout ratio is calculated by
(a) Profit/earning per share
(b) Retained earning/profit
(c) Dividend per share/earning per share
(d) Earning per share/dividend share

752. ₹ 331 received from a customer is debited to his account as ₹ 313. What is the effect?
(a) Debit increase by ₹ 313
(b) Credit increase by ₹ 313
(c) Debit increase by ₹ 331
(d) Credit increase by ₹ 331

753. If Opening stock is ₹ 16,000, Purchases of ₹ 12,000 and Closing stock ₹ 2,000. What is the cost of goods sold?
(a) ₹ 30,000 (b) ₹ 12,000
(c) ₹ 28,000 (d) ₹ 26,000

754. Which is a revenue expenditure?
(a) Wages paid
(b) Heavy advertisement
(c) Machinery purchased
(d) None of the above

755. A cinema makes his picture curtain as cinemascope. This expenditure is
(a) Capital
(b) Revenue
(c) Deferred revenue
(d) None of the above

756. If a person pay off all its creditors. The effect on balance sheet is
(a) increase assets and increase liability.
(b) decrease liability and decrease assets.
(c) increase assets and increase owners equity.
(d) None of the above.

757. What is the amount of profit when capital at the end is ₹ 1,50,000, capital in the beginning ₹ 75,000 and capital introduced ₹ 20,000 and capital withdrawn ₹ 25,000?
(a) ₹ 50,000 (b) ₹ 40,000
(c) ₹ 80,000 (d) ₹ 75,000

758. Find out the capital at the beginning. Profit during the year ₹ 60,000, capital at the end ₹ 2,00,000, Withdrawn ₹ 40,000, Introduced ₹ 25,000
(a) ₹ 1,00,000 (b) ₹ 60,000
(c) ₹ 1,50,000 (d) ₹ 1,55,000

759. XYZ Co. Ltd. forfeited 10 shares of ₹ 10 each ₹ 7 called up, ₹ 5 paid on application, the amount to be forfeited is
(a) ₹ 70 (b) ₹ 50
(c) ₹ 100 (d) ₹ 120

760. Issue of 10,000 shares @ ₹ 10 per share. Purchase of 500 debentures @ ₹ 100 per debenture and purchase of furniture ₹ 30,000, What is the source of fund?
(a) 30,000 (b) 50,000
(c) 10,000 (d) 20,000

761. X and Y are partners in the ratio of 2: 1. Z joints the firm for 1/4 share. The new profit sharing ratio
(a) 3 : 1 : 2 (b) 3 : 1 : 1
(c) 2 : 1 : 2 (d) 2 : 1 : 1

762. In the above question what is the sacrificing ratio?
(a) 1 : 2 (b) 1/2 : 1/2
(c) Equal (d) 2 : 1

763. R, M and P are partners. P dies in an accident, it is a case of
(a) Dissolution of partnership
(b) Dissolution of firm
(c) Both (a) and (b)
(d) None of the above

764. What is the credit sales when cash sales ₹ 10,000. Collected from debtors ₹ 4,00,000. Bad debts ₹ 25,000. Opening Balance ₹ 25,000, Closing Balance ₹ 75,000?
(a) ₹ 4.00,000 (b) ₹ 4,50,000
(c) ₹ 3,00,000 (d) ₹ 4,75,000

765. ₹ 5,000 spent on repairing of second hand machinery purchased is transferred to Repairs A/c. It is an error of
(a) Principle (b) Omission
(c) Commission (d) All of the above

766. From the following, determine the amount of subscription received during the year shown in Income and Expenditure A/c ₹ 5,000, Subscription outstanding ₹ 500. Received in advance ₹ 750, Subscription of the year received during last year ₹ 300.
(a) 4,950 (b) 4,350
(c) 5,550 (d) 5,300

767. What will be the answer if it is also given that subscription of the last year received during this year is ₹ 600?
(a) 4,350 (b) 4,950
(c) 5,300 (d) 5,550

768. From the following calculate the amount of subscription to be shown in Income and Expenditure A/c. Subscription received ₹ 5,000, Subscription outstanding ₹ 750, Subscription received in advance ₹ 700.
(a) ₹ 4,950 (b) ₹ 3,550
(c) ₹ 6,450 (d) ₹ 5,050

769. Trial balance is a proof that
(a) books are authentically and correctly written.
(b) every transaction is recorded twice.
(c) no error remains undetected.
(d) None of the above.

770. Letter of probate is to be demanded in the transmission of shares when a person
(a) has died
(b) is declared insolvent
(c) Both (a) and (b)
(d) None of the above

771. Blue chips means
(a) Shares giving consistent high rate of return.
(b) Shares guaranted by the Government.
(c) Shares listed in the stock exchange.
(d) None of the above.

772. Return of allotment of shares must be filed with the Registrar of Companies within
(a) 45 days (b) 60 days
(c) 21 days (d) 30 days

773. In the Balance Sheet of a company, assets are arranged in the order of their
(a) Permanence (b) Market value
(c) Liquidity (d) Book value

774. Outstanding wages is an example of
(a) Nominal A/c (b) Personal A/c
(c) Real A/c (d) All of the above

775. The unpaid amount on shares which can only be called up on the winding up of the company is known as
(a) Called up capital (b) Capital Reserve
(c) Paid up capital (d) Reserve capital

776. Which of the following is not required to be prepared under statue?
(a) Balance Sheet
(b) Funds Flow statement
(c) Profit and Loss A/c
(d) None of the above

777. Working Capital can be used for the purchase of
(a) Furniture (b) Stock
(c) Plant (d) All of these

778. Purchase of machinery and equipment for cash by a firm
(a) decreases the total assets.
(b) increase the total assets.

(c) increases the liabilities of the firm.
(d) keeps total assets unchanged.

779. A credit sale of goods to Shivendra should be debited to
(a) Purchase account
(b) Sales account
(c) Goods account
(d) Shivendra account

780. Valuing the stock in trade at market price or cost price, whichever is less, is an example of the convention of
(a) Knowing the value
(b) Consistency
(c) Disclosure
(d) None of the above

781. Double entry principle means
(a) writing all the entries twice in the book.
(b) having debit for every credit and similarly, credit for each debit.
(c) writing two times the same entry.
(d) maintaining the double account for all business transactions.

782. A sale of goods to Vaibhav Deep for cash should be debited to
(a) Sale of goods A/c
(b) Vaibhav's A/c
(c) Cash A/c
(d) None of the above

783. A withdrawal of cash from business by the proprietor of the firm should be credited to
(a) Drawing account
(b) Proprietor's account
(c) Capital account
(d) Cash account

784. A cheque received and deposited in the bank on the same day is recorded in the
(a) debited in the cash book.
(b) cash column of the cash book.
(c) bank column of the cash book.
(d) credited in the cash book.

785. Petty cash may be used to pay
(a) salaries and wages to the minial staff.
(b) the expenses relating to postages and conveyance.
(c) for the purchase of furniture and fittings.
(d) None of the above.

786. The term current assets does not include
(a) Advance payment
(b) Stock
(c) Furniture
(d) Cash

787. Secret reserves may result by
(a) providing excessive depreciation.
(b) creating general reserve.
(c) undervaluation of liabilities.
(d) overvaluation of stocks.

788. Which of the following is created by debiting the Profit and Loss Account?
(a) Sinking fund for redemption of debentures
(b) Dividend equalisation fund
(c) Provision
(d) All of the above

789. The payment side of cash book is undercast by ₹ 200 when overdraft as per pass book is the starting point
(a) no effect will be in the pass book
(b) ₹ 200 will be deducted
(c) ₹ 200 will be added
(d) None of the above

790. An amount of ₹ 300 is debited twice in the pass book when overdraft as per the cash book is the starting point
(a) ₹ 600 will be deducted
(b) no effect will be in the cash book
(c) ₹ 600 will be added
(d) None of the above

791. Expenditure incurred by a publisher for acquiring copyrights is a
(a) deferred revenue expenditure
(b) capital expenditure
(c) revenue expenditure
(d) None of the above

792. Immediately after purchasing a new truck ₹ 1000 is paid to have the name of the company and other advertising material painted on the truck. This ₹ 1000 is a
(a) revenue expenditure
(b) capital expenditure
(c) deferred revenue expenditure
(d) All of the above

793. A Return Inwards Book is kept to record
(a) returns of goods purchased.
(b) returns of goods sold.
(c) returns of anything sold.
(d) returns of anything purchased.

794. Bills receivable book is a part of the
(a) Journal
(b) Ledger
(c) Balance sheet
(d) Profit and Loss Account

795. A sale of ₹ 2000 wrongly entered in the purchase book
(a) increases the gross profit by ₹ 2000.
(b) increases the gross profit by ₹ 4000.
(c) decreases the gross profit by ₹ 2000.
(d) None of the above.

796. Which of the following is an operating expenses?
(a) Expired insurance
(b) Depreciation of plant
(c) None of the above
(d) All of the above

797. Which of the following are current assets?
(a) Account receivable
(b) Bank loan for three years
(c) Debentures sinking fund investments
(d) Long term investments

798. Insurance unexpired accounts is a
(a) Nominal account
(b) Real account
(c) Personal account
(d) None of the above

799. Trading account is a
(a) Nominal account
(b) Real account
(c) Personal account
(d) None of the above

800. Goodwill account is a
(a) Real account
(b) Personal account
(c) Nominal account
(d) None of the above

801. Bank overdraft account is a
(a) Real account
(b) Nominal account
(c) Personal account
(d) All of the above

802. Contingent liability is shown due to
(a) dual aspect concept
(b) convention of conservatism
(c) convention of conservatism
(d) convention of full disclosure

803. Which item is shown on the debit side of a trial balance?
(a) Over expenses by the firm
(b) Rent outstanding
(c) Prepaid expenses
(d) Purchase returns

804. Purchases for office furniture on account is recorded in
(a) Purchases Book (b) Sale Book
(c) General Journal (d) Cash Book

805. Sales on account is recorded in
(a) General Journal (b) Sales Book
(c) Cash Book (d) Journal

806. The credit balance in the bank account is
(a) A Liability (b) An expense
(c) Capital (d) An Asset

807. Cash sales are recorded in
(a) Journal (b) Purchase Book
(c) Sales Book (d) Cash Book

808. Error of commission do not permit
(a) correct the total of balance sheet.
(b) correct totalling of trial balance.
(c) the trial balance to agree.
(d) None of the above.

809. Sales to Shyam of ₹ 500 not recorded in the books would affect
(a) Sales return account
(b) Shyam's account
(c) Sales account
(d) Sales account and Shyam's account

810. Profit and loss account of business shows the
(a) gross profit earned
(b) balance of all accounts
(c) capital employed in business
(d) net profit earned

811. Purchase of office equipment results in
(a) increase in assets.
(b) increase in capital.
(c) decrease in capital.
(d) decrease in liability.

812. If a receipt of ₹ 200 from Rajesh (our debtor) has not been recorded in the books the profit would show
(a) neither an increase nor a decrease.
(b) an increase of ₹ 200.
(c) a decrease of ₹ 200.
(d) None of the above.

813. Unearned income account is
(a) an expense (b) an income
(c) an asset (d) a liability

814. Bills receivable account is
(a) an assets account
(b) an expense account
(c) a revenue account
(d) a liability account

815. Repayment of loan results into
(a) application of fund
(b) source of fund
(c) no flow of fund
(d) All of the above

816. Sale of building results into
(a) application of fund
(b) source of fund
(c) no flow of fund
(d) None of the above

817. The term 'funds' as used in 'funds flow statement' means
(a) Current liabilities
(b) Cash
(c) Current assets – Current liabilities
(d) Current assets

818. If a company issues 1000 equity shares of ₹ 10 each will be legally all right if it asks on application
(a) ₹ 4.50 (b) ₹ 5.00
(c) ₹ 2.50 (d) ₹ 3.50

819. If a share of ₹ 10 issued at a premium of ₹ 1, on which ₹ 9 (including premium) have been called and ₹ 7 (including premium) paid is forfeited the capital account should be debited by
(a) ₹ 7 (b) ₹ 6
(c) ₹ 8 (d) ₹ 9

820. Interest on calls in advance is paid by the Company according to Table A is
(a) 8% (b) 10%
(c) 5% (d) 6%

821. If vendors are issued fully paid shares of ₹ 1,00,000 in consideration of net assets

of ₹ 120000, the balance of ₹ 20000 will be credited to
(a) Capital reserve account
(b) Vendor's account
(c) Goodwill account
(d) None of the above

822. Partner's salaries to be debited to
(a) Profit and Loss Appropriation Account
(b) Profit and Loss Account
(c) Trading Account
(d) None of the above

823. In the absence of any partnership deed, interest on partner's loan will be allowed at the rate of
(a) 9% (b) 12%
(c) 5% (d) 6%

824. On the admission of a new partner the decrease in the value of assets is debited to
(a) Old partner's Capital Account
(b) Revaluation Account
(c) Assets Account
(d) New partner's Capital Account

825. X, Y and Z are partners in the ratio of 1/2 : 2/5 : 1/10, what will be the new ratio of the remaining partners if X retires
(a) 5 : 1 (b) 3 : 1
(c) 2 : 1 (d) 4 : 1

826. Goodwill of a firm of A and B is valued at ₹ 30000. It is appearing in the books at ₹ 12000. C is admitted for 1/4 share. What amount he is supposed to bring for goodwill?
(a) 4500 (b) 3000
(c) 10500 (d) 7500

827. A and B are partners in the Ratio of 2 : 1. They admit C for 1/4 share who contributes for ₹ 3000 for his share of goodwill. The total value of goodwill of the firm is
(a) ₹ 12000 (b) ₹ 15000
(c) ₹ 3000 (d) ₹ 9000

828. At the time of dissolution, an unrecorded asset taken by Mr. X a partner should be debited to
(a) Assets A/c
(b) Mr. X's Capital A/c
(c) Realisation A/c
(d) None of the above

829. In Garner V. Murray the deficiency of the insolvent partners is borne by other partner in the
(a) ratio of their capital
(b) equal share by each
(c) profit sharing ratio
(d) None of the above

830. The loss of a firm when all the partners are insolvent is to be borne by
(a) Government (b) Creditors
(c) Partners (d) None

831. A new partner may be admitted to partnership
(a) with the consent of any one partner.
(b) with the consent of all the old partners.
(c) with the consent of three fourth of the old parnters.
(d) with the consent of two thirds of the old partners.

832. When goods are purchased for the joint venture out of joint Bank A/c the amount is debited to
(a) Purchases Account
(b) Joint Bank A/c
(c) Joint Venture A/c
(d) None of the above

833. Bills receivable endorsed are debited to
(a) Bills receivable Account
(b) Debtor's Account
(c) Creditor's Account
(d) Bills Payable Account

834. Subscription received during the year were ₹ 800 for the current year, ₹ 100 for the previous year and ₹ 100 in the next year. In the receipts and payments account, the receipts from subscriptions would appear at
(a) ₹ 900 (b) ₹ 1000
(c) ₹ 700 (d) ₹ 800

835. Unclaimed dividend is shown in the balance sheet under the heading as
(a) Reserves and surplus
(b) Current liabilities
(c) Unsecured Loans
(d) None of the above

836. If the rate of gross profit is 25% on cost of goods sold and the sales are ₹ 200000 the amount of goods profit will be
(a) ₹ 40000 (b) ₹ 45000
(c) ₹ 50000 (d) None of these

837. The remuneration payable to a whole-time director of the company should not exceed
(a) 6% of the net profits
(b) 5% of the net profits
(c) 10% of the net profits
(d) 7% of the net profits

838. Vishal Motor Ltd., takes over Ashoka Motor Ltd., with the exception of creditors and agrees to pay ₹ 50 lacs to the shareholders of Ashoka Motor Ltd. Creditors stood at ₹ 10 lacs. The purchase consideration is to be taken as
(a) ₹ 50 lacs (b) ₹ 60 lacs
(c) ₹ 40 lacs (d) None of these

839. Quick ratio is a good indicator of the liquid position of a concern. The ideal quick ratio is
(a) 3 : 1 (b) 4 : 1
(c) 2 : 1 (d) 1 : 1

840. The equation for the Debt Equity Ratio is
(a) $\dfrac{\text{Current assets}}{\text{Current liabilities}}$
(b) $\dfrac{\text{Net profits}}{\text{Net sales}}$
(c) $\dfrac{\text{Long – term debt}}{\text{Equity capital}}$
(d) $\dfrac{\text{Liquid assets}}{\text{Current liabilities}}$

841. The liabilities of shareholders of a public company is limited to the extent of
(a) called up value of the share.
(b) paid up value of the share.
(c) the face value of the share.
(d) All of the above.

842. A public company having a share capital
(a) may file a statement in lieu of prospectus.
(b) must issue a prospectus.
(c) cannot file a statement in lieu of prospectus.
(d) None of the above.

843. What is irredeemable preference shares?
(a) which are repayable after a specified period.
(b) which are not repayable during the life of the company.
(c) which become equity shares after a specified period.
(d) None of the above.

844. The minimum subscription is to be received in
(a) 130 days (b) 45 days
(c) 120 days (d) 65 days

845. Interest receivable on investments by a charitable institution will be shown on

(a) liability side of the Balance Sheet.
(b) Dr. side of income and expenditure A/c.
(c) assets side of Balance Sheet.
(d) None of the above.

846. There are 500 members of a club, each paying an annual subscription of ₹ 20 each. Subscription received during a year amount to ₹ 10750, including arrears of previous year ₹ 750. What amount should be shown in the Income and Expenditure Account?
(a) ₹ 750 (b) ₹ 9,250
(c) ₹ 10,000 (d) ₹ 10,750

847. Arrears of preference dividends (cumulative) will be shown in the balance sheet of a company as
(a) Current liability
(b) Contingent liability
(c) Unclaimed dividend
(d) None of the above

848. Contingent liability is shown in the Balance Sheet due to
(a) convention of conservation.
(b) convention of full disclosure.
(c) going concern concept.
(d) convention of materiality.

849. When all partners are insolvent, the loss is then borne by
(a) Creditors (b) Partners
(c) Government (d) All of the above

850. In partnership, who among the following can step out easily?
(a) Widow
(b) Retiring partner
(c) Infant
(d) None of the above

851. What does water in Balance Sheet indicate?
(a) Over trading
(b) Excess of liquidity
(c) Part of capital not represented by assets
(d) Under trading

852. "Higher the ratio, the more favourable it is" does not apply to
(a) operating profit ratio
(b) stock turnover ratio
(c) gross profit ratio
(d) operating ratio

853. An equipment is imported at original price of ₹ 50,000, for shipping ₹ 5,000, for freight ₹ 5,000 wages for erecting the plant ₹ 1,000. What should be debited as the cost of equipment?
(a) ₹ 60,000 (b) ₹ 61,000
(c) ₹ 50,000 (d) ₹ 55,000

854. Z Ltd. forfeited 20 shares of ₹ 10 each, on which ₹ 4 share were paid. What is the minimum price for reissue of these shares as fully paid?
(a) ₹ 4 per share (b) ₹ 2 per share
(c) ₹ 8 per share (d) ₹ 6 per share

855. Admission fees received by a Sports club is a
(a) Deferred receipt
(b) Revenue receipt
(c) Capital receipt
(d) None of the above

856. Balance Sheet audit is useful when
(a) internal check is weak
(b) concern is very large
(c) concern is small one
(d) All of the above

857. The 'fund' in fund flow statement means
(a) net working capital
(b) cash
(c) current assets
(d) current liabilities

858. A diversified firm has the following budget data for the year ending December 31, 2010.

Budgeted Sales ₹ 5,00,000
Budgeted Variable Costs ₹ 3,00,000
Budgeted Fixed Costs ₹ 1,00,000

The BEP (₹) for the firm will be

(a) ₹ 2,30,000 (b) ₹ 2,00,000
(c) ₹ 1,50,000 (d) ₹ 2,50,000

859. The following information is available
1. 2,000,10% preference shares of ₹ 100 each ₹ 2,00,000
2. 10,000 equity shares of ₹ 100 each ₹ 60 per share paid up 6,00,000
3. Expected profit per year before tax ₹ 3,20,000
4. Rate of tax 50%
5. Transfer to general reserve every year 20% of net profit
6. Normal rate of earnings 15%

The value of equity shares as per yield value method would be

(a) ₹ 72 (b) ₹ 64
(c) ₹ 120 (d) ₹ 93-32

860. A company's reported current profit is ₹ 70,000 after in corporating the following.

Loss on sale of investments ₹ 10,000; premiums redemption of debentures ₹ 1500; depreciation on machinery and plant ₹ 20,000, goodwill and preliminary expenses written off ₹ 30,000; gain from sale of no current assets ₹ 40,000

The net inflow of funds from the operation would be

(a) ₹ 70,000 (b) ₹ 59.500
(c) ₹ 91,500 (d) ₹ 80,000

Directions: Questions 861 to 915 are of multiple statement type. Choose the correct answers from the codes given below.

861. Arrange the following.
1. Financial Accounting.
2. Cost Accounting.
3. Management Accounting.

Codes:

(a) 3, 2, 1 (b) 2, 3, 1
(c) 1, 2, 3 (d) 2, 1, 3

862. Dividend can be paid out of
1. Profit 2. Reserve
3. Share premium

Codes:

(a) 1 and 2 (b) 2 and 3
(c) Both (a) and (b) (d) All of the above

863. Rearrange the following heads of assets in the Balance Sheet of a company
1. Fixed Assets
2. Miscellaneous Expenditure
3. Current Assets
4. Lans and Advances
5. Investments

Codes:

(a) 5, 1, 3, 4, 2 (b) 1, 5, 3, 4, 2
(c) 1, 3, 4, 5, 2 (d) 1, 5, 2, 3, 4

864. In what order the following items are shown on the liability side of the balance sheet?
1. Share capital
2. Debentures
3. Sundry creditors
4. Proposed dividends

Codes:

(a) 2, 3, 4, 1 (b) 1, 4, 2, 3
(c) 1, 2, 3, 4 (d) 1, 3, 2, 4

865. If a company is wound up, the following debtors have to be paid.
1. Bank loan
2. Preference capital
3. Debentures holders
4. Equity share holders

Codes:

(a) 1, 3, 2, 4 (b) 3, 2, 1, 4
(c) 1, 2, 3, 4 (d) 4, 1, 3, 2

866. Which of the following are capital expenditure?

1. Purchase of machinery
2. Wages paid for erection of machinery
3. Repairing of old machinery to make it usable
4. Registrarion charges for purchase of building

Codes:

(a) 1 and 4 (b) 1, 2, 3, 4
(c) 1, 3, 4 (d) 1, 2, 3

867. How the following items are shown in the balance sheet of a company?

1. Company Liabilities
2. Share Capital
3. Debentures
4. Reserves and Surplus

Codes:

(a) 2, 1, 4, 3 (b) 4, 3, 2, 1
(c) 2, 4, 3, 1 (d) 1, 2, 3, 4

868. How the following items are shown in the Balance Sheet of a Bank?

1. Investments
2. Cash
3. Money at call and short notice
4. Furniture and fittingss

Codes:

(a) 2, 3, 1, 4 (b) 1, 2, 3, 4
(c) 4, 1, 2, 3 (d) 2, 1, 3, 4

869. Given below are some of the assets.

1. Cash 2. Goodwill
3. Building 4. Stock
5. Prepaid expenses 6. Loose tools
7. Work in progress 8. Preliminary expenses
9. Motor vehicles

Codes:

(a) 2, 3, 8, 9 (b) 1, 2, 3, 4
(c) 1, 4, 5, 7 (d) 1, 4, 6, 9

870. Which of the following statements are appropriate in respect of partnership accounts?

1. In the absence of any provision in the partnership agreement to the contrary, partners can charge interest at 6% per annum on loans given by them to the partnership firm.
2. An ordinary partnership firm can have not more than 50 partners.
3. A banking partnership firm can have not more than 10 partnership.
4. In the absence of any provision in the partnership agreement to the contrary, profits and losses are shared by the partners in the ratio of their capitals.

Codes:

(a) 2, 3 and 4 (b) 1, 3 and 4
(c) 1 and 2 (d) 1 and 3

871. What is the correct sequence of the following action required for the preparation of final accounts?

1. Preparation of Trial Accounts
2. Balancing of Accounts
3. Preparation of Annual Financial Statements
4. Making Adjusting Entries.

Codes:

(a) 2, 1, 4, 3 (b) 4, 2, 3, 1
(c) 4, 2, 1, 3 (d) 2, 4, 3, 1

872. Which of the following items should be entered in the receipts and payments account of a club?

1. Sale of old newspapers
2. Loss on sale of some asset
3. Payments for investment

Codes:

(a) 1 and 2 (b) 2 and 3
(c) 1,2 and 3 (d) 1 and 3

873. In what order the following items in respect of share capital are shown in the balance sheet of a company?

1. Paid up capital
2. Issued capital

3. Authorised capital
4. Subscribed capital

Codes:

(a) 3, 2, 4, 1 (b) 4, 3, 1, 2
(c) 4, 1, 3, 2 (d) 3, 4, 2, 1

874. Some of the liabilities are given as under.
1. Bank overdraft
2. Debentures
3. Loan from financial institutions
4. Outstanding wages
5. Creditors

Codes:

(a) 1, 4 and 5 (b) 4 and 5
(c) 3, 4 and 5 (d) All of the above

875. Various items appearing in a funds flow statements are
1. Sale of furniture
2. Funds from operations
3. Purchase of building
4. Redemption of debentures
5. Payment of dividend
6. Issue of equity share capital

Codes:

(a) 2, 3 and 5 (b) 3, 4, 5 and 6
(c) 1, 2 and 6 (d) All of the above

876. Which of the following assets would be taken into account for current ratio?
1. Stock 2. Creditor
3. Mortgage 4. Cash
5. Bills payable 6. Bank

Codes:

(a) 1, 3, and 5 (b) 2, 3, and 5
(c) 1, 4, and 5 (d) 1, 4, and 6

877. Consider the following statemnts. Redeemable Preference Shares can be redeemed
1. out of the proceeds of new issue of shares for the purpose.
2. out of profits available for dividend.
3. out of sale proceeds of the assets.
4. out of the grants received from the government.

Codes:

(a) 1, 2, 3 and 4 (b) 1 and 3
(c) 1 and 2 (d) 3 and 4

878. Consider the following adjusting entries.
1. Outstanding expenses : Expense A/c Dr To outstanding expense A/c
2. Prepaid expenses : Expense A/c Dr To outstanding income A/c
3. Income earned and not received : Income A/c Dr To outstanding income A/c
4. Income received in advance : Income A/c Dr To prepaid in come A/c

Codes:

(a) 1 only (b) 1, 2, 3 and 4
(c) 1 and 4 (d) 2 and 3

879. Income and Expenditure account of a college is credited with which of the following?
1. Tuition fees paid by the students
2. Cost of science laboratory equipments
3. Fines realized by the authority from students
4. Price of prizes

Codes:

(a) 1 and 3 (b) 2 and 4
(c) 1 and 2 (d) 2 and 3

880. Consider the following statements.
"Teaming and lapping" method of fraud is committed by
1. Concealment of a shortage by delaying the recording of cash receipts.
2. When a cheque is received, it is not credited to customers but misappropriated.

3. When another customer sends a cheque, it is credited to first customer's account.
4. Inflating the payment vouchers.

Codes:

(a) 1, 2 and 3 (b) 1 and 4
(d) 3 and 4 (d) 2 and 4

881. The steps used to derive the deduction approach in accounting are as under
1. developing the techniques of accounting.
2. selecting the postulates—the basic accounting propositions or premises.
3. specifying the objectives of financial statements.
4. deriving the principles of accounting.

Codes:

(a) 4, 2, 3, 1 (b) 3, 1, 4, 2
(c) 4, 1, 3, 2 (d) 3, 2, 4, 1

882. Consider the following statements about balance sheet of a company.
1. It is always prepared from the point of view of the firm, company or business, and not from that of its owners, creditors, directors or employees.
2. The financial relationship of the business to its owners is shown in the amount of capital, reserves and undistributed profits.
3. It always relates to a particular period of time.

Codes:

(a) 1 and 2 (b) 1, 2 and 3
(c) 2 only (d) 1 only

883. For which of the following purposes can the share premium of the company be used in case the company issues share at premium?
1. For the cost of underwriting and distributing the share capital.
2. For the issues of fully paid bonus shares to the members of the company.
3. For writing off preliminary expenses of the company.
4. For providing premium payable on the redemption of any redeemable preference shares or debentrues of the company.

Codes:

(a) 1 and 4 (b) 2, 3 and 4
(c) 1, 2 and 3 (d) 1, 2 and 4

884. To test the liquidity of a concern, which of the following ratios are useful?
1. Acid test ratio
2. Capital turnover ratio
3. Bad debts to sales ratio
4. Inventory turnover ratio

Codes:

(a) 2 and 4 (b) 2 and 3
(c) 1 and 3 (d) 1 and 4

885. In the case of a company making a public issue, 'Minimum Subscription' must provide for which of the following?
1. Investments to be made
2. Preliminary expenses
3. Repayment of money borrowed for preliminary expenses
4. Working capital
5. Any other expenditure if it is specifically stated.

Codes:

(a) 1,2 and 4
(b) 2, 3, 4 and 5
(c) 1, 2, 3, 4 and 5
(d) 1, 3 and 5

886. Company accounting conforms more to dual aspect concept than to incomplete recording system because
1. Companies Act insists upon the adoption of double entry system of book-keeping.
2. Balance sheet could not be prepared u/s 211 of Companies Act according to the incomplete recording system.

3. To show true and fair view of the affairs of the company.
4. To ensure adequate disclosure.

Codes:

(a) 2 and 3 (b) 1 and 2
(c) 1, 2 and 3 (d) 2, 3 and 4

887. What is the correct sequence of the following in the preparation of periodical financial statements?
1. Preparation of balance sheet
2. Preparation of funds flow statements
3. Preparation of trial balance
4. Preparation of profit/loss statement

Codes:

(a) 2, 4, 3, 1 (b) 1, 3, 2, 4
(c) 4, 2, 1, 3 (d) 3, 4, 1, 2

888. Which one of the following item/items will be included in income and expenditure account?
1. Accrued expenses
2. Credit purchases
3. Prepaid expenses
4. Opening cash balance

Codes:

(a) 2 and 3 (b) 3 and 4
(c) 1 (d) 1 and 2

889. In financial statements, adequate disclosure the ensured by companies, as per the requirements of
1. management polices
2. materiality concept
3. disclosure concept
4. relevant provisions of the Companies Act
5. internal control

Codes:

(a) 1, 2 and 3 are correct
(b) 1 and 3 are correct
(c) 2, 3 and 4 are correct
(d) 2, 3 and 5 are correct

890. Bonus shares may be issued out of
1. Profit
2. Share Premium
3. Capital Reserve
4. General Reserve

Codes:

(a) 2, 3 and 4 (b) 1, 2, 3 and 4
(c) 1, 3, and 4 (d) 3 and 4

891. Which of the following expenditures are to be treated as revenue expenditure?
1. Interest paid on money borrowed during construction period.
2. Cost of patent right.
3. Loss of uninsured stock due to fire.
4. Retirement gratuity paid to an employee.

Codes:

(a) 2, 3 and 4 (b) 1, 2 and 3
(c) 1 and 2 (d) 3 and 4

892. In what order the following items are shown on the liability side of the balance-sheet?
1. Share capital
2. Debentures
3. Sundry creditors
4. Proposed dividends

Codes:

(a) 2, 3, 4, 1 (b) 1, 4, 2, 3
(c) 1, 2, 3, 4 (d) 1, 3, 2, 4

893. Dividend may be paid out of
1. Profit earned
2. Capital redemption reserve
3. Share premium A/c
4. General reserve

Codes:

(a) 1 and 4 (b) 1, 2, 3 and 4
(c) 1 and 3 (d) 1, 3 and 4

894. What is the order of the following assets in the balance sheet of a company?
1. Investments
2. Fixed Assets

3. Current Assets
4. Profit and Loss A/c (Dr.)

Codes:

(a) 2, 1, 4, 3 (b) 1, 3, 2, 4
(c) 1, 2, 4, 3 (d) 3, 2, 1, 4

895. The following are some of the types of errors.
1. Error of omission
2. Error of commission
3. Error in posting from journal to ledger
4. Error in totalling
5. Error of principle

Codes:

(a) 3 and 4 (b) 1, 2 and 5
(c) 1, 2 and 4 (d) All of the above

896. If a company is wound up, the following debtors have to be paid
1. Bank loan
2. Preference capital
3. Debentures holders
4. Equity shareholders

Codes:

(a) 1, 3, 2, 4 (b) 3, 2, 1, 4
(c) 1, 2, 3, 4 (d) 4, 1, 3, 2

897. Which of the following are considered for calculating working capital.
1. Cash in hand
2. Bills Receivable
3. Book debts
4. Bank OD

Codes:

(a) 1, 3 and 4 (b) 1, 2 and 3
(c) 1 and 4 (d) All of the above

898. Which group of the following items are application of funds?
1. Loss from operations
2. Loan from financial institutions
3. Redemption of debentures
4. Sale of fixed assets
5. Payment of dividends

Codes:

(a) 1, 2 and 4 (b) 3, 4 and 5
(c) 1, 3 and 4 (d) 1, 3 and 5

899. A Ltd. was taken over by B Ltd. as from 1st April, 2009 upon the following terms
1. B Ltd. to assume the liabilities and taken over all the assets at book value.
2. B Ltd. to discharge the debentures in A Ltd. at 105% by the issue of new debentures at 8% in B Ltd.
3. B Ltd. to pay the shareholders in A Ltd. ₹ 10 per share of ₹ 10 each were considered as being at par.

Purchase consideration is

Codes:

(a) ₹ 20,00,000 (b) ₹ 1,20,00,000
(c) ₹ 19,00,000 (d) ₹ 19,50,000

900. From the following statements related insolvency account mark your answer according to the answer code given
1. List A contains particulars relating to unsecured creditors.
2. All taxes due are considered preferential creditors.
3. Properties held by the insolvent in the fiduciary capacity can be distributed amongst his creditors.
4. List D contains the particulars relating to assets and properties.

Codes:

(a) 2 and 4 are correct
(b) 1 and 4 are correct
(c) 1 and 3 are correct
(d) 1 and 2 are correct

901. Consider the following statement.
1. Operational loss is a source of fund.
2. Decrease in working capital is a source of fund.
3. Additions to fixed assets are an application of fund.
4. Fresh introduction of capital is an application of funds.

Which of the above statements are applicable while preparing the funds flow statements?

Codes:

(a) 2 and 3 (b) 1, 3 and 4
(c) 1 and 2 (d) 1 and 3

902. The current ratio of a company is 2 : 5 : 1 which of the following suggestions would improve, reduce and net change it?

1. Payment to trade creditors
2. Sell machinery for cash
3. Purchased goods for cash
4. Issue of equity shares

Codes:

(a) No effect, Increase, Decrease, Increase
(b) Decrease, Increase, Increase, No effect
(c) Increase, No effect, Decrease, Increase
(d) Increases, Increase, No effect, Increase

903. Which of their following assets would be taken into account for working capital turnover ratio?

1. Plant 2. Stock
3. Mortgage 4. Sales
5. Reserve 6. Bank

Codes:

(a) 2, 4, and 6 (b) 3, 5, and 6
(c) 1, 5, and 6 (d) 4, 5, and 6

904. Consider the following information.

1. Gross sales ₹ 20,00,000
2. Sales tax 7% on gross sales
3. Income tax 40%
4. Profit before tax 400,000

What is net profit before tax ratio?

Codes:

(a) 23.5% (b) 24.5%
(c) 21.5% (d) 22.5%

905. Consider the following ratios.

1. Acid test ratio
2. Capital turnover ratio
3. Bad debts to sales ratio
4. Inventory turnover ratio

Which of these ratios are more appropriate for testing the liquidity of a concern?

Codes:

(a) 2 and 4 (b) 2 and 3
(c) 1 and 3 (d) 1 and 4

906. Consider the given data.

1. Proprietary ratio = 0.75
2. Current ratio = 2:1
3. Proprietary fund = ₹ 60,000
4. Fixed assets = ₹ 50,000

The working capital will be computed as

Codes:

(a) ₹ 20,000 (b) ₹ 25,000
(c) ₹ 10,000 (d) ₹ 15,000

907. Which of the following transactions will improve the current Ratio?

1. Bills receivable Dishonoured
2. Cash collected from customers
3. Issue of new shares
4. Payment of preliminary expenses by way of equity shares

Codes:

(a) 3 only (b) 2 and 4
(c) 1, 2 and 3 (d) 4 only

908. Which of the following statements are appropriate in respect of partnership accounts?

1. In the absence of any provision in the partnership agreement to the contrary, partners can charge interest as 6% per annum on loans given by them to the partnership firm.
2. An ordinary partnership firm can have not more than 50 partners.
3. A banking partnership firm can have not more than 10 partnership.
4. In the absence of any provision in the partnership agreement to the contrary, profits and losses are shared by the partners in the ratio of their capitals.

Codes:

(a) 1 and 3 (b) 1, 3 and 4
(c) 1 and 2 (d) 2, 3 and 4

909. A low inventory turnover ratio may be the result of

1. Obsolescence of some of the stock
2. Slow moving inventory
3. Frequent stock-outs
4. Fast moving inventory of these Statements

Codes:

(a) 4 only (b) 2 and 3
(c) 1 and 2 (d) 2 only

910. What is the amount of goodwill in the following case? Three year's purchase of the last four year's average profits. The profits and losses for the last four years are

1. Year ₹ 5,000
2. Year ₹ 8,000
3. Year ₹ 3,000 (Loss)
4. Year ₹ 6,000

Codes:

(a) ₹ 11,000 (b) ₹ 12,000
(c) ₹ 9,000 (d) ₹ 10,000

911. Given the following data.

Net profit during the year	₹ 30,000
Total purchase	₹ 70,000
Creditors in the begining	₹ 24,000
Creditors at the end	₹ 36,000

Cash from operations is

Codes:

(a) ₹ 22,000 (b) ₹ 42,000
(c) ₹ 100,000 (d) ₹ 30,000

912. A few statements are given below. Select whether it is True of False.

1. Trade discount is not recorded in the books of account.
2. Cash discount can be recorded through journal or through cash book.
3. Two column cash book has an extra column for discount on the debit side.
4. No posting is required in personal accounts for cash discount.
5. Discount columns in the cash book are not balanced they are merely totalled.

Codes:

(a) True, False, True, False, False
(b) True, True, True, True, False
(c) True, True, False, False, True
(d) True, False, True, False, True

913. Fill in the blanks with suitable word or words.

1. The balances of assets accounts are usually ______ balances.
2. The balance of liability accounts are always ______ balances.
3. The capital account generally has ______ balances.
4. The revenue and expenses accounts are closed by transferring the balance to ______.

(a) (1) Debit (2) Debit (3) Credit (4) Trading and Profit and Loss
(b) (1) Debit (2) Debit (3) Debit (4) Trading and Profit and Loss
(c) (1) Credit (2) Debit (3) Debit (4) Trading and Profit and Loss
(d) (1) Debit (2) Credit (3) Credit (4) Trading and Profit and Loss

914. Fill in the blanks with suitable word or words.

1. Credit vouchers are prepared for ______ receipts.
2. Credit vouchers are prepared on the basis of ______ vouchers.
3. The title of a particular account is written in the credit voucher against the word ______.
4. In credit vouchers debiting of account ______ is implied.

(a) (1) Cash (2) Supporting
(3) Credit (4) Cash
(b) (1) Cash (2) Cash
(3) Debit (4) Bank
(c) (1) Advance (2) Supporting
(3) Credit (4) Cash
(d) (1) Advance (2) Supporting
(3) Debit (4) Bank

915. A few errors committed in Ahluwalia's books of account are given below. State which errors would affect the Trial Balance.

(a) Sales of ₹ 950 to Ram completely omitted from books of account
(b) Purchases of ₹ 720 from Shyam entered in the purchases journal as ₹ 700
(c) Purchases Journal is overcast by ₹ 1,000
(d) Sales returns journal is undercast by ₹ 200
(e) Amount paid to Agarwal wrongly posted to the debit to Mittal's account.
(f) Bank overdraft shown under debit column in the Trial Balance.
(g) Sales of ₹ 500 to Sadiq entered in sales journal as sales to Mushtaq.
(h) Wages paid for installation of machinery debited to wages account.

Codes:
(a) c, d, e, and h (b) c, d, f and h
(c) a, c, and g (d) c, d and f

Directions: Questions 916 to 958 are of matching type. Match List I with List II and select the correct answer using the codes given below the list.

916. **List I** **List II**
A. Liquidity Ratio 1. Current Ratio
B. Profitability Ratio 2. Debt Equity Ratio
C. Solvency Ratio 3. G/P Ratio

Codes:	A	B	C
(a)	1	3	2
(b)	2	1	3
(c)	1	2	3

917. **List I (Item)**
A. Brand equity
B. Plant and machinery
C. Advances to suppliers
D. Deferred revenue expenditure

List II (Type of asset)
1. Tangible 2. Current
3. Intangible 4. Fictitious

Codes:	A	B	C	D
(a)	1	3	4	2
(b)	3	1	4	2
(c)	3	1	2	4
(d)	1	3	2	4

918. **List I**
A. G.P. Ratio B. Cash budget
C. E.O.Q. D. Provision for bad debts

List II
1. Convention of conservatism
2. Profitability
3. Inventory management
4. Management of liquid assets

Codes:	A	B	C	D
(a)	4	2	1	3
(b)	2	4	3	1
(c)	2	4	1	3
(d)	4	2	3	1

919. **List I**
A. Mutual fund
B. Public issue of capital
C. Forward trading
D. Option pricing

List II
1. Stock exchange
2. Assets management company

3. Merchant banking
4. Forex market

Codes:	A	B	C	D
(a)	2	3	1	4
(b)	2	3	4	1
(c)	3	2	4	1
(d)	3	2	1	4

920. **List I**

A. Partner's current accounts
B. Goodwill account
C. Partner's drawings accounts
D. Profit and Loss adjustment account

List II

1. Dissolution of partnership
2. Revaluation of assets on the admission of a partner
3. Fixed capitals of partners
4. Goods taken by partners for private consumption

Codes:	A	B	C	D
(a)	3	1	4	2
(b)	3	1	2	4
(c)	1	3	2	4
(d)	1	3	4	2

921. **List I**

A. Loss on realisation
B. Profit on realisation
C. Assets sold
D. Creditors paid

List II

1. Debits partner's capital A/c
2. Credit realisation A/c
3. Credit partner's capital A/c
4. Debit realisation A/c

Codes:	A	B	C	D
(a)	3	1	4	2
(b)	1	3	2	4
(c)	1	3	4	2
(d)	3	1	2	4

922. **List I**

A. Preliminary expense
B. Travelling expenses of the salesman
C. Profit on sale of a part of the business building
D. Nazrana paid on the purchase of land for business

List II

1. Capital expenditure
2. Revenue expenditure
3. Capital gain
4. Deferred revenue expenditure

Codes:	A	B	C	D
(a)	2	4	3	1
(b)	2	4	1	3
(c)	4	2	3	1
(d)	4	2	1	3

923. **List I**

A. Heavy amount of premium on redemption.
B. Excess of sale proceeds of fixed assets over their original cost.
C. Cost of installation of an old machine.
D. Freight paid on purchase of raw material.

List II

1. Capital expenditure
2. Deferred revenue expenditure
3. Capital gain
4. Revenue expenditure

Codes:	A	B	C	D
(a)	2	3	1	4
(b)	2	3	4	1
(c)	3	2	1	4
(d)	3	2	4	1

924. **List I (Functions)**

A. Audit work is carried on almost simultaneously with the recording of transactions.
B. Auditor starts his work when the final accounts have been prepared.

C. Audit conducted in between two annual audits.
D. Some of the books and records of the whole period or specific period are audited.

List II (Types)
1. Balance Sheet
2. Continuous Audit
3. Interim Audit
4. Partial Audit

Codes:	A	B	C	D
(a)	2	3	1	4
(b)	2	1	3	4
(c)	4	3	1	2
(d)	4	1	3	2

925. **List I (Forms of memorandum of association)**
A. Table B B. Table C
C. Table D D. Table E

List II (Type of company)
1. Company limited by guarantee not having share capital
2. Company limited by guarantee having share capital
3. Unlimited liability company
4. Company limited by shares

Codes:	A	B	C	D
(a)	4	1	2	3
(b)	4	3	2	1
(c)	2	3	4	1
(d)	2	1	4	3

926. **List I (Accounting concepts)**
A. Consistency B. Comparability
C. Conservatism D. Disclosure

List II (Principle involved)
1. Losses are anticipated and accounted for in advance but prof. its are not accounted for until realized.
2. All the relevant financial information should be summarised and presented in the accounting statements
3. Accounting procedures in an entity should be followed uniformly from period to period
4. Accounting statements of different periods of an entity and those of different entites of a period shou'd be based on the same accounting principles and procedures
5. Personal judge ment of accountants should not influence accounting statements.

Codes:	A	B	C	D
(a)	1	5	2	3
(b)	4	5	1	3
(c)	1	3	2	5
(d)	4	3	1	5

927. **List I (Provision of partnership act)**
A. Interest must be allowed @ 6% p.a.
B. No interest shall be paid
C. No interest shall be charged
D. Must be shared equally by all the partners unless otherwise agreed

List II (Matter with which the provisions are related)
1. Drawings of partners
2. Net loss of the firm for an accounting year
3. Capital contributed by the partners
4. Loan given by a partner to the firm

Codes:	A	B	C	D
(a)	1	3	4	2
(b)	4	2	1	3
(c)	1	2	4	3
(d)	4	3	1	2

928.

List I (Item)	List II (Nature of Item)
A. Cash	1. Shareholder's equity
B. Profits	2. Fixed asset
C. Discount on issue of shares	3. Current asset

D. Plant and machinery	4. Fictious asset
	5. Intangible asset

Codes:	A	B	C	D
(a)	1	3	4	2
(b)	3	4	5	1
(c)	3	1	4	2
(d)	2	5	1	3

929. List I

A. EAIT No. of equity shares outstanding
B. Debt equity performance
C. FA Long-term funds
D. CA CL

List II

1. Liquidity
2. Solvency
3. Capital structure
4. Overall

Codes:	A	B	C	D
(a)	4	3	1	2
(b)	4	3	2	1
(c)	2	3	4	1
(d)	2	3	1	4

930. List I (Items of balance sheets of company)

A. Profit prior to incorporation
B. Proposed dividend
C. Interest paid
D. Unclaimed dividend

List II (Headings of balance sheet)

1. Provisions
2. Miscellaneous expenditure
3. Current liabilities
4. Reserves and Surplus

Codes:	A	B	C	D
(a)	1	4	3	2
(b)	1	4	2	3
(c)	4	1	2	3
(d)	4	1	3	2

931. List I

A. Income measurement
B. Expense recognition
C. Basis for realisation in accounting
D. Recognised revenue

List II

1. Accrues to owners equity
2. Revenue recognition
3. Matching revenues and expenses
4. Accounting period

Codes:	A	B	C	D
(a)	2	3	4	1
(b)	2	3	1	4
(c)	3	4	2	1
(d)	3	4	1	2

932. List I

A. Compensating errors
B. Errors of ommission
C. Errors of principle
D. Errors of commission

List II

1. Not recording a business transaction
2. Charging a Revenueitem to capital
3. Writing a debit item on the credit side and a credit item on the debit side of equal amount
4. Posting a correct amount to a wrong Account

Codes:	A	B	C	D
(a)	b	a	c	d
(b)	c	a	d	b
(c)	b	a	d	c
(d)	c	a	b	d

933. List I

A. Company X buys up company and shareholders of Y get shares in X.
B. Company X and company Y join to form company Z.

C. Company X buys 51% of shares in Company X.
D. Company X and company Y have the same directors.

List II
1. Amalgamation
2. Absorption
3. Cartel
4. Holding company
5. Community of interest

Codes:	A	B	C	D
(a)	2	1	4	5
(b)	1	2	5	4
(c)	1	2	4	5
(d)	2	1	4	3

934. **List I (Financial ratios)**
A. Debt Service Ratio
B. Preference Dividend Coverage Ratio
C. Cash to Debt Service Ratio
D. Gross Profit Ratio
E. Administrative Expenses Ratio

List II (Their formulae)

1. $\dfrac{\text{Net Income before Charging Interest and Income Tax}}{\text{Fixed Interest Charges}}$

2. $\dfrac{\text{Net Income after Interest and Income Tax}}{\text{Preference Dividend}}$

3. $\dfrac{\text{Annual Cash Flow before Interest and Taxes}}{\text{Interest} + \dfrac{\text{Sinking Fund appropriation on Debt}}{1 - \text{Tax}}}$

4. $\dfrac{\text{Gross Profit}}{\text{Net Sales}} \times 100$

5. $\dfrac{\text{Administrative Costs}}{\text{Sales}} \times 100$

Codes:	A	B	C	D	E
(a)	1	4	3	2	5
(b)	1	2	3	4	5
(c)	5	4	3	2	1
(d)	4	5	3	2	1

935. **List I (Type of capital)**
A. Authorised capital
B. Issued capital
C. Subscribed capital
D. Paid-up capital

List II (Their explanation)
1. A registered capital
2. Which is issued for public
3. Which is purchased by the capital
4. That part has been paid by the shareholders

Codes:	A	B	C	D
(a)	2	3	4	1
(b)	1	4	3	2
(c)	4	3	2	1
(d)	1	2	3	4

936. **List I (Purchase consideration method)**
A. Net Payment
B. Net Assets
C. Share Proportion
D. Contract

List II (Formula)
1. Purchase Consideration = Payment to Shareholders in shares + Debentures + Cash
2. Purchases Consideration = Total of Assets taken over – Total of Liabilities taken over
3. 5% Equity share of Total purchase Consideration and Remaining in Preference Shares
4. Assets or Payment

Codes:	A	B	C	D
(a)	2	1	3	4
(b)	1	2	3	4

(c)	4	1	3	2
(d)	2	3	4	1

937. **List I (Expenses)**
A. Depreciation
B. Priliminary Expenses
C. Directors Fee
D. Selling Expenses

List II (Allocation basis)
1. Time
2. Pre-Incorporation
3. Post Incorporation
4. Sales

Codes:	A	B	C	D
(a)	1	3	2	4
(b)	1	2	3	4
(c)	3	4	1	2
(d)	2	1	3	4

938. **List I (Expenses)**
A. Discount allowed
B. Advertisement expenses
C. Rent
D. Wages

List II (Allocation basis)
1. Turnover 2. Turnover
3. Time 4. Time

Codes:	A	B	C	D
(a)	2	1	3	4
(b)	4	1	2	3
(c)	1	2	3	4
(d)	2	1	3	4

939. **List I (Questions)**
A. At BEP, the total cost is equal ____
B. Excess of actual sales over breake even sales is called ____
C. Contribution is the difference between sales and _____
D. The total cost of fixed cost and profit is called _____

List II (Answers)
(1) Sales
(2) Margin of Safety
(3) Variable Cost
(4) Contribution

Codes:	A	B	C	D
(a)	2	3	4	1
(b)	1	2	3	4
(c)	4	3	1	2
(d)	3	1	2	4

940. **List I (Accounting concept)**
A. Objectivity Concept
B. Realisation Concept
C. Matching Concept
D. Cost Concept

List II (Fact)
1. All accounting transactions should be evidenced and supported by business documents i.e. vouchers and invoice
2. The concept revolves around the determination of the point of time when revenues are earned.
3. It is necessary to match the expenses incurred during the accounting period with the revenues recognised during the same period
4. Fixed assets are recorded in the account books at the price at which they are acquired

Codes:	A	B	C	D
(a)	3	2	1	4
(b)	1	2	3	4
(c)	2	1	3	4
(d)	4	3	2	1

941. **List I**
A. Current Assets-Current liabilities
B. Fixed assets-long term funds
C. Debit-Equity
D. Earnings after interest and taxes number of shares issued

List II
1. Performance of equity capital
2. Short term solvency
3. Capital structure
4. Overall performance
5. Long term solvency

Codes:	A	B	C	D
(a)	1	2	3	4
(b)	2	5	3	4
(c)	1	2	4	3
(d)	2	5	4	3

942. List I
A. Acid test ratio
B. Gearing ratio
C. Working capital
D. Return on capital employed

List II
1. Liquidity ratio
2. Profitability ratio
3. Leverage ratio turnover ratio
4. Long term solvency ratio
5. Activity ratio

Codes:	A	B	C	D
(a)	2	5	1	3
(b)	1	3	5	2
(c)	5	3	4	1
(d)	1	5	3	2

943. List I
A. EAIT No. of Liquidity Shares outstanding
B. Debt Equity
C. FA long term funds
D. CA CL

List II
1. Equity
2. Solvency
3. Capital structure
4. Overall performance

Codes:	A	B	C	D
(a)	4	3	1	2
(b)	4	3	2	1
(c)	2	3	d	1
(d)	2	3	1	4

944. List I
A. Trading on Equity
B. Efficiency of inventory control
C. Overall Efficiency
D. Immediate solvency

List II
1. Earning per share
2. Liquidity Ratio
3. Capital Gearing
4. Stock turnover Ratio

Codes:	A	B	C	D
(a)	3	4	1	2
(b)	2	1	4	3
(c)	2	4	1	3
(d)	3	1	4	2

945. List I
A. Debt service coverage Ratio
B. Turnover of Receivables
C. Proprietary Ratio
D. Capital Turnover credit

List II
1. Solvency Ratio
2. Structural Ratio
3. Activity Ratio
4. Efficiency of credit and collection policy

Codes:	A	B	C	D
(a)	4	1	3	2
(b)	1	4	3	2
(c)	4	1	2	3
(d)	1	4	2	3

946. List I
A. Leverage Ratio
B. Acid Test

C. Turnover Ratio
D. Current Ratio

List II

1. Liquidity position
2. Efficiency of assets management
3. Management of working Capital
4. Debt and equity relationship

Codes:	A	B	C	D
(a)	2	3	1	4
(b)	4	1	2	3
(c)	4	1	3	2
(d)	2	4	1	3

947. **List I**

A. Debt-Equity Ratio
B. Proprietary Ratio
C. Capital Gearing
D. ROI

List II

1. $\frac{\text{External Equity}}{\text{Owner's Equity}}$
2. $\frac{\text{Test shareholders funds}}{\text{Total Assets}}$
3. $\frac{\text{Equity capital}}{\text{Total Debt capital profit before}}$
4. $\frac{\text{Interest and Tax}}{\text{Net Assets}}$

Codes:	A	B	C	D
(a)	3	2	1	4
(b)	3	2	4	1
(c)	2	3	1	4
(d)	2	3	4	1

948. **List I** | **List II**

A. Financial coverage — 1. Efficiency
B. Quick Ratio — 2. Profitability
C. Stock Turnover Ratio — 3. Risk
D. Margin on sales — 4. Liquidity

Codes:	A	B	C	D
(a)	4	3	2	1
(b)	3	4	2	1
(c)	3	4	1	2
(d)	4	3	1	2

949. **List I (Names of accounting ratios)**

A. Capital gearing statement ratio
B. Stock velocity ratio
C. Debtors velocity ratio
D. Dividend yield ratio

List II (Nature of accounting ratios)

1. Revenue ratio
2. Coverage ratio
3. Market price ratio
4. Balance sheet ratio
5. Balance sheet and revenue statement combined ratio

Codes:	A	B	C	D
(a)	1	5	4	2
(b)	3	2	5	1
(c)	4	1	5	3
(d)	5	4	2	1

950. **List I**

A. Cooperative Society
B. Joint Hindu Family
C. Joint Stock company
D. Partnership firm

List II

1. Collective business
2. Purchase/Trnasfer of shares
3. By virtue of Birth
4. Common mutual interest
5. Mutual contract

Codes:	A	B	C	D
(a)	5	4	1	3
(b)	1	3	2	5
(c)	4	1	2	3
(d)	4	3	2	5

951. List I

A. Partners current account
B. Goodwil account
C. Partners drawings account
D. Profit and Loss

List II

1. Dissolution of partnership
2. Revaluation of assets on the admisstionofa partner.
3. Fixed capitals of partners
4. Goods taken by partners for private consumption

Codes:	A	B	C	D
(a)	3	1	4	2
(b)	1	3	4	2
(c)	3	1	2	4
(d)	1	3	4	2

952. List I

A. Interest must be allowed @ 6% p.a.
B. No interest shall be allowed.
C. No interest shall be charged.
D. Must be shared equally by all the partners unless otherwise agreed.

List II

1. Drawings of partners.
2. Net loss of the firm for an accounting year.
3. Capitals contributed by the partners.
4. Loan given by a partner to the firm.

Codes:	A	B	C	D
(a)	4	3	1	2
(b)	1	3	2	4
(c)	3	2	4	1
(d)	4	3	2	1

953. List I

A. Loss on realisation
B. Profit on realisation
C. Assets sold
D. Creditors paid

List II

1. Debits partner's capital A/C
2. Credit realisation A/C
3. Credit Partner's A/C
4. Debit realisation A/C

Codes:	A	B	C	D
(a)	3	1	2	4
(b)	1	3	2	4
(c)	1	3	4	2
(d)	3	1	4	2

954. List I

A. Heavy amount of premium on redemption of preference shares
B. Excess of sale proceeds of fixed assets over their original cost
C. Cost of installation of an old machine
D. Freight paid on purchase of raw material

List II

1. Capital expenditure
2. Deferred revenue expenditure
3. Capital gain
4. Revenue expenditure

Code:	A	B	C	D
(a)	3	2	4	1
(b)	2	3	4	1
(c)	3	2	1	4
(d)	2	3	1	4

955. List I

A. Preliminary expenses
B. Travelling expenses of the salesman
C. Profit on sale of a part of the business building
D. Nazranapaid on the purchase of Land for business

List II

1. Capital expenditure
2. Revenue expenditure
3. Capital gain
4. Deferred revenue expenditure

Codes:	A	B	C	D
(a)	2	4	3	1
(b)	4	2	3	1
(c)	2	4	1	3
(d)	4	2	1	3

956. List I | List II

List I	List II
A. Debit and Credit Vouchers are also called	1. Non-cash transactions transactions
B. Credit vouchers are prepared for	2. Cash payment of the business
C. Transfer Vouchers are prepared for	3. Cash Vouchers
D. Debit Vouchers are prepared for	4. Cash receipts of the business

Codes:	A	B	C	D
(a)	4	3	2	1
(b)	3	4	1	2
(c)	3	1	2	4
(d)	1	2	3	4

957. List I

A. Compensation paid to retrenched workers of the factory for the loss of service
B. Legal expenses incurred in connection with the purchase of a plot of land
C. Compensation from the Government for the compulsory removal of a business premises to another place
D. Sale proceeds of marchandise (goods)

List II

1. Capital expenditure
2. Capital receipt
3. Revenue Expenditure
4. Revenue receipt

Codes:	A	B	C	D
(a)	1	3	2	4
(b)	3	1	4	2
(c)	3	1	2	4
(d)	1	3	4	2

958. List I

A. Premium paid for a leesehold property
B. Insurance premium paid for risks against accidental losses of properties (Fixed assets)
C. Amount realised from the sale of securities (investments) purchased earlier.
D. Huge sales promotion expenses

List II

1. Revenue expenditure
2. Capital receipt
3. Deferred revenue
4. Capital expenditure

Codes:	A	B	C	D
(a)	3	2	1	4
(b)	4	1	2	3
(c)	3	1	2	4
(d)	4	2	1	3

Directions: Questions 959 to 973 consist of two statements, one labelled as 'Assertion (A)' and the other as 'Reason (R)'. You have to examine these two statements carefuly and decide if the Assertion (A) and the Reason (R) are individually true and if so, whether the Reason is a correct explanation of the Assertion. Select your answer to these items using the codes given below.

(a) Both A and R are true and R is the correct explanation of A.
(b) Both A and R are true and R is not the correct explanation of A.
(c) A is true but R is false.
(d) A is false but R is true.

959. **Assertion (A):** Management Accounting provides management with information for decision-making.

Reason (R): Management Accounting is a branch of financial accounting.

960. **Assertion (A):** Materiality concept refers to the state of ignoring relatively small items and values from accounts.

Reason (R): The effort involved in allocating the cost of a small item over a long period should be justified in terms of the benefit derived from this operation. Therefore cost of such items may be treated as expenses for the period in which they are acquired.

961. **Assertion (A):** Accounting is the language of business.

Reason (R): Accounting provides all information needed by a businessman.

962. **Assertion (A):** The investors in the capital market have been showing a decisive shift in favour of fixed income instruments.

Reason (R): The debt instruments have active secondary market.

963. **Assertion (A):** A transferee of shares cannot sue the promoters of a company for misinformation in the prospectus.

Reason (R): The information provided by the company promoters in the prospectus is addressed only to the original allottees.

964. **Assertion (A):** An agreement of a trial balance is not a conclusive evidence of accuracy of ledger posting.

Reason (R): A ledger may contain mistakes relating to errors of commission.

965. **Assertion (A):** In a fund flow statement, and issue of shares for an asset is to be disclos d on its both sides.

Reason (R): The fund flow statement discloses what is not disclosed by the balance sheet.

966. **Assertion (A):** The companies prefer to issue debt securities in their private placements.

Reason (R): It helps them to go for trading on equity.

967. **Assertion (A):** The liability of shareholders of a private limited company is limited to the amount unpaid on shares.

Reason (R): The number of shareholders of a private limited company is limited to fifty.

968. **Assertion (A):** Amount realised on the disposal sale of a discarded machine of the factory should be treated as revenue receipt.

Reason (R): Sale proceeds are usually of revenue in nature.

969. **Assertion (A):** An accounting principle is that the relatively small item and values should be ignored from accounts.

Reason (R): The cost of the effort in the allocation of small items over a long period does not justify the benefit derived from this operation and the cost of such items is treated as expense for the period in which they are in incurred.

970. **Assertion (A):** The Responsibility Accounting classifies costs and revenues according to the responsibility centers.

Reason (R): For each responsibility centre, the extent of responsibility should be defined.

971. **Assertion (A):** Ratio analysis is an important tool of judging the financial soundness of the company.

Reason (R): Ratio analysis is the only guide to an investor for deciding about investing or not investing in a company

972. **Assertion (A):** "Share Premium can not be utilised for any purpose other than

mentioned in Sec. 78 of the Companies Act."

Reason (R): "Share Premium is a Capital receipt."

973. **Assertion (A):** Accounting is a continuous process in any business undertaking.

Reason (R): This is an Accounting period concept.

ANSWERS

1. (c)	2. (b)	3. (b)	4. (b)	5. (c)	6. (c)
7. (c)	8. (b)	9. (d)	10. (c)	11. (c)	12. (a)
13. (c)	14. (b)	15. (b)	16. (b)	17. (b)	18. (c)
19. (c)	20. (b)	21. (c)	22. (b)	23. (c)	24. (d)
25. (b)	26. (d)	27. (b)	28. (b)	29. (c)	30. (b)
31. (a)	32. (c)	33. (c)	34. (b)	35. (d)	36. (c)
37. (a)	38. (c)	39. (b)	40. (b)	41. (c)	42. (d)
43. (b)	44. (d)	45. (b)	46. (a)	47. (c)	48. (d)
49. (a)	50. (a)	51. (a)	52. (d)	53. (c)	54. (a)
55. (c)	56. (a)	57. (c)	58. (d)	59. (b)	60. (c)
61. (a)	62. (a)	63. (b)	64. (b)	65. (d)	66. (c)
67. (d)	68. (d)	69. (a)	70. (a)	71. (d)	72. (d)
73. (c)	74. (a)	75. (a)	76. (b)	77. (d)	78. (d)
79. (c)	80. (a)	81. (c)	82. (b)	83. (d)	84. (a)
85. (a)	86. (b)	87. (b)	88. (c)	89. (d)	90. (c)
91. (c)	92. (a)	93. (a)	94. (c)	95. (c)	96. (a)
97. (c)	98. (b)	99. (d)	100. (a)	101. (d)	102. (b)
103. (b)	104. (d)	105. (b)	106. (b)	107. (b)	108. (a)
109. (a)	110. (c)	111. (b)	112. (c)	113. (a)	114. (b)
115. (b)	116. (b)	117. (a)	118. (c)	119. (a)	120. (d)
121. (c)	122. (b)	123. (c)	124. (a)	125. (d)	126. (d)
127. (c)	128. (c)	129. (d)	130. (a)	131. (b)	132. (a)
133. (a)	134. (c)	135. (b)	136. (a)	137. (d)	138. (d)
139. (b)	140. (c)	141. (d)	142. (c)	143. (d)	144. (c)
145. (c)	146. (d)	147. (b)	148. (d)	149. (c)	150. (c)
151. (a)	152. (b)	153. (a)	154. (a)	155. (b)	156. (c)
157. (c)	158. (d)	159. (b)	160. (b)	161. (c)	162. (a)
163. (a)	164. (a)	165. (b)	166. (c)	167. (c)	168. (c)

169. (d)	170. (d)	171. (a)	172. (d)	173. (a)	174. (c)
175. (b)	176. (a)	177. (b)	178. (d)	179. (b)	180. (b)
181. (c)	182. (c)	183. (d)	184. (a)	185. (b)	186. (d)
187. (c)	188. (c)	189. (b)	190. (d)	191. (c)	192. (d)
193. (d)	194. (d)	195. (d)	196. (c)	197. (c)	198. (a)
199. (a)	200. (b)	201. (c)	202. (c)	203. (d)	204. (d)
205. (d)	206. (c)	207. (c)	208. (c)	209. (c)	210. (d)
211. (d)	212. (c)	213. (a)	214. (a)	215. (c)	216. (c)
217. (a)	218. (c)	219. (c)	220. (b)	221. (b)	222. (c)
223. (c)	224. (b)	225. (c)	226. (a)	227. (c)	228. (d)
229. (a)	230. (a)	231. (a)	232. (c)	233. (a)	234. (b)
235. (c)	236. (b)	237. (d)	238. (b)	239. (a)	240. (c)
241. (a)	242. (a)	243. (c)	244. (b)	245. (d)	246. (c)
247. (b)	248. (d)	249. (c)	250. (b)	251. (a)	252. (c)
253. (a)	254. (c)	255. (b)	256. (c)	257. (d)	258. (b)
259. (c)	260. (c)	261. (c)	262. (a)	263. (b)	264. (d)
265. (c)	266. (c)	267. (d)	268. (d)	269. (d)	270. (d)
271. (a)	272. (b)	273. (d)	274. (a)	275. (d)	276. (b)
277. (a)	278. (d)	279. (b)	280. (d)	281. (c)	282. (c)
283. (b)	284. (c)	285. (c)	286. (d)	287. (a)	288. (b)
289. (c)	290. (c)	291. (a)	292. (a)	293. (d)	294. (d)
295. (b)	296. (c)	297. (c)	298. (b)	299. (d)	300. (c)
301. (c)	302. (c)	303. (d)	304. (c)	305. (b)	306. (c)
307. (b)	308. (a)	309. (b)	310. (c)	311. (c)	312. (b)
313. (a)	314. (c)	315. (a)	316. (b)	317. (d)	318. (a)
319. (a)	320. (c)	321. (a)	322. (a)	323. (b)	324. (a)
325. (d)	326. (d)	327. (d)	328. (a)	329. (d)	330. (a)
331. (d)	332. (b)	333. (d)	334. (b)	335. (c)	336. (c)
337. (d)	338. (a)	339. (c)	340. (c)	341. (a)	342. (d)
343. (b)	344. (b)	345. (d)	346. (b)	347. (d)	348. (d)
349. (d)	350. (d)	351. (d)	352. (d)	353. (d)	354. (c)
355. (c)	356. (c)	357. (c)	358. (c)	359. (c)	360. (b)
361. (c)	362. (d)	363. (c)	364. (c)	365. (c)	366. (c)
367. (c)	368. (c)	369. (b)	370. (d)	371. (d)	372. (d)

373. (d)	374. (b)	375. (c)	376. (b)	377. (c)	378. (d)
379. (b)	380. (c)	381. (c)	382. (c)	383. (c)	384. (c)
385. (c)	386. (c)	387. (c)	388. (c)	389. (c)	390. (d)
391. (d)	392. (d)	393. (d)	394. (d)	395. (c)	396. (c)
397. (d)	398. (c)	399. (d)	400. (b)	401. (b)	402. (c)
403. (d)	404. (d)	405. (d)	406. (a)	407. (d)	408. (d)
409. (d)	410. (d)	411. (d)	412. (d)	413. (b)	414. (c)
415. (a)	416. (c)	417. (b)	418. (d)	419. (b)	420. (b)
421. (b)	422. (d)	423. (a)	424. (d)	425. (d)	426. (d)
427. (b)	428. (d)	429. (d)	430. (b)	431. (c)	432. (d)
433. (d)	434. (b)	435. (c)	436. (a)	437. (a)	438. (c)
439. (a)	440. (b)	441. (d)	442. (d)	443. (c)	444. (b)
445. (b)	446. (c)	447. (d)	448. (b)	449. (b)	450. (b)
451. (d)	452. (d)	453. (d)	454. (b)	455. (c)	456. (b)
457. (d)	458. (c)	459. (d)	460. (b)	461. (c)	462. (c)
463. (c)	464. (c)	465. (d)	466. (c)	467. (c)	468. (c)
469. (a)	470. (a)	471. (d)	472. (d)	473. (a)	474. (a)
475. (a)	476. (c)	477. (b)	478. (b)	479. (b)	480. (d)
481. (a)	482. (b)	483. (a)	484. (c)	485. (a)	486. (a)
487. (b)	488. (c)	489. (c)	490. (d)	491. (a)	492. (b)
493. (d)	494. (c)	495. (b)	496. (d)	497. (d)	498. (a)
499. (a)	500. (b)	501. (c)	502. (c)	503. (a)	504. (a)
505. (b)	506. (a)	507. (d)	508. (d)	509. (b)	510. (d)
511. (c)	512. (c)	513. (c)	514. (d)	515. (c)	516. (a)
517. (a)	518. (d)	519. (a)	520. (a)	521. (b)	522. (a)
523. (a)	524. (a)	525. (a)	526. (d)	527. (d)	528. (d)
529. (a)	530. (c)	531. (a)	532. (d)	533. (a)	534. (c)
535. (a)	536. (d)	537. (a)	538. (b)	539. (a)	540. (c)
541. (b)	542. (b)	543. (c)	544. (a)	545. (b)	546. (c)
547. (c)	548. (b)	549. (b)	550. (b)	551. (b)	552. (c)
553. (a)	554. (b)	555. (a)	556. (b)	557. (d)	558. (a)
559. (a)	560. (c)	561. (a)	562. (d)	563. (a)	564. (b)
565. (d)	566. (b)	567. (c)	568. (c)	569. (c)	570. (d)
571. (a)	572. (d)	573. (a)	574. (a)	575. (c)	576. (b)

577. (d)	578. (a)	579. (d)	580. (c)	581. (d)	582. (b)
583. (d)	584. (a)	585. (b)	586. (d)	587. (c)	588. (a)
589. (b)	590. (a)	591. (a)	592. (d)	593. (a)	594. (c)
595. (a)	596. (c)	597. (d)	598. (d)	599. (a)	600. (d)
601. (c)	602. (c)	603. (c)	604. (d)	605. (a)	606. (d)
607. (c)	608. (a)	609. (b)	610. (d)	611. (b)	612. (d)
613. (d)	614. (d)	615. (a)	616. (a)	617. (a)	618. (c)
619. (d)	620. (c)	621. (a)	622. (a)	623. (d)	624. (b)
625. (d)	626. (d)	627. (a)	628. (d)	629. (c)	630. (b)
631. (c)	632. (b)	633. (d)	634. (a)	635. (b)	636. (a)
637. (d)	638. (b)	639. (a)	640. (d)	641. (a)	642. (c)
643. (a)	644. (b)	645. (b)	646. (d)	647. (c)	648. (d)
649. (d)	650. (a)	651. (b)	652. (d)	653. (a)	654. (b)
655. (b)	656. (b)	657. (b)	658. (b)	659. (a)	660. (d)
661. (a)	662. (c)	663. (a)	664. (c)	665. (d)	666. (a)
667. (d)	668. (a)	669. (d)	670. (b)	671. (d)	672. (a)
673. (d)	674. (d)	675. (c)	676. (a)	677. (b)	678. (a)
679. (b)	680. (b)	681. (a)	682. (a)	683. (d)	684. (c)
685. (c)	686. (d)	687. (b)	688. (a)	689. (a)	690. (b)
691. (d)	692. (b)	693. (b)	694. (a)	695. (d)	696. (a)
697. (c)	698. (b)	699. (a)	700. (c)	701. (a)	702. (c)
703. (d)	704. (a)	705. (a)	706. (a)	707. (c)	708. (a)
709. (d)	710. (a)	711. (b)	712. (c)	713. (c)	714. (a)
715. (a)	716. (c)	717. (c)	718. (a)	719. (b)	720. (a)
721. (b)	722. (a)	723. (a)	724. (b)	725. (c)	726. (b)
727. (a)	728. (c)	729. (a)	730. (b)	731. (a)	732. (d)
733. (b)	734. (a)	735. (c)	736. (b)	737. (c)	738. (a)
739. (d)	740. (a)	741. (c)	742. (b)	743. (b)	744. (b)
745. (a)	746. (c)	747. (c)	748. (a)	749. (d)	750. (c)
751. (c)	752. (a)	753. (d)	754. (a)	755. (c)	756. (b)
757. (c)	758. (d)	759. (b)	760. (d)	761. (d)	762. (d)
763. (a)	764. (a)	765. (a)	766. (a)	767. (d)	768. (d)
769. (b)	770. (a)	771. (a)	772. (d)	773. (a)	774. (b)
775. (d)	776. (b)	777. (d)	778. (d)	779. (d)	780. (c)

781. (b)	782. (c)	783. (d)	784. (c)	785. (b)	786. (c)
787. (a)	788. (c)	789. (b)	790. (c)	791. (b)	792. (a)
793. (b)	794. (a)	795. (b)	796. (d)	797. (a)	798. (c)
799. (a)	800. (a)	801. (c)	802. (d)	803. (b)	804. (c)
805. (b)	806. (a)	807. (d)	808. (c)	809. (d)	810. (d)
811. (a)	812. (a)	813. (d)	814. (a)	815. (a)	816. (b)
817. (c)	818. (b)	819. (c)	820. (d)	821. (a)	822. (a)
823. (d)	824. (b)	825. (d)	826. (a)	827. (a)	828. (b)
829. (a)	830. (b)	831. (b)	832. (c)	833. (c)	834. (b)
835. (b)	836. (a)	837. (b)	838. (c)	839. (d)	840. (c)
841. (c)	842. (a)	843. (a)	844. (c)	845. (c)	846. (c)
847. (b)	848. (b)	849. (a)	850. (c)	851. (d)	852. (d)
853. (b)	854. (d)	855. (c)	856. (b)	857. (a)	858. (d)
859. (a)	860. (c)	861. (c)	862. (a)	863. (b)	864. (c)
865. (a)	866. (b)	867. (c)	868. (a)	869. (c)	870. (d)
871. (a)	872. (d)	873. (a)	874. (a)	875. (c)	876. (d)
877. (c)	878. (a)	879. (a)	880. (a)	881. (d)	882. (a)
883. (b)	884. (d)	885. (a)	886. (b)	887. (d)	888. (c)
889. (c)	890. (b)	891. (d)	892. (c)	893. (a)	894. (d)
895. (a)	896. (a)	897. (c)	898. (d)	899. (c)	900. (a)
901. (a)	902. (d)	903. (a)	904. (c)	905. (c)	906. (d)
907. (a)	908. (a)	909. (c)	910. (b)	911. (b)	912. (c)
913. (d)	914. (a)	915. (d)	916. (a)	917. (c)	918. (b)
919. (b)	920. (a)	921. (b)	922. (c)	923. (a)	924. (b)
925. (a)	926. (d)	927. (d)	928. (c)	929. (b)	930. (c)
931. (c)	932. (d)	933. (a)	934. (b)	935. (d)	936. (b)
937. (b)	938. (c)	939. (b)	940. (b)	941. (d)	942. (b)
943. (b)	944. (a)	945. (d)	946. (b)	947. (c)	948. (c)
949. (c)	950. (d)	951. (d)	952. (a)	953. (b)	954. (d)
955. (b)	956. (b)	957. (c)	958. (b)	959. (a)	960. (a)
961. (a)	962. (c)	963. (a)	964. (a)	965. (d)	966. (d)
967. (b)	968. (b)	969. (a)	970. (a)	971. (a)	972. (b)
973. (c)					

3

Business Economics

1. The collective demand of all persons in the market is referred as
   (a) market demand schedule
   (b) demand curve
   (c) Both (a) and (b)
   (d) None of the above
2. When the demand of a commodity also depends upon prices of the substitutes and complementaries or relative prices then it is called
   (a) Cross demand
   (b) Price-demand
   (c) Income-demand
   (d) None of the above
3. The fall in the price of one commodity leads to fall in demand for other commodity and vice versa for
   (a) Complementaries
   (b) Substitutes
   (c) Both (a) and (b)
   (d) None of the above
4. The fall in the price of one commodity leads to increase in demand for other commodity is called
   (a) Complementaries
   (b) Substitutes
   (c) Both (a) and (b)
   (d) None of the above
5. When a No. of goods are required collectively for one purpose, it is called
   (a) composite demand
   (b) derived demand
   (c) joint demand
   (d) None of the above
6. When a commodity with many uses is demanded then it is called
   (a) direct demand
   (b) composite demand
   (c) joint demand
   (d) None of the above
7. Decrease or fall in the price of commodity leads to increase in demand because of
   (a) income effect *i.e.* Consumer becomes better off.
   (b) substitution effect *i.e.* Relatively cheaper than related goods.
   (c) Both (a) and (b)
   (d) None of the above
8. Who has given four major exceptions to the law of demand?
   (a) Samuelson
   (b) Beham
   (c) Giffen
   (d) None of the above
9. When quantity demanded changes only due to change in price then it is called
   (a) contraction in demand
   (b) extension in demand
   (c) Both (a) and (b)
   (d) None of the above
10. When quantity demanded changes due to factors other than price, it is called
    (a) decrease in demand
    (b) increase in demand

(c) Both (a) and (b)
(d) None of the above

11. In case of contraction or extension in demand, the movement is along a demand curve whereas in case of increase or decrease, the demand curve will move
(a) Upward
(b) Downward
(c) Any of the above
(d) None of the above

12. Proportionate method of measurement of elasticity of demand is also known as
(a) ratio method
(b) arithmetic method
(c) flux method
(d) All of the above

13. Under total outlay or total expenditure method, the elasticity of demand can be measured as

(a) $\dfrac{\dfrac{\Delta p}{q_1 + q_2}}{\dfrac{\Delta p}{p_1 + p_2}}$ (b) $1 - \dfrac{\Delta Exp}{\chi \Delta p}$

(c) $\dfrac{\Delta Q}{\Delta P}$ (d) $\dfrac{\Delta p}{\Delta q} \times \dfrac{p}{q}$

14. The law of variable proportions is
(a) wider and includes law of increasing returns, law of decreasing returns and law of constant return as three phases.
(b) also called law of non-proportional returns.
(c) also called law of proportionality.
(d) All of the above.

15. Which of the following economies accrue all the firm in an industry?
(a) Economies of concentration
(b) Managerial economies
(c) Marketing economies
(d) Labour economies

16. For the relationship between AC and MC, which of the following statement is wrong?
(a) If AC rises, MC also rises.
(b) Both AC and MC are calculated from TC.
(c) For the minimum point of AC, average cost is equal to marginal cost.
(d) If AC Falls, MC will rise.

17. Marginal cost is the addition to total cost due to the addition of one unit of output is represented by

(a) $MC = \dfrac{\Delta TC}{\Delta q}$

(b) $MCq = TCq - TCq - 1$
(c) Both (a) and (b)
(d) None of the above

18. Total Revenue (TR) is best represented by
(a) $TR = AR \times q$

(b) $TRn = \sum_{i=1}^{n} p_i q_i$

(c) $TRn = \sum_{i=1}^{n} MR_i$

(d) All of the above

19. A market situation in which there are only few sellers and each seller can influence its price-output policy is called
(a) Duopoly (b) Monopolistic
(c) Monopoly (d) Oligopoly

20. The concept of imperfect competition was developed by
(a) Mrs. Lillian Gilbreth
(b) Joan Robinson
(c) Jevons
(d) Marshall

21. The perfect competition is characterised by

(a) firms selling identical products.
(b) presence of many firms.
(c) seller as price taker.
(d) All of the above.

22. The monopolist faces
(a) a downward sloping demand curve.
(b) a downward sloping average revenue curve.
(c) Both (a) and (b).
(d) None of the above.

23. Two conditions are required to be there for the equilibrium under monopoly. These are
(a) MC = MR and MR cuts the MC from below.
(b) MR = MC and MC cuts the MR from above.
(c) MR = MC and MC cuts the MR from below.
(d) MC = AR and MC cuts the MR from below.

24. Utility theory is not able to explain the reason for
(a) normal goods
(b) precious goods
(c) giffen goods
(d) inferior goods

25. Ordinal measure of utility is required in
(a) indifference curve
(b) revealed preference
(c) utility
(d) None of the above

26. Demand curve was drawn with empirical evidence by
(a) indifference curve
(b) utility
(c) revealed preference
(d) None of the above

27. The appropriate objective of an enterprise is
(a) maximisation of owner's wealth.
(b) maximisation of profits.
(c) maximisation of sales.
(d) None of the above.

28. The term 'revealed preference' was introduced in the book by
(a) Foundations of Economic Analysis
(b) Das Capital
(c) Affluent Society
(d) None of the above

29. The job of a finance manager is confined to
(a) management of cash.
(b) raising of funds and their effective utilisation.
(c) raising of funds.
(d) None of the above.

30. MRS_{xy} is the slope of
(a) indifference curve
(b) demand curve
(c) iso-costline
(d) None of the above

31. P_x/P_y is the slope of
(a) demand curve
(b) indifference curve
(c) iso-costline
(d) None of the above

32. Shape of indifference curve in case of complementary goods is
(a) V (b) L
(c) U (d) S

33. In case of giffen goods, price effect is
(a) Positive (b) Zero
(c) Negative (d) None of these

34. In case of inferior goods, price effect is
(a) Positive (b) Negative
(c) Zero (d) None of these

35. Positive income effect is greater than negative substitution effect in case of

(a) luxury goods (b) giffen goods
(c) normal goods (d) inferior goods

36. Reason behind goods could not be explained by
(a) indifference curve
(b) utility theory
(c) Both (a) and (b)
(d) None of the above

37. Willingness to pay actual payment is equal to
(a) consumer's surplus
(b) producer's surplus
(c) supplier's surplus
(d) None of the above

38. In case of utility theory, as income increases, marginal utility of money
(a) Increases (b) Constant
(c) Decreases (d) None of these

39. A consumer's demand curve can be obtained from
(a) PCC (b) Engel curve
(c) ICC (d) Lorenz curve

40. A consumer's income curve can be obtained from
(a) Lorenz curve (b) Engel curve
(c) PCC (d) ICC

41. If demand curve is horizontal, then e_p is equal to
(a) 1 (b) ∞
(c) 0 (d) 2

42. If demand curve is vertical, then e_p is equal to
(a) ∞ (b) 2
(c) 0 (d) 1

43. If demand curve is rectangular hyperbola, e_p is equal to
(a) 1 (b) ∞
(c) 0 (d) 2

44. If as a result of increase in price, total outlay on the commodity remains same, then the e_p is equal to
(a) ∞ (b) 2
(c) 1 (d) 0

45. In case of giffen goods, demand curve will slope
(a) Horizontal (b) Vertical
(c) Upward (d) Downward

46. In case of veblen goods, demand curve will slope
(a) Vertical (b) Horizontal
(c) Downward (d) Upward

47. Relationship between the income level and the quantity of commodity purchased by the consumer is represented by which curve?
(a) Engel curve (b) Lorenz curve
(c) Demand curve (d) None of these

48. All giffen goods are inferior, but all inferior goods are not giffen goods. The statement is
(a) Sometimes true (b) False
(c) True (d) None of these

49. Of the following commodities, which has the lowest elasticity of demand?
(a) Tea (b) House
(c) Car (d) Salt

50. Cross elasticity of demand between tea and sugar is
(a) Zero (b) Infinity
(c) Positive (d) Negative

51. Cross elasticity of demand, between tea and coffee is
(a) Zero (b) Negative
(c) Positive (d) Infinity

52. These communications are much freer and therefore much less distorted. The reference is to

(a) Incoming (b) Outgoing
(c) Formal (d) Informal

53. Total utility is maximum when marginal utility is
(a) Zero (b) Rising
(c) Positive (d) Negative

54. Gosen's first law is related to
(a) Demand
(b) Diminishing marginal utility
(c) Elasticity
(d) Supply

55. Consumer reaches a saturation point for a product when MU is
(a) Zero (b) Positive
(c) Negative (d) None of these

56. Indifference curves are parallel
(a) Sometimes (b) Never
(c) Always (d) None of these

57. Indifference curve is always
(a) Concave (b) Convex
(c) Vertical line (d) L-shaped

58. Increase in demand because of decrease in price is called
(a) Contraction (b) Decrease
(c) Extension (d) Increase

59. Increase in demand because of increase in income is called
(a) Contraction (b) Extension
(c) Decrease (d) Increase

60. In case of $e_p = \infty$, demand curve will be
(a) upward sloping
(b) horizontal
(c) vertical
(d) downward sloping

61. Demand curve is related to
(a) marginal revenue
(b) MU curve
(c) Both (a) and (b)
(d) None of the above

62. Demand curved can be derived from
(a) PGG (b) MU curve
(c) Both (a) and (b) (d) None of these

63. In case of demand curve, if lower segment is greater than upper segment, then e_p will be
(a) 3
(b) 2
(c) greater than one
(d) lower than one

64. At the mid point of the demand curve, e_p is equal to
(a) 2 (b) 3
(c) 0 (d) 1

65. In the calculation of elasticity, there is error in case of
(a) Point elasticity
(b) Arc elasticity
(c) Both (a) and (b)
(d) None of the above

66. The exception to law of demand are
(a) giffen goods (b) beblen goods
(c) Both (a) and (b) (d) None of these

67. Demand for a product should have the following pre-requisite
(a) Willingness (b) Need
(c) Ability to buy (d) All of these

68. Cross elasticity of demand between two perfect substitutes will be
(a) High (b) Infinity
(c) Low (d) Zero

69. Business finance deals with
(a) financial controls
(b) acquisition of funds
(c) use and allocation of funds
(d) All of the above

70. In the above question, slope of the demand curve is
(a) –1 (b) –2
(c) 0 (d) 1

71. At what price, elasticity will be equal to 1?
(a) 35 (b) 40
(c) 10 (d) 25

72. At elasticity of 1, marginal revenue is equal to
(a) Infinity (b) One
(c) Zero (d) None of these

73. Total revenue is maximum when elasticity of demand is
(a) 1 (b) 3
(c) 0 (d) 0.5

74. Market demand is aggregation of individual demand
(a) Horizontally (b) Vertically
(c) Both (a) and (b) (d) None of these

75. Dynamic theory of profit was introduced by
(a) Walras (b) Marshall
(c) Both (a) and (b) (d) None of these

76. Study of demand over two periods is called
(a) Dynamic
(b) Static
(c) Comparative static
(d) None of the above

77. Cobwell theory of demand is related to
(a) Comparative static
(b) Dynamic
(c) Static
(d) None of the above

78. Impact of change in demand in one sector on other sectors is studied by
(a) partial equilibrium
(b) general equilibrium
(c) Both (a) and (b)
(d) None of the above

79. Industry with few firms is termed as
(a) Perfect competition
(b) Monopoly
(c) Oligopoly
(d) None of the above

80. Homogeneity of product is characteristic of
(a) Perfect competition
(b) Monopoly
(c) Oligopoly
(d) None of the above

81. This is the mechanism by which the system controls its own operation. The reference is to
(a) Processing (b) Feedback
(c) Input (d) Output

82. Letters, Notices, Bulletins, Rules, etc. are examples of
(a) implied written communication.
(b) implied oral communication.
(c) express oral communication.
(d) express written communication.

83. Which of the following dimensions is external to the leaders?
(a) Relations (b) Task
(c) Attitude (d) Style

84. The demand curve of the monopolist is X= 50 - 0.5 P and cost function is C = 50 + 40X.
Find marginal revenue at maximum profit.
(a) 60 (b) 80
(c) 20 (d) 40

85. In the above question, what is price at maximum profit?
(a) 40 (b) 50
(c) 60 (d) 70

86. In the above question what is the maximum profit?
(a) 400 (b) 300
(c) 600 (d) 500

87. What is the slope of MR curve in case of above question?
(a) –5 (b) –6
(c) –3 (d) –4

88. If the company is following profit maximisation then impact of lump sum tax will be
(a) no effect
(b) increase in price
(c) decrease in price
(d) None of the above

89. In case of perfect competition, elasticity will be
(a) 3 (b) Infinity
(c) 0 (d) 2

90. Cartel is a part of
(a) Oligopoly
(b) Monopoly
(c) Perfect competition
(d) Monopolistic competition

91. A firm will close down in short run if AR is less than
(a) AVC (b) AC
(c) MC (d) None of these

92. In case of oligopoly, number of firms is
(a) One (b) Large
(c) Few (d) Infinite

93. Imperfect competition was introduced by
(a) Keynes (b) Marshall
(c) Chamberlin (d) None of these

94. Which type of competition leads to exploitation of consumer?
(a) Monopolistic competition
(b) Monopoly
(c) Oligopoly
(d) All of the above

95. Market with one buyer and one seller is called
(a) Monopoly
(b) Bilateral monopoly
(c) Monopsony
(d) None of the above

96. How many sellers are present in duopoly?
(a) 3 (b) 4
(c) 1 (d) 2

97. Which of the following is an important dynamic variable?
(a) Organisational nature
(b) Superior's style and behaviour
(c) Cultural variables
(d) The task structure

98. Factors responsible for creating conditions for emergence and growth of monopoly are
(a) Licensing
(b) Control over strategic raw materials
(c) Patents
(d) All of the above

99. Selling costs have to be incurred in case of
(a) imperfect competition
(b) perfect competition
(c) monopolistic competition
(d) None of the above

100. For maximisation of profit in the short run, the condition is
(a) MR = AR (b) MC = AC
(c) AR = AC (d) MR = MC

101. Under perfect competition, price of the product
(a) can be controlled within certain limit.
(b) can be controlled.
(c) cannot be controlled.
(d) None of the above.

102. Which one is not normally possible in case of monopoly?
(a) MR = AR (b) MR = P
(c) MC = MR (d) AC = AR

103. In the case of monopolistic competition
(a) the short run supply curve cannot be defined.
(b) MR curve cannot be defined.

(c) AR curve cannot be defined.
(d) None of the above.

104. In case of monopoly, a firm in the long run can have
(a) Profit (b) Breakeven
(c) Loss (d) All of the above

105. A situation in which the number of competing firms is relatively small is known as
(a) Monopsony
(b) Monopoly
(c) Oligopoly
(d) Perfect competition

106. A situation where there is only one buyer is called
(a) Monopsony
(b) Monopoly
(c) Perfect competition
(d) Oligopoly

107. A market in which only two firms exist is called
(a) Duopsony (b) Oligopsony
(c) Oligopoly (d) Duopoly

108. The kinked demand curve explains
(a) Demand rigidity
(b) Price rigidity
(c) Demand flexibility
(d) Price flexibility

109. 'The term group equilibrium' is related to
(a) Perfect competition
(b) Duopoly
(c) Oligopoly
(d) Monopolistic competition

110. The equilibrium is unstable and indeterminate under
(a) Sweezy model
(b) Pareto model
(c) Edgeworth model
(d) Cournot model

111. Each seller determines his price on the assumption that his rival will keep his price constant under
(a) Bertrand's model
(b) Cournot model
(c) Edgeworth model
(d) Price leadership

112. "The equilibrium prices of duopoly model are obtained at the intersection of their reaction curves". It is correct in the case of
(a) Bertrand's duopoly
(b) Edgeworth model
(c) Sweezy model
(d) None of the above

113. The upper portion of the kinked demand curve is relatively
(a) Inelastic (b) Less elastic
(c) More elastic (d) More inelastic

114. 'Excess capacity' is the resort of free entry of firms with no price competition, according to
(a) Marshall (b) Keynes
(c) J. Hicks (d) Joan Robinson

115. Which of the following curve is not U-shaped?
(a) AC (b) MC
(c) AVC (d) AFC

116. In his book *Countervailing Power,* J.K. Galbraith stated that monopoly power will be countered by any institution which is
(a) Government
(b) Trade union
(c) Consumer agency
(d) None of the above

117. Under MRTP Act, dominant firm is one which has market share of
(a) 25% (b) 30%
(c) 10% (d) 20%

118. Efficient allocation of resources is achieved to greatest extent under
(a) Oligopoly
(b) Monopolistic competition
(c) Monopoly
(d) Perfect competition

119. 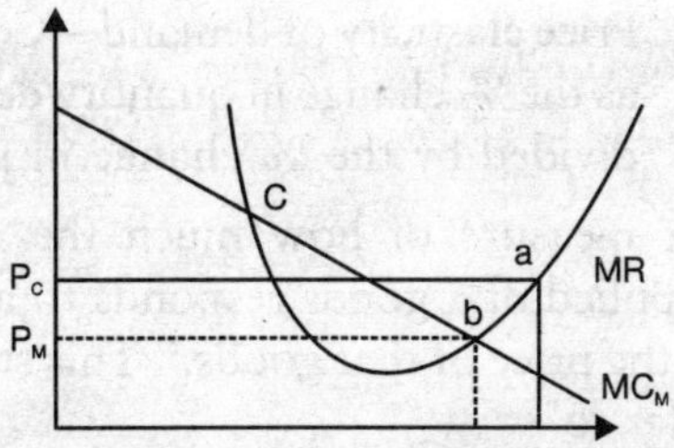

In the above figure, the equilibrium of the firm in case of perfect competition is at point
(a) c (b) a
(c) b (d) None of these

120. In the above figure, the equilibrium of the firm in case of monopoly is
(a) b (b) c
(c) a (d) None of these

121. In the above figure, the equilibrium price in case of monopoly is
(a) P_c (b) P_m
(c) Both (a) and (b) (d) None of these

122. In the above figure, the equilibrium price in case of perfect competition is
(a) P_m (b) P_c
(c) Both (a) and (b) (d) None of these

123. Marginal cost curve cuts the average cost curve from below at
(a) right of the lowest point.
(b) its lowest point.
(c) the left of the lowest point.
(d) All of the above.

124. If the demand curve confronting an individual firm is perfectly elastic, then firm is
(a) Adjust price (b) Price taker
(c) Adjust output (d) All of the above

125. A firm's marginal revenue
(a) positive at point at which the total revenue is maximum.
(b) is always negative.
(c) can be positive.
(d) is always positive.

126. In the short period, monopolist firm's equilibrium is at
(a) AR > AC
(b) AR < AC
(c) break even point
(d) All of the above

127. Concentration of monopoly is implemented under
(a) IDRA (b) FEMA
(c) FERA (d) MRTP

128. Which economist stated the positive impact of monopoly?
(a) Joseph Schumpeter
(b) Marshall
(c) Pigou
(d) Adam Smith

129. Study of collusive agreement is
(a) Monopoly
(b) Collusive oligopoly
(c) Non-collusive oligopoly
(d) All of the above

130. Cartels is a form of
(a) Monopoly
(b) Non-collusive oligopoly
(c) Collusive oligopoly
(d) None of the above

131. An economy that allocates resources through the decentralized decisions of man firms and households as they interact in markets for goods and services called
(a) Business economy
(b) Market economy

(c) Social economy
(d) None of the above

132. In a _____, the decisions of a central planner are replaced by the decisions of millions of firms and households. Which answer will be suitable for the blank?
(a) social economy
(b) market economy
(c) business economy
(d) None of the above

133. Which of the following statement is not correct?
(a) Externality—The impact of one person's actions on thv'ell being of a bystander.
(b) Market power—The ability of a single economic actor to have a substantial influence on market prices.
(c) Market failure—A situation in which a market left on its own fails to allocate resources efficiently.
(d) None of the above.

134. Which of the following statement is correct?
(a) Inflatio—An increase in the over all level of prices in the economy.
(b) Phillips curve—A curve that show the short-run trade off between inflation and unemployment.
(c) Productivity—The amount of goods and services produced from each hour of a worker's time.
(d) All of the above.

135. Calculate elasticity of demand given that a 20% increase in the price of an Breed cone causes the amount of breed you buy to fall by 40%
(a) .5 (b) 6
(c) 2 (d) 4

136. Which one of the formula is wrong?
(a) Total revenue—Computed as the price of the good times the quantity sold.
(b) Income elasticity of demand—Computed as the % change in quantity demanded dividend by the % change in income.
(c) Price elasticity of demand—Computed as the % change in quantity demanded divided by the change in price.
(d) Price elasticity of demand—Computed as the % change in quantity demanded divided by the % change in price.

137. "A measure of how much the quantity supplied of a goods responds to a change in the price of that goods." This statement refer to
(a) mode elasticity of demand
(b) cost elasticity of supply
(c) price elasticity supply
(d) None of the above

138. Computed as the % change in quantity supplied divided by the % change in price. This formula indicate to
(a) cross price elasticity of demand
(b) income elasticity of demand
(c) price elasticity of supply
(d) None of the above

139. Which formula used for computed cross price elasticity of demand?

(a) $\dfrac{\text{\% Change in quantity supplied}}{\text{\% Change in price}}$

(b) $\dfrac{\text{\% Change in quantity demanded in goods X}}{\text{\% Change in the price of goods Y}}$

(c) $\dfrac{\text{\% Change in quantity supplied}}{\text{Change in price}}$

(d) $\dfrac{\text{Change in quantity}}{\text{\% Change in the price of goods}}$

140. Calculate the price elasticity of supply. Given—suppose that an increase in the

price of wheat from ₹ 2.85 to ₹ 3.15 a ton increases the amount the food farmers produce from 9000 to 11000 ton per month. Using the mid point method calculate above said

(a) 0.2 (b) 2.0
(c) 1.2 (d) 1.30

141. Which curve is related with elastic supply—Elasticity is greater than 2.

(a) 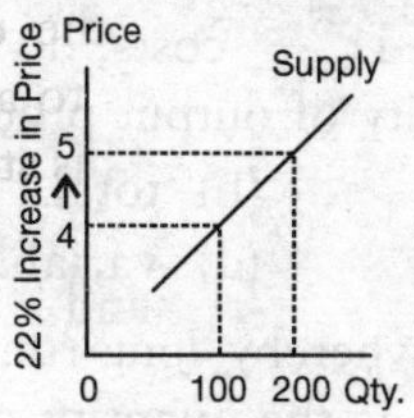

(b) 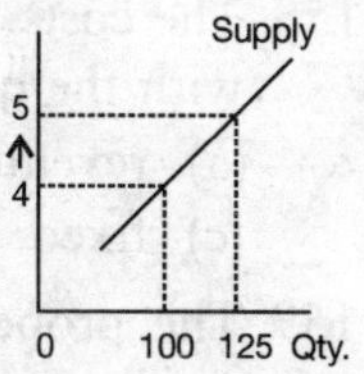

(c) 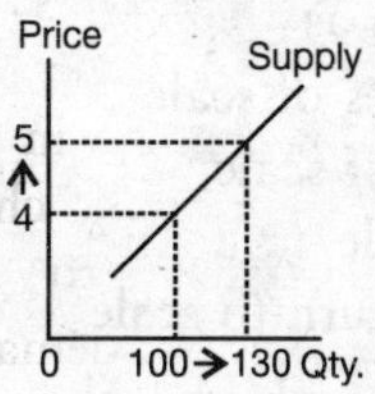

(d) 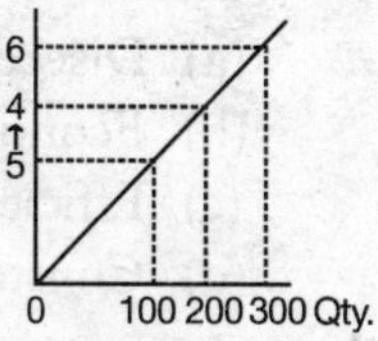

142. A firm that is the sole seller of a product without close substitutes called

(a) Competition (b) Bureaucracy
(c) Monopoly (d) Oligopoly

143. Which one of the following is not fundamental causes of monopoly arises?

(a) The government gives a single firm executive right to product some goods or services.
(b) A key resources is owned by a single firm.
(c) A key resources is owned by a number of firms.
(d) The cost of production make a single producer more efficient than a large number of producers.

144. A monopolist's marginal revenue is always ____ than the price of its goods.

(a) higher (b) greater than
(c) less (d) None of these

145. When the firm is producing 3 tons of sugar. It receives total revenue of ₹ 24. Raising production to 4 tons increases total revenue to ₹ 28. Thus marginal revenue is

(a) ₹ 28 (b) ₹ 52
(c) ₹ 4 (d) ₹ 8

146. Which one of the statement is not true?

(a) In monopolised markets, price exceeds marginal cost.
(b) In competitive markets, price equals marginal cost.
(c) Profit = Total price – Total cost.
(d) Profit = Total revenue – Total cost.

147. Which is not part of market structure?

(a) Oligopoly
(b) Monopoly
(c) Perfect competition
(d) None of the above

148. Which of the following statement is incorrect?

(a) Monopolistic competition—A market structure in which many firms sell products that are similar but not identical.
(b) Oligopoly—A market structure in which only a few seller offer similar or identical products.
(c) Cartel—A group of the person acting in union.
(d) Cartel—A group of firms acting in union.

149. An agreement among firms in a market about quantities to produce or prices to change is called

(a) Monopolies (b) Oligopoly
(c) Collusion (d) Cartel

150. Profit = Total revenue – (?). Choose the suitable answer for blank.

(a) Total price (b) Total sale
(c) Total cost (d) None of these

151. Which of the following statement is true?
   (a) The market value of the inputs of a firm uses in production called total cost
   (b) Profit = Total revenue – Total cost
   (c) The amount received by an organisation for the sale of its product or service called total revenue
   (d) All of the above

152. Total revenue minus total cost called
   (a) Contribution (b) MOS
   (c) Profit (d) Loss

153. The input costs that require an outlay of money by the organisation called
   (a) Implicit costs
   (b) Explicit costs
   (c) Total cost
   (d) Replacement cost

154. The input costs that do not require an outlay of money by the concern called
   (a) Marginal cost
   (b) Implicit costs
   (c) Explicit costs
   (d) Replacement cost

155. Which one of the following statement is incorrect?
   (a) Marginal Product—The decrease in output that arises from an additional unit of input.
   (b) Marginal Product—The increase in output that arises from an additional unit of input.
   (c) Accounting Profit = Total revenue – Total explicit cost.
   (d) Economic Profit = Total revenue – Total cost, including both explicit and implicit costs.

156. The relationship between quantity of inputs used to make a goods and the quantity of output of that goods called
   (a) Economic function
   (b) Production function
   (c) Marginal function
   (d) Manufacturing function

157. The firm's costs, called costs, change as the firm alters the quantity of output produced.
   (a) Fixed costs
   (b) Marginal less profit
   (c) Revenue profit
   (d) Variable costs

158. The costs, called ____ costs, do not vary with the quantity of output produced.
   (a) revenue (b) total
   (c) fixed (d) variable

159. The property whereby long-run average total cost falls as the quantity of output increases known as
   (a) Diseconomies of scale
   (b) Economies of scale
   (c) Efficient scale
   (d) Constant return to scale

160. A curve on which the various combinations of labour and capital show the same output, is called
   (a) Capital
   (b) Isoquant/Isoproduct
   (c) Factor
   (d) Cost

161. The neo-classical utility analysis refers to
   (a) budgeting.
   (b) cost.
   (c) variable cost.
   (d) the theory of consumer demand as built by Marshall, Pigon and Sieon.

162. Which is the assumption of utility analysis?
   (a) Utility is a price
   (b) There are substitutes
   (c) Utility is measurable in terms of money
   (d) None of the above

163. Which cost known as periodical cost?
(a) Revenue cost (b) Marginal cost
(c) Fixed cost (d) Variable cost

164. A competitive market called a
(a) Monopoly
(b) Oligipoly
(c) Perfectly competitive market
(d) None of the above

165. Which one of the characteristics is not of competitive market?
(a) The goods offered by the various sellers are largely the same.
(b) There are many buyers and many sellers in the market.
(c) Firms cannot freely enter or exit the market.
(d) Firms can freely enter or exit the market.

166. A market with many buyers and sellers trading identical products so that each buyer and seller is a price taker, is called as a
(a) Perfect market
(b) Competitive market
(c) Full market
(d) All of the above

167. Total revenue divided by the quantity sold called
(a) Average revenue
(b) Total revenue
(c) Revenue
(d) None of the above

168. The change in total revenue from an additional unit sold called as
(a) Revenue
(b) Marginal revenue
(c) Average revenue
(d) Profit

169. The firm shuts down if the _____ that it would get from producting is less than its variable costs of production.
(a) cost (b) profit
(c) revenue (d) price

170. A cost that has already been committed and cannot be recovered known as
(a) Full cost (b) Variable cost
(c) Sunk cost (d) Total cost

171. The competitive Firm's long run supply curve is the portion of its _____ curve that lies above average total cost.
(a) Fixed cost (b) Marginal cost
(c) Revenue cost (d) None of these

172. The firm exists the market if the revenue it would get from producing is ____ than its total cost.
(a) Higher (b) Equal
(c) Less (d) None of these

173. Which one of the is not properties of the Big-Bof's cost curves?
(a) The average total cost curve is U-shaped.
(b) The marginal cost curve crosses the average total cost curve at the minimum of average total cost.
(c) The average total cost curve is T-shaped.
(d) Marginal cost eventually rises with the quantity of output.

174. Whenever ______ is greater than average total cost, average total cost is rising.
(a) fixed cost (b) full cost
(c) marginal cost (d) variable cost

175. The claim that, other things equal, the quantity supplied of a goods rises when the price of goods rises known as
(a) law of demand
(b) law of economic
(c) law of supply
(d) All of the above

176. The amount of a goods that sellers are willing and able to sell called

(a) Quantity demanded
(b) Quantity supplied
(c) Control of sale
(d) Market force

177. A graph of the relationship between the price of a goods and the quantity supplied called
(a) Demand curve (b) Supply curve
(c) MOS curve (d) Normal curve

178. The supply schedule shows the quantity supplied at each price called
(a) Supply schedule
(b) Ben's supply schedule
(c) Ren's supply schedule
(d) None of the above

179. Supply schedule is a table that shows the relationship between the price of a goods and
(a) Supply
(b) Demand
(c) Purchased
(d) Quantity supplied

180. Demand curve is a graph of the relationship between the price of a goods and the
(a) Demand
(b) Supply
(c) Quantity supplied
(d) Quantity Demanded

181. Two goods for which an increase in the price of one leads to an increase in the demand for the other called
(a) Substituted (b) Replacement
(c) Sub-goods (d) All of the above

182. Per-capita income for 2011 is computed by

(a) $= \dfrac{\text{National income}}{2}$

(b) $= \dfrac{\text{National income for 2011}}{\text{Population in 2011}}$

(c) $= \dfrac{\text{National income}}{100}$

(d) None of the above

183. A goods for which, other things equal an increase in income lends to a decrease in demand, is known as
(a) Capital goods (b) Sub-goods
(c) Inferior goods (d) None of these

184. The demand schedule shows the demanded at each price known as
(a) Okha's Demand Schedule
(b) Catherin's Demand Schedule
(c) Ponter's Supply Shedule
(d) None of the above

185. A graph of the relationship between the price of a goods and the quantity demanded, called
(a) Demand curve (b) Market curve
(c) Supply curve (d) None of these

186. The marginal revenue equation can be derived from the
(a) Supply equation
(b) Demand equation
(c) Price equation
(d) Cost equation

187. Marginal revenue is the change in revenue associated with one unit change in
(a) Input
(b) Output
(c) Both (a) and (b)
(d) None of the above

188. Marginal revenue is at the quantity that generates maximum total revenue and negative beyond that point.
(a) One (b) Zero
(c) −1 (d) +1

189. For a linear demand curve, the absolute value of the slope of the marginal revenue curve is twice that of the

(a) Supply curve (b) Price curve
(c) Demand curve (d) All of the above

190. Which one of the formula may be used for the price elasticity of demand?

(a) $\dfrac{\text{Percentage change in price}}{\text{Percentage change in quantity demanded}}$

(b) $\dfrac{\text{Percentage change in quantity demanded}}{\text{Percentage change in price}}$

(c) $\dfrac{\text{Percentage change in quantity demanded}}{2} \times 100$

(d) $\dfrac{\text{Percentage change in quality}}{\text{Percentage change in quantity demanded}}$

191. Suppose that a firm increases the price of its product by 4% and quantity demanded subsequently decreases by 6 per cent. The price elasticity would be

(a) 1.2 (b) 2
(c) 1.5 (d) 10

192. Arc elasticities are appropriate for analysing that effect of discrete change in

(a) Quality (b) Quantity
(c) Price (d) Cost

193. Which formula related with computing Arc elasticity?

(a) $\dfrac{\text{Percentage change in price}}{2}$

(b) $\dfrac{\text{Percentage change in price}}{\text{Price}}$

(c) $\dfrac{\text{Price}}{\text{Percentage change in price}}$

(d) $\dfrac{\text{Percentage change in price}}{1+2} \times 100$

194. Suppose the market demand for playing cards is given by the equation

Q = 600,0000 – 1000000 P

where Q is the number of cards demanded each year and P is the price in ₹ for a price increase from ₹ 2 to ₹ 3 per deck. What is the arc price elasticity?

(a) 0.61 (b) 0.71
(c) 0.91 (d) None of these

195. Price elasticity is defined as the percentage change in _____ that results from a 1 per cent change in price.

(a) supply demanded
(b) quantity demanded
(c) supply
(d) quantity

196. Point elasticity is used where the price change is very small. Arc elasticity is appropriate for a change in price.

(a) Lower (b) Equal
(c) Larger (d) None of these

197. Demand is _____ where marginal revenue is positive, unitary elastic when marginal revenue is zero and inelastic if marginal revenue is negative.

(a) inelastic
(b) elastic
(c) Both (a) and (b)
(d) None of the above

198. Demand tends to be less elastic if

(a) expenditures on the goods or service account for a small proportion of total expenditures
(b) consumers have not yet had time to adjust fully to change in price
(c) there are few goods substitute available
(d) All of the above

199. Income elasticities can be

(a) Double
(b) Equal

(c) Negative or positive
(d) None of the above

200. Goods with negative income elasticities are defined as
(a) Competitive goods
(b) Inferior goods
(c) Selective goods
(d) All of the above

201. Normal goods and services have positive ______ elasticities.
(a) cost (b) price
(c) income (d) expenditure

202. Luxuries are goods and services for which
(a) $e_1 + 1$ (b) $e_1 < 1$
(c) $e_1 > 1$ (d) All of the above

203. Negative income elasticities denote
(a) Inferior goods
(b) Substitute goods
(c) Complete goods
(d) All of the above

204. Demand is also influenced by prices of other goods and
(a) Services
(b) Employee and service
(c) Both (a) and (b)
(d) All of the above

205. Cross elasticity defined as

(a) $\dfrac{\text{Percentage change in quantit demanded of one goods caused by a 1 per cent}}{\text{Change in the price of some other goods}}$

(b) $\dfrac{\text{Percentage change in quantity}}{1+\text{Price}}$

(c) $\dfrac{\text{Price}+1}{\text{Change in quantity demanded}}$

(d) $\dfrac{1+\text{Price}}{\text{Percentage change in quantity}}$

206. Cross elasticities are used to classify the relationship between
(a) Goods and services
(b) Substitute
(c) Goods
(d) All of the above

207. The income elasticity determines whether a product is a necessity or a
(a) Luxury
(b) Compulsory
(c) Both (a) and (b)
(d) None of the above

208. Cross elasticities are ______ for substitutes and negative for complements.
(a) Negative (b) Luxury goods
(c) Positive (d) None of these

209. Pricing decisions are affected by the ______ in which the firm operates?
(a) Economic environment
(b) Political environment
(c) Demand
(d) Business

210. In market where there are a large number of small buyers and individual firm, have little control over price.
(a) Firm (b) Market
(c) Buyer (d) Seller

211. By differentiating its product, a firm can gain some control over
(a) Quantity (b) Quality
(c) Cost (d) Price

212. If it is easy for ______ to enter an industry, existing firms may have little freedom in their pricing decisions.
(a) New firms (b) New buyer
(c) Old firm (d) All of the above

213. Which is not a feature of perfect competition?
(a) Many small sellers
(b) No sellers

(c) No buyers
(d) All of the above

214. Which is a type of market structure?
(a) Monopoly (b) Zeropoly
(c) Duopoly (d) All of the above

215. If one input is variable and all other inputs are fixed the firm's production function exhibits the
(a) Law of capital
(b) Law variable
(c) Law of demand
(d) Law of supply

216. Which of the following is/are characteristic(s) of market structure?
(a) Conditions of entry and exit.
(b) Number and size distribution of sellers.
(c) Number and size distribution of buyers.
(d) All of the above.

217. Which of the following is/are the characteristic(s) of perfect competition?
(a) Many small buyers
(b) Product undifferentiated
(c) Many small sellers
(d) All of the above

218. The firm in perfect competition maximizes profit by producing at the rate of output where price equals
(a) Revenue (b) Marginal cost
(c) Revenue cost (d) Marginal profit

219. In the managers of a firm should shut down the operation if price is below average
(a) short run, fixed cost
(b) long run, variable cost
(c) short run, variable cost
(d) short run, cost

220. If price is greater than average but less than average total cost, the firm should continue to produce in the short run because a contribution can be made to fixed cost.
(a) Variable cost (b) Price
(c) Fixed cost (d) Cost

221. In the long run, economic profit is eliminated by the entry of
(a) Incoming firm (b) Old firm
(c) Outgoing firm (d) New firm

222. Which is/are method(s) of measuring national income?
(a) Expenditure method
(b) Product method
(c) Income Method
(d) All of the above

223. Consumers who would have been willing to pay more than the receive a consumer surplus when they buy the product.
(a) Cost (b) Market
(c) Market price (d) Price

224. In perfectly competitive markets
(a) Average cost curve.
(b) The value of last unit exchanged equals the opportunity cost of producing it.
(c) Capital moves to its highest valued use.
(d) Production takes place at the minimum point on the average cost curve.

225. As the only seller, a monopolist faces the _____ curve.
(a) cost (b) quantity
(c) market demand (d) price

226. The profit maximizing output is determined by the point where marginal revenue equals
(a) Fixed cost (b) Total cost
(c) Marginal cost (d) Cost

227. If entry by other firm is difficult, even in the long run, the monopolist can earn _____ profits.
(a) traditional (b) business
(c) economic (d) All of the above

228. Profits are maximized by choosing quantity where marginal revenue equals
(a) Full cost (b) Marginal cost
(c) Fixed cost (d) All of the above

229. ___ pricing results in allocative inefficiency not enough output is produced.
(a) Oligopoly
(b) Perfect competition
(c) Monopoly
(d) All of the above

230. _____ pricing also causes a redistribution of income from consumers to the owners of the monopoly.
(a) Oligopoly
(b) Perfect competition
(c) Monopoly
(d) All of the above

231. Which of the following statement is true?
(a) Rent seeking involves the use of resources to acquire or maintain monopoly profits.
(b) Rent seeking involves a dead weight loss to society because no additional goods or services are produced.
(c) If a firm has market power and there is separation of ownership from control technical inefficiency may result because of the failure of managers to minimise cost.
(d) All of the above.

232. Which of the following statement(s) is/are true?
(a) Firm in monopolistic competition have some control over price because where product are differentiated.
(b) Perfect competition serves as a bench mark and a guide for public policy.
(c) The monopoly model may be applicable in situations where a producer has some power over price.
(d) All of the above.

233. When demand are interrelated, insight into managerial decisions can be gained by considering the marginal revenue equation for the products, consider a firm that produces only two goods, X and Y. Assume that sales of X have an impact on the demand for Y and vice versa. In terms of marginal revenue. This assumption can be stated mathematically as

(a) $MR_Y = \frac{dTR_X}{dQ_X} + \frac{dTR_Y}{dQ_X}$,

$MR_Y = \frac{dTR_Y}{dQ_Y} + \frac{dTR_X}{dQ_Y}$

(b) $MR_X = \frac{dTR_X}{dQ_X} + \frac{dTR_Y}{dQ_X}$,

$MR_Y = \frac{dTR_Y}{dQ_Y} + \frac{dTRX}{dQ_Y}$

(c) $MR = \frac{TR_X}{R_Y} + \frac{TRM}{R_X}, MR = \frac{dTR_Y}{dQ_Y}$

(d) $R_Y = \frac{TR_Y}{d_X} + \frac{dR_Y}{MR_Y}$,

$MR_X = \frac{TR_Y}{dQ} + \frac{R_X}{Q_Y}$

234. If a firm produces two goods that are substitutes, the optional rate of output for each good is less than the rate would ________ if there were no demand interdependence.
(a) maximise cost (b) revenue
(c) maximise profit (d) maximise loss

235. If a firm produces complementary goods, the optional rates of output are greater than if there were no
(a) Interdependence
(b) Dependence
(c) Both (a) and (b)
(d) None of the above

236. For products complementary goods, the optional rates of output are ______ than if there were no interdependence.
(a) equal (b) greater
(c) lower (d) All of thė above

237. For products produced jointly in fixed proportions, output should be increased until the sum of the marginal revenues equals the of the product package.
(a) Marginal Revenues
(b) Fixed cost
(c) Marginal cost
(d) All of the above

238. Despite the problems, many businesses make extensive use of a practice called pricing.
(a) Full cost
(b) Normal cost
(c) Fully distributed cost
(d) All of the above

239. For an electric utility, expenses associated with high voltage transmission are referred to as
(a) Allocating cost
(b) Common cost
(c) Total cost
(d) Distribution cost

240. A firm's common costs are those that cannot be to any single product or service.
(a) Delegates (b) Transfer
(c) Assigned (d) None of these

241. Which of the following statement is true?
(a) A simple version of Ramsey pricing specifies that price deviations from marginal cost should be inversely related to the elasticity of demand.
(b) The use of fully distributed costs can lead to poor pricing decisions. A product can be profitably produced. If its price exceeds incremental costs of supplying the product.
(c) Ramsey pricing is a second best alternative that can be used when marginal cost pricing is not feasible.
(d) All of the above.

242. If there is a perfectly competitive external market for an intermediate goods, market force will cause the price of the goods to approach and no marginal pricing decision will be necessary.
(a) Fixed cost
(b) Marginal Revenue
(c) Marginal cost
(d) All of the above

243. In the absence of an external market, profit maximisation requires that the price of each intermediate goods be set equal to its
(a) Full cost
(b) Marginal cost
(c) Fixed cost
(d) Marginal Revenue

244. The most common type of price descrimination is degree discrimination.
(a) First degree (b) Second degree
(c) Third degree (d) All of the above

245. Third degree discrimination involves separating consumers or markets in terms of their
(a) cost elasticity of demand.
(b) demand elasticity.
(c) price elasticity of demand.
(d) All of the above.

246. Cost plus pricing is widely used by managers and involves a mark-up over the of acquiring or producing a product.
(a) Full cost (b) Average cost
(c) Total cost (d) None of these

247. Price discrimination occurs when variation in prices for a product in different markets does not reflect variation in

(a) Price (b) Demand
(c) Costs (d) All of the above

248. The three criteria for successful price discrimination are market power, separable markets and variation in demand elasticity among
(a) Buyers (b) Sellers
(c) Market (d) Firm

249. Which of the following statement is true?
(a) Second degree discrimination, prices are based on the quantity purchased by consumers.
(b) Third degree discrimination usually requires selling a higher price in markets with less elastic demand.
(c) First degree price discrimination consists of charging the maximum price for each unit.
(d) All of the above.

250. Which of the following statement(s) is/are true?
(a) Pure bundling involves selling two or more products together for the same price.
(b) If reservation prices are negatively correlated, bundling can increase profits by capturing part of the consumer surplus.
(c) Market may be segmented on the basis of geography, use of the product, or personal characteristics of consumers of the product.
(d) All of the above.

251. Peak-load pricing can be used to reduce costs and increase profits if
(a) Demand characteristics vary from period to period.
(b) The same facilities are used to provide a product or service at different periods of time.
(c) The product or services is not storable.
(d) All of the above.

252. Cost plus pricing may stabilize price and provide a justification for price
(a) Sets (b) Changes
(c) Fixed (d) All of the above

253. Cost plus pricing may simply represent for decision rule used by managers in pursuit of
(a) Loss maximisation
(b) Profit maximisation
(c) Normal loss
(d) None of the above

254. A complete forecast should be based on a thorough demand analysis, although this does not imply that demand analysis is useful only in forecasting. Is this statement true?
(a) Can not say (b) No
(c) Yes (d) All of the above

255. If a full demand analysis support the forecast, the likelihood that changes in the constant factors will be detected earlier is greater than if the forecast is not buttressed by a
(a) Cost analysis
(b) Price analysis
(c) Demand analysis
(d) All of the above

256. Which is most important concept of demand analysis?
(a) Quality (b) Elasticity
(c) Cost (d) All of the above

257. Which is the sensitivity of change in the quantity of a product demanded to change in a variable?
(a) Elasticity of price
(b) Elasticity of supply
(c) Elasticity of demand
(d) None of the above.

258. The principal variable involved when
(a) Income (in the case of income elasticity).

(b) The price of a substitute product in the case of substitute product elasticity which is usually called cross elasticity.

(c) Demand elasticity is discussed are the price of that goods (in the case of price elasticity).

(d) All of the above.

259. Elasticity is commonly stated in the form of

(a) 5 per cent change

(b) 5 per cent

(c) 1 per cent change

(d) All of the above

260. Elasticity of demand is numerically measured as the ratio of the

(a) $\frac{\text{Change in quantity of product demanded}}{1+\text{Demand}}$

(b) $\frac{\text{Relative change in quantity of product demanded}}{\text{Relative change in the variable}}$

(c) $\frac{\text{Price elasticity of Demand}}{1+E_p}\times 100$

(d) $\frac{\text{Relative change in the variable}}{2}\times 100$

261. Which formula is relative with price elasticity of demand?

(a) $E_P = \dfrac{\dfrac{(Q_1-Q_2)}{P_1}}{\dfrac{(P_1-P_2)}{1}}$

(b) $E_P = \dfrac{\dfrac{(Q_1-Q_2)}{Q_1}}{\dfrac{(P_1-P_2)}{2}}$

(c) $E_P = \dfrac{\dfrac{(Q_1-Q_2)}{P_1}}{\dfrac{(P_1-Q_2)}{P+Q}}$

(d) $E_P = \dfrac{\dfrac{(Q_1-P_2)}{P_1-Q_2}}{\dfrac{Q_1}{(P_1-P_2)}}$

262. Income elasticity of demand is defined as

(a) $\frac{\text{A small change in income}}{100}\times 1+1$

(b) $\frac{\text{A small change in quantity demanded}}{\text{A small change in income}}$

(c) $\frac{\text{Price change in market}}{100+1}$ $\times$ A small change in income

(d) $\frac{\text{A small change in quantity demanded}}{\text{Quantity}+100}$

263. Income elasticity of demand is expressed mathematically as

(a) $E_i = \dfrac{\dfrac{Q_1-Q_2}{Q_1}}{\dfrac{I_1-I_2}{I_1}}$

(b) $E_i = \dfrac{\dfrac{(Q_1-Q_2)}{I_1-I_2}\times\dfrac{Q_1}{I}}{I_1+I_2}$

(c) $E_i = \dfrac{\dfrac{(Q_1+Q_2)}{P_1}}{\dfrac{P_1+P_2}{100}} \times i$

(d) $E_i = \dfrac{\dfrac{Q_1-I_2}{I+Q_1}}{\dfrac{100-1}{Q_1+Q_2}} \times 100$

264. Cross (price) elasticity (E_c) is expressed mathematically as

(a) $E_c = \dfrac{\dfrac{Q_1-Q_{A2}}{Q_{A1}+_{A2}}}{\dfrac{P_{B1}-P_2}{100}} \times i$

(b) $E_c = \dfrac{\dfrac{(Q_1-Q_2)}{Q_{A1}}}{\dfrac{(P_{B1}+P_{B2}}{P_{B1}}}$

(c) $E_c = \dfrac{\dfrac{Q_1-Q_2}{A_1+P_2}}{\dfrac{C_1+P_2}{100}} \times \dfrac{i+100}{2}$

(d) $E_c = \dfrac{\dfrac{Q_{A1}-Q_{A2}}{P_{B1}-P_{B2}}}{\dfrac{100}{Q_1-Q_2}}$

265. Cross (price) elasticity E_c is defined as

(a) $\dfrac{\text{Change in quantity demanded of product 'B'}}{100}$

(b) $\dfrac{\text{Change in quantity demanded of product 'A'}}{\text{Change in price of product 'B'}}$

(c) $\dfrac{\text{Change in price of product 'B'}}{\text{Change in quantity demand of product 'A'}} \times 100 + 1$

(d) $\dfrac{100}{\text{Change in quantity demanded}} \times 100$

266. In the case of income elasticity of demand, E_i will have a positive sign when the goods is
(a) Inferior
(b) Substitute
(c) Superior
(d) All of the above

267. In a partnership business if there is no specific agreement among partners, profit is distributed in the:
(a) Ratio to be decided by the Court
(b) Equal ratio*
(c) Ratio of capital contributions
(d) Ratio of time spent in the business

268. The elasticity of substitution can be defined as

(a) E_S = Percentage in ratio

$= \dfrac{\dfrac{\text{Quantity demanded of X}}{\text{Quantity demanded of Y}}}{\text{Percentage change in ratio } \dfrac{\text{Price X}}{\text{Price Y}}}$

(b) E_S = Percentage change in ratio

$= \dfrac{\dfrac{\text{Quantity demanded of X}}{\text{Quantity of Y}}}{\dfrac{100+1}{\text{Price change in X}}}$

(c) E_S = Percentage change in ratio

$= \dfrac{\dfrac{\text{Quantity demanded of X}}{\text{Quantity demanded of Y}}}{\dfrac{1+100}{2}}$

(d) E_S = Percentage change in ratio

$$= \frac{\dfrac{\text{Quantity demanded of Y}}{\dfrac{P+100}{2}}}{\text{Percentage in ratio of } \dfrac{\text{Price X}}{\text{Price Y}}} \times 100$$

269. The three types of elasticity of demand is
(a) Gross (b) Price
(c) Income (d) All of the above

270. Elasticity can then be measured directly as the slope of the line
(a) $\frac{\Delta X}{\Delta Y}$ (b) $\frac{\Delta + X}{\Delta + Y}$
(c) $\frac{\Delta Y}{\Delta X}$ (d) All of the above

271. Producing equation may be stated in an additive form such as
(a) Y = 2(X + Z) (b) Y = (X + Z)
(c) Y = F(X + Z) (d) All of the above

272. Producing equation may be stated in multiplicative form such as
(a) Y = (X – Z)
(b) Y = F(X – Z)
(c) Y = 2(2 + X – Z)
(d) All of the above

273. According to Roos which one of the following is not defined classification of product?
(a) Consumers durable goods
(b) Dual
(c) Consumer's perishable goods
(d) Consumers semidurable goods

274. According to Roos which one of the following is not refined classification of goods?
(a) Capital goods
(b) Construction materials
(c) Fuels
(d) Trend goods

275. Products are frequently classified as
(a) Consumer's durable goods
(b) Producers goods
(c) Consumer's non-durable goods
(d) All of the above

276. Purchases of consumer non-durable and semidurable goods frequently are significantly determined by
(a) Price
(b) Population and its characteristics
(c) Secular per capita consumption of the product
(d) All of the above

277. The quantity demanded of consumer durables frequently is partially determined by
(a) disposable income and discretionary income.
(b) the number of households.
(c) credit terms.
(d) All of the above.

278. Demand for consumer durable classified as
(a) average age or durability of stock
(b) price
(c) existing stock of goods
(d) All of the above

279. Purchases of consumer durable goods differ significantly as to demand determinants from the determinants of consumer non-durable.
(a) Services
(b) Goods
(c) Both (a) and (b)
(d) None of the above

280. Quantity demanded in the case of capital goods frequently is significantly determined by

(a) depreciation and obsolescence situation.
(b) margin of unused capacity.
(c) profit picture of the industry buying.
(d) All of the above.

281. Quantity demanded in the case of capital goods frequently is significantly determined by
(a) price of the equipment.
(b) long term interest rate.
(c) prices of the goods produced by equipment.
(d) All of the above.

282. Suppose equation 1 is such that demand is partially determined by real income. This can then be written.
(a) $d = \frac{a+b+m}{y}$
(b) $d = a + bp + ey + m$
(c) $\frac{y_1 + y_2}{100} \times \text{income}$
(d) $d_1 = \frac{a_1 + b_2 + c_2}{100} \times \text{income}$

283. A market is defined in term of the cross elasticities of demand and supply between one ____ and another.
(a) firm (b) market
(c) seller (d) All of the above

284. The degree of freedom which sellers or buyers have in acting with respect to price is ____ by constraints.
(a) price limited
(b) frequently limited
(c) factor
(d) None of the above

285. The consideration of the rate of return aspect in pricing policy has come to be known as
(a) Transfer pricing
(b) Maximum
(c) Target pricing
(d) All of the above

286. Price discrimination is a _____ word.
(a) Target (b) Slippery
(c) Dopplery (d) All of the above

287. Consumers' surplus is defined as the excess of the price a consumer is willing to pay for a product over the price he is charged for the
(a) Labour (b) Firm
(c) Product (d) Service

288. Load factor, strictly speaking, is the ratio between to the peak output of a system.
(a) Full output
(b) Fixed output
(c) Average output
(d) All of the above

289. Given—where P_x = ₹ 400, P_y = ₹ 500, E_w = 40,00,000,1 = ₹ 10,000, Á = ₹ 50,000 and Q_x = 30,000, income elasticity of demand is
(a) 0-67 (b) 0-47
(c) 0-87 (d) All of the above

290. Which of the following is/are the assumptions of perfect competition?
(a) There are no artificial interevences with the activities of the buyers and sellers.
(b) There is a very large number of buyers and selers in the market.
(c) The product of each seller is identical to that of every other seller.
(d) All of the above.

291. Which of the following is/are the assumptions of perfect competition?
(a) Homogeneous product.
(b) There is freedom of entry into or exit from the industry.
(c) All buyers and sellers have perfect knowledge of market conditions and

any changes in market conditions that do occur.

(d) All of the above.

292. In the market place, the demand curve for the homogeneous product of a perfectly competitive industry is determined by the

(a) Firm
(b) Salary
(c) Preferences of consumers
(d) All of the above

293. One market structure which is less than perfectly competitive and as a result, draws on the tools of monopoly analysis is the case called

(a) Oligopoly
(b) Perfect competition
(c) Monopolistic competition
(d) All of the above

294. Economist have settled on the term oligopoly to describe product market situation that are characterised by relatively

(a) Many Buyers (b) Few sellers
(c) Many sellers (d) All of the above

295. Oligopoly analysis is difficult because it tries to deal with some of the most complex interfirm relationship encountered in the real world, especially since many of these structure are characterised by

(a) Certainty
(b) Uncertainty
(c) Both (a) and (b)
(d) All of the above

296. Cournot model was developed by

(a) Frenchman Dupoly
(b) Kinked Togo
(c) Augustin Cournot
(d) None of the above

297. Cournot was criticized even in his own time for the quantity assumptions.

(a) Adequate (b) Price
(c) Constant (d) Inconstant

298. A market structure characterized by Havi only one buyer and one seller of a particular goods or service is known as

(a) Oligopoly
(b) Bilateral monopoly
(c) Monopoly
(d) All of the above

299. Profit per unit of output is known as

(a) Profit
(b) Maximize profit
(c) Average profit
(d) All of the above

300. The additional cost that will be incurred by the firm if it undertake a new project or produces an additional batch of output known as

(a) Fixed cost (b) Variable cost
(c) Incremental cost (d) All of the above

301. The rate of change of total revenue with respect to quantity sold known as

(a) Profit
(b) Fixed revenue
(c) Marginal revenue
(d) All of the above

302. Average profit is found by

(a) $\frac{\text{Profit}}{\text{Quantity}} \times 100$

(b) $\frac{\text{Total profit}}{\text{Quantity of output}}$

(c) $\frac{\text{Quantity of output}}{\text{Total profit}}$

(d) $\frac{\text{Profit}}{2}$

303. Average fixed cost is equal to total fixed cost divided by
   (a) level of price
   (b) level of output
   (c) level of service
   (d) All of the above

304. Average benefit cost ratio calculated as
   (a) $\frac{\text{Total differential costs of a project}}{100}$
   (b) $\frac{\text{Total differential benefits}}{\text{Total differential costs of a project}}$
   (c) $\frac{\text{Total differential benefit}}{\frac{100}{2} \times \text{income}}$
   (d) $\frac{\text{Cost of project}}{100} \times \text{quantity}$

305. Average product is
   (a) $\frac{\text{Total output}}{100 + \text{Number of use quantity}}$
   (b) $\frac{\text{Total output}}{\text{The number of units of the input in use}}$
   (c) $\frac{\text{Total output}}{\frac{2}{100} \times \text{Total number of input}}$
   (d) $\frac{\text{Total output}}{\frac{100}{2} \times \text{Total number of input}}$

306. Cost per unit of output known as
   (a) $\frac{100}{\text{Output}} \times \text{Total cost}$
   (b) Average cost
   (c) $\frac{\text{Cost} + 2}{100}$
   (d) $\frac{\text{Total cost}}{2}$

307. Average cost is equal to
   (a) Average fixed cost + Average variable cost
   (b) $\frac{\text{Total cost}}{\text{Quantity of output}}$
   (c) Both (a) and (b)
   (d) None of the above

308. Average revenue is equal to
   (a) $\frac{\text{Average revenue}}{2}$
   (b) $\frac{\text{Total revenue}}{\text{Quantity sold}}$
   (c) $\frac{\text{Average quantity}}{\text{Quantity sold}} \times 2$
   (d) $\frac{\text{Total revenue}}{100}$

309. Incremental revenue minus incremental cost resulting from an activity of the firm is known as
   (a) Incremental loss
   (b) Incremental profit
   (c) Revenue
   (d) Fixed profit

310. The additional revenue which a firm will receive by undertaking a particular project known as
   (a) Profit
   (b) Incremental revenue
   (c) Revenue
   (d) All of the above

311. A product or service with a negative income elasticity of demand known as
(a) Complete goods
(b) Inferior goods
(c) Goods
(d) All of the above

312. A product or service with a positive income elasticity of demand known as
(a) Inferior goods
(b) Normal goods
(c) Abnormal goods
(d) All of the above

313. A market structure characterised by having only one buyer of a product or service known as
(a) Negligence (b) Oligopoly
(c) Monopsony (d) Monopoly

314. A pricing technique where by a contain percentage of cost of goods sold or of price is added to cost of goods sold to obtain the market price known as
(a) Product pricing
(b) Mark-up pricing
(c) Monopoly pricing
(d) None of the above

315. Marginal private cost + Marginal external costs defined as
(a) Variable cost
(b) Marginal Social cost
(c) Social cost
(d) All of the above

316. The Marginal private benefit of a goods or service plus any marginal external or third party benefits expressed as
(a) Social cost
(b) Marginal social benefit
(c) Social profit
(d) All of the above

317. Marginal profit expressed as
(a) $\frac{100}{2} \times \text{Total output}$
(b) $\frac{\text{The rate change of total profit}}{\text{Change in the level of the firm's output}}$
(c) $\frac{\text{The rate change of output of profit}}{100}$
(d) $\frac{100+2}{\text{Change in the level of the firm's output}}$

318. Indicate the various combinations of two inputs that would enable a firm to produce a particular level of output known as
(a) Isocost (b) Isocurve
(c) Isoquants (d) All of the above

319. A measure of the relative responsiveness of the quantity demanded of a product to changes in income known as
(a) Income elasticity of price
(b) Income elasticity of demand
(c) $\frac{\text{Income} \times \text{income}}{100}$
(d) Cost of profit Income × income

320. Total revenue – Total costs (including opportunity cost) expressed as
(a) Profit (b) Net profit
(c) Total profit (d) All of the above

321. Total ₹ sales value of a firm, which is equal to price times quantity sold can be defined as
(a) Profit (b) Total revenue
(c) Revenue (d) All of the above

322. Total amount of costs that vary with the level of output express as
(a) Total cost
(b) Fixed cost
(c) Total variable cost
(d) All of the above

323. Those costs which vary with the level of a firm's output can be expressed as
(a) Normal cost (b) Variable cost
(c) Fixed cost (d) All of the above

324. Accounting price charged one division of a firm for a product which is produced by another division of the same firm known as
(a) Transfer cost
(b) Transfer price
(c) Delegation cost
(d) All of the above

325. The loss bearing capacity of issuers affects partially revealing arising from different information regimes
(a) Market competition
(b) Market equilibria
(c) Market diversification
(d) Traditional

326. The contract structure underlying the securitization transaction affords issuers to dispose of all default loss in excess of the enhancement.
(a) Reference portfolio
(b) Market economics
(c) Mandatory credit
(d) Default premium

327. Market value added seeks to measure a firm's value creation, and is the difference between the market value of the firm's equity and the
(a) Equity's book value
(b) Initial investment
(c) Both (a) and (b)
(d) Creating value

328. Market value added = Equity Market value?
(a) Economic profit
(b) Cost of equity
(c) Equity book value for profit
(d) Equity book value

329. Economic profit is profit after less equity book value.
(a) General Reserve
(b) Statutory Reserve
(c) Tax
(d) Common profit

330. Economic profit can be calculated by
(a) E_{Pt} = Profit after general reserve – Equity book value × Commission on equity
(b) E_{Pt} = Profit after tax – Equity market value × Commission on equity
(c) $E_{pt} = \frac{\text{Profit after tax} \times \text{Equity book value}}{\text{Cost of equity}}$
(d) E_{Pt} = Profit after tax – Equity book value × Cost of equity

331. Which of the following is/are not the issue of macroeconomics?
(a) Issues related to foreign trade
(b) Issues related to government policies
(c) Issues related to macro variables
(d) None of the above

332. Microeconomic theories includes
(a) theory of production
(b) theory of profit
(c) theory of demand
(d) All of the above

333. Which one of the following statement is not meaningful statement regarding the demand for a commodity?
(a) The price at which a commodity is demanded.
(b) The time period over which a commodity is demanded.
(c) The quantity demanded.
(d) None of the above.

334. The annual demand for watch in Jaipur at an average price of ₹ 5000 a piece is 20,000 is a meaningful statement in your opinion

(a) No (b) Yes
(c) Perhaps (d) Can't say

335. The concept of utility can be looked upon from two angle, wh ich is
(a) from the consumer's angle
(b) from the commodity angle
(c) Both (a) and (b)
(d) None of the above

336. Marginal utility may be expressed as
(a) $\frac{\text{Total utility}}{100} \times 12$
(b) $\frac{\text{Total utility}}{\text{Change in quantity consumed by one unit}}$
(c) $\frac{\text{Total utility}}{2} \times 100$
(d) $\frac{\text{Marginal utility}}{\text{Variable cost} + \text{fixed cost}}$

337. The law of diminishing marginal utility is based on
(a) Concept (b) Principle
(c) Assumptional (d) All of the above

338. The utility gained from a unity of a commodity depends on the intensity of the desire for it. Is this statement true?
(a) False (b) May be
(c) True (d) All of the above

339. Which of the following is included in the assumptions of law of diminishing marginal utility?
(a) The consumer's taste or preference must be remain the same during the period of consumption.
(b) These must be continuity in consumption.
(c) The unit of the consumer goods must be a standard one.
(d) All of the above.

340. Cardinal concepts of utility involves
(a) it has a measurability.
(b) utility is psychological phenomenon.
(c) it is a felling of satisfaction, pleasure or happiness.
(d) All of the above.

341. Who is the best followers of cardinal utility approach?
(a) De'sauza (b) Hongrey
(c) Alfred Marshall (d) All of the above

342. Who is the best followers of ordinal utility approach?
(a) Alfred Marshall (b) J.R. Hicks
(c) Batliboy (d) All of the above

343. Which of the following is the approaches to consumer demand analysis?
(a) ordinal utility approach
(b) cardinal utility approach
(c) Both (a) and (b)
(d) None of the above

344. Which one of the following is not the cardinal utility approach to consumer analysis?
(a) Recko
(b) Rationality
(c) Maximization of satisfaction
(d) Limited money income

345. Which one of the following is not the cardinal utility approach to consumer analysis?
(a) Constant marginal utility of money
(b) Utility is cardinals measurable
(c) Domentry of law
(d) Diminishing marginal utility

346. In cardinal utility approach, the consumer has a utility function which may expressed as
(a) $U = F(X_1^3 + X_2^3)$
(b) $U = F(X_1 X_2 X_3 \ldots X_3)$

(c) $\frac{U + F_1X_2}{100 + 2}$

(d) $U = \frac{F + X_2 + X_3}{2}$

347. In which case the law of demand does not apply?
(a) Status goods
(b) Giffen goods
(c) Expectations regarding further prices
(d) All of the above

348. A Giffen goods may be inferior commodity much than its superior substitutes, consumed by the poor house holds as an essential commodity.
(a) Greater (b) Cheaper
(c) Higher (d) All of the above

349. Which of the following assumptions involves in assumptions of ordinal utility theory?
(a) Non-funding (b) Rationality
(c) Ordinal utility (d) All of the above

350. The price effect may be derived as the total change in the quantity consumed of a commodity due to a in its price.
(a) Fixed
(b) Change
(c) Both (a) and (b)
(d) None of the above

351. Which curve is expressed as 'Indifference curve'?

(a) 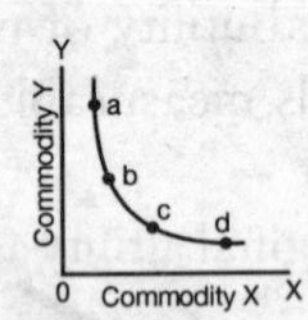

(b) 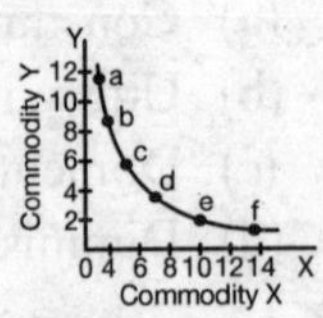

(c) 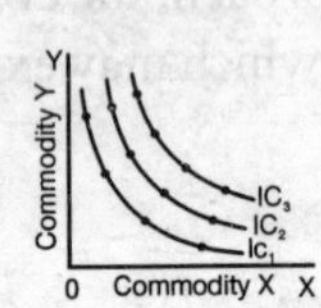

(d) 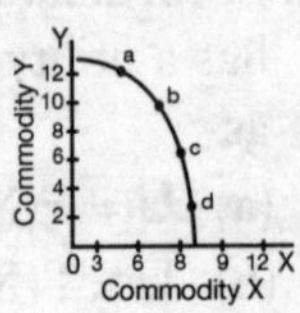

352. Indifference curve have which basic properties?
(a) Indicate a higher levels of satisfaction
(b) A negative slope
(c) Convex to the origin
(d) All of the above

353. Samuelson's revealed perference hypothesis is based on the which straight forward assumptions?
(a) Consistency (b) Rationality
(c) Transitivity (d) All of the above

354. Which one of the following is not most appropriate base of analysis of market demand?
(a) Elasticities of demand.
(b) The factors which determine the size of demand.
(c) Minimum levels of sales.
(d) Possibility of sales promotion through manipulation of price.

355. The market demand is the sum of individual demand for a product at a price per unit of
(a) Quantity (b) Time
(c) Demand (d) All of the above

356. The aggregate of individual demand for a product is called for the product.
(a) Market supply
(b) Market price
(c) Market demand
(d) All of the above

357. Which of the following is the determinants of market demand for a product?
(a) Level of consumer's income
(b) Price of the product
(c) Price of the substitutes goods
(d) All of the above.

358. Which one of the following is not a types of the goods?
(a) Complements goods
(b) Substitute goods

(c) First goods
(d) Supplements goods

359. Which of the following is/are the determinants of market demand for a product?
(a) Advertisement of the product
(b) Consumer's taste and preference
(c) Consumer credit facility
(d) All of the above.

360. That goods which are demanded in increasing quantities as consumer's income rises?
(a) Substitute goods (b) Inferior goods
(c) Normal goods (d) All of the above

361. The degree of responsiveness of demand to the change in its determinants is called
(a) Price elasticity
(b) Quality elasticity
(c) Elasticity of demand
(d) All of the above

362. The price elasticity coefficient of demand for its product at levels of its price provides the answer to this question (price elasticity and total revenue).
(a) Fare (b) Different
(c) Same (d) All of the above

363. The price elasticity of demand at any point on a linear demand curve is equal to
(a) $e_p = \frac{\text{Upper segment}}{\text{Lower segment}}$
(b) $e_p = \frac{\text{Lower segment}}{\text{Upper segment}}$
(c) $e_p = \frac{\text{Lower segment}}{100} \times \text{Price change}$
(d) $e_p = \frac{\text{Lower segment}}{\text{Price}}$

364. The case of infinitely elastic demand represented by a horizontal straight line is
(a) Easy (b) Rare
(c) Old (d) All of the above

365. Which of the following is/are the determinants of price elasticity of demand?
(a) Weightage in the total consumption
(b) Availability of substitutes
(c) Nature of commodity
(d) All of the above

366. Which one of the formula expressed as a cross elasticity of demand?
(a) $\frac{\text{Percentage change in demand for Chikoo } (Q_t)}{100} \times \text{Income}$
(b) $\frac{\text{Percentage change in demand for Chikoo } (Q_t)}{\text{Percentage change in price of Banana } (P_c)}$
(c) $\frac{100}{\text{Percentage change in price of Banana } (P_c)} \times \text{Income}$
(d) $\frac{\text{Percentage change in demand for Chikoo } (Q_t)}{2+100}$

367. Advertisement elasticity (e_A) of sales may be defined by formula.
(a) $\frac{\Delta S + S}{\frac{\Delta A + A}{2}} = \frac{A}{5}$
(b) $\frac{\Delta S / S}{\Delta A / A} = \frac{\Delta S}{\Delta A} - \frac{A}{5}$

(c) $\frac{\Delta}{5} = \frac{\Delta S / S}{\Delta S}$

(d) $\frac{\Delta S / S}{\frac{A}{5}} = \frac{\Delta A}{\Delta S}$

368. Which of the following is the determinants of advertisement elasticity?
(a) Advertisement by rival firms
(b) Cumulative effect of past advertisement
(c) The level of total sales
(d) All of the above

369. The concept of price expectation elasticity was devised and popularised by
(a) J.R. Docks in 1930
(b) J.R. Hicks in 1913
(c) J.R. Hopy in 1940
(d) All of the above

370. Which of the following statement is true?
(a) If price elasticity < 1, MR < 0
(b) If price elasticity = 1, MR = 0
(c) If price elasticity > 1 . MR > 0
(d) All of the above

371. Supposing price of capital, P_k = ₹ 2 and price of labour, P_1 = ₹ 5 and Q = 20 find out the slope of cost.
(a) 2-40 (b) 2-60
(c) 2-5 (d) 2-45

372. Which is/are the essential of competition?
(a) Homogeneous product.
(b) Perfect mobility of factors of productions.
(c) A large number of sellers and buyers.
(d) All of the above.

373. Which is the essential of the perfect competition?
(a) Absence of collusion or artificial restraint.
(b) Free entry and free exit of firm.
(c) Perfect knowledge.
(d) All of the above.

374. Which is the essential of the perfect competition?
(a) Restruction on entry.
(b) Imperfect mobility of factors of production.
(c) No government intervention.
(d) None of the above.

375. Price determination under perfect competition is analysed under
(a) Long run (b) Market period
(c) Short run (d) All of the above

376. Which one of the following curve is related with supply determined price in market period?

(a) 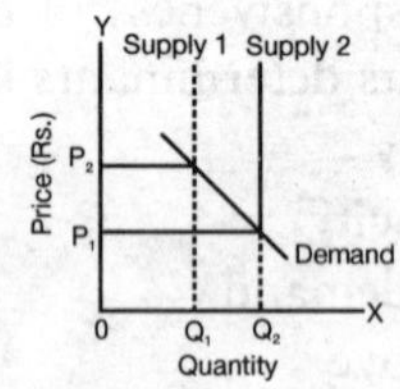

(b) 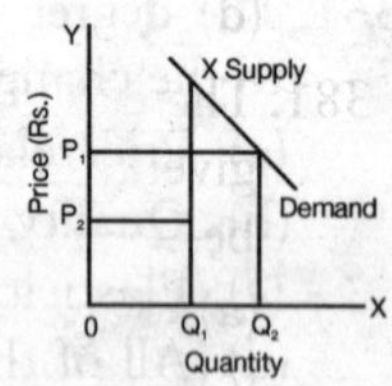

(c) 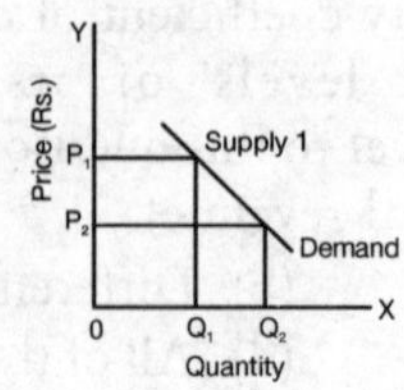

(d) 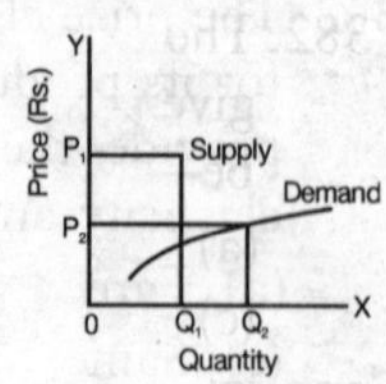

377. Which is true?
(a) If AR < AC, though only a theoretical possibly the firm makes losses.
(b) If AR > AC, there is economic profit for the firm.
(c) If AR = AC, the firm earns only normal profit.
(d) All of the above.

378. Which of the following is necessary condition for price discrimination?
(a) There must be imperfect competition in the market.
(b) Different market must be separable for a seller to be able to practice discriminatory pricing.

(c) The elasticity of demand must be different in different markets.
(d) All of the above.

379. The third degree price discrimination may be suitable practised between
(a) Transport barriers
(b) Cost of transportation
(c) Two or more markets
(d) All of the above

380. The total costs of production of a firm are divided into total variable cost and
(a) total operating cost
(b) total profit cost
(c) total fixed cost
(d) None of the above

381. The demand function yield price function given below. The price for market A will be— ($P_a = 32 - 2Q_a$)
(a) 30 (b) 23
(c) 24 (d) None of these

382. The demand function yield price function given below. The price for market will be— ($Pfo = 22 - Q_h$)
(a) 20 (b) 25
(c) 19 (d) None of these

383. The short run equilibrium condition gives following data:

Equilibrium output = 30

$P_1 (= AR_1) = 140$

LAC = 72.08

Supernormal profit will be
(a) 70-42 (b) 67-92
(c) 67 (d) All of the above

384. Monopoly power may be expressed by the
(a) $\frac{P-MC}{MR}$ (b) $\frac{MR}{MC-P}$
(c) $\frac{P-MC}{P}$ (d) $\frac{P-MC}{P}\times 100$

385. Which is not feature of monopolistic competitions?
(a) Perfect factor mobility
(b) Large number of sellers
(c) Free entry and free exit
(d) None of the above

386. Which is not sources of oligopoly?
(a) Economic of scale
(b) Patent of rights
(c) Huge Capital Investment
(d) None of the above

387. Which of the following is included in the feature of oligopoly?
(a) Barriers to entry
(b) Small number of sellers
(c) Interdependence of decision making
(d) All of the above

388. Contribution is a combination of
(a) Fixed cost + Loss
(b) Fixed cost + Profit
(c) Latest variable cost
(d) Fixed cost + Variable cost

389. Variable cost + contribution both are expressed as
(a) Loss (b) Fixed cost
(c) Sales (d) Profit

390. Business economics is based on
(a) Real and unreal assumptions both
(b) Real assumptions
(c) Unreal assumptions
(d) None of the above

391. Which of the following confirm to proportionality rule?
(a) $\frac{MU_A}{MU_B} = \frac{P_A}{P_B}$
(b) $\frac{MU_A}{\text{Rupees worth of A}} = \frac{MU_B}{\text{Rupees worth of B}}$

(c) $\frac{MU_A}{P_A} = \frac{MU_B}{P_B} = \frac{MU_C}{P_C}$

(d) All of the above

392. Which of the following is not the characteristics of oligopoly?

(a) There is a great importance of advertising.

(b) There are so many sellers of a commodity.

(c) There is very difficult to determine the fix theory of pricing.

(d) None of the above.

393. The rule that "A fall in price results in a tendency for the consumer to buy more of the good since it has becomes cheaper and less of it when it becomes dearer" is

(a) Substitution effect

(b) Income effect

(c) Law of demand

(d) None of the above

394. Which of the following is not the cause of downward sloping demand curve?

(a) Income effect

(b) Law of diminishing marginal utility

(c) Substitution effect

(d) None of the above

395. The relation between income and quantity of a commodity demanded is explained by

(a) Demonstration effect

(b) Income elasticity

(c) Law of demand

(d) Cross elasticity

396. The indifference curve analysis explains consumer's behaviour in terms of his

(a) Demand (b) Income

(c) Price (d) Preferences

397. Which among these is not an assumption of ordinal theory (Indifference curve analysis)?

(a) Consumer behaves irrationally.

(b) An IC is negatively sloped downwards.

(c) IC moves upward to the right.

(d) The market prices of two goods are given.

398. Which among the following is the condition for consumer's equilibrium under IC analysis

(a) The income and expenditure becomes constant.

(b) The IC and budget line should be parallel to each other.

(c) No relationship between income and expenditure.

(d) The budget line should be tangent to IC.

399. The utility received by every successive unit is known as

(a) Marginal Utility

(b) Initial Utility

(c) Total Utility

(d) None of the above

400. Perfectly inelastic demand exist when

(a) ed < 1 (b) ed > 1

(c) ed = 0 (d) ed = 1

401. Modern economists, explain the equilibrium of producers with the help of

(a) isoquants

(b) law of increasing proportion

(c) law of decreasing proportion/ diminishing proportion

(d) returns to scale

402. Under isocost approach a producer is in equilibrium when

(a) producer produces desired output laleast possible cost.

(b) law of increasing returns operates.

(c) producer selling the product at maximum price.

(d) law of diminishing cost operates.

403. Total cost, marginal cost, average costs are example of
(a) Real costs
(b) Accounting costs
(c) Economic costs
(d) Production costs

404. Average variable costs or AVC =
(a) $\frac{TVC + TFC}{Qty}$ (b) $\frac{TC}{Qty}$
(c) $\frac{AC + MC}{Qty}$ (d) $\frac{TVC}{Qty}$

405. In long run
(a) all costs are variable
(b) all costs are fixed
(c) only two costs exist-fixed, variable
(d) None of the above

406. Following concept is considered as myth
(a) Oligopoly
(b) Monopolistic competition
(c) Monopoly
(d) Perfect competition

407. The law of demand sets relationship between
(a) price and demand of the commodity.
(b) supply and price of the commodity.
(c) consumption and supply of the commodity.
(d) None of the above.

408. There are ____ types of price discrimination.
(a) 5 (b) 4
(c) 2 (d) 3

409. The percentage change in demand due to a change in consumer's income is
(a) price elasticity of demand
(b) income elasticity of demand
(c) cross elasticity of demand
(d) None of the above

410. If cross elasticity of demand is positive the goods are
(a) Giffen goods
(b) Substitutes
(c) Complementary
(d) None of the above

411. For all normal goods, income elasticity of demand is
(a) Equal to unity (b) Positive
(c) Negative (d) None of these

412. A 'Good' is a necessity when income elasticity of demand is
(a) Zero
(b) Positive
(c) Greater than zero but less than unity
(d) None of the above

413. The maximum price that a buyer will agree to pay for a commodity will not exceed
(a) Marginal utility
(b) Average utility
(c) Total utility
(d) None of the above

414. The theory of "Paradox of value".
(a) Why some less useful commodities sell at high value?
(b) How the value of a good is fixed?
(c) Why necessities are not demanded more when their price declines?
(d) None of the above.

415. What will be the effect of a imposition of sales tax or excise tax on equilibrium price and output?
(a) The equilibrium price increases while equilibrium output falls.
(b) The equilibrium price will fall and output will rise.
(c) The equilibrium point shifts.
(d) None of the above.

416. "Floor Price" refers to the
(a) minimum price limit fixed by the Govt.
(b) ordinary prices prevailing in the market.
(c) maximum price limit fixed by the Govt.
(d) None of the above.

417. When the supply is inelastic, the entire burden of sales tax or excise tax is borne by
(a) government (b) consumer
(c) producer (d) None of these

418. When the supply is perfectly elastic, the _____ bears the entire burden of tax.
(a) government (b) consumer
(c) producer (d) None of these

419. When change in demand is great than change in price of a commodity, it is pointed as
(a) less elastic demand
(b) highly inelastic demand
(c) highly elastic demand
(d) perfectly elastic demand

420. Utility is
(a) want satisfying power of a commodity
(b) synonymous to consumption
(c) Both (a) and (b)
(d) None of the above

421. Which of the following is not an exception to the law of diminishing marginal utility
(a) early stages of consumption
(b) articles of conspicuous consumption
(c) articles of distinction
(d) None of the above

422. According to J.R. Hicks, the utility
(a) cannot be measured
(b) can be measured
(c) Both (a) and (b)
(d) None of the above

423. Engel curve states
(a) that as the income increases demand also increases.
(b) relationship between income of a consumer and the quantity of commodity purchased.
(c) Both (a) and (b).
(d) None of the above.

424. According to Mrs. Joan Robinson elasticity of demand
(a) $\frac{\text{Proportionate Change in Demand}}{\text{Proportionate Change in Price}}$
(b) $\frac{\text{Proportion Change in Cost}}{\text{Proportion Change in Price}}$
(c) $\frac{\text{Proportionate Change in Price}}{\text{Proportionate Change in Demand}}$
(d) None of the above

425. In case of inferior goods income effect is
(a) Perfectly elastic (b) More
(c) Negative (d) None of these

426. Engel's law says that
(a) the expenditure on food remains constant irrespective of an increase or decrease in consumer's income.
(b) as the income of a consumer increases, the expenditure on food decreases.
(c) as the income of a consumer increases the expenditure on food increases.
(d) None of the above.

427. Price effect is the sum of
(a) production and consumption
(b) consumer's income and savings
(c) income effect and substitution effect
(d) None of the above

428. A grant of food or cash subsidy
(a) does not effect him
(b) shifts the consumers to a higher indifference curve

(c) Both (a) and (b)
(d) None of the above

429. The major difference between Hicks' and Slutsky's substitution effect is that
(a) Slutsky's consumer gets more satisfaction.
(b) Hicks' consumer remains on same indifference curve while Slutsky's consumer shifts to higher indifference curve.
(c) Hicks' consumer gets more satisfaction.
(d) None of the above.

430. The relationship between the inputs to the production process and resulting output is described by
(a) production function
(b) marginal rate of technical substitution
(c) capital-labour ratio
(d) None of these above

431. Factor intensity means
(a) capital labour ratio
(b) capital input ratio
(c) capital factor ratio
(d) None of the above

432. Which among these is false about isoquants?
(a) Isoquants intersect each other
(b) Isoquants are convex to the origin
(c) Isoquants are negatively sloped
(d) None of the above.

433. The value of a resource in a foregone employment is called
(a) opportunity costs
(b) social cost
(c) sunk cost
(d) None of the above

434. Which among these is true?
(a) TFC + TVC = TC
(b) TFC = TVC + TC
(c) TFC – TC = TVC
(d) TFC – TVC = TC

435. The market form in which every seller influences and is influenced by the behaviour of other firms is called
(a) perfect market
(b) oligopoly
(c) monopolistic competition
(d) None of the above

436. In perfect oligopoly
(a) all firms are into non-price competition.
(b) all firms produce identical goods.
(c) all firms produce different goods.
(d) None of the above.

437. The demand curve facing a firm in a perfectly competitive market is
(a) Horizontal
(b) Vertical
(c) Downward sloping
(d) None of the above

438. The demand curve faced by a monopolist has
(a) horizontal slope
(b) negative slope
(c) a positive slope
(d) None of the above

439. Per unit price of a commodity is called
(a) marginal cost
(b) average cost
(c) average Revenue
(d) None of the above

440. Break even point is a point in which
(a) profit just starts accruing
(b) losses are being incurred by the firm
(c) no profit and no loss is earned
(d) None of the above

441. When total utility is maximum marginal utility is
(a) Positive (b) Negative
(c) Zero (d) None of these

442. The point where marginal utility is zero is called the
(a) Negative utility
(b) Point of satisfy
(c) Both (a) and (b)
(d) None of the above

443. Two goods are substitutes when
(a) they satisfy the same need of the consumer.
(b) they are highly elastic.
(c) their elasticity of demand is positive.
(d) None of the above.

444. Marginal rate of technical substitution is equal to
(a) elasticity of technical substitution
(b) relative marginal utilities of factors
(c) Both (a) and (b)
(d) None of the above

445. Which 'Law' of Economics says

$$\frac{MU_1}{P_1} = \frac{MU_2}{P_2} = \frac{MU_3}{P_3} \ldots\ldots \frac{MU_n}{P_n}$$

(a) law of proportionality
(b) law of diminishing marginal utility
(c) law of equimarginal utility
(d) None of the above

446. In which of the following are as the law of equimarginal utility cannot be applied
(a) Production (b) Distribution
(c) Public finance (d) None of these

447. Determinate solutions to price and output problems under oligopoly are reached by
(a) predicting rival's action
(b) ignoring interdependence
(c) Both (a) and (b)
(d) None of the above

448. Which among these is not a feature of monopolistic competition?
(a) Barriers to the entry in the market.
(b) Large number of firms which are not interdependent.
(c) Differentiated products.
(d) None of the above.

449. What is the name given to the cost which is incurred by the firm to alter the position or shape of the demand curve?
(a) Fixed cost
(b) Advertising costs
(c) Selling costs
(d) None of the above

450. Price elasticity of demand

(a) $\dfrac{\text{Proportionate Change in Demand}}{\text{Proportionate Change in Price}}$

(b) $\dfrac{\text{Proportion Change in Cost}}{\text{Proportion Change in Price}}$

(c) $\dfrac{\text{Proportionate Change in Demand}}{\text{Proportionate Change in income}}$

(d) None of the above

451. Which change in demand is less than change in price of a commodity, it is named as
(a) less elasticity of demand
(b) highly elasticity of demand
(c) perfectly inelasticity of demand
(d) perfectly elasticity of demand

452. The law of variable proportion is not applicable in
(a) agriculture sector
(b) construction sector
(c) industrial sector
(d) None of the above

453. In perfect completion price is determined with the help of
(a) dynamic equilibrium
(b) static equilibrium
(c) Both (a) and (b)
(d) None of the above

454. Which among these is not a condition of perfect competition?

(a) Small number of producer and sellers.
(b) Free entry and exit of firms.
(c) Homogeneous product.
(d) None of the above.

455. The 'Standard Costing' is a tool or method of
(a) budgetary control
(b) cost control
(c) ratio analysis
(d) cost reduction

456. Which costs are also known as social cost?
(a) Fixed cost (b) Real cost
(c) Economic cost (d) Product cost

457. Which of the following is/are part of Economic costs?
(a) Accounting cost
(b) Economic cost
(c) Money cost
(d) All of the above

458. Fixed cost is related with
(a) Price (b) Time
(c) Cost (d) Production

459. TVC + TFC =
(a) TFC (b) TC
(c) FC (d) VC

460. A market in which only two firms exist is called
(a) Duopsony (b) Oligopsony
(c) Oligopoly (d) Duopoly

461. The kinked demand curve explains
(a) Demand rigidity
(b) Price rigidity
(c) Demand flexibility
(d) Price flexibility

462. The term group equilibrium is related to
(a) Duopoly
(b) Perfect competition
(c) Oligopoly
(d) Monopolistic competition

463. The equilibrium is unstable and indeterminate under
(a) Cournot model
(b) Edgeworth model
(c) Pareto model
(d) Sweezy model

464. Each seller determines his price on the assumption that his rival will keep his price constant under
(a) Cournot model
(b) Edgeworth model
(c) Price leadership
(d) Bertrand's model

465. "The equilibrium prices of duopoly model are obtained at the intersection of their reaction curves." It is correct in the case of
(a) Bertrand's duopoly
(b) Edgeworth model
(c) Sweezy model
(d) None of the above

466. The upper portion of the kinked demand curve is relatively
(a) Inelastic
(b) Less elastic
(c) More elastic
(d) More inelastic

467. 'Excess capacity' is the resort of free entry of firms with no price competition, according to
(a) Joan Robinson (b) J. Hicks
(c) Keynes (d) Marshall

468. Which of the following curve is not unshaped?
(a) AC (b) MC
(c) AVC (d) AFC

469. Efficient allocation of resources is achieved to greatest extent under
(a) Perfect competition
(b) Oligopoly

(c) Monopolistic competition
(d) Monopoly

470. Marginal cost curve cuts the average cost curve form below at
(a) the left of the lowest point
(b) right of the lowest point
(c) its lowest point
(d) All of the above

471. If the demand curve confronting an individual firm is perfectly elastic, then firm is
(a) adjust price (b) price taker
(c) adjust output (d) All of the above

472. A firm's marginal revenue
(a) positive at point at which the total revenue is maximum.
(b) is always negative.
(c) can be positive.
(d) is always positive.

473. In the short period, monopolist firm's equilibrium is at
(a) AR > AC
(b) AR < AC
(c) Break even point
(d) All of the above

474. Concentration of monopoly is implemented under
(a) IDRA (b) FEMA
(c) FERA (d) MRTP

475. Which economist stated the positive impact of monopoly?
(a) Pigou
(b) Joseph Schumpeter
(c) Adam Smith
(d) Marshall

476. The theory which deals with the Comparative statistics and positive equilibrium is called
(a) Modern economics
(b) Micro economics
(c) Macro economics
(d) None of the above

477. The definition that economics is concerned with an enquiry into the nature and causes of wealth of nations is given by
(a) Adam Smith (b) A.E. Cairens
(c) Karl Marx (d) All of the above

478. "Economics is the study of administration of scarce resources and of the determinants of income and employment", was the definition for economics given by
(a) Keynes (b) Marshall
(c) Robbinson (d) All of the above

479. The profit which the firm must earn if they are to remain in the industry is called
(a) marginal profit
(b) some profit
(c) normal profit
(d) All of the above

480. Price = Marginal cost = Minimum average cost equation occurs when there is
(a) Equilibrium in the short run
(b) Equilibrium in the long run
(c) Both (a) and (b)
(d) None of the above

481. The price at which demand and supply are equal is called
(a) optimum price
(b) normal price
(c) equilibrium price
(d) All of the above

482. In the short period, the national income is determined by
(a) Aggregate demand and aggregate supply
(b) Aggregate demand and price
(c) Aggregate supply and price
(d) None of the above

483. Equilibrium levels of national income is determined when
(a) Intended investment = Intended saving
(b) Aggregate demand = Aggregate supply
(c) Both (a) and (b)
(d) None of the above

484. When consumption and investment spending together is greater than full employment GNP level it creates
(a) deflationary gap
(b) inflationary gap
(c) deficit financing
(d) None of the above

485. The low of substitution has no place when the resources are
(a) Constant (b) Limited
(c) Unlimited (d) None of these

486. The Law of Equi-Marginal Utility is also known as
(a) Law of Substitution
(b) Law of Demand
(c) Law of Supply
(d) None of the above

487. Demand price is identical with
(a) Average Revenue
(b) Marginal Income
(c) Both (a) and (b)
(d) None of the above

488. Generally, the Demand Curve slopes
(a) Remain constant
(b) Upwards
(c) Downwards
(d) All of the above

489. Giffen paradox is theory of
(a) Karl Marx (b) Sir Robert
(c) Marshall (d) All of the above

490. Giffen paradox speaks about
(a) Rising Demand Curve
(b) Falling Demand Curve
(c) Both (a) and (b)
(d) None of the above

491. Demand Law states that demand varies
(a) Inversely with the price
(b) Remains Constant of the Price is constant
(c) Conversely with the price
(d) None of the above

492. Law of Demand is based upon
(a) The Law of Marginal Utility
(b) The Law of Diminishing Returns
(c) The Law of Equilibrium
(d) None of the above

493. When we analyse the problems of economy as a whole it is a study of
(a) Macro Economics
(b) Micro Economics
(c) Both (a) and (b)
(d) None of the above

494. Price theory is
(a) Macro Economics
(b) Micro Economics
(c) Both (a) and (b)
(d) None of the above

495. "Full Employment" assumption is generally made in
(a) Macro Economics
(b) Employment theory
(c) Micro Economics
(d) None of the above

496. The study of aggregates of economy is done through
(a) Macro Economics
(b) Theory of population
(c) Micro Economics
(d) None of the above

497. Deductive, Analytical, Abstract method is used by
(a) Modern school
(b) Classical school

(c) Neo-classical school
(d) None of the above

498. After having been disturbed if an object reverts back to the original position it is called
(a) Neutral Equilibrium
(b) Stable Equilibrium
(c) Unstable Equilibrium
(d) None of the above

499. When the object acquires newer and newer positions with each disturbance and never returns back to the original position it is called
(a) Stable equilibrium
(b) Unstable equilibrium
(c) Neutral equilibrium
(d) None of the above

500. When the disturbing positions do not bring back to, nor drive it from the original position it is called
(a) Neutral equilibrium
(b) Stable equilibrium
(c) Both (a) and (b)
(d) None of the above

501. The Equilibrium of a single consumer is
(a) Partial equilibrium
(b) General equilibrium
(c) Both (a) and (b)
(d) None of the above

502. The necessary condition for the resources to be employed is the existence of
(a) General equilibrium
(b) Abundant resources
(c) Exploitation of resources
(d) None of the above

503. Marginal utility analysis assumes
(a) that utility is static.
(b) that utility can be measured.
(c) that utility cannot be quantified.
(d) None of the above.

504. Marginal utility analysis assumes that the marginal utility of money
(a) varies according to price fluctuations.
(b) remains constant.
(c) varies according to consumer behaviour.
(d) None of the above.

505. The total utility of a quantity of a commodity is maximum when the marginal utility is
(a) Zero (b) Maximum
(c) Minimum (d) All of these

506. With every diminution of one's stock the marginal utility will go on
(a) Remain constant (b) Decreasing
(c) Increasing (d) All of the above

507. The marginal utility falls when the quantity of the commodity with the consumer
(a) Remain constant (b) Increasing
(c) Decreases (d) None of these

508. The Law of Diminishing Marginal Utility holds goods if the persons are
(a) Eccentric (b) Normal
(c) Irrational (d) All of the above

509. A consumer goes on purchasing a commodity till the marginal utility is
(a) equal to price
(b) less than the price
(c) zero
(d) None of the above

510. The change in the total utility resulting from a one unit change in the total consumption of a commodity per unit of time is called
(a) Diminishing Marginal Utility
(b) Marginal Utility
(c) Both (a) and (b)
(d) None of the above

511. Change in total utility/Change in quantity consumed
(a) Equi-Marginal Utility
(b) Diminishing Marginal Utility
(c) Marginal Utility
(d) All of the above

512. Law of Diminishing Marginal Utility does not apply to
(a) spending of money
(b) earning of money
(c) Both (a) and (b)
(d) None of the above

513. The Marginal Utility of money goes on increasing
(a) with the decrease of money.
(b) with the desire for money remaining constant.
(c) with the increasing of money.
(d) None of the above.

514. Marginal utility is a function of
(a) Supply (b) Demand
(c) Both (a) and (b) (d) None of these

515. The Marginal Utility curve of a commodity is
(a) downwards sloping curve
(b) upwards curve
(c) Both (a) and (b)
(d) None of the above

516. A consumer buying two commodities, attains a position of equilibrium when the marginal utility of both the commodities are
(a) Equal or proportional to their prices
(b) Equal
(c) Unequal
(d) None of the above

Directions: Questions 517 to 519 of multiple statement type. Choose the correct answers from the codes given below.

517. Among following which are conditions of perfect competition?
1. There are restriction on any type either buyer or seller side.
2. There are no restriction between any type of movement of goods.
3. There are no restriction on movement of any type factor of production.

Codes:
(a) (1) and (2) (b) (2) and (3)
(c) (1) and (3) (d) None of these

518. Among following which are conditions of price discrimination
1. market must be segmentable
2. price elasticity of demand is different in different markets
3. income desparity exist

Codes:
(a) 1 and 2 (b) only 2
(c) All of these (d) None of these

519. Consider the following elements.
1. Indicators
2. Objectives
3. Controls
4. Key Result Areas
5. Roles and Missions
6. Action Plans

Codes:
(a) 4, 5, 2, 1, 3, 6 (b) 5, 4, 2, 1, 3, 6
(c) 4, 5, 1, 2, 6, 3 (d) 5, 4, 1, 2, 6, 3

Directions: Questions 520 to 548 are of matching type. Match List I with List II and select the correct answer using the codes given below the list.

520. **List I (Economist)**
A. Boston
B. Baumal W.J.
C. Augustine Cournot
D. R.L. Hall

List II (Books)
1. *Microeconomics Decisions*
2. *Economic Theory and Operation Analysis*

3. *Research into the Mathematical Principles of Theory of Wealth*
4. *Price Theory and Price Behaviour*

Codes:	A	B	C	D
(a)	3	4	1	2
(b)	1	2	3	4
(c)	2	1	3	4
(d)	4	1	3	2

521. **List I (Authors)**

A. Finnerty, Joseph and Hun park
B. Don M. Chance
C. Altzner P.F. Delbaen, T.M. Eber and D. Heath
D. Allen, Michael

List II (Books)

1. *Stock Index futures — Doses the Tail wag the Dog*
2. *Essays in Derivatives*
3. *Coherent Measure of Risk*
4. *Building a Role Model*

Codes:	A	B	C	D
(a)	4	3	1	2
(b)	1	4	3	2
(c)	1	2	3	4
(d)	1	3	4	2

522. **List I (Type of market structure)**

A. Perfect competition
B. Monopolistic competition
C. Oligopoly
D. Monopoly

List II (Nature of industry)

1. Financial Markets
2. Manufacturing
3. Cars
4. Transport

Codes:	A	B	C	D
(a)	4	3	1	2
(b)	4	2	1	3
(c)	3	1	4	2
(d)	1	2	3	4

523. **List I (Type of market structure)**

A. Perfect competition
B. Monopolistic competition
C. Oligopoly
D. Monopoly

List II (Control over price)

1. No
2. Some
3. Partially some
4. Usually

Codes:	A	B	C	D
(a)	2	3	4	1
(b)	1	2	3	4
(c)	3	1	2	4
(d)	2	1	4	3

524. **List I (Consumer goods)**

A. Essential goods
B. Comforts
C. Luxuries
D. Prestige goods

List II (Effect on sale)

1. Less than proportionate change in sale
2. Almost proportionate change in sale
3. More than proportionate increase in sale
4. Increase in sale

Codes:	A	B	C	D
(a)	2	1	3	4
(b)	1	2	3	4
(c)	3	1	2	4
(d)	2	4	1	3

525. **List I (Elasticity co-efficient)**

A. $e = 0$ B. $e < 1$
C. $e = 1$ D. $e = \infty$

List II (Change in total revenue)

1. Increase
2. Decrease
3. No change
4. Decrease to zero

Codes:	A	B	C	D
(a)	1	3	4	2
(b)	1	2	3	4
(c)	4	3	1	2
(d)	2	1	3	4

526. **List I (Elastic coefficient)**

A. e = 0 B. e < 1
C. e = 1 D. e > 1

List II (Change in price)

1. Increase 2. Decrease
3. Increase 4. Decrease

Codes:	A	B	C	D
(a)	4	1	2	3
(b)	1	2	3	4
(c)	3	1	2	4
(d)	2	1	3	4

527. **List I (Economist)**

A. K.E. Boulding
B. W.L. Baumol
C. E.K. Browing and J.M. Browing
D. D.N. Dwivedi

List II (Books)

1. *Economic Analysis—Microeconomic*
2. *Economic Theory and Operations Analysis*
3. *Microeconomic—Theory and Application*
4. *Microeconomic Theory*

Codes:	A	B	C	D
(a)	2	1	3	4
(b)	1	2	3	4
(c)	4	1	3	2
(d)	1	3	2	4

528. **List I (Economist)**

A. E. Mansfield
B. M.H. Spencer and Seigelmen
C. Evan J. Douglas
D. Ronnie Davis and Semoon Chary

List II (Books)

1. *Marginal Economics and Operations Research*
2. *Managerial Economics*
3. *Managerial Economics—Analysis and Strategy*
4. *Principles of Managerial Economics*

Codes:	A	B	C	D
(a)	4	3	1	2
(b)	1	2	3	4
(c)	4	2	1	3
(d)	2	4	1	3

529. **List I (Economists)**

A. E.H. Chamberlin
B. Paul Sweezy
C. Stackelberg
D. Leonard W. Weiss

List II (Books)

1. *The Theory of Monopolistic Competition*
2. *The Kinked Demand Curve*
3. *Supply and demand Under Condition of Oligopoly*
4. *Case Studies in American Industry*

Codes:	A	B	C	D
(a)	2	1	4	2
(b)	1	2	3	4
(c)	1	4	3	2
(d)	3	1	2	4

530. **List I (Classification price)**

A. Elastic B. Inelastic
C. Unitary elastic D. Fully elastic

List II (Effect of price change on total revenue)

1. Increase in price lower. Total revenue, decrease in price raise total revenue
2. Increase in price raise total revenue: Decrease in price lowers total revenue

3. Price change does not effect, total revenue
4. $|e_p| > 1$

Codes:	A	B	C	D
(a)	4	2	3	1
(b)	1	2	3	4
(c)	2	3	4	1
(d)	4	3	1	2

531. **List I (Economist)**
   A. C. Hoods and T.C. Koopmans
   B. H. Theil
   C. Homewood
   D. P.W. Hoguet

List II (Books)
1. *Studies in Econometric Methods*
2. *Estimation of Parameters of Econometric Models*
3. *Managerial Economics*
4. *Business and Economic Forecasting*

Codes:	A	B	C	D
(a)	3	4	1	2
(b)	1	2	3	4
(c)	3	1	2	4
(d)	2	1	3	4

532. **List I (Economists)**
   A. L.W. Weiss
   B. A.D.H. Kaplan, J.B. Dirlam and R.F. Lanrillophi
   C. William Fellner
   D. A.R. Oxenfeldt

List II (Books)
1. *Economics and American Industry*
2. *Pricing in Big Business*
3. *Competition Among the Few*
4. *Industrial Pricing and Market Practices*

Codes:	A	B	C	D
(a)	4	2	3	1
(b)	1	2	3	4
(c)	3	1	2	4
(d)	4	1	3	2

533. **List I (Economist)**
   A. Charles Roos
   B. Menlo park
   C. M-Janet Hansen
   D. P.H. Duglas

List II (Books)
1. *Dynamics of Economic Growth*
2. *Stanford Research Institute*
3. *Production Trends in the US Through*
4. *A Theory of Production*

Codes:	A	B	C	D
(a)	2	1	3	4
(b)	1	2	3	4
(c)	4	3	2	1
(d)	3	1	4	2

534. **List I**
   A. H. Wold and L. Jurren
   B. A.C. Harberger
   C. Cobb. H. Douglas
   D. Henry Schultz

List II
1. Demand analysis
2. The demand for durable goods
3. A theory of production
4. Theory and measurement of demand

Codes:	A	B	C	D
(a)	2	3	1	4
(b)	1	2	3	4
(c)	2	1	3	4
(d)	2	1	4	2

535. **List I (Market structure)**
   A. Number and size of distribution of sellers.
   B. Number and size of distribution of buyers.
   C. Product differentiation.
   D. Conditions of entry and exit.

List II (Characteristics of monopoly)

1. Single seller
2. Unspecified
3. No close substitutes
4. Entry prohibited

Codes:	A	B	C	D
(a)	4	1	3	2
(b)	3	2	1	4
(c)	2	1	3	4
(d)	1	2	3	4

536. **List I (Characteristics of perfect competition)**

A. Many small sellers
B. Many small buyers
C. Product undifferentiated
D. Easy entry and exit

List II (Explanations)

1. No seller is able to exert a significant influence over price.
2. No buyer is able to exert a significant influence over price.
3. Decisions to buy are made on the basis of price.
4. Resources are easily transferable among industries.

Codes:	A	B	C	D
(a)	1	2	3	4
(b)	3	1	2	4
(c)	1	3	4	2
(d)	2	3	4	1

537. **List I (Principles)**

A. Total revenue
B. Average revenue
C. Marginal revenue
D. Profit

List II (Formulas)

1. Price × Quantity
2. $\dfrac{\text{Total Revenue}}{\text{Quantity}}$
3. $\dfrac{\text{\% Change in Total Revenue}}{\text{\% Change in quantity}}$
4. Total Revenue – Total Cost

Codes:	A	B	C	D
(a)	4	3	1	2
(b)	1	2	3	4
(c)	3	4	1	2
(d)	4	3	1	2

538. **List I**

A. Total cost
B. Average fixed cost
C. Average variable cost
D. Average total cost

List II

1. Fixed cost + Variable cost
2. $\dfrac{\text{Fixed cost}}{\text{Quantity of output}}$
3. $\dfrac{\text{Variable cost}}{\text{Quantity of output}}$
4. $\dfrac{\text{Total cost}}{\text{Quantity of output}}$

Codes:	A	B	C	D
(a)	1	2	3	4
(b)	4	3	2	1
(c)	3	4	1	2
(d)	2	3	4	1

539. **List I (Cost)**

A. Average total cost
B. Average fixed cost
C. Average variable cost
D. Marginal cost

List II (Descriptions)

1. Total cost divided by the quantity of output
2. Fixed costs divided by the quantity of output

3. Variable costs divided by the quantity of output
4. The increase in total cost that arises from an extra unit of production

Codes:	A	B	C	D
(a)	1	4	3	2
(b)	1	2	3	4
(c)	3	4	1	2
(d)	2	3	1	4

540. **List I (Concept)**

A. Diminishing marginal product
B. Economic v/s Accountants
C. Fixed costs
D. Variable costs

List II (Explanation)

1. The property whereby the marginal product of an input declines as the quantity of the input increase
2. Economists include all opportunity costs when analysing a firm, whereas accountants measure only explicit costs. Therefore, economic profit is similar than accounting profit
3. Costs that do not vary with the quantity of output produced
4. Costs that do vary with quantity of output produced

Codes:	A	B	C	D
(a)	3	4	1	2
(b)	2	3	1	4
(c)	4	3	1	2
(d)	1	2	3	4

541. **List I**

A. Non equilibrium
B. Game theory
C. Prisoners' dilemma
D. Dominant strategy

List II

1. A situation in which economic actors interacting with one another each choose their best strategy given the strategies that all the other actors have chosen.
2. The study of how people behave in strategic situations.
3. A particular 'game' between two captured prisoners that illustrates why cooperation is difficult to maintain even when it is mutually beneficial.
4. A strategy that is best for a player in a game regardless of the strategies chosen by the other players.

Codes:	A	B	C	D
(a)	1	2	3	4
(b)	2	3	4	1
(c)	3	4	2	1
(d)	4	3	1	2

542. **List I (Concept)**

A. An oligopoly Game
B. An Arms Race Game
C. An Advertising Game
D. A Common Resources Game

List II (Definition)

1. In this game between members of an oligopoly the profit that each earns depends on both its production decision and the production decision of the other oligopolist.
2. In this game between two countries, the safety and power of each country depends on both its decision whether to arm and the decision made by the other country.
3. In this game between firm selling similar type of products (consumable and non-consumable) the profit that each earns, depends on both its own advertising decision and the advertising decision of the other firm.
4. In this game between firms pumping oil from a common pool, the profit that each earns depends on both the numbers of wells it drills and the number of wells drilled by the other firm.

Codes:	A	B	C	D
(a)	1	2	3	4
(b)	1	2	4	3
(c)	2	3	4	1
(d)	4	3	2	1

543. List I

A. Elasticity
B. Price elasticity of demand
C. Total revenue
D. Income elasticity of demand

List II

1. A measure of the responsiveness of quantity demanded or quantity supplied to one of its determinants.
2. A measure of how much the quantity demanded of a goods responds to a change in the price of that goods.
3. The amount paid by buyers and received by sellers of a goods.
4. A measure of how much the quantity demanded of a goods responds to a change in consumers income.

Codes:	A	B	C	D
(a)	2	1	3	4
(b)	1	2	3	4
(c)	3	4	2	1
(d)	4	3	2	1

544. List I

A. Complementary
B. Higher indifference curve
C. Slope of the indifference curve
D. Compensatory variation

List II

1. L-shaped curve
2. Higher satisfaction level
3. Relativemarginal utility
4. To remove income effect

Codes:	A	B	C	D
(a)	2	1	3	4
(b)	1	2	3	4
(c)	4	3	1	2
(d)	3	1	2	4

545.

List I	List II
A. Car	1. Giffen
B. Coarse cereals	2. Elastic
C. Salt	3. Inelastic

Codes:	A	B	C
(a)	3	2	1
(b)	1	2	3
(c)	2	3	1
(d)	2	1	3

546. List I

A. Indifference curve
B. Utility
C. Revealed preference

List II

1. Cardinal 2. Empirical
3. Ordinal

Codes:	A	B	C
(a)	3	2	1
(b)	3	1	2
(c)	1	2	3
(d)	2	1	3

547. List I

A. Law of equi-marginal utility
B. Consumer's surplus
C. Law of demand

List II

1. Optimum allocation
2. Inverse relation between price and quantity
3. Tax policy

Codes:	A	B	C
(a)	3	1	2
(b)	2	1	3
(c)	1	3	2
(d)	3	2	1

548. List I

A. Utility theory
B. Indifference curve
C. Revealed preference

List II

1. Stating the preference
2. Constant MUm
3. Convexity

Codes:	**A**	**B**	**C**
(a)	3	2	1
(b)	1	2	3
(c)	2	1	3
(d)	2	3	1

Directions: Questions 549 to 553 consists of two statements, one labelled as 'Assertion (A)' and the other as 'Reason (R)'. You have to examine these two statements carefuly and decide if the Assertion (A) and the Reason (R) are individually true and if so, whether the Reason is a correct explanation of the Assertion. Select your answer to these items using the codes given below.

(a) Both A and R are true and R is the correct explanation of A.
(b) Both A and R are true and R is not the correct explanation of A.
(c) A is true but R is false.
(d) A is false but R is true.

549. **Assertion (A):** Break-even chart merely depicts the relationship between sales and expenses in such a way as to show at what volume revenues exactly cover expenses.

Reason (R): The break-even chart shows that at any lesser volume of sale, the company would suffer a loss, and at a greater volume of sale it would enjoy a profit.

550. **Assertion (A):** The demand for the product of the firm under oligopoly is at prices higher than the prevailing market prices.

Reason (R): The oligopolistic firm faces a kinked demand curve.

551. **Assertion (A):** Utility will be maximised when the marginal unit of expenditure in each direction brings the same increment of utility.

Reason (R): A consumer will try to maximise his utility.

552. **Assertion (A):** Grant of cash subsidy is better than food subsidy.

Reason (R): Cost of cash subsidy is lower.

553. **Assertion (A):** The excess price which a man is willing to pay rather than go without the thing, over that he actually does pay is the consumer's surplus.

Reason (R): The basic reason for consumer's surplus is Law of Diminishing Marginal Utility.

ANSWERS

1. (a)	2. (a)	3. (b)	4. (a)	5. (c)	6. (b)
7. (c)	8. (b)	9. (c)	10. (c)	11. (c)	12. (d)
13. (b)	14. (d)	15. (a)	16. (d)	17. (c)	18. (d)
19. (d)	20. (b)	21. (d)	22. (c)	23. (c)	24. (c)
25. (a)	26. (c)	27. (b)	28. (a)	29. (a)	30. (a)
31. (c)	32. (b)	33. (a)	34. (b)	35. (b)	36. (b)
37. (a)	38. (b)	39. (a)	40. (d)	41. (b)	42. (c)
43. (a)	44. (c)	45. (c)	46. (d)	47. (a)	48. (c)

49. (d)	50. (d)	51. (c)	52. (b)	53. (a)	54. (b)
55. (a)	56. (c)	57. (b)	58. (c)	59. (d)	60. (b)
61. (c)	62. (c)	63. (c)	64. (d)	65. (b)	66. (c)
67. (d)	68. (b)	69. (d)	70. (a)	71. (d)	72. (b)
73. (a)	74. (a)	75. (c)	76. (c)	77. (b)	78. (b)
79. (c)	80. (a)	81. (d)	82. (c)	83. (d)	84. (d)
85. (d)	86. (a)	87. (d)	88. (a)	89. (b)	90. (a)
91. (a)	92. (c)	93. (c)	94. (d)	95. (b)	96. (d)
97. (d)	98. (d)	99. (c)	100. (d)	101. (c)	102. (a)
103. (a)	104. (d)	105. (d)	106. (d)	107. (d)	108. (b)
109. (d)	110. (c)	111. (a)	112. (a)	113. (c)	114. (d)
115. (d)	116. (b)	117. (a)	118. (d)	119. (b)	120. (a)
121. (d)	122. (b)	123. (b)	124. (b)	125. (a)	126. (d)
127. (d)	128. (a)	129. (b)	130. (c)	131. (b)	132. (b)
133. (d)	134. (d)	135. (c)	136. (c)	137. (c)	138. (c)
139. (b)	140. (b)	141. (a)	142. (c)	143. (c)	144. (c)
145. (c)	146. (c)	147. (d)	148. (c)	149. (c)	150. (c)
151. (d)	152. (c)	153. (b)	154. (b)	155. (a)	156. (b)
157. (d)	158. (d)	159. (b)	160. (b)	161. (d)	162. (c)
163. (c)	164. (c)	165. (c)	166. (b)	167. (a)	168. (b)
169. (c)	170. (c)	171. (b)	172. (c)	173. (c)	174. (c)
175. (c)	176. (b)	177. (b)	178. (b)	179. (d)	180. (d)
181. (a)	182. (b)	183. (c)	184. (b)	185. (a)	186. (b)
187. (b)	188. (b)	189. (c)	190. (b)	191. (c)	192. (c)
193. (b)	194. (b)	195. (b)	196. (c)	197. (b)	198. (d)
199. (c)	200. (b)	201. (c)	202. (c)	203. (a)	204. (b)
205. (a)	206. (a)	207. (a)	208. (c)	209. (a)	210. (d)
211. (d)	212. (a)	213. (a)	214. (a)	215. (b)	216. (d)
217. (d)	218. (b)	219. (c)	220. (a)	221. (d)	222. (d)
223. (c)	224. (a)	225. (c)	226. (c)	227. (c)	228. (b)
229. (c)	230. (c)	231. (c)	232. (d)	233. (c)	234. (c)
235. (a)	236. (b)	237. (c)	238. (c)	239. (b)	240. (c)
241. (b)	242. (d)	243. (b)	244. (c)	245. (c)	246. (d)
247. (c)	248. (c)	249. (c)	250. (d)	251. (d)	252. (b)

253. (b)	254. (c)	255. (c)	256. (b)	257. (c)	258. (c)
259. (c)	260. (c)	261. (b)	262. (b)	263. (b)	264. (a)
265. (b)	266. (c)	267. (b)	268. (c)	269. (b)	270. (d)
271. (c)	272. (b)	273. (b)	274. (d)	275. (c)	276. (d)
277. (b)	278. (d)	279. (d)	280. (c)	281. (d)	282. (c)
283. (b)	284. (b)	285. (c)	286. (b)	287. (c)	288. (c)
289. (c)	290. (d)	291. (d)	292. (c)	293. (c)	294. (b)
295. (b)	296. (c)	297. (c)	298. (b)	299. (c)	300. (c)
301. (c)	302. (b)	303. (b)	304. (b)	305. (b)	306. (b)
307. (b)	308. (b)	309. (b)	310. (b)	311. (b)	312. (b)
313. (c)	314. (b)	315. (b)	316. (b)	317. (b)	318. (c)
319. (a)	320. (c)	321. (b)	322. (c)	323. (b)	324. (b)
325. (b)	326. (c)	327. (d)	328. (d)	329. (c)	330. (d)
331. (d)	332. (d)	333. (d)	334. (b)	335. (d)	336. (b)
337. (c)	338. (c)	339. (d)	340. (d)	341. (c)	342. (b)
343. (c)	344. (a)	345. (c)	346. (b)	347. (d)	348. (b)
349. (d)	350. (b)	351. (b)	352. (d)	353. (d)	354. (c)
355. (b)	356. (c)	357. (d)	358. (c)	359. (d)	360. (c)
361. (c)	362. (c)	363. (b)	364. (b)	365. (d)	366. (b)
367. (b)	368. (d)	369. (b)	370. (d)	371. (c)	372. (d)
373. (d)	374. (c)	375. (d)	376. (a)	377. (d)	378. (d)
379. (d)	380. (c)	381. (c)	382. (a)	383. (b)	384. (c)
385. (d)	386. (d)	387. (d)	388. (b)	389. (c)	390. (b)
391. (d)	392. (b)	393. (b)	394. (d)	395. (b)	396. (d)
397. (a)	398. (b)	399. (a)	400. (c)	401. (d)	402. (a)
403. (d)	404. (d)	405. (a)	406. (d)	407. (a)	408. (d)
409. (b)	410. (b)	411. (b)	412. (c)	413. (a)	414. (a)
415. (a)	416. (c)	417. (c)	418. (b)	419. (c)	420. (a)
421. (a)	422. (a)	423. (b)	424. (a)	425. (c)	426. (b)
427. (c)	428. (b)	429. (b)	430. (a)	431. (a)	432. (a)
433. (a)	434. (b)	435. (b)	436. (b)	437. (a)	438. (b)
439. (c)	440. (c)	441. (c)	442. (b)	443. (a)	444. (b)
445. (c)	446. (b)	447. (c)	448. (a)	449. (c)	450. (a)
451. (a)	452. (a)	453. (b)	454. (a)	455. (b)	456. (b)

457. (d)	458. (b)	459. (b)	460. (d)	461. (b)	462. (d)
463. (b)	464. (d)	465. (a)	466. (c)	467. (a)	468. (d)
469. (a)	470. (c)	471. (b)	472. (a)	473. (d)	474. (d)
475. (b)	476. (b)	477. (a)	478. (a)	479. (c)	480. (b)
481. (b)	482. (a)	483. (c)	484. (b)	485. (c)	486. (a)
487. (a)	488. (c)	489. (b)	490. (a)	491. (a)	492. (b)
493. (a)	494. (a)	495. (c)	496. (c)	497. (b)	498. (b)
499. (b)	500. (a)	501. (a)	502. (a)	503. (b)	504. (b)
505. (a)	506. (c)	507. (b)	508. (b)	509. (a)	510. (a)
511. (c)	512. (b)	513. (c)	514. (a)	515. (a)	516. (a)
517. (c)	518. (a)	519. (b)	520. (b)	521. (c)	522. (d)
523. (b)	524. (b)	525. (b)	526. (b)	527. (c)	528. (b)
529. (b)	530. (b)	531. (b)	532. (b)	533. (c)	534. (b)
535. (d)	536. (a)	537. (b)	538. (a)	539. (b)	540. (b)
541. (a)	542. (a)	543. (b)	544. (b)	545. (d)	546. (b)
547. (c)	548. (d)	549. (a)	550. (b)	551. (a)	552. (a)
553. (a)					

4

Business Statistics and Data Processing

1. If b_{xy} is positive, then b_{yx} will be
   (a) positive
   (b) negative
   (c) either negative or positive
   (d) None of the above
2. A sample is a study of
   (a) only representative items
   (b) 51 items
   (c) whole population
   (d) None of the above
3. Choose the methods of sampling.
   (a) Non-probability sampling or non-random sampling
   (b) Probability sampling or random sampling
   (c) Both (a) and (b)
   (d) None of the above
4. The Graphical method can be used to solve
   (a) A linear programming problem with two decision variables.
   (b) A linear programming problem with all integer data base.
   (c) Any linear programming problem.
   (d) A transportation problem with two origins and two destinations.
5. Among the following methods, which is not the probability sampling method?
   (a) Cluster sampling
   (b) Systematic sampling
   (c) Quota sampling
   (d) Stratified sampling
6. Among the following methods, which is not the non-probability sampling method?
   (a) Judgement sampling
   (b) Convenient sampling
   (c) Systematic sampling
   (d) Quota sampling
7. External data is stored in the
   (a) forecast allocation file
   (b) customer file
   (c) market forecast file
   (d) None of the above
8. A store manager is trying to explore the relationship between percentage fat content (Y) and price (X) of various dairy products. He finds that the coefficient of determination is 0.4624 and the estimated regression line is Y = 0.5 – 0.02 X. The coefficient of correlation would be
   (a) – 0.01 (b) 0.2446
   (c) 0.54 (d) – 0.68
9. Data items in the fixed asset record of a newly purchased asset that a well-designed application programme could obtain automatically include
   (a) source
   (b) estimated disposal data
   (c) first cost
   (d) All of the above
10. File key of the fixed assets file includes the
    (a) acquisition date
    (b) asset identification number

(c) depreciation account number
(d) fixed asset account number

11. The journal voucher file includes
(a) date of entry
(b) rupees post to each account
(c) general ledger accounts involved
(d) All of the above

12. In statistics, ______ classification groups the data according to locational differences among the items.
(a) alphabetical (b) regional
(c) chronological (d) geographical

13. Data integrity refers to the
(a) privacy of data
(b) simplicity of data
(c) security of data
(d) validity of data

14. Personnel activity reports are produced from the
(a) applicant file
(b) jobs files
(c) personnel transactions file
(d) employee file

15. Computing systems most often facilitate planning because they
(a) enable an appropriate data processing system to provide answers quickly.
(b) make it possible to take into account many possibilities in an uncertain situation.
(c) make it possible to solve complex problems.
(d) All of the above.

16. If a hypothesis is tested at a significant level of 5%, then it means that
(a) there is 95% probability that the alternative hypothesis will be false.
(b) there is 5% probability that the null hypothesis will be true.
(c) there is 5% probability that the null hypothesis will be false.
(d) there is 5% probability that the null hypothesis will be rejected though it is true.

17. Critical path of the PERT chart is
(a) path which takes the shortest time to complete the project.
(b) path which takes the longest time to complete the project.
(c) the shortest path.
(d) None of the above.

18. PERT and CPM are
(a) project evaluation techniques.
(b) network techniques.
(c) assignment techniques.
(d) All of the above.

19. Hungarian method is a way of solving operation research problems in
(a) transportation method
(b) linear programming by graphical method
(c) simplex method
(d) assignment method

20. The degree of randomness of selection would depend upon the process of selecting the items from the ______.
(a) sample (b) data
(c) population (d) region

21. The following methods is (Care) used in transportation models of operations research.
(a) Least cost method
(b) Vogel's approximation method
(c) North west corner method
(d) All of the above

22. In the graphical model of linear programming, the region defined by the constraints and the non-negative restriction is the

(a) feasible solution region
(b) constraints
(c) objective function
(d) non-negativity restrictions

23. A model in which one physical property is used to represent another physical property is known as
(a) ionic model
(b) decision theory model
(c) deterministic model
(d) analog model

24. A machine on the average produces 5% defective items. What are the mean and variance in a set of 32 items?
(a) 4, 16 (b) 16, 4
(c) 16, 8 (d) None of these

25. Benefits from a computerised MIS include
(a) lower rates of interest.
(b) higher returns on short-term investment.
(c) less frequent and smaller short-term loans.
(d) All of the above.

26. The relationship between the computer and quantitative techniques can be said to be a
(a) Synergistic (b) Symbiotic
(c) Synthetic (d) Syntactical

27. A popular technique for forecasting is
(a) linear programming
(b) correlation analysis
(c) regression analysis
(d) None of the above

28. Econometric models include techniques from
(a) Economics (b) Mathematics
(c) Statistics (d) All of the above

29. The method of sampling, in which the choice of sample items depends exclusively on the judgement of the investigator is termed as ______.
(a) Systematic sampling
(b) Convenience sampling
(c) Judgement sampling
(d) Quota sampling

30. The order entry subsystem creates a file of order records that are input to the
(a) control subsystem
(b) quality subsystem
(c) production subsystem
(d) inventory subsystem

31. Data collection terminals gather data for use by the
(a) cost subsystem
(b) inventory subsystem
(c) production subsystem
(d) All of the above

32. Average inventory level is reduced by
(a) decreasing the order quantity.
(b) lowering the reorder point.
(c) decreasing the vendor lead time.
(d) increasing the usage rate.

33. The numerical value given to the likelyhood of the occurrence of an event is called
(a) Regression (b) Probability
(c) Correlation (d) None of these

34. Marketing research data is gathered by
(a) controlled experiment
(b) observation
(c) in-depth interviews
(d) All of the above

35. The most structured marketing problems are likely to be those dealing with
(a) Promotion (b) Product
(c) Price (d) Place

36. Linear programming models solve problems dealing with
(a) rupees and percentages.
(b) dispersions and similarities.
(c) routes and mixes.
(d) relatives and absolutes.

37. The manager of inventory would most likely be found in the
    (a) marketing function
    (b) finance function
    (c) information system function
    (d) manufacturing function
38. The integration of the computer with manufacturing is called
    (a) Computer Integrated Manufacturing
    (b) CAM
    (c) CAD
    (d) All of the above
39. A set of events are said to be _____ if the occurrence of one of them excludes the possibility of the occurrence of the other.
    (a) independent
    (b) mutually exclusive
    (c) not mutually exclusive
    (d) None of the above
40. The latest time that the event can be delayed without delaying the completion of the entire project in PERT chart is
    (a) latest pass
    (b) earliest pass
    (c) latest allowable time
    (d) earliest allowable time
41. If r = 0.9, coefficient of determination is
    (a) 81% (b) 75%
    (c) 91% (d) 82%
42. In the financial decision-making system, which of the following is not a transaction processing system input?
    (a) Cash issues
    (b) Warehouse requisition slip
    (c) Cash receipts
    (d) Cash returns
43. Quantitative techniques used to solve business problems are called
    (a) operation science
    (b) operation management
    (c) operation research
    (d) None of the above
44. Relation between two variables is determined by
    (a) Dispersion (b) Correlation
    (c) Mean (d) Regression
45. If plotted points in a scatter diagram lie on a straight line vertical to the Y-axis, then r = _____.
    (a) +2 (b) –0
    (c) 0 (d) None of these
46. Maximum value of correlation is
    (a) 1 (b) 0
    (c) 2 (d) 1.5
47. Minimum value of correlation is
    (a) –1 (b) 0
    (c) –1.5 (d) –2
48. In case there is no relation between two variables, value of coefficient of correlation will be
    (a) 0 (b) +2
    (c) +1 (d) –2
49. Coefficient of correlation measures
    (a) degree of the relation
    (b) direction of the relation
    (c) Both (a) and (b)
    (d) None of the above
50. Geometric mean of regression coefficients will be _______
    (a) Coefficient of determination
    (b) Coefficient of non-determination
    (c) Coefficient of correlation
    (d) None of the above
51. Independent variable is represented along
    (a) z-axis
    (b) y-axis
    (c) x-axis
    (d) None of the above

52. Dependent variable is represented along
    (a) y-axis
    (b) z-axis
    (c) x-axis
    (d) None of the above
53. Range of the coefficient of correlation is
    (a) +1 (b) 0.25
    (c) +2 (d) 0.5
54. As the value of x increases, if y also increases, then coefficient of correlation will be
    (a) Zero (b) Negative
    (c) Positive (d) None of these
55. In correlation analysis, the formulae $1-r^2$ is used to compute the value of _____
    (a) Coefficient of alienation
    (b) Coefficient of correlation
    (c) Coefficient of determination
    (d) Coefficient of non-determination
56. As the value of x increases, if value of y decreases, then coefficient of correlation will be
    (a) Negative (b) Positive
    (c) Zero (d) None of these
57. In case, coefficient of correlation is positive, the curve representing the relation will be
    (a) Vertical
    (b) Upward sloping
    (c) Horizontal
    (d) Downward sloping
58. Vertical curve represents the value of coefficient of correlation to be
    (a) Negative (b) Zero
    (c) Positive (d) All of the above
59. Horizontal curve represents the value of coefficient of correlation to be
    (a) Positive (b) Zero
    (c) Negative (d) All of the above
60. In case, coefficient of correlation is negative, the curve representing the relation will be
    (a) Downward sloping
    (b) Vertical
    (c) Horizontal
    (d) Upward sloping
61. In case of simple correlation, the number of variables involved are
    (a) 2 (b) 3
    (c) 4 (d) 1
62. If all the dots of a scatter diagram lie on a straight line falling from the upper left-hand corner to the lower right hand corner, the correlation is said to be _____
    (a) High degree of negative correlation
    (b) Perfect negative correlation
    (c) Perfect positive correlation
    (d) Zero correlation
63. In case of multiple correlation, the number of variables involved are greater than
    (a) 2 (b) 1
    (c) 3 (d) 4
64. Relationship of two or more variables is examined excluding some other variables in case of
    (a) Multiple correlation
    (b) Total correlation
    (c) Partial correlation
    (d) None of the above
65. Partial correlation is a type of
    (a) Multiple correlation
    (b) Simple correlation
    (c) Both (a) and (b)
    (d) None of the above
66. Scatter diagram is
    (a) positional method of finding out correlation.
    (b) graphic method of finding out correlation.

(c) mathematical method of finding out correlation.
(d) None of the above.

67. The quantitative measure of correlation between two variables is known as ____
(a) Coefficient of determination
(b) Coefficient of regression
(c) Coefficient of correlation
(d) All of the above

68. When variations in the values of two variables have a constant ratio, there will be
(a) non-linear correlation
(b) zero correlation
(c) linear correlation
(d) None of the above

69. Graph of variables having linear relation will be
(a) Hyperbola (b) Straight line
(c) Curved (d) None of these

70. Graph of variables having non-linear relation will be
(a) Hyperbola (b) Curved
(c) Straight line (d) None of these

71. Karl Pearson's coefficient of correlation method of measuring correlation is
(a) Positional (b) Graphic
(c) Mathematical (d) None of these

72. If coefficient of correlation is more than _____ of its P.E., correlation is significant.
(a) 8 times (b) 4 times
(c) 6 times (d) None of these

73. Karl Pearson's coefficient of correlation's formula is
(a) $\frac{cov(x, y)\,\sigma y}{\sigma x}$ (b) $\frac{cov(x, y)}{\sigma x\,\sigma y}$
(c) $\frac{cov(x, y)\,\sigma x}{\sigma y}$ (d) None of these

74. Karl Pearson's coefficient of correlation is based on the assumption by
(a) Platykurtic (b) Leptokurtic
(c) Normality (d) None of these

75. $R = 0.6745\ \frac{1 - r^3}{\sqrt{n}}$. R is
(a) Probable error
(b) Correlation error
(c) Standard error
(d) None of the above

76. $R = \frac{1 - r^2}{\sqrt{N}}$, where R is
(a) Correlation error
(b) Standard error
(c) Probable error
(d) None of the above

77. While analysing the relationship between variables, independent variable is also called ______
(a) Explained variable
(b) Explanatory variable
(c) Variable
(d) None of these

78. Coefficient of correlation is equal to
(a) $\sqrt{bxy.byx}$ (b) bxy/byx
(c) bxy + byx (d) bxy – byx

79. Coefficient of correlation is independent of
(a) Change of scale
(b) Change of origin
(c) Both (a) and (b)
(d) None of the above

80. Probable error and standard error is equal to
(a) 2/3 (b) 3/2
(c) 1 (d) 2

81. Spearman's method of calculating coefficient of correlation is based on

(a) Actual pictures
(b) Position
(c) Rank
(d) None of the above

82. The method of calculating coefficient of correlation by
(a) Karl Pearson
(b) Irvin Fischer
(c) Charles Spearman
(d) Lorenz

83. If X and Y are independent, the value of regression coefficient byx = ______.
(a) 0
(b) 1
(c) Greater than 1
(d) Any negative value

84. Coefficient of correlation in case of frequency distribution could not be calculated in case of
(a) Least square method
(b) Karl Pearson
(c) Spearman
(d) None of the above

85. Correlation between price and demand is
(a) Positive (b) Negative
(c) Zero (d) None of these

86. Correlation between price and supply is
(a) Positive (b) Zero
(c) Negative (d) None of these

87. Correlation between income and demand is
(a) Zero (b) Positive
(c) Negative (d) None of these

88. Correlation between rainfall and population is
(a) Zero (b) Negative
(c) Positive (d) None of these

89. Which is the most widely used method of calculating correlation?
(a) Charles Spearman's
(b) Scatter diagram
(c) Karl Pearson's
(d) None of the above

90. Test of hypothesis and ____ are the two branches of statistical inference.
(a) estimation
(b) statistical analysis
(c) alternative hypothesis
(d) None of these

91. Age of applicants of life insurance and the premium of insurance is
(a) Zero correlation
(b) Negatively correlated
(c) Positively correlated
(d) None of the above

92. In the field of management, some of the important techniques, relate to budgeting, cost accounting, planning and control are through
(a) budgetary control
(b) operational research
(c) financial administration
(d) PERT and CPM

93. A series of actions or operations that convert inputs into outputs is known as
(a) Data (b) Information
(c) Facts (d) Processing

94. ______ is the original hypothesis.
(a) Statistical analysis
(b) Probability
(c) Null hypothesis
(d) None of these

95. The collection of integrated and related master files is known as
(a) Record (b) Field
(c) Database (d) Table

96. In which files records are stored one after another in an ascending or descending order determined by the key field of the records?

(a) Sequential files (b) Direct files
(c) Both (a) and (b) (d) None of these

97. The advantages of sequential files are
(a) there is no overhead in address generation. Locating in a particular record requires only the specification of the key field.
(b) relatively inexpensive I/O media and devices can be used for the storage and processing of such files.
(c) easy to organise, maintain and understand.
(d) All of the above.

98. While applying chi-square test, the frequency in any cell should not be ____
(a) Less than 5 (b) Less than 15
(c) More than 5 (d) More than 15

99. In which files, the records organised in such way that it is possible for the computer to directly locate the key of the desired record without having to search through a sequence of other records?
(a) Sequential files (b) Direct files
(c) Both (a) and (b) (d) None of these

100. In which files, the records are organised in sequence and an index table is used to speed up access to the records without requiring a search of the entire file?
(a) Indexed sequential files
(b) Direct files
(c) Sequential files
(d) None of the above

101. To arrange records within a file in some defined sequence. This process is known as
(a) Merging (b) Copying
(c) Sorting (d) Searching

102. The process of scanning of file to find a particular record is known as
(a) Searching (b) Sorting
(c) Copying (d) Merging

103. In a 4×4 contingency table, degree of freedom is
(a) 18 (b) 4
(c) 9 (d) 16

104. The process of combining of records from two or more ordered files into a single ordered file is known as
(a) Copying (b) Merging
(c) Searching (d) Sorting

105. Files held on a storage device are identified by a special block of data held as the first block on the file. This block called the
(a) File maintenance (b) File lable
(c) File scratch (d) None of these

106. ______ is the term given to any system of reorganisation of data items within a file, where the reorganisation is independent of the information content of the file.
(a) Merging (b) Printing
(c) Maintenance (d) Copying

107. The amount of a certain product sold to a certain customer in a past period can be obtained from the
(a) Inventory file
(b) Customer file
(c) Sales history file
(d) All of the above

108. Scatter diagram is also called
(a) Dot chart
(b) Correlation graph
(c) Zero correlation
(d) None of the above

109. Computing system designed to supply supervisory information include
(a) Payroll systems
(b) Process control systems
(c) Invoicing systems
(d) All of the above

110. If all the points of a scatter diagram lie on a straight line falling from the lower left-

hand corner to the upper right-hand corner, the correlation is said to be
(a) Perfect negative correlation
(b) Zero correlation
(c) Perfect positive correlation
(d) High degree of positive correlation

111. An optional facilitates location programme can be used to study
(a) warehouse location alternative.
(b) plant location alternative.
(c) factory location alternative.
(d) All of the above.

112. Data collection terminals
(a) record employee attendance.
(b) track the flow of materials from one production area to another.
(c) All of the above.
(d) None of the above.

113. Coefficient of correlation is independent of
(a) Scale (b) Origin
(c) Both (a) and (b) (d) None of these

114. The files required to maintain general ledger records include
(a) charts of accounts file
(b) inventory file
(c) detail posting file
(d) None of the above

115. When three or more variables are studied simultaneously for correlation analysis it is called
(a) Partial correlation
(b) Multiple correlation
(c) Simple correlation
(d) All of the above

116. The formula for computing Karl Pearson's coefficient
(a) $\frac{\Sigma xy}{\sqrt{\Sigma x^2}}$ (b) $\frac{\Sigma xy}{\sqrt{\Sigma x^2 \Sigma y^2}}$
(c) Both (a) and (b) (d) None of these

117. The probable error of the coefficient of correlation is obtained as
(a) $0.6745\frac{1+N^2}{\sqrt{r}}$ (b) $0.6547\frac{1-r^2}{\sqrt{N}}$
(c) $0.6745\frac{1-r^2}{\sqrt{N}}$ (d) $0.6745\frac{1-N^2}{\sqrt{r}}$

118. In the Spearman's rank correlation coefficient when the ranks are equal, the formula is
(a) $1-\frac{6\left[\Sigma D^2+\frac{1}{2}(m^3-m)+\frac{1}{2}(m^3-m)+...\right]}{N^3-N}$
(b) $1-\frac{\frac{1}{2}\left[(m^3-m)+\frac{1}{2}(m^3-m)+...\right]}{N^3-N}$
(c) $1-\frac{\left[6\Sigma D^2+\frac{1}{2}(m^2-m)+\frac{1}{2}(m^2-m)+...\right]}{N^3-N}$
(d) None of the above

119. The concept of regression was developed by
(a) Marshall in 1890
(b) Sir Frencis Galton in 1877
(c) R.A. Fisher in 1823
(d) None of the above

120. If the plotted points of a scatter diagram fall on a narrow band, it indicates a ____ degree of correlation.
(a) high (b) low
(c) Both (a) and (b) (d) None of these

121. A statistical tool used to estimate the unknown values of one variable from the known values of another variable, is known as
(a) Test of Significance
(b) Correlation
(c) Regression
(d) Probability

122. A line representing the average relationship between two variables is called
(a) Regression line
(b) Functional line
(c) Probable line
(d) None of the above

123. If one regression coefficient is positive, the other is ____
(a) Negative (b) Positive
(c) Both (a) and (b) (d) None of these

124. What is a flow chart?
(a) A chart showing the rate of return on investments.
(b) A diagrammatic representation of sequence of events.
(c) A chart showing profit/loss of the company.
(d) All of the above.

125. Franking machine is used for
(a) fixing stamps
(b) duplicating documents
(c) making arithmetic calculation
(d) All of the above

126. Memory unit in an electronic computer performs the function of
(a) Co-ordination (b) Controlling
(c) Calculation (d) Storage

127. Every indecomposable outcome of a random experiment is called ____
(a) Sample point (b) Probability
(c) Sample space (d) None of these

128. Mimeography is a
(a) process of blue printing.
(b) process of electrical photography.
(c) method of photocopying.
(d) method of stencil duplication.

129. When probability is revised on the basis of all the available information, it is called ____
(a) Posterior probability
(b) Continuous
(c) Priori probability
(d) None of these

130. Is card indexing system and improvement over simple indexing system?
(a) No, because the cards wanted for reference cannot be taken out without holding up the work of recording of information as the other cards are left behind.
(b) Yes, because it facilitates location of any name of subject with the minimum of searching as the cards are arranged in an alphabetical order.
(c) No, because the system has a limited capacity for expansion as the number of drawers cannot be increased as desired.
(d) Yes, because the cards can be arranged in a particular order and the order cannot be changed at will.

131. Sample point is also called ____
(a) Elementary outcome
(b) Event
(c) Sample space
(d) All of these

132. According to Graicunas' theory, total number of relations among superiors and subordinates can be found by the formula
(a) $n(2^{n-1}/2 + n + 1)$ (b) $n(2^n/2 + n - 1)$
(c) $n(2^{n-1}/2 + n - 1)$ (d) $n(2^n/n + n + 1)$

133. Organisation and methods aim at simplification of office procedures through
(a) allowing existing procedures to continue without adding any new procedures or amendments.
(b) discarding all the records and treating each work on merit.
(c) elaboration of specification work processes for better implementation.

(d) elimination of all unnecessary work, minimising the number of forms and direct communication.

134. The latest generation of personal computers (PCs) being used in an office setup is
(a) PC Pentium (b) PC XT
(c) PC 486 (d) PC AT

135. The height of persons in a country is a _____ random variable.
(a) continuous
(b) discrete
(c) Both (a) and (b)
(d) None of the above

136. When the output of one department becomes the input for the other department, the relationship between the two departments is called
(a) Reciprocal interdependence
(b) Pooled interdependence
(c) Mutual interdependence
(d) Sequential interdependence

137. In this method, the objective, the constraints and the different influences in the decision area are expressed in the form of mathematical equations and inequalities.
(a) The Model (b) Experience
(c) Experiment (d) Any of the above

138. In Poisson distribution, the value of 'e' = _____.
(a) 2.718 (b) 2.871
(c) 2.178 (d) 2.817

139. This method gives a purely objective solution as objective and truthful as the input data with which the equations of the system are formulated.
(a) Experiment (b) The Model
(c) Experience (d) Any of the above

140. A basic limitation of this method is that it is sometimes difficult to master all the data with the degree of precision required by the mathematical equations.
(a) The Model (b) Experience
(c) Experiment (d) Any of the above

141. This decisioning approach puts the decisioning area in the perspective of 'dynamics'.
(a) Limiting factor analysis
(b) The marginal analysis
(c) The differential analysis
(d) Cost-benefit analysis

142. The technique of analysis of variance is developed by
(a) Frank wilcoxon (b) James Bernoulli
(c) R.A. Fischer (d) Kruskal

143. This approach to decision-making is referred to as the 'with or without principle'.
(a) Cost-benefit analysis
(b) Differential analysis
(c) Factor analysis
(d) Marginal analysis

144. This approach is similar to the marginal analysis except that it takes a total view of the plus and minus of the two alternatives after the decision is taken.
(a) Cost-benefit analysis
(b) Differential analysis
(c) Limiting factor analysis
(d) None of the above

145. Although this method is treated as a distinct approach and analytical tool for decision making, it constitutes the basic principle running through all choice-techniques.
(a) The differential analysis
(b) The marginal analysis
(c) The limiting factor analysis
(d) The cost-benefit analysis

146. The two major dimension, viz. (i) the peripheral dimesnsion, and (ii) the time dimension are relevant in this approach.

(a) The cost-benefit analysis
(b) The limiting factor analysis
(c) The marginal analysis
(d) The differential analysis

147. Chi-square test was developed by
(a) William Gosset (b) Kruskal
(c) R.A. Fischer (d) Karl Pearson

148. A management step which is already systematised, pre-determined by rules, regulations or procedures is better known as.
(a) an unprogrammed decision
(b) a management decision
(c) an act of management
(d) a programmed decision

149. Managerial decision-making refers to
(a) information system
(b) programmed decisions
(c) operational research
(d) unprogrammed decisions

150. These decisions are original and the product of managerial wisdom. These decisions are known as
(a) unprogrammed decision
(b) programmed decision
(c) top-level decisions
(d) middle-level decisions

151. In a normal curve, the significance level is usually termed as
(a) Critical region
(b) Acceptance region
(c) Level of acceptance
(d) None of these

152. In the types of decisions, the choice area is prominent, rival alternatives clamour for selection, environment plays a role. These decisions are
(a) top-level decisions
(b) decisions by the chief executive
(c) unprogrammed decisions
(d) programmed decisions

153. Almost all decisions need to be preceded by the same set of logical analyses. This is known as
(a) process of logic
(b) universality of decision-making process
(c) logic of decision-making
(d) decision-making process

154. For planning and decision-making, the method that consists in consulting the past is known as
(a) Experiment (b) The Model
(c) Experience (d) None of these

155. ____ describes the magnitude of difference between observed frequencies and expected frequencies.
(a) F-value
(b) t-value
(c) z-value
(d) Chi-square value

156. For planning and decision-making, the method that consists in trying out alternatives is known as
(a) The Model (b) Experience
(c) Experiment (d) None of these

157. ____ are distribution free tests.
(a) Parametric tests
(b) Level of acceptance
(c) Non-parametric tests
(d) None of the above

158. It is the value assigned to the expected benefits for desirable national gains.
(a) Shadow price
(b) Cost price
(c) Opportunity cost
(d) Real price

159. This approach makes comparison of alternatives possible for planners and decision makers to reach objective solutions.

(a) The limiting factor analysis
(b) The marginal analysis
(c) The cost-benefit analysis
(d) The differential analysis

160. Chi-square test was first used by
(a) Frank Wicoxon
(b) Karl Pearson
(c) Simeon Denis Poisson
(d) R.A. Fischer

161. It is the variable that sets limit to achieving the goal or extending the goal horizon.
(a) Cost factor
(b) Marginal factor
(c) Differential factor
(d) Limiting factor

162. This approach states that once the key factor is located, management can plan matching resources which together then constitute the system.
(a) The cost-benefit approach
(b) The marginal approach
(c) The limiting factor approach
(d) The differential approach

163. Chi-square value ranges from 0 to
(a) –1 (b) +1
(c) 10 (d) Infinity

164. It is the application of mathematics and the laws and methods of physical science to the sphere of business and enterprise management.
(a) Operations analysis
(b) Management science
(c) Operations research
(d) All of the above

165. It is a business situation in a capsule form. Its purpose is to reduce the complex reality into smaller and manageable dimensions without mutilating the character of the reality.
(a) System
(b) Political variables
(c) Economic variables
(d) OR model

166. _____ is the simplest and most widely used non-parametric test.
(a) K-S test
(b) Wilcoxon matched paired test
(c) Sign test
(d) Chi-square test

167. Andrew W. Halpirfs study had made use of
(a) LNPK method (b) LJPK method
(c) LBDQ method (d) LOQ method

168. Ohil state model suggests the following as the best leader-behaviour.
(a) High concern both for production and people.
(b) Low structure and low consideration.
(c) High structure and high consideration.
(d) Low concern both for production and people.

169. Computer system accessile to non-specialists to assist in planning and decision-making is called
(a) Expert System
(b) Disk Operating System
(c) Management Information System
(d) Decision Support System

170. What is Mimeography?
(a) A process of blue printing.
(b) A method of photocopying.
(c) A process of digintal photography.
(d) A method of stencil duplication.

171. The continuous process of comparing organisational strategies, products or processes with those of the best in class organisations is
(a) Benchmarking (b) Quality circle
(c) TQM (d) Kaizen

172. ______ is used as a test of goodness of fit.
(a) Mann-whitney U-test
(b) Chi-square test

(c) Run test
(d) Wilcoxon test

173. While evaluating the internal control system, which one of the following stages is not required?
(a) Evaluating the system
(b) Ascertaining the system
(c) Formulating the internal control questionnarie
(d) Formulating the internal control schemes

174. Internal check serves the purpose of
(a) detection and prevention of errors.
(b) detection of errors.
(c) prevention of errors.
(d) None of the above

175. Mimeograph is a
(a) Accounting machine
(b) Calculating machine
(c) Duplicating machine
(d) Dictating machine

176. Non-parametric test
(a) Does not make assumption about the form of distribution
(b) Not concerned with parameter
(c) Distribution free statistical test
(d) All the above

177. Memory unit is an electronic computer performs the function of
(a) Making calculations
(b) Storing the data
(c) Giving out the end product
(d) Controlling the other operating units

178. Franking machine is used for
(a) fixing stamps on outward letters and envelopes.
(b) producing a typewritten document in multiple copies.
(c) printing addresses on envelopes, wrap pers, etc.
(d) None of the above.

179. Which of the following is not a non-parametric test?
(a) t-test
(b) Chi-square test
(c) Run test
(d) Sign test

180. Vertical filing is used in
(a) Medium size offices
(b) Big offices
(c) Small offices
(d) All of the above

181. Indexing is an important
(a) aid to filing.
(b) method of filing.
(c) method of keeping statistical records.
(d) method of keeping account books.

182. Computer hardware refers to
(a) punch cards, magnetic tapes or paper tapes.
(b) data required for processing.
(c) the end product obtained from computer.
(d) all the equipment required for proper functioning of a programme.

183. Signed rank test was developed by
(a) Kolmogrov
(b) Frank Wilcoxon
(c) Karl Pearson
(d) Kruskal

184. Below are given some points.
1. It is automatic and uniform given identical situations.
2. It can be assigned to clerical or routine managerial levels.
3. The more of an organisation's decision making areas are programmed, the more it leaves the senior management free to concentrate on larger decision areas.
4. It helps the communication process as everybody seems to know the

outcome of a certain set of conditions or situation.
5. It minimises eraticism or the subjective element in management decision.

These are all the qualities of
(a) a top-level management
(b) a programmed decision
(c) a middle-level management
(d) an unprogrammed decision

185. 1. Feedback.
2. Evaluation.
3. Identification of discrepancies.
4. Correcting the system to reality.

Above are the features of
(a) Application of a model
(b) Formulation of a model
(c) Testing a model
(d) Monitoring a model

186. Below are given three methods
1. Experience
2. Experiment
3. The Model

These three models relate to
(a) decision-making
(b) planning and decision-making
(c) planning
(d) None of the above

Directions: Questions 187 to 194 are of multiple statement type. Choose the correct answer from the codes given below.

187. Consider the following steps.
1. Analysis of variances
2. Initiating corrective action
3. Measurement of actual performance
4. Establishment of standards

Codes:
(a) 3, 1, 2, 4 (b) 4, 3, 1, 2
(c) 1, 2, 3, 4 (d) 2, 3, 1, 4

188. Coefficient of determination of a regression model:
1. Explains the proportion of total variation in the values of the dependent variable.
2. It can be used to derive the estimate of the extent of variation in the value of Y that is explained by the random factors.
3. Direction of inter-relation between the dependent and independent variables.
4. It explains the influence of the intercept on the dependent variable.

Codes:
(a) 1, 2 (b) 1, 2, 3, 4
(c) 2, 4, 3 (d) 4, 1, 3

189. Following are the ingredients of management by exception. What should be their correct logical sequence?
1. Measurement 2. Observation
3. Projection 4. Comparison
5. Selection 6. Decision-making

Codes:
(a) 5, 2, 6, 3, 1, 4 (b) 1, 3, 5, 2, 4, 6
(c) 1, 2, 5, 3, 4, 6 (d) 5, 3, 6, 2, 1, 4

190. Mathematical solutions suffer from some limitations which are often classified as inherent limitations and empirical limitations. Below are given a few important limitations.
1. It is almost impossible to identify and incorporate all the variables of the reality situation into the model.
2. There are many intangible variables to which only national values can be assigned.
3. The functional relations between the variables are often too vague and elusive for precision and qualification.
4. The mathematical tools should not choose the real-life problems.
5. The communication gap between the manager and the O.R. specialist is difficult to bridge.

6. The level of basic management in most enterprises is still crude and unrefined.
7. Imprecision in the input information spoils the precision of the mathematical solution.
8. The data and information base available is often inadequate.

Codes:

(a) 3, 4, 5 and 6 (b) 4, 5, 6 and 7
(c) 1, 2, 5 and 6 (d) 1, 2, 3 and 4

191. Identify the correct chronology of the following:

1. Fisher's test of significance of differences between means of three or more samples.
2. Kendal's partial rank correlation.
3. Gossest's T test of significance between means of two samples.
4. Chi-Square test of goodness of fit of the curve and randomness of the sample values.

Codes:

(a) 3, 1, 2, 4 (b) 1, 2, 3, 4
(c) 4, 3, 2, 1 (d) 1, 2, 4, 3

192. Which of the following advatages accrue from vertical filing?

1. The system has universal application, as all types of papers and documents can be filed.
2. It provides ample scope for the expansion of the filing facility.
3. It is comparatively a cheap method.
4. The papers are kept in a chronological order.

Codes:

(a) 2, 3 and 4 (b) 1, 2, 3 and 4
(c) 1 and 3 (d) 1 and 2

193. Determine the order in which the following were developed

1. Fisher's F test of significance of differences between the means of more than two samples.
2. Gosset's t-test of difference between the means of two samples.
3. Pearson's correlation coefficient.
4. Spearman's rank correlation coefficient.

Codes:

(a) 1, 2, 3, 4 (b) 2, 1, 3, 4
(c) 3, 2, 1, 4 (d) 4, 1, 2, 3

194. Which of the following advantages could be derived from the use of Franking machine?

1. It saves time because of its speed
2. Valuable facts and figures can be obtained
3. It is very convenient to use
4. In ensures much greater accuracy.

Codes:

(a) 1 and 2 (b) 2 and 3
(c) 1 and 4 (d) 1 and 3

Directions: Questions 195 to 203 are of matching type. Match List I with List II and select the correct answer using the codes given below the list.

195. **List I (Systems)**

A. Procedural Test
B. Stratified Random
C. Substantive Test
D. Depth Test

List II (Events)

1. Population is divided into two or more than two groups
2. Verification of sampling procedures and their implementation
3. Tracing through the system all aspects of a transaction
4. Obtaining an evi-dence as to the completeness and accuracy of data

Codes:	A	B	C	D
(a)	4	3	2	1
(b)	2	1	4	3
(c)	4	1	2	3
(d)	2	3	4	1

196. **List I (Reports)**
   A. Routing Reports
   B. Special Reports
   C. Statutory Reports
   D. Technical Reports

   List II (Examples)
   1. Project Report
   2. Market Research Report
   3. Production Report
   4. Auditor's Report

Codes:	A	B	C	D
(a)	4	2	3	1
(b)	3	1	4	2
(c)	4	1	3	2
(d)	3	2	4	1

197. **List I**
   A. Poisson distribution has the property that
   B. Normal distribution is
   C. Chi-square distribution is
   D. Binomial distribution has the property that

   List II
   1. Its mean is greater than Variance
   2. Symmetric distribution
   3. Positively skewed distribution
   4. Its mean and variance are equal.

Codes:	A	B	C	D
(a)	4	2	1	3
(b)	4	2	3	1
(c)	1	2	3	4
(d)	2	4	3	1

198.

List I	List II
A. Portable Disk	1. Selection and movement of files and objects
B. RAM	2. Data entry
C. Key Board	3. Floppy drive
D. Mouse	4. Speed

Codes:	A	B	C	D
(a)	3	4	2	1
(b)	3	1	2	4
(c)	2	1	3	4
(d)	2	4	3	1

199. **List I**
   A. Karl Pearson method
   B. Spearman's Method
   C. Concurrent deviation method

   List II

   1. $\dfrac{\sum(x-\overline{x})(y-\overline{y})}{\sqrt{\dfrac{\sum(x-\overline{x})^2}{n}}\sqrt{\dfrac{\sum(y-\overline{y})^2}{n}}}$

   2. $\pm\sqrt{\dfrac{\pm 2C-N}{N}}$

   3. $1-\dfrac{6\sum d^2}{N^3-N}$

Codes:	A	B	C
(a)	2	3	1
(b)	3	2	1
(c)	1	2	3
(d)	1	3	2

200.

List I	List II
A. Probable error	1. $\sqrt{bxy.byx}$
B. Standard error	2. $1-r^3/\sqrt{N}$
C. Correlation	3. $\frac{2}{3}(1-r^3/\sqrt{N})$

Codes:	A	B	C
(a)	2	3	1
(b)	2	1	3
(c)	3	2	1
(d)	1	2	3

201. **List I**

A. Relation between price standard
B. Relation between income and demand
C. Relation between rainfall and population

List II

1. Negative
2. Positive
3. Zero

Codes:	**A**	**B**	**C**
(a)	2	1	3
(b)	3	2	1
(c)	2	3	1
(d)	1	2	3

202. **List I**

A. Scatter diagram
B. Pearson method
C. Spearman

List II

1. Actual figures
2. Graphic method
3. Ranking method

Codes:	**A**	**B**	**C**
(a)	2	3	1
(b)	3	2	1
(c)	1	2	3
(d)	2	1	3

203.

List I	**List II**
A. Perfect positive	1. 0
B. Perfect Negative	2. +1
C. No correlation	3. –1

Codes:	**A**	**B**	**C**
(a)	2	1	3
(b)	1	2	3
(c)	2	3	1
(d)	3	1	2

Direction: Question 204 consists of two statements, one labelled as 'Assertion (A)' and the other as 'Reason (R)'. You have to examine these two statements carefuly and decide if the Assertion A and the Reason R are individually true and if so, whether the Reason is a correct explanation of the Assertion. Select your answer to these items using the codes given below.

(a) Both A and R are true and R is the correct explanation of A.
(b) Both A and R are true but R is not the correct explanaton of A.
(c) A is true but R is false.
(d) A is false but R is true.

204. **Assertion (A):** Programmed decisions are under conditions of certainty.

Reason (R): Conditions of certainty provide reliable information about consequences of alternatives.

ANSWERS

1. (a)	2. (a)	3. (c)	4. (a)	5. (c)	6. (d)
7. (c)	8. (d)	9. (d)	10. (b)	11. (a)	12. (d)
13. (d)	14. (c)	15. (b)	16. (d)	17. (b)	18. (a)
19. (c)	20. (a)	21. (d)	22. (a)	23. (d)	24. (d)
25. (d)	26. (a)	27. (c)	28. (d)	29. (c)	30. (d)
31. (d)	32. (a)	33. (b)	34. (d)	35. (d)	36. (c)
37. (d)	38. (a)	39. (b)	40. (c)	41. (a)	42. (b)
43. (c)	44. (b)	45. (c)	46. (a)	47. (a)	48. (a)

49. (c) 50. (c) 51. (c) 52. (a) 53. (a) 54. (c)
55. (d) 56. (a) 57. (b) 58. (b) 59. (b) 60. (a)
61. (a) 62. (b) 63. (a) 64. (c) 65. (a) 66. (a)
67. (c) 68. (c) 69. (b) 70. (b) 71. (c) 72. (c)
73. (b) 74. (c) 75. (a) 76. (c) 77. (b) 78. (a)
79. (c) 80. (a) 81. (c) 82. (c) 83. (a) 84. (c)
85. (b) 86. (a) 87. (b) 88. (a) 89. (c) 90. (a)
91. (c) 92. (d) 93. (d) 94. (c) 95. (c) 96. (a)
97. (d) 98. (a) 99. (b) 100. (a) 101. (c) 102. (a)
103. (c) 104. (b) 105. (b) 106. (c) 107. (a) 108. (c)
109. (a) 110. (c) 111. (d) 112. (c) 113. (c) 114. (c)
115. (b) 116. (b) 117. (c) 118. (a) 119. (b) 120. (a)
121. (c) 122. (a) 123. (b) 124. (b) 125. (a) 126. (d)
127. (a) 128. (d) 129. (a) 130. (a) 131. (a) 132. (b)
133. (d) 134. (a) 135. (a) 136. (d) 137. (a) 138. (a)
139. (b) 140. (a) 141. (b) 142. (c) 143. (d) 144. (b)
145. (d) 146. (a) 147. (a) 148. (d) 149. (d) 150. (a)
151. (a) 152. (c) 153. (b) 154. (c) 155. (d) 156. (c)
157. (c) 158. (a) 159. (c) 160. (b) 161. (d) 162. (c)
163. (d) 164. (d) 165. (d) 166. (d) 167. (c) 168. (c)
169. (d) 170. (d) 171. (a) 172. (b) 173. (d) 174. (c)
175. (c) 176. (c) 177. (b) 178. (a) 179. (a) 180. (b)
181. (a) 182. (d) 183. (b) 184. (b) 185. (d) 186. (b)
187. (b) 188. (a) 189. (b) 190. (d) 191. (a) 192. (d)
193. (c) 194. (d) 195. (b) 196. (d) 197. (b) 198. (a)
199. (d) 200. (c) 201. (d) 202. (d) 203. (d) 204. (a)

5

Business Management

1. An organisation structure is effective if it enables individuals to contribute to the objectives of the enterprise. This is known as
   (a) principle of unity of objectives.
   (b) scalar principle.
   (c) principle of functional definition.
   (d) None of the above.
2. Which one of the following orders indicates the correct logical order of managerial functions?
   (a) Planning, directing, organising, staffing, control and coordination.
   (b) Organising, planning, directing, staffing, coordination and control.
   (c) Organising, planning, staffing, directing, control and coordination.
   (d) Planning, organising, staffing, directing, control and coordination.
3. Which one of the following formulae is used to calculate "Cross Relationship" under span of control?
   (a) n(2n/2 + n – 1) (b) n(n – 1)
   (c) n(2n/2 – 1) (d) None of these
4. The main difference between delegation and decentralisation is that
   (a) delegation of authority can take place without decentralisation whereas there cannot be decentralisation without delegation of authority.
   (b) delegation refers primarily to transfer of authority from one individual to another while decentralisation refers to systematic delegation of authority to all units in an organisation.
   (c) delegation may take place due to administrative, technical and routine reasons while decentralisation involves deliberate action for the smooth functioning of the organisation.
   (d) delegation represents sharing of excessive burden of key managerial personnel while decentralisation refers to division of top managerial operations.
5. Management by exception introduces
   (a) requirement of full reports on performance.
   (b) selective, responsibility-oriented reporting.
   (c) computation of actuals in different spheres of performance.
   (d) reporting of significant variances.
6. The potential disadvantage of MBO is
   (a) the additional commitment to the organisation.
   (b) its inability to control progress of work and achievement of results.
   (c) the absence of short-term and long-term planning.
   (d) its over-emphasis on production and productivity.
7. Which one of the following statements regarding 'skill-mix' of management is correct?

(a) Middle-level management requires more technical skills than others.
(b) Top management requires more human relations skill than others.
(c) Top management requires more conceptual skill than others.
(d) Supervisory level men require less technical skill than others.

8. From the point of view of functional organisation, which one of the following cannot be claimed to be an advantage?
(a) It leads to a higher degree of efficiency.
(b) It ensures a greater division of labour.
(c) It facilitates small scale production.
(d) It helps in the assignment of specific responsibilities.

9. Attracting the proper and suitable type of candidate for the post to be filled constitutes.
(a) Recruitment (b) Performance
(c) Appointment (d) Appraisal

10. Organisation theory deals with
(a) structure of an organisation.
(b) industrial relations.
(c) incentives and wage policy.
(d) forms of business organisation.

11. Which one of the following statements is correct?
(a) Delegation does not bestow an obligation on the part of the delegatee.
(b) Responsibility of the delegatee cannot be greater than the authority delegated.
(c) Delegation frees the delegator of the responsibility.
(d) Delegation merely the division of work.

12. Delegation of authority is linked to
(a) scientific management.
(b) managerial planning.
(c) management coordination.
(d) management control.

13. Span of management may be larger in the case of
(a) loyal subordinates.
(b) centralised works and less responsibility.
(c) repetitive work and clear responsibility.
(d) hard working subordinates.

14. "Management is the art of getting things done through people". Who said this?
(a) F.W. Taylor
(b) Mary Parker Follett
(c) George R. Terry
(d) Henri Fayol

15. Five M's of management are
(a) Man, Money, Materials, Machinery and Methods
(b) Manager, Muscle, Machinery, Methods and Marketing
(c) Marketing, Monitoring, Motivation, Machinery and Methods
(d) Marketing, Manpower, Muscle power, Motivation and Methods

16. Read the following definition:
"Planning is that function of a manager in which he decides in advance what he will do. It is an intellectual process in which creative thinking and imagination are essential". Who has given this definition?
(a) Maslow
(b) Koontzand O'Donnell
(c) Haynes and Massie
(d) George R. Terry

17. "Administration is a part of management", this view is held by
(a) William Newman
(b) American experts in management

(c) British School of Thought
(d) Henri Fayol

18. Which of the following functions is known as the essence of management?
(a) Co-ordinating (b) Control
(c) Planning (d) Organising

19. The process of grouping activities into units for the purpose of administration may be referred to as
(a) Co-ordination
(b) Departmentalisation
(c) Specialisation
(d) Decentralisation

20. Which of the following is not true in respect of planning?
(a) Planning function is not performed by the top management.
(b) Planning is an intellectual activity.
(c) Planning is related to objectives.
(d) Planning is forward-looking.

21. The main advantage of functional organisation is
(a) Expert advice (b) Experience
(c) Specialisation (d) Simplicity

22. Which of the following is the top administrative organ of the company?
(a) Board of Directors
(b) Shareholders
(c) Managing Director
(d) General Manager

23. It is an element which sets the enterprise in motion, which infuses the otherwise dead structure with life, metamorphoses it towards a richer and more satisfying existence.
Which is this element?
(a) Communication (b) Motivation
(c) Leadership (d) Management

24. The famous book *General and Industrial Management* was written by
(a) Elton Mayo (b) Maslow
(c) Henri Fayol (d) Oliver Sheldon

25. Management is
(a) a science (b) an art
(c) Both (a) and (b) (d) None of these

26. While delegating, a superior delegates
(a) authority and responsibility but not accountability.
(b) authority, responsibility and accountability.
(c) authority and responsibility.
(d) only authority.

27. In line and staff organisation, the staff performs the function of
(a) advising the management.
(b) assigning responsibility.
(c) management.
(d) None of the above.

28. Which of the following skills is equally important at all levels of management?
(a) Conceptual skill
(b) Technical skill
(c) Human relation skill
(d) All of the above

29. Which of the following is not an advantage of MBO?
(a) Better appraisal
(b) Success without planning
(c) Self-control
(d) Employee commitment

30. Activity analysis, decision analysis, and relations analysis are done with a view
(a) to devise a suitable strategy to beat the competition.
(b) to exercise effective control.
(c) to find out what kind of organisation structure is needed to attain the objectives of an enterprise.
(d) to determine the objectives of the enterprises.

31. The managerial function of organisation is
    (a) determining the manpower requirements of the organisation and of filling the various managerial and non-managerial positions with competent people.
    (b) designing the structure of organisational activities, authority responsibility relationship among the members.
    (c) to make planning, keeping in view the environmental changes.
    (d) to organise the workforce in the form of trade unions.
32. Which of the following is true with respect to planning function?
    (a) Monitoring whether the things allocated are done properly.
    (b) To make a blue print of ideas and work.
    (c) To tell the work allocation to all.
    (d) None of the above.
33. Planning function is mainly performed at
    (a) middle management level.
    (b) lower management level.
    (c) top management level.
    (d) None of the above.
34. Functional approach to management was developed by
    (a) Payol (b) Louis Allen
    (c) Taylor (d) Terry
35. Esprit de corps principle of management states that
    (a) labour turnover should be minimised.
    (b) there is a need for teamwork.
    (c) there should be only one superior for each subordinate.
    (d) discipline should be maintained.
36. In Taylor's functional organisation, gang boss
    (a) compiles cost of production.
    (b) inspects the quality of work done.
    (c) issues instructions to workers.
    (d) sets up tools and machines for work.
37. Repeated use plans or standing plans include
    (a) procedures and methods
    (b) rules
    (c) objectives and policies
    (d) All of the above
38. Overall and strategic planning is done by the
    (a) middle level management
    (b) supervisory level management
    (c) top management
    (d) All of the above
39. Difference between policy and rule is/are
    (a) a policy is flexible and gives some discretion to the executives concerned whereas a rule is rigid and does not leave any scope for discretion.
    (b) a policy is a general statement of a management decision whereas a rule is a specific statement.
    (c) a policy is a less specific type of standing plan whereas a rule constitutes the most specific type of standing plan.
    (d) All of the above.
40. Leadership is a function of all the following factors except
    (a) Leader
    (b) Workgroup
    (c) Situation
    (d) Product or service
41. In a functional organization,
    (a) the organization is divided into functions with specialists having authority.
    (b) the entire organization is divided into functions with specific role for specialists.

(c) there are no advisers, the executive alone having the authority and competence.
(d) there are specialist advisers having no authority.

42. MBO is a technique which required that the objectives of the enterprise
(a) be defined in terms of measurable results.
(b) be written and defined in broad terms.
(c) lay down the time period for achieving the desired results.
(d) include a plan of action for achieving the desired result.

43. Which one of the following principles states that recurring decisions should be handled in a routine manner by lower level managers whereas problems involving unusual matters only should be referred to higher levels?
(a) Scalar principle
(b) Principle of exception
(c) Principle of commitment
(d) Principle of unity of command

44. The process of grouping activities into units. For the purpose of administration may be referred to as
(a) Decentralization
(b) Co-ordination
(c) Specialisation
(d) Departmentalisation

45. 'Matrix organisation' refers to a term of
(a) mathematical arrangement of events in columns and rows.
(b) organisation where authority and responsibility coexist.
(c) organisation in which two or more basic types of departmentation are combined.
(d) None of the above.

46. If a general manager asks the sales manager to recruit some salesman on his behalf, it is an instance of
(a) delegation of authority.
(b) division of authority.
(c) delegation of responsibility.
(d) decentralisation of authority.

47. Effective direction does not depend on the
(a) ability of the manger.
(b) communication process.
(c) deployment of human resources.
(d) forces at the subordinate level.

48. Planning refers to
(a) looking and actual performance to decide action to be taken.
(b) looking backward.
(c) looking forward.
(d) looking forwarding and backward.

49. Which one of the following defines coordination?
(a) Orderly arranged of group effort to provide unity of action in the pursuit of a common purpose.
(b) Actuating force which inspires a person to put his best for the fulfilment of a task.
(c) Process of determining what is to be accomplished and what has been accomplished and if necessary applying corrective measures.
(d) Process of transmitting information from one person to another or form one unit to another.

50. A written statement of the main duties and responsibilities which a particular job entails is called
(a) Job evaluation
(b) Job analysis
(c) Job specification
(d) Job description

51. Selection process in any organization is usually proceeded by the preparation of
    (a) human resources accounting
    (b) human resources inventory
    (c) human resources audit
    (d) operations audit

52. Which one of the following monitors critical inputs and suggest preventive measures in the form of corrective action to correct inputs and processes?
    (a) Operational control
    (b) Feedback control
    (c) Feedforward control
    (d) Budgetary control

53. If the span of control is narrow, a number of managers would be required in each unit of the organization and there would be many managerial levels or layers, such an organizational structure is referred to as
    (a) Fall structure
    (b) Project structure
    (c) Flat structure
    (d) Matrix structure

54. Which one of the following statement is correct?
    (a) Controlling is a part of the planning process.
    (b) A control process is meaningless without pre-set goals.
    (c) Planning and controlling are essentially one and the same.
    (d) Controlling is a substitute for planning.

55. When jobs are broadened in scope and complexity so that the person's overall area of job responsibility increases, it is a case of
    (a) Job enrichment
    (b) Job rotation
    (c) Job enlargement
    (d) Job specification

56. Techniques of managerial control are useful in
    (a) identifying appropriate technology.
    (b) selection of plant location.
    (c) conducting shareholders' meetings.
    (d) profit planning.

57. Which one of the following is the oldest form of organization?
    (a) One and staff organization
    (b) Functional organization
    (c) Departmentation
    (d) Line and staff organization

58. Each subordinate should have only one superior whose command he has to obey. This is known as
    (a) exception principle
    (b) scalar principle
    (c) authority-responsibility principle
    (d) unity of commercial principle

59. Motivational process and not the motivators as such is associated with the
    (a) ERG theory
    (b) expectancy theory
    (c) need hierarchy theory
    (d) two-factor theory

60. Delegation of authority takes place when a manager thinks that
    (a) he needs to punish his subordinate.
    (b) the job is too difficult and hazardous.
    (c) the job requires the high skill that he does not possess.
    (d) he cannot lookafter all the demanding tasks by himself.

61. One of the steps that may be required for achieving effective coordination is
    (a) making an honest appraisal and initiating rewards/punishments.
    (b) transmission of messages in a full line communication channel.

(c) training in leadership and supervising abilities of controllers of activity.
(d) reporting on performance and taking remedial measures.

62. According to the principle of "span of control", there is
(a) no limit to the number of subordinates a supervisor can supervise.
(b) a tendency of overload supervisors with too much of work.
(c) a limit to delegation of authority to the subordinate.
(d) a limit to the number of subordinates a supervisor can effectively supervise.

63. Perceived equity in reward results in satisfy which one of the following motivation theories take this into account?
(a) Herzberg's two-factor theory
(b) Porter and lower model
(c) Victor Vroom's expectancy model
(d) F.W. Taylor's incentive scheme

64. Establishment of management by objectives presupposes
(a) that the employees are provided with result expected.
(b) that limits of authority are not defined.
(c) unlimited freedom to set goals.
(d) unlimited freedom to operate in the assigned task.

65. An important aspect of control is that the
(a) manager sets as effective management information system.
(b) plans are checked before implementation against predetermined measures of performance.
(c) performance is checked against predetermined standards.
(d) manager motivates his subordinates to give better performance.

66. According to the Peter principle, managers tend to
(a) lose their competence with successive promotions.
(b) work late as they go higher up the hierarchy.
(c) work even beyond their retirement age.
(d) get promoted to the level of their incompetence.

67. Understanding control does not signify understanding
(a) who controls.
(b) how one controls.
(c) what is controlled.
(d) what is meant by control.

68. Which one of the following may not necessarily be an advantage of coordination?
(a) Unity of direction
(b) Effective supervision
(c) Summarisation of all management functions
(d) Creative force

69. According to Graicunas' theory, total number of relations among superiors and subordinates can be found by the formula
(a) $n(2^{n-1}/2 + n + 1)$
(b) $n(2^{n}/2 + n - 1)$
(c) $n(2^{n}/n + n + 1)$
(d) $n(2^{nl}/2 + n - 1)$

70. Which one of the following clearly defines 'organisation' as a function?
(a) Controlised authority in the hands of an individual to achieve business goals.
(b) Management of business.
(c) Process of assigning duties to individuals to achieve specific ends effectively.
(d) Accomplishment of goals through means.

71. According to need hierarchy theory of Moslow, human needs arise in which one of the following order?
    (a) Physiological needs, Social needs, Ego needs, Safety needs, Self actualisation needs.
    (b) Physiological needs, Social needs, Safety needs, Ego needs, Self actualisation needs.
    (c) Physiological needs, Safety needs, Ego needs, Social needs, Self actualisation needs.
    (d) Physiological needs, Safety needs, Social needs, Ego needs, Self actualisation needs.
72. Scalar principle of organisation implies that
    (a) line of authority is defined clearly.
    (b) all subordinates have only one supervisor.
    (c) the subordinates need not necessarily have a supervisor.
    (d) manager can directly supervise only a limited number of persons.
73. Consider the following Organisation Chart.

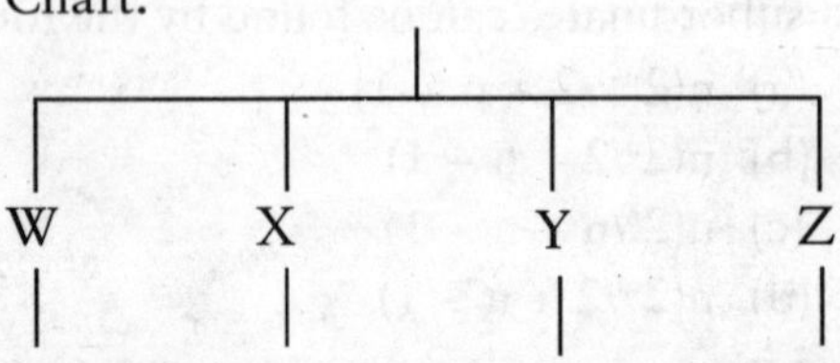

Which one of the following is indicated by this chart?
    (a) Multiple levels of supervision
    (b) Wide span
    (c) Decentralisation
    (d) Narrow span
74. To indicate the functions of management, the catch word POSDCORB was coined by
    (a) Henri Fayol
    (b) Ernest Dale
    (c) Luther Gulik
    (d) None of the above
75. Scalar principle refers to the
    (a) existence of a clear line of authority in all parts of the organization.
    (b) responsibility of a subordinate to a superior.
    (c) delegation of authority at all levels of an organization.
    (d) conflict of instructions from two or more superiors.
76. The primary function of an office is
    (a) carrying out the management policies.
    (b) making, using and preserving records.
    (c) safeguarding of company's assets.
    (d) remunerating personal.
77. In a small company, who acts as an office supervisor
    (a) Accountant
    (b) Secretary
    (c) Director
    (d) Managing Director
78. Office layout aims at
    (a) providing larger accommodation.
    (b) optimum utilisation of space.
    (c) providing larger space for the office manager.
    (d) providing larger open space.
79. Franking machine is used for
    (a) accounting work
    (b) duplicating
    (c) stamp fixing
    (d) punching cards
80. Outward mail means
    (a) personal mail received by the employees.
    (b) mail received in the office.
    (c) personal mail sent by the employees.
    (d) mail sent out to customers.

81. In which of the following types of office organisation expert advisers are engaged to advise the executive?
   (a) Committee organisation
   (b) Line and staff organisation
   (c) Functional organisation
   (d) Line organisation

82. A good layout results in
   (a) smoother flow of work.
   (b) installation of expensive office equipment.
   (c) open space for all employees.
   (d) All of the above.

83. Decentralisation of authority means
   (a) conveying what the subordinate is expected to do.
   (b) giving permission to the subordinate to do his work.
   (c) departmentalising activities.
   (d) delegating responsibility.

84. An open office has the advantage of
   (a) avoidance of noise
   (b) inflexibility
   (c) economy
   (d) privacy

85. The internal mail implies
   (a) the letters posted within India.
   (b) the written messages transmitted within the organisation.
   (c) the letters posted in the same city.
   (d) None of the above.

86. Centralisation of mailing services means
   (a) all mailing operations are handled at one place.
   (b) incoming and outgoing mailing operations are separated.
   (c) each department handles its own mail.
   (d) None of the above.

87. One of the primary functions of an office is to
   (a) appoint workers.
   (b) appoint the company secretary.
   (c) provide the requisite information.
   (d) provide training facilities.

88. Inward mail means
   (a) personal mail received by these employees.
   (b) mail received in the office.
   (c) mail sent out to customers.
   (d) None of the above.

89. In which of the following type of organisation, the office work is concentrated?
   (a) Decentralised organisation
   (b) Functional organisation
   (c) Centralised organisation
   (d) None of the above

90. The main benefit of decentralisation is that
   (a) top executive is relieved of much of his burden.
   (b) operating cost of decentralized organisation is low.
   (c) burden on the top executive is increased.
   (d) co-ordination of various office activities becomes difficult.

91. Which of the following statements explains the relationship between office and other departments?
   (a) Office provides clerical services to the other departments.
   (b) Office provides expert advice to the other departments.
   (c) Other departments provide information required by office.
   (d) The activities of other departments are secondary to the activities of office.

92. Xerography is process of
   (a) fixing stamps
   (b) electrical photography

(c) printing addresses
(d) blueprinting

93. Which method of filing is described as the best?
(a) Box files
(b) Pigeon hole system
(c) Vertical filing
(d) Horizontal filing

94. The main advantage of centralised office organisation is
(a) the low cost of its operation.
(b) that secrecy of business affairs is maintained.
(c) that it leads to employment of larger number of supervisors.
(d) that wide dispersal of authority is possible.

95. Indexing is an important
(a) method of maintaining statistical books.
(b) aid to filing.
(c) method of maintaining account books.
(d) method of filing.

96. O and M refers to
(a) office work measurement.
(b) overall efficiency of business.
(c) efficiency of office and administrative work.
(d) None of the above.

97. Blue printing is also known as
(a) Diazo
(b) Lithography
(c) Xerography
(d) Micro filming

98. In which of the methods of filing, files or folders are kept in a standing upright position?
(a) Flat files
(b) Pigeon hole system
(c) Horizontal files
(d) Vertical files

99. The heart of a computer system is
(a) output device
(b) central processing unit
(c) input device
(d) None of the above

100. Which of the following methods of filing do you recommend for a large size undertaking?
(a) Vertical filing
(b) Pigeon hole system
(c) Spike files
(d) Box files

101. In vertical filing system, files or folders are kept
(a) in standing upright position.
(b) in packets on large envelopes.
(c) in a cupboard, divided into a number of small compartments.
(d) one upon the other.

102. Which of the following is the latest communication device?
(a) Speaking tubes (b) P.B.X.
(c) Telephone (d) Fax

103. Mimeograph is a
(a) method of photocopying.
(b) stencil duplicator.
(c) process of blue printing.
(d) process of electrical photography.

104. In which of the methods of filing, files or folders are kept in a horizontal position?
(a) Suspension filing
(b) Vertical filing
(c) Box files
(d) Lateral filing system

105. Memory unit is a part of
(a) electronic data processing.
(b) punched card system.
(c) both electronic data processing and punched card system.
(d) both punched card system and manually operated accounting machines.

106. The computations in a computer are performed by
(a) Output unit (b) Control unit
(c) Logical unit (d) Memory unit

107. "Memory Unit" performs the function of
(a) giving out the end product.
(b) calculations at a very high speed.
(c) storing the data.
(d) controlling all the operating units.

108. Output unit is an electronic computer performs the functions of
(a) controlling all the operating units.
(b) calculations at a very high speed.
(c) storing the data.
(d) giving out the end product.

109. The first electronic computer system was developed in
(a) 1930 (b) 1920
(c) 1950 (d) 1940

110. The concept of punched cards was invented by
(a) Blaise Pascal (b) Howard Aiken
(c) Hollerith (d) Babbage

111. A company in need of computer service may
(a) obtain a computer on hire.
(b) hire computer service.
(c) purchase a computer outright.
(d) Any of the above.

112. Computer 'hardware' refers to
(a) punched cards, punched paper tape or magnetic tapes.
(b) all of the equipment required for proper functioning of a programme.
(c) the end-product of final information obtained from the computer.
(d) data required for immediate working.

113. In order to get the fastest results in electronic computer, which of the following input media should be used?
(a) Magnetic tape
(b) Punched paper type
(c) Punched cards
(d) None of the above

114. Logical unit in an electronic computer performs the function of
(a) controlling all the operating units.
(b) calculations at a very high speed.
(c) storing the data.
(d) giving out the end-product.

115. An analogue computer makes
(a) measurements but not calculations.
(b) calculations but not measurement.
(c) both measurements and calculations.
(d) None of the above.

116. Which of the following is not a function, of an office?
(a) Keep a check on the quality of goods produced.
(b) Purchase of office furniture and machines.
(c) Handling communication system.
(d) Arranging for meetings and conferences.

117. In an electronic computer, the device used to transform the information from common language into machine language is
(a) arithmetic unit (b) input device
(c) interpreter unit (d) key punch

118. The use of office machine cannot
(a) save labour
(b) enhance production
(c) relieve monotony
(d) promote accuracy

119. The latest generation of personal computers (PCs) being used in an office set up is
(a) PC AT (b) PC 486
(c) PC XT (d) PC Pentium

120. Various filing equipment used includes
 (a) folders (b) flat tiles
 (c) lever arch files (d) cabinets

121. Office management is generally speaking the responsibility area of
 (a) Chief Executive
 (b) Corporate Controller
 (c) Works Manager
 (d) Chairman, Board of Directors

122. Which one of the following is the latest and the most reliable form of communication?
 (a) Fax (b) E-mail
 (c) Speed post (d) Telex

123. Liability of partners in respect of the firm's debt is
 (a) unlimited.
 (b) limited upto the amount of guarantee given by the partner.
 (c) limited upto the amount of his capital in the business.
 (d) limited upto the amount of his capital and loan to the firm if any.

124. The oldest form of business organisation is
 (a) co-operative undertaking
 (b) joint stock company
 (c) sole proprietorship
 (d) partnership

125. Partnership may come into existence
 (a) by an express agreement only.
 (b) by the operation of the law.
 (c) by inheritance of property.
 (d) by an express or implied agreement only.

126. In which of the following forms of business organisation registration is legaly compulsory?
 (a) Partnership
 (b) Sole properietorship
 (c) Co-operative undertaking
 (d) Joint stock company

127. A partner in a firm
 (a) can transfer his share to an outsider with the consent of all other partners.
 (b) can transfer his share to an outsider without the consent for any other partner.
 (c) can transfer his share to an outsider with the consent of majority partners.
 (d) cannot transfer his share to an outsider.

128. The liability of a role is
 (a) limited to the extent of the value of business assets and his all private assets.
 (b) limited to the extent of his capital invested in the business.
 (c) limited to the extent of the value of business assets.
 (d) None of the above.

129. A manager with a share in the profits
 (a) becomes a partner from status.
 (b) becomes a partner by implied agreement.
 (c) becomes a partner by the operation of law.
 (d) is only a servant of the firm.

130. Individual proprietorship form of business organisation is not advisable for the enterprises which
 (a) need personal attenion to customers.
 (b) require small amount of capital.
 (c) do not involve heavy risk.
 (d) are large in size.

131. Dissolution of partnership must take place when
 (a) a partner dies.
 (b) a partner misbehaves.
 (c) a partner becomes of unsound mind.
 (d) business is running at a loss.

132. The minimum number of partners in firm for a general business is
(a) 20 (b) 50
(c) 8 (d) 10

133. The agreement of partnership
(a) must be in writing on a stamp paper.
(b) must be oral.
(c) must be in writing.
(d) can be either oral or in writing.

134. The maximum number of partners in firm for a general business is
(a) 50 (b) 20
(c) 8 (d) 10

135. An association of persons becomes partnership
(a) when its purpose is to carry on business for profit motive.
(b) when its purpose is to carry on some charitable work.
(c) when its purpose is to render services for general welfare of mankind.
(d) All of the above.

136. The maximum number of partner in a firm has been specified by
(a) the Contract Act, 1986
(b) the Partnership Act, 1932
(c) the Companies Act, 1956
(d) None of the above

137. The maximum number of members in a public limited company is
(a) 80 (b) 40
(c) 20 (d) Unlimited

138. A partner has an implied authority to
(a) enter into a partnership on behalf of firm.
(b) to borrow money on behalf of the firm.
(c) acquire immovable property on behalf of the firm.
(d) None of the above.

139. The minimum number of members in a public limited company is
(a) 7 (b) 10
(c) 2 (d) 3

140. The minimum number of directors in a private limited company is
(a) 7 (b) 1
(c) 2 (d) 3

141. Registration of partnership is
(a) compuslory under the Indian Partnership Act.
(b) compulsory under the Income Tax Act.
(c) optional.
(d) None of the above.

142. The maximum number of members in a private limited company is
(a) 50 (b) 10
(c) 20 (d) unlimited

143. If a firm is not registered with the registrar of a firm,
(a) it introduces certain liabilities which make registration necessary at one time of the other.
(b) the members of the unregistered firm can enforce their rights between themselves.
(c) the members of the unregistered firm can file suit against third parties.
(d) it has to pay penalty for non-registration.

144. Limited partnership form of business organisation means
(a) the liability of some partners is limited.
(b) the number of partners is limited.
(c) the amount of capital that can be raised is limited.
(d) the liability of all partners is limited.

145. A nominal partner is
(a) entitled to equal share in the pofits unless there is an agreement to any other profit showing ratio.
(b) not liable to third parties.

(c) not entitled to share the profits of the concern.
(d) not liable for the acts of other partners.

146. Limited partnership organisation device is
(a) not provided by status in India.
(b) quite common in India.
(c) not common in India.
(d) None of the above.

147. The court may dissolve a firm where
(a) business has incurred huge loss in the current year.
(b) the firm of partnership has expired.
(c) a partner becomes of unsound mind.
(d) any one partner is declared insolvent.

148. Dissolution of firms takes place
(a) by the retirement of any one partner.
(b) by the death or insolvency of any one partner.
(c) by the insolvency of all but one partner.
(d) by the expiry of the term.

149. In the co-operative organisation, the voting rights of members are
(a) equal irrespective of amount of capital contribution.
(b) in proportion to the normal value of capital held by each member.
(c) in proportion to the capital paid by each member.
(d) None of the above.

150. The minimum number of directors in a public limited company is
(a) 7 (b) 10
(c) 2 (d) 3

151. A company is called an artificial person because
(a) it cannot be used in the court of law.
(b) it is invisible and intangible.
(c) it exists only in contemplation of law.
(d) it does not have the shape of natural persons.

152. The liability of shareholder of a public company is limited to the
(a) amounts called up.
(b) content of their private assets.
(c) nominal value of shares.
(d) paid-up value of shares.

153. The existence of a joint stock company is interrupted by
(a) the transfer of shares by members.
(b) the death of its members.
(c) the death of its directors.
(d) None of the above.

154. The most important advantage of a joint stock company form of business organisation is that
(a) members can conveniently transfer their share.
(b) the liability of its members is limited.
(c) it mobilises vast amount of financial resources.
(d) it offers infinite scope for expansion.

155. In the case of companies with ability limited by guarantee, the liability of members is limited
(a) to the additional amount payable in addition to the amount of share as laid down in the Memorandum of Association needs to arise.
(b) to the nominal values of shares.
(c) to the called up value of shares.
(d) None of the above.

156. A government company is one in which
(a) 50% of capital is held by central government and the remaining 50% by one or more state governments.
(b) at least 51% of the capital is held by central and/or state governments.

(c) the entire share capital is held by the central and/or state governments.
(d) None of the above.

157. A private limited company
(a) may not place any restriction on the transfer of its shares.
(b) must place some restrictions on the transfer of its share.
(c) must make its shares non-transferable.
(d) must not place any restrictions on the transfer of its shares.

158. A private limited company
(a) may not issue a prospectus, but in that case it must file a statement in lieu of prospectus.
(b) must issue a prospectus.
(c) must issue a prospectus and also file a statement in lieu of prospectus.
(d) may neither issue a prospectus nor file a statement in lieu of prospectus.

159. A private limited company
(a) must hold a statutory meeting within six months of certificate of incorporation.
(b) must hold a statutory meeting within one year of certificate of incorporation.
(c) need not hold a statutory meeting.
(d) must hold a statutory meeting within three months of certificate of incorporation.

160. A private limited company can commence business
(a) only when it receives both, the certificate of incorporation and certificate of commencement of business.
(b) immediately on receiving a certificate of incorporation.
(c) only when it receives certificate of commencement of business.
(d) without receiving a certificate of incorporation.

161. No person can hold at the same time as director in more than
(a) 10 companies (b) 20 companies
(c) 5 companies (d) 7 companies

162. The liability of members of a co-operative society is
(a) limited or unlimited depending upon what the society has opted for.
(b) limited to the amount of normal value of capital held.
(c) limited to the amount of paid up value of the capital held.
(d) unlimited.

163. Reserve Bank of India is a
(a) a company limited by guarantee.
(b) statutory corporation.
(c) an unlimited company.
(d) a company limited by shares.

164. The minimum number of members required for registration of a co-operative society is
(a) 10 (b) 20
(c) 2 (d) 7

165. The life of a co-operative society is
(a) affected by the insolvency of a member.
(b) affected by the withdrawal by a member from membership.
(c) not affected by death, insolvency, etc. of members.
(d) affected by the death of member.

166. The basic objective of co-operative society is to
(a) organise some essential service for the benefit of its members.
(b) earn profits.
(c) arrange for enough of quality goods for the community at large.
(d) organise essential services for the community at large.

167. Trading in a consumer's co-operative store is
(a) that credit facilities are available for both members and non-members.
(b) on cash basis only.
(c) on cash basis for non-member and credit facilities for members.
(d) None of the above.

168. Co-operative and public companies are similar in respect of
(a) the minimum number of members.
(b) the liability of member.
(c) the minimum number of members required for registration.
(d) None of the above.

169. A member of co-operative society can value the society by
(a) transferring no share to another person with the consent of the managing committee.
(b) transferring his share to another person without any body's consent.
(c) withdrawing his capital from the society.
(d) transferring his share to a fellow member.

170. Profits earned by a co-operative society are distributed
(a) to members in the ratio of capital held by them.
(b) by declaring divident at a specific rate and transferring remaining to general reserves.
(c) by providing a nominal rate of interest on capital contribution by members and remaining the ratio of purchases made by members.
(d) to members in the ratio of purchases made by them.

171. Management of a co-operative organisation is in the hands of
(a) an elected body by the members.
(b) the promoters of the co-operative organisation.
(c) persons nominated by the registrar of co-operative societies.
(d) None of the above.

172. Which of the following is an example of a company incorporated by a special act of Parliament?
(a) Industrial Finance Corporation of India Ltd.
(b) Delhi Cloth and General Mills Ltd.
(c) Swadeshi Cotton Mills Ltd.
(d) Tata Iron and Steel Co. Ltd.

173. Every co-operative has to get units accounts audited by
(a) any person approved by a managing committee of the co-operative society.
(b) an auditor from the co-operative department.
(c) a qualified chartered accountant.
(d) qualified chartered or cost accountant.

174. The articles of association establishes relationship between
(a) company and its members and members interse.
(b) company and its members.
(c) company and outsiders.
(d) None of the above.

175. 'Table A' of companies Act gives
(a) a model articles of association.
(b) a model form of balance sheet.
(c) a model minute book.
(d) a model memorandum of association.

176. Companies which need not frame their own articles of association are
(a) companies limited by guarantee.
(b) public companies limited by shares.
(c) unlimited companies.
(d) private companies limited by shares.

177. Which of the following is the most important documents of the company?
(a) Annual Report
(b) Memorandum of Association
(c) Articles of Association
(d) Prospectus

178. A shareholder in a company
(a) cannot be its debenture-holder.
(b) can be its denture-holders.
(c) Both of the above.
(d) None of the above.

179. Which of the following documents contains rules and regulations for internal management of the company?
(a) Articles of Association
(b) Prospectus
(c) Memorandum of Association
(d) None of the above

180. Which of the following documents defines the relation of the companies with outside world?
(a) Articles of Association
(b) Prospectus
(c) Memorandum of Association
(d) None of the above

181. Dividend on preference capital will be paid
(a) even if there are no profits.
(b) only when there are profits and when directors recommend.
(c) only when there are profits.
(d) None of the above.

182. Which of the following documents defines the scope of the company's activities?
(a) Articles of Association
(b) Memorandum of Association
(c) Statuary Declaration
(d) Prospectus

183. When at least 8% of the share capital is held by government, then it is called
(a) government company
(b) public corporation
(c) public interprise
(d) public company

184. A company is said to have been registered when
(a) it gets certificate of incorporation from registrar of companies.
(b) it filed with the registrar of companies certain documents, like memorandum and articles of association.
(c) it actually starts its business.
(d) it gets certificate of commencement of business from registrar of companies.

185. A private company
(a) cannot issue shares with disproportionate voting rights.
(b) can issue deferred shares with disproportionate voting rights.
(c) Both of the above.
(d) Neither (a) nor (b).

186. Name of a company can be changed by
(a) a special resolution.
(b) an ordinary resolution.
(c) a special resolution and under approval of the central government.
(d) an approval of the central government.

187. A change in the registered office of the company from one state to another can be effected by
(a) an ordinary resolution.
(b) a resolution of the board of directors.
(c) a special resolution and confirmation from the company law board.
(d) a special resolution.

188. So far as internal proceedings of a company are concerned, any outside dealing with the company is entitled to assume that

(a) regularity of the internal proceedings must be enquired into before dealing with the company.
(b) everything has been regularly done.
(c) everything has not been regularly done.
(d) None of the above.

189. Which of the following documents need not be prepared and registered with the registrar of companies in public limited companies?
(a) Articles of Association
(b) Statutory Declaration
(c) Director's undertaking to take up and pay for qualification shares
(d) Memorandum of Association

190. Any person dealing with the company is deemed to have a knowledge of its
(a) Memorandum as well as Articles.
(b) need not have knowledge of Memorandum of Articles.
(c) Memorandum of Association.
(d) Articles of Association.

191. Which of the following companies can adopt 'Table A' in place of Articles of Association?
(a) Public limited companies
(b) Unlimited companies
(c) Private limited companies
(d) All of the above

192. Which of the following companies must file a statement in lieu of prospectus?
(a) A public company which has not issued a prospectus.
(b) A private limited company.
(c) A company which has issued as prospectus.
(d) All of the above.

193. Which of the following can be changed with reprospective effect?
(a) Articles of Association
(b) Prospectus
(c) Memorandum of Association
(d) None of the above

194. The value of qualification shares of directors need not exceed
(a) ₹ 8,000 (b) ₹ 10,000
(c) ₹ 1,000 (d) ₹ 2,000

195. 'Objects clause' of the memorandum can be altered by
(a) special resolution and confirmation by company law board.
(b) ordinary resolution.
(c) special resolution.
(d) special resolution and confirmation by registrar of companies.

196. Which of the following types of alternative in Articles of Association is permitted?
(a) An alteration which is contrary to the provisions of the companies Act.
(b) An alteration which may not be in the interest of the company on a whole.
(c) An alteration which in consistent with the Memorandum of Association.
(d) An alteration that increases the liability of member without his written consent.

197. When the Articles of Association does not authorise the change in the capital then order to alter the capital of a companies.
(a) Permission of the registrar of companies should be obtained.
(b) Table 'A' should be adopted.
(c) 'Article' should be attended.
(d) None of the above.

198. While incorporating a company, a statutory declaration should be made by
(a) an advocate
(b) a Chartered Accountant

(c) a person named in the articles as Director
(d) Any of the above

199. A company deemed to be public company as per Sec. 43A must have at least
(a) three directors (b) two directors
(c) five directors (d) four directors

200. Which of the following is not an economic activity?
(a) Vocation (b) Sports
(c) Business (d) Social Work

201. Which of these is an international agency for worker's education?
(a) ILO (b) NLI
(c) GLI (d) CLI

202. Which chapter of Factories Act provide for working hours of adults?
(a) VII (b) VIII
(c) VI (d) All of the above

203. Fencing of machinery comes under
(a) education programme
(b) welfare programme
(c) health programme
(d) safety programme

204. Control is a complimentary function to
(a) Controlling (b) Determine
(c) Organising (d) Planning

205. Grapevine is also called
(a) Upward communication
(b) Downward communication
(c) Organising
(d) Informal communication

206. Grievances resulting from management policy are
(a) Company rules
(b) Wage payment and job rates
(c) Both (a) and (b)
(d) None of the above

207. Horizontal communication is the communication in between members of different work groups at
(a) different organisation level
(b) inter-departmental level
(c) same organisation level
(d) None of the above

208. Flow of information from managers to its subordinates is
(a) downward communication
(b) horizontal communication
(c) vertical communication
(d) upward communication

209. Development of an organisation without changing its structure is done by
(a) MD (b) MBO
(c) OD (d) None of these

210. Expand MBO
(a) Management by Objectives
(b) Management of Business Organisation
(c) Management of Business Officials
(d) Management by Observations

211. Need theory of motivation is formulated by
(a) Varoom (b) McClelland
(c) Maslow (d) Herzberg

212. Mathematical formula to calculate human $n\left(\frac{2^n}{2}+n-1\right)$. Here n is
(a) Employees
(b) Executives
(c) Authority
(d) No. of subordinates

213. Who offered general principle of Management over scientific management
(a) O'Donell
(b) Koontz
(c) Henry Fayol
(d) F. Winslow Taylor

214. RBI comes under
(a) Departmental organisations
(b) Govt. Company
(c) Multinational Company
(d) Public Corporation

215. The state shall direct its policy towards securing that there is equal pay for equal work for both men and women, comes under
(a) Article 39 (b) Article 33
(c) Article 41 (d) Article 43

216. Company created by special Act of Parliament
(a) Statutory Company
(b) Chartered Company
(c) Public Company
(d) Registered Company

217. A company making any issue of shares or debentures must receive a minimum of subscription before making any allotment
(a) 80% (b) 90%
(c) 50% (d) 70%

218. Complete the steps involved in the process of communication, Ideation, Encoding, Transmission, ______, Decoding, Acting.
(a) Rejecting (b) Receiving
(c) Repeating (d) Reporting

219. Which of the following is true with respect to planning function?
(a) Monitoring whether the things allocated are done properly.
(b) To make a blue print of ideas and work.
(c) To tell the work allocation to all.
(d) All of the above.

220. Which meeting is held only once during the life time of the company?
(a) Annual general meeting
(b) Creditor's's meeting
(c) Statutory meeting
(d) Extraordinary meeting

221. The articles of association establishes relationship between
(a) company and its members
(b) members interse
(c) company and outsiders
(d) Both (a) and (b)

222. A statutory meeting need not be held by
(a) company limited by guarantee
(b) public company
(c) private company
(d) All of the above

223. Experts of specialists are attached to managers in
(a) functional organisation
(b) line organisation
(c) line and staff organisation
(d) All of the above

224. Planning function is mainly performed at
(a) middle management level
(b) lower management level
(c) top management level
(d) None of the above

225. Functional approach to management was developed by
(a) Fayol (b) Louis Allen
(c) Taylor (d) Terry

226. Which theory of motivation assumes that average human being dislikes to work
(a) Equity theory
(b) McGregor's theory X
(c) Theory Y
(d) Maslow's theory

227. The company secretary is appointed by the
(a) board of directors.
(b) board of directors with approval from the central government.
(c) shareholders in general meeting.
(d) central government.

228. In the case of private companies—quorum for company meetings is ____ members personally present in the meeting.
(a) 5 (b) 4
(c) 3 (d) 2

229. Which of the following is the top administrative organ of the company?
(a) Managing director
(b) General manager
(c) Board of directors
(d) Shareholders

230. Converting public company into a private ltd., company requires
(a) special resolution and central government approval.
(b) special resolution.
(c) special resolution and company law board approval.
(d) All of the above.

231. The founder of modern scientific management is
(a) Dickinson (b) Henry Fayol
(c) Mc. Farland (d) F.W. Taylor

232. In the field of management some of the important techniques, relate to budgeting, cost according, planning and control through
(a) PERT and CPM
(b) budgetary control
(c) financial administration
(d) operational research

233. Economic oligarchy, fraudulent practices, bureaucratic management and difficulty in formation are the limitations of a
(a) partnership firm.
(b) sale propertory concern.
(c) co-operative society.
(d) joint stock company.

234. Combination of printing and dyeing companies is a type of
(a) horizontal combination
(b) circular combination
(c) allied combination
(d) vertical combination

235. If the Brooke Bond Company merges with the Lipton company, it would be an example of
(a) horizontal combination
(b) vertical combination
(c) diagonal intergration
(d) lateral integration

236. Leadership is a function of all of the following factors except
(a) Situation
(b) Leader
(c) Product or Service
(d) Work group

237. Which one of the following is not related to the trait theory of leadership?
(a) Intelligence and extroversion.
(b) Physical factors such as height.
(c) Training and experience of employees.
(d) Self-confidence and ambition.

238. The process of grouping activities into units for the purpose of administration may be referred to as
(a) Specialisation
(b) Departmentalisation
(c) Decentralisation
(d) Co-ordination

239. Span of control means that
(a) every subordinate has one superior.
(b) a manager can supervise only limited number of subordinates.
(c) an organisation consists of various departments.
(d) each person's authority is clearly defined.

240. Which one of the following principle states that recurring decisions should be

handled in a routine manner by lower level managers whereas problems involving unusual matters only should be referred to higher levels?

(a) Principle of commitment
(b) Principle of unity of command
(c) Scalar principle
(d) Principle of exception.

241. M.B.O. is a technique which requires that the objectives of the enterprise
(a) lay down the time period for achieving the results.
(b) be written and defined in broad terms.
(c) be defined in terms of measurable results.
(d) include a plan of action for achieving the desired result.

242. Job specification is
(a) a statement of the skills and abilities needed in the performance of a job.
(b) the specifications required for the job.
(c) the manner in which the job is to be performed.
(d) a statement of the duties and responsiblities of job.

243. Which one of the following is the correct sequence of 'records management process'?
(a) Utilisation, creation, retrieval, disposition, storage.
(b) Creation, retrieval, utilisation, storage, disposition.
(c) Retrieval, creation, utilisation, disposition, storage.
(d) Creation, utilisation, storage, retrieval, disposition.

244. 'Work Study is a part of Motion Study' is a statement that is
(a) false, but the reverse is true.
(b) true, and vice versa too.
(c) false, as it is part of Time Study also.
(d) true, as work cannot be studied without action.

245. Perpetuity and separate legal entity are the two most important distinctive features of
(a) Partnership
(b) Sole proprietorship form of business
(c) Joint Hindu family firm
(d) Company

246. Which one of the following is the oldest form of organisation?
(a) Line and staff organisation
(b) Functional organisation
(c) Departmentation
(d) Line organisation

247. Management audit is conducted by
(a) government auditors
(b) cost auditors
(c) the statutory auditors
(d) None of the above

248. System of internal check is said to exist in an organisation when
(a) the departmental head checks the work of his subordinate.
(b) an employee is specifically deputed to check the work of another employee.
(c) another employee of the same department check.
(d) some outside experts check the work of employees.

249. Management audit is
(a) a statutory requirement.
(b) an independent appraisal of the total management process.
(c) an independent appraisal of competitiveness of business.
(d) an investigation into the conduct of director.

250. Setting the mission which empasses objectives, policies and goals in known as
(a) strategic planning
(b) operational planning
(c) contingency planning
(d) tractical planning

251. Minimum wages are fixed by the
(a) employers
(b) trade unions
(c) courts of law
(d) state governments

252. Brainstorming is used by the management for
(a) generating alternative for problem solving.
(b) work allocation on the shop floor.
(c) training employees.
(d) the promotion or research and development.

253. Which one of the following statements is correct?
(a) Minutes contain a much more detailed account of all matters of the meeting where as reports have fewer details.
(b) There is very little difference between the minutes and reports except that one is brief and cotains only action points while the other (reports) contains details including pros and cons of a particular decision.
(c) Minutes has the legal recognition by virtue of the provisions contained in the Companies Act, while reports have no such legal sancity.
(d) Minutes have no legal sancity but reports have legal sancity by virtue of the provisions contained in the Companies Act.

254. Rate of consumption of materials is one of the most important factors while fixing
(a) maximum level and reorder level.
(b) maximum level.
(c) maximum level, minimum level and reorder level.
(d) minimum level and reorder level.

255. Which one of the following may not necessarily be an advantage of co-ordination?
(a) Unity of direction
(b) Effective supervision
(c) Summarisation of all management functions
(d) Creative force

256. In the last-in-first-out (LIFO) method, the closing stock is valued at
(a) a price which is paid for the earlier consignments.
(b) an average price of all the consignments.
(c) a price which is paid for the last consignment.
(d) None of the above.

257. Any organization that employs a multiple command structure but also related support mechanisms and an associated organisational culture and behaviour pattern, is known as
(a) Flat structure
(b) Project organization
(c) Tall structure
(d) Matrix organization

258. A process of combining a series of tasks into a new, broader job that provides the worker with greater work variety and a greater sense of responsibility is known as
(a) Job analysis
(b) Job enlargement
(c) Job simplification
(d) Job enrichment

259. Scalar principle in management is also known as
(a) Chain of command
(b) Unity of command

(c) Esprit de corps
(d) Management by exception

260. Which one of the following defines co-ordination?
(a) Process of determining what is to be accomplished and what has been accomplished.
(b) Actuating force which inspires a person to put his best for the fulfilment of a task.
(c) Orderly arrangement of group effort to provide unity of action in the pursuit of a common goal.
(d) Process of transmitting information from one person to another or from one unit to another.

261. The formal procedure for obtaining consensus of a number of expert through a series of questionnaires is
(a) Synectics
(b) Delphi technique
(c) Brainstorming
(d) Nominal group technique

262. Which of the following motivational theories states that the average human being avoids responsibility and needs to be controlled and directed by his superiors?
(a) Herzberg's theory
(b) Maslow's theory
(c) Theory X
(d) Theory Y

263. Communication between departments of an organization that generally follows the work flow rather than the chain of command is termed as
(a) Grapevine chains
(b) Informal communication
(c) Vertical communication
(d) Lateral communication

264. Which one of the following is not related to the trait theory of leadership?
(a) Intelligence and extroversion
(b) Physical factors such as height
(c) Training and experience of employees
(d) Self-confidence and ambition

265. Leaders who guide their followers in the direction of established goals by clarifying role and task requirements are known as
(a) Charismatic leaders
(b) Transactional leaders
(c) Autocratic leaders
(d) Transformational leaders

266. In Taylor's functional organisation, what does the gangboss perform?
(a) He sets up tools and machines for the workers.
(b) He inspects the quality of work done.
(c) He compiles cost of production.
(d) He issues instructions to workers.

267. Broad organisational goals, based on planning premises, which justifies an organization's existence, is called
(a) Operational plan
(b) Vision statement
(c) Mission statement
(d) Strategic plan

268. The plans that establish a required method of handling future activities are called
(a) Objectives (b) Mission
(c) Programs (d) Procedures

269. Span of control also described as
(a) Span of co-ordination
(b) Span of attention
(c) Span of subjugation
(d) Span of authority

270. Who is the great supporter of the principle of unity of command?
(a) H. Fayol
(b) Pfiffner and Presthus

(c) H. Simon
(d) Secklor-Hudson

271. Which one of the following is considered as the first principle of organisation?
(a) Co-ordination
(b) Delegation
(c) Supervision
(d) Unity of command

272. Which one of the following is considered as first principle of management?
(a) Line, staff, auxilliary agencies
(b) Co-ordination
(c) Supervision
(d) Delegation

273. Who said, "Co-oridnation is much more than collective action and means synchronization of efforts"?
(a) M.P. Follett (b) Appleby
(c) Seckier-Hudson (d) Terry

274. Find out the correct answer.
(a) Co-ordination is not a distinct function, but the very essence of management.
(b) Heart of co-ordination is unity of actions.
(c) Co-ordination is the basic responsibility of management.
(d) All of the above.

275. The human realtions theory rejects
(a) Informal functioning
(b) Formal institutionalisation
(c) People
(d) Human motivation

276. Find the odd one out
(a) Structural theory
(b) Human relations theory
(c) Informal functioning
(d) Humanistic theory

277. This type of informal overlay describes the pattern of relationships growing out of the feelings of social attraction or rejection that people have each other
(a) Socio-metric overlay
(b) Communication overlay
(c) Decision overlay
(d) Power overlay

278. This type of informal overlay refers to contacts such as those between the staff specialist and those in the organisation who directly seek his guidance or co-operation outside the formal channels
(a) Functional overlay
(b) Socio-metric overlay
(c) Power overlay
(d) Decision overlay

279. This type of overlay describes the relationship based on going directly to the people who have the real influence in reaching a decision and by passing the formal lines
(a) the power overlay
(b) the communication overlay
(c) the functional overlay
(d) the decision overlay

280. This type of informal overlay indicates the key people who can accomplish something because they know the ropes:
(a) the functional overlay
(b) the communication overlay
(c) the power overlay
(d) the decision overlay

281. This type of informal overlay reveals the acutal pattern of pathways which information such as correspondence takes in moving through an organisation
(a) Communication overlay
(b) Power overlay
(c) Decision overlay
(d) Functional overlay

282. One who passes unfavourable information about his colleagues to the superior is called

(a) A cheater (b) A squealer
(c) A rate buster (d) A chiseller

283. The greatest weakness of the informal organisation is
(a) its behaviour can be predicted
(b) it does not change
(c) its utter instability
(d) All of the above

284. If a leader is seen to possess certain traits, his leadership index can be read off a leadership meter. This statement relates to
(a) Attitude approach
(b) Criterion approach
(c) Administrative approach
(d) Trait approach

285. Michigan leadership studies are based on the following approach to the study of leadership
(a) Attitude criterion
(b) Behaviour approach
(c) Situational approach
(d) Trait approach

286. McGregor's Theory 'X' approximates to
(a) Production orientation
(b) Input orientation
(c) Employee orientation
(d) Employment orientation

287. Theory 'Y' approximates to
(a) Production orientation
(b) Employee orientation
(c) Input orientation
(d) Employment orientation

288. The authoritarian leadership style goes with
(a) Theory Z (b) Theory X
(c) Theory Y (d) None of these

289. The democratic leadership style goes with
(a) Theory Y (b) Theory Z
(c) Theory X (d) None of these

290. "In this style, the leader consults his team and drives them to the goal which is well defined and set with common constant." The reference is to
(a) low-high management style
(b) low-low management style
(c) high-low management style
(d) high-high management style

291. In this style, the leader is authoritarian, task-oriented, derives power from his authority position and levels his team with instructions and discipline. The leadership style is known as
(a) high-high management style
(b) high-low management style
(c) low-low management style
(d) low-high management style

292. In this system, the leader keeps his team in good humour, underplays problems, pleases, often placates followers to get things done as best as the team will allow
(a) high-high management style
(b) high-low management style
(c) low-low management style
(d) low-high management style

293. The ultimate aim of all leadership theories and models is to build
(a) a process that leads to optimisation.
(b) a postulate for maximising benefits.
(c) a cause and effect relationship.
(d) a leadership model.

294. For planning and decision-making, the method that consists in analysing and stimulating is known as
(a) The model (b) Experience
(c) Experiment (d) Any of the above

295. "Leadership is the activity of influencing people to strive willingly for group objectives". Leadership has been so defined by
(a) George R. Terry
(b) Carry O' Donnel

(c) Fred Massarik
(d) Irving R. Weschler

296. Who of the following did not argue for small 'Span of Control'?
(a) V.A. Graicunas
(b) L. Urwick
(c) I. Hamilton
(d) H. Simon

297. The word administration is derived from the Latin word ad + ministration, which means
(a) to advise the government.
(b) to look after people to manage affairs.
(c) to add to the resources of the ministries.
(d) to advertise ministerial efforts.

298. The scientific management movement gave a great fillip to the use of this method in the development of effective techniques of organisation and management and of budgeting and supply.
(a) True (b) Can't say
(c) It is debatable (d) False

299. The overall goal of scientific management is
(a) maximisation of social welfare.
(b) higher industrial efficiency.
(c) maximisation of employment.
(d) None of the above.

300. Who used for the first time the term scientific management?
(a) F.W. Taylor (b) Max Weber
(c) Louis Braudies (d) V.D. Gournay

301. How many principles of organisation propounded by Henry Fayol?
(a) 7 (b) 14
(c) 6 (d) 20

302. According to the Taylor's scientific management theory, the main motivator for workers was
(a) The power
(b) Self development
(c) The prestige
(d) The money

303. F.W. Taylor called "the Military type of foreman" to
(a) unity of command
(b) span of control
(c) delegated legislature
(d) department

304. The ultimate goal of OD is to
(a) reduce the levels of uncertainty in managerial decision-making throughout the organization.
(b) create an internal environment which is conducive to self-expression.
(c) structure the organizational environment so that managers and employees can use their developed skills and abilities to the fullest.
(d) None of the above.

305. Formal rewards provided by oragnizations that do not lend themselves to being related to performance include all of the following except
(a) Paid holidays (b) Paid vacations
(c) Retirement plans (d) Merit plans

306. In Taylor's functional foremanship, the repairs and maintenance of machine is looked after by
(a) gang boss (b) inspector
(c) speed boss (d) repair boss

307. Examination of alternative courses of action is an activity which falls under
(a) control function
(b) direction function
(c) organisation function
(d) planning function

308. Effective supervision is an activity of
(a) direction function
(b) control function

(c) staffing function
(d) organisation function

309. This analysis helps in improved decision making where scarce economic resources have to be employed among competing projects. Setting priorities, in effectively done through this analysis.
(a) The cost-benefit analysis
(b) The marginal analysis
(c) The limiting factor analysis
(d) The differential analysis

310. It is the process of appraising a situation within an environment in the midst of a number of opportunities and constraints with the object of optimising the goal.
(a) Cost-benefit approach
(b) The differential approach
(c) Marginal analysis
(d) Management planning

311. Motivation is an element of
(a) direction function
(b) planning function
(c) organisation function
(d) control function

312. The principle that a subordinate should receive order and be responsible to only one boss is known as
(a) span of control
(b) unity of command
(c) unity of direction
(d) None of the above

313. The delegation of authority depends on the subordinate's
(a) ability and potential.
(b) training.
(c) educational qualifications.
(d) None of the above.

314. Span of control is narrow than the
(a) posts in the middle management increases.
(b) posts in the top management are few.
(c) Both (a) and (b).
(d) None of the above.

315. Delegation of authority is effective when
(a) dual subordination is avoided.
(b) the concern is doing business in different branches.
(c) responsibility is avoided.
(d) All of the above.

316. In equity theory, the employees are not motivated when
(a) reward is more than the expectation.
(b) the reward falls below the expectation.
(c) the reward is not proportionate to the work.
(d) None of the above.

317. Superior-subordinate relationship on the basis of personal likes, dislikies, attitudes and prejudices results in
(a) informal organisation
(b) formal organisation
(c) no organisation
(d) All of the above

318. In the organisation, authority flows in a vertical line
(a) from the bottom upward
(b) from the top downward
(c) Both ways downward and upward
(d) None of the above

319. Grapevine is a term used in relation to
(a) informal communication.
(b) formal communication.
(c) this term is not used related to communication.
(d) Both (a) and (b).

320. Effort-reward relationship is considered in
(a) McClelland's theory of motivation.
(b) Equity theory of motivation.
(c) Varoom's theory of motivation.
(d) None of the above.

321. Which of the following is an important dynamic variable?
(a) The task structure
(b) Superior's style and behaviour
(c) Cultural variables
(d) Organisational nature

322. It is desire to maximize one's potential and to become what one is capable of becoming. The reference is to
(a) self-actualization needs
(b) self-esteem needs
(c) security needs
(d) physiological needs

323. Its basic premise is that the behaviour of human beings is determined by the sum of external environmental factors and not by internal needs, desires and wants. The reference is to
(a) Skinner's Operant Theory of Motivation.
(b) Adam's Equity Theory of Motivation.
(c) Vroom's Contingency Model of Motivation.
(d) All of the above.

324. A management step which is already systematised, pre-determined by rules, regulations or procedures is better known as
(a) An unprogrammed decision
(b) A management decision
(c) A programmed decision
(d) An act of management

325. Simon observes that serious blockades may occur at three levels of communication. Which of the following is not one of them?
(a) Transmission (b) Reception
(c) Initiation (d) Noise

326. Which of the following is not important hinderance to effective communication?
(a) Resistance to change
(b) Language difficulties
(c) Employee's relationship with the management
(d) Status distance

327. One person gets some infection and passes it on to everyone he meets. The reference is to ______ grapevine.
(a) gossip (b) single-strand
(c) cluster chain (d) probability chin

328. Managerial grid suggests the following as the best leader-behaviour.
(a) High structure and high consideration.
(b) Low structure and low consideration.
(c) High concern both for production and people.
(d) Low concern both for production and people.

329. "Superiors with the best records of performance focus their primary attention on the human aspects of their subordinates' problems and on endeavouring to build effective work groups with high performance goals." The observation has been made by
(a) Ohio State University
(b) Rensis Likert
(c) Michigan Model
(d) Andrew W. Halpin

330. Likert believed the following types of leaders to be more effective.
(a) Task-oriented
(b) Job-centred
(c) People-centred
(d) Production-oriented

331. Effective leadership behaviour is a result of following variable.
(a) Consideration (b) Environment
(c) Structure (d) All of the above

332. Structure variable is synonymous with
(a) Style (b) Attitude
(c) Task (d) Relations

333. Consideration is synonymous with
(a) Relations (b) Attitude
(c) Task (d) Style

334. Environment is synonymous with
(a) Relations
(b) Task
(c) Situational variables
(d) People

335. Which of the following is not an important factor in decision-making?
(a) Attitude of superiors and subordinates.
(b) The name of the organisation.
(c) Competence and morale of the decision-making.
(d) Relevant facts gathered by the staff agencies.

336. Who says, that "the necessary production of leaders to the population has greatly increased"?
(a) M.P. Follett
(b) C.I. Barnard
(c) Seckler-Hudson
(d) H.C. Metcaff

337. Which one of the following leadership is based on organisational status?
(a) Diplomatic leadership
(b) Informal leadership
(c) Bureaucratic leadership
(d) Charismatic leadership

338. The traditional theory of organisation is based on
(a) Specialization
(b) Principle of hierarchy
(c) Both (a) and (b)
(d) None of the above

339. Which of the following theories provides a criticism of the classical theory of organisation?
(a) Human Relations theory
(b) Scientific Management theory
(c) Bureaucratic theory
(d) Administration theory

340. Which of the following principles of organisation stipulates a worker to receive orders from one superrior only?
(a) Unity of Command
(b) Unity of Direction
(c) Hierarchy
(d) Co-ordination

341. Hierarchy has been described as the 'Scalar process' by
(a) P.H. Appleby
(b) L.D. White
(c) Gullick and Urwick
(d) Mooney and Reiley

342. "Hierarchy consists in the universal application of the superior-subordinate relationship through a number of levels of responsibility reaching from the top to the bottom of the structure."
This observaion is attributed to
(a) T.D. Mooney
(b) L. Gullick
(c) Lyndal Urns CR.
(d) L.D. White

343. 'Focus on Social Environment' is related to
(a) Delegation
(b) Unity of Command
(c) Human Relations
(d) Unity of Direction

344. The term 'General System Theory' owes its origin to
(a) John A. Verg
(b) Max Weber
(c) Taylor
(d) Lundurg Von Bertalanffy

345. ______ has been defined as the means of "conferring authority from one executive of organisation unit to another".

(a) Staff (b) Delegation
(c) Decentralization (d) Hierarchy

346. It is "the orderly arrangement of group efforts, to provide unity of action in pursuit of a common purpose". This statement refers to
(a) Hierarchy (b) Delegation
(c) Co-ordination (d) None of these

347. The "right to give orders and the power to exact obedience" is known as
(a) Authority (b) Power
(c) Responsibility (d) Accountability

348. Which of the following is not a staff agency?
(a) Cabinet Secretariat
(b) Planning Commission
(c) PM's Secretariat
(d) None of the above

349. A Line agency does not have
(a) Independent Staff
(b) Advisory and Co-ordinating functions
(c) Operatting Unit
(d) None of the above

350. According to Pfiffner, which one of the following is not a type to staff?
(a) Auxiliary (b) Technical
(c) Specialist (d) General

351. Who calls 'Auxiliary agency' as 'House keeping' one?
(a) Willonghby (b) White
(c) Seekler Hudson (d) Pfiffner

352. It only implies the transfer of functions and not of authority. The reference is to
(a) Co-ordination (b) Delegation
(c) Decentralization (d) None of these

353. "The right adjustment between line and staff constitutes one of the most different areas of management". Who said it?
(a) Weber and Marx
(b) Fayol and Taylor
(c) Dimock and Kocing
(d) None of the above

354. Henri Fayol supports the
(a) Mechanistic approach
(b) Humanistic approach
(c) Scientific approach
(d) Organic approach

355. Who authored the book *Policy and Management*?
(a) Dimock (b) Appleby
(c) Gladden (d) Weber

356. Under this plan those who produce above standards receive higher wages than those producing below standards.
(a) Follott's differential piecework plan
(b) Fayol's differential piecework plan
(c) Taylor's differential piecework plan
(d) None of the above

357. The direction of its goal proceeds straight towards the enterprising goal. This element is to be found in
(a) the Line function
(b) the Staff function
(c) Both (a) and (b)
(d) None of the above

358. Staff explosion refers to explosion of people manning the function. This is also known as
(a) The Graicunas Law
(b) The Creep Effect
(c) The Riggrian Law
(d) The Parkinson Law

359. The most logical criterion to distinguish a line function from staff is
(a) The Authority relationship
(b) The Functional relationship
(c) The Grouping
(d) The Departmentalisation

360. A study on the subject had concluded "effective or desirable leadership behaviour

is characterised by high scores on both imitating structure and consideration conversely, ineffective or undesirable leadership behaviour is marked by low scoreson both dimensions".
Who had conducted this study?
(a) Andrew W. Halpin
(b) Ohio State University
(c) Cartwright and Zander
(d) Tannebau and Schimdt

361. The calculation of expected outcomes is intended to help the manager.
(a) evaluate solutions
(b) idenfiy problems
(c) identify solutions
(d) All of the above

362. Which of the following is considered to be a systematised cyclic pattern of communication?
(a) Management Information System
(b) Formal Information System
(c) Informal Information System
(d) All of the above

363. Who of the following is related to path goal theory of leadership?
(a) Abraham Maslow
(b) R. Likert
(c) Chester Bernard
(d) Douglas McGregor

364. A leader who commands skill and experience not shared by any other possess what may be called?
(a) Autocratic power
(b) Dominant power
(c) Monopoly power
(d) Coercive power

365. In Likert's system approach which of the following characteristics is not trust in system?
(a) Fear is the main motivator.
(b) There is free communication between the leader and the subordinate.
(c) The leader does not trust the subordinates and closely supervises them.
(d) The leader defines the work in great detail.

366. Which of the following is not correct about the essential features of the internal communication process in an organisation?
(a) Communication involves people.
(b) Communication involves shared meaning.
(c) Communication requires instruments like radio telephone or television, etc.
(d) Communication is symbolic.

367. Oral communication in an organisation is:
(a) Discretionary Communication
(b) Formal Communication
(c) Informal Communication
(d) All of the above

368. Which of the following statement about the basic characteristics of the phenomenon of motivation is not correct?
(a) Like needs, the goals also originate within the individual only.
(b) It derives people's behaviour towards goals that are pay-offs or incentives.
(c) Achievement of goals creates satisfaction which in turn reinforce perpetuation of the needs.
(d) An internal need within the individual creates a desire or drive.

369. To study an individual consumer's behaviour, we need
(a) Consumer behaviour science
(b) Micro economics
(c) Macro economics
(d) None of the above

370. The motion of men implicit in the classical theory lends to generate a kind of employee psyche, which may be described as

(a) Aggressive
(b) Submissive
(c) Deficiency-oriented
(d) Self-development oriented

371. The main focus of Human Relations theory is on
(a) Participatory decision-making
(b) Individual
(c) Informal organisation
(d) Formal organisation

372. Who described the phenomenon that each employee engaged in a staff function creates work for his colleagues
(a) Parkinson (b) W. Wilson
(c) Creep (d) D. Waldo

373. Theory is the formulation of universal principles of organisation
(a) Scientific Management
(b) Classical theory
(c) Human Relations theory
(d) Bureaucratic theory

374. Accent of Human Relation theory is
(a) Hierarchy-oriented
(b) Organisation-oriented
(c) Action-oriented
(d) None of the above

375. According to Fayol, activities in an organisation may be divided into _____ elements.
(a) 5 (b) 4
(c) 9 (d) 6

376. Human Relations theory treats an organisation as
(a) An open system
(b) An non-existing system
(c) A closed system
(d) None of the above

377. The Human Relations theory rejects
(a) Formal institutionalisation
(b) People
(c) Human motivation
(d) Informal functioning

378. What is PERT in management?
(a) A refinement of what Alwin Toffler envisioned as an "Electronic Cottage" with computer terminals installed at home.
(b) A refinement of the original Gantt Charts.
(c) A refinement of Critical Path Method (CPM).
(d) A refinement of what Dr. Taylor said.

379. Theory Z refers to which one of the following?
(a) Selected Russian managerial practices adapted to Chinese environment.
(b) Selected German managerial practices adapted to Japan's environment.
(c) Selected Japanese managerial practices adapted to the environment of the USA.
(d) Selected Indian managerial practices adapted to the environment of the UK.

380. A positive leader is one who motivates people by
(a) threatening the employees.
(b) centralising authority.
(c) increasing the satisfaction.
(d) creating fear.

381. In line and staff organisation, the staff performs the function of
(a) assigning responsibility
(b) management
(c) advising the management
(d) None of the above

382. Board meetings must be held at least once in
(a) six months (b) each month
(c) three months (d) each year

383. According to which of the following theories human needs are arranged in the hierarchy of importance?
(a) Varoom's theory
(b) Masloy's theory
(c) McGregor's theory
(d) Herzberg's theory

384. The functions of management that are more closely related are
(a) planning and control
(b) planning and staffing
(c) planning and organising
(d) planning and co-ordination

385. The main advantages of functional organisation is
(a) Expert advice (b) Experience
(c) Specialisation (d) Simplicity

386. Theory 'Y' states that
(a) workers exercise self-control and self-direction.
(b) workers have inherent liking for work.
(c) workers prefer to be directed.
(d) None of the above.

387. A speculator in the stock exchange who expects the price to rise is known as
(a) Bear (b) Stag
(c) Bull (d) None of these

388. Minutes of company meeting should be prepared within
(a) 30 days of the meeting
(b) 21 days of the meeting
(c) 45 days of the meeting
(d) 40 days of the meeting

389. Hunting is an example of
(a) Manufacturing industry
(b) It is not an industry
(c) Extractive industry
(d) Genetic industry

390. ABC technique of inventory control is
(a) selective control
(b) always best control
(c) always better control
(d) None of the above

391. Which one of the following statements is correct?
(a) Controlling is a part of the planning process.
(b) Planning and controlling are essentially one and the same.
(c) A control process is meaningless without pre-set goals.
(d) Controlling is a substitute for planning.

392. When jobs are broadened in scope and complexity so that the person's overall area of job responsibility increases, it is a case of
(a) job enrichment.
(b) job rotation.
(c) job enlargement.
(d) job specification.

393. Techniques of managerial control are useful in
(a) identifying appropriate technology.
(b) selection of plant location.
(c) conducting shareholders meetings.
(d) profit planning.

394. Motivational process and not the motivators as such is associated with the
(a) Two-factor theory
(b) ERG theory
(c) Expectancy theory
(d) Need hierarchy theory

395. "Perceived equity in reward results in satisfaction." Which one of the following motivation theories take this into account?
(a) Victor Vroom's Expectancy mode
(b) Porter and Lowler model
(c) Herzberg's Two-factor theory
(d) F.W. Taylor's incentive scheme

396. One of the steps that may be required for achieving effective coordination is

(a) training in leadership and supervisory abilities of controllers of acitvity.
(b) reporting on performance and taking remedial measures.
(c) making an honest appraisal and initiating rewards' punishments.
(d) transmission of messages in a full line communication channel.

397. An important aspect of control is that the
(a) manager sets as effective management information system.
(b) manager motivates his subordinates to give better performance.
(c) performance is checked against predeter mined standards.
(d) plans are checked before implementation against predetermined measures of performance.

398. Delegation of authority takes place when a manager thinks that
(a) the job requires the high skill that he does not possess.
(b) the job is too difficult and hazardous.
(c) he needs to punish his subordinate.
(d) he cannot look after all the demanding tasks by himself.

399. According to the principle of "span of control", there is
(a) a limit to the number of subordinates a supervisor can effectively supervise.
(b) a tendency to overload supervisors with too much of work.
(c) a limit to delegation of authority to the subordinate.
(d) no limit to the number of subordinates a supervisor can supervise.

400. Establishment of management by objectives presupposes
(a) unlimited freedom to set goals.
(b) unlimited freedom to operate in the assigned task.
(c) that the employees are provided with result expected.
(d) that limits of authority are not defined.

401. Each subordinate have only one superior whose command he has to obey. This is known as
(a) Exception principle.
(b) Scalar principle.
(c) Authority-responsibility principle.
(d) Utility of command principle.

402. Inventory is valued at
(a) Market price
(b) Cost price
(c) (a) or (b) or whichever is less
(d) (a) or (b) or whichever is higher

403. The role of staff in line and staff organisation is
(a) Executive (b) Advisory
(c) Both (a) and (b) (d) None of these

404. The principle that a subordinate should receive order from and be responsible to only one superior is known as
(a) Span of control
(b) Unity of command
(c) Unity of direction
(d) None of the above

405. Theory X and theory Y was originated by
(a) McClelland (b) Herzberg
(c) Maslow (d) McGregor

406. A.C.C. is an example of
(a) Vertical combination
(b) Federation
(c) Horizontal combination
(d) None of the above

407. Grapevine is also known as
(a) Downward communication
(b) Horizontal communication
(c) Internal communication
(d) Upward communication

408. In the field of management some of the important techniques, relate to budgeting, cost accounting, planning and control through
   (a) Budgetary Control
   (b) Operational Research
   (c) Financial Administration
   (d) PERT and CPM

409. Which of the following is true with respect to planning function?
   (a) To tell the work allocation to all.
   (b) Monitoring whether the things allocated are done properly.
   (c) To make a blue print of ideas and work.
   (d) All of the above.

410. The idea of MBO originally come from
   (a) P.F. Drucker (b) McGregor
   (c) Maslow (d) Taylor

411. In line and staff organisation, the authority lies in
   (a) Staff (b) Line
   (c) Both (a) and (b) (d) All of the above

412. Decentralisation
   (a) decreases the importance of superiors.
   (b) increases the importance of superior.
   (c) decreases the importance of subordinates.
   (d) increases the importance of subordinates.

413. Consider the following statements.
   1. There is a clear hierarchy of offices
   2. The functions are clearly specified
   3. There is a career structure
   4. There is a money salary

   The above are the characteristics of
   (a) The Administration
   (b) The Government
   (c) The Bureaucracy
   (d) All of the above

414. Below are given four different theories
   1. Trait approach
   2. Attitude criterion
   3. Behaviour approach
   4. Situational approach

   These are identified with
   (a) Administrative approaches
   (b) Leadership index
   (c) Organisational behaviour
   (d) Administrative behaviour

415. Three necessary and sufficient conditions that must be satisfied if traits should be unique determinants of the Leadership Index are
   1. the trait quality should follow a descending order as one traverses from the highest to the lowest levels.
   2. there must be a high correlation between the level of traits and the level of success.
   3. the achievement trait curve should be convex to the trait axis as one travels from the low to the high trait terminals.

   The above coniditions have been suggested by
   (a) Elton Mayo
   (b) F.W. Taylor
   (c) Dorvvin Cartwright
   (d) Edwin E. Ghiselli

416. Given the following variables that determine leadership
   1. Followers (F)
   2. The goal (G)
   3. A measure of willingness (W)
   4. A given situation (S)
   5. Leadership (L)

   The leadership function may be described as
   (a) G=f(F, L, w, s) (b) S=f(F, L, w, g)
   (c) F=f(L, g, w, s) (d) L=f(F, g, w, s)

Directions: Questions 417 to 474 are of multiple statement type. Choose the correct answer from the codes given below.

417. Consider the following factors:
   1. Enterprise management is conceived as a sub-system.
   2. Enterprise management necessarily works within a socio-economic environment which forms the system.
   3. The management of the enterprise is concerned with the manipulation of a series of interrelated variables working wihtin the sub-system.
   4. The environment functions with its own variables which interacts with the variables of the sub-system.
   5. The management has an objective carved out of the dynamics of interaction between the management sub-system and the environmental system.
   6. It is the function of the management to optimise the objective.

   Codes:
   (a) all forms of administration
   (b) the marginal analysis
   (c) all forms of executive
   (d) all forms of legislation

418. Maslow's Theory of motivation has classified the human needs into five categories as follows:
   1. Safety needs
   2. Social needs
   3. Physiological needs
   4. Esteem needs
   5. Self realisation needs

   Codes:
   (a) 1, 3, 2, 4, 5 (b) 5, 4, 3, 2, 1
   (c) 1, 2, 3, 4, 5 (d) 3, 1, 2, 4, 5

419. The delegation of authority results in
   1. Decentralisation of branches at places.
   2. Avoiding responsibility by top management.
   3. Delegation of authority by top management without avoiding responsibility.

   Codes:
   (a) 2 only (b) 1 and 2
   (c) 1 and 3 (d) 1, 2 and 3

420. What is the order of the performance of the following functions of management?
   1. Planning 2. Directing
   3. Organising 4. Controlling

   Codes:
   (a) 1, 3, 2, 4 (b) 1, 3, 4, 2
   (c) 1, 2, 3, 4 (d) 1, 4, 2, 3

421. Essential elements of rationalisation are:
   1. Business combination
   2. Modernisation
   3. Research
   4. Specialisation

   Codes:
   (a) 2, 3, 4 (b) 1, 3, 4
   (c) 1, 2, 3 (d) All of the above

422. Staffing function of management includes
   1. Training 2. Appraisal
   3. Placement 4. Directing

   Codes:
   (a) 1, 2, 3 and 4 (b) 1, 2 and 3
   (c) 1 and 2 (d) 3 and 4

423. Consider the following statements.
   1. It is only advisory in character
   2. It has the monopoly of execution
   3. It can issue commands

   Codes:
   (a) 1 only (b) 2 only
   (c) 1 and 2 (d) 2 and 3

424. Directing function of management implies
   1. Planning 2. Staffing
   3. Leadership 4. Motivation

   Codes:
   (a) 3 and 4 (c) 2, 3 and 4
   (b) 1 and 2 (d) 2 and 4

425. Which of the following functions of management are closely related?
 1. Planning 2. Coordination
 3. Motivation 4. Control

Codes:
(a) 3 and 4 (b) 1, 2 and 4
(c) 1 and 2 (d) 2 and 4

426. Consider the following statements.
 1. Management auditor makes the audit of planning and policies of the company.
 2. Statutory auditor makes the comments on the financial position statements of the company.
 3. The work of statutory auditor begins with the end of management auditor's work.
 4. Statutory auditor comments on the operational areas of the concern.

Codes:
(a) 3 and 4 (b) 1 and 2
(c) 2, 3 and 4 (d) 1, 2 and 3

427. Consider the following steps.
 1. Assignment of duties
 2. Authorisation for actions
 3. Creation of obligation
 4. Determination of results expected

Codes:
(a) 4, 1, 2 and 3 (b) 3, 2, 1 and 4
(c) 4, 2, 1 and 3 (d) 3, 1, 2 and 4

428. Following are the steps in designing an organization structure.
 1. Grouping of activites
 2. Delegation of authority
 3. Identification of activities
 4. Assignment of duties

Codes:
(a) 4, 1, 3, 2 (b) 3, 2, 4, 1
(c) 4, 2, 3, 1 (d) 3, 1, 4, 2

429. In the context of social responsibility of business, the enlightened self-interest concept refers to which of the following?
 1. Treating natural resources as the property of future generations.
 2. Considering long term survival interests of business.
 3. Contributing to community development.
 4. Enhancing profit prospects of business.

Codes:
(a) 1, 2 and 3 (b) 3 and 4
(c) 1 and 2 (d) 4 only

430. The three main objectives of Scientific Management are
 1. Standardization of working conditions
 2. Standardization of working methods
 3. Planning of large daily tasks
 4. Maximisation of employment

Codes:
(a) 2, 3 and 4 (b) 1, 2 and 4
(c) 1, 2 and 3 (d) 1, 3 and 4

431. Dorwin Cartwright and Alvin Zander identified the following two variables
 1. Employee-oriented
 2. Production-oriented
 3. Goal-oriented
 4. Group-oriented

Codes:
(a) 3 and 4 (b) 1 and 4
(c) 1 and 2 (d) 2 and 3

432. A leader uses the following methods.
 1. Uses criticism
 2. Encourages growth
 3. Sets objectives
 4. Gives orders and directions

Codes:
(a) 1, 2 and 4 (b) 2 and 3
(c) 1 and 2 (d) 3 and 4

433. Michigan leadership studies defined two variables. These were
1. Employee orientation
2. Employment orientation
3. Input orientation
4. Production orientation

Codes:
(a) 1 and 4 (b) 1 and 3
(c) 1 and 2 (d) 2 and 4

434. An informal organisation is
(a) not written and manualised.
(b) not portrayed in organisational charts.
(c) a set of work relationship that grow out of the mutual interactions of persons working together over a period of time.
(d) customary, not enacted.

Codes:
(a) 1, 2 and 3 (b) 1, 2, 3 and 4
(c) 1 only (d) 1 and 2

435. The human relations theory does not lay emphasis on
1. Principles
2. People
3. Human motivations
4. Informal group functions

Codes:
(a) 1, 2 and 3 (b) 1, 2, 3 and 4
(c) 1 only (d) 1 and 2

436. Which of the following are devices to bring about co-ordination
1. Cabinet Committees
2. Union Government
3. Zonal Councils
4. National Development Council

Codes:
(a) 2 only (b) 1 and 2
(c) 1, 2, 3 and 4 (d) 1, 3 and 4

437. The strategic approach to total compensation involved splitting the total compensation into three parts as under
1. Variable pay 2. Indirect pay
3. Base pay

Codes:
(a) 1, 2 and 3 (b) 2 and 3
(c) 1 only (d) 1 and 2

438. Which of the following is/are the reason(s) for centralization of authority in an organization?
1. Specialized skills, talent and technology are neither affordable nor practical in multiple locations.
2. Decentralization usually results in an increase in overhead and staff.
3. Recent improvements in communication technology facilitate the movement of money, credit information and data processing from a single centre of authority.

Codes:
(a) 1 and 2 (b) 1, 2 and 3
(c) 3 only (d) 1 and 3

439. Consider the following statements about Management by Objectives (MBO)
1. Effective MBO programmes usually start with the top managers who determine the organization's strategy and set preliminary goals.
2. Employees enjoy wide autonomy in implementation of plans.
3. Managers and employees periodically meet to review progress towards the objectives.

Codes:
(a) 1 only (b) 1, 2 and 3
(c) 2 and 3 (d) 1 and 3

440. In the process of controlling office management, certain steps are normally taken. These include
1. analysing the actual performance
2. finding out the reasons for discrepancies

3. evaluating the performance
4. establishing the standards of work performance.

Codes:

(a) 1, 4, 3, 2 (b) 4, 1, 3, 2
(c) 4, 1, 2, 3 (d) 1, 4, 2, 3

441. The basic flow of activities of a business firm follows a certain cyclical sequence. A business would like to have as many such cycles as possible during a given time period, say a year. What will be the sequential flow of some of these activities in the cycle?

1. Financing decision
2. Investment decision
3. Disposal of output
4. Acquisition of resources

Codes:

(a) 2, 3, 1, 4 (b) 1, 3, 4, 2
(c) 4, 1, 2, 3 (d) 2, 1, 4, 3

442. Consider the following statements regarding indian industries.

1. Industrial modernisation has not come up even in a modest way.
2. A support system and a regulatory framework has been developed so as to encourage and direct the industrial houses to modernise their plants.
3. Considerable advances have been made in the fields of managerial and technological skills in the country.
4. No effort has so far been made towards attaining the goal of self-reliance in the manufacture of consumer items.

Codes:

(a) 2 and 3 are correct
(b) 1 and 2 are correct
(c) 1 and 4 are correct
(d) 3 and 4 are correct

443. Decentralization of an organisation is commended on account of which of the following advantages?

1. Reduced burden on top executives
2. Executive development
3. Improvement of morale
4. Solves problems of coordination.

Codes:

(a) 1, 2 and 3 (b) 3 and 4
(c) 2 and 3 (d) 1, 2 and 4

444. Consider the following statements.

1. MBO is a control technique in which managers devote time only on the areas of deviation.
2. MBO integrates the individual with the organisation and the organisation with the environment.
3. In MBO the control over people is shifted to control over operations.
4. The MBO principle must be accompanied in practice by the principle of critical-point control.

Codes:

(a) 3 and 4 are correct
(b) 1 and 4 are correct
(c) 1 and 2 are correct
(d) 2 and 3 are correct

445. Consider the following statements. Strategic management process comprises

1. goal setting, strategy formulation, administration and strategic control.
2. setting courses of action attaining objective, process of seeking key areas and strategy formulation.
3. integrating the organisation with culture.
4. strategic planning and acting on these plans.

Codes:

(a) 1, 3 and 4 are correct
(b) 1, 2 and 4 are correct

(c) 2, 3 and 4 are correct
(d) 1, 2 and 3 are correct

446. Which of the following constitute manpower planning?
1. Determining human resource requirements both quantitatively and qualitatively.
2. Finding the sources of talented individuals.
3. Planning for the human resource needs of an organisation.
4. Reaching out to the right source for procuring the right people.

Codes:

(a) 1 and 3 (b) 1, 2, 3 and 4
(c) 1, 2 and 4 (d) 2 and 3

447. Consider the following statements. The social responsibility of business is to
1. do a business as per the public policy.
2. obey all the rules and regulations of the government.
3. make payment of the taxes imposee by the government.
4. provide not necessarily adequate but good quality of goods.

Codes:

(a) 1 and 4are correct.
(b) 2 and 3 are correct.
(c) 1, 2, 3 and 4 are correct.
(d) 1, 2 and 3 are correct.

448. Control refers to
1. estblishment of standards.
2. measurement of actual performance against the set standards.
3. Correction for deviation from standards.

Codes:

(a) 3 alone is correct
(b) 1 alone is correct
(c) 1, 2 and 3 are correct
(d) 1 and 2 are correct

449. Which of the following pairs are correctly matched?
1. Henri Fayol — Administration Industrial et Generale
2. F.W. Taylor — The Functions of the Executive
3. Douglas McGregor — The Human side of Enterprise
4. Peter Drucker — Management: Tasks, Responsibilities and Practices

Codes:

(a) 3 and 4 (b) 2 and 4
(c) 1 and 3 (d) 1, 2, 3 and 4

450. Staffing function of management includes
1. Training 2. Recruitment
3. Placement 4. Appraisal

Codes:

(a) 2, 3 and 4 (b) 1, 2, 3 and 4
(c) 1, 2 and 4 (d) 1, 2 and 3

451. What is the order of the performance of the following functions of management?
1. Planning 3. Organising
2. Directing 4. Controlling

Codes:

(a) 1, 3, 2, 4 (b) 1, 3, 4, 2
(c) 1, 2, 3, 4 (d) 1, 4, 2, 3

452. Job analysis involves
1. developing training skills, knowledge and personal traits of the worker necessary for a specific job.
2. identifying machines, tools and equipment to be used for the job.
3. identification of the task to be performed by an individual.
4. determination of the materials, products or services needed.

Codes:

(a) 2, 3, 4, 1 (b) 2, 3, 1, 4
(c) 3, 2, 4, 1 (d) 3, 2, 1, 4

453. Consider the following statements.
 1. Authority flows downward but responsibility flows upward.
 2. Authority should be equal to responsibility.
 3. Both authority and responsibility are divisible.
 4. If delegation is the end, then decentralization should be the means.

Codes:
(a) 1, 2 and 3 are correct
(b) 2, 3 and 4 are correct
(c) 1 and 2 are correct
(d) 3 and 4 are correct

454. Following are the steps in the process of delegation of authority.
 1. Assignment of task
 2. Creation of responsibility
 3. Granting authority
 4. Fixing accountability

Codes:
(a) 1, 3, 4, 2 (b) 1, 2, 3, 4
(c) 1, 3, 2, 4 (d) 1, 4, 2, 3

455. Consider the following statements.
 1. Planning is looking ahead
 2. Controlling is looking back
 3. Delegation multiplies leadership
 4. Life insurance is a contract of indemnity.

Codes:
(a) 1, 3 and 4 are correct
(b) 1, 2 and 4 are correct
(c) 2, 3 and 4 are correct
(d) 1, 2 and 3 are correct

456. What is the correct sequence of the following functions of a manager in an organisation?
 1. Motivation 2. Controlling
 3. Organising 4. Planning

Codes:
(a) 3, 4, 2, 1 (b) 3, 4, 1, 2
(c) 4, 3, 2, 1 (d) 4, 3, 1, 2

457. The basic flow of activities of a business firm follows a certain cyclical sequence. A business during a given time period, say a year, what will be the sequential flow of some of these activities in the cycle?
 1. Financing decision
 2. Investment decision
 3. Disposal of output
 4. Acquisition of resources

Codes:
(a) 2, 3, 1, 4 (b) 1, 3, 4, 2
(c) 4, 1, 2, 3 (d) 2, 1, 4, 3

458. Consider the following statements.
 1. MBO is a control technique in which managers devote time only on the areas of deviation.
 2. MBO integrates the individual with the organization and the organization with the environment.
 3. In MBO the control over people is shifted to control over operations.
 4. The MBO principle must be accompanied in practice by the principle of critical point control.

Codes:
(a) 3 and 4 are correct
(b) 1 and 4 are correct
(c) 2 and 3 are correct
(d) 1 and 2 are correct

459. In the process of controlling office management certain steps are normally taken.

These include
 1. analysing the actual performance.
 2. finding out the reasons for discrepancies.

3. evaluating the performance.
4. establishing the standards of work performance.

Codes:
(a) 1, 4, 3, 2 (b) 4, 1, 3, 2
(c) 4, 1, 2, 3 (d) 1, 4, 2, 3

460. Which of the following constitute manpower planning?
1. Determining human resource requirements both quantitatively and qualitatively.
2. Finding the sources of talented individuals.
3. Planning for the human resource needs of an organization.
4. Reaching out to the right source for procuring the right people.

Codes:
(a) 1, 2, 3 and 4 (b) 1 and 3
(c) 2 and 3 (d) 1, 2 and 4

461. Directing function of management implies
1. Planning 2. Staffing
3. Leadership 4. Motivation

Codes:
(a) 2 and 4 (b) 2, 3 and 4
(c) 1 and 2 (d) 3 and 4

462. Consider the following steps.
1. Analysis of variances
2. Initiating corrective action
3. Measurement of actual performance
4. Establishment of standards

Codes:
(a) 3, 1, 2, 4 (b) 4, 3, 1, 2
(c) 1, 2, 3, 4 (d) 2, 3, 1, 4

463. Consider the following elements.
1. Indicators
2. Objectives
3. Controls
4. Key Result Areas
5. Roles and Missions
6. Action Plans

Codes:
(a) 4, 5, 2, 1, 3, 6 (b) 4, 5, 1, 2, 6, 3
(c) 5, 4, 2, 1, 3, 6 (d) 5, 4, 1, 2, 6, 3

464. Which one of the following pairs are correctly matched?
1. Planning — Sets out the objectives and complete set of policies.
2. Organisation — Enables the owner or top executive of a business to arrange men, money, materials and methods.
3. Coordination — Orderly arrangement of group effort to provide unity of action.
4. Control — Verifying whether every thing occurs in conformity with the plan adopted, the instructions issued and principles established.

Codes:
(a) 1, 3 and 4 (b) 1, 2 and 3
(c) 2, 3 and 4 (d) 2 and 4

465. Consider the following elements in a feedback loop.
1. Identification of deviations
2. Measurement of actual performance
3. Actual performance
4. Comparison of actual against standards

Codes:
(a) 2, 3, 1, 4 (b) 2, 3, 4, 1
(c) 3, 2, 1, 4 (d) 3, 2, 4, 1

466. The following steps are involved in the process of organizing.
1. Forming supportive objectives
2. Delegating to the head of each group the authority
3. Necessary to perform the activities
4. Establishing enterprise objectives

Codes:

(a) 1, 3, 4, 2 (b) 1, 3, 2, 4
(c) 3, 1, 2, 4 (d) 3, 1, 4, 2

467. The following steps are involved in managing by objectives.
   1. Preliminary setting of objectives at the top
   2. Setting subordinate's objectives
   3. Tying resources with the goals
   4. Clarifying the organizational step is

Codes:

(a) 1, 3, 2, 4 (b) 1, 4, 2, 3
(c) 1, 2, 3, 4 (d) 1, 2, 4, 3

468. Consider the following office equipments used in various offices.
   1. Fax 2. Typewriter
   3. Dictaphone 4. Letter opener

Codes:

(a) 2, 4, 3, 1 (b) 3, 2, 4, 1
(c) 1, 2, 3, 4 (d) 4, 3, 2, 1

469. Consider the following basic steps involved in the process of control.
   1. Identifying the strategic control points.
   2. Establishment the standards.
   3. Measuring performance against standards.
   4. Correcting deviations from the standards.

Codes:

(a) 2, 1, 3, 4 (b) 2, 3, 1, 4
(c) 1, 4, 3, 2 (d) 4, 3, 2, 1

470. Decentralisation of an organization is commanded on account of which of the following advantages?
   1. Reduced burden on top executives
   2. Executive development
   3. Improvement of morale
   4. Solves problems of coordination

Codes:

(a) 1, 2 and 3 (b) 3 and 4
(c) 2 and 3 (d) 1, 2 and 4

471. Taylor whose thoughts go under the name of scientific management made two assumptions. The correct ones are
   1. The application of the methods of science to organisational problems lead to higher industrial efficiency.
   2. The incentive of high wage will promote the mutuality of interests between workers and managers which, in its turn, will lead to higher productivity.
   3. The staff members are personally free, observing only the impersonal duties of their offices.
   4. There is a clear hierarchy of offices.

Codes:

(a) 1 and 3 (b) 3 and 4
(c) 1 and 2 (d) 2 and 3

472. The following steps are involved in managing by objectives
   1. preliminary setting of objectives at the top.
   2. setting subordinates objectives.
   3. tying resources with the goals.
   4. clarifying the organisational roles.

Codes:

(a) 1, 4, 2, 3 (b) 1, 3, 2, 4
(c) 1, 2, 4, 3 (d) 1, 2, 3, 4

473. Following are some of the statements related with management.
   1. Management is essential in all organisations as well as at all levels of an organisation.
   2. Management makes policy and administration carries it out.
   3. In modern times, management can be replaced by the computer.
   4. Top management is also known as administrative management.

Codes:

(a) 1 and 4 (b) 3 and 4
(c) 1 and 2 (d) 2 and 3

474. Consider the following statements
1. Decentralisation and delegation are closely interrelated.
2. Delegation and decentralisation both desirable.
3. Decentralisation is not suitable for large organisation.
4. Delegation is not possible in the case of small organisations.

Codes:
(a) 2 and 3 are correct
(b) 1 and 2 are correct
(c) 1, 3 and 4 are correct
(d) 1 and 4 are correct

Directions: Questions 475 to 498 are of matching type. Match List I with List II and select the correct answer using the codes given below the list.

475. **List I**
A. Uses praise
B. Uses criticism
C. Negative approach
D. Positive approach

List II
1. Autocratic leade
2. Theory X
3. Theory Y
4. Democratic leader

Codes:	**A**	**B**	**C**	**D**
(a)	4	1	3	2
(b)	2	3	4	1
(c)	3	2	1	4
(d)	1	2	4	3

476. **List I**
A. Trust
B. Merger
C. Holding Company
D. Amalgamation

List II
1. Compare A holding more than 51% share capital of Company B
2. Existing companies A and B are merged into company C
3. Business of a number of firms is entrusted to the care of Board of trustees
4. Company A takes over the business of company B and company A contin ues

Codes:	**A**	**B**	**C**	**D**
(a)	3	4	1	2
(b)	1	2	3	4
(c)	3	4	2	1
(d)	3	2	1	4

477. **List I**
A. Scientific Management
B. M.B.O.
C. Funcitonal Approach to Management
D. Behavioural Approach

List II
1. Henry Fayol
2. Taylor
3. P.F. Drucker
4. Elton Mayo

Codes:	**A**	**B**	**C**	**D**
(a)	2	3	1	4
(b)	1	3	4	2
(c)	3	2	4	1
(d)	2	1	3	4

478. **List I**
A. Fayol
B. Taylor
C. Weber
D. Mooney and Reilley

List II
1. Economy and Society
2. General & Industrial Administration
3. Principles of Organisation
4. Shop Management

Codes:	**A**	**B**	**C**	**D**
(a)	2	4	1	3
(b)	3	4	1	2
(c)	4	3	2	1
(d)	1	3	2	4

479. List I

A. Structure
B. Concern for production
C. Production orientation
D. Group goal
E. Task orientation

List II

1. Tannebau and Schimdt
2. Cartwright and Zander
3. Ohio Study
4. Managerial Grid
5. Michigan Studies

Codes:	A	B	C	D	E
(a)	1	2	3	4	5
(b)	3	4	5	2	1
(c)	4	3	2	1	5
(d)	2	3	4	5	1

480. List I

A. Staff executives B. Directing
C. Line executives D. Staffing

List II

1. Advisory function
2. Manpower development
3. Guiding function
4. Managerial authority

Codes:	A	B	C	D
(a)	2	3	4	1
(b)	2	1	3	4
(c)	1	3	4	2
(d)	1	4	3	2

481.

List I	List II
(A) Hygine Theory	1. Abraham H. Maslow
(B) Theory 'X' and Theory 'Y'	2. Victor Vroom
(C) Expectancy	3. Fredrick Herzberg theory
	4. Douglas Mc Gregor

Codes:	A	B	C
(a)	1	2	4
(b)	3	2	4
(c)	1	4	2
(d)	3	4	2

482. List I

A. To check the quality of work
B. To see that work is completed in time
C. To check absenteeism of workers
D. To issue instructions regarding method of work

List II

1. Speed boss
2. Inspector
3. Instruciton card clerk
4. Shop disciplinarian

Codes:	A	B	C	D
(a)	2	1	4	3
(b)	3	2	1	4
(c)	4	3	1	2
(d)	2	1	3	4

483. List I

A. High consideration and low structure
B. Low structure and low consideration
C. High structure and high consideration
D. High structure and low consideration

List II

1. Team 2. Task
3. Impoverished 4. Country club

Codes:	A	B	C	D
(a)	4	3	1	2
(b)	1	2	4	3
(c)	4	2	1	3
(d)	1	3	4	2

484. List I (Name)

A. Kurt Lewin B. H.J. Leeavitt
C. Larry Greiner D. Floyd C. Mann

List II (Model)

1. Action Research Process Model
2. Sequential Process Model

3. System Model
4. Three-step Model

Codes:	A	B	C	D
(a)	1	4	3	2
(b)	1	2	3	4
(c)	4	3	2	1
(d)	3	2	1	4

485. List I
A. Line authority
B. Staff authority
C. Functional authority
D. Formal authority

List II
1. Some people in an organisation are vested with primary source of authority
2. Some people in an organisation have legitimate right to expert influence on others
3. Some people in an organisation lack independent, formal authority
4. Some people have right to control activities of other departments as they relate to specific staff

Codes:	A	B	C	D
(a)	2	3	4	1
(b)	1	3	4	2
(c)	2	4	3	1
(d)	1	2	3	4

486. List I
A. Span of control
B. M.B.O.
C. M.B.E.
D. Delegation of authority

List II
1. The superior helps, through continuous guidance, the subordinate to reach his goals.
2. Numerical limit of subordinates to be supervised by an executive.
3. Subordinate remains account able to his superior and the superior has the authority to demand accountability from his subordinate.
4. The management will concern itself and confine its activities to those areas and operations where the actual performance is short of the target.

Codes:	A	B	C	D
(a)	2	1	3	4
(b)	2	1	4	3
(c)	1	2	4	3
(d)	1	2	3	4

487.

List I	List II
A. Mayo	1. Functions of Management
B. Maslow	2. Behavioural Approach
C. Fayol	3. Theory of Motivation
D. Weber	4. Theory of Location

Codes:	A	B	C	D
(a)	2	4	1	3
(b)	3	2	1	4
(c)	2	3	1	4
(d)	4	3	1	2

488.

List I	List II
A. Planning	1. Training
B. Staffing	2. Forecasting
C. Directing	3. Evaluating
D. Controlling	4. Motivating
	5. Grouping

Codes:	A	B	C	D
(a)	3	5	1	2
(b)	3	1	4	5
(c)	2	5	1	3
(d)	2	1	4	3

489.

List I	List II
1. Communication system	A. Hectograph
2. Filing system	B. Telex

3. Duplicate copies — C. Franking machine
4. Fixing stamps — D. Pigeon holes

Codes:	A	B	C	D
(a)	3	4	2	1
(b)	3	1	4	2
(c)	2	1	3	4
(a)	4	2	1	3

490.

List I	List II
A. Premium Plan	1. Gantt
B. Efficiency Bonus	2. Emerson Plan
C. Points Premium	3. Bedaux Plan
D. Task and Bonus	4. Taylor Plan

Codes:	A	B	C	D
(a)	1	2	3	4
(b)	1	2	3	4
(c)	4	3	2	1
(d)	1	2	3	4

491. List I

A. Line authority
B. Staff authority
C. Functional authority
D. Formal authority

List II

1. Some people in an organization have.
2. Some people in an organization have legitimate right to expert influence on others.
3. Some people in an organization lack independent formal authority.
4. Some people have right to control activities of other departments as they relate to specific staff.

Codes:	A	B	C	D
(a)	1	3	4	2
(b)	1	2	3	4
(c)	2	3	4	1
(d)	2	4	3	1

492. List I

A. Blue Chip
B. Deep Discount Bonds
C. Commercial paper
D. Debentures

List II

1. Issued by a private limited company
2. Highly profitable investments in a stock exchange
3. Issued by finally sound companies
4. Small investments yielding a big sum after a long term
5. Issued by companies having large reserves.
6. Issued in lieu of loans

Codes:	A	B	C	D
(a)	2	3	1	5
(b)	2	1	3	6
(c)	2	4	3	6
(d)	1	4	6	5

493. List I (Management thinkers)

A. Elton Mayo
B. Frederick W. Taylor
C. Henri Fayol
D. Mary Parker Follet

List II (Contribution work)

1. Importance of integrating the company's and employees goal
2. Social problems of industrial civilization
3. General and industrial management
4. Principles of scientific management

Codes:	A	B	C	D
(a)	3	4	1	2
(b)	1	4	3	2
(c)	4	3	2	1
(d)	2	4	3	1

494.

List I	List II
A. Planning	1. Training
B. Staffing	2. Forecasting

C. Directing 3. Evaluating
D. Controlling 4. Motivating

Codes:	A	B	C	D
(a)	3	4	1	2
(b)	2	4	1	3
(c)	3	1	4	2
(d)	2	1	4	3

495. **List I (Management experts)**
A. Newman and Summer
B. Henri Fayol
C. Luther Gulick
D. Koontz and O'Donnell

List II (Sequences of functions advocated by them)
1. Organising, planning, leading and controlling.
2. Planning, organising, commanding, coordinating and controlling.
3. Planning, organising, staffing, directing and controlling.
4. 'POSDCORB'.

Codes:	A	B	C	D
(a)	2	1	3	4
(b)	1	2	4	3
(c)	2	1	4	3
(d)	1	2	3	4

496. **List I (Managerial function)**
A. Planning B. Staffing
C. Directing D. Controlling

List II (Activity)
1. Regulating the ongoing activities of the organisation to ensure that they are in conformity with the established plans.
2. Mobilising individual and group efforts through motivation, communication, leadership and supervision.
3. Filling the various managerial and non-managerial positions.
4. Determining the organisational objectives and the formulation of strategies, policies and programmes for achieving them.

Codes:	A	B	C	D
(a)	4	3	1	2
(b)	4	3	2	1
(c)	1	3	4	2
(d)	1	3	2	4

497.

List I	List II
A. Forecasting	1. Controlling
B. Communication	2. Planning
C. Selection of managers	3. Leading
D. Establishing performance standards	4. Staffing

Codes:	A	B	C	D
(a)	2	4	3	1
(b)	1	3	4	2
(c)	2	3	4	1
(d)	1	2	4	3

498.

List I	List II
A. F.W. Taylor	1. MBO
B. Henri Fayol	2. Scientific Management
C. Elton Mayo	3. Fourteen Principles of Management
D. Peter F. Drucker	4. Hawthorne Experiments

Codes:	A	B	C	D
(a)	3	2	4	1
(b)	2	3	4	1
(c)	1	2	4	3
(d)	2	3	4	1

Directions: Questions 499 to 520 consist of two statements one labelled as 'Assertion A' and the other labelled as 'Reason R'. You are to examine these two statements carefully and decide if the Assertion A and the Reason R are individually true and if so, whether the Reason is a correct explanation of the Assertion select your answers to these items using the codes given below and mark your answer sheet accordingly.

(A) Both A and R are true and R is the correct explanation of A.
(B) Both A and R are true but R is not a correct explanation of A.
(C) A is true but R is false.
(D) A is false but R is true.

499. **Assertion (A):** In accounting, a distinction is made between the business and the owner.

Reason (R): Accounting concepts are based on adjectivity and not on subjectivity.

500. **Assertion (A):** A minor can be admitted to the benefits of partnership with the consent of all the partners.

Reason (R): This liability is confined only to the extent of his share in the profits and property of the firm.

501. **Assertion (A):** Social responsibility of business is an idea that cannot be put into practice by most of the business.

Reason (R): There are no norms to measure the extent of responsibility towards each segment of the society.

502. **Assertion (A):** The auditor should examine the 'Objects' clause of the Memorandum of Association.

Reason (R): This would ensure that the company is carrying on business as specified in the Memorandum of Association.

503. **Assertion (A):** Improvement in the social environment benefit both society and business.

Reason (R): Society must pay for the social environment of business through higher prices.

504. **Assertion (A):** Matters which cannot be decided because of limitiation of authority may be referred to superiors.

Reason (R): Maintenance of intended delegation requires that decisions without authority of individual be made by them.

505. **Assertion (A):** Delegation of authority does not reduce the work load of a superior executive.

Reasoning (R): Authority can be delegated but responsibility cannot be delegated.

506. **Assertion (A):** The top management in an organisation should be mainly concerned with very important and complex problems and not with day-to-day problems.

Reasoning (R): This is started by the scalar principle of organisation.

507. **Assertion (A):** The span of management at upper levels of management is generally narrow while at lower level span is wide.

Reasoning (R): Tasks allocated to subordinates at lower levels of management are more specific and precise and thus making supervision easy and simple.

508. **Assertion (A):** Management is a continuous operation or process involving the interaction of all functions.

Reason (R): Manager first plan, then organize and finally perform the function of controlling.

509. **Assertion (A):** When the span of control is wide, coordination and control becomes difficult.

Reason (R): In a narrow span levels of authority decrease.

510. **Assertion (A):** The agenda helps systematic transacton of business at the meeting without omission of any item of importance.

Reason (R): The routine matters in the agenda are put first in order and the contentious matters later.

511. **Assertion (A):** Management by exception is not a control technique.

Reason (R): The principles of management by exception was first propounded by F.W. Taylor.

512. **Assertion (A):** Co-ordination implies the avoidance of all splintering efforts.

Reason (R): One of the four benefits of co-ordination is unity of direction.

513. **Assertion (A):** Management by Exception is not a control technique.

Reason (R): The Principles of Management by Exception was first propounded by F.W. Taylor.

514. **Assertion (A):** Effective motivation is moderated by organisational complexity and conflicts.

Reason (R): An individual's motives may be complex and conflicting.

515. **Assertion (A):** According to theory X all employees dislike work and must be coerced, controlled or threatened to make them work.

Reason (R): Theory X makes an assumption about the basic human nature which is relevant to the employees also.

516. **Assertion (A):** A manager delegates authority.

Reason (R): Manager wants to shirk his responsibility.

517. **Assertion (A):** Everything that goes to increase the importance of the subordinate's role is decentralization.

Reason (R): When the degree of delegation of authority is more than the degree of reservation of authority. It is a case of decentralization.

518. **Assertion (A):** MBO is effective way of planning and organizing the work.

Reason (R): Employees participate in setting the objectives.

519. **Assertion (A):** Shares must be listed on all the stock exchanges.

Reason (R): Stock exchange listing provides liquidity to shares.

520. **Assertion (A):** Commercial banks in India are treated as social banks.

Reason (R): They provide finance for the upliftment of the downtrodden.

ANSWERS

1. (a)	2. (d)	3. (b)	4. (b)	5. (d)	6. (d)
7. (c)	8. (c)	9. (a)	10. (a)	11. (b)	12. (d)
13. (b)	14. (b)	15. (a)	16. (c)	17. (c)	18. (a)
19. (b)	20. (a)	21. (c)	22. (a)	23. (c)	24. (c)
25. (c)	26. (d)	27. (a)	28. (c)	29. (b)	30. (c)
31. (b)	32. (b)	33. (c)	34. (a)	35. (b)	36. (d)
37. (d)	38. (c)	39. (d)	40. (d)	41. (a)	42. (a)

43. (b)	44. (d)	45. (a)	46. (a)	47. (a)	48. (a)
49. (c)	50. (d)	51. (b)	52. (c)	53. (a)	54. (b)
55. (c)	56. (d)	57. (a)	58. (d)	59. (b)	60. (d)
61. (b)	62. (d)	63. (b)	64. (a)	65. (c)	66. (b)
67. (b)	68. (b)	69. (b)	70. (d)	71. (d)	72. (a)
73. (a)	74. (c)	75. (a)	76. (b)	77. (a)	78. (b)
79. (c)	80. (d)	81. (b)	82. (a)	83. (c)	84. (c)
85. (b)	86. (a)	87. (c)	88. (b)	89. (c)	90. (a)
91. (a)	92. (b)	93. (c)	94. (a)	95. (b)	96. (c)
97. (a)	98. (d)	99. (b)	100. (a)	101. (a)	102. (d)
103. (b)	104. (c)	105. (a)	106. (c)	107. (c)	108. (d)
109. (d)	110. (c)	111. (d)	112. (b)	113. (a)	114. (b)
115. (a)	116. (c)	117. (b)	118. (b)	119. (d)	120. (d)
121. (a)	122. (b)	123. (a)	124. (c)	125. (d)	126. (d)
127. (a)	128. (d)	129. (d)	130. (d)	131. (a)	132. (a)
133. (d)	134. (d)	135. (a)	136. (c)	137. (d)	138. (b)
139. (a)	140. (c)	141. (c)	142. (a)	143. (a)	144. (a)
145. (c)	146. (a)	147. (c)	148. (c)	149. (a)	150. (c)
151. (c)	152. (c)	153. (b)	154. (c)	155. (a)	156. (b)
157. (b)	158. (d)	159. (c)	160. (b)	161. (b)	162. (a)
163. (b)	164. (a)	165. (c)	166. (a)	167. (b)	168. (a)
169. (c)	170. (c)	171. (a)	172. (a)	173. (b)	174. (a)
175. (a)	176. (b)	177. (b)	178. (b)	179. (a)	180. (b)
181. (b)	182. (b)	183. (a)	184. (a)	185. (b)	186. (c)
187. (c)	188. (b)	189. (c)	190. (a)	191. (a)	192. (a)
193. (a)	194. (a)	195. (a)	196. (c)	197. (c)	198. (d)
199. (b)	200. (d)	201. (a)	202. (d)	203. (d)	204. (d)
205. (d)	206. (a)	207. (c)	208. (a)	209. (a)	210. (a)
211. (b)	212. (d)	213. (c)	214. (d)	215. (a)	216. (a)
217. (b)	218. (b)	219. (b)	220. (c)	221. (d)	222. (c)
223. (c)	224. (c)	225. (a)	226. (b)	227. (a)	228. (d)
229. (c)	230. (a)	231. (d)	232. (a)	233. (d)	234. (b)
235. (a)	236. (c)	237. (c)	238. (b)	239. (b)	240. (d)
241. (c)	242. (c)	243. (d)	244. (b)	245. (d)	246. (b)

247. (d)	248. (c)	249. (b)	250. (a)	251. (d)	252. (a)
253. (c)	254. (a)	255. (b)	256. (a)	257. (d)	258. (b)
259. (a)	260. (c)	261. (b)	262. (c)	263. (d)	264. (c)
265. (b)	266. (a)	267. (c)	268. (d)	269. (b)	270. (a)
271. (a)	272. (b)	273. (d)	274. (d)	275. (b)	276. (a)
277. (a)	278. (a)	279. (d)	280. (c)	281. (a)	282. (b)
283. (c)	284. (d)	285. (a)	286. (a)	287. (b)	288. (b)
289. (a)	290. (d)	291. (b)	292. (d)	293. (c)	294. (a)
295. (a)	296. (d)	297. (b)	298. (a)	299. (b)	300. (c)
301. (b)	302. (d)	303. (a)	304. (c)	305. (d)	306. (d)
307. (d)	308. (a)	309. (a)	310. (d)	311. (a)	312. (b)
313. (a)	314. (b)	315. (a)	316. (c)	317. (a)	318. (b)
319. (a)	320. (b)	321. (b)	322. (a)	323. (a)	324. (c)
325. (d)	326. (c)	327. (a)	328. (c)	329. (b)	330. (c)
331. (d)	332. (c)	333. (a)	334. (c)	335. (b)	336. (b)
337. (c)	338. (c)	339. (a)	340. (a)	341. (d)	342. (d)
343. (c)	344. (d)	345. (b)	346. (c)	347. (a)	348. (d)
349. (d)	350. (c)	351. (a)	352. (b)	353. (c)	354. (a)
355. (b)	356. (c)	357. (b)	358. (d)	359. (a)	360. (a)
361. (a)	362. (a)	363. (b)	364. (c)	365. (b)	366. (c)
367. (c)	368. (a)	369. (b)	370. (b)	371. (b)	372. (a)
373. (b)	374. (c)	375. (d)	376. (a)	377. (a)	378. (c)
379. (c)	380. (c)	381. (c)	382. (c)	383. (b)	384. (a)
385. (c)	386. (a)	387. (c)	388. (a)	389. (c)	390. (a)
391. (c)	392. (c)	393. (d)	394. (c)	395. (b)	396. (d)
397. (c)	398. (d)	399. (a)	400. (c)	401. (d)	402. (c)
403. (a)	404. (b)	405. (d)	406. (c)	407. (c)	408. (d)
409. (c)	410. (a)	411. (b)	412. (d)	413. (c)	414. (b)
415. (d)	416. (d)	417. (a)	418. (d)	419. (c)	420. (a)
421. (d)	422. (b)	423. (d)	424. (d)	425. (b)	426. (b)
427. (a)	428. (d)	429. (a)	430. (c)	431. (a)	432. (b)
433. (a)	434. (b)	435. (c)	436. (c)	437. (c)	438. (b)
439. (d)	440. (b)	441. (c)	442. (a)	443. (d)	444. (d)
445. (b)	446. (a)	447. (c)	448. (c)	449. (c)	450. (b)

451. (a)	452. (c)	453. (c)	454. (b)	455. (d)	456. (d)
457. (c)	458. (c)	459. (b)	460. (b)	461. (d)	462. (b)
463. (c)	464. (d)	465. (c)	466. (d)	467. (c)	468. (d)
469. (d)	470. (a)	471. (c)	472. (c)	473. (a)	474. (b)
475. (b)	476. (d)	477. (a)	478. (a)	479. (b)	480. (c)
481. (d)	482. (a)	483. (a)	484. (c)	485. (b)	486. (a)
487. (c)	488. (d)	489. (d)	490. (b)	491. (a)	492. (c)
493. (a)	494. (d)	495. (b)	496. (b)	497. (c)	498. (b)
499. (b)	500. (b)	501. (b)	502. (a)	503. (c)	504. (a)
505. (d)	506. (c)	507. (a)	508. (a)	509. (c)	510. (a)
511. (d)	512. (b)	513. (d)	514. (d)	515. (b)	516. (b)
517. (a)	518. (c)	519. (c)	520. (a)		

6

Marketing Management

1. In the traditional sense marketing is ________ oriented.
   (a) sales (b) production
   (c) Both (a) and (b) (d) None of these
2. In the modern sense marketing is ________ oriented.
   (a) product (b) sales
   (c) consumer (d) All of the above
3. Marketing occupies an important place in ______.
   (a) society (b) business
   (c) Both (a) and (b) (d) None of these
4. Marketing creates ______ for goods and services.
   (a) product (b) customer
   (c) demand (d) All of the above
5. Marketing involves ______ and need for requirements of consumers.
   (a) competition (b) ascertaining
   (c) Both (a) and (b) (d) None of these
6. Role of marketing has become vital because of changes and increased ______.
   (a) competition (b) technological
   (c) Both (a) and (b) (d) None of these
7. In the modern sense emphasis of marketing is on ______ satisfaction.
   (a) market (b) sales
   (c) consumer (d) customer
8. Marketing is essentially a ______ activity.
   (a) selling (b) production
   (c) management (d) All of the above
9. Marketing starts with identification of ________ needs.
   (a) goods (b) sale
   (c) consumer (d) customer
10. Advertising creates ________ among customers.
    (a) positive affects (b) confusion
    (c) clearity (d) awareness
11. Marketing distributes ______ and services among ______.
    (a) consumers (b) goods
    (c) Both (a) and (b) (d) None of these
12. Marketing designs and develop goods and ________.
    (a) quality (b) services
    (c) consumer (d) All of the above
13. Pricing activity is ________ of product prices.
    (a) taxation (b) fixation
    (c) Both (a) and (b) (d) None of these
14. Promotional activities include
    (a) sales promotion
    (b) publicity
    (c) Advertising/selling
    (d) All of the above
15. Distributional activities involve decisions regarding
    (a) decision-making
    (b) channels of distribution
    (c) Both (a) and (b)
    (d) None of the above

16. Promotional activities involve establishing contact with the ______ and ______ customers.
(a) prospective (b) existing
(c) Both (a) and (b) (d) None of these

17. Two important considerations in price fixation are ______ and ______.
(a) capacity of consumers to pay
(b) Product costs
(c) Both (a) and (b)
(d) None of the above

18. Marketing involves decisions regarding ______ and ______.
(a) promotion of product
(b) distribution of product
(c) product design
(d) pricing

19. Assembly of goods means bringing goods to a ______ place.
(a) corner (b) central
(c) Both (a) and (b) (d) None of these

20. Sales of good involves transfer of ownership of goods and services from the seller to the buyer for a consideration known as
(a) Price (b) Production
(c) Transfer (d) Ownership

21. Marketing research is a ______ method of solving marketing problems.
(a) practical (b) logical
(c) theoratical (d) None of these

22. Marketing research ______ records and analyses facts to make rational decisions.
(a) analyses (b) gathers
(c) Both (a) and (b) (d) None of these

23. Price of a product affects its
(a) customer (b) demand
(c) production (d) All of the above

24. Transport involves ______ goods from their place of origin to the place of their consumption.
(a) distributing (b) sending
(c) taking (d) None of these

25. Storage involves making ______ for maintaining goods in a desirable state.
(a) suitable arrangements
(b) economical arrangements
(c) Both (a) and (b)
(d) None of the above

26. In credit sales payment of price is postponed for ______ after the sale takes place.
(a) one year (b) five year
(c) postponed (d) a period

27. Grading means ______ products into different classes.
(a) integrating (b) separating
(c) different (d) None of these

28. Risk management is an important function of ______.
(a) controling (b) planning
(c) marketing (d) selling

29. Marketing is an ______ found in all types of business organisations.
(a) strategic function
(b) universal function
(c) Both (a) and (a)
(d) None of the above

30. The scope of marketing is
(a) limited (b) undefined
(c) unlimited (d) All of the above

31. The goods may be consumer goods or ______ goods durable goods or non-durable goods.
(a) buyer (b) producer
(c) customer (d) None of these

32. Business organisation are engaged in providing goods and services to ______.
(a) customers (b) goods
(c) consumers (d) None of these

33. Business organisation try to satisfy _______ needs of customers through the provision of services.
(a) general (b) specific
(c) Both (a) and (a) (d) None of these

34. Products are more identified by their _________ name.
(a) company (b) goods
(c) brand (d) None of these

35. Plastic jars are now-a-days quite popular for _________.
(a) storing (b) collecting
(c) packaging (d) bundlling

36. ______ refers to the division concerning product line or which product will be offered in different markets.
(a) Market mix (b) Ratio analysis
(c) Product mix (d) None of these

37. Services which are provided with the product and may be before or after sale are known as _____.
(a) product support services
(b) goods support services
(c) Both (a) and (b)
(d) None of the above

38. Different stages through which the sale of a product passes over a period of time denote?
(a) Product mix (b) Product life
(c) Marketing mix (d) None of these

39. For industrial goods _____ gets maximum weightage.
(a) advertisement
(b) sales promotion
(c) personal selling
(d) None of the above

40. ________ is more effective for non technical and low cost goods.
(a) Production (b) Selling
(c) Advertisement (d) None of these

41. No-cost tools of promotion mix is ________.
(a) marketing (b) advertisement
(c) incentives (d) publicity

42. The effect of _______ is temporary and short lived.
(a) product promotion
(b) sales promotion
(c) Both (a) and (b)
(d) None of the above

43. A channel of distribution is the along which goods move from producers to consumers.
(a) route (b) path
(c) either (a) or (b) (d) None of these

44. Banks are not included in the
(a) finance distribution
(b) channel of distribution
(c) Both (a) and (b)
(d) None of the above

45. Retailer acts as a ________ between the wholesaler and consumers.
(a) salesman (b) middleman
(c) Both (a) and (b) (d) None of these

46. Role of the middlemen is to _______ out buyers and sellers and match goods to the requirements of market.
(a) find (b) search
(c) Both (a) and (b) (d) None of these

47. Some businessmen (middlemen) indulge in activities.
(a) social (b) sports
(c) antisocial (d) All of the above

48. A wholesaler forcasts the _____ for the goods.
(a) production (b) quality
(c) selling (d) demand

49. A wholesaler gives name to the products packed and graded by him.
(a) company (b) brand
(c) Both (a) and (b) (d) None of these

50. A wholesaler provides financial help to manufacturer by for cash.
(a) providing in depth
(b) selling goods
(c) purchasing goods
(d) None of the above

51. Some retailers provide free home delivery service to their
(a) consumers (b) customer
(c) Both (a) and (b) (d) None of these

52. Retailer provides feedback to wholesalers and ______ about consumers preferences.
(a) retailers (b) customers
(c) manufacturers (d) None of these

53. Sales promotion includes all promotional activities other than advertising personal selling and ______.
(a) advertisement (b) production
(c) publicity (d) All of the above

54. The basic object of sales promotion is to increase the buying response of ultimate
(a) retailer (b) wholesaler
(c) consumers (d) All of the above

55. The object of sales promotion is to improve ______ share.
(a) stock (b) market
(c) Both (a) and (b) (d) None of these

56. Informing buyers of new brand and new package is the ______ of sales promotion.
(a) application (b) objective
(c) method (d) None of these

57. Free samples are given to customers to introduce a new ______.
(a) market (b) business
(c) product (d) interest

58. Coupon is a certificate that reduces the ______ of the product.
(a) sales (b) demand
(c) price (d) All of the above

59. Price-off gives a temporary ______ to the consumers.
(a) free sample (b) discount
(c) Both (a) and (b) (d) None of these

60. Producers of garments often ____ organise shows to promote their products.
(a) fashion (b) movie
(c) charity (d) archestra

61. Retail demonstrations are supplied by manufacturers for preparing and distributing the products as retail
(a) price (b) sample
(c) products (d) None of these

62. Goods are produced these days on a large scale in anticipation of ______ demand.
(a) more (b) less
(c) future (d) post

63. The objective of advertising in case of competition is to see that the _____ for the firm's product is maintained at the existing level, (price demand).
(a) demand (b) production
(c) price (d) sales

64. In advertising the business firms highlight the importance they attach to ______ satisfaction, (consumer, producer).
(a) retailer (b) wholesaler
(c) consumer (d) producer

65. In the absence of advertising firms can not reach the consumers in
(a) few number (b) large number
(c) Both (a) and (b) (d) None of these

66. By advertising copy is meant the ______, contents, colour and presentation of the message of advertisement.
(a) shape (b) size
(c) quality (d) None of these

67. The advertising copy may make use of different form of ______ depending on the media used.

(a) expressions (b) colaboration
(c) presentation (d) conversation

68. Advertising copy refers to the form of presentation of ______ and its contents.
(a) summary (b) message
(c) contents (d) None of these

69. Advertising media means the ______ of communication through which advertisement message is sent to the customers.
(a) channel (b) medium
(c) distribution (d) All of the above

70. Different media of advertising are ______ for different products.
(a) unsuitable (b) stable
(c) suitable (d) None of these

71. Newspapers happen to be suitable media for advertising ______ products used by masses.
(a) wholesaler (b) retailer
(c) consumer (d) customer

72. Magazines and Journals are suitable for advertising ______ products of type purchased by only a particular section of society.
(a) specific (b) general
(c) special (d) None of these

73. Television is not suitable for ______ advertising products.
(a) consumer (b) homemade
(c) natural (d) industrial

74. Personal selling is an art and ______ of presentation of goods to the prospective buyer and persuading him to buy it.
(a) commerce (b) science
(c) Both (a) and (b) (d) None of these

75. A salesman helps the consumers to match their needs with the
(a) products (b) quality
(c) price (d) discount

76. Salesman explains to the customers by giving a ______ of how to use it.
(a) demonstration (b) action
(c) Both (a) and (b) (d) None of these

77. Salesman passes on the ______ regarding the needs and taste of the consumers to the manufacturers.
(a) message (b) information
(c) Both (a) and (b) (d) None of these

78. Salesman creates more ______ which makes planned and regular mass production possible.
(a) price (b) consumer
(c) demand (d) sales

79. Marketing consists which concept?
(a) Modern concept
(b) Continuity concept
(c) Old concept
(d) All of the above

80. Which concept of marketing is/are product oriented?
(a) Entity concept of business
(b) Old concept of marketing
(c) Modern concept of marketing
(d) All of the above

81. Which concept of marketing is/are customer oriented?
(a) Entity concept of business
(b) Modern concept of marketing
(c) Old concept of marketing
(d) All of the above

82. Which concept of marketing is based on 'customer satisfaction' key point?
(a) Entity concept of business
(b) Modern concept of marketing
(c) Old concept of marketing
(d) All of the above

83. Modern concept of marketing consists of
(a) co-ordination (b) responsibility
(c) decision (d) All of the above

84. Marketing refers to the
(a) goods distribution
(b) sale of product
(c) goods and services are exchanged to each other
(d) All of the above

85. Functions of marketing management consists
(a) marketing planning
(b) marketing organisation
(c) determination the marketing objects
(d) All of the above

86. Which of the following is/are not factors of the demand variable, according to Philip Kotler?
(a) Competition variable
(b) Environment variable
(c) Customer variable
(d) All of the above

87. Which of the following factors affects to the planning of marketing programme?
(a) Marketing strategy
(b) Demand variable
(c) Marketing mix
(d) All of the above

88. Which one of the step is not included under the step of marketing programming process?
(a) Selection of market targets
(b) Setting objectives
(c) Market response
(d) Developing the marketing mix

89. Marketing mix involves
(a) service mix
(b) product mix
(c) promotional mix
(d) All of the above

90. Marketing planning consists
(a) marketing programme
(b) determination of policies
(c) setting objectives
(d) All of the above

91. Sub-dividation marketing is called as
(a) Allocation of marketing
(b) Decision of market
(c) Only segmentation
(d) Market segmentation

92. Which of the following point is responsible for effective market segmentation?
(a) Easy accessibility
(b) Measurability
(c) Substantiality
(d) All of the above

93. Which of the following is/are the function of marketing as a managerial?
(a) Environmental scanning and market opportunity analysis.
(b) Undeistandmg consumer needs.
(c) Development of a competitive marketing plan and strategy such that an organisation is able to satisfy not only the consumers needs but also achieve its own objectives.
(d) All of the above.

94. The concept of marketing mix involves a deliberate and careful choice of organisation, product, price, promotion and place strategies and
(a) Concept (b) Planning
(c) Policies (d) All of the above

95. Corporate goals involves
(a) Production objectives
(b) Marketing objectives
(c) Research and development
(d) All of the above

96. Which one of the following is/are not element of marketing mix?
(a) Product (b) Promotion
(c) Place (d) None of these

97. The choice of marketing mix depends upon
(a) marketing objectives.
(b) marketing organisation structure and information system.

(c) the marketing environment of the organisation.
(d) All of the above.

98. Which of the following statement is true?
(a) Marketing orientation is philosophy, which has to pervade the organisation structure.
(b) Marketing is also a managerial function involving analysis planning and control marketing activities in an organisation.
(c) The essence of marketing is a transaction an exchange.
(d) All of the above.

99. The role of marketing in modern organisation is ____ with marketing offers to lend a competitive edge and marketing tasks to match the demand and supply.
(a) responding (b) integrative
(c) non-Integrative (d) All of the above

100. Socio-economic forces consist of
(a) Competition (b) Customer
(c) Substitutes (d) All of the above

101. The market environment consists of
(a) Competition (b) Technology
(c) Socio-economic (d) All of the above

102. Sources of verbal information include
(a) customers and consultants
(b) radio and television reports
(c) financial institutions
(d) All of the above

103. Which of the following steps are not involved in the environmental scanning (Scenario Building) technique?
(a) Analysis of each of the key variable separately.
(b) Analysis of the decision.
(c) Identification of key decision factors.
(d) None of the above

104. Which of the following statement is/are true?
(a) Technology factor involves understanding technological change affecting the firm's products, process and systems and its capacity to respond faster to the customer. The technological development in the industry creats an opportunity for a market to develop new products the consumer also tends to benefit from these developments.
(b) Environmental analysis and diagnosis involve understanding the five forces, namely socio-economic, competition, technology, government policies and suppliers.
(c) Understanding the socio-economic forces is important as they determine the demand for a product or service at any given time. This involves an analysis of structural changes in the population and economic change in the society.
(d) All of the above.

105. Buying situations may be caused by
(a) customer is able to evaluate and decide on his choice.
(b) awareness about competing brands in a product group.
(c) customer has a decision criteria.
(d) All of the above.

106. Service value is the assistance customer seek in purchasing a product?
(a) Value (b) Facilities
(c) Service (d) All of the above

107. Values of society involves
(a) Educational institute
(b) Family
(c) Religious institutions
(d) All of the above

108. CRM refers to the
(a) Cost rate money
(b) Cost reserve money

(c) Customer relationship management
(d) None of the above

109. Which of the following statement is/are true?
(a) There are three types of buying situations—straight rebuy, modified rebuy and new task.
(b) The buyer is motivated by economic and psychological factors.
(c) Buyer behaviour differs across product groups and hence it is necessary to know that consumer products can be categorised into high involvement and low involvement products depending upon the time spent by the buyer in considering the alternatives.
(d) All of the above.

110. The marketing concept involves
(a) competition orientation
(b) customer orientation
(c) goal achievement
(d) All of the above

111. Buy phase refers to
(a) Brand building strategy on the net today has to be coordinated with the firm's real market place strategy.
(b) The buyer can compare prices across multiple suppliers at the same time and select the one that best suits his budget.
(c) Different stages in organisational buying decisions.
(d) None of the above.

112. "All communication are action oriented." is this statement true?
(a) Can't say (b) Perhaps
(c) Yes (d) No

113. Which one of the statement is not true?
(a) In marketing, promotion menas all those tools that a marketer uses to take his product from the factory to the customer and hence involves advertising, sales promotion, personal selling, public relation publicity and merchandizing.
(b) Rational appeals, these are the appeals that are directed at the rational thinking and evaluation of the customer.
(c) Promotion is a term taken from Latin word promoverer, it means moving from one end to another.
(d) The social channel of communication this refers to a one-to-one communication and involves a person or two person addressing a group of person.

114. Personal channel consists of
(a) Advocate (b) Social
(c) Expert (d) All of the above

115. The effectiveness of marketing communication has to be measured on
(a) Connative levels
(b) Behavioural levels
(c) Cognitive levels
(d) All of the above

116. A firm select a mix of promotional tools to effectively communicate with their target _____ group.
(a) firm (b) marketer
(c) customer (d) None of these

117. The promotion mix involves to
(a) Personal selling
(b) Advertising
(c) Public relation
(d) All of the above

118. The factors that guide a marketer's decision in selecting a promotion mix which are
(a) buyer readiness stage.
(b) nature of the product market.
(c) overall marketing strategy.
(d) All of the above.

119. Which of the following is/are elements of marketing planning?
   (a) It involves an analysis of part events and projection of future events.
   (b) Marketing planning is managerial function.
   (c) In envisages determination of the future course of marketing action.
   (d) All of the above.

120. Programme consists of
   (a) Rule (b) Budget
   (c) Procedure (d) All of the above

121. Which one of the following is not step of process of the marketing planning?
   (a) Accepting and rejecting.
   (b) Analysis and interpretation of marketing opportunities and problems.
   (c) Establishing marketing objective.
   (d) Programming sub-functional operations.

122. Sales forecasting is a method of estimating ______ volume that a company can expect to attain within plan period.
   (a) purchases
   (b) sales
   (c) product or service
   (d) product

123. Merket control process consists of
   (a) plan reformulation
   (b) formulation of performance standards
   (c) performance appraisal
   (d) All of the above

124. A good control system should active corrective action no sooner ____ occur.
   (a) controllable (b) deviations
   (c) flexible (d) None of these

125. Which of the following is/are marketing oriental?
   (a) Decentralised
   (b) Consumer consideration dominate
   (c) Broad product line
   (d) All of the above

126. Marketing orientation consists of
   (a) emphasis on market price rather than cost.
   (b) external influences dominate objectives.
   (c) market research.
   (d) All of the above.

127. Marketing orientation is combination of
   (a) controller.
   (b) flexibility in production.
   (c) style and appearance prime consideration.
   (d) All of the above.

128. Which of the following is/are production oriented?
   (a) Centralised
   (b) Company consideration dominate
   (c) Narrow product line
   (d) All of the above

129. Production oriented involves
   (a) performance and applications prime consideration.
   (b) technical research.
   (c) production less flexible.
   (d) All of the above.

130. "The marketing concept is a customer orientation backed by integrated marketing aimed at generating customer satisfaction as the key to satisfying organisational goals." Who said it?
   (a) Swarteze Honda
   (b) L.G. Peter
   (c) P. Kotler
   (d) None of the above

131. "Marketing concept is the recognition on the part of management that all business decisions of the firm must be made in the light of customer needs and wants, hence,

that all marketing activities must be under one supervision and that all activities of a firm must be co-ordinated at the top, in the light of market requirements." Who refers it?

(a) R.L. King
(b) Lazo and Corbin
(c) C.P. Mc Namara
(d) All of the above

132. The marketing concept as a corporate state of mind that insists on the integration and coordination of all marketing functions which, in the turn, are welded with all other corporate functions, for the basic objective of producing maximum long-range corporate profits." Who said this statement?

(a) Peter L.G. (b) Felton P.
(c) P. Kotler (d) None of these

133. Management must think of itself not as producing products but a providing customer creating value

(a) Disapproval (b) Demand
(c) Forcing (d) Satisfactions

134. Consumer behaviour consists of all human ____ that go in making purchase decisions.

(a) tradition (b) behaviour
(c) code of conduct (d) character

135. The sociological aspects which help marketers to understand consumer behaviour include

(a) Reference group
(b) Opinion leader
(c) Family
(d) All of the above

136. Which of the following statement is/are true?

(a) Product item is a specific version of a product that has a separate name or designation in the seller's list.
(b) Product mix also referred to as product portfolio, product mix, is the composite of products offered for sale by a firm or a business unit.
(c) Product line is a group of closely related to products which are able to satisfy a class of need, to be used together, to be sold to the same customer groups to be moved through the same distribution channels, or fall within given price ranges.
(d) All of the above.

137. The process of commercialisation involves the

(a) building up a appropriate marketing mix.
(b) introducing product in the market.
(c) deciding product characteristics and package.
(d) All of the above.

138. Product life cycle characteristics consists of

(a) Channel (b) Advertising
(c) Customers (d) All of the above

139. Product market integration may be defined as a state wherein both product image and consumer self image are in focus, there is a match between product attributes and consumer expectations both economic and

(a) Political (b) Social
(c) Non-economic (d) None of these

140. Which of the following condition is true about determinants and strengths of positioning strategy?

(a) The market segment should be able to effectively receive communication ness-ages transmitted by the company.
(b) There should be competition warranting positioning.
(c) The market segment to be served should be sizeable and profitable.
(d) All of the above.

141. Corporate strengths includes
(a) a centrally located expendable plant.
(b) an aggressive and experienced top management team.
(c) extensive modern manufacturing facilities.
(d) All of the above.

142. e-marketing also referred to as
(a) Internet marketing
(b) Online marketing
(c) Internet advertising
(d) All of the above

143. Criteria for simplification, consists
(a) sales volume decreasing as a percentage of the firm's is total sales.
(b) declining absolute sales volume.
(c) decreasing market share.
(d) All of the above.

144. Which of the following statement is/are true?
(a) A brand is usually composed of a name and a mark of a product.
(b) A brand name is a part of a brand which can be vocalised.
(c) Brand means a name term and symbol or a mix thereof used to identify the product of one firm and to distinguish it from the competitive products.
(d) All of the above.

145. Which of the following statement is/are true?
(a) Sorting out involves breaking a heterogeneous supply into separate lots which are relatively homogeneous through grading or inspection.
(b) Distribution channels play a very important role in achieving the marketing objectives of a company.
(c) Distribution channel is a path way though which products and services flow from producer to consumers.
(d) All of the above.

146. Internet marketing is the marketing of products or series over
(a) TV (b) Radio
(c) Internet (d) All of the above

147. Elements of marketing planning is/are
(a) It involves an analysis of past events and projection of future events.
(b) Marketing planning is a managerial function.
(c) In envisages determination of the future course of marketing action.
(d) All of the above

148. Marketing objectives covers
(a) to win the loyalty and co-operation of dealers.
(b) to market at profit product of maximum value to consumer both current and potential.
(c) to develop and maintain product leadership.
(d) All of the above.

149. Sales promotion includes
(a) sales promotion and personnel selling
(b) publicity
(c) advertising
(d) All of the above

150. Communications model is a representation of the flow of information in a message from its sources to ______ and of the audience's reaction to the message.
(a) customers (b) business firms
(c) audiences (d) None of these

151. The communication model provides a very useful framework for understanding
(a) planning (b) promotion
(c) publicity (d) None of these

152. Promotion media are the various vehicles that corporation can use to carry their promotional message to
(a) owners (b) audiences
(c) managers (d) None of these

153. Promotion program involves
   (a) Promotion budget
   (b) Promotion objectives
   (c) Message design
   (d) All of the above

154. Pricing objectives consist of
   (a) targeted rate of return
   (b) price stabilisation
   (c) skim the cream
   (d) All of the above

155. Which of the following statement is true?
   (a) The promotion program is desi to support the marketing plan in the red way, and the cost of the promotion program is set by the budget required to implement the marketing plan.
   (b) Promotion objectives should be set before message content, layout and delivery decision are made.
   (c) Advertising is particularly difficult to evaluate because it include so many different types of delivery vehicles.
   (d) All of the above.

156. Which of the following is pricing objectives?
   (a) Market share
   (b) Market penetration
   (c) Competition
   (d) All of the above

157. Pricing objectives is combination of
   (a) Product line promotion
   (b) Profit maximisation
   (c) Cash recovery
   (d) All of the above

158. "Price policies provide the guidelines within which pricing strategy is formulated and implemented" who said it?
   (a) Scoffe
   (b) Cundiff and still
   (c) P. Kataler
   (d) All of the above

159. Which of the following cost may be used for pricing decision?
   (a) Average cost (b) Fixed cost
   (c) Variable cost (d) All of the above

160. Which one of the formula may be used for setting prices under cost plus pricing method?
   (a) Selling price = Unit total cost + Selling expenses
   (b) Selling price = Unit total cost + Desired unit profit
   (c) Selling price = Unit total cost + Profit
   (d) None of the above

161. Which one of the following is not method of selling prices?
   (a) First in-first out cost method
   (b) Cost plus pricing method
   (c) Break-even-pricing method
   (d) Marginal cost pricing method

162. Discount policies covers
   (a) trade discount policy
   (b) cash discount policy
   (c) quantity discount policy
   (d) All of the above

163. "The expected price for a product is the price at which customers consciously or unconsciously value the product, it is what they think the product is worth." Who said this statement?
   (a) William J. Holl
   (b) P. Kotler
   (c) Stanton
   (d) None of the above

164. Which of the following may be apply for government regulation on pricing?
   (a) Monopolies and Restrictive Trade Practices Act, 1969
   (b) Essential Commodities Act, 1955

(c) Industries Development and Regulation Act, 1951
(d) All of the above

165. Channels of distribution is known as
(a) Proper channel
(b) Trade channel
(c) Path channel
(d) None of these

166. Which of the following is/are the functions of distribution channel?
(a) Promotional activities
(b) Fixing prices
(c) Routinization of decisions
(d) All of the above

167. Which of the following is/are not a functions of distribution channel?
(a) Aiding communication
(b) Minimizing total transactions
(c) Managing finances
(d) None of the above

168. Direct distribution system involves
(a) Own salesman (b) Mail order
(c) Own sales (d) All of the above

169. Which of the following channels of distribution is correct?
(a) Manufacturer → Agents → Retailers → Ultimate consumer
(b) Manufacturer → Wholesaler → Retailers → Consumer
(c) Manufacturer → Agents → Consumer
(d) All of the above

170. Which is the primary aim of social marketing?
(a) Service
(b) Maximization of profit
(c) Minimization of loss
(d) Social of goods

171. "Wholesalers sells to retailers or other merchants and or industrial, institutional and commercial users but they do not sell in significant amounts to ultimate consumers." This statement refer by
(a) William J. Stanton
(b) Cundiff and Still
(c) American Marketing Association
(d) None of the above

172. "An agent middlemen negotiated purchase or sales or both, but does not take title to the goods in which he deals." This statement is
(a) Mc Carthy
(b) Cundiff and Still
(c) Stanton
(d) None of the above

173. Retailing includes all activities incident to selling to the ultimate
(a) Agents (b) Wholesaler
(c) Consumer (d) Firm

174. "A departmental stores is a large retail establishment having in the same building a number of department each of which confines its activities to one particular branch of trade and from a complete unit itself" who said it?
(a) Clark and Clark
(b) Jemes Stephenson
(c) S.L. Thomas
(d) None of the above

175. Product lines covers
(a) departmental stores
(b) general retailer
(c) one price retailer
(d) All of the above

176. Retailing middlemen on the basis of ownership covers
(a) contract chains
(b) independent stores
(c) corporate chain stores
(d) All of the above

177. Which one of the formula may be use for cost of service in case physical distribution?
   (a) Total freight cost proposed system.
   (b) Total fixed warehouse cost of proposed system.
   (c) Total freight cost of proposed system + Total fixed warehouse cost of proposal system + total variable warehouse cost of proposed system + total cost of lost sales due to average delivery delay under proposed system.
   (d) None of the above

178. Which of the following decision areas includes in management of physical distribution?
   (a) Warehousing
   (b) Size of inventory
   (c) Size of the order
   (d) All of the above

179. Which factors determines the building up of a sales organisation?
   (a) Size of the unit
   (b) Nature of the product
   (c) Traditions and customs
   (d) All of the above

180. Relationship marketing is influenced by
   (a) Price (b) Product
   (c) Re-engineering (d) Cost

181. Which is not the concept of marketing?
   (a) Marketing strategy
   (b) Capital budgeting
   (c) Branding
   (d) Market deminance

182. The promotional content of marketing is/are
   (a) Public relations
   (b) Direct marketing
   (c) Branding
   (d) All of the above

183. Which of the following statements is/are true?
   (a) Sales organisation is planning, direction and control of personal selling including recruiting, selecting, training, equipping, assigning, routine supervising paying and motivating as these tasks apply to the personal sales force.
   (b) The line and staff type is one in which the sales manager is given a staff of specialists in such fields as planning, research, statistics, engineering, promotion and training to advice him in administering the sales of the company.
   (c) A sales organisation, like any organisation is a group of individuals striving jointly to reach certain common goals, and bearing informal as well as certain formal relations to each other.
   (d) All of the above.

184. Form of sales organisation consists
   (a) line and staff type sales organisation.
   (b) line type sales organisation.
   (c) committee type sales organisation.
   (d) All of the above.

185. Field organisation of sales department involves
   (a) branch office type organisation.
   (b) head office type organisation.
   (c) divisional and branch office and crew type organisation.
   (d) All of the above.

186. "Decentralisation refers to the systematic efforts to delegate to the lowest levels all authority except that which can be exercised at central points." Who said it?
   (a) Still and Scwaff
   (b) Lavis A. Allen

(c) Stanton
(d) None of the above

187. Management of sales force involves
(a) remuneration to salesman.
(b) selection of salesman.
(c) supervision and control of the salesman.
(d) All of the above.

188. Which of the following is/are a outside sources of salesman recruitment?
(a) Attracting from other units
(b) Training and educational institutions
(c) Employment exchanges
(d) All of the above

189. Process selection of salesman consists
(a) Application form
(b) Advertisement
(c) Interview
(d) All of the above

190. Individual training involves
(a) Job rotation
(b) Training on the job
(c) Individual training conferences
(d) Correspondence training

191. Group training consists of
(a) Sales demonstration
(b) Lecturers
(c) Sales training conference
(d) All of the above

192. Which of the following method may be used for remuneration to salesmen?
(a) Commission method.
(b) Straight salary method.
(c) Drawing account and commission method.
(d) All of the above.

193. Organisations are comprised of structure
(a) People (b) Processes
(c) Culture (d) All of the above

194. Which of the following statement is true?
(a) Organisation structure is the collection of beliefs, expectations and values shared by employees.
(b) Functional organisations are divided into specialised marketing functions such as advertising, selling and marketing research.
(c) Structure is the formal arrangements of people's roles and relationship so as to achieve corporate and marketing objectives.
(d) All of the above.

195. Product based organisations are divided into units that specialize in marketing certain products or types of
(a) Firm (b) Channel
(c) Product (d) Service

196. Organisation's culture includes
(a) the extent to which employees protect their turf and control information flow.
(b) the freedom of individual employees to make significant decisions without multilevel approvals.
(c) whether major career risks are associated with risk laden decisions.
(d) All of the above.

197. Marketing characteristics is are
(a) need based marketing strategy.
(b) product market segmentation.
(c) profit orientation.
(d) All of the above.

198. Market oriented consists of
(a) highlights the factor that influence customers' buying decisions.
(b) product application and economic benefits.
(c) diagnosis and interprets the strategy, assumption, cost structure and objectives of major components.
(d) All of the above.

199. Marketing environment systems covers
(a) monitoring and control system
(b) marketing planing system
(c) marketing information system
(d) All of the above

200. The tertiary environment has a territorial phenomenon comprising
(a) Technology
(b) Demography
(c) Economic Issues
(d) All of the above

201. The marketing process involves
(a) Demand flow (b) Human needs
(c) Exchange (d) All of the above

202. Customer driven consists of
(a) Appraisal (b) Vision
(c) Mission (d) All of the above

203. Marketing management is the process of product planning, pricing, promotion and ______ along with the services to generate transaction that satisfies the organisational and user objectives.
(a) reward (b) goals
(c) distribution (d) None of these

204. Market planning consists of
(a) Market segmentation
(b) Distribution network
(c) Product positioning
(d) All of the above

205. Which one of the following is not theories of buying behaviour?
(a) Consumer variable v/s product variable
(b) Inhierent v/s learned motives
(c) Emotional v/s rational motives
(d) All of the above

206. Which of the following is group of consumers according to buying behaviour?
(a) Emotional reactors group
(b) Habit determined group
(c) Cognitive group
(d) All of the above

207. Basic needs consist of
(a) Safety needs — Insurance
(b) Physical needs — Food, drink
(c) Goodwill/reputation needs — Honour
(d) All of the above

208. Which of the following is not motivation models?
(a) Psycho-analytic model
(b) Economic model
(c) Learning model
(d) All of the above

209. "Motivational research is a form of market research that attempts to discover the deepest reasons why people buy." Who said it?
(a) Stanton
(b) Still and Scweff
(c) Manson and Rath
(d) None of the above

210. Which techniques may be used for studying buyer behaviour?
(a) Questionnaire technique
(b) Projective techniques
(c) Experience and knowledge technique
(d) All of the above

211. Projective techniques consist of
(a) Word association test
(b) Thematic apperception test
(c) Sentence completion test
(d) All of the above

212. "Motivation research is the currently popular term used to describe the application of psychiatric psychological techiniques to obtain a better understanding of why people respond as they do to products, advertisements and various other marketing situations." Who gave this statement?

(a) William J. Stanton
(b) Lawrence C. Lockley
(c) Manson and Rath
(d) All of the above

213. Which of the following is not discount policy?
(a) Trade discount policy
(b) Quantity discount policy
(c) Discount cash policy
(d) All of the above

214. Quantity discount policy consists of
(a) Off season discount policy
(b) Comulative quantity discount
(c) Non-cumulative quantity discount
(d) All of the above

215. "The expected price for a product is the price at which consciously or unconsciously value the product, it is what they think the product is worth." Who refer this statement?
(a) R.S. Dawar
(b) Stanton
(c) Philip Kotler
(d) Manson and Rath

216. Which statement is/are true about the marketing functions?
(a) Marketing consists of all those activities which are meant to ensure the flow of goods and services from the producer or the manufacturer to the consumer.
(b) Marketing consists of those efforts which effect transfers in ownership of goods and care for their physical distribution.
(c) Mraketing is the process by which products are made available to the ultimate consumers from their point of origin.
(d) All of the above.

217. The major instruments of marketing in the hands of management are
(a) Promotion (b) Price
(c) Product (d) All of the above

218. Facilitating functions of the marketing process consists which functions
(a) Pricing (b) Risk-taking
(c) Financing (d) All of the above

219. Which of the following is/are a mode of purchasing?
(a) By sample
(b) By description
(c) By inspection
(d) All of the above

220. Which of the following statements is/are true?
(a) Production under the modern industrial set-up is carried on in anticipation of consumer demand.
(b) The concept of marketing research is related to the consumer oriented modern concept of marketing.
(c) Pricing is a marketing function whose importance is acknowledged even more easily than that of other functions.
(d) All of the above.

221. Transportation performs this essential function of marketing. Proper arrangements for the transportation of products to markets is, of course, vital to the process of
(a) Selling (b) Transportation
(c) Marketing (d) Pricing

222. The provision of funds is essential for meeting the various requirements of
(a) Transportation (b) Marketing
(c) Pricing (d) All of the above

223. The marketing concerns requires both fixed capital and

(a) Flexible capital
(b) Working capital
(c) Long term capital
(d) Share capital

224. A marketing concern generally taps three sources for financing its activities there are
(a) Owned capital (b) Bank credit
(c) Trade credit (d) All of the above

225. Grading is an important process in the function of
(a) Equalisation
(b) Standardization
(c) Specialisation
(d) None of the above

226. Grading consists of
(a) it assures goods of standard quality to the consumers.
(b) it enables the manufacture to produce standardized goods.
(c) it removes the element of speculation from buying and enables the seller to secure a better price for his produce.
(d) All of the above

227. Broker are those mercantile agents who obtain neither the possession nor the ____ of the goods but only serve to bring the buyers and sellers together.
(a) right of lien (b) title
(c) ownership (d) None of these

228. The mercantile agents who adopt the auction method of selling goods on behalf of their principles are called
(a) Auctioneers
(b) Common carriers
(c) Brokers
(d) All of the above

229. The commission agents is an agent who sell goods on behalf of the
(a) Government (b) Consumers
(c) Sellers (d) Buyers

230. The marketing manager have to carry out their responsibilities integrating all these factors in the management
(a) Objectives (b) Opportunity
(c) Process (d) Goals

231. Business opportunity involves
(a) Distribution network
(b) Pruduct characteristics
(c) Segmented markets
(d) All of the above

232. The procedure for segmenting the industrial markets is different than the
(a) Business markets
(b) Industrial markets
(c) Consumer markets
(d) All of the above

233. Marketing segmentation should be followed by the targeting and product positioning activities for effective planning and implementation of the
(a) Marketing process
(b) Marketing plans
(c) Business control
(d) None of the above

234. The physical distribution involves which activities?
(a) Retail warehousing
(b) Customer service
(c) Sales force costing
(d) All of the above

235. Which of the following activities involves under physical distribution?
(a) Distribution planning
(b) Outward transportation
(c) Packaging
(d) All of the above

236. The distribution planning may invariably be based on the market survey carried out at the time of preparing the
(a) Demand concentration
(b) Product distribution

(c) Distribution channel
(d) Business plan

237. Which of the following statement is/are true?
(a) Product line—a group of products that are closely related either because they satisfy a class of need, are used together are sold to the same customer groups, are marketed through the same types of outlets, or fall within given price ranges.
(b) Product mix—the composite of product offered for sale by a firm or a business unit.
(c) Test marketing is the stage where the entire product and marketing programming is tried out for the first time in a small number of well chosen and authentic sales environments.
(d) All of the above.

238. Which of the following statement is/are true?
(a) The life cycle of a product has many points of similarity with the human life cycle, the product is bom, grown lustily, attains dynamic maturity, then enters its declining years.
(b) A brand is a name, term or design which is intended to identify the goods or services of one seller or group of sellers and to differentiate them those of competitors.
(c) The current product mix is said to be optimal if no adjustment would enhance the company's chances of achieving the objectives.
(d) All of the above.

239. Marketing is the management function which organises and directs all those activities involved in assessing and converting customer purchasing power into effective demand for specific product or service and in moving the product or service to the final consumer or use so as to active the ______ or other objective set by a company.
(a) sales target (b) pricing
(c) profit target (d) None of these

240. Marketing is the managerial process by which products are matched with market and through which transfers of ____ are affected.
(a) price (b) ownership
(c) product (d) All of the above

241. Which of the following statement is true?
(a) Just as marketing does not begin at the end of the production line it does not and with the final sale—Stanton.
(b) The objective of marketing as of all production activities is to supply human wants—Converse, Huegy and Mitchell.
(c) Marketing is the set of human activities directed at facilitating and consumating exchanges.
(d) All of the above.

242. Which one of the following is not controllable variable of marketing management?
(a) Psychological environment
(b) Social environment
(c) Cultural environment
(d) Competitive environment

243. Which one of the following is not controllable variable of marketing management?
(a) Competitive environment
(b) Economic environment
(c) Technological environment
(d) Science environment

244. Which one of the following is controllable variable of marketing management?

(a) Advertisement
(b) Political Environment
(c) Packaging
(d) Legal Environment

245. "A marketing policy is a statement of a course of action which will be followed under a given set of circumstances." Who said it?
(a) Manson and Rath
(b) Me Crathy
(c) Stanton
(d) None of the above

246. An appropriate pricing policy has a positive impact on profit making and
(a) Controlling
(b) Purchasing
(c) Sales realisation
(d) None of the above

247. The advantage of a high profit under the value pricing approach is ____ in the long run when there is a consumer segmentation for the product with a high recognition.
(a) motivated (b) oriented
(c) anticipated (d) inspired

248. Which of the following is included under store retailers?
(a) Super markets
(b) Discount store
(c) Departmental store
(d) All of the above

249. Which of the following is included under store retailers?
(a) Convenience store
(b) Superstore
(c) Hypermarkets
(d) All of the above

250. A departmental store offers a wide range of products in an organised fashion and is easily accessible to the
(a) Firm (b) Suppliers
(c) Consumers (d) Governments

251. The exclusive stores involves
(a) Limited line stores
(b) Super speciality stores
(c) Single line store
(d) All of the above

252. Super markets are retail stores which handle relatively a large volume of goods and services at ______ high margin principle of retailing.
(a) low cost
(b) high cost
(c) no profit-no loss
(d) None of the above

253. The catlog stores is new generation super stores which deal with a variety of goods and services of
(a) Wide range (b) Firm
(c) Low range (d) None of these

254. Advertising is an instrument of ____ which is applied in practice both as a science and an art generated by creative devices.
(a) firm (b) salesmen
(c) marketing (d) All of the above

255. The process of advertising in bussiness begins with market situation analysis conducted to assess the marketing ____ for the product in the existing state of business in the market.
(a) assessibility (b) functioning
(c) opportunities (d) difficulty

256. The environmental factors of advertising are
(a) Legal factors
(b) Economic factors
(c) Social and cultural factors
(d) All of the above

257. Advertising process involves
(a) Media use plan
(b) Target audience

(c) Research
(d) All of the above

258. Which of the following functions covers under advertising classification?
(a) Primary advertising
(b) Selective advertising
(c) Product advertising
(d) All of the above

259. Cost data are need to make decisions such as
(a) Make or Buy (b) Replacement
(c) Pricing (d) All of these

260. Which cost are known as periodical cost?
(a) Variable cost (b) Sunk cost
(c) Fixed cost (d) Total cost

261. Cost is
(a) measured in monetary terms.
(b) a foregoing or sacrifice.
(c) to achieve a specific purpose.
(d) All of the above.

262. Expired cost, the monetary value of the resources that have already been used in
(a) Producing revenue
(b) Producing cost
(c) Goods
(d) Producing unit

263. Future costs are based on
(a) Per unit cost (b) Advertising
(c) Forecasts (d) Production

264. When costs are accumulated for an organizational unit or department, it is called
(a) A cost benefit
(b) Cost of production
(c) Unit
(d) A cost centre

265. _____ are those cost items which can be traced logically and conveniently, in their entirety, to a cost object.
(a) Fixed costs (b) Make cost
(c) Direct costs (d) Indirect costs

266. _____ are those cost items which cannot be traced or identified directly with a cost object.
(a) Indirect costs (b) Full costs
(c) Direct costs (d) Fixed costs

267. The sum of direct materials and direct labour costs is called
(a) Overhead cost (b) Prime cost
(c) Full cost (d) Factory cost

268. The sum of direct materials cost, direct labour cost and factory overhead is called
(a) Factory cost
(b) Full cost
(c) Total factory cost
(d) None of the above

269. When products have been manufactured and are on saleable condition, the selling function
(a) Reduced (b) Starts
(c) Increased (d) Drop

270. ______ are those costs which are incurred to perform the marketing functions.
(a) Full costs
(b) Sale of goods
(c) Transfer cost
(d) Distribution costs

271. Distribution costs are also called
(a) Selling costs
(b) Marketing costs
(c) Both (a) and (b)
(d) Full costs

272. Order-getting costs are incurred to affect
(a) Cost of product
(b) Sales of product
(c) Transfer cost
(d) Distribution cost

273. Those cost items which attach or using to units of finished goods are called
(a) Fixed costs (b) Variable costs
(c) Product costs (d) Full costs

274. When total cost changes in direct proportion to changes in volume, it is called a
(a) Sunk cost (b) Full cost
(c) Total cost (d) Variable cost

275. Variable costs vary in a proportionate and paralleled manner with
(a) Quality (b) Factory
(c) Time (d) Volume

276. When fixed cost remains non-variable to changes in volume, it is called a
(a) Fixed cost (b) Variable cost
(c) Transfer cost (d) Full cost

277. Fixed cost remain at the same level irrespective of change in
(a) Quality (b) Centres
(c) Volume (d) Cost

278. Shut down sales can be find out as

(a) $\dfrac{\text{Contribution ratio}}{\text{Fixed costs} - \text{Variable cost}}$

(b) $\dfrac{\text{Fixed costs} - \text{Avoidable costs on shut down}}{\text{Contribution ratio}}$

(c) $\dfrac{\text{Fixed costs}}{100} \times \text{Variable cost}$

(d) $\dfrac{\text{Contribution ratio}}{\text{Fixed costs}} \times 100$

279. If Fixed cost are expected to remain unaltered, that would be irrelevant in
(a) Sales planning
(b) Product mix decision
(c) Production decision
(d) The make or buy decision

280. The contribution approach to pricing is based on the incremental
(a) Cost force (b) Cost principle
(c) Trade customs (d) Cost systems

281. Fixed costs, in the short run, are ______ therefore, they are irrelevant in pricing special order.
(a) Controllable (b) Flexible
(c) Uncontrollable (d) Variable

282. The net profit will be maximised when
(a) Contribution is maximised
(b) Contribution is minimised
(c) Fixed cost remains same
(d) Fixed cost is increased

283. Decision-making is a future oriented activity. It involves forecasting and planning. The function of decision-making is to choose alternatives for the
(a) Profit (b) Loss
(c) Future (d) Present

284. Marketing manager may be classified in the category of
(a) middle level management
(b) lower level of management
(c) top level management
(d) None of the above

Directions: Questions 285 to 302 are of multiple statement type. Choose the correct answer from the codes given below.

285. Which one of the following is not views regarding marketing concept?
1. The distribiution of goods and services concept
2. The creation of utilities concept
3. Delivery of standard of living concept
4. System approach concept
5. Consumer satisfaction concept

Codes:
(a) 1, 2, 3 and 5 (b) 1, 2 and 4
(c) 1 and 3 (d) None of these

286. Which of the following is/are not stage of the marketing management process?
1. Assessment of business opportunity
2. Organising research market surveys
3. Selecting target markets
4. Strategy formulation
5. Planning marketing programmes
6. Implementation
7. Controlling marketing efforts
8. Accounting information system

Codes:
(a) 1, 4 and 6 (b) 1, 2 and 4
(c) 8 only (d) None of these

287. The market process involves which functions?
1. Buying 2. Transporting
3. Storing 4. Selling
5. Grading 6. Financing
7. Risk-bearing 8. Dividing

Codes:
(a) 1, 3, 4, 5, 6 and 7
(b) 1, 3, 5, 6, 7 and 8
(c) 1, 2, 3, 6, and 7
(d) All of the above

288. Which of the following production is/are not considered on the basis of psychology?
1. Prestige product
2. Maturity product
3. Anxiety product
4. Function products
5. Hedonic products

Codes:
(a) 1, 3, 4 and 5 (b) 1, 2, 3 and 5
(c) 1, 2, 3, 4 and 5 (d) None of these

289. The marketing begins with human needs which may be classified as under
1. Essential needs
2. Economic needs
3. Social needs
4. Conspicuous needs
5. Risk needs
6. Product utility

Codes:
(a) 2, 3 and 4 (b) 1, 2, 3, 4
(c) 1, 2, 3 and 6 (d) None of these

290. Which of the following may be considered for evaluation of salesman's performance?
1. Report on completed activities
2. Report on future activities
3. Report on expenses
4. Report on lost business
5. Report on new business

Codes:
(a) 1, 2, 3, 4 and 5 (b) 5 only
(c) 3 only (d) 4 and 5

291. Which of the following factors affects to the choice of channels of distribution?
1. Size of manufacturer
2. Desire to control the channel
3. Perishability of product
4. Weight of product
5. Number of customers

Codes:
(a) 3 and 4 (b) 4 and 5
(c) 2 only (d) All of the above

292. MRTP Act, 1969 covers
1. Establishement of monopolies and restrictive trade practice commission.
2. Control on monopolistic trade practices.
3. Registration of restrictive trade practices agreements.
4. Prevention of concentration of economic power.
5. Prohibition for maintaining re-sale prices.
6. Power to obtain information and appoint inspectors.

Codes:
(a) 2, 3, 4, 5 and 6
(b) 1, 2, 3, 4 and 5

(c) 1, 3, 4 and 6
(d) 1, 2, 3, 4, 5 and 6

293. Which of the four criteria may be use by managers typically to determine the role of each promotion program?
1. Cost of reaching an audience member.
2. Ability to reach target audiences with little leakage to persons not included in them.
3. Ability to deliver a complicated message.
4. Ability to engage in interchanges with the target audiences.

Codes:

(a) 3 only (b) 1, 2, 3 and 4
(c) 2 and 4 (d) None of these

294. Which of the following factor that affects to pricing decisions?
1. Demand of the product
2. Product characteristics
3. Cost of the product
4. Distribution channels of the product
5. Customers characteristics

Codes:

(a) 3 and 4 (b) 1 only
(c) 3 only (d) All of the above

295. A marketing plan is composed of three basic components, namely
1. Objective 2. Policies
3. Program 4. Procedure
5. Hints 6. Decision
7. Command 8. Periodic
9. Diversify

Codes:

(a) 5, 7 and 9 (b) 6, 7 and 8
(c) 1, 2 and 3 (d) 2, 3 and 9

296. Which of the following statement is/are true?
1. The social environment serves as a noncommercial source of consumer information and influence which is not under the direct control of the firm.
2. Social environment included reference groups and individuals, family members, social class and castes, culture and the like.
3. Consumer behaviour is influenced not only by the current disposable personal income available but also by the future income expectations of a consumer.
4. Consumer buying behaviour is also influenced by the level of the consumer's liquid assets.
5. Liquid assets refer to those assets that are in cash or may be easily converted into cash when desired like that stock Bank Balance and B/R.
6. The economic theories and condition of a consumer is determined by economic factors.

Codes:

(a) 1, 2, 3, 4, 5 and 6
(b) 1, 2, 4, 5 and 6
(c) 1, 3, 4, 5 and 6
(d) 2, 4, 5 and 6

297. Which of the following channel is/are related with conventional distribution channels?
1. Manufacturer → Customer (Consumer)
2. Manufacturer → Retailers → Customers (Consumer)
3. Manufacturer → Wholesaler → Retailers → Consumer
4. Manufacturer → Wholesaler

Codes:

(a) 1, 2, 3 and 4 (b) 2 and 3
(c) 1 only (d) None of these

298. Which of the following are the merits of marketing planning?

1. Identification of future development.
2. Consideration of opportunities and problems.
3. Focus on objectives.
4. Profitable employment of resources.
5. Management by exception becomes possible.

Codes:

(a) 3 only (b) 1 only
(c) 5 only (d) 1, 2, 3, 4 and 5

299. Which of the following attitudes and behaviour influenced by culture are
1. Sense of self and space
2. Communication and language
3. Dress and appearance
4. Food and feeding habits
5. Mental processes and learning

Codes:

(a) 5 only
(b) 3 and 4
(c) 1, 2, 3, 4 and 5
(d) 3 and 5

300. Which of the following function involved under marketing management's functions?
1. Collection of marketing sources
2. Marketing co-ordination
3. Marketing controlling
4. Marketing direction

Codes:

(a) 2 and 3 (b) 1, 2, 3 and 4
(c) 1 only (d) 2 only

301. Which of the following is not an economic factor?
1. Gross National Product
2. Per capita income
3. Balance of payment position
4. Fiscal policies and prime rate of interest charged to commercial banks
5. Trends in the price of goods and services

Codes:

(a) 1, 3 and 5 (b) 1, 2, 3 and 4
(c) 1, 2, 3, 4 and 5 (d) None of these

302. Which of the following steps are covered under the process of marketing programme?
1. Setting objectives
2. Selection of marketing
3. Developing the marketing mix
4. Physical and Human Resources
5. Mobilization of Resources

Codes:

(a) 1, 3, 4 and 5 (b) 1, 2, 3, 4 and 5
(c) 1, 2, 3 and 4 (d) 1, 2, 4 and 5

Directions: Questions 303 to 369 are of matching type. Match List I with List II and select the correct answer using the codes given below the list.

303. **List I**

A. Pyle
B. Tousley and Clark
C. Huegy and Mitchell
D. Edward and David

List II

1. Marketing comprises both buying and selling activities.
2. Marketing consists of those effects which effect transfers in the ownership of goods and services and which provide for physical distribution.
3. Marketing includes activities involved in the flow of goods and services from production to consumption.
4. Marketing is the economic process by means of which goods and services are exchanged and their values determined in terms of money price.

Codes:	A	B	C	D
(a)	2	1	3	4
(b)	3	4	1	2

(c) 4 2 1 3
(d) 1 2 3 4

304. **List I (Thinkers of marketing management)**

A. A.P. Felton
B. P. Kotler
C. Lewis K. Johnson
D. L.K. Johnson

List II (Their statements)

1. Marketing concept is a coiporate state of mind that insists on the integration and co-ordination of all marketing functions which, in turn, are welded with all other corporate functions, for the basic objectives of producing maximum long- range corporate profits.
2. The marketing concept is customer-oriented backed by integrated marketing aimed at generating customer satisfaction as the key to satisfying organisational goods.
3. Specifically marketing management includes within its scope, the analysis, formulation and execution of plans concerning the product, the markets to be covered, the distributive methods to be used, the type of organisation of the sales division, the functions of sales management, the advertising compaign, sales promotion work and the techniques of sales control.
4. Marketing management is the field of business activity involving the establishment and execution of the plans of all phases or step of complete sales compaign.

Codes:	A	B	C	D
(a)	3	1	4	2
(b)	1	3	2	4
(c)	3	1	2	4
(d)	1	2	3	4

305. **List I (Marketing management thinkers)**

A. W.J. Stanton
B. Paul Mazur
C. H.L. Hansen
D. E. Jerome Mc Carthy
E. Malcolm Menair

List II (Statements)

1. Marketing is a total system of interacting business activities designed to plan, price, promote and distribute want satisfying products and services to present and potential customers.
2. Marketing is the delivery of a standard of living.
3. Marketing is the process of discovering and translating consumer needs and wants into product and service specifications, creating demand for these products and services and then in turn expanding this demand.
4. Marketing is the responses of businessmen to the need to edjust production capabilities to the requirements of consumer demands.
5. Marketing is the creation and delivery of a standard of living.

Codes:	A	B	C	D
(a)	4	2	3	1
(b)	1	2	4	3
(c)	1	2	3	4
(d)	2	1	3	4

306. **List I (Market segmentation)**

A. Geographic B. Demographic
C. Psychographic D. Behavioural

List II (Factors)

1. Territory 2. Age
3. Race 4. User status

Codes:	A	B	C	D
(a)	3	1	2	4
(b)	1	2	3	4

(c)	2	3	1	3
(d)	3	1	4	2

307. **List I (Marketing management thinkers)**
   A. F.J. Borch
   B. St. Thomas
   C. E.F.L. Breach
   D. Paul T. Cherigntor

   List II (Their statements)
   1. Marketing is the fundamental business philosophy.
   2. Marketing is a way of managing a business so that each critical business decision is made with full knowledge of the impact of that decision on the customer.
   3. Marketing is the process of determining consumer demand for a product or service, motivating its sale and distributing it into ultimate consumption of profit.
   4. The function of marketing is the establishment of contract.

Codes:	A	B	C	D
(a)	2	3	1	4
(b)	1	2	3	4
(c)	2	3	1	4
(d)	3	1	2	4

308. **List I (Bases of segmenting industrial markets)**
   A. Physical
   B. Operational
   C. Purchase
   D. Personal
   E. Situational

   List II (Variables for segmenting industrial markets)
   1. Type of industry
   2. Logistics policy
   3. Purchase policy
   4. Brand loyalty
   5. Legal binding

Codes:	A	B	C	D	E
(a)	2	1	3	4	5
(b)	1	2	3	4	5
(c)	4	2	1	3	5
(d)	3	1	2	4	5

309. **List I (Bases of segmenting industrial markets)**
   A. Physical
   B. Operational
   C. Purchase
   D. Situational
   E. Personal

   List II (Variables for segmenting industrial markets)
   1. size of industry
   2. logistics policy
   3. lobby status
   4. specific order
   5. risk factor

Codes:	A	B	C	D	E
(a)	4	5	1	2	3
(b)	2	3	1	4	5
(c)	5	1	2	3	4
(d)	1	2	3	4	5

310. **List I (Marketing sub-plan)**
   A. Baseline research
   B. Technical plan
   C. Organisational plan
   D. Contingency plan

   List II (Variables of marketing sub-plan)
   1. Customer service
   2. Packaging
   3. Regulation
   4. Risk management

Codes:	A	B	C	D
(a)	2	3	1	4
(b)	1	3	2	4
(c)	4	2	3	1
(d)	1	2	3	4

311. **List I (Marketing sub-plan)**
A. Contingency plan
B. Organisational plan
C. Technical plan
D. Baseline research

List II (Variables of marketing sub-plan)
1. Diversification
2. Public relations
3. Quality control
4. Customer service

Codes:	A	B	C	D
(a)	1	2	3	4
(b)	1	3	2	4
(c)	4	2	3	1
(d)	2	4	3	1

312. **List I (Market segmentation)**
A. Geographic B. Demographic
C. Psychographic D. Behavioural

List II (Factors of segmentation)
1. Habitat
2. Sex
3. Nationality
4. Personal preferences

Codes:	A	B	C	D
(a)	2	3	1	4
(b)	1	2	3	4
(c)	2	1	3	4
(d)	2	1	4	3

313. **List I (Market segmentation)**
A. Geographic B. Demographic
C. Psychographic D. Behavioural

List II (Factors of segmentation)
1. Identity 2. Education
3. Social Class 4. Attitude

Codes:	A	B	C	D
(a)	1	2	3	4
(b)	1	2	4	3
(c)	3	1	2	4
(d)	2	3	1	4

314. **List I (Market segmentation)**
A. Psychographic B. Demographic
C. Behavioural D. Geographic

List II (Factors of segmentation)
1. Personality groups
2. Occupation
3. Brand loyalty
4. Population size

Codes:	A	B	C	D
(a)	1	2	3	4
(b)	2	1	3	4
(c)	4	2	1	3
(d)	1	3	2	4

315. **List I (Type of wholesalers)**
A. Manufacturer wholesalers
B. Retailer wholesalers
C. Wholesalers proper
D. Single line wholesalers

List II (Their qualities)
1. A wholesaler who engage in manufacturing activities to some extent.
2. These wholesalers purchase goods in large parcle from the manufacturers and retail them to the consumers through their own shops.
3. The wholesalers who are, however, those merchants who concentrate entirely on the functions of buying and selling in large lots, and do not engage in the manufacturing or retailing activities.
4. The wholesalers deal in different varieties in a particular line of goods and sell goods to many types of buyers of such goods.

Codes:	A	B	C	D
(a)	2	1	3	4
(b)	1	2	3	4
(c)	2	3	1	4
(d)	3	4	1	2

316. List I (Functions of a marketing process)
A. Functions of exchanges
B. Transfer of ownership
C. Functions of physical supply
D. Facilitating functions

List II (Their sub-functions)
1. Selling
2. Buying and selling
3. Transportation
4. Financing

Codes:	A	B	C	D
(a)	2	3	1	4
(b)	1	2	3	4
(c)	4	2	3	1
(d)	3	1	2	4

317. List I (Instrument of marketing)
A. Product B. Promotion
C. Price D. Place

List II (Their qualities)
1. Shape, design
2. Advertising, publicity
3. Discount, policies regarding pricing
4. Layout of stores, location

Codes:	A	B	C	D
(a)	2	1	3	4
(b)	1	2	3	4
(c)	2	3	1	4
(d)	3	4	1	2

318. List I (Management thinkers)
A. Philip Kotler
B. Cundiff, Still and Govoni
C. Stanton
D. Mc Carthy

List II (Their statements)
1. Every producer seeks to link together the set of marketing intermediaries that best fulfil the firm's objectives. The set of marketing intermediaries is called the marketing channel.
2. Marketing channels are the distribution network through which producers products flow to the market.
3. Physical distribution involves the management of the physical flow of products and the establishment and operation of flow system.
4. Physical distribution is the actual handling and moving of goods within individual firms and along channel systems.

Codes:	A	B	C	D
(a)	2	3	1	4
(b)	1	2	3	4
(c)	1	3	2	4
(d)	2	3	4	1

319. List I (Marketing management thinkers)
A. Stanton
B. Cundiff and Still
C. Stewart
D. Philip Kotler

List II (Books and articles)
1. *Fundamental of Marketing*
2. *Basic Marketing*
3. *Principles of Marketing*
4. *Marketing Management*

Codes:	A	B	C	D
(a)	2	3	1	4
(b)	1	2	3	4
(c)	4	3	1	2
(d)	2	1	3	4

320. List I (Marketing management thinker)
A. Tousley, Clark and Clark
B. Stanton
C. Richard Buskrik
D. Mc Carthy

List II (Their statements)
1. Re-sale price maintenance is the marketing policy under which the

manufacturer or owner of a commodity by brand trademark, copyright, or patent, places restrictions on the price at which that commodity shall be sold by purchasers and sub-purchasers.

2. A channel of distribution for a product is the route taken by the title to the goods as they move from the producer to the ultimate consumer or industrial user.
3. Distribution channels are systems of economic institutions, through which a producer of goods delivers them into the hands of their users.
4. Any sequence of institutions from the producer to the consumer, including one or any number of middlemen, is called a channel of distribution.

Codes:	A	B	C	D
(a)	1	2	3	4
(b)	1	2	4	3
(c)	3	1	2	4
(d)	4	3	1	2

321. **List I (Marketing management thinkers)**

A. P. Kotler
B. Stanton
C. Karl H. Tietjen
D. Mason and Rath

List II (Their statements)

1. Planning is deciding in the present what to do in future.
2. Product planning embraces all activities which enable producers and middlemen to determine what should constitute a company's line of product.
3. Product planning may be defined as the act of marketing out and supervising the search, screening development and commercialisation of new products, the modification of existing lines and the discontinuance of marginal or unprofitable items.
4. The planning, direction and control of all stages in the life of a product from the time of its creation to the time of its removal from the company's line of product is known as product planning.

Codes:	A	B	C	D
(a)	2	1	3	4
(b)	4	3	1	2
(c)	1	2	3	4
(d)	3	4	1	2

322. **List I**

A. Johnson
B. Stanton
C. Cipson and Darling
D. Richard Buskirk

List II

1. Product planning determines the characteristics of product best meeting the consumer's numerous desire, characteristics that add sale ability to product and in corporates these characteristics into the finished product.
2. Product planning is the starting point for the entire marketing programme in a firm.
3. Product development involves the adding, dropping and modification of item specification in the product line for a given period of time usually one year.
4. The marketing management philosophy of business operation makes it mandatory that the fundamental responsibility for product planning rests in the marketing division and not in the production or engineering divisions.

Codes:	A	B	C	D
(a)	3	1	2	4
(b)	4	2	1	3

(c)	1	2	3	4
(d)	1	3	2	4

323. List I (Motivation models)

A. Economic model
B. Learning model
C. Psycho anlytic model
D. Organisational model

List II (Elements)

1. Attractive design 2. Inspiration
3. Sex 4. Cost of product

Codes:	**A**	**B**	**C**	**D**
(a)	1	2	3	4
(b)	1	2	4	3
(c)	1	3	2	4
(d)	2	1	4	3

324. List I (Product on the basis of psychology)

A. Prestige products
B. Maturity products
C. Anxiety product
D. Hedonic product

List II (Products)

1. Ownership on the car, bus, house
2. Bidi, cigareatte, cold drink
3. Soap, Blades
4. Biscuit, double-roti, bread and butter

Codes:	**A**	**B**	**C**	**D**
(a)	2	1	3	4
(b)	1	2	3	4
(c)	4	3	1	2
(d)	1	2	4	3

325. List I (Determinants of buyer behaviour)

A. Psychological factors
B. Economic factors
C. Security needs
D. Physical needs

List II (Factors)

1. Basic needs 2. Family income
3. Insurance 4. Apples, food

Codes:	**A**	**B**	**C**	**D**
(a)	2	1	3	4
(b)	1	2	3	4
(c)	1	3	2	4
(d)	3	4	1	2

326. List I

A. Bertrand R. Canfield
B. Edwin B. Flippo
C. Dale S. Beach
D. M.J. Jucious

List II

1. Good salesman are not born but made by properly organised and directed sales training programmes.
2. Training is the act of increasing the knowledge and skill of an employee for doing a particular job.
3. Training is the organised procedure by which people learn knowledge and skill for a definite purpose.
4. The term training is used how to indicate only process by which the aptitude skills and abilities of employees to perform specific jobs are increased.

Codes:	**A**	**B**	**C**	**D**
(a)	1	3	2	4
(b)	1	2	3	4
(c)	3	4	1	2
(d)	2	1	3	4

327. List I (Field organisation of sales department)

A. Head office type organisation
B. Branch office type organisation
C. Divisional and branch office type organisation
D. Divisional, branch offices and crew type organisation

List II (Their expression)

1. Head office → Salesman
2. Head office → Branch office → Salesman
3. Head office → Divisional offices → Branch office → Salesman
4. Head office → Divisional office → Branch offices → Crew manager → Salesman

Codes:	A	B	C	D
(a)	1	2	4	3
(b)	1	2	3	4
(c)	1	4	2	3
(d)	1	3	2	4

328. **List I (Marketing management educationist)**

A. B.R. Canfield
B. Still and Cundiff
C. Franklin G. Moore
D. Bertrand R. Canfield

List II (Their statements)

1. The line and staff type is one in which the sales manager is given a staff of specialists in such field as planning, research statistics, engineering, promotion and training to advice him in administering the sales of product/services of the company.
2. The line and staff provides the chief sales executive the assistance of a group of specialists.
3. Authority is the right to decide and the power to act to carry out decisions.
4. Authority is the right to command or act.

Codes:	A	B	C	D
(a)	3	1	2	4
(b)	1	2	3	4
(c)	3	2	3	1
(d)	3	1	4	2

329. **List I (Classification of retailing middlemen)**

A. On the basis of sales
B. On the basis of product lines
C. On the basis of ownership
D. On the basis of method of operation

List II (Middlemen)

1. Large retailer
2. Single line retailer
3. Consumer stores
4. Vending machine

Codes:	1	2	3	4
(a)	1	2	3	4
(b)	1	2	4	3
(c)	3	2	1	4
(d)	2	3	1	4

330. **List I (Marketing management thinkers)**

A. Mason and Rath
B. Cundiff and Still
C. William J. Stanton
D. James Stephenson

List II (Books and articles)

1. *Marketing and distribution*
2. *Basic Marketing*
3. *Fundamental of marketing*
4. *Principles and practice of commerce*

Codes:	A	B	C	D
(a)	1	2	3	4
(b)	2	1	3	4
(c)	3	1	2	4
(d)	1	2	4	3

331. **List I (Marketing management thinkers)**

A. Stanton
B. Cundiff and Still
C. Mc Crathy
D. Wendell M. Stewart

List II (Their statements)

1. Physical distribution involves the management of the physical flow of

products and the establishment and operation of flow system.
2. Physical distribution involves the actual movement and storage of goods after they are produced and before they are consumed.
3. Physical distribution is the actual handling and moving of goods whithin individual firms and along channel systems.
4. Physical distribution is the science of business logistics whereby the proper amount of the right kind of product is made available at the place where demand for it exists, viewed in this light, physical distribution is the keylink between manufacturing and demand creation.

Codes:	A	B	C	D
(a)	2	1	3	4
(b)	1	2	3	4
(c)	4	1	2	3
(d)	2	3	1	4

332. **List I (Marketing management thinkers)**
A. Mason and Rath
B. Cundiff and Still
C. Mc Carthy
D. Stanton

List II (Their statements)
1. A person or firm that buys merchandise and resale it either to retailers for subsequent resale to the consumer or to business firm for industrial and business use is called a wholesaler.
2. Wholesalers buy and resell merchandise to retailers and other merchants and to industrial institutional and commercial users but do not sell in significant amount to ultimate consumers.
3. Retailing is selling final consumer products to house holders.
4. Retailing includes all activities directly related to the sale of goods or services to the ultimate consumer of personal non business use.

Codes:	A	B	C	D
(a)	1	2	3	4
(b)	1	2	4	3
(c)	2	4	1	3
(d)	2	1	4	3

333. **List I (Factors affecting choice of channels of distribution)**
A. Manufacturers considerations
B. Product considerations
C. Market considerations
D. Middlemen considerations

List II (Elements)
1. Managerial Experience and Ability
2. Technical Nature
3. Customer's Buying Habits
4. Service

Codes:	A	B	C	D
(a)	1	3	4	2
(b)	2	3	1	4
(c)	3	1	2	4
(d)	1	2	3	4

334. **List I (Factors affecting choice of channels of distribution)**
A. Manufacturers considerations
B. Product considerations
C. Market considerations
D. Middlemen considerations

List II (Elements)
1. Size of manufacturer
2. Weight of product
3. Number of customers
4. Sales possibilities

Codes:	**A**	**B**	**C**	**D**
(a)	1	3	2	4
(b)	1	2	3	4
(c)	2	3	1	4
(d)	2	3	4	1

335. **List I (Distribution systems)**
   - A. Direct distribution system
   - B. Indirect distribution system
   - C. Dual distribution system
   - D. Direct distribution system

   List II (Meant of distribution system)
   1. Own sales shops
   2. Agent
   3. Retailers and Telephone
   4. Chain stores

Codes:	**A**	**B**	**C**	**D**
(a)	1	2	3	4
(b)	1	3	2	4
(c)	3	1	2	4
(d)	2	3	1	4

336. **List I (Marketing management thinkers)**
   - A. McCarthy
   - B. P. Kotler
   - C. Cundiff, Still and Govoni
   - D. Mason and Rath

   List II (Their statements)
   1. Any sequence of institutions from the producer to the consumer, including one or any number of middlemen, is called a channel of distribution.
   2. Every producer seeks to link together the set of marketing intermediaries that best fulfil the firm's objectives. This set of marketing intermediaries is called the marketing channel (also trade channel and channel of distribution).
   3. Marketing channels are the distribution network through which producers products flow to the market.
   4. A person or firm that buy merchandise and results it either to retailers for subsequent resale to the consumer or to business firm for industrial and business use is called a wholesaler.

Codes:	**A**	**B**	**C**	**D**
(a)	2	3	4	1
(b)	1	2	3	3
(c)	1	3	2	3
(d)	4	3	1	2

337. **List I (Marketing management thinkers)**
   - A. John Robinson
   - B. Tousley, Clark and Clark
   - C. Stanton
   - D. Richard Buskrik

   List II (Statements)
   1. The act of selling the same article, product under a single control, at different prices to different buyers is known as price discrimination.
   2. Resale price maintenance is the marketing policy under which the manufacturer or owner of a commodity identified by brand trade mark, copyright or patent, places restrictions on the price at which that commodity shall be sold by purchasers and sub purchasers.
   3. A channel of distribution for a product is taken by the firm for the title of the goods as they move from the producer to the ultimate consumer or industrial user.
   4. Distribution channels are systems of economic institution through which producer of goods delivers them into the hands of their users.

Codes:	**A**	**B**	**C**	**D**
(a)	2	1	3	4
(b)	1	2	3	4
(c)	4	3	1	2
(d)	3	4	1	2

338. **List I (Promotion mix tools)**

A. Advertising
B. Sales Promotion
C. Personal selling
D. Publicity

List (Sources of message)

1. Print ads 2. Couponing
3. Telemarketing 4. Print media

Codes:	**A**	**B**	**C**	**D**
(a)	3	1	2	4
(b)	1	2	3	4
(c)	3	2	4	1
(d)	2	3	1	4

339. **List I (Sources of communication flow)**

A. Source credibility
B. Source attractiveness
C. Message content
D. Message format

List II (Their characteristics)

1. The source's trust worthiness and expertise with respect to the content of the message, as perceived by audience.
2. The sources which is refers to the physical attractiveness of a sources as perceived by the audience, or the degree to which the audience sees the sources as being similar to itself in age, interests values, or other characteristics.
3. The information provided by promotion can include facts opinions and persuasive arguments.
4. The way that a message is presented the arrangement of text and visual displays in such a way as to capture an audience's attention and convey the message.

Codes:	**A**	**B**	**C**	**D**
(a)	2	3	1	4
(b)	1	2	3	4
(c)	1	2	4	3
(d)	2	3	4	1

340. **List I (Promotion mix tools)**

A. Personal selling
B. Publicity
C. Sales Promotion
D. Advertising

List II (Sources of message)

1. Telemarketing
2. News stories
3. Trade shows
4. Billboard ads

Codes:	**A**	**B**	**C**	**D**
(a)	2	3	4	1
(b)	1	2	3	4
(c)	1	4	3	2
(d)	2	1	3	4

341. **List I (Marketing management thinkers)**

A. Gulick Luther
B. Smith W.R.
C. Koontz H. and C.O. Donnell
D. W.H. Newman

List I (Books and articles)

1. *Administrative Reflections from World War II*
2. *The Role of Planning in Marketing*
3. *Principles of Management*
4. *Administration Action*

Codes:	**A**	**B**	**C**	**D**
(a)	1	2	4	3
(b)	2	3	1	4
(c)	3	4	1	2
(d)	1	2	3	4

342. **List I (Merchant intermediaries)**

A. Wholesaler
B. Retailer
C. Full function wholesaler
D. Drop seller/ Shipper

List II (Role and functions)

1. A merchant wholesaler may be defined as that intermediary who buys goods in bulk from manufacturers and sells them largely to subsequent intermediaries participating in the channel, namely, semi wholesalers and retailers and, some times, to large consumers in relatively smaller lots.
2. A merchant intermediary who buys products from preceding channel members in small assorted lots and sells them to consumers in still smaller assorted lots to suit individual consumer requirements.
3. A merchant intermediary who buys and sells products in his own account, carries stock, organises selling, extends credit, assembles products from many sources in bulk, sell.es in smaller lots and renders counsel and advice to his buyers.
4. A merchant wholesaler who neither stores products or services nor delivers/ renders them to buyers from his own stock but he books orders and directs manufacturers to despatch products to buyers at the places and times indicated in the orders so booked.

Codes:	A	B	C	D
(a)	3	4	1	2
(b)	1	2	3	4
(c)	3	1	2	4
(d)	1	3	2	4

343. **List I (Marketing management thinkers)**

A. Kotler P.
B. R.S. Alexander
C. Ansoff H.I.
D. Berenson C.

List II (Books and Articles)

1. *Phasing Out Weak Product*
2. *The Death and Burial of 'Sick' Products*
3. *A model for Diversification*
4. *Proning the Product Line*

Codes:	A	B	C	D
(a)	3	1	4	2
(b)	2	1	3	4
(c)	1	3	2	4
(d)	1	2	3	4

344. **List I (Marketing management thinkers)**

A. Sherif C.W. and M. Sherif
B. Walter C.G. and G.W. Paul
C. Mc Neal, J.V.
D. D.M. Mc Gregor

List II (Books and Articles)

1. *Attitude, Ego-Involvement and Change*
2. *Consumer Behaviour*
3. *Dimensions of Consumer Behaviour*
4. *Leadership and Motivation*

Codes:	A	B	C	D
(a)	1	3	2	4
(b)	2	4	3	1
(c)	3	2	1	4
(d)	1	2	3	4

345. **List I (Product category)**

A. Bread B. Biscuits
C. Butter D. Soap

List II (Brand name)

1. Modern 2. Britannia
3. Amul 4. Lux

Codes:	A	B	C	D
(a)	3	4	1	2
(b)	1	2	4	3
(c)	1	2	3	4
(d)	2	1	3	4

346. **List I (Classification of product)**

1. Consumer product
2. Durable product
3. Convenience product
4. Speciality product

List II (Explanation)

1. Consumer products are those products which are destined for use by ultimate consumers or households and in such form that they can be used without further commercial processing.
2. Durable products are those tangible products which normally survive many use like, for example car, motor and furniture.
3. Convenience products are those consumer goods which a customer usually purchases frequently, immediately and with the minimum of effort in comparison and buying for example soap and bread.
4. Speciality products are those consumer goods with unique characteristics and/ or brand identification for which a significant group of buyers are habitually willing to make a special purchasing effort, as for example ice cream.

Codes:	A	B	C	D
(a)	3	1	4	2
(b)	1	2	3	4
(c)	4	3	1	2
(d)	2	1	3	4

347. **List I (Product category)**

A. Ties B. Tooth past

C. Pen D. Lock

List II (Brand name)

1. Zodiac 2. Colgate

3. Ronalds 4. Herison

Codes:	A	B	C	D
(a)	3	1	4	2
(b)	3	1	2	4
(c)	2	1	3	4
(d)	1	2	3	4

348. **List I (Product category)**

A. Soap B. Scooter

C. Car D. Cold drinks

List II (Brand name)

1. Rexona 2. Bajaj

3. Maruti 4. Pepsi

Codes:	A	B	C	D
(a)	1	3	2	4
(b)	2	1	3	4
(c)	1	3	4	2
(d)	1	2	3	4

349. **List I (Product category)**

A. Tea B. Vanspati Ghee

C. Cold drinks D. Biscuits

List II (Brand name)

1. Lipton 2. Dalda

3. Limca 4. Parle Glucose

Codes:	A	B	C	D
(a)	4	3	1	2
(b)	3	1	2	4
(c)	1	2	3	4
(d)	2	3	1	4

350. **List I (Marketing management educationist)**

A. Kaldor A.G.

B. Mckitterick J.B.

C. Levitt. T.

D. Lazo H. and A. Corbin

List II (Books and Articles)

1. *Imbricative Marketing*
2. *What is the Marketing Management Concept?*
3. *Innovation in Marketing*
4. *Management in Marketing*

Codes:	A	B	C	D
(a)	1	2	3	4
(b)	2	3	1	4
(c)	1	3	4	2
(d)	3	1	2	4

351. **List I (Bases for market segmentation)**

A. Geographic B. Demographic

C. Socio-economic D. Psychographic

List II (Sub-dividation of market)
1. Region
2. Age
3. Income levels
4. Compulsiveness

Codes:	A	B	C	D
(a)	4	2	3	1
(b)	1	2	3	4
(c)	2	3	1	4
(d)	1	3	2	4

352. **List I (Bases for market segmentation)**
A. Market conditions
B. Psychographic
C. Socio-economic
D. Geographic

List II (Sub-dividation of market)
1. Distribution channel
2. Autonomy Dependent Independent
3. Religion
4. Climate

Codes:	A	B	C	D
(a)	1	2	3	4
(b)	1	3	2	4
(c)	4	3	1	2
(d)	2	3	1	4

353. **List I (Bases for market segmentation)**
A. Demographic
B. Socio-economic
C. Psychographic
D. Marketing conditions

List II (Sub-dividation of market)
1. Family size
2. Consumption levels
3. Ambitiousness high achiever, low achiever
4. Intensity of competition

Codes:	A	B	C	D
(a)	2	3	4	1
(b)	4	2	3	1
(c)	1	2	3	4
(d)	2	3	1	4

354. **List I (Marketing management thinkers)**
A. Haley R.I. B. Frank R.E.
C. Pandey S.M. D. Gupta D.B.

List II (Books and Articles)
1. *Benefit Segmentation A Decision Oriented Research Tool*
2. *Correlates of Buying Behaviour for Grocery Products*
3. *Nature and Determinates of Urbanisation in Developing Economy*
4. *Consumption Pattern in India*

Codes:	A	B	C	D
(a)	3	4	2	1
(b)	3	1	2	1
(c)	2	1	3	3
(d)	1	2	3	4

355. **List I (Management thinkers)**
A. Mcnamara C.P.
B. Lazo H. and A. Corbin
C. King R.L.
D. Schwartz G.

List II (Books)
1. *The Present Status of the Marketing Concept*
2. *Management in Marketing*
3. *The Marketing Concept*
4. *Science in Marketing*

Codes:	A	B	C	D
(a)	3	1	2	4
(b)	1	2	3	4
(c)	1	3	2	4
(d)	4	3	1	2

356. **List I (Management thinkers)**
A. Alderson W. B. Kotler P.
C. W.H. Newman D. Brion J.M.

List II (Books)
1. *Marketing Behaviour and Executive Action*
2. *Marketing Management*
3. *Administrative Action*
4. *Corporate Marketing Planning*

Codes:	A	B	C	D
(a)	3	4	1	2
(b)	1	2	3	4
(c)	4	3	1	2
(d)	2	3	1	4

357. **List I (Type of personal channel of communication)**

A. Expert channel
B. Advocate channel
C. Social channel
D. Personal channel

List II (Subject matter)

1. The expert channel consists of acknowledged individuals, experts, promoting the company's products.
2. Advocate channel is one where a person hired by the company advocates its cause or the product.
3. The social channel refers to the word of mouth communication that takes place among persons.
4. Personal channel refers to a one-to-one communication and involves a person or two persons addressing a group of persons.

Codes:	A	B	C	D
(a)	3	4	1	2
(b)	2	3	1	4
(c)	1	2	4	3
(d)	1	2	3	4

358. **List I (Management thinkers)**

A. Newman W.H.
B. Koontz H. and C.O. Donnell
C. Smith W.R.
D. Gulick L.

List II (Books)

1. *Administrative Action*
2. *Principles of Management*
3. *The Role of Planning in Marketing*
4. *Administrative Reflections from World War II*

Codes:	A	B	C	D
(a)	4	3	1	2
(b)	1	3	4	2
(c)	4	1	3	2
(d)	1	2	3	4

359. **List I (Management thinkers)**

A. Burnett Leo, David A. Aaker and John G. Myers
B. Ogilvy David, David A. Aaker and John G. Myers
C. Everett M. Rogers
D. Lavidge Robert J. and Steiner Gary A.

List II (Books)

1. *Advertising Management*
2. *Principles of Advertising Management*
3. *Diffusion of Innovations*
4. *A Model for Predictive Measurements of Advertising Effectiveness*

Codes:	A	B	C	D
(a)	4	3	1	2
(b)	2	3	1	4
(c)	3	1	2	4
(d)	1	2	3	4

360.

List I	List II
A. Highest Reach	1. Publicity
B. Most persuasive	2. Advertising
C. Immediate effect on sale	3. Personal selling
D. No cost involved	4. Sales promition

Codes:	A	B	C	D
(a)	4	1	2	3
(b)	1	2	3	4
(c)	2	1	3	4
(d)	2	3	4	1

361. **List I (Management thinkers)**

A. Webstar, Frederick E. Jr. and Wind, Yaram
B. Nrus, James, A. and Anderson James C.

C. Festinger Leon
D. Wells, William D.

List II (Books)

1. *Organisational Buying Behaviour*
2. *Turn Your Industrial Distributors in Partners*
3. *A Theory of Cognitive Dissonance*
4. *Psychographic a Critical Review*

Codes:	A	B	C	D
(a)	1	3	4	2
(b)	1	2	3	4
(c)	4	1	3	2
(d)	3	1	2	4

362. **List I (Management thinkers)**

A. R. Honston Franklin
B. H. Neil Borden
C. Kotler Philip
D. Kotler Philip and J. Levy Sidney

List II (Books and Articles)

1. *The Marketing Concept; What it is and What it is not*
2. *The Concept of Marketing Mix*
3. *The Major Tasks of Marketing Management*
4. *Demarketing Yes Demarking, Harward Business Review*

Codes:	A	B	C	D
(a)	2	1	3	4
(b)	1	2	3	4
(c)	4	2	1	3
(d)	4	3	1	2

363.

List I	List II
A. Consumer	1. Advantage
B. Product	2. Profit
C. Earning	3. Development
D. Competitive	4. Satisfaction

Codes:	A	B	C	D
(a)	2	3	4	1
(b)	3	1	4	2
(c)	1	2	3	4
(d)	4	3	2	1

364.

List I	List II
A. Growth in	1. Goodwill
B. Creation of	2. Customer Loyalty
C. Sustaining	3. Sales

Codes:	A	B	C
(a)	3	2	1
(b)	1	2	3
(c)	3	1	2
(d)	2	3	1

365. **List I**

A. Channels of distribution and physical distribution
B. Manufacturer to consumer
C. Person/Agent between manufacturer and consumer
D. Warehouses with cold storage arrangements

List II

1. Middleman/Intermediary
2. Components of place-mix
3. Perishable goods
4. Direct channel

Codes:	A	B	C	D
(a)	2	4	1	3
(b)	1	4	3	1
(c)	3	1	2	4
(d)	1	2	3	4

366. **Statement (A):** The marketing concept is a philosophy of business states that the consumer's want satisfaction is the economic and social justification of a company's existence, consequently all company activities in production, engineering and finance, as well as in marketing, must be devoted to, first determining what the customer's wants

are end thus satisfying their wants while still making a reasonable profit.

Statement (B): Above statement referred by Stanton.

Statement (C): Above statement is related with marketing concept.

Statement (D): Statement 'A' has been defined under the book of *Fundamentals of Marketing*.

Codes:

(a) Statement A, B, C and D are false
(b) Statement A, B, C and D are true
(c) Statement B, C and D are true
(d) Only statement A is true

367. **Statement (A):** Selling is important not merely for increasing the profits of businessmen, but also for making goods and services available to the consumers in society.

Statement (B): It is the process whereby goods and services finally flow to the consumers who need them and the firm performs its function of distributing its products among consumers.

Codes:

(a) Statement A and statement B both are true.
(b) Statement A is true but statement B is not true.
(c) Statement A is not true but statement B is true.
(d) Statement A and B are true, but statement B is the reason of statement A.

368. **Statement (A):** "Relatively permanent a homogeneous division in a society into which individuals or families showing similar values, life styles, interests and behaviour can) be categorized."

Statement (B): This is social class.

Codes:

(a) Statement A is true. But statement B is not true.
(b) Statement A and statement B. Both are true.
(c) Statemetn A is not true but statement B is true.
(d) Only statement A is true.

369. **Statement (A):** Marketing occupies an important position in the organisation.

Statement (B): Marketing is the function of business concerned with creation of a consumer.

Codes:

(a) Statement A is true but statement B is not true.
(b) Statement A and statement B both are true.
(c) Statement A is not true but statement B is true.
(d) Statment A and B both are untrue.

370. Marketing aims at providing consumer satisfaction.

(a) False (b) True

371. Product development means production of goods.

(a) True (b) False

372. Marketing helps business in earning profits.

(a) False (b) True

373. Marketing does not create goodwill for firm.

(a) True (b) False

374. Product development means developing new and better products.

(a) False (b) True

375. Marketing-mix is a onetime decision.

(a) True (b) False

376. Marketing-mix consists of four elements.
(a) False (b) True

377. External environment does not affect marketing-mix.
(a) False (b) True

378. Marketing-mix needs continuous review.
(a) False (b) True

379. Marketing-mix should be so planned that it fulfills the needs of consumer as well as the organisation.
(a) False (b) True

380. Cost is the main consideration while setting the price of a product.
(a) False (b) True

381. Govt. policies have no influence on the price fixation policy of a company.
(a) True (b) False

382. Both internal as well as external factors affect price fixation.
(a) False (b) True

383. Under cost-based approach only the variable costs of a product are considered.
(a) False (b) True

384. Competition-based approach of price fixation forces a company to supply the product at existing prices.
(a) True (b) False

385. Mail order business house is known as institutional retailer.
(a) False (b) True

386. Vedlars are known as institutional retailers
(a) False (b) True

387. Perishable goods require short channel of distribution.
(a) False (b) True

388. If the market size is large business firm must have many channels of distribution.
(a) False (b) True

389. A business house desiring to exercise greater control over channel will not prefer a shorter channel of distribution.
(a) True (b) False

390. Advertising is a personal communication of messages.
(a) False (b) True

391. The massage advertised may be oral or in writing.
(a) False (b) True

392. Advertising is done by wholesalers only.
(a) False (b) True

393. The aim of sending a message in any advertisement is to inform the customers about the availability of product.
(a) True (b) False

394. There is only one medium of advertising, i.e. newspapers.
(a) False (b) True

395. Good advertising is one which is able to achieve its objectives.
(a) False (b) True

396. An advertisement which goes unnoticed by potential customers, is waste of money.
(a) False (b) True

397. The function of advertising is not to educate the customer but only to create demand for the product.
(a) False (b) True

398. The object of advertising is to achieve its aims at the least costs.
(a) False (b) True

399. Ascertaining performance means to ascertain the effectiveness of advertising programme.
(a) False (b) True

400. Advertising copy affects the success of advertising capaign.
(a) False (b) True

401. Drafting an advertising copy does not require lots of imagination of the part of advertiser.
(a) False (b) True

402. Advertising copy should have only attention value.
(a) False (b) True

403. In order that the customer is able to remember the name of the product, it is frequently used in the advertisement copy.
(a) False (b) True

404. The name of the product should be given in the advertisement in an attractive manner.
(a) False (b) True

405. Newspapers are most suitable for advertising consumer products.
(a) False (b) True

406. Television is suitable for advertising products used by special class of people such as doctors, lawyers, etc.
(a) False (b) True

407. Cinema advertising is suitable for advertising goods and services that are locally consumed.
(a) False (b) True

408. Advertising on radio is losing importance in comparison with television.
(a) False (b) True

409. Knowledge of product is not necessary to make one a good salesman.
(a) False (b) True

410. A good salesman should have imagination, initiatives, alertness, etc.
(a) False (b) True

411. Honesty and integrity need not be there in a salesman.
(a) True (b) False

412. A salesman becomes good if he has the ability to persuade the customer to buy the products.
(a) False (b) True

413. To become a good salesman one need not be courtous and cooperative.
(a) True (b) False

ANSWERS

1. (c)	2. (c)	3. (c)	4. (c)	5. (b)	6. (c)
7. (c)	8. (c)	9. (c)	10. (d)	11. (c)	12. (b)
13. (b)	14. (d)	15. (b)	16. (c)	17. (c)	18. (a)
19. (b)	20. (a)	21. (b)	22. (b)	23. (b)	24. (c)
25. (a)	26. (d)	27. (c)	28. (c)	29. (b)	30. (c)
31. (b)	32. (b)	33. (a)	34. (c)	35. (c)	36. (c)
37. (c)	38. (b)	39. (c)	40. (c)	41. (d)	42. (c)
43. (c)	44. (b)	45. (b)	46. (c)	47. (d)	48. (d)
49. (b)	50. (b)	51. (c)	52. (c)	53. (c)	54. (c)
55. (b)	56. (b)	57. (c)	58. (c)	59. (b)	60. (a)
61. (b)	62. (c)	63. (a)	64. (c)	65. (b)	66. (c)

67. (a)	68. (b)	69. (a)	70. (c)	71. (c)	72. (a)
73. (d)	74. (b)	75. (a)	76. (a)	77. (b)	78. (c)
79. (c)	80. (b)	81. (b)	82. (b)	83. (d)	84. (d)
85. (d)	86. (d)	87. (d)	88. (c)	89. (d)	90. (d)
91. (d)	92. (d)	93. (d)	94. (c)	95. (d)	96. (d)
97. (d)	98. (d)	99. (b)	100. (d)	101. (d)	102. (d)
103. (d)	104. (d)	105. (d)	106. (c)	107. (d)	108. (c)
109. (d)	110. (d)	111. (c)	112. (c)	113. (d)	114. (d)
115. (d)	116. (c)	117. (d)	118. (d)	119. (d)	120. (d)
121. (a)	122. (b)	123. (d)	124. (b)	125. (d)	126. (d)
127. (d)	128. (d)	129. (d)	130. (c)	131. (b)	132. (b)
133. (d)	134. (b)	135. (d)	136. (d)	137. (d)	138. (d)
139. (c)	140. (d)	141. (d)	142. (d)	143. (d)	144. (d)
145. (d)	146. (c)	147. (d)	148. (d)	149. (d)	150. (c)
151. (b)	152. (b)	153. (d)	154. (d)	155. (d)	156. (d)
157. (d)	158. (b)	159. (d)	160. (b)	161. (a)	162. (d)
163. (c)	164. (d)	165. (b)	166. (d)	167. (d)	168. (c)
169. (d)	170. (d)	171. (c)	172. (b)	173. (c)	174. (c)
175. (d)	176. (d)	177. (c)	178. (d)	179. (d)	180. (c)
181. (b)	182. (d)	183. (d)	184. (d)	185. (d)	186. (b)
187. (d)	188. (d)	189. (d)	190. (c)	191. (d)	192. (d)
193. (d)	194. (d)	195. (c)	196. (d)	197. (d)	198. (d)
199. (d)	200. (d)	201. (d)	202. (d)	203. (c)	204. (d)
205. (d)	206. (d)	207. (d)	208. (d)	209. (c)	210. (d)
211. (d)	212. (b)	213. (d)	214. (d)	215. (b)	216. (d)
217. (d)	218. (d)	219. (d)	220. (d)	221. (c)	222. (b)
223. (b)	224. (d)	225. (b)	226. (d)	227. (c)	228. (a)
229. (c)	230. (c)	231. (d)	232. (c)	233. (b)	234. (d)
235. (d)	236. (d)	237. (d)	238. (d)	239. (c)	240. (b)
241. (d)	242. (a)	243. (b)	244. (c)	245. (c)	246. (c)
247. (c)	248. (d)	249. (d)	250. (c)	251. (d)	252. (a)
253. (a)	254. (c)	255. (c)	256. (d)	257. (d)	258. (d)
259. (d)	260. (c)	261. (d)	262. (a)	263. (c)	264. (d)
265. (c)	266. (a)	267. (b)	268. (d)	269. (b)	270. (d)

271. (c)	272. (b)	273. (c)	274. (d)	275. (d)	276. (a)
277. (c)	278. (b)	279. (d)	280. (b)	281. (c)	282. (b)
283. (c)	284. (a)	285. (d)	286. (c)	287. (d)	288. (d)
289. (b)	290. (a)	291. (d)	292. (d)	293. (b)	294. (d)
295. (c)	296. (a)	297. (a)	298. (d)	299. (c)	300. (b)
301. (c)	302. (b)	303. (d)	304. (d)	305. (c)	306. (b)
307. (b)	308. (b)	309. (d)	310. (d)	311. (b)	312. (b)
313. (a)	314. (a)	315. (b)	316. (b)	317. (b)	318. (b)
319. (b)	320. (a)	321. (c)	322. (c)	323. (a)	324. (b)
325. (b)	326. (b)	327. (b)	328. (b)	329. (a)	330. (a)
331. (b)	332. (a)	333. (d)	334. (b)	335. (b)	336. (b)
337. (b)	338. (b)	339. (b)	340. (b)	341. (d)	342. (b)
343. (d)	344. (d)	345. (c)	346. (b)	347. (d)	348. (d)
349. (c)	350. (a)	351. (b)	352. (a)	353. (c)	354. (d)
355. (b)	356. (b)	357. (d)	358. (d)	359. (d)	360. (d)
361. (b)	362. (b)	363. (d)	364. (c)	365. (a)	366. (b)
367. (d)	368. (b)	369. (b)	370. (b)	371. (b)	372. (b)
373. (b)	374. (b)	375. (b)	376. (b)	377. (a)	378. (b)
379. (b)	380. (b)	381. (b)	382. (b)	383. (a)	384. (b)
385. (b)	386. (a)	387. (b)	388. (b)	389. (b)	390. (a)
391. (b)	392. (a)	393. (a)	394. (a)	395. (b)	396. (b)
397. (a)	398. (b)	399. (b)	400. (b)	401. (a)	402. (a)
403. (b)	404. (b)	405. (b)	406. (a)	407. (b)	408. (b)
409. (a)	410. (b)	411. (b)	412. (a)	413. (b)	

7

Financial Management

1. Generally there are ______ types of business finance.
(a) four (b) five
(c) three (d) two

2. Long-term finances required to be invested for a period of above ______ years.
(a) three (b) five
(c) two (d) four

3. Public deposit is a source of
(a) long-term finance
(b) short-term finance
(c) medium-term finance
(d) None of the above

4. Short-term financial requirements are also known as capital requirements.
(a) Working (b) Fixed
(c) Both (a) and (b) (d) None of these

5. Long-term finance is required for the purchase of ______ assets.
(a) intangible (b) fixed
(c) tangible (d) None of these

6. Overdraft limit is granted on the basis of credit worthiness of
(a) Retailer (b) Wholesaler
(c) Customer (d) Consumer

7. Banks ask for ______ security while granting cash credit.
(a) fixed (b) collateral
(c) bilateral (d) None of these

8. While making payment on discounted bill, banks deduct ______ which is equal to the amount of interest for the period of bill.
(a) discount (b) deposit
(c) Both (a) and (b) (d) None of these

9. When supplier extend credit to the buyer, it is called
(a) Instalment credit
(b) Trade credit
(c) Both (a) and (b)
(d) None of the above

10. Under trade credit and instalment credit does not flow in
(a) Cash Credit (b) Trade credit
(c) Bank credit (d) None of these

11. Raising funds for short-term purposes is
(a) Beneficial (b) Costly
(c) Economical (d) None of these

12. Short-term finance may serve
(a) middle-term purpose
(b) short-term purpose
(c) long-term purpose
(d) All of the above

13. Trade credit is for a ______ period of time but bank credit may be extended.
(a) specific (b) uncertain
(c) Both (a) and (b) (d) None of these

14. Payment after a specific date is ______ in case of bank credit.
(a) not compulsory (b) undefined
(c) compulsory (d) None of these

15. Discounting of bill _____ cash immediately,
    (a) does not provide
    (b) depending upon situation
    (c) provides
    (d) None of the above
16. Which of the following is the source of short-term finance?
    (a) Bank credit
    (b) Loans from co-operatives
    (c) Trade credit
    (d) All of the above
17. Enumerate the various points of difference between cash credit and bank overdraft.
    (a) The amount of credit in case of cash credit depends upon the value of securities offered. But overdraft limits is decided on the average balance of the customers in his account.
    (b) Overdraft is granted without the security of tangible assets. But for cash credit security of tangible assets is an essential requirement.
    (c) In case of cash credit, the amount of credit is placed in a separate account of the borrower. Overdraft limit is generally granted to an existing account of the customer.
    (d) All of the above.
18. The merits of customers is/are
    (a) Money received as advance is not to be refunded. Hence there are no repayment obligations.
    (b) Amount offered as advance is interest free. Hence funds are available without involving financial burden.
    (c) The seller is not required to deposit any tangible security while seeking advance from the customers. Thus assets remain free of change.
    (d) All of the above.
19. Long-term finance is required for
    (a) Intangible assets (b) Current assets
    (c) Fixed assets (d) None of these
20. Long-term sources of finance are also required for _____ of working capital.
    (a) temporary part
    (b) permanent part
    (c) Both (a) and (b)
    (d) None of the above
21. Investment in machines require
    (a) long-term finance
    (b) short-term finance
    (c) Both (a) and (b)
    (d) None of the above
22. Fixed capital requirement is more in _____ business.
    (a) manufacturing (b) selling
    (c) controlling (d) All of the above
23. A part of profits of the company that is used as capital is known as
    (a) Shares
    (b) Retained earning
    (c) Debentures
    (d) Public deposits
24. Savings of the public invested in companies for safety and interest earning is
    (a) Debentures
    (b) Shares
    (c) Public deposits
    (d) Retained earnings
25. Available to a company as ownership capital
    (a) Public deposits
    (b) Retained earning
    (c) Debentures
    (d) Shares
26. Long-term loans from the public is called
    (a) Shares
    (b) Debentures

(c) Public deposits
(d) Retained earning

27. In case of good profits, company pays higher dividend.
(a) Merits to management
(b) Demerits to management
(c) Merits to shareholders
(d) Demerits to shareholders

28. Benefit of trading on equity will not be available.
(a) Demerits to management
(b) Merits to shareholders
(c) Demerits to shareholders
(d) Merits to management

29. It helps in creating more confidence among the investors and creditors.
(a) Demerits to management
(b) Merits to management
(c) Demerits to shareholders
(d) Merits to shareholders

30. No certainty of payment of dividends.
(a) Merits to shareholders
(b) Demerits to management
(c) Demerits to shareholders
(d) Merits to management

31. Public deposits are
(a) Secured (b) Unsecured
(c) Both (a) and (b) (d) None of these

32. Public deposits ______ any charge on the assets of the company.
(a) do not involve
(b) partially involve
(c) involve
(d) None of the above

33. Advertisement is required for inviting
(a) government deposits
(b) shareholders
(c) public deposits
(d) money donors

34. Public deposit cannot be for more than
(a) one year (b) two year
(c) three year (d) four year

35. Capital budgeting is also known as
(a) Planning capital expenditure
(b) Investment decision making
(c) Capital expenditure decision
(d) All of the above

36. Pay-back period is calculated as
(a) $\frac{\text{Original cost of the asset}}{\text{Annual cash inflows}}$
(b) $\frac{\text{Initial outlay of the project}}{\text{Annual cash inflows}}$
(c) $\frac{\text{Cash outlay of the project}}{\text{Annual cash inflows}}$
(d) All the the above

37. Which of the following is a method for accounting of risk in capital budgeting?
(a) Sensitivity technique
(b) Probability technique
(c) Decision tree analysis
(d) All of the above

38. Working capital is also called
(a) Circulating capital
(b) Revolving capital
(c) Both (a) and (b)
(d) None of the above

39. A business concern should not have
(a) excess working capital
(b) inadequate working capital
(c) Both of the above
(d) None of the above

40. Requirements of working capital depend upon
(a) credit policy adopted
(b) operating cycle involved
(c) size of the business
(d) All of the above

41. Main motives for holding cash are
(a) Speculation (b) Transaction
(c) Precaution (d) All of the above

42. Cost of capital is the _____ rate of return expected by the investors.
(a) average (b) minimum
(c) maximum (d) None of these

43. Generally, if the risk involved in a firm is higher,
(a) cost of capital will be higher.
(b) cost of capital is neutral.
(c) cost of capital will be lower.
(d) None of the above.

44. The concept of cost of capital is useful in
(a) capital structure decisions.
(b) capital budgeting decisions.
(c) Both of the above.
(d) None of the above.

45. Working capital management is concerned with the problems that arise in attempting to manage
(a) current assets, current liabilities and interrelationship between them.
(b) current assets and fixed liabilities.
(c) fixed assets and fixed liabilities.
(d) fixed assets and current liabilities.

46. Operating cycle refers to
(a) collection of debtors and making payment to creditors.
(b) sale of product either for cash or credit.
(c) the time duration to convert sales into cash.
(d) acquisition of resources such as raw materials, labour, fuel, etc.

47. Which of the factors do not influence the level of working capital?
(a) Operating capital
(b) Nature of business
(c) Profit
(d) Sales

48. The better and broader objective of financial management is
(a) wealth maximisation
(b) profit maximisation
(c) finance maximisation
(d) None of the above

49. Which of the following cannot be a consideration in forming a dividend policy?
(a) Access to capital market
(b) Shareholder's expectation
(c) Capital
(d) Stable dividends

50. Cost of perpetual debt =
(a) $K_p = \dfrac{d}{P_0(1-f)}$ (b) $K_d = \dfrac{D_1}{P_0} + g$
(c) $K_d = \dfrac{I}{SV}(1-t)$ (d) None of these

51. Capital budgeting refers to the
(a) raising of capital.
(b) demand and supply of capital.
(c) managerial technique of planning capital expenditures of the company.
(d) overall cost of capital.

52. Discounted cash flow technique involves
(a) accounting rate of return
(b) net present value
(c) payback method
(d) None of the above

53. Operating leverage results from
(a) variable costs
(b) fixed costs
(c) operating profit
(d) operating expenses

54. Financial average is related to
(a) fixed financial charges
(b) financing activities of the firm
(c) operating losses
(d) operating expenses

55. Trading on equity refers to
    (a) smaller borrowings and larger profits.
    (b) using debt capital along with own capital.
    (c) selling of equity shares.
    (d) 100% dividend payout ratio.
56. Which of the following is not a theory of capital structure?
    (a) Weighted average cost of capital
    (b) Net income approach
    (c) Net perating income approach
    (d) None of the above
57. Which of these is not an essential element of optimum or ideal capital structure?
    (a) Minimum risk
    (b) Flexibility
    (c) Simplicity
    (d) Minimum control
58. The average of all the costs of each source of funds employed by the firm is known as
    (a) Average cost of sales
    (b) Average cost of production
    (c) Average cost of capital
    (d) None of the above
59. The distribution of capital in favour of more acceptable proposals is known as
    (a) Capital raising
    (b) Cost of capital
    (c) Capital budgeting
    (d) Capital rationing
60. What is the rate which equates the present value of expected future cash flows with the cost of investment?
    (a) Average rate of return
    (b) External rate of return
    (c) Internal rate of return
    (d) Return on investment
61. Capital budgeting is also known as
    (a) Long-run-planning process of capital.
    (b) Short-run-planning process of capital.
    (c) Both of the above.
    (d) None of the above.
62. The minimum amount of current assets needed to conduct a business even during the dullest season of that year is known as
    (a) variable working capital
    (b) fixed working capital
    (c) net working capital
    (d) gross working capital
63. Under which theory, the optional capital structure of a firm occurs at the point at which it can no longer take advantage of a favourable financial leverage?
    (a) Variable cost of equity capital theory.
    (b) Combined cost of equity capital theory.
    (c) Fixed cost of equity capital theory.
    (d) None of the above.
64. If the inventory turnover is high, the working capital requirements will be
    (a) Low (b) High
    (c) Medium (d) None of these
65. Which among the following capital structure theories say that the firm can increase its value by increasing its proportion of debt in the capital structure?
    (a) Net Operating Income Approach
    (b) Net Income Approach
    (c) Traditional Approach
    (d) None of the above
66. The net income approach supports the view
    (a) Perfect capital market
    (b) Capital does not matter
    (c) Capital structure matters for value of the firm
    (d) None of the above
67. The third stage of change in capital structure shows the

(a) Constant value
(b) Declining value
(c) Optimum value
(d) Increasing value

68. The net income approach was suggested by
(a) Ezra Solomon
(b) Walter
(c) Modigliani-Miller
(d) Durand

69. Financial leverage is zero when
(a) A firm uses equity
(b) A firm uses no debt
(c) A firm uses debt
(d) None of the above

70. Which of the following is not an assumption of net income approach?
(a) Cost of debt is more than capitalization rate.
(b) Use of debt does not change the risk perception of investors.
(c) There are no taxes.
(d) None of the above.

71. According to net operating income (NOI) approach, the capital structure decision of the firm is
(a) Irrelevant
(b) Relevant
(c) Sometimes relevant otherwise non-relevant
(d) Neutral

72. Which among the following is an assumption of the NOI approach?
(a) The cost of capital is dynamic.
(b) The capitalisation rate is constant.
(c) The value of equity is not a residual value.
(d) All of the above.

73. Chandrika Ltd. by investing ₹ 1,00,000 gets net annual cash inflow of ₹ 20,000 before depreciation but after tax for 8 years. Here, Pay-Back Period will be
(a) 5 years (b) 22 years
(c) 4 years (d) 10 years

74. The term 'leverage' refers to
(a) the employment of an asset or source of funds for which the firm has to pay a fixed cost.
(b) use of debt capital to purchase assets.
(c) operating profits.
(d) All of the above.

75. Operating leverage depicts the firm's ability to use fixed operating cost to magnify the effect of change in sales on
(a) the earnings after interest and taxes.
(b) its earnings before interest and taxes.
(c) the creditors.
(d) None of the above.

76. Operating costs of the firm include
(a) those costs which vary directly with the sales volume.
(b) those costs which are partly fixed and partly variable.
(c) those costs which do not vary with sales volume.
(d) All of the above.

77. Financial leverage implies
(a) use of non-fixed charge sources of funds to purchase assets.
(b) use of fixed financial charges to magnify the effect of changes in EBIT.
(c) Both (a) and (b).
(d) None of the above.

78. High operating leverage is bad when
(a) EBIT is rising
(b) Sales revenues are falling
(c) Sales revenues are rising
(d) None of the above

79. The indifference point for financial leverage is the point at which

(a) The EPS is different for all financial plans.
(b) The EBTT does not change.
(c) The EPS/market price is the same for all financial plans.
(d) None of the above.

80. Total leverage is a combination of
(a) Financial leverage and EPS
(b) Financial and Operating Leverage
(c) Various costs
(d) None of the above

81. The DCL or degree of combined leverage measures the
(a) change in EPS due to change in debt funds.
(b) change in EPS due to change in costs.
(c) change in EPS due to change in sales.
(d) None of the above.

82. Financial leverage can be measured in
(a) flow term
(b) stock term
(c) Both (a) and (b)
(d) None of the above

83. In flow terms, the financial leverage can be measured
(a) by ratio of cash flow to interest payment.
(b) by ratio of EBIT to interest payment.
(c) Either (a) or (b).
(d) None of the above.

84. Cost of capital means
(a) the present value of a past investment.
(b) the expected cash inflows.
(c) the minimum rate of return that a firm must earn on its investments.
(d) None of the above.

85. The cost of capital can be
(a) Implicit
(b) Explicit
(c) Both (a) and (b)
(d) None of the above

86. The explicit cost of capital is associated with
(a) internal financing
(b) opportunity cost
(c) raising of funds
(d) None of the above

87. Which among these is not a specific cost?
(a) Cost of retained earnings
(b) Cost of an asset
(c) Cost of debt
(d) None of the above

88. The measurement of cost of debt depends on
(a) the irredeemable nature of debt
(b) the redeemable nature of debt
(c) Both of the above
(d) None of the above

89. The two approaches to the measurement of cost of equity capital are
(a) NOI and NI Approach
(b) CAPM and dividend valuation model
(c) PERT and CPM
(d) None of the above

90. CAPM refers to
(a) capital asset pricing model
(b) critical analysis of preference model
(c) critical asset pricing model
(d) None of the above

91. The measurement of overall cost of capital depends upon
(a) appropriate weight choices.
(b) historical costs.
(c) combination of preference and equity share capital.
(d) None of the above.

92. Historical weights takes into account
(a) the past benefits accruing due to investment in assets.
(b) the long-term implications of firm's current finaricing.

(c) the market value of assets.
(d) None of the above.

93. The Average Rate of Return (ARR) method of capital budgeting is unsatisfactory because
(a) it ignores the time value of money.
(b) it is based on accounting profits.
(c) it does not helps in determining the feasibility of an investment.
(d) None of the above.

94. The Pay-Back Period shows
(a) recovery period of original investment outlay.
(b) the time value of money.
(c) the cash outflows.
(d) None of the above.

95. These are corporate bonds, issued in the country of denomination, by a firm based outside that country
(a) Convertible bonds
(b) Foreign bonds
(c) Euro bonds
(d) Putable bonds

96. Which among these is not a discounted cash flow technique?
(a) Pay-back method
(b) Internal rate of return
(c) Net present value
(d) None of the above

97. Which of the following pairs will give consistent results in terms of acceptance or rejection of an investment proposal?
(a) ARR: Profitability Index
(b) IRR and NPV (Net Present Value)
(c) Pay-back: IRR (Internal Rate of Return) Method
(d) None of the above

98. ______ are corporate bonds whose issuers are regarded by bond credit rating agencies as being of high risk
(a) Euro bonds (b) Foreign bonds
(c) Junk bonds (d) None of these

99. Under APR method, a project would be accepted if
(a) the ARR is more than minimum desired ARR.
(b) the cash inflows are more than cash outflows.
(c) the ARR is more than cash outflows.
(d) None of the above.

100. The decision rule under net present value method is
(a) NPV < zero reject
(b) NPV > zero accept
(c) Both (a) and (b)
(d) None of the above

101. The capital rationing involves
(a) resolving the conflicts between the results of NPV or IRR.
(b) finding ways to reduce time disparity in value of investment.
(c) choice of combination of available projects in a way to maximise the total NPV.
(d) None of the above.

102. Which of these is not a determinant of dividend policy?
(a) Capital market situations
(b) Inflation
(c) Stability of dividends
(d) All of the above

103. ______ is a form of fixed income security, but the dividends is at the discretion of the company's board.
(a) Preferred stock (b) Debenture
(c) Debt capital (d) None of these

104. A stable dividend policy refers to
(a) same dividend to be paid every year.
(b) shareholder's wishes regarding dividends.

(c) the consistency or lack of variability in the stream of dividends.
(d) None of the above.

105. Once a dividend declaration has been made, the dividend warrants must be posted within
(a) 42 days (b) 7 days
(c) 24 hours (d) None of these

106. In operating cycle method of working capital, the first step will be taken as
(a) estimation of total amount of annual operating expenses.
(b) estimation of required working.
(c) computation of duration of the operating cycle.
(d) None of the above.

107. Which factor is responsible for overcapitalization?
(a) Liberal dividend policy
(b) High promotion expenses
(c) Wrong estimate of earning at the time of promotion
(d) All of the above

108. Which among these is not an operating expense?
(a) Fuel and power
(b) Tax and dividend
(c) Purchase of raw materials
(d) Direct labour cost

109. Depreciation and write off intangible assets are included in
(a) non-cash expenses
(b) operating expenses
(c) capital expenses
(d) None of the above

110. The duration of operating cycle is computed in
(a) Weeks (b) Days
(c) Years (d) Months

111. Capital gearing means
(a) Fixation of a proper ratio between two or more type securities
(b) Proper capitalization
(c) Watered capital
(d) Trading on equity

112. In operating cycle method, the estimation of working capital can be calculated as follows

(a) $\dfrac{\text{Annual Capital Expenses}}{\text{Number of Operating Cycles}}$

(b) $\dfrac{\text{Annual Operating Expenses}}{\text{Number of Operating Cycles}}$

(c) $\dfrac{\text{Annual Total Expenses}}{\text{Number of Operating Cycles}}$

(d) None of the above

113. Stable Divided Policy is also known as
(a) Long-term policy
(b) Short-term policy
(c) Both (a) and (b)
(d) None of the above

114. Dividend is a part of
(a) Retained earnings
(b) Divisible profit
(c) Both (a) and (b)
(d) None of the above

115. Dividend is distributed to the
(a) bankers of a company
(b) shareholders of a company
(c) debenture holders of a company
(d) All of the above

116. A bearer of a share warrant of a company is
(a) A member subject to certain condition
(b) A creditor of the company
(c) A member of the company
(d) Not a member of the company

117. Dividend policy of a company to a large extent affects the
(a) Corporate liquidity
(b) Growth of the company
(c) Financial structure
(d) All of the above

118. The most important and common form of dividend is
(a) Bond dividend
(b) Stock dividend
(c) Scrips dividend
(d) Cash dividend

119. The dividend which is paid without preparing final accounts of the company is called as
(a) Bond dividend
(b) Scrips dividend
(c) Interim dividend
(d) None of the above

120. Which of the following is/are the assumption of Gordon's model?
(a) The firm has perpetual life.
(b) There are no corporate taxes.
(c) In the firm R and K remain unchanged.
(d) All of the above.

121. Which factors affected to the working capital?
(a) Credit policy
(b) Production policy
(c) Nature of business
(d) All of the above

122. The rate of dividend of preference share is decided at the time of
(a) allotment of share
(b) winding up
(c) issue of share
(d) None of the above

123. In which method amount of depreciation decreases every year?
(a) Annuity method
(b) Sinking fund method
(c) Straight line method
(d) Sum of years digit method

124. Ratio of net profit after tax and preference shares dividend to number of equity shares is known as
(a) Earnings per share
(b) Financial position ratio
(c) Solvency ratio
(d) Overall profitability ratio

125. According to Companies Act, a company must have a whole time secretary if its paid up share capital is
(a) ₹ 1 crore
(b) ₹ 10 lakhs or more
(c) ₹ 25 lakhs or more
(d) ₹ 50 lakhs or more

126. Major repairs of plant and machinery is
(a) capital expenditure
(b) revenue expenditure
(c) deferred revenue expenditure
(d) None of the above

127. Which of the following is a capital expenditure?
(a) Preliminary expenses of a company.
(b) Amount spent on extension and thus increasing the seating capacity of picture hall.
(c) Depreciation of a picture hall building.
(d) All of the above.

128. Principle of subrogation in insurance applies
(a) only to fire and marine insurance.
(b) to all types of insurance.
(c) only to life insurance.
(d) All of the above.

129. Watered capital means
(a) Excessive capital
(b) Over capitalization
(c) Part of the capital not represented by assets
(d) Under capitalization

130. Average clause in a fire policy is to check the
(a) over insurance
(b) under insurance
(c) Both (a) and (b)
(d) None of the above

131. Continuous forward selling to depress prices of securities in stock exchange is known as
(a) bear hammering
(b) bear squeeze
(c) short selling
(d) All of the above

132. Sinking fund for depreciation is created
(a) to provide funds for replacement of asset.
(b) to write off depreciation.
(c) to provide for increased price of new asset to be purchased.
(d) All of the above.

133. Trading on thin equity means
(a) Restricted transactions on equity shares in stock exchange
(b) Trading in equity shares of small face value
(c) Transaction between its company and its minority shareholders
(d) A relatively smaller equity capital than borrowed capital

134. Arrears of preference dividends (cumulative) will be shown in the balance sheet of a company as
(a) current liability
(b) contingent liability
(c) unclaimed dividend
(d) None of the above

135. Internal audit helps in
(a) audit in depth
(b) internal control
(c) internal check
(d) statutory audit

136. ₹ 5,000 paid for purchase of furniture is charged to repairs. It is an error of
(a) Principle (b) Clerical error
(c) Omission (d) Commission

137. Insurance unexpired is a
(a) real account
(b) nominal account
(c) personal account
(d) All of the above

138. Ploughing back of profit means
(a) transferring a part of profit to reserves
(b) Earning of black money
(c) Re-investment of earnings
(d) Unclaimed dividends

139. Under the diminishing balance method of depreciation, depreciation at a fixed rate is calculated on the
(a) original cost less scrap value
(b) written down value
(c) original cost
(d) All of the above

140. The term depletion is used in relation to
(a) stock in trade
(b) plant and machinery
(c) mines
(d) goodwill

141. Depreciation charge goes on decreasing year after year in
(a) production units method
(b) original cost method
(c) sum of years digit method
(d) machine hour rate method

142. Stock valuation at cost or market price whichever is less is based on principle of
(a) cost principle (b) full disclosure
(c) materiality (d) conservation

143. The long-run objective of financial management is to:
(a) Maximize the value of the firm's common stock.
(b) Maximize earnings per share.

(c) Maximize market share.
(d) Maximize return on investment.

144. When debentures are redeemed, the balance left in the debenture redemption fund account is transferred to
(a) general reserve account
(b) debenture redemption investment account
(c) debenture account
(d) capital redemption reserve account

145. In times of rising prices, which of the following methods of inventory valuation results in lower inventory value
(a) Moving simple average
(b) First in first out
(c) Last in first out
(d) Simple average

146. In a highly geared company,
(a) major part of finance is raised by debentures.
(b) only ordinary capital is raised.
(c) major part of finance is raised by equity capital.
(d) only debentures are issued.

147. Accounting Rate of return net of interest on the book value of the shareholders' investment in the asset is ______
(a) Return on investment
(b) Opportunity cost of capital
(c) Return on Capital Employed
(d) None of the above

148. Which of the following carry voting rights at the general meetings?
(a) Debentures
(b) Equity shares
(c) Preference shares
(d) All of the above

149. Interest dividend is payable even if there is a loss in the case of
(a) Preference shares
(b) Debentures
(c) Equity shares
(d) All of the above

150. A person insured his property worth ₹ 2,00,000 for ₹ 1,50,000 against fire. His actual loss is ₹ 1,00,000. His claim is
(a) ₹ 1,50,000 (b) ₹ 1,00,000
(c) ₹ 2,00,000 (d) Nil

151. A Variable interest rate changing in response to changes in a specified index of market rates of interest is termed as
(a) Floating rate (b) Forward rate
(c) Fixed rate (d) None of these

152. Working capital is increased by
(a) issue of shares
(b) bills receivable realised
(c) cash received from debtors
(d) None of the above

153. Heavy advertisement in the initial years is a
(a) deferred revenue expenditure
(b) revenue expenditure
(c) capital expenditure
(d) None of the above

154. Given—Face value of share = ₹ 10
No. of shares issued = ₹ 20,000
Total net profit = ₹ 40,000
Dividend paid = 10%
What is EPS?
(a) ₹ 3 (b) ₹ 5
(c) ₹ 1 (d) ₹ 2

155. Risk that translation effects of unexpected changes in exchange rates could increase tax liabilities is known as
(a) Economic exposure
(b) Finance Exposure
(c) Tax exposure
(d) None of the above

156. Stock of semi-finished goods is a
(a) working capital
(b) fixed capital

(c) watered capital
(d) liquid capital

157. Purchase of machinery and equipment for cash by a firm
(a) keeps total assets unchanged.
(b) increase the total assets.
(c) increases the liabilities of the firm.
(d) decreases the total assets.

158. A credit sale of goods to Shivendra should be debited to
(a) Goods account
(b) Sales account
(c) Purchase account
(d) Shivendra account

159. Which of the following assets does not depreciate?
(a) Patents
(b) Machinery and equipment
(c) Furniture
(d) Land

160. The factors affecting to P/E multiple are
(a) Required return and expected growth rate
(b) Dividend pay-out ratio and required return
(c) Dividend pay-out ratio, required return and expected growth rate
(d) Dividend pay-out ratio and expected growth rate

161. Valuing the stock in trade at market price or cost price, whichever is less, is an example of the convention of
(a) Knowing the value
(b) Consistency
(c) Disclosure
(d) None of the above

162. Purchase of furniture for cash would
(a) reduce the fixed assets and increase the current assets.
(b) increase the fixed assets and reduce the current assets.
(c) increase total asstes.
(d) Both (a) and (b).

163. Petty cash may be used to pay
(a) for the purchase of furniture and fittings.
(b) the expenses relating to postage and con veyance.
(c) salaries and wages to the staff.
(d) None of the above.

164. Buying the company's shares from its shareholders instead of using the cash to pay them dividends is called as
(a) Right share
(b) Sweet equity
(c) Buy back of shares
(d) None of the above

165. The term current assets does not include
(a) Furniture
(b) Stock
(c) Cash
(d) Advance payment

166. Which of following is not a capital reserve?
(a) Dividend equalisation reserve
(b) Profit on sale of fixed assets
(c) Profits prior to incorporation
(d) All of the above

167. Charging of capital expenditure to revenue results in
(a) revenue reserve
(b) capital reserve
(c) secret reserve
(d) None of the above

168. Secret reserves serve the purpose of
(a) increasing the working capital.
(b) enabling the directors to tide over unfavourable times.
(c) meeting exceptional losses.
(d) None of the above.

169. The time that elapses between the purchase of raw materials and the collection of cash for sales is referred as
(a) Organisation cycle
(b) Cash cycle
(c) Operating cycle
(d) Production cycle

170. A provision is a
(a) specific reserve (b) capital reserve
(c) general reserve (d) None of these

171. The payment side of cash book is undercast by ₹ 200 when overdraft as per pass book is the starting point
(a) ₹ 200 will be added
(b) No effect will be in the pass book
(c) ₹ 200 will be deducted
(d) None of the above

172. Working capital refers to the capital mobilised for meeting
(a) To meet the future financial requirements of the company
(b) Long-term financial needs of the company
(c) To meet day-to-day financial obligations of the company
(d) None of the above

173. An amount of ₹ 300 is debited twice in the pass book when overdraft as per the cash book is the starting point
(a) ₹ 600 will be deducted
(b) ₹ 600 will be added
(c) No effect will be in the cash book
(d) None of the above

174. Closing stock is valued at
(a) cost price or market price whichever is higher.
(b) market price.
(c) cost price.
(d) cost price or market price whichever is lower.

175. Depreciation is provided on
(a) fictitious assets (b) fixed assets
(c) current assets (d) liquid assets

176. Contract granting the right without obligation to engage in a future transaction on terms specified in the contract is termed as
(a) Future (b) Option
(c) Swaps (d) Forward

177. Payment of interim dividend is a
(a) application of fund
(b) source of fund
(c) no flow of fund
(d) All of the above

178. If a company issues 1000 equity shares of ₹ 10 each it will be legally all right if it asks on application
(a) ₹ 4.50 (b) ₹ 5.00
(c) ₹ 2.50 (d) ₹ 3.50

179. Interest on calls in advance paid by the company according to Table A is
(a) 8% (b) 10%
(c) 5% (d) 6%

180. If on a share of ₹ 100 and called up capital is ₹ 90 while the company received ₹ 80, the capital account should be credited with
(a) ₹ 80 (b) ₹ 70
(c) ₹ 100 (d) ₹ 90

181. In production control, scheduling includes
(a) Estimating the time to be consumed in these departments.
(b) How much time will be taken in transferring production from one department to another.
(c) Deciding about the time when the production will reach various departments.
(d) All of the above.

182. Unclaimed dividend is shown in the balance sheet under the heading as
(a) unsecured loans
(b) reserves and surplus
(c) current liabilities
(d) None of the above

183. Quick ratio is a good indicator of the liquid position of a concern. The ideal quick ratio is
(a) 3 (b) 4
(c) 2 (d) 1

184. The equation for the debt equity ratio is
(a) $\frac{\text{Long-term Debt}}{\text{Equity Capital}}$
(b) $\frac{\text{Liquid Assets}}{\text{Current Liabilities}}$
(c) $\frac{\text{Current Assets}}{\text{Current Liabilities}}$
(d) $\frac{\text{Net Profits}}{\text{Net Sales}}$

185. The proportions of different forms of debt and equity constituting a company's total capital is termed as
(a) Capital Structure
(b) Financial leverage
(c) Operating leverage
(d) None of the above

186. When at an annual general meeting of a company, no auditor is appointed or reappointed. In that case
(a) the board of directors appoints a person to fill the vacancy.
(b) the managing director of the company appoints a person to fill that vacancy.
(c) the central government appoints a person to fill the vacancy.
(d) None of the above.

187. Charging a period for the proportionate cost of an intangible asset is termed as
(a) Amortisation (b) Expiration
(c) Depreciation (d) Diminution

188. A policy which provides the holder with a regular stream of payments from some specified date until death is
(a) Term assurance policy
(b) Annuity
(c) Endowment policy
(d) None of these

189. Obsolescence means decline in the value due to
(a) innovations and inventions.
(b) fall in the market price.
(c) efflux of time.
(d) physical wear and tear.

190. If the total charge of depreciation and maintenance is considered, the method which would provide a uniform charge is
(a) Straight line method
(b) Annuity method
(c) Insurance policy method
(d) Diminishing balance method

191. Provision for discount on debtors shall be made on
(a) book debts after incurring bad debt and after providing for bad debt.
(b) book debts before incurring bad and before providing for bad debt.
(c) book debts after incurring bad debt but before providing for bad debt.
(d) book debts before incurring bad debt but after providing for bad debt.

192. A policy, normally requiring regular contributions, which makes a payment to a named survivor only on the death of the insured is
(a) Endowment policy
(b) Term assurance policy

(c) Annuity
(d) Whole life policy

193. Closing stock appearing in trial balance will be taken to
(a) trading account and balance sheet.
(b) trading account only.
(c) profit and loss account only.
(d) balance sheet only.

194. Whenever debentures are cancelled, any profit on cancellation is transferred to
(a) sinking fund account
(b) profit and loss account
(c) capital reserve account
(d) capital redemption reserve account

195. Bonus shares are issued by the companies because
(a) there are heavy accumulated general reserves.
(b) surplus cash is available.
(c) they have high gross profit ratio.
(d) there is heavy competition from similar companies.

196. If the stock turnover ratio is 4 times and the collection period is 30 day, the operating cycle would be
(a) 90 days (b) 120 days
(c) 30 days (d) 60 days

197. The bonds denominated in Euros and issued in the euro currency area
(a) Euro bonds
(b) Convertible bonds
(c) Putable bonds
(d) Callable bonds

198. Depreciation is
(a) a use of fund.
(b) a source of fund.
(c) partly a source and partly an application of fund.
(d) neither a source nor a use of fund.

199. A company issue 10,000 shares of ₹ 10 each at a discount of 10% payable as follows:
On application ₹ 2.50
On allotment ₹ 3.00
On first and final call ₹ 3.50
A holder of 100 share did not pay the final call and his shares were forfeited. Share Capital account will be debited by
(a) ₹ 1,000 (b) ₹ 900
(c) ₹ 650 (d) ₹ 850

200. Given
Fixed assets ₹ 10,00,000
Current assets ₹ 6,00,000
Total net profit ₹ 2,60,000
Current liabilities ₹ 3,00,000
Which one of the following will be the correct ROI?
(a) 25% (b) 26%
(c) 16.5% (d) 20%

201. Net working capital of a firm is the
(a) capital borrowed from banks.
(b) effective capital of the company when the business is in full swing.
(c) capital provided by shareholders only.
(d) difference between the current assets and current liabilities.

202. Corporate bonds issued with the option for holders to convert into some other asset on specified terms at a future date is
(a) Convertible bonds
(b) Callable bonds
(c) Putable bonds
(d) None of the above

203. If

Capital at the end	= ₹ 7,000
Capital introduced	= ₹ 5,000
Drawings	= ₹ 8,000
Loss	= ₹ 10,000

then capital in the beginning is equal to

(a) ₹ 20,000 (b) ₹ 30,000
(c) ₹ 12,000 (d) ₹ 16,000

204. A policy requiring regular contributions which pays a specified sum on a specified date or on the death of the insured if this should occur earlier is
(a) Annuity
(b) Term assurance policy
(c) Endowment policy
(d) None of the above

205. The purpose of depreciation is to
(a) reduce fixed assets to nil as soon as possible.
(b) reduce fixed assets to market value each year.
(c) allocate the cost of fixed assets to expense over their working lives.
(d) save income tax and wealth tax.

206. The amount of depreciation under straight line method vis-à-vis written down value method, when the rate of depreciation is same, would be
(a) equal in the first year but higher in subsequent years.
(b) equal in all years.
(c) lower in the first year but equal in subsequent years.
(d) equal in the year but lower in subsequent years.

207. If on January 1, 1983 a plant is purchased for ₹ 1,20,000, its estimated life is ten years and its salvage value is ₹ 10,000 under which one of the following methods would the 1983 depreciation be the largest?
(a) Double-declining balance method.
(b) Straight line method.
(c) 15% on original cost.
(d) Sum of-the-years digits method.

208. An intermediary who undertakes to issue new securities on behalf of a borrower is
(a) Stock broker (b) Bank
(c) Issuing House (d) None of these

209. Cost of carrying inventory implies
(a) cost of economic lot size.
(b) the acquisition cost of the items as per invoice.
(c) moving average of cost of the items.
(d) risk of obsolescence and interest.

210. A company has inadvertently overstated its ending inventory. This will
(a) decrease the income of the current year.
(b) increase the income of the succeeding year.
(c) decrease the income of the succeeding year.
(d) have no effect on the income of the succeeding year.

211. An intermediary who holds stocks of securities and quotes a price at which each of the securities may be bought and sold is
(a) Arbitrager (b) Broker
(c) Market maker (d) None of these

212. If the carrying cost of average inventory *(i)* goes up, other things remaining the same, EOQ would
(a) go down in inverse proportion to *(i)*.
(b) go up in proporiton to *(i)*.
(c) go down in inverse proportion to square root of *(i)*.
(d) go up in proporiton to square root of *(i)*.

213. In a preiod of inflation, which inventory method would be considered suitable by the accountant?
(a) Average cost (b) Standard cost
(c) LIFO (d) FIFO

214. Modern Leasing Co. Ltd. has debt equity ratio 8 : 1. It has decided to issue bonus shares in the ratio of 1 : 2. The debt-equity ratio after the issue would be
(a) 1 : 8 (b) 1 : 4
(c) 8 : 1 (d) 4 : 1

215. The bonds where the coupon can be adjusted at pre-determined intervals is
(a) Convertible bonds
(b) Floating rate bonds
(c) Euro bonds
(d) Putable bonds

216. Which one of the following ratios is the indicator of the long term solvency of the firm?
(a) Debt-equity ratio
(b) Time interest earned ratio
(c) Acid test ratio
(d) None of the above

217. Trading on thin equity means
(a) a relatively smaller equity capital than borrowed capital.
(b) trading in equity shares of small face value.
(c) restricted transactions on equity shares in stock exchanges.
(d) transactions between the company and its minority shareholders.

218. Which one of the following is least suited for measuring return on investment?
(a) $\frac{\text{Income}}{\text{Invested capital}}$
(b) $\frac{\text{Net operating income before interest and taxes}}{\text{Average total assets}}$
(c) $\frac{\text{Net income after interest but before taxes}}{\text{Average total shareholder quity}}$
(d) Operating income ratio × Total assets turn over

219. A type of bond can be redeemed at the issuer's discretion prior to the specified redemption date
(a) Callable bonds
(b) Putable bonds
(c) Convertible bonds
(d) None of the above

220. An asset is purchased for ₹ 50,000 on which depreciation is to be provided annually according to the straight line method. The useful life of the asset is 10 years and the residual value is ₹ 10,000. The rate of depreciation is
(a) 18% (b) 8%
(c) 20% (d) 10%

221. During a period of declining prices, which one of the following inventory pricing methods will result in lower cost of goods sold?
(a) LIFO
(b) FIFO
(c) Inflated price method
(d) Simple average method

222. ______ is someone who brings together two parties with a coincidence.
(a) Arbitrager (b) Market maker
(c) Broker (d) None of these

223. If a company adepts Table 'A', the company is required to pay interest on calls in advance at the rate of
(a) 6% (b) 5%
(c) 8% (d) 7%

224. The speed and convenience with which an asset can be converted into money for a certain value is
(a) Liquidity (b) Solvency
(c) Profitability (d) None of these

225. A particular firm provided the following data for an accounting year:

Current ratio : 2.5 : 1
Liquid ratio : 1.5 : 1
Net Working capital : ₹ 6,00,000

Current assets and current liabilites of the firm are, respecitvely

(a) ₹ 7,50,000 and ₹ 1,50,000
(b) ₹ 9,00,000 and ₹ 3,00,000
(c) ₹ 8,50,000 and ₹ 2,50,000
(d) ₹ 10,00,000 and ₹ 4,00,000

226. Which one of the following reflects the overall efficiency with which capital is used?

(a) Investment turnover ratio
(b) Return on shareholders funds
(c) Operating ratio
(d) Earning per share

227. The following journal entry appears in the books of X Co. Ltd.

	Dr. ₹	Cr. ₹
Bank A/c	96,000	
Loss on issue of debentures A/c	10,000	
To 8% debentures A/c		1,00,000
To premium on redemption of debentures A/c		6,000

The debentures have been issued at

(a) premium of 6%
(b) discount of 10%
(c) discount of 4%
(d) discount of 6%

228. A ratio of reserves to deposits which banks can choose for themselves in the light of their own experience is called

(a) A prudential reserve ratio
(b) SLR
(c) CRR
(d) None of these

229. A limited company has to redeem redeemable preference shares of the value of ₹ 1,00,000 for which the company has issued 3000 equity shares of ₹ 10 each at a premium of 10%. The amount to be transferred to capital redemption reserve account will be

(a) ₹ 70,000 (b) ₹ 67,000
(c) ₹ 1,00,000 (d) ₹ 97,000

230. X Ltd. issued 1,000 9% preference shares of ₹ 100 each at a premium of 10%, redeemable at par after 5 years. What is the cost of preference capital of the company?

(a) 5.3% (b) 7.6%
(c) 3.5% (d) 6.7%

231. A firm employs ₹ 10,00,000 as capital. Investors expect an income of 15%. The actual profits (likely to be continued) is ₹ 2,00,000. What will be the value of Goodwill of the firm according to Super Profit method if it is to be valued at 3 years purchase?

(a) ₹ 2,00,000 (b) ₹ 2,15,000
(c) ₹ 50,000 (d) ₹ 1,50,000

232. The balances in the books of X, a sole proprietor were: Opening stock ₹ 17,000, Purchases ₹ 52,000; Wages ₹ 46,500; Fuel ₹ 15,000; Sales ₹ 1,45,000 and Closing stock on hand ₹ 25,000 whose net realisable value was ₹ 28,000.

The gross profit calculated would be

(a) ₹ 54,500 (b) ₹ 57,000
(c) ₹ 39,500 (d) ₹ 42,500

233. In sinking fund method of depreciation, the amount of depreciation

(a) decreases year after year.
(b) increases year after year.
(c) sometimes increases and sometimes decreases.
(d) remains constant over the years.

234. On 1.4.2002, the position of X Company Ltd. was as follows.

(Figures in '000)

Liabilities	₹	Assets	₹
Loan	200	Fixed assets	150
Creditors	50	Stock	40
		Debtors	50
		Cash	5
		Bank	5
	250		250

On 31.3.2003, the company's ship sank and all records and the cash were sunk. However, it was revealed that creditors and debtors were 20% more than at 1.4.2002 position. Stock and Bank was at the same level. The current ratio had always been 2. What was the amount of cash sunk on 31.3.2003?

(a) ₹ 15,000 (b) ₹ 20,000
(c) ₹ 5,000 (d) ₹ 10,000

235. Which one of the following statements is correct?

While conducting audit, the auditor should ensure that the stock is valued at

(a) cost or market price whichever is lower.
(b) cost price.
(c) cost or market price whichever is higher.
(d) market price.

236. The following is the Balance Sheet of Z company:

Liabilities	₹	Assets	₹
Sundry creditors	4,000	Cash	500
Bank overdraft	500	Bill receivables	5,000
Bills payable	1,000	Debtors	3,000
Provision for taxation	500	Stock	4,000
Outstanding expenses	500		
Reserves and Funds	6,000		
	12,500		12,500

What is the absolute liquidity ratio of the company?

(a) 0.92 : 1 (b) 1.90 : 1
(c) 2 : 1 (d) 1.06 : 1

237. When net profit is ₹ 2,25,000; taxes ₹ 25,000; and net worth ₹ 10,00,000. What is the rate of return on shareholders equity?

(a) 20%
(b) 25%
(c) 22.5%
(d) Cannot be calculated

238. The following information relates to an organization.

Equity share capital ₹ 10,00,000;
18% debentures ₹ 8,00,000;
10% preference share capital ₹ 5,00,000;
Current liabilities ₹ 3,00,000;
Loan at 15% (Long term) ₹ 1,40,000;
General Reserve ₹ 8,00,000;
Current Assets ₹ 3,50,000.

What is the Capital gearing ratio of the organization?

(a) 1.2 (b) 0.5
(c) 1.6 (d) 0.8

239. The conversion of funds lent for a short period into loans of longer duration is called

(a) Diversification
(b) Maturity transformation
(c) Risk transformation
(d) None of the above

240. A machinery costs ₹ 1,00,000 and has no scrap value at the end of its estimated life of 10 years. What is the amount of accumulated depreciation at the end of 6 years?

(a) ₹ 60,000 (b) ₹ 1,00,000
(c) ₹ 40,000 (d) None of these

241. Which of the following transactions will have no effect on the current ratio?
(a) Old motor car sold for cash.
(b) Goods purchased on credit.
(c) Machinery purchased for cash.
(d) Equity shares issued.

242. Net worth of a business means
(a) Total assets
(b) Equity capital
(c) Fixed assets minus current assets
(d) Total assets minus liabilities

243. Commission payable on the issue of shares can not exceed
(a) 4% (b) 2%
(c) 5% (d) 3%

244. A company has issued shares of ₹ 10 each at a premium of ₹ 2 each. The whole of the amount has been called up but the shares has been forfeited for non-payment of ₹ 4, the share capital account will be debited by
(a) ₹ 8 (b) ₹ 6
(c) ₹ 12 (d) ₹ 10

245. A new company cannot issue shares at a
(a) Premium
(b) Discount
(c) Premium or Discount
(d) None of the above

246. X Ltd. forfeited 20 shares of ₹ 10 each, ₹ 7 called up on which Ram has paid application and allotment money of ₹ 5 per share. Of these 15 shares were re-issued to Shyam as fully paid up for ₹ 6 per share. The amount to be transferred to capital reserve is
(a) ₹ 75 (b) ₹ 105
(c) ₹ 15 (d) ₹ 30

247. "Higher the ratio, the lower the profitability" is applicable to
(a) Operating ratio (b) ROI
(c) Net profit ratio (d) None of these

248. Ploughing back of profit means
(a) unclaimed dividends.
(b) earning of black money.
(c) transferring a part of profits to reserves.
(d) re-investment of earnings.

249. Which of the following is a capital expenditure?
(a) Heavy advertisement paid when a new product is introduced.
(b) Wages paid for manufacturing goods.
(c) Wages paid for installation of a new machine.
(d) Repairs of plant and machinery.

250. On using reducing balance method on an asset of ₹ 20,000 at the rate of 10% per annum, depreciation of 3rd year will be
(a) ₹ 1,620 (b) ₹ 2,000
(c) ₹ 6,000 (d) ₹ 1,800

251. Having re-issued all forfeited shares, the credit balance remaining in forfeited shares account is transferred to
(a) capital reserve (b) general reserve
(c) reserve capital (d) None of these

252. The holding of many assets leads to a reduction in risk is called
(a) Diversification
(b) Maturity transformation
(c) Risk transformation
(d) None of the above

253. Which one of the following is capital expenditure?
(a) Purchase of machine oil
(b) Cost of advertisement
(c) Purchase of a delivery van
(d) Purchase of raw material

254. Which one of the following depreciation methods is most suitable for a coal mine?
(a) Depletion method
(b) Diminishing balance method

(c) Sum of years' digits method
(d) Fixed instalment method

255. A business concern provides the following details.

Cost of goods sold	₹ 1,50,000
Sales	₹ 2,00,000
Opening stock	₹ 60,000
Closing stock	₹ 40,000
Debtors	₹ 45,000
Creditors	₹ 50,000

The concern's purchases would amount to (in ₹)
(a) 2,60,000 (b) 2,90,000
(c) 1,30,000 (d) 2,20,000

256. Rights issue refers to the shares issued to
(a) Existing directors (b) Employees
(c) Public (d) None of these

257. Given that the current ratio is 2 : 1, if the net working capital is ₹ 60,600, then the amount of current liabilities would be
(a) ₹ 1,21,200 (b) ₹ 90,900
(c) ₹ 30,300 (d) ₹ 60,600

258. The time and/or money used in carrying out the exchange of assets, goods or services is
(a) Transaction cost
(b) Managerial cost
(c) Implicit cost
(d) None of the above

259. Project Engineering Ltd. has an adverse current ratio. Which one of the following would improve this ratio?
(a) Collection of some of the current accounts receivables.
(b) Sale of fixed assets for cash.
(c) Collection from sundry debtors.
(d) Use of cash to pay off some long-term debts.

260. XYZ Ltd. incurs a net loss of ₹ 5,000 during an accounting year. Depreciation for the relevant year amounts to ₹ 1,000, preliminary expenses written off during the accounting year is ₹ 3,000 and a loss of ₹ 4,000 is due to sale of plant and machinery. Based on this data, funds from operations would amount to
(a) ₹ 5,000 (b) ₹ 4,000
(c) ₹ 3,000 (d) ₹ 2,000

261. Which of the following is correct?
(a) Internal check and internal audit are the same.
(b) Internal control is a part of internal check.
(c) Internal control is a part of internal audit.
(d) Internal audit is a part of internal control.

262. Preference shares to be redeemed ₹ 1,00,000. Shares issued of ₹ 50,000 at a premium of 10%. The amount to be transferred to capital redemption reserve will be
(a) 45,000 (b) 1,00,000
(c) 50,000 (d) 55,000

263. Preference shares to be redeemed ₹ 2,00,000 at a premium of 5%. Shares issued of ₹ 1,000,000 at a premium of 10%. The amount to be transferred to capital redemption reserve is
(a) 1,10,000 (b) 1,00,000
(c) 1,05,000 (d) 2,00,000

264. For debentures, underwriting commission cannot exceed
(a) 5% (b) 4%
(c) 7% (d) 2%

265. In single entry system,
(a) part of the transaction is recorded.
(b) only one book is maintained.
(c) only one account is maintained.
(d) None of the above.

266. Working capital is the excess of
(a) fixed assets over fixed liabilities.
(b) current assets over current liabilities.
(c) fixed assets over current liabilities.
(d) total assets over total liabilities.

267. FIFO is advisable in case
(a) Constant prices (b) Rising prices
(c) Falling prices (d) None of these

268. In which of the following methods of capital budgeting annual returns of the future years are discounted to their present value?
(a) Pay-back period
(b) Internal rate of return
(c) Present value method
(d) Both (b) and (c)

269. In which of the following methods, the assets appears at its original cost throughout its life?
(a) Annuity
(b) Machine hour rate
(c) Straight line
(d) Depriciation fund

270. Cost of machine ₹ 1,00,000, scrap value ₹ 10,000. Life 4 years. What will be the amount of depriciation according to sum of years digit method in the first year?
(a) 36,000 (b) 25,000
(c) 40,000 (d) 60,000

271. The underwriting commission on share capital should not exceed
(a) 4% (b) 7%
(c) 5% (d) 2%

272. Under which method of deprication, the value of machinery never comes to zero?
(a) Diminishing value
(b) Straight line
(c) Sinking fund
(d) Sum of years digit

273. Goodwill is
(a) Intangible asset (b) Wasting asset
(c) Fixed asset (d) Fictitious asset

274. Depletion method is used in respect of
(a) Wasting asset (b) Fixed asset
(c) Current asset (d) Tangible asset

275. Depreciation is provided on
(a) fictitious assets (b) fixed assets
(c) current assets (d) liquid assets

276. Which of the following is not a capital reserve?
(a) Dividend equalisation reserve
(b) Profit on sale of fixed assets
(c) Profits prior to incorporation
(d) All of the above

277. Charging of capital expenditure to revenue results in
(a) Capital reserve (b) Secret reserve
(c) Revenue reserve (d) None of these

278. Secret reserves serve the purpose of
(a) meeting exceptional losses.
(b) increasing the working capital.
(c) enabling the directors to tide over unfavourable times.
(d) None of the above.

279. A provision is a
(a) Specific reserve (b) Capital reserve
(c) General reserve (d) None of these

280. Capital gearing is the ratio between
(a) equity capital and preference capital.
(b) equity capital and fixed interest securities.
(c) equity capital and debentrues.
(d) All of the above.

281. Liabilities in a company are ₹ 80,000 and owner's equity is ₹ 70,000. What is the amount of total equity?
(a) ₹ 10,000 (b) ₹ 1,50,000
(c) ₹ 80,000 (d) ₹ 70,000

282. Major repairs of plant and machinery is
(a) deferred revenue expenditure
(b) capital expenditure
(c) revenue expenditure
(d) All of the above

283. Which of the following is a capital expenditure?
(a) Preliminary expenses of a company.
(b) Amount spent on extention and thus increasing the seating capacity of picture hall.
(c) Depreciation of a picture hall building.
(d) All of the above.

284. Sinking fund for depreciation is created
(a) to provide funds for replacement of asset.
(b) to write off depreciation.
(c) to provide for increased price of new asset to be purchased.
(d) None of the above.

285. What is quick ratio?
(a) Immediate realisable assets/current liabilities.
(b) Current assets/immediately realisable liabilities.
(c) Current assets/current liabilities.
(d) None of the above.

286. ROI is the relation between
(a) Investment and profit
(b) Net profit and capital employed
(c) Turnover and capital employed
(d) None of the above

287. Which of the following types of companies should avoid issue of debentures?
(a) Companies where earnings are not stable.
(b) Companies which are able to earn a higher rate of profit than rate of interest payable on debentures.
(c) Companies with stable earnings.
(d) All of the above.

288. If total sources of funds ₹ 50,000 and total applications ₹ 20,000, the net increase in working capital is:
(a) ₹ 20,000 (b) ₹ 30,000
(c) ₹ 70,000 (d) ₹ 50,000

Directions: Questions 289 to 304 are of multiple statement type. Choose the correct answer from the codes given below.

289. Consider:
1. Cash in hand 2. Bills Receivable
3. Book debts 4. Bank OD

Which of the above are considered for calculating working capital?

Codes:
(a) 1, 3 and 4 (b) 1, 2 and 3
(c) 1 and 4 (d) 1, 2, 3 and 4

290. Which of the following increases the working capital?
1. Cash received from debtors
2. B/R realised
3. Issue of debenture
4. Issue of shares
5. Conversion of debenture into shares

Codes:
(a) 3, 4, 5 (b) 1, 2, 3
(c) 3 and 5 (d) All of the above

291. Which of the following is not the correct symptom of over-capitalisation?
1. When a company earns less than what it should have earned as a fair-rate of return on its capital.
2. When book value of shares is lower than their real value.
3. When earnings do not justify the amount of capital invested.

Codes:
(a) 1 and 2 (b) 2 and 3
(c) 1 only (d) 2 only

292. Consider the following items:
1. Debentures 2. Prepaid rent
3. Accrued interest 4. Bank overdraft

Current liabities would include

Codes:

(a) 3 and 4 (b) 1, 2, 3 and 4
(c) 2, 3 and 4 (d) 1, 2 and 3

293. The Tax shield would result in

1. increase in tax liability
2. increase in EPS
3. decrease in EPS
4. decrease in tax liability

Codes:

(a) 2 and 4 (b) 1 and 3
(c) 1 and 4 (d) 3 and 4

294. Which of the following ratios are used for measuring profitability of a business?

1. Acid test ratio
2. ROI
3. Net profit ratio
4. Interest coverage ratio

Codes:

(a) 2 and 3 (b) 1, 2, 3 and 4
(c) 3 only (d) 1 and 3

295. By adopting which of the following tactics, return on investment of a company can be enhanced?

1. Postponing the replacement.
2. Valuing closing stock on LIFO basis during rising prices.
3. Providing less depreciation.
4. Making higher provisions.

Codes:

(a) 1, 3 and 4 (b) 1, 2, 3 and 4
(c) 1 and 3 (d) 2 and 4

296. Consider the following statements.

As per section 46AA of the Companies (Second Amendment) Act, 2002, sick industrial company means an industrial company which has

1. the accumulated losses in any financial year equal to fifty per cent or more of its average net worth during four years immediately preceding such financial year.
2. failed to repay its debts within any three consecutive quarters on demand made in writing for its repayments by a creditor or creditors of such company.

Codes:

(a) 1 only (b) 2 only
(c) Neither 1 or 2 (d) Both 1 and 2

297. Consider the steps in Risk Management.

1. Risk Evaluation
2. Risk Avoidance
3. Risk Identification
4. Risk Elimination
5. Risk Reduction
6. Risk Financing

Codes:

(a) 3, 4, 2, 5, 6, 1 (b) 4, 1, 2, 3, 5, 6
(c) 2, 4, 5, 1, 6, 3 (d) 3, 1, 2, 4, 5, 6

298. Consider the following conditions to be fulfilled by a company regarding issue of sweat equity shares.

1. The issue of sweat equity shares is authorised by an ordinary resolution passed by the company in the general meeting.
2. Not less than 6 months should have, at the date of the issue elapsed since the date on which the company was entitled to commence business.
3. All the limitations shall be applicable to such sweat equity shares.

Codes:

(a) 3 only (b) 1, 2 and 3
(c) 1 only (d) 1 and 2

299. Which of the following statements are true?

1. Dividend can be paid out of capital profits if only Article of Association of the company permits.
2. Goodwill taken over may be written off out of profit prior to incorporation.

3. Dividend can be paid out of current profits in spite of unprovided depreciation for past years.
4. Capital redemption reserve can be used for issuing fully paid bonus shares to the shareholders according to Company's Act.

Codes:

(a) 2 and 4 (b) 3 and 4
(c) 1 and 2 (d) 1, 2 and 3

300. Rate of return on investment is meaningful to

1. Shareholders 2. Creditors
3. Management

Codes:

(a) 1 and 3 are true
(b) 1 alone is true
(c) 1, 2 and 3 are true
(d) 2 and 3 are true

301. To test the liquidity of a concern which of the following ratios are useful?

1. Acid test ratio
2. Capital turnover ratio
3. Bad debts to sales ratio
4. Inventory turnover ratio

Codes:

(a) 2 and 4 (b) 2 and 3
(c) 1 and 3 (d) 1 and 4

302. While calculating the net present value under discounted cash flow method of return on investement analysis, the operations involved are

1. Cash outflow
2. Discounted net cash flow
3. Cash inflow
4. Net present value

The correct sequence of these operations is

(a) 4, 1, 3, 2 (b) 3, 1, 4, 2
(c) 1, 2, 3, 4 (d) 1, 3, 2, 4

303. A low inventory turnover ratio may be the result of

1. obsolescence of some of the stock.
2. slow moving inventory.
3. frequent stock-outs.
4. fast moving inventory.

Codes:

(a) 2 and 3 are correct
(b) 1 and 2 are correct
(c) 2 alone is correct
(d) 4 alone is correct

304. In a trial balance, debtors appear at ₹ 45,000. Provision for doubtful debts at 5% is to be made after considering the following adjustments.

1. An amount of ₹ 1,000 is included in debtor who is bankrupt and his estate is expected to realise 50 paise in the rupee.
2. Debtor include an account of ₹ 2,000 for goods supplied to proprietor.
3. Bills receivable include a dishonoured bill for ₹ 1,000.
4. Goods sold in, 'Sale of Return' basis not approval by the customer for ₹ 5,000 recorded as sale.
5. Debtor includes as amount of ₹ 500 from a customar whose financial position is doubtful.

The total provision to be made for doubtful debts is

(a) ₹ 2,250 (b) ₹ 2,425
(c) ₹ 1,900 (d) None of these

Directions: Questions 305 to 311 are of matching type. Match List I with List II and select the correct answer using the codes given below the list.

305. **List I (Appointment of auditor)**

A. First auditor of a non-government limited company
B. Reappointment of a retiring auditor of a non-government limited company

C. Auditor of a Government company
D. Auditor of a non-Government limited company, when shareholders fail to appoint or reappoint an auditor

List II (Appointing authority)

1. Shareholders of the company
2. Board of Directors of the company
3. Central Government on the advice of the Comptroller and Auditor General of India
4. Central Government

Codes:	A	B	C	D
(a)	1	2	3	4
(b)	2	1	4	3
(c)	1	2	4	3
(d)	2	1	3	4

306. **List I**

A. Net present value method
B. Average rate of return
C. Internal rate of return
D. Pay back method

List II

1. Inflow after interest and tax
2. Discounted cash flow
3. Traditional method
4. Decision based on cut-off rate

Codes:	A	B	C	D
(a)	4	1	2	3
(b)	4	3	2	1
(c)	2	1	4	3
(d)	1	3	4	2

307. **List I (Type of manual fund)**

A. Open-ended fund
B. Income fund
C. Close-ended fund
D. Growth fund

List II (Features)

1. Maximises short-term return to investros
2. Can sell ultimited number of units
3. The units are not redeemable at their NAV
4. Maximises long-term return to investors

Codes:	A	B	C	D
(a)	3	4	1	2
(b)	3	4	2	1
(c)	2	1	3	4
(d)	2	1	4	3

308.

List I	List II
A. Shares	1. Fixed capital
B. Land and Building	2. Period of medium-term finance
C. Public deposits	3. Source of long-term finance
D. One to five years	4. Short-term finance
E. Meeting of day-to-day requirements	5. Source of medium-term finance

Codes:	A	B	C	D	E
(a)	3	1	5	2	4
(b)	2	3	5	1	4
(c)	4	2	3	4	5
(d)	1	2	4	3	5

309. **List I**

A. Convertible debenture
B. Secured debentures
C. Interest on debentures
D. Irredeemable debentures

List II

1. Holders have the right to recover their money from the sale of assets of the company.
2. Deducted from the profits of the company.
3. Permanent liability on the company.
4. The holders of such debentures are given the option to exchange then for shares.

Codes:	A	B	C	D
(a)	3	4	2	1
(b)	2	4	1	3
(c)	1	2	3	4
(d)	4	1	3	2

310. **List I**

A. Balance of debenture redemption fund account.

B. Balance of sinking fund account for replacement of an asset.

C. On dissolution of a firm, the provisions made for doubtful debts appearing in balance sheet.

D. Financial consequences of business operations.

List II

1. Realisation account
2. Funds-flow statement
3. General reserve
4. Asset account

Codes:	A	B	C	D
(a)	1	2	4	3
(b)	3	4	2	1
(c)	1	2	3	4
(d)	3	4	1	2

311.

List I	List II
A. They provide ownership capital	1. Share
B. Return on these is called interest	2. Debentures
C. Return on these is called dividend	
D. Holders enjoy voting rights	

Codes:	A	B	C	D
(a)	1	2	1	1
(b)	2	2	2	2
(c)	2	2	1	1
(d)	1	1	1	2

Directions: Questions 312 to 320 consist of two statements, one labelled as 'Assertion (A)' and the other as 'Reason (R)'. You have to examine these two statements carefuly and decide if the Assertion A and the Reason R are individually true and if so, whether the Reason is a correct explanation of the Assertion. Select your answer to these items using the codes given below.

(a) Both A and R are true and R is the correct explanation of A.

(b) Both A and R are true but R is not the correct explanaton of A.

(c) A is true but R is false.

(d) A is false but R is true.

312. **Assertion (A):** The floating policy protects the policy holder against errors and omissions.

Reason (R): Goods are insured even if the policy holder fails to reports that goods have already been forwarded from the place of shipment.

313. **Assertion (A):** "Service Hours Method" is applied to depreciate aircraft.

Reason (R): The useful life of an aircraft is measured in terms of machine hours.

314. **Assertion (A):** Current ration is generally an acceptable measure of short-term solvency of a business unit.

Reason (R): Current ratio indicates the extent to which the business unit can meet its short-term obligations with short-term resources available with it.

315. **Assertion (A):** The matching concept requires that costs should be recognised as expenses in the period in which revenue is realised.

Reason (R): There may not be a matching between expenditure and expense over a short period.

316. **Assertion (A):** Share premium amount can be refunded in cash to equity shareholders.

Reason (R): Share premium is usually collected when the market price of the shares is higher than the face value of the share.

317. **Assertion (A):** Shares can be issued at a discount by a company at any time if the articles so provide and a special resolution to that effect is passed.

Reason (R): Usually discount is given so as to ensure that the issue is fully subscribed.

318. **Assertion (A):** A company can pay interest out of the capital prior to commencement of its business.

Reason (R): Interest is part of the cost of construction of building, plant and machinery.

319. **Assertion (A):** High capital gearing leads to greater speculation.

Reason (R): Proportion of equity share capital in relation to the total capital comprising the other securities is small leading to capitalisation being highly geared.

320. **Assertion (A):** Financial leverage is beneficial only when the rate of earning is higher than the cost of debt.

Reason (R): Debt-equity ratio indicates the short-term financial soundness of a business concern.

321. Purchase of fixed assets is a day-to-day expense.

(a) False (b) True

322. Business finance means money and credit employed in business firms.

(a) False (b) True

323. Business finance deals only with investment of money.

(a) False (b) True

324. Business finance is concerned with funds, raising of funds from different sources and their investment in different types of activities.

(a) False (b) True

325. Without adequate finance, business may run into difficulties.

(a) False (b) True

326. Limit in case of cash credit is generally less than that is case of bank overdraft.

(a) False (b) True

327. Bank overdraft is granted on the basis of credit-worthiness of customers.

(a) False (b) True

328. The method of charging interest is same in case of bank overdraft and cash credit.

(a) False (b) True

329. Banks do not open separate account while advancing cash credit.

(a) True (b) False

330. Besides personal security of borrower, banks insist upon the security of tangible goods while granting loan.

(a) False (b) True

331. Instalment credit facilities purchase of assets and equipments.

(a) False (b) True

332. Customers' advances do not make cash immediately available.

(a) False (b) True

333. Loans from co-operative banks are easily available to farmers for productive purposes.

(a) False (b) True

334. Repayment is not made in case of customer's advances.
(a) False (b) True

335. Co-operative credit facilitates replacements and renovation.
(a) False (b) True

336. Debenture holders are the creditors of the company.
(a) False (b) True

337. Debenture holders have the right to vote in the meetings of the company.
(a) False (b) True

338. Interest at a fixed rate is paid on debentures.
(a) False (b) True

339. Debentures carry more risk than shares.
(a) False (b) True

340. Debentures are generally redeemable after a fixed period.
(a) False (b) True

341. Retained earning is the portion of profit which is not distributed among share holders as dividend.
(a) False (b) True

342. A company can create reserves even if it is running at a loss.
(a) False (b) True

343. Heavy expenses are incurred to raise capital through retained earnings.
(a) False (b) True

344. Retained earnings are useful for shareholders because it brings stability in the rate of dividend and leads to capital appreciation.
(a) False (b) True

345. Retained earning means ploughing back of profits.
(a) False (b) True

346. The system of public deposits is economical.
(a) False (b) True

347. Public deposits are secured.
(a) False (b) True

348. Rate of interest on public deposits is not fixed.
(a) False (b) True

349. Public deposits helps in the growth of a sound capital market in the country.
(a) False (b) True

350. Public deposit is a method which has become popular only recently.
(a) False (b) True

351. Commercial banks do not grant long-term loans.
(a) False (b) True

352. Short-term loans grant by commercial banks can become long term loan.
(a) False (b) True

353. Commercial banks charge high rate of interest while giving loans to small-scale industries and industrial units set up in villages.
(a) False (b) True

354. No guarantee or pledge of assets are to be made borrowing from commercial banks.
(a) False (b) True

ANSWERS

1. (c)	2. (c)	3. (c)	4. (a)	5. (b)	6. (c)
7. (b)	8. (a)	9. (b)	10. (b)	11. (c)	12. (c)
13. (a)	14. (a)	15. (c)	16. (d)	17. (d)	18. (d)

19. (c)	20. (b)	21. (a)	22. (a)	23. (b)	24. (c)
25. (a)	26. (b)	27. (c)	28. (a)	29. (c)	30. (c)
31. (b)	32. (a)	33. (c)	34. (c)	35. (d)	36. (d)
37. (d)	38. (c)	39. (c)	40. (d)	41. (d)	42. (b)
43. (a)	44. (c)	45. (a)	46. (c)	47. (a)	48. (a)
49. (d)	50. (c)	51. (c)	52. (a)	53. (d)	54. (b)
55. (b)	56. (a)	57. (d)	58. (c)	59. (d)	60. (c)
61. (a)	62. (b)	63. (c)	64. (a)	65. (b)	66. (b)
67. (b)	68. (d)	69. (b)	70. (a)	71. (a)	72. (b)
73. (a)	74. (a)	75. (b)	76. (d)	77. (b)	78. (b)
79. (c)	80. (b)	81. (c)	82. (c)	83. (c)	84. (c)
85. (c)	86. (c)	87. (b)	88. (c)	89. (b)	90. (a)
91. (a)	92. (b)	93. (a)	94. (a)	95. (b)	96. (a)
97. (b)	98. (c)	99. (a)	100. (c)	101. (c)	102. (d)
103. (a)	104. (c)	105. (a)	106. (a)	107. (d)	108. (b)
109. (a)	110. (b)	111. (a)	112. (b)	113. (a)	114. (b)
115. (b)	116. (d)	117. (d)	118. (d)	119. (c)	120. (d)
121. (d)	122. (c)	123. (d)	124. (a)	125. (c)	126. (c)
127. (b)	128. (a)	129. (c)	130. (a)	131. (b)	132. (a)
133. (c)	134. (b)	135. (b)	136. (a)	137. (c)	138. (c)
139. (b)	140. (c)	141. (c)	142. (d)	143. (a)	144. (a)
145. (c)	146. (a)	147. (a)	148. (b)	149. (b)	150. (b)
151. (a)	152. (a)	153. (a)	154. (d)	155. (c)	156. (a)
157. (a)	158. (d)	159. (d)	160. (c)	161. (b)	162. (b)
163. (b)	164. (c)	165. (c)	166. (a)	167. (c)	168. (a)
169. (c)	170. (a)	171. (c)	172. (c)	173. (b)	174. (d)
175. (b)	176. (b)	177. (a)	178. (b)	179. (d)	180. (d)
181. (d)	182. (c)	183. (d)	184. (c)	185. (a)	186. (c)
187. (a)	188. (b)	189. (a)	190. (a)	191. (a)	192. (d)
193. (a)	194. (c)	195. (a)	196. (b)	197. (a)	198. (d)
199. (a)	200. (d)	201. (d)	202. (a)	203. (a)	204. (c)
205. (c)	206. (a)	207. (d)	208. (c)	209. (d)	210. (c)
211. (c)	212. (c)	213. (a)	214. (c)	215. (b)	216. (a)
217. (a)	218. (a)	219. (a)	220. (b)	221. (d)	222. (c)

223. (a)	224. (a)	225. (d)	226. (a)	227. (c)	228. (a)
229. (a)	230. (d)	231. (d)	232. (c)	233. (d)	234. (a)
235. (a)	236. (a)	237. (a)	238. (d)	239. (b)	240. (a)
241. (b)	242. (d)	243. (c)	244. (d)	245. (b)	246. (c)
247. (a)	248. (d)	249. (c)	250. (a)	251. (a)	252. (a)
253. (c)	254. (a)	255. (c)	256. (d)	257. (d)	258. (a)
259. (b)	260. (c)	261. (d)	262. (a)	263. (b)	264. (d)
265. (a)	266. (b)	267. (c)	268. (d)	269. (d)	270. (a)
271. (c)	272. (a)	273. (a)	274. (a)	275. (b)	276. (a)
277. (b)	278. (d)	279. (a)	280. (b)	281. (b)	282. (a)
283. (b)	284. (a)	285. (a)	286. (b)	287. (a)	288. (b)
289. (d)	290. (c)	291. (d)	292. (a)	293. (a)	294. (a)
295. (c)	296. (d)	297. (d)	298. (a)	299. (a)	300. (b)
301. (d)	302. (d)	303. (b)	304. (c)	305. (d)	306. (c)
307. (c)	308. (a)	309. (d)	310. (a)	311. (a)	312. (d)
313. (a)	314. (d)	315. (c)	316. (d)	317. (d)	318. (a)
319. (c)	320. (c)	321. (a)	322. (b)	323. (a)	324. (b)
325. (b)	326. (a)	327. (b)	328. (b)	329. (b)	330. (b)
331. (b)	332. (a)	333. (b)	334. (b)	335. (a)	336. (b)
337. (a)	338. (b)	339. (a)	340. (b)	341. (b)	342. (a)
343. (a)	344. (b)	345. (b)	346. (b)	347. (a)	348. (a)
349. (a)	350. (a)	351. (a)	352. (b)	353. (a)	354. (a)

8

Human Resource Management

1. Recruitment is
   (a) negative process
   (b) neutral
   (c) positive process
   (d) None of the above
2. Selection refers to the negative process of eliminating all those who appear uncompromising from all the candidates considered for possible employment was stated by
   (a) George R. Terry
   (b) Dale Yoder
   (c) Edwin B. Flippo
   (d) E.F.L. Brech
3. The interview in which pressure is deliberately put on the applicant is known as
   (a) Directed interview
   (b) Patterned interview
   (c) Non-directed interview
   (d) None of the above
4. The training imparted to a new employee to induct him into new social setting of his work, is called
   (a) Promotional training
   (b) Orientation training
   (c) Job training
   (d) Corrective training
5. Which one of the following formula was given by F.A. Halsey for determination of wages?
   (a) $T \times R$
   (b) $T \times R + (S - T) \times R\%$
   (c) $T \times R + \dfrac{S - T}{T} \times T \times R$
   (d) $T \times R + \dfrac{S - T}{S} \times T \times R$
6. Which of the following is not a phase of the job design process?
   (a) The specification of the measurement of performance of each task.
   (b) The combination of individual tasks into specific jobs.
   (c) The specification of individual tasks.
   (d) The specification of the method of performing each task.
7. Which of the following should be carefully considered before using the socio-teachnical approach to job design?
   (a) Number of people in the work group.
   (b) The role of each employee in the socio technical system.
   (c) The nature of the tasks performed.
   (d) The a utonomy of the work group.
8. Data obtained from job analysis has utility for all but which of the following human resource management activities?
   (a) Labour relations
   (b) Selection
   (c) Training
   (d) Job redesign

9. Which of the following is not one of the potential uses of job evaluation information?
   (a) To provide a base for measuring individual performance.
   (b) To provide incentives for employees.
   (c) To provide information for wage negotiations.
   (d) To provide input to job design programmes.

10. When assigning weights to factors, sub factors and degrees
   (a) judgement plays a major role.
   (b) there is one best technique.
   (c) the weights assigned must stay constant from job to job.
   (d) the weights assigned should reflect the minimum number of points allocated.

11. Pay refers to
   (a) the rewards that employees receive as a result of their employment.
   (b) all the extrinsic rewards that employees receive.
   (c) the actual money that employees receive in exchange for their work.
   (d) only the base wage or salary that employees receive.

12. Policies for a successful compensation system must address which of the following issues?
   (a) Perceived long term opportunities.
   (b) Style and quality of leadership.
   (c) Social relationships.
   (d) None of the above.

13. Which of the following is not an action that can be expected when an individual desire for more money increases?
   (a) Looking for another job.
   (b) Joining a union.
   (c) Performing better.
   (d) Increased thrift.

14. Which of the following is not a recommendation to help avoid the problems associated with wage and salary surveys?
   (a) Correlate survey data with adjustment periods.
   (b) Comparemore than base wage or salary.
   (c) Make comparisons of the participating companies for comparability.
   (d) Generate survey data at the beginning of the calendar year.

15. Which of the following statements concerning individual incentive system is false?
   (a) The primary advantage of individual incentive system is that employees can readily see the relationship between what they do and what they get.
   (b) Individual plans can sometimes cause undesirable competition between peers.
   (c) Individual incentive plans, while used more frequently than organisation based plans are used less frequently than group based systems.
   (d) None of the above.

16. Scientific management movement popularised the search for universal generalisation on administrative procedure.
   (a) Debatable (b) Can't say
   (c) No (d) Yes

17. The Human Relations theory focuses on
   (a) Man
   (b) Informal organisation
   (c) Individual
   (d) System

18. The Human Relations theory can be termed as

(a) Socio-economic theory
(b) Humanistic theory
(c) Either (a) or (b)
(d) Both (a) and (b)

19. The Human Relations theory respects
(a) Human motivation
(b) Formal institutionalisation
(c) Informal functioning
(d) None of the above

20. HRD systems or processes may include the following process mechanisms or sub systems.
(a) Performance appraisal, motivation & grievance handling.
(b) Career planning, manpower planning and collective bargaining.
(c) Training and developments, communication and quality of work life.
(d) Performance appraisal, career planning organisation development.

21. Common use of information generated via performance appraisal include all of the following except
(a) organisational training and development programme to job content evaluation.
(b) administrative I personnel decisions.
(c) valuation of selection devices.
(d) input to job content evaluation.

22. Successful career planning and development requires action from
(a) a variety of sources both internal and external to the organisation.
(b) the organisation, his employees immediate manager and the employee.
(c) the employee with some assistance / guidance from his or her immediate manager.
(d) the employee and his/her immediate manager.

23. The ultimate goal of OD is to
(a) do none of the above.
(b) structure the organisational environment so that managers and employees can use their developed skills and abilities to the fullest.
(c) reduce the levels of uncertainity in managerial decision making through out the organ isation.
(d) create an internal environment which is conducive to self expression the cost of quality.

24. The purpose of any human resource information system is to
(a) provide data and data summaries (statistical analysis) that are error free.
(b) replace human decision making with computerised decision making.
(c) reduce the number of low-level support staff.
(d) assist managers in decision making.

25. Designing an integrated HRD system requires a thorough understanding of the following in an organisation.
(a) Organisation culture, organisational conflicts and organisation development.
(b) Development needs, job design and industrial relations.
(c) Organisation culture, existing HRD practices, development climate.
(d) Productivity, manpower planning, incentive systems.

26. Human resources development systems often include the following.
(a) Human resources development employee benefits and welfare, performance appraisal.
(b) Personnel environment, training and development, individual relations.

(c) Manpower planning, potential appraisal, industrial relations.
(d) Personnel administration, human resources development and industrial relations.

27. It is useful to look upon human resources department as providing three types of assistance.
(a) Specific services, advice and coordination.
(b) Specific services, management development and employee evaluations.
(c) Advice, management development and organisational maintenance.
(d) None of the above.

28. Which of the following is not a reason for the increased use of human resources department in the strategic planning process?
(a) A workforce that is becoming most demanding with regard to job satisfaction and the quality of work life.
(b) Changes in the composition of work force.
(c) The societal shift towards greater conservation.
(d) None of the above.

29. The primary goal of human resources management is to
(a) influence internal constituencies.
(b) eliminate non-automated operative positions.
(c) facilitateorganisational performance.
(d) None of the above.

30. Methods for forecasting human resource needs can be classified as either
(a) judgementally or mathematically based.
(b) judgementally or contingency based.
(c) situationally or mathematically based.
(d) None of the above.

31. A frequently used method for determining training need involves
(a) observation analysis conducted by training experts.
(b) individual skill assessment by supervisors.
(c) group discussion with employee group.
(d) None of the above.

32. One advantage of on the job training involves
(a) the fact that trainee is being productive.
(b) the relaxed pace inherent to the procedure.
(c) environmental control.
(d) short time horizons for learning.

33. One advantage of the use of job rotation, a development tool is that
(a) it is relatively easy to perceive factual information.
(b) the learner is encouraged to make mistakes.
(c) the time horizons are usually short.
(d) the training is practical.

34. Sensitivity training
(a) focuses primarily on decision making.
(b) usually involves 2 or 3 participants.
(c) is used frequently in practice.
(d) None of the above.

35. Personnel policy deals with
(a) setting of disputes
(b) employment of new persons
(c) working of employees
(d) None of the above

36. Recruitment is the process of
(a) employing new persons.
(b) placing persons properly.

(c) searching for prospective candidates.
(d) None of the above.

37. Internal sources of recruitment include
(a) promotions from within.
(b) employment through exchanges.
(c) employment through contractors.
(d) None of the above.

38. Which of the following is the external source of recruitment?
(a) Unsolicited applicants.
(b) Promotion from within.
(c) Transfer of employees.
(d) None of the above.

39. Casual callers are appointed to meet ______ needs.
(a) middle term
(b) short term
(c) long term
(d) None of the above

40. Selection process
(a) prepares employers for training.
(b) helps in locating candidates.
(c) determines the suitability of the candidate.
(d) None of the above.

41. Scrutiny of applications is the
(a) third step in selection process.
(b) last step in selection process.
(c) first step in selection process.
(d) None of the above.

42. Blank application form is supplied after
(a) preliminary interview.
(b) scrutiny of application.
(c) medical examination of applications.
(d) None of the above.

43. Dexterity tests are used to judge the
(a) physical movements of the candidate.
(b) proficiency of the candidate.
(c) training of the candidate.
(d) None of the above.

44. Intelligence tests measure
(a) personality traits
(b) overall intelligence
(c) training expertise
(d) None of the above

45. Orientation is generally given to
(a) supervisory staff
(b) new entrants
(c) previous employees
(d) None of the above

46. Off-the job training is given
(a) on the days
(b) outside the factory gate
(c) in the class room
(d) None of the above

47. When trainees are attached to senior workers, it is called
(a) Apprenticeship training
(b) Vestibule training
(c) Refresher training
(d) None of the above

48. Vestibule training is provided
(a) training department
(b) on the job
(c) in the class room
(d) None of the above

49. Minimum wages are not guaranteed under
(a) Piece wage system
(b) Incentive plan
(c) Time wage system
(d) None of the above

50. Piece wage system is suitable when
(a) quality is more important.
(b) quantity is more important.
(c) Both are important.
(d) None of the above.

51. Incentive plan of wage payment can be introduced when
(a) work is of repetitive nature.
(b) work can be standardised.

(c) work is of easy nature.
(d) None of the above.

52. Which of them is time based incentive plan?
(a) Profit sharing plan
(b) Halsey plan
(c) Priestman's plan
(d) None of the above

53. In Emerson plan
(a) minimum wages are guaranteed.
(b) payments are on the basis of output.
(c) minimum wages are not guaranteed.
(d) None of the above.

54. Under worker's participation scheme
(a) worker increase their output.
(b) workers participate in decision making process.
(c) workers get more benefits.
(d) None of the above.

55. Works committees are formed where
(a) more than 20 workers are employed.
(b) more than 50 workers are employed.
(c) 100 or more workers are employed.
(d) None of the above.

56. Joint management councils are formed where
(a) more than 500 workers are employed.
(b) more than 100 workers are employed.
(c) more than 200 workers are employed.
(d) None of the above.

57. Marginal utility theory was conceptualised by
(a) Alfred Marshall (b) Allen
(c) Keynes (d) J.R. Hicks

58. The type of leader who welcomes the participation of the group in the formulation of policies and decisionmaking is
(a) democratic leader
(b) laissez-faire leader
(c) autocratic leader
(d) None of the above

59. The process of searching for prospective employees and stimulating them to apply for jobs in organisation is
(a) Promotion (b) Selection
(c) Recruitment (d) None of these

60. The process in which candidates for employment are divided into two classes those who are to be offered employment and those who are not is
(a) Selection (b) Recruitment
(c) Transfer (d) None of these

61. Personality tests aim at
(a) measuring the candidate's intelligence.
(b) measu ring the basic make up of the individual.
(c) measuring the candidate's knowledge and skill.
(d) None of the above.

62. The practice of placing a candidate at the right job is
(a) Interview (b) Selection
(c) Placement (d) None of these

63. Behavioural factors consist
(a) Physical fitness
(b) Personal attitudes
(c) Behaviour patterns and work habits
(d) None of the above

64. Personnel management is not possible
(a) large-sized concern.
(b) number of workers is so large.
(c) where the work force is too less.
(d) None of the above.

65. Recruitment is made
(a) through different departments
(b) by centralised office
(c) Both of the above
(d) None of the above

66. The sources of recruitment is/are
    (a) internal as well as external
    (b) internal
    (c) external
    (d) None of the above
67. The management of personnel is also called
    (a) Co-ordinating
    (b) Staffing
    (c) Controlling
    (d) None of the above
68. Job analysis should always be done
    (a) at the time of placement
    (b) before recruitment
    (c) after recruitment
    (d) None of the above
69. Employment exchanges are very good sources of
    (a) direct recruitment
    (b) external recruitment
    (c) internal recruitment
    (d) None of the above
70. Recruitment at the factory gate is generally done in case of
    (a) skilled as well as unskilled labour
    (b) skilled labour
    (c) unskilled labour
    (d) None of the above
71. The procedure in which people learn knowledge and/or skill for a definite purpose is
    (a) Training
    (b) Education
    (c) Both of the above
    (d) None of the above
72. In which training the worker is trained in the course of his work?
    (a) Vestibule training
    (b) On-the-job training
    (c) Apprenticeship training
    (d) None of the above
73. The purpose of induction of training is
    (a) to receive the earlier learning in the minds of employees.
    (b) to enable the trainee to overcome nervousness and get the best out of training.
    (c) to finalise the new entrants to the organisation, its objectives, rules and working conditions.
    (d) None of the above.
74. Normally, permanent employees are appointed on
    (a) probation basis
    (b) ad-hoc basis
    (c) confirmed basis
    (d) None of the above
75. Training is required for
    (a) skilled labour only
    (b) unskilled labour only
    (c) both skilled and unskilled labour
    (d) None of the above
76. Training adds to
    (a) Nothing
    (b) Knowledge
    (c) Practical efficiency
    (d) None of the above
77. Training and accidents have
    (a) no relationship
    (b) negative relationship
    (c) positive relationship
    (d) None of the above
78. Where the work can't be measured the working force can be easily controlled the wage payment must be
    (a) according to time
    (b) according to pieces
    (c) Any of the above
    (d) None of the above
79. More job security is available in
    (a) piece wages
    (b) time wages

(c) Both of the wages
(d) None of the above

80. The important feature of piece rate system is the worker
(a) Who produced more will be rewarded more.
(b) Who works for more time, will be rewarded more.
(c) Both of the above.
(d) None of the above.

81. F.W. Taylor advocated for
(a) differential wage rates
(b) time rate system
(c) piece rate system
(d) None of the above

82. Wages are paid for the use of
(a) Labour (b) Land
(c) Capital (d) None of these

83. Incentives given on psychological base
(a) monetary and non-monetary
(b) are not financial
(c) are financial
(d) None of the above

84. Which of the following is not non-monetary?
(a) Effective communication
(b) Bonus
(c) Job security
(d) None of the above

85. Man can't live on bread alone, he wants
(a) due recognition
(b) better wages and due recognition
(c) better wages
(d) None of the above

86. Management is bound for labour welfare
(a) outside the factory only
(b) within the factory only
(c) both the above
(d) None of the above

87. Where the wage policy is the most complex, there
(a) strike never happens
(b) strike happens
(c) Both (a) and (b)
(d) None of the above

88. "No temptation to increase the quantity at the cost of quality" is
(a) piece rate system
(b) time rate system
(c) Both of the above
(d) None of the above

89. 'Piece wages' provides
(a) nothing to them.
(b) encouragement to efficient hard workers.
(c) discouragement to efficient and hard workers.
(d) None of the above.

90. In which of the following respects the Human Relations theory differs from the Classical theory?
(a) Emphasis on human aspects as against mechanical aspects.
(b) Emphasis on social environment as against on physical environment.
(c) Viewing organisations as sociological entitles rather than legal-rational entities.
(d) None of the above.

91. What may be called the starting points of the Human Relations theory?
(a) Administrative principles of Henry Fayol.
(b) Hawthorne experiment.
(c) Herbert Simon's work on decision making.
(d) Herzberg's work on motivation.

92. The Human Relations theory has been criticised on the ground that

(a) the psychological inducements offered to workers constituted another instrument of exploitation.
(b) if fails to take into consideration the inherent conflict between management and workers.
(c) the theory over-emphasises the human aspects of the organisation.
(d) All of the above.

93. Human resource can be valued like any other asset.
(a) False
(b) True
(c) Both (a) and (b)
(d) None of the above

94. Human resource planning is the responsibility of both the line and staff manager.
(a) False
(b) True
(c) Only staff manager
(d) Only line manager

95. Job analysis includes the preparation of
(a) job descriptions and job specifications.
(b) experience and responsibilities.
(c) qualification and abilities.
(d) None of the above.

96. Groupings of workers who produce entire products or components of products is termed as
(a) Organisation unit
(b) Production cells
(c) Control group
(d) None of the above

97. "Human Relations approach or theory" to management was originated by
(a) Elton Mayo (b) F.W. Taylor
(c) Peter F. Drucker (d) Henry Fayol

98. The Human Relations theory does not lay emphasis on
(a) Human motivations
(b) Principles
(c) Informal group
(d) Peoplefunctions

99. Human resource can be thought of as "the total knowledge, skill, creative abilities, talents and attitudes of an organisation's work force as well as the values, attitudes and beliefs of the individuals involved." Who gave this statement?
(a) Merton
(b) Koteler
(c) D. Philopho
(d) Leon C. Megginson

100. Under _____ employees are used for the multiple mutual benefit of the organisation, employees and their family members.
(a) personnel management
(b) human resource management
(c) performance management
(d) functional management

101. "_____ is a responsibility of all those who manage people as well as bring a description of the work of those who are employed as specialists. It is that part of management which is concerned with people at work and with their relationships within an enterprise. It applies not only to industry and commerce but to all fields of employment."
(a) Human resource management
(b) Personnel management
(c) Functional management
(d) Performance management

102. Which one of the following does not include under the functions of human resource management?
(a) Recruitment (b) Profitability
(c) Planning (d) Organising

103. Human relations consists
(a) Communication (b) Motivation
(c) Morale (d) All of the above

104. Compensation management consists
(a) wages and salary administration
(b) job evaluation
(c) fringe benefits
(d) All of the above

105. Human resource development consists
(a) career planning and development
(b) performance appraisal
(c) training
(d) All of the above

106. Recruitment deals with
(a) identification of new sources of applicants.
(b) identification of existing sources of applicants and developing them.
(c) creation of new sources of applicants.
(d) All of the above.

107. Selection includes
(a) checking of references.
(b) formulating interviewing techniques.
(c) framing and developing application blanks.
(d) All of the above.

108. Training involves
(a) developing suitable training programmes.
(b) evaluating the effectiveness of training programmes.
(c) identification of training needs of the individuals and the company.
(d) All of the above.

109. The rate of separation will be found as

(a) $\frac{100+1}{\text{Total number of employee}} + \frac{\text{Recruitment made in the year} - 100}{2}$

(b) $\frac{\text{Total number of workers leaving per month}}{\text{Total pay-roll for a month}} \times 100$

(c) $\frac{\text{Total pay-roll in a month}}{\text{Total number of workers leaving per month}} \times 100$

(d) $\frac{\text{Total number of workers leaving per month}}{\text{Average number of workers on pay-roll for a month}} \times 100$

110. Labour Productivity can be expressed as
(a) Production of labour

$$= \frac{\text{Output in terms of value / quantity / units / standard time for actual output}}{\text{Number of man-hours spent on production}}$$

(b) $\frac{\text{Number of man-hours spent on production}}{\text{Output in terms of standard time}} \times 100$

(c) Productivity of labour

$$= \frac{\text{Output in terms of units or quantity of value or standard time}}{\text{Number of man-hours}}$$

(d) $\frac{\text{Output in term of unit}}{\text{Number of man-hours}} \times 100 - 1$

111. Man-hours calculated as

(a) $\frac{\text{Number of hours worked}}{\text{Number of workers employed on production}} \times 100$

(b) Number of workers empioved in production × Number of hours worked

(c) $\frac{\text{Productivity of labour}}{100} \times \text{Man-hours spent on standard work}$

(d) $\frac{\text{Number of workers employed on production}}{\text{Number of hours worked}}$

112. Productivity can be expressed as

(a) $\text{Productivity} = \dfrac{\text{Input}}{\text{Output}}$

(b) $\text{Productivity} = \dfrac{\text{Output}}{\text{Input}}$

(c) $\text{Productivity} = \dfrac{\text{Output}}{100} \times (100 - \text{Input})$

(d) $\dfrac{\text{Productivity}}{100+1} = \dfrac{\text{Input}}{\text{Output}}$

113. Physical condition of work includes
(a) Lighting (b) Temperature
(c) Ventilation (d) All of the above

114. Technological development includes
(a) Raw Materials (b) Plant size
(c) Job layout (d) All of the above

115. Which of the following statement is true?
(a) A condition of low morale is on the other hand, characterised by an attitude of indifference or hostility towards the work in hand and lack of a co-operate spirit.
(b) Morale is basically a matter of human behaviour.
(c) The Howthrone experiment is related with morale.
(d) All of the above.

116. "Morale as a readiness to co-operate warmly in the tasks and purposes of a given group or organisation." Who gave this statement?
(a) Ackooff (b) Viteles
(c) Alldrich (d) None of these

117. Which of the following factors connected with working conditions?
(a) Work environment
(b) Fair wages
(c) Security and opportunity to rise
(d) All of the above

118. Which of the following types is/are fatigue?
(a) Nervous fatigue
(b) Industrial fatigue
(c) Muscular or Physiological fatigue
(d) All of the above

119. Mental fatigue arises due to a feeling of tiredness that drops up in a person while working continuously on a ___ operation.
(a) standing (b) repetitive
(c) performance (d) industrial

120. Human resource management policy consists of
(a) developing collaborative and problem solving approaches in human resources management.
(b) ensuring congruence between individual and organisational goals and objectives and setting high standard of productivity, efficiency and quality of working life.
(c) enriching employee commitment and role effectiveness through sharing of information regarding matural rights, obligations and the philosophy underlying man management policies and systems.
(d) All of the above.

121. Human resource planning includes
(a) creating a climate of opportunity and professional challenge.
(b) improvement in the quality of working life.
(c) recognition of excellence in performance.
(d) All of the above.

122. Redressal of employee grievances covers
(a) positive attitude towards employee grievances and readiness to help.
(b) institutionalising an expeditious machinery for resolving employees grievances.

(c) Both (a) and (b).
(d) Equitable wages and salary system.

123. 'On the job training' can be provided through
(a) distance education
(b) mobile teacher
(c) non-formal education
(d) All of the above

124. The Industrial relations in the 21st century are not going to be between two groups—haves or havenots or managers and managed or employers and
(a) Customers (b) Suppliers
(c) Employees (d) Firm

125. The organisation systems that were strengthened were
(a) planning and scheduling
(b) plant and machinery function
(c) tender monitoring
(d) All of the above

126. Organisation and development consists
(a) awareness of organisation and development being along-drawn out process, whose benefits are raped only over a period of time.
(b) top management commitment for the organisation development process, continued education.
(c) involvement of line and operational staff in its implementation.
(d) All of the above.

127. A number of decisions have been taken to strengthen recruitment and improve the quality of management
(a) Assignees (b) Trainees
(c) Programmes (d) Company

128. Which one of the following statement is not true?
(a) The introduction and operation of a good performance appraisal system is among the most difficult of all organisational process.
(b) Initiating human resources development has been a reactive step for most organisation in our country when every things else second to fail.
(c) Systematic identification of training is not done through performance appraisal.
(d) Organisations need to find ways to tap this potential and motivate them for improved performance.

129. Job description consists
(a) performance appraisal to make the rate/expectations clear both to assessors and assessees
(b) potential appraisal to evaluate suitability of the individual on the higher position
(c) recruitment of right people for the right job
(d) All of the above

130. The human resource development initiatives have a significant role to play in terms of
(a) training and development effort attendant upon technological changes to upgrade skill and managerial ability.
(b) rationalisation of organisation and of manpower along with increase in production, capacity and investment in new technology.
(c) improvement in work culture as a prerequisite for improvements in other areas and to tune up the organisation for modernisation.
(d) All of the above.

131. Human resource management includes
(a) man power planning and recruitment.
(b) motivation, communication and team building.

(c) training and development.
(d) All of the above.

132. Qualitative changes in the attitudes of employees involves
(a) employees have begun to think positively about the company.
(b) there is a greater awareness among officers, workers and associations.
(c) communication process is more effective.
(d) All of the above.

133. Industrial relations consists
(a) job analysis
(b) supervision
(c) recruitment and placement
(d) All of the above

134. Feedback and counselling involves
(a) discuss the steps the employee can take for improvement.
(b) give critical and supporting feedback.
(c) provide support.
(d) All of the above.

135. Organisation and development includes
(a) team building
(b) organisational diagnosis
(c) job-enrichment
(d) All of the above

136. Performance appraisal includes
(a) check reviews done by the superiors.
(b) send summary information for central storage and use.
(c) review his performance in relation to the objectives and other behaviours.
(d) All of the above.

137. Training central system includes
(a) real time review of specific projects.
(b) annual review of years training plans.
(c) monthly review of budget and plans.
(d) All of the above.

138. Man power planning system include
(a) man power inventory
(b) corporate plan
(c) man power wastage forecast
(d) All of the above

139. Action plan includes
(a) Reporting
(b) Budgeting and control
(c) Red employment
(d) Utilization and audit

140. Man power inventory includes
(a) category of employee
(b) number of employees
(c) age of the employee
(d) All of the above

141. Man power audit system covers
(a) by examining if the systems are being followed and identifying the bottlenecks.
(b) by recording the component of all the systems relating to manpower in the organisation and see that all important activities have been covered by the systems.
(c) by examining the structure and content of the systems to see if the activities are controlling to the fulfilment of objectives.
(d) All of the above.

142. The Industrial Employment (standing orders) Act was enacted in
(a) 1946 (b) 1947
(c) 1950 (d) 1960

143. Administration of standing orders covers
(a) attendance and late-coming
(b) grievance machinery
(c) stoppage and shut down of work
(d) All of the above

144. Disciplined behaviour of employees is a condition of efficient performance in

(a) Communication
(b) Industrial enterprises
(c) Sample units
(d) Personnel department

145. Traditionally discipline is understood as nothing more than obedient and orderly behaviour and as a means of maintaining proper
(a) Communication
(b) Department
(c) Subordination
(d) Firmly

146. In dealing with cases of indiscipline management can resort to five possible approaches namely
(a) the human relations approach
(b) the judicial approach
(c) the group discipline approach
(d) All of the above

147. Penalties for the misconducts also assigned in the _______ of the units.
(a) fluctious orders
(b) law order
(c) standing orders
(d) All of the above

148. "The procedure for dealing with cases of misconduct is a major portion of the standing orders of all the units." Is this statement true?
(a) No (b) Yes
(c) Can't say (d) May be

149. The successive steps in disciplinary action are
(a) suspension of the offender in grave cases.
(b) preparing and serving the charge sheet.
(c) time to be given for the dependent's explanation.
(d) All of the above

150. Grievance is affecting one or more individual workers in respect of their conditions of work and not disputes over matters of general applicability to all
(a) Information (b) Claims
(c) Complaint (d) Order

151. Which of the following statement is true?
(a) The job should be the primary means for training and development.
(b) A definition of grievance common to all the grievance procures of the units under study can be outlined as any complaint affecting an individual workman in regard to payment of wages, overtime, leave, transfer, promotion, non-extension or any welfare amenities of benefits due under the rules, but does not include representation concerning matters of policy and grievances arising out of punishments imposed in accordance with the standing orders.
(c) Peter Drucker's, *The Practice of Management* published in 1954 helped popularise the MBO approach.
(d) All of the above.

152. Aptitude test includes
(a) skill test
(b) intelligence test
(c) psychomotor tests
(d) All of the above

153. Intelligence quotient can be calculated as
(a) $\frac{\text{Actual Age}}{\text{Standard Age}} \times 100$
(b) $\frac{\text{Mental Age}}{\text{Actual Age}} \times 100$
(c) Actual Age × Mental Age
(d) $\frac{100}{\text{Actual Age}}(100 - \text{Mental Age})$

154. Which of the following is/are a type of skill test?
(a) Achievement test
(b) Interest test
(c) Situational test
(d) All of the above

155. Personality test includes
(a) Objective tests
(b) Projective tests
(c) Training method
(d) Both (a) and (b)

156. "Selection of personnel to man the organisation is a crucial complex and continuing function." Is this statement true?
(a) No (b) Yes
(c) Can't say (d) May be

157. The objective of the selection decision is to choose the individual who can most successfully perform the job from the pool of
(a) unqualified candidates
(b) qualified candidates
(c) qualified expert
(d) qualified correspondent

158. The human resource system covers under training and development
(a) train and develop
(b) job design and evaluation
(c) recruit and select
(d) All of the above

159. Training and development refers to the total structure of on the job and off the job training systems used by the
(a) Candidates (b) Government
(c) Organistaion (d) Expert

160. The career planning and development process is also part of comprehensive organisation development
(a) Communication (b) Process
(c) Finn (d) Project

161. Methods for training and development involve various job techniques such as expanded responsibility, job rotation, assistant to positions and other
(a) Project (b) System
(c) Techniques (d) Firms

162. The components of the information systems should be made up only of information units which enhance effective
(a) personnel management decision
(b) human resources decision
(c) project
(d) None of the above

163. The executive's total compensation package consists of
(a) short term incentives
(b) basic salary
(c) perquisites
(d) All of the above

164. Objectives of training is
(a) awareness of the problems.
(b) better work decisions.
(c) increase in employee morale, confidence skill and productivity.
(d) All of the above.

165. Which of the following includes under techniques of training?
(a) Role playing method
(b) On the job training method
(c) Informal training
(d) All of the above

166. On the job training methods includes
(a) Training at training centre
(b) Guidance
(c) Job rotation method
(d) All of the above

167. Off the job training methods includes
(a) Conference method
(b) Role playing method
(c) Lecture method
(d) All of the above

168. Off the job training method consists
(a) Programmed training
(b) Role playing method
(c) Group discussion seminar
(d) All of the above

169. Executive employee training method consists
(a) Basket training method
(b) Position rotation training
(c) Management game method
(d) All of the above

170. Executive employee training method involves
(a) Transactional analysis training method
(b) Management game method
(c) Understudy
(d) Programme training method

171. Which one is not a training method?
(a) Recruitment method
(b) Management role playing
(c) Workshop
(d) Multiple management

172. Understudy training means
(a) Roundtable conference/meetings
(b) Under the executives
(c) Special meetings
(d) None of the above

173. The basket training method means
(a) Development of institute
(b) Development of decision skilled
(c) Development of production
(d) Development or resources

174. Apprenticeship Training Act passed on
(a) 1961 (b) 1971
(c) 1941 (d) 1951

175. On the job training method means
(a) To arrange Conference/Meetings
(b) Providing study matters
(c) To work on the site
(d) Development of Institute

176. Introduction training method provided to the
(a) Freshers/newcomers employees
(b) Present employees
(c) Ex-employees
(d) Retired employees

177. The main objects of training methods is
(a) For loan obtaining
(b) Introduction of new technology
(c) To earn money
(d) To obtain property

178. Types of interview includes
(a) Non-directive interview
(b) Patterned interview
(c) Group interview
(d) All of the above

179. Which of the following is/are not a type of interview?
(a) Interview rating form
(b) Panel interview
(c) Productive interview
(d) Depth interview

180. Type of selection test consists
(a) Interest test
(b) Personality test
(c) Mental ability test
(d) All of the above

181. Role of personnel managers is
(a) Advisory role
(b) Conversion agent role
(c) Mediator role
(d) All of the above

182. Management functions of personnel management includes
(a) Motivation
(b) Grouping
(c) Controlling
(d) Personnel planning

183. Advisory functions of personnel managers includes
(a) advising to the top management
(b) advising to the departmental officers
(c) training and development
(d) Both (a) and (b)

184. Executive functions of personnel managers involves
(a) Job description
(b) Wages and salary administration
(c) Job evaluation
(d) All of the above

185. Process of manpower planning consists of
(a) Controlling
(b) Development implementation
(c) Forecasting
(d) All of the above

186. An extent to which an organisation achieves its predetermined objectives within given resources and without undue strain to its members
(a) Organization behavior
(b) Organizational culture
(c) Organizational spirit
(d) Organizational effectiveness

187. Utility of job analysis includes
(a) Training of employee
(b) Performance appraisal
(c) Guidance to the new employee
(d) Work study

188. Which of the following is the internal sources of recruitment?
(a) Transfer (b) Trainees
(c) Promotion (d) All of the above

189. Internal sources of recruitment involves
(a) Extension of service
(b) Internal advisement
(c) Informal search
(d) All of the above

190. External sources of recruitment consists of
(a) Advertisement
(b) Through employment exchange
(c) Recommendations of existing employees
(d) All of the above

191. What are the benefits of human resource planning?
(a) Achieve economies in hiring new workers.
(b) Improve the utilization of human resources.
(c) Match personnel activities and future organisation objectives efficiently.
(d) All of the above.

192. Developments in the organisation environment are difficult for personnel specialists to predict in the short run and sometimes impossible to estimate in the run.
(a) Short (b) Long
(c) Faster (d) Equal

193. What influence the demand for people?
(a) Budgets
(b) Technology
(c) Social-political legal
(d) All of the above

194. Work-force involves
(a) Terminations (b) Retirement
(c) Resignations (d) All of the above

195. When new venture complicate employment planning, planners can use new venture analysis?
(a) Can't say (b) Yes
(c) No (d) None of these

196. "Indexation is a method of estimating future employment needs by matching employment growth with some index." Is this statement true?

(a) No (b) Yes
(c) Can't say (d) None of these

197. The internal supply of human resources consists of present employees who can be to fill expected opening.
(a) Transferred (b) Demoted
(c) Promoted (d) All of the above

198. Human resource audits summarize each employee's skill and
(a) Evidence (b) Life
(c) Abilities (d) Property

199. Management inventory information consists of
(a) Duties of subordinates
(b) Number of employee supervised
(c) Management training received
(d) All of the above

200. Present performance is determined largely from
(a) Job
(b) Appraisal evaluation
(c) Supervisory evaluation
(d) Advisory evaluation

201. Jobs are the link between the people and the
(a) Auditor (b) Manager
(c) Organisation (d) Supervisor

202. Organisational elements of job design are concerned with
(a) Approach (b) Techniques
(c) Firm (d) Efficiency

203. People with a strong desire to satisfy higher order needs perform their best when placed on jobs that were high on certain
(a) Circumstances (b) Dimensions
(c) Performance (d) Issues

204. Autonomy is having responsibility for what one does. It is the freedom to control one's response to the
(a) Partner (b) Environment
(c) Organisation (d) Employer

205. Job enlargement expands the number of related tasks in the
(a) Identity (b) Range
(c) Job (d) Work

206. Effective job design seeks a trade off between efficiency are behavioural elements. Is this statement true?
(a) No (b) Yes
(c) Can't say (d) None of these

207. Which of the following challengers faced by recruiters?
(a) Affirmative action plans
(b) Job requirements
(c) Environmental conditions
(d) All of the above

208. Recruiters must be sensitive to the constraints on the process.
(a) Appointment (b) Employment
(c) Recruitment (d) Environment

209. Which of the following statement is/are true?
(a) Quality control in personnel means feedback.
(b) The selection process depend heavily upon inputs such as job analysis, human resource plan, and recruits.
(c) The evaluatory may provide this feedback through several approaches, tell and said, tell and listen and problem solving.
(d) All of the above.

210. The appraisal process is designed by the personnel
(a) Factory (b) Management
(c) Department (d) Workshop

211. Which of the following is/are not benefits of training and development?

(a) Makes the organisation a better place to work and live.
(b) Improve communication between groups and individuals.
(c) Development is a sense of growth in learning.
(d) None of the above.

212. Which of the following is/are the benefits of the training and development?
(a) Creates an appropriate climate for growth and communication.
(b) Helps people identify with organisational goals.
(c) Improve the morale of the work force.
(d) All of these.

213. Factors which have contributed to the slow progress of arbitration have identified by the National Commission on Labour as
(a) The fact that in law no appeal was competent against an arbitrator's award
(b) Absence of recognised unions which could bind workers to common agreements
(c) Absence of a simplified procedure to be followed in voluntary arbitration
(d) All of the above

214. Which of the following statement is/are true?
(a) The formation centre-cum-industry and national industrial federations should be encouraged.
(b) Industrial disputes refer to difference that affect groups of employees and employers engaged in an industry.
(c) The minimum membership fee of a union should be raised and statutorily fixed.
(d) All of the above.

215. The Industrial Dispute Act came into force on
(a) 1950 (b) 1960
(c) 1947 (d) 1940

216. Three major schemes of workers' participation in management in India have been introduced which are
(a) Shop councils
(b) Works committees
(c) Joint management councils
(d) All of the above

217. The industrial policy resolution came into force on
(a) 1947 (b) 1956
(c) 1966 (d) 1970

218. The joint management councils includes
(a) In some others, the management is expected to share information with the council.
(b) In a set of functions administrative responsibilities have to be give...to it.
(c) The Council is entitled to be consulted on certain specified matters.
(d) All of the above.

219. The joint management council scheme started as an experimental measure in 1958 in undertaking.
(a) 23 (b) 24
(c) 25 (d) 30

220. A scheme for worker's participation in industry at the shop-floor and plant levels was introduced in
(a) October 1980 (b) October 1985
(c) October 1970 (d) October 1975

221. Which of the following statement is/are true?
(a) The code of discipline, requiring employers and workers to utilise the existing machinery for the settlement

of disputes and avoiding direct action, was evolved at the Indian labour conference in 1958.
(b) Industrial relations are as old as industry itself.
(c) In the highest form of discipline, all are self-regulated and all are free.
(d) All of the above.

222. Productivity of machine calculated by
(a) $\frac{100}{\text{Total workers}} \times \text{Machine hours worked}$
(b) $\frac{\text{Total production in length, weight etc.}}{\text{Machine hour worked}}$
(c) $\frac{\text{Total worker}}{\text{Total Machine hour worked}} \times 100$
(d) $\frac{\text{Machine hours worked}}{\text{Total production in length, weight etc.}}$

223. Productivity of material can be expressed as
(a) $\frac{\text{Total raw material used}}{\text{Weight or volume or number of finished goods}} \times 100$
(b) $\frac{100}{\text{Total raw material}} \times \text{Total finished goods}$
(c) $\frac{\text{Weight or volume or number or length of finished goods}}{\text{Weight, volume, number or length of raw material used}}$
(d) $\frac{100}{\text{Weight or volume or number finished goods}} \times \text{Total raw material used}$

224. Productivity of land can be calculated as
(a) $\frac{\text{Total production}}{\text{Area of land used}}$
(b) $\frac{\text{Total Machine}}{\text{Total property}} \times 100$
(c) $\frac{\text{Total Machine used}}{\text{Total production}} \times 100$
(d) $\frac{\text{Area of land used}}{\text{Total production}} \times 100$

225. The Hawthorne experiments showed that physical conditions of work were not directly and necessarily related to
(a) Employee (b) Motivation
(c) Input (d) Output

226. Employees' job performance consists
(a) Ability—knowledge (Education, Experience).
(b) Physical condition work.
(c) Formal organisation—structure, policies and efficiency.
(d) All of the above.

227. Which of the following factors affecting to the productivity?
(a) Employees' job performance
(b) Technological developments
(c) Physical condition of work
(d) All of the above

228. Physical conditions of work involves
(a) Rest pauses (b) Lighting
(c) Temperature (d) All of the above

229. Which of the following is not the chief agencies of labour welfare?
(a) Central government
(b) Government TOPSO management Institute
(c) Employee's organisation
(d) State government

230. Which of the following is/are central organisation of workers?
   (a) Indian National Trade Union Congress
   (b) United Trade Union Congress
   (c) Trade Union Co-ordination Centre
   (d) All of the above

231. The Trade Union activity in India made a beginning even before the end of the century.
   (a) 16th (b) 20th
   (c) 18th (d) 19th

232. Who started an agitation to draw the attention of the Government to the deplorable condition of women and child labour in Indian industry?
   (a) Mahatma Gandhi
   (b) Mr. Sorabjee Shapurjee
   (c) Madan Mohan Malviya
   (d) Pt. Jawaharlal Nehru

233. When was organised first meeting of workers in India?
   (a) In 1870 (b) In 1816
   (c) In 1890 (d) In 1980

234. Who started a paper known as 'Dinbandhu' for the working class and organised Bombay Mill Hands Union in 1890?
   (a) Mr. Sorabjee Shapurjee
   (b) Mr. N.M. Lokhande
   (c) Dr. B.R. Ambedker
   (d) Mr. Raghu Nath Chatterjee

235. When the Society of Railway servants was established?
   (a) In 1897 (b) In 1890
   (c) In 1870 (d) In 1990

236. The Society of Railway Servants was registered under the
   (a) Industrial Dispute Act, 1947
   (b) The Factory Act, 1947
   (c) Worker Trade Union Act
   (d) Indian Companies Act

237. When Postal Union was organised?
   (a) In 1908 (b) In 1920
   (c) In 1909 (d) In 1907

238. In _____ textile workers were organised in Madras.
   (a) 1930 (b) 1950
   (c) 1918 (d) 1917

239. Which of the problems is not of the trade unions in India?
   (a) Performance
   (b) Inter Union
   (c) Size of the Unions
   (d) Weak Finance of the Unions

240. Objects of trade unions includes
   (a) To protect a part of the increased prosperity of Industry for their members in the form of bonus.
   (b) To secure better wages for the workers in keeping with the prevailing standard of living and cost of living in the nation.
   (c) To strive for better working conditions for the workers in the form of shorter working hours, leave with pay, social security benefits and other welfare facilities.
   (d) All of the above.

241. Which Article lays down that a directive principle of state policy that "The state shall endeavour to secure _______ to all workers a living wages, conditions of work ensuring decent standard of life, full employment social and cultural opportunities."
   (a) Article 70 (b) Article 23
   (c) Article 43 (d) Article 46

242. The National Government accepted the recommendations of the Tripartite

Industrial Conference held in ____ regarding the need for paying fair wages to labour.

(a) December 1947 (b) March 1940
(c) December 1948 (d) March 1947

243. When a Tripartite Committee on fair wages was appointed?

(a) In 1949 (b) In 1950
(c) In 1948 (d) In 1947

244. The Tripartite Committee on fair wages examined the question of fare wages at length and adopted its draft report on the

(a) 6th of July 1949
(b) 6th of September 1949
(c) 6th of June 1949
(d) None of the above

245. The concept of wages is

(a) Fair wages (b) Living wages
(c) Minimum wages (d) All of the above

246. Payment of Bonus Act came into force on

(a) 1970 (b) 1948
(c) 1960 (d) 1965

247. The Government of India gave effect to the major recommendations of the Bonus Commission by introducing a Bill which was passed by Parliament and became the Payment of _____ Act, 1965.

(a) dividends (b) salary
(c) wages (d) bonus

248. The provisions of the Payment of Bonus Act, 1965 take effect from the accounting year commencing on

(a) 7th July 1965
(b) 6th April 1966
(c) 7th August 1960
(d) Any day in 1964

249. One of the problems, faced by employee at work in industry is

(a) Transfer (b) Demotion
(c) Accidents (d) Retirement

250. When was introduced Factories Act?

(a) 1950 (b) 1961
(c) 1948 (d) 1949

251. Which of the following is/are causes of accidents?

(a) Natural Event
(b) Unsafe Act
(c) Unsafe condition
(d) All of these

252. The concept of luck is used in explaining human behaviour only when the real cause factors are

(a) Collateral (b) Known
(c) Unknown (d) None of these

253. Which of the following statement is/are true?

(a) The human capital cannot be purchased or owned by the firm and it would not be recognised as assets.
(b) The labour cannot be treated as assets since it has no service potential extending after a given period.
(c) When an individual employee is found consistently to experience more accidents than the average employee, he may be called an accident prone employee.
(d) All of the above.

254. How to reduce accidents at work in Industry?

(a) By safety programme
(b) By proper training
(c) By safety propaganda work
(d) All of the above

255. Elimination of hazardous conditions involves

(a) Insufficient work space
(b) Placement hazard
(c) Use of improper tools
(d) All of the above

256. Body is to be protected against
(a) Chemical hazards
(b) Fire
(c) Minor mishaps
(d) All of the above

257. Which precautions shall have to be taken by the industry or employee in case of fire at work?
(a) Exit door shall not be locked.
(b) Every window, door or other exit, a means of escape in case of fire shall be marked in a language understood by majority of workers or any other symbol.
(c) Exit door to escape in case of fire shall be provided.
(d) All of the above.

258. When was started The Employees' State Insurance Act?
(a) 1947 (b) 1950
(c) 1940 (d) 1948

259. Social security (minimum standards) convention covers
(a) Sickness benefit
(b) Unemployment benefit
(c) Medical care
(d) All of the above

260. Social security (minimum standards) convention includes
(a) Employment injury benefit
(b) Invalidity benefit
(c) Survivors' benefits
(d) All of the above

261. The Assam Tea Plantations Provident Fund Act came into force in
(a) 1955 (b) 1960
(c) 1970 (d) 1968

262. The Assam Tea Plantations Employees' Welfare Fund Act started from
(a) 1960 (b) 1970
(c) 1950 (d) 1959

263. The Dock Workers (Regulation of Employment) Act introduced from
(a) 1950 (b) 1960
(c) 1948 (d) 1949

264. The Iron Ore Mines Labour Welfare Cess Act started from
(a) 1947 (b) 1967
(c) 1961 (d) 1960

265. The Mica Mines Labour Welfare Fund Act introduced from
(a) 1970 (b) 1963
(c) 1946 (d) 1960

266. The Industrial Disputes (Amendment) Act came into force from
(a) 1953 (b) 1980
(c) 1960 (d) 1940

267. Satisfaction is an attitude of mind and it is not the same as
(a) Communication (b) Performance
(c) Motivation (d) None of these

268. Equity theory of work motivation has been developed by
(a) R. Thesis (b) Dr. L.N. Koli
(c) J. Stacy Adams (d) J. Arun Kaul

269. Work Motivation theory covers
(a) Process Models (b) Conet Models
(c) Vroom (d) All of the above

270. Work Motivation theory involves
(a) Herzberg
(b) Human Relations
(c) Maslaw
(d) All of the above

271. The human relations movement emphasises the importance of providing the employees with conditions that permit and

(a) denote self-actualisation
(b) a suitable change in the individual
(c) promote self-actualisation
(d) All of the above

272. The main object of training is to induce a suitable change in the
(a) experienced employee
(b) individual concerned
(c) performance of the employer
(d) firm

273. Apprentice Act started from
(a) 1965 (b) 1970
(c) 1961 (d) 1960

274. Horizontal job rotation refers to
(a) Lateral promotion
(b) Lateral motivation
(c) Lateral transfer
(d) All of the above

275. Which of the following statement is/are false?
(a) The trainer should certainly be varychary of transferring attitude and approaches which are both appropriate and necessary for group instruction session.
(b) Seminars differ from the discussion.
(c) The Apprenticeship Act started from 1970.
(d) Planning the programme is a good essentials of training programme.

276. When was established the Indian Institute of Social Welfare and Business Management in Calcutta?
(a) 1960 (b) 1945
(c) 1980 (d) 1947

277. Which of the following institutes run management training course with specialised course of study?
(a) The South Indian Textile Coimbatore Research Association.
(b) Sri Ram centre for Industrial Relations, Delhi.
(c) Vaikunth Metita National Institute of Cooperative Management, Poona.
(d) All of the above.

278. Which of the following steps are taken at the time of training programme?
(a) Evaluation of the programme
(b) Getting ready for the job
(c) Follow up
(d) All of the above

279. The object of employees appraisal is
(a) To help determine promotions and transfers.
(b) To identify areas which require further training.
(c) To improve job performance.
(d) All of the above

280. The management development programme should be based on a definite strategy which should spell out the type coverage and objective of
(a) Human planning (b) Firm
(c) Work (d) Programme

281. Marginal Productivity theory is mainly concerned with predicting the pay level
(a) Entrepreneurs (b) Employees
(c) Executives (d) Productive

282. "Human resources management policies as a of proposals and actions that act as a reference point for mangers in their dealings with employees." Who refers this statement?
(a) A. Ronalads
(b) Browster and Richbell
(c) Homgreen L.H.
(d) S. Rohardall I

283. Procedure of organisational structure includes
(a) Political
(b) External environment

(c) Legal
(d) All of the above

284. Which of the following is a source of content for formulating human resource management policies?
(a) Organisational policies.
(b) Past experience of the organisation.
(c) Existing practices and experiences in other organisations of the same nature or in the same geographical area or in the entire nation.
(d) All of the above.

285. Management style includes
(a) Benevolent (b) Autocratic
(c) Laissez-Faire (d) All of the above

286. Formal relation of human resources policies are divided into
(a) Line relations
(b) Staff relations
(c) Both (a) and (b)
(d) Functional relations

287. The functions of personnel manager includes
(a) Development (b) Employment
(c) Training (d) All of the above

288. Which of the following attributes should be possess by the personnel manager?
(a) Educational skill
(b) Discriminating skills
(c) Intelligence
(d) All of the above

289. The All India Trade Union Congress was formed in
(a) 1919 (b) 1920
(c) 1940 (d) 1930

290. When the Printers Union was established in Calcutta?
(a) 1919 (b) 1907
(c) 1905 (d) 1906

291. When the Postal Union was established in Bombay?
(a) 1937 (b) 1927
(c) 1917 (d) 1907

292. When Factory Labour Commission submitted its report to the Government of India?
(a) 1909 (b) 1998
(c) 1907 (d) 1908

293. Which of the following functions attend by Shop Councils?
(a) Assist in maintaining a general discipline in the shop.
(b) Assisting management in achieving production targets.
(c) Do not attend to the physical conditions of working, such as lighting, ventilation, noise, dust, etc., and increase of fatigue.
(d) To adopt safety measures.

294. When Emphasis has been shifted to human resources development?
(a) 1970 (b) 1960
(c) 1995 (d) 1965

295. When The Payment of Wages Act (Regulation the deductions from wages) was passed?
(a) 1936 (b) 1963
(c) 1980 (d) 1970

296. When Indian Labour Conference was held?
(a) 1960 (b) 1972
(c) 1942 (d) 1940

297. Which of the following is not the features of the shop councils scheme?
(a) A shop council, once formed, will function for a period of six month.
(b) The scheme is applicable to industrial units employing 500 or more worker.

(c) Each shop council consists of an equal number of representative of employers and workers, the employers' representatives are nominated by the management.
(d) The representatives of workers must belong to the department or shop concerned.

298. The Bombay Trade Disputes Conciliation Act was passed in
(a) 1937 (b) 1947
(c) 1934 (d) 1936

299. When Tripartite Labour Conference represe-nting government, employees and labour became a regular feature of labour policy?
(a) 1945 (b) 1960
(c) 1942 (d) 1940

300. When the Contract Labour (Regulation and Abolition) Act was passed?
(a) 1960 (b) 1980
(c) 1970 (d) 1965

301. When National Commission on labour submitted its report?
(a) 1989 (b) 1969
(c) 1970 (d) None of these

302. Steps of job enrichment involves
(a) providing wider scope, more sequence and increased pace of the works.
(b) all owing the employees to set their own standards or targets.
(c) increasing the responsibility of the activity.
(d) All of the above.

303. Procurement is the first operative function of
(a) human resource management
(b) performance management
(c) personnel management
(d) None of the above

304. Job description includes
(a) relation to other jobs
(b) contains information and facts about
(c) job summary
(d) All of the above

305. Job description involves
(a) condition of work
(b) accident hazards
(c) machine tools
(d) All of the above

306. Job description includes
(a) sitting
(b) material used
(c) location of work
(d) All of the above

307. Job specification consists of
(a) Emotional characteristics
(b) Judgement
(c) Physical effort
(d) All of the above

308. Procedures of collection of data for job analysis includes
(a) Maintenance of long record
(b) Direct observations
(c) Interviews
(d) All of the above

309. Procedures of collection of data for job analysis includes
(a) Questionnaires
(b) Direct Observations
(c) Critical incident
(d) All of the above

310. Alexander Leighton enumerates five major determinants of morale, which are
(a) Confidence of different members of group in the leadership and the ability to the leadership.
(b) Confidence to the individual members in their fellow-workers.

(c) Confidence individual members in the purpose of the group.
(d) Conditions in the group and working conditions.

311. The contents of job description involves
(a) organisational location of the job
(b) job title
(c) location of work
(d) All of the above

312. Job specification information includes
(a) mental specification
(b) physical specification
(c) social specification
(d) All of the above

313. Social specification includes
(a) Dominance (b) Maturity
(c) Job grade (d) All of the above

314. Which of the following point is/are not important for Job Analysis?
(a) Promotion and transfer
(b) Performance appraisal in the organisation
(c) Organisation audit
(d) All of the above

315. Role of job analysis covers
(a) Safety (b) Discipline
(c) Health (d) All of the above

316. Role of job analysis covers
(a) Implementation of collective bargaining
(b) Induction
(c) Wages and salary administration
(d) All of the above

317. Job analysis is the basis for
(a) Bargaining
(b) Job evaluation
(c) Performance appraisal
(d) All of the above

318. Which of the following is a benefit of human resource planning?
(a) It provides scope for advancement and development of employers through training and development.
(b) It checks the corporate plan of the firm.
(c) It helps to anticipate the cost of salary.
(d) All of the above.

319. The process of wages and salary administration is influenced by several challenges including union power, the productivity of workers, the company's compensation policies, and government on pay.
(a) Approaches (b) Productivity
(c) Constraints (d) All of the above

320. Workers compensation programms have a serious defect. They are after-the-fact efforts. These laws attempt to compensate employees for accidents and illnesses that have already
(a) Claimants (b) Occurred
(c) Permanent (d) All of the above

321. Laboratory training is a form of group training primarily to enhance
(a) Displays
(b) Development
(c) Obsolescence in a changing world
(d) Interpersonal skills

322. Unemployment compensation pays the worker a modest income to reduce the hardships of losing a
(a) Records (b) Job
(c) Enforcement (d) All of the above

323. Human resource development is an effective way to meet several challenges faced by most large
(a) Firm (b) Company
(c) Organisation (d) All of the above

324. What is the main idea of group discussion?
(a) To see personality
(b) To see communication ability
(c) To tap leadership quality
(d) None of the above

Directions: Questions 325 to 349 are of multiple statement type. Choose the correct answer from the codes given below.

325. Which of the following is/are the benefits of labour welfare schemes?
   1. Workers' efficiency is considerably enhanced.
   2. Workers begin to feel interested in their work when they find that they are being well looked after by their employers. Thus their morale is raised and industrial relations improve.
   3. Labour turnover and absenteeism rates decline when the workers find the workplace congenial and the employer is sympathetic towards them.
   4. On humanitarian grounds too, labour welfare is commendable, because it show faith in the basic human values in life.
   5. From the social stand point, labour welfare ensure healthier and more enlightened citizens.

   Codes:

   (a) 5, 1, 2, 3, 4 (b) 1, 2, 3, 4, 5
   (b) 2, 3, 1, 4, 5 (d) 1, 3, 2, 4, 5

326. Job specification covers
   1. Education 2. Experience
   3. Judgement 4. Initiative
   5. Physical skills 6. Responsibilities

   Codes:

   (a) 1, 2, 3, 4, 5 and 6
   (b) 1, 2, 3, 4 and 5
   (c) 4, 5 and 6
   (d) 2, 3, 4 and 6

327. Which of the following statements are true?
   1. The difficulties experienced in processing safety equipment for installation in establishments mainly relates to their inadequacy and deficiency in quality.
   2. Morale is basically a matter of human behaviour.
   3. The problem of morale was not as complicated in the industry of medieval age as it is now under the modem factory set up.
   4. The Constitution of India, which came into force on 26th January, 1950, has given due place to the question of wages policy.

   Codes:

   (a) 2, 3 and 4 (b) 1, 2 and 4
   (c) 1, 2, 3 and 4 (d) 1, 3 and 4

328. Industrial accident may be traced by
   1. Fatigue
   2. Disturbed rental state of the worker
   3. Unsafe practices associated with the job
   4. Faulty equipment
   5. Unsafe part of worker
   6. Uncomfortable working condition

   Codes:

   (a) 2, 3, and 4 (b) 2, 3 and 6
   (c) 1, 2, 3 and 4 (d) All of the above

329. Which of the following are not central organisations of workers?
   1. Indian National Trade Union Congress
   2. Hind Mazdoor Shabha
   3. Bhartiya Mazdoor Sangh
   4. United Trade Union Congress
   5. SAFTA
   6. COSEFA

   Codes:

   (a) 1, 4, 5 and 6 (b) 5 and 6
   (c) 2, 3, 4 and 6 (d) 1, 2, 3 and 5

330. Which of the following is/are not central organisations of workers?
   1. All India Trade Union Congress
   2. Centra] of India Trade Unions
   3. National Labour Organisation

4. National Front of Indian Trade Unions
5. FICCI
6. DURA

Code:

(a) 5 and 6 (b) 1, 2, 3, 4 and 5
(c) 2, 3, 4 and 6 (d) None of these

331. Which of the following are the suggestions to strengthen the Union Movement?
   1. Measures should be taken on several forms to strengthen forces building up internal leadership.
   2. The minimum number required for starting a new union should be raised.
   3. Establishing a convention that no union office bearer will concurrently hold office in a political party.
   4. Trade unions should not be more fighting organisation of workers, but should be co-operating bodies to promote the cause of workers.

Codes:

(a) 1, 2, 3 and 4 (b) 2, 3 and 4
(c) 1, 2 and 4 (d) 1, 2 and 3

332. Methods of securing workers' participation in management involves
   1. Co-partnership
   2. Suggestions scheme
   3. Joint consultation
   4. Employees representations on the Board of Directors

Codes:

(a) 1, 2, 3 and 4 (b) 1, 2 and 4
(c) 1, 3 and 4 (d) 2, 3 and 4

333. Which of the following statements are true?
   1. Jobs cannot be designed by using only those element is that aid efficiency.
   2. The acceptability of a job's design is also influenced by the expectations of society.
   3. Behavioral elements of job design tell personnel specialists to add more autonomy, variety, task identity, task significance, and feedback.
   4. A lack of variety may cause boredom.

Codes:

(a) 1, 2, 3 and 4 (b) 1, 2 and 4
(c) 1, 2 and 3 (d) 2, 3 and 4

334. Which of the following statements is/are true?
   1. The design of a job reflects the organisational, environmental, and behavioural demands placed on it.
   2. The design of the jobs provides individual employee's full responsibility for groups of accounts.
   3. Poorly designed jobs not only lead to low productivity, but they can also cause employee turnover, absenteeism, complaints, sabotage, unionization, resignations and other problems.
   4. Organisational elements of job design are concerned with efficiency.

Codes:

(a) 1, 2 and 4 (b) 1, 2, 3 and 4
(c) 2 only (d) 2, 3 and 4

335. Which of the following statements are true?
   1. Job analysis systematically collects evaluates and organises information about jobs.
   2. Knowledge about jobs and their requirements must be collected through job analysis.
   3. A job description is a written statement that explains the duties, working conditions and other aspects of a specified job.
   4. A job description explains working conditions.

Codes:

(a) 1, 2, 3 and 4 (b) 2, 3 and 4
(c) 1, 3 and 4 (d) 1, 2 and 3

336. Which of the following statements are true?
   1. Annual planning budgeting process includes human resource needs.
   2. Managers discuss goals, plans, and thus types and numbers of people needed in the short run.
   3. The personnel department may contribute of these estimates through the use of psychological tests, interviews, and other methods of assessment.
   4. Replacement charts are a visual representation of who will replace whom in the event of a job opening.

Codes:
(a) 2, 3 and 4 (b) 1, 2 and 4
(c) 1, 2 and 3 (d) 1, 2, 3 and 4

337. Which of the following statements are true?
   1. The demand for human resources is modified by such employee actions as retirements resignations and terminations.
   2. Human resources forecasts are attempts to predict an organisation's future demand for employees.
   3. Expert forecast are based on the judgements of those who are knowledgeable of future human resource needs.
   4. Major organisational decisions affect the demand for human resources.

Codes:
(a) 2 and 4 (b) 1, 3 and 4
(c) 1, 2, 3 and 4 (d) 2, 3 and 4

338. Which organisational decisions affect the demand for human resources?
   1. Strategic plan 2. Budgets
   3. Sales and production forecasts
   4. New ventures 5. Organisation
   6. Job designs

Codes:
(a) 1, 2, 4, 5 and 6
(b) 1, 2, 3, 4, 5 and 6
(c) 2, 3 and 4
(d) 2, 3, 4 and 6

339. Which of the following points is/are not important for training?
   1. Reduction in supervision
   2. Reduction in cost and wastage
   3. Increased stability and flexibility
   4. Convenience in co-ordination
   5. Improvement in Industrial Relations

Codes:
(a) 1 only (b) 5 only
(c) 3 and 4 (d) All of the above

340. Which of the following statements are true?
   1. Job analysis is the process of getting information about jobs.
   2. Job analysis indicates the specific duties to be performed by the worker and the circumstance under which these duties are to be performed.
   3. A job description is a written record of the duties, responsibilities and conditions of the job.
   4. The objective of job evaluation is to price the job rather than the man.

Codes:
(a) 2, 1 and 4 (b) 1, 2 and 3
(c) 2, 3 and 4 (d) 1, 2, 3 and 4

341. Which one of the following is/are true?
   1. Training is required at different levels namely, for unskilled workers, semiskilled workers, skilled workers, office staff, supervisory staff and managerial.
   2. Semi-skilled workers are selected amongst the unskilled workers who have made themselves conversant with the handling of the machine.

3. Management training has become an essential activity of every firm.
4. Training programme should be periodically evaluated to determine its effectiveness.

Codes:
(a) 1, 2, 3 and 4 (b) 1, 2 and 4
(c) 1, 3 and 4 (d) 1, 2 and 3

342. Methods of training is
1. the telling method
2. the showing method
3. the role playing method
4. the discussion technique

Codes:
(a) 2 and 3 (b) 2 only
(c) 1, 2 and 3 (d) 1, 2, 3 and 4

343. McGehee and Thayer recommend which of the following three tier approach to determine the training needs?
1. Organisational analysis
2. Operational analysis
3. Man analysis
4. Assets analysis
5. Inventory analysis

Codes:
(a) 1, 2 and 3 (b) 4 and 5
(c) 1, 3 and 5 (d) 2 and 3

344. Which of the following need is/are not fall under needs of training and development?
1. Technological advances
2. Organisational complexity
3. Organisational tenure
4. Human relation movement
5. Performance evaluation

Codes:
(a) 3 only (b) 2 only
(c) 4 and 5 (d) 1, 2, 3 and 4

345. Mechanism of human resource development includes
1. job redesign
2. rewards
3. human resource information system
4. system development
5. research

Codes:
(a) 1 only (b) 2 only
(c) 3 and 4 (d) All of the above

346. Training Information System included
1. training resources
2. internal and external faculty
3. training aids
4. training needs
5. opportunities

Codes:
(a) 1 only (b) 2 only
(c) 3 and 4 (d) All of the above

347. Which of following statements are true?
1. Human resource management is a strategic management function.
2. Under human resource management employee is treated as a tesovitct.
3. Human resource management is the management of employee's skills, talents and abilities.
4. Human resource management function is treated as only an auxiliary.

Codes:
(a) 1, 2 and 3 (b) 2, 3 and 4
(c) 1, 2, 3 and 4 (d) None of these

348. Alexander of Leighton enumerates five major determinants of morale which are
1. Confidence of the individual members in the purpose of the group.
2. Confidence of the different member of the group in the leadership and the ability of the leadership.

3. Confidence of the individual members in their fellow workers.
4. Organisational efficiency.
5. Conditions in the group and working conditions.

Codes:

(a) 1, 2, 4 and 5 (b) 2, 3, 4 and 5
(c) 1, 2, 3, 4 and 5 (d) 1, 3, 4 and 5

349. Human resource management includes
1. Dynamic human resource
2. Trade unions
3. Down sizing
4. Non-union organisation
5. Motivation

Codes:

(a) 2 only (b) 3 and 4
(c) 4 and 5 (d) All of the above

Directions: Questions 350 to 376 are of matching type. Match List I with List II and select the correct answer using the codes given below the list.

350. **List I (Management educationist)**
A. William P. Anthony
B. Richard W. Woodman and John J. Sherwood
C. Jean Jones, and Thomas A. De caltis
D. Herbert G. Zollitsch and Adolph

List II (Their books)
1. *The Human Resource Information System*
2. *A comprehensive Look at Job Design*
3. *Job Analysis—National Survey Finding*
4. *Wages and Salary Administration*

Codes:	A	B	C	D
(a)	3	1	2	4
(b)	4	2	1	3
(c)	1	2	4	3
(d)	1	2	3	4

351. **List I**
A. Harry Levinson
B. James M. McFillen and Patric G. Deckor
C. Thomas C. Alenine
D. J. Peter Graves

List II
1. Appraisal of what Performance
2. Building meaning into Appraisal
3. Performance Appraisals and Performance Standings
4. Let's put Appraisal Back in Performance Appraisal

Codes:	A	B	C	D
(a)	2	3	1	4
(b)	3	1	2	4
(c)	4	3	1	2
(d)	1	2	3	4

352. **List I (Management thinkers)**
A. Elizabeth M. Kaplan and Emery L. Cowen
B. James A. Behoblar and Paul O. Popp.
C. William B. Werther
D. Marthen Glenn Cox and Jame Covey Brown

List II (Books)
1. *Interpersonal Helping Behaviour of Industrial Foremen*
2. *Making Employee Discipline Work*
3. *Productivity Improvement through People*
4. *Quality of Work Life*

Codes:	A	B	C	D
(a)	4	3	1	2
(b)	1	2	3	4
(c)	2	3	1	4
(d)	3	1	2	4

353. **List I (Authors management)**
A. Leland C. Nichols and Joeseph Hudson
B. John B. Miner

C. Allan N. Nash and Stephen J. Carrall
D. William A. Evans

List II (Books)

1. *Dual Role Assessment Centre—Selection and Development*
2. *Management Appraisal—A Review of Procedures and Practices*
3. *The Management of Compensation Monetary*
4. *Pay for Performance—Fact or Feeble*

Codes:	A	B	C	D
(a)	2	3	1	4
(b)	1	2	3	4
(c)	2	1	3	4
(d)	3	1	2	4

354. **List I (Year)**

A. 1995 B. 1985
C. 1939 D. 1937

List II (Growth of HRM in India)

1. Emphasis has been shifted to human resources development
2. Ministry of Human Resource Development
3. Industrial code under Bombay Industrial Disputes Act
4. Provincial Labour Legislation

Codes:	A	B	C	D
(a)	4	2	3	1
(b)	1	2	3	4
(c)	3	1	2	4
(d)	2	4	3	1

355. **List I (Year)**

A. 1923 B. 1918
C. 1901 D. 1890

List II (Growth of HRM in India)

1. Workmen's Compensation Act passed
2. Massive industrial unrest prevailed following the end of world war I
3. The Mines Act
4. The First Labour Organisation

Codes:	A	B	C	D
(a)	4	3	1	2
(b)	3	1	2	4
(c)	1	2	3	4
(d)	1	3	2	4

356. **List I (Year)**

A. 1948 B. 1959
C. 1961 D. 1972

List II (Growth of HRM in India)

1. Factories Act was implemented
2. The Employment Exchange (Compulsory Notification of vacancies) Act was passed
3. The Maternity Benefit Act was passed
4. Payment of Gratuity Act was passed

Codes:	A	B	C	D
(a)	1	2	3	4
(b)	2	1	3	4
(c)	2	4	3	1
(d)	2	3	1	4

357. **List I (Year)**

A. 1907 B. 1860
C. 1890 D. 1922

List II (Growth of HRM in India)

1. Factory Labour Commission
2. Employer's and Workmen's
3. The Bombay Mill Hands Association
4. Social Service League in Bombay

Codes:	A	B	C	D
(a)	1	2	3	4
(b)	1	3	2	4
(c)	4	3	2	1
(d)	1	4	2	3

358. **List I (Nature of development)**

A. The All India Trade Unions Congress
B. The Indian Factory Act passed on
C. The Postal Union
D. The Assam Labour Acts

List II (Year of formation)

1. 1919 2. 1911
3. 1907 4. 1863

Codes:	A	B	C	D
(a)	4	3	2	1
(b)	4	3	1	2
(c)	3	1	2	4
(d)	1	2	3	4

359. **List I (Nature of development)**

A. All India Industrial Welfare Conference
B. The Union of Throstte Department Workers
C. Calico Mills in Ahmedabad
D. Factory Labour Commission's Report

List II (Year of formation)

1. 1922 2. 1920
3. 1915 4. 1907

Codes:	A	B	C	D
(a)	2	3	1	4
(b)	4	3	1	2
(c)	1	2	3	4
(d)	3	1	2	4

360. **List I (Thinkers of management)**

A. Omit Oscar
B. Myers C.A.
C. T.K. Richardson
D. Institute of Personnel Management

List II (Their books/articles)

1. *Jobs and Workers*
2. *Industrial Relation in India*
3. *Industrial Relations*
4. *Personnel Management in India*

Codes:	A	B	C	D
(a)	1	2	3	4
(b)	1	2	4	3
(c)	4	3	1	2
(d)	2	3	1	4

361. **List I (Factors of productivity)**

A. Labour productivity
B. Machine productivity
C. Productivity of material
D. Productivity of land

List II (Their formulae)

1. $\dfrac{\text{Units or value or standard time for actual output}}{\text{Number of man hours spent on production}}$

2. $\dfrac{\text{Total production in weight}}{\text{Machine hours worked}}$

3. $\dfrac{\text{Weight or units of finished goods}}{\text{Weight, length of raw material used}}$

4. $\dfrac{\text{Total production}}{\text{Area of land used}}$

Codes:	A	B	C	D
(a)	1	2	3	4
(b)	1	4	2	3
(c)	4	2	3	1
(d)	2	3	1	4

362. **List I (Management educationist)**

A. Borbara Garson
B. J.R. Hackman and E.E. Lawer
C. Paul Sheibar
D. Jerrold Markowitz

List II (Their books/articles)

1. *Luddites in Landstown*
2. *Employee Reactions to Job Characteristics*
3. *A Simple Selection System called—Job Match*
4. *Four Methods of Job Analysis*

Codes:	A	B	C	D
(a)	2	4	1	3
(b)	2	3	1	4

(c)	3	1	2	4
(d)	1	2	3	4

363. **List I (Management educationists)**

A. Bruce H. Johnson, Gegory Moorhead and Rick W. Girffin
B. Jon L. Piere and Randall B
C. Edward E. Lawler III
D. Freednck Herzberg, Bernard Musner and Barbara Synderman

List II (Their books/articles)

1. *Integration of Job Design Variables into a Human Resource Information System*
2. *Task Design—A Literature Review*
3. *Job Attitudes and Employee Motivation*
4. *The Motivation to Work*

Codes:	**A**	**B**	**C**	**D**
(a)	1	2	3	4
(b)	3	4	2	1
(c)	2	1	3	4
(d)	1	2	4	3

364. **List I (Type of skill test)**

A. Aptitude test
B. Achievement test
C. Situational test
D. Personality test

List II (Sub-type of test)

1. Skill test
2. Job knowledge test
3. Group discussion
4. Projective test

Codes:	**A**	**B**	**C**	**D**
(a)	3	4	2	1
(b)	1	2	3	4
(c)	3	2	4	1
(d)	3	1	2	4

365. **List I (Component of human resource planning)**

A. Demographics
B. Community attitudes
C. Replacement summaries
D. Human resource planning

List II (Their qualities)

1. Demographic trends are another long term development that affects the availability of external supply
2. Community attitudes also affect the nature of the labour market
3. The list likely replacements for each job and indicate their relative strengths and weeknesses
4. The planning requires considerable time, staff and financial resources

Codes:	**A**	**B**	**C**	**D**
(a)	2	3	4	1
(b)	1	2	3	4
(c)	4	3	1	2
(d)	2	4	3	1

366. **List I (Management educationist)**

A. James W. Walker
B. George T. Milkovich and Thomas A. Wahoney
C. Eddie C. Smith
D. Herbert Heneman and G. Seltzer

List II (Their books)

1. *Linking Human Resource Planning and Strategic Planning, Human Resources Planning.*
2. *Human Resource Planning Models-perspective.*
3. *Strategic Business Planning and Human Resources.*
4. *Employer Manpower Planning and Forecasting.*

Codes:	A	B	C	D
(a)	3	1	2	4
(b)	2	1	3	4
(c)	4	3	1	2
(d)	1	2	3	4

367. **List I**
   A. Elmar H. Burak
   B. Smith and Walker
   C. Richard B. Frantzerb
   D. Douglas B. Gehrman

   List II
   1. *Strategies for Manpower Planning and Programming.*
   2. *Business Planning is People Planning.*
   3. *Human Resource Planning—Forecasting Manpower Needs.*
   4. *Objective Based Human Resource Planning.*

Codes:	A	B	C	D
(a)	4	2	3	1
(b)	1	3	2	4
(c)	1	2	3	4
(d)	3	1	2	4

368. **List I (Functions of personnel management)**
   A. Management function
   B. Advisory function
   C. Executive function
   D. Management function

   List II (Main functions)
   1. Human resource planning
   2. Advise to the departmental officers
   3. Appointment of labour and employee
   4. Personnel planning

Codes:	A	B	C	D
(a)	4	2	3	1
(b)	3	1	2	4
(c)	1	2	3	4
(d)	2	3	1	4

369. **List I (Methods of training)**
   A. On the job training method
   B. Off the job training method
   C. Executive employees training method
   D. At the job training method

   List II (Sub-methods)
   1. Training at Training Centre
   2. Lecturer Method
   3. In basket Training Method
   4. Coaching or Guidance

Codes:	A	B	C	D
(a)	4	3	1	2
(b)	3	1	2	4
(c)	1	2	3	4
(d)	2	4	3	1

370. **List I (Specific training methods)**
   A. On-the-job training
   B. Off-the-job training
   C. Understudy method
   D. Role playing method

   List II (Their qualities)
   1. Mostly the executive training is done on the job. An executive is expected to learn his work while working.
   2. That method can also be used to train the executives.
   3. The method under this executive is assigned an understudy or an assistant who, in addition to his regular duties, is expected to acquire some familiarity with the tasks and practices of his superior.
   4. The method under which an employee learn by playing a role in drammatic setting which corresponds to his work.

Codes:	A	B	C	D
(a)	4	2	3	1
(b)	2	3	1	4
(c)	1	2	3	4
(d)	1	2	4	3

371. **List I (Business games)**

A. Case study B. Role play
C. Sensitivity D. Simulations

List II (Their utility)

1. Analytical
2. Human relations skills
3. Tolerance for individual difference
4. Encountering skills

Codes:	**A**	**B**	**C**	**D**
(a)	4	2	3	1
(b)	3	1	2	4
(c)	1	3	2	4
(d)	1	2	3	4

372. **List I**

A. Man power planning
B. Selection and placement
C. Reinforcement and advancement
D. Industrial relations

List II

1. Forecast man power needs based on the policies and strategies of the company trend
2. Use the criteria and measures developed for selection procedures and placement
3. Promotion
4. Job analysis

Codes:	**A**	**B**	**C**	**D**
(a)	2	1	3	4
(b)	1	2	3	4
(c)	1	3	2	4
(d)	3	1	4	2

373. **List I (Psychologist needs)**

A. Physiological B. Security
C. Social D. Ego
E. Self-realisation

List II (Basic needs)

1. Eating 2. Accidents
3. Need for association with other
4. Reputation 5. Confidence

Codes:	**A**	**B**	**C**	**D**	**E**
(a)	3	1	2	4	5
(b)	4	2	3	1	5
(c)	1	2	4	3	5
(d)	1	2	3	4	5

374. **List I**

A. Melmen Seymour
B. Leighton
C. R.W. Revans
D. Aldrich

List II

1. Dynamic factors in industrial productivity.
2. Human relation in changing world.
3. Essay in human relations and modern management.
4. The principles and practice of management.

Codes:	**A**	**B**	**C**	**D**
(a)	3	1	2	4
(b)	1	2	3	4
(c)	4	2	3	1
(d)	2	3	4	1

375. **List I**

A. Need for team work and health interpersonal relationships
B. Right man in the right place
C. Justice tempered with kindness
D. One head one plan

List II

1. Unity of direction
2. Equity
3. Order
4. Espirit de corps

Codes:	**A**	**B**	**C**	**D**
(a)	4	3	2	1
(b)	3	4	1	2
(c)	1	2	3	4
(d)	2	3	4	1

376. **List I (Component of human resource management)**

A. Human resource development
B. Compensation management
C. Human relations
D. Human resource accounting

List II (Function of human resource management)

1. Training
2. Job-evaluation
3. Motivation
4. Man Power evaluation

Codes:	A	B	C	D
(a)	2	1	3	4
(b)	1	2	3	4
(c)	4	3	1	2
(d)	2	3	1	4

377. **Statement (A):** Training is for present jobs.

Statement (B): Development is for future jobs.

Statement (C): Orientation is not enough for employee.

Statement (D): Training help employees to their present job.

Codes:
(a) Statement 'A', 'B' and 'C' are true
(b) Statement 'B', 'C' and 'D' are true
(c) Statement 'A', 'C' and 'D' are true
(d) Statement 'A', 'B', 'C' and 'D' are true
(e) Only statement 'B' is true

378. **Statement (A):** Human Resource Management is a Line Responsibility.

Statement (B): Human Resource Management is a line manager's Responsibility but a staff function.

Codes:
(a) Statement 'A' is false but statement 'B' is true
(b) Statement 'A' and statement 'B' both are false
(c) Statement 'A' is true but statement 'B' is not true
(d) Statement 'A' and statement 'B' both are true
(e) Only statement 'B' is true
(f) Only statement 'A' is true

379. **Statement (A):** Reinforcement and expectancy theory states that a response followed by a reward is more likely to secure in the future.

Statement (B): According to this theory, high employee performance followed by a monetary reward will result in high performance in the future.

Codes:
(a) Statement 'A' is true but statement 'B' is false
(b) Statement 'A' and statement 'B' both are false
(c) Statement 'A' and statement 'B' both are true
(d) Statement 'A' is false but statement B is true

380. **Statement (A):** The most important aspects of the training programme is a correct assessment of the training needs.

Statement (B): This is a assessment of training needs.

Codes:
(a) Statement 'A' and statement 'B' both are false
(b) Statement 'A' and statement 'B' both are true
(c) Statement 'A' is true but statement 'B' is false
(d) Statement 'A' is false but statement 'B' is true

381. **Statement (A):** The Apprentice Act started from 1961.

Statement (B): This Act is meant to regulate and control the training of apprentices in trades and matters connected therewith.

Codes:

(a) Statement 'A' and 'B' both are true but statement 'B' is reason of the statement 'A'
(b) Statement 'A' and statement 'B' both are not true
(c) Statement 'A' and statement 'B' both are true
(d) Statement 'A' and 'B' both are true but statement 'B' is not reason of the statement 'A'

382. **Statement (A):** The introduction of the new employee to the job is known as induction.

Statement (B): Induction is the process by which new employee are introduced to the practices, policies and purposes of the organisation.

Codes:

(a) Statement 'A' is true but statement 'B' is not true
(b) Statement 'A' and statement 'B' both are false
(c) Statement 'A' and statement 'B' both are true
(d) Statement 'A' is untrue but statement 'B' is true
(e) Only statement 'A' is true
(f) Only statement 'B' is true

383. **Statement (A):** Semi-skilled employees are selected amongst the unskilled employees.

Statement (B): In me telling method, lectures are delivered similar to the classroom session.

Codes:

(a) Statement 'A' is true but statement 'B' is not true
(b) Statement 'A' and statement 'B' both are false
(c) Statement 'A' and statement 'B' both are true
(d) Statement 'A' is partially true but statement 'B' is true

384. **Statement (A):** Performance appraisal is a critical activity of personnel management.

Statement (B): Its goal is to provide an accurate picture of a past and future employee performance.

Codes:

(a) Statement 'A' and statement 'B' both are true
(b) Statement 'A' is true but statement 'B' is explanation of statement 'A'
(c) Statement 'A' and statement 'B' both are false
(d) Statement 'A' is true but statement 'B' is not explanation of statement 'B'

385. **Statement (A):** A job description defines what the Job is it is a profile of the job.

Statement (B): A job specification describes what the job demands of employees who do it and the human skills that are required.

Codes:

(a) Only statement 'A' is true
(b) Statement 'A' is true but 'B' is not true
(c) Statement 'A' and 'B' are true
(d) Statement 'A' is not true but statement B is true

386. **Statement (A):** Organisational policies sect to achieve uniformity, economic, public relations benefits, or other objectives that are sometimes unrelated to recruiting.

Statement (B): Promote from within policies are intended to give present employees the first opportunity for job openings.

Codes:

(a) Statement 'A' is true but statement 'B' is false
(b) Statement 'A' and statement 'B' is true
(c) Statement 'A' is untrue but statement 'B' is true
(d) Only statement 'A' is true
(e) Only statement 'B' is true

387. **Statement (A):** Job analysis information provides the foundations of an organisation's human resource information sysiem.

Statement (B): The job analysis information can be collected through interviews, juries of experts, mail questionnaires, employee logs, direct observation, or some combination of these techniques.

Codes:

(a) Statement 'A' and statement 'B' both are false
(b) Statement 'A' and statement 'B' both are true
(c) Statement 'A' is true but statement 'B' is false
(d) Statement 'B' is false but statement 'A' is true

ANSWERS

1. (c)	2. (b)	3. (d)	4. (b)	5. (b)	6. (d)
7. (a)	8. (a)	9. (d)	10. (a)	11. (c)	12. (d)
13. (d)	14. (d)	15. (c)	16. (d)	17. (b)	18. (c)
19. (b)	20. (d)	21. (d)	22. (b)	23. (b)	24. (d)
25. (c)	26. (d)	27. (a)	28. (a)	29. (c)	30. (d)
31. (d)	32. (a)	33. (d)	34. (d)	35. (c)	36. (c)
37. (a)	38. (a)	39. (b)	40. (c)	41. (a)	42. (b)
43. (a)	44. (b)	45. (b)	46. (c)	47. (a)	48. (b)
49. (a)	50. (b)	51. (b)	52. (b)	53. (a)	54. (b)
55. (c)	56. (a)	57. (a)	58. (a)	59. (c)	60. (a)
61. (b)	62. (c)	63. (c)	64. (c)	65. (b)	66. (a)
67. (b)	68. (b)	69. (b)	70. (c)	71. (a)	72. (b)
73. (c)	74. (a)	75. (c)	76. (c)	77. (b)	78. (a)
79. (b)	80. (a)	81. (a)	82. (a)	83. (c)	84. (b)
85. (b)	86. (c)	87. (b)	88. (b)	89. (b)	90. (a)
91. (b)	92. (d)	93. (d)	94. (b)	95. (a)	96. (c)
97. (c)	98. (b)	99. (d)	100. (b)	101. (b)	102. (b)
103. (d)	104. (d)	105. (d)	106. (d)	107. (d)	108. (d)
109. (d)	110. (a)	111. (b)	112. (b)	113. (d)	114. (d)
115. (d)	116. (c)	117. (d)	118. (d)	119. (b)	120. (d)

121. (d)	122. (c)	123. (d)	124. (c)	125. (d)	126. (d)
127. (b)	128. (c)	129. (d)	130. (d)	131. (d)	132. (d)
133. (d)	134. (d)	135. (d)	136. (d)	137. (d)	138. (d)
139. (c)	140. (d)	141. (d)	142. (a)	143. (d)	144. (b)
145. (c)	146. (d)	147. (c)	148. (b)	149. (d)	150. (c)
151. (d)	152. (d)	153. (b)	154. (d)	155. (d)	156. (b)
157. (b)	158. (d)	159. (c)	160. (b)	161. (c)	162. (b)
163. (d)	164. (d)	165. (d)	166. (d)	167. (d)	168. (d)
169. (d)	170. (d)	171. (a)	172. (b)	173. (b)	174. (a)
175. (c)	176. (a)	177. (b)	178. (d)	179. (c)	180. (d)
181. (d)	182. (b)	183. (d)	184. (d)	185. (d)	186. (d)
187. (d)	188. (d)	189. (d)	190. (d)	191. (d)	192. (b)
193. (d)	194. (d)	195. (b)	196. (b)	197. (d)	198. (c)
199. (d)	200. (c)	201. (c)	202. (d)	203. (b)	204. (b)
205. (c)	206. (b)	207. (d)	208. (c)	209. (d)	210. (c)
211. (d)	212. (d)	213. (d)	214. (d)	215. (c)	216. (d)
217. (b)	218. (d)	219. (a)	220. (d)	221. (d)	222. (b)
223. (c)	224. (a)	225. (d)	226. (d)	227. (d)	228. (d)
229. (b)	230. (d)	231. (d)	232. (b)	233. (c)	234. (b)
235. (a)	236. (d)	237. (d)	238. (c)	239. (a)	240. (d)
241. (c)	242. (b)	243. (c)	244. (c)	245. (d)	246. (b)
247. (d)	248. (d)	249. (c)	250. (c)	251. (d)	252. (c)
253. (d)	254. (d)	255. (d)	256. (d)	257. (d)	258. (d)
259. (d)	260. (d)	261. (a)	262. (d)	263. (c)	264. (c)
265. (c)	266. (a)	267. (c)	268. (c)	269. (d)	270. (d)
271. (c)	272. (b)	273. (c)	274. (c)	275. (c)	276. (b)
277. (d)	278. (d)	279. (d)	280. (d)	281. (c)	282. (b)
283. (b)	284. (d)	285. (d)	286. (c)	287. (d)	288. (d)
289. (a)	290. (c)	291. (d)	292. (c)	293. (c)	294. (c)
295. (a)	296. (c)	297. (a)	298. (c)	299. (c)	300. (c)
301. (b)	302. (d)	303. (c)	304. (d)	305. (d)	306. (d)
307. (d)	308. (d)	309. (d)	310. (d)	311. (d)	312. (d)
313. (d)	314. (d)	315. (d)	316. (d)	317. (b)	318. (d)
319. (c)	320. (b)	321. (d)	322. (b)	323. (d)	324. (c)

325. (b)	326. (a)	327. (c)	328. (d)	329. (b)	330. (a)
331. (a)	332. (a)	333. (a)	334. (b)	335. (a)	336. (d)
337. (c)	338. (b)	339. (d)	340. (d)	341. (a)	342. (d)
343. (a)	344. (d)	345. (d)	346. (d)	347. (a)	348. (c)
349. (d)	350. (d)	351. (d)	352. (b)	353. (b)	354. (b)
355. (c)	356. (a)	357. (a)	358. (a)	359. (c)	360. (a)
361. (a)	362. (d)	363. (a)	364. (b)	365. (b)	366. (d)
367. (c)	368. (c)	369. (c)	370. (c)	371. (d)	372. (b)
373. (d)	374. (b)	375. (c)	376. (b)	377. (d)	378. (d)
379. (c)	380. (b)	381. (a)	382. (c)	383. (c)	384. (b)
385. (c)	386. (b)	387. (b)			

9

Banking and Financial Institutions

1. In India, the first bank of limited liability managed by Indians and founded in 1881 was
   (a Punjab National Bank
   (b) Punjab and Sindh Bank
   (c) Hindustan Commercial Bank
   (d) Oudh Commercial Bank
2. IDBI serves as the institution for term finance to industries.
   (a) IIT (b) APEX
   (c) CAT (d) None of these
3. When was Indian Banking Act come into force?
   (a) 1946 (b) 1947
   (c) 1948 (d) 1949
4. One of the functions of IDBI is to assist other financial institutions by _____ of loans granted for exports.
   (a) refinancing (b) planning
   (c) Both (a) and (b) (d) None of these
5. The primary objective of IDBI is to regulate and supervise the working of other financial institutions like IFCI, SFCs, UTI.
   (a) Planning (b) Co-ordinate
   (c) Control (d) None of these
6. The IDBI can grant and advances to other financial institutions.
   (a) Loans (b) Line of credit
   (c) Both (a) and (b) (d) None of these
7. When was Ombuds Men Scheme first introduced?
   (a) June 1995 (b) December 1997
   (c) January 2005 (d) March 1999
8. The IDBI underwriters and the shares and debentures of industrial concerns
   (a) subscribes to (b) targets
   (c) imposses on (d) None of these
9. How many banks were nationalized in the first phases in India?
   (a) 14 (b) 12
   (c) 8 (d) 18
10. All India Financial Institutions are
    (a) Industrial Credit and Investment Corporation of India (ICICI).
    (b) Industrial Development Bank of India (IDBI).
    (c) Industrial Finance Corporation of India (IFCI).
    (d) All of the above.
11. State-level financial institutions are
    (a) State Industrial Investment Corporations (SIIC).
    (b) State Financial Corporations (SFCs).
    (c) State Industrial Development Corporations (SIDI).
    (d) All of the above.
12. When was the second phase of nationalization of banks done in India?
    (a) 15th April, 1980
    (b) 18th April, 1968

(c) 25th July 1982
(d) 10th July, 1970

13. The importance of SFIs may be attributed to
(a) they have helped new and small entrepreneurs in setting up industry.
(b) they have played an important role is the development of (a) small-scale industry, (b) projects is backward areas.
(c) they constitute an important source of long-term finance to industry.
(d) All of the above.

14. The main objective of IDBI is to
(a) planning, promotion and development of key industries and diversifications of industrial growth.
(b) co-ordination, regulation and supervision of the working of other financial institutions such as IFCI, ICICI, UTI, LIC, commercial banks and SFCs.
(c) supplementing there sources of other financial institution and thereby widening the scope of their assistance.
(d) All of the above.

15. The main functions of UTI are
(a) to invest the savings so mobilised in corporate securities such as shares and debentures, etc.
(b) to serve unit holders along the length and breadth of the country.
(c) to mobilise the sayings of the community through sale of units.
(d) All of the above.

16. When was Lead Bank Scheme introduced?
(a) 1969 (b) 1962
(c) 1965 (d) 1975

17. The ICICI has been established to achieve the objectives
(a) to stimulate and promote the participation of private capital (both Indian and foreign) in such industrial units.
(b) to assist in the formation, expansion and modernisation of industrial units in the private sector.
(c) Both (a) and (b).
(d) None of the above.

18. The functions of SFCs are
(a) guaranteeing loans raised by industrial concerns which are repayable within a period not exceeding 20 years.
(b) grant of loans and advances to or subscribe to debentures of industrial concerns repayable within a period not exceeding 20 years, with option of conversion into shares or stock of industrial concern.
(c) Both (a) and (b).
(d) None of the above.

19. Expansion of deposit through expanding loans and advances by commercial banks is known as ______
(a) Trade discount
(b) Credit creation
(c) Bank advances
(d) Deposit

20. State Financial Corporation have been established by
(a) Any private organisation
(b) State Government
(c) Central Government
(d) None of the above

21. Bank places certain restriction on withdrawal for ______ deposit.
(a) current account
(b) savings deposit
(c) fixed deposit
(d) demand deposit

22. The financial institute IFCI established in
(a) 1950 (b) 1949
(c) 1948 (d) 1947

23. The UTI was established in
(a) 1964 (b) 1965
(c) 1962 (d) 1963

24. The ICICI was formed in
(a) 1954 (b) 1955
(c) 1953 (d) 1952

25. Banks can avail refinance against loans made to industrial units from
(a) ECGC (b) IDBI
(c) DI and CGC (d) NABARD

26. The loan facility where neither ownership nor possession of asset is transferred as security to the bank is called?
(a) Hypothecation
(b) Property security
(c) Mortgage
(d) Pledge

27. Which of the following are the objectives and functions of IDBI?
(a) To undertake market and investment research and surveys as also technical and economic studies in connection with development of industry.
(b) To act as lender of last resort and to finance projects that are in conformity with national priorities.
(c) To provide technical and administrative assistance for promotion or expansion of industry.
(d) All of the above.

28. Which of the following schemes are operated by IDBI?
(a) Equipment finance scheme
(b) Modernisation assistance scheme
(c) Technical development fund scheme
(d) All of the above

29. If interest is changed on full amount of loan (principal) throughout the entire tenure of the loan is
(a) Flat rate (b) Float rate
(c) Diminishing rate (d) Fixed rate

30. The Reserve Bank of India is
(a) an institution owned by Indian Banks' Association.
(b) a department of Central Government under Ministry of Finance.
(c) a body corporate, having perpetual succession and common seal.
(d) None of the above.

31. Which of the following is a statement of objectives (a type of plan)?
(a) Reduce products prices to capture market.
(b) Make more profits.
(c) Reduce costs by 5 per cent.
(d) Reduce costs as much as possible.

32. The concept of scientific management is developed by
(a) Marx (b) Fayol
(c) Taylor (d) None

33. EFT is also known as
(a) Paperless Banking
(b) Exchange Fund Transfer
(c) Maintenance Fund Transfer
(d) Easy Fund Transfer

34. According to Fayol, the terms "Management" and "Administration" are
(a) different
(b) he did not consider it all
(c) same
(d) None of the above

35. Industrial Development Bank of India is
(a) public limited company.
(b) wholly-owned government of India undertaking.

(c) wholly-owned subsidiary of Reserve Bank of India.
(d) a corporation and owned by government of India and public sector banks.

36. The first public bank was
(a) Rural Bank (b) SBI
(c) Bank of Venice (d) PNB

37. Creation of derivative deposit out of the money from primary deposit is called?
(a) Credit Creation
(b) Cash Credit
(c) Loan and Advances
(d) Lending Money

38. Italian moneylenders were known as Banechi or Banacheri because
(a) they kept a special type of table to transact their business.
(b) they had a lot of money.
(c) they had a money bank.
(d) None of the above.

39. Which was the first bank to be established in 1157?
(a) CBI
(b) SBI
(c) Case De Sangiorgio
(d) Reserve bank

40. In which year BOV was established?
(a) 1157 (b) 1158
(c) 1150 (d) 1156

41. The regulator of Indian Capital Market is
(a) Commercial Bank (b) SEBI
(c) RBI (d) SBI

42. The statement of Banking Definition is given by
(a) Whitehead (b) Kinley
(c) T.G. Hart (d) All of the above

43. The statement "A banker is a person or corporation which holds it self out to receive from the public, deposit payable on demand on cheque" is given by
(a) T.G. Hart (b) Findlayshirras
(c) Walterleaf (d) Kinley

44. The interest computed on the principal for the entire period of borrowings?
(a) Flat Rate Interest
(b) Compound Interest
(c) Floating Rate Interest
(d) Simple Interest

45. How many types of bank are there on the basis of ownership?
(a) 4 type (b) 3 type
(c) 2 type (d) 5 type

46. Bank classifications according to law are
(a) Scheduled bank
(b) Non-schedule banks
(c) Private bank
(d) Both (a) and (b)

47. Bank classification is possible according to
(a) Function (b) Ownership
(c) Law (d) All of the above

48. The statement "commercial banks are the institutions that make short-term loans to business and in the process create money" is given by
(a) Reed and Gill (b) Kineley
(c) Chandler (d) Culbertson

49. In which year the first central bank in the world was established?
(a) 1680 (b) 1668
(c) 1660 (d) 1670

50. In RTGS minimum amount to be remitted is
(a) ₹ 1,50, 000 (b) ₹ 2,00,000
(c) ₹ 1,70,000 (d) ₹ 10,000

51. In which year saving banks were first established in Hamberg city of Germany?

(a) 1763 (b) 1776
(c) 1765 (d) 1764

52. "A bank not only accept money on deposit, but it also lends money and creates and lands its own credit." Is this statement true?
(a) Can't say (b) Yes
(c) No (d) None of these

53. "A dealer is debts his own and of other people." Who said it?
(a) De-landger (b) Crowther
(c) Lindley (d) None of these

54. ECS payment ______ code is essential.
(a) IFSC (b) CTS
(c) MICR (d) RTGS

55 When introduced Banking Companies Act?
(a) 1949 (b) 1970
(c) 1950 (d) 1960

56. The word 'bank' originated from ____ language.
(a) Sanskrit (b) Urdu
(c) Italy (d) Hindi

57. Which one of the following bank was the first public banking institution in world?
(a) Bank of Venice
(b) Bank of Japan
(c) Bank of England
(d) Bank of Hindustan

58. CTS was introduced RBI in _____
(a) February 2008 (b) December 2006
(c) July 2002 (d) February 1998

59. "Cash credit granted to a customer is drawn by him as and when needed and not all at once." Are you agree with this?
(a) Can't say (b) No
(c) Yes (d) None of these

60. Which are two types of bank deposits?
(a) Demand deposits
(b) Time deposits
(c) Both (a) and (b)
(d) Fixed deposits

61. When the Bank of Japan was set up in
(a) 1982 (b) 1910
(c) 1810 (d) 1890

62. The Balance Sheet of a banking company contains _____ schedules.
(a) 9 (b) 12
(c) 16 (d) 11

63. ______ is also called virtual banking or anywhere banking.
(a) Internet banking
(b) Hi-tech banking
(c) Off shore banking
(d) None of the above

64. Reserve and Surplus shown under
(a) 2 schedule (b) 8 schedule
(c) 4 schedule (d) 6 schedule

65. Deposits consists
(a) demand deposits account
(b) savings deposits account
(c) fixed deposits account
(d) All of the above

66. Banking Regulation Act was introduced in?
(a) 1940 (b) 1956
(c) 1935 (d) 1949

67. Off-shore banking units by Indian Banks in ______
(a) London (b) India
(c) Geneva (d) U.S.

68. Which bank is known as a Central Bank of India?
(a) Punjab National Bank
(b) Reserve Bank of India
(c) State Bank of India
(d) All of the above

69. When the Reserve Bank of India Act was passed?
(a) March 6, 1934 (b) March 6, 1930
(c) March 6, 1937 (d) March 6, 1935

70. RBI introduced 14-day intermediate treasury bills and 14-day treasury bills on?
(a) 1995 (b) 1984
(c) 1997 (d) 1975

71. The initial capital of RBI is
(a) ₹ 5 crore (b) ₹ 10 crore
(c) ₹ 1 crore (d) ₹ 2 crore

72. The Governor of RBI appointed by
(a) President of India
(b) State Government
(c) Finance Minister of India all
(d) Central Government of India

73. The Deposit Insurance Corporation was setup on
(a) 1 July 1962
(b) 1 January 1962
(c) 1 June 1980
(d) 1 March 1970

74. The RBI introduced the Bill Market Scheme in
(a) 1970 (b) 1980
(c) 1952 (d) 1960

75. System of banking is guided by the Islamic Law called?
(a) Shariat
(b) Banking Regulation Act
(c) Islamic Banking
(d) Islamic Guide

76. The issue of paper money is the most important function of a Bank.
(a) SBI (b) Pill
(c) UTI (d) RBI

77. The RBI was nationalised in
(a) 1948 (b) 1950
(c) 1940 (d) 1942

78. The Unit Trust of India was established on
(a) March 1, 1964
(b) February 1, 1964
(c) March 1, 1965
(d) February 1, 1965

79. RBI introduced ______ scheme in 1969.
(a) Lead Bank
(b) DIRE
(c) SAA
(d) Village Adaptation

80. Merchant banker invested his accumulated _____ in all kinds of promising activities.
(a) profits
(b) loss
(c) depreciation
(d) proposed, dividend

81. The RBI is the king pin of the Indian ______ market.
(a) capital (b) vegetable
(c) money (d) gold

82. Industrial bank is a ______ bank.
(a) commercial
(b) common
(c) contractual Banks
(d) special

83. Who introduced micro credit system in social banking segment?
(a) N.D. Thiwari
(b) Banking Regulation Act 1949
(c) D.R. Gadgil
(d) Mohammed Yunus

84. Deposit banks lend money for a period between ______ months.
(a) 5 to 10 (b) 9 to 12
(c) 1 to 6 (d) 3 to 6

85. Which types of banks are formed for savings?
(a) Agricultural bank
(b) Exchange bank
(c) Saving bank
(d) Deposits bank

86. In branch banking there is a better control co-ordination of the

(a) ICICI
(b) Reserve Bank of India
(c) State Bank of India
(d) Union Bank of India

87. Apex bank for rural credit is
(a) LDB (b) NABARD
(c) RRB (d) PACS

88. The State Bank of India was set up in
(a) July 1, 1955 (b) July 1, 1960
(c) July 1, 1950 (d) July 1, 1952

89. The scheduled of Banking Act is related with
(a) Fixed Assets (b) Interest
(c) Capital (d) Investments

90. The Industrial Reconstruction Corporation of India Ltd. (IRCI) was set up in
(a) May 1981 (b) June 1970
(c) April 1971 (d) May 1980

91. RBI subscribed ₹ 2.5 crore in capital
(a) State Bank of India
(b) IDBI
(c) UTI
(d) RBI

92. Membership of a credit information company is not mandatory for
(a) housing finance company
(b) another credit information company
(c) private sector bank
(d) an urban co-operative Bank

93. IDBI contributed _____ of the share capital of IRCI.
(a) 50% (b) 60%
(c) 70% (d) 79%

94. The Banking of Agricultural Training College was set up by the RBI at
(a) Udaipur
(b) Purse
(c) Chouth Ka Barwara (SWM)
(d) Jaipur

95. Which financial body issues mutual fund eyes pension in the capital market?
(a) RBI (b) UTI
(c) SBI (d) LIC

96. CRAR means
(a) Capital Reserve Adequacy Ratio
(b) Capital to Risk weighted Asset Ratio
(c) Capital Reserve Asset Ratio
(d) Credit Reserve Asset Ratio

97. Which of the following is the name of the asset reconstruction company created by various banks in India?
(a) SBI (b) HCR
(c) AMFI (d) ARCIL

98. Advancing loans consist of
(a) term loans
(b) consumer credit
(c) Both (a) and (b)
(d) agency services

99. The financial position of a commercial bank is reflected in its
(a) Cash Flow Statement
(b) Profit and Loss Account
(c) Fund Flow Statement
(d) Balance Sheet

100. The Head office of _______ is in Basel.
(a) BIS (b) IDBI
(c) DRT (d) IFC

101. Investment policy of banks consists of
(a) Security (b) Diversify
(c) Profitability (d) Liquidity

102. The authorised capital of NABARD is
(a) ₹ 600 crore (b) ₹ 700 crore
(c) ₹ 50 crore (d) ₹ 500 crore

103. What is the issued share capital of SBI?
(a) ₹ 6340 crore (b) ₹ 5625 crore
(c) ₹ 7340 crore (d) ₹, 5630 crore

104. When was the 20-point economic programme of the Government of India announced for the first time?

(a) July 1, 1976
(b) March 15, 1930
(c) July 1, 1960
(d) July 1, 1975

105. BIS was established in
(a) 1920 (b) 1930
(c) 1940 (d) 1950

106. Group Banking System originated in
(a) England (b) Japan
(c) America (d) India

107. The Chain Banking System originated in
(a) 1920 America (b) 1925 Italy
(c) 1930 India (d) 1930 Japan

108. The head office of RBI located at
(a) Mumbai (b) Kolkata
(c) Chennai (d) New Delhi

109. The authorised capital of SBI is
(a) ₹ 526.3 crore (b) ₹ 2100 crore
(c) ₹ 152.24 crore (d) ₹ 1000 crore

110. Which of the following organizations is meant for promoting small scale industries at district level?
(a) SFCs (b) NABARD
(c) SIDBI (d) DIC

111. SBI is
(a) a commercial bank
(b) a industrial bank
(c) a foreign exchange bank
(d) a co-operative bank

112. The head office of SBI is located at
(a) Mumbai (b) Kolkata
(c) New Delhi (d) Jaipur

113. The Chairman of NABARD is appointed by
(a) The State Bank of India
(b) Central Government
(c) The President of India
(d) The Reserve Bank of India

114. Rate of interest fluctuates according to market lending rate in
(a) Floating rate
(b) Compound interest
(c) Flat rate interest
(d) Simple interest

115. Which of the following is a primary function of bank?
(a) To accept the deposits from the public
(b) Credit creation
(c) Both (a) and (b)
(d) Advancing of loans

116. The first joint stock bank in India?
(a) Allahabad Bank
(b) Imperial Bank
(c) ICICI
(d) IDBI

117. Which bank started merchant banking first time in India?
(a) State Bank of India
(b) Reserve Bank of India
(c) Unit Trust of India
(d) Union Bank of India

118. Bank note of one rupee issued by
(a) Reserve Bank of India
(b) Finance Commission
(c) Government of India
(d) State Government

119. Banker has _______ lien.
(a) general (b) primary
(c) particular (d) special

120. Exchanger who operated internationally engaged in
(a) provision of long-term capital for public borrowers.
(b) raising foreign exchange.
(c) bill broking.
(d) All of the above.

121. In the United Kingdom, merchant banks came on the scene in the late
(a) 21th century (b) 20th century
(c) 19th century (d) 18th century

122. Advancing loans includes
(a) Discounting trade bills
(b) Cash credit
(c) Overdraft
(d) All of the above

123. When was the Bank of England set-up?
(a) 1950 (b) 1970
(c) 1694 (d) 1940

124. "A Central bank is not primarily a profit seeking enterprise." Is this statement true?
(a) Yes (b) Can't Say
(c) No (d) None of these

125. Banker can exercise the right of set off
(a) Even if the customers dues are payable at a future date.
(b) If the account is joint account and the debt due is from a single account holder.
(c) After the garnishee order if received.
(d) If the two accounts are in the same name and same right.

126. Federal Reserve Bank was formed in
(a) 1930 (b) 1194
(c) 1914 (d) 1915

127. Banks prepare the accounts for the
(a) Financial year (b) Diwali year
(c) Calender year (d) None of these

128. Bank show provision for income tax under the head
(a) Other accounts
(b) Contingent liabilities
(c) Other liabilities and provisions
(d) Contingency accounts

129. Current account is also called _____
(a) Demand deposit account
(b) Term deposit account
(c) Savings account
(d) Time deposit account

130. The posting of entires is done in bank from
(a) Book (b) Records
(c) Vouchers (d) Slips

131. Schedule IX is related to
(a) Advance (b) Borrowings
(c) Cash (d) Fixed Assers

132. Schedule 3 consists of
(a) Advance (b) Deposits
(c) Borrowing (d) Cash

133. The minimum period for which a commercial bank can accept term deposit is _______
(a) 5 days (b) 7 days
(c) 30 days (d) 25 days

134. The Refinance Corporation for Industry Private Limited was set-up by the RBI in
(a) 1958 (b) 1985
(c) 1890 (d) 1895

135. Every bank wishing to commence banking business in India is required to obtain a licence from the
(a) State Bank of India
(b) Reserve Bank of India
(c) Central Government of India
(d) President of India

136. The RBI was set up as a _______ Bank
(a) Creditor Bank
(b) Employee's Bank
(c) Rural Bank
(d) Shareholder Bank

137. The minimum investment of recurring deposit varies _______
(a) 100 (b) 1500
(c) 1000 (d) 25000

138. The Bank of Poland was set up in
(a) 1920 (b) 1919
(c) 1930 (d) 1924

139. The IFCI takes loans from
(a) RBI
(b) Central Government
(c) IDBI
(d) All of the above

140. The paid up capital of NABARD is
(a) ₹ 100 crore (b) ₹ 30 crore
(c) ₹ 2000 crore (d) ₹ 400 crore

141. The time limit allowed under ombudsman scheme for a customer is ______
(a) 6 months (b) 1 year
(c) 3 years (d) 5 years

142. The paid up capital of NABARD contributed by
(a) Reserve Bank of India
(b) State Bank of India
(c) Both (a) and (b) in equal proportions
(d) Central Bank of India

143. Who announced the 20-point economic programme of the Government of India for the first time?
(a) Shri N. Rao
(b) Smt. Indira Gandhi
(c) Shri Rajeev Gandhi
(d) Shri Atal Bihari Vajpai

144. The bankers' debt is known as
(a) Advances (b) Deposit
(c) Cash reserve (d) None of these

145. Foreign Exchange Act performed by
(a) HDFC Bank
(b) Co-operative Bank
(c) HUDCO Bank
(d) Exchange Bank

146. Unit Banking System originated in the
(a) India
(b) England
(c) Japan
(d) United States of America

147. The National Bank for Agricultural and Rural Development was set up on
(a) 12 July 1932
(b) 21 March 1930
(c) 12 July 1928
(d) 12 July 1930

148. Which of the following is restricted fund of RBI?
(a) Interest on dept
(b) Lending to bank
(c) Bank not issue
(d) Credit control

149. A cheque crossed by drawing two transverse parallel lines through top left corner of the cheque is called
(a) Special crossing
(b) General crossing
(c) Post dated cheque
(d) Crossed cheque

150. The SBI was set-up in
(a) 1935 (b) 1955
(c) 1921 (d) 1949

151. The origin of merchant banking is to be traced to ______ in late medieval times.
(a) Italy (b) Sanskrit
(c) Hindi (d) French

152. The origin of banking, in the modern sense, is traced to
(a) French (b) Italy
(c) Sanskrit (d) Hindi

153. The Deposit Insurance Corporation has been renamed as the Deposit Insurance and
(a) Credit Gurantee Corporation
(b) Flexible Rate Insurance Corporation
(c) Guarantee Corporation Corporation
(d) Central and Audit Corporation

154. ______ is a person who becomes the possessor or payee of a negotiable instrument for a consideration.
(a) Holder in due course
(b) Holder

(c) Holder of the instrument
(d) Electronic cheque

155. The Bank of England was nationalised in
(a) 1946 (b) 1945
(c) 1949 (d) 1947

156. The Bank of France was nationalised in
(a) 1947 (b) 1948
(c) 1945 (d) 1940

157. The Board of Directors of IFCI is guided on questions of policy by
(a) The IDBI (b) The RBI
(c) The UTI (d) The SBI

158. Introduced first of all by the Refinance Corporation for Industry in
(a) 1980 (b) 1970
(c) 1960 (d) 1958

159. ______ means signing on the back of a negotiable instrument with a view to transfer the title of the instrument to another person.
(a) Instrument (b) Endorsement
(c) Underwriting (d) Document

160. ______ is the first specialist institution to be established in India soon after indepdence, in July 1948.
(a) General Insurance Corporation
(b) State Bank of India
(c) The Industrial Finance Corporation of India
(d) Reserve Bank of India

161. Which of the following is not helpful in controlling money supply?
(a) CRR
(b) Free market policy
(c) Change in margin requirement
(d) Bank Rate

162. Operating expenses are shown in schedule
(a) 16 (b) 20
(c) 17 (d) 19

163. The banking system which combines commercial banking with investment banking is known as
(a) Mixed banking
(b) Multiple banking
(c) Group banking
(d) All of these

164. Accounting entries are made by a banking company according to
(a) Single entry system
(b) Only slip system
(c) Slip system and double entry system
(d) Only double entry system

165. Unit Banking means a system of banking under which banking services are provided a single banking organisation. Are you agree with this statement?
(a) Sometimes (b) Can't say
(c) No (d) Yes

166. ______ is called primary reserve of bank.
(a) Cash
(b) Retained earnings
(c) Investment
(d) Goodwill

167. Which of the following is not cooperative bank or institution?
(a) Deposit Insurance Corporation of India
(b) Credit Guarantee Corporation of India
(c) Central Cooperative Banks
(d) Cooperative Agricultural Credit

168. What is the CRR minimum limit for commercial bank to be deposited with RBI?
(a) 5% (b) 6%
(c) 3% (d) 10%

169. Deposit are secondary or derived from the primary deposits is known as
(a) Multiple credit creation
(b) Derivative deposit

(c) Credit creation
(d) Single credit creation

170. Controls the monetary system and the over all credit operation of the banks.
(a) Reserve Bank of India
(b) Central Government
(c) Finance Minister
(d) State Bank of India

171. The RBI is the apex institution of the monetary and ____ system of the country.
(a) banking (b) liquidity
(c) solvency (d) All of the above

172. When the Imperial Bank of India was set-up?
(a) In 1921 (b) In 1930
(c) In 1919 (d) In 1918

173. When did the Royal Commission of Indian Currency and Finance Commission suggest the establishment of the Reserve Bank of India?
(a) In 1930 (b) In 1935
(c) In 1920 (d) In 1926

174. DFHI stands for
(a) Discount and Finance House of India Ltd.
(b) Discount and Finance Housing investment Ltd.
(c) District Finance House of India Ltd.
(d) Direct Finance House of India Ltd.

175. Reserve Fund known as
(a) Statutory Reserve Fund
(b) General Reserve
(c) Proposed Dividend
(d) All of the above

176. The RBI acts as banker of the Central and
(a) President of India
(b) State Bank of India
(c) Comptroller and Auditor General of India
(d) State Government

177. The Agricultural Refinance and Development Corporation (ARDC) was set-up as subsidiary of the Reserve Bank of India in
(a) 1961 (b) 1963
(c) 1950 (d) 1960

178. Which of the following is not part of World Bank Group?
(a) ADB (b) IDA
(c) IFC (d) IBRD

179. RBI introduced a _____ operated through repo and reverse repo.
(a) SRR (b) CRAR
(c) LAF (d) CRR

180. A foreign company means
(a) a company incorporated in India but doing business outside India.
(b) a company incorporated outside India but doing business in India.
(c) Both (a) and (b).
(d) None of the above.

181. Working of a stock exchange is governed by
(a) controller of capital issue.
(b) governing board of that stock exchange.
(c) Government of India.
(d) All of the above.

182. If a person buys shares at one market and sells at another at a higher price, it is called
(a) Arbitrage
(b) Badla transaction
(c) Inside trading
(d) Bull liquidation

183. NPA is defined as a credit facility in respect which the interest and/or instalment of principal has remained overdue for _____ days.
(a) 75 (b) 125
(c) 90 (d) 365

184. The accounting year of banks ends on
(a) 31st December (b) 30th November
(c) 31st March (d) 30th June

185. With the special permission of registrar, the financial year of a company may be extended to
(a) 21 months (b) 24 months
(c) 15 months (d) 18 months

186. Kerb dealings means
(a) dealing in shares outside the stock exchange official trading hours.
(b) dealing in shares not list in stock exchange.
(c) dealing in shares outside the stock exchange buildings.
(d) All of the above.

187. FCNR deposits are _____ operated by NRIs in Indian bank for a fixed period in major foreign currencies
(a) term deposit (b) NRE deposit
(c) recurring deposit (d) time deposit

188. The principle of indemnity does not apply to
(a) general insurance
(b) life insurance
(c) fire insurance
(d) marine insurance

189. A speculator in the stock exchange who expects the prices of shares to fall is called
(a) Lame duck (b) Stag
(c) Bear (d) Bull

190. Option dealings in stock exchange is
(a) Illegal (b) Void
(c) Legal (d) None of these

191. The maker of a cheque is called the
(a) Drawee (b) Payee
(c) Drawer (d) All of the above

192. An establishment insured its property worth ₹ 50 lacs for ₹ 30 lacs against fire. The actual loss due to fire was ₹ 40 lacs. The firm can get
(a) ₹ 40 Lacs (b) ₹ 30 Lacs
(c) ₹ 50 Lacs (d) None of these

193. When an insurance company (other than Life Insurance Corporation) pays for the total loss to the insured it has a right to take overall right and remedies, the insured may have against the third parties. This right of an insurance company is based on
(a) contract of indemnity
(b) scientific and actuarial calculation
(c) subrogation
(d) causa proxima

194. Which one of the following does not constitute the purpose of setting up SEBI?
(a) To promote the development of the securities' markets.
(b) To protect the interests of the investors in securities.
(c) To deal with matters connected with fraudulent and unfair trade practices relating to securities' markets.
(d) To regulate the global securities markets.

195. Which one of the following types of companies deals with only its shareholders for their benefit?
(a) Chit fund company
(b) Banking company
(c) Private limited company
(d) Nidhi company

196. Which one of the following best supports the theory that the stock exchange is a secondary market?
In a stock exchange
(a) securities are dealt in for dual purposes investment and speculation.
(b) no new investment is created.

(c) an existing holder of securities can dispose of the holdings to another investor who intends to buy then.
(d) securities are bought and sold by way of transfer.

197. Under the Companies Act, 1956, the 'financial year' of a company
(a) may be more or less than a calendar year, but it shall not exceed 20 months.
(b) may be more or less than a calendar year, but it shall not exceed 20 months.
(c) must be exactly 12 months.
(d) must not be less than 12 months.

198. Which one of the following is not a commercial risk?
(a) Change in the exchange rate
(b) Insolvency of the buyer
(c) New restrictions placed on import-export trade
(d) Damage to goods in transit

199. The average clause in a fire policy states that the insured can get back
(a) the entire amount of the total loss suffered.
(b) the entire amount of partial loss suffered.
(c) a fixed percentage of loss suffered.
(d) only that portion of the actual loss suffered as the sum insured bears to total value.

200. The first development financial institution in India that has got merged with a bank is
(a) IDFC (b) UTI
(c) IDBI (d) ICICI

201. In option dealings, speculation means
(a) agreeing to illegitimate trading in securities outside the reorganised stock exchange.
(b) buying in one market at cheaper price and selling the same in another at a higher price.
(c) postponing the payment to and delivery of securities if market conditions turn adverse.
(d) acquiring right to buy or sell a certain quantity of security at a stated price within a prescribed time.

202 The insurer will pay proportionately and the insured will be his own insurer for the balance if the value of the subject matter is greater than the insured amount in
(a) declaration policy
(b) valued policy
(c) consequential loss policy
(d) average policy

203. Average clause in a fire policy
(a) penalises under insurance.
(b) average the claim on the different policies taken by the insured.
(c) insures the property at average premium paid for the last three years.
(d) insures the property at the average rate of premium received.

204. The rate of which discounting the bills of first class banks is done by RBI is called
(a) Discounting Rate
(b) Bank Rate
(c) Prime Lending Rate
(d) Loan Rate

205. According to the principle of subrogation.
(a) the actual amount of loss, not exceeding the amount of the policy, shall be paid.
(b) the insured must take all necessary steps to minimise the loss.
(c) on making good the loss, the insurer is entitled to succeed to all the rights of the insured regarding the subject matter of insurance.
(d) the actual amount of loss, should be distributed among the different insurers of the same risk.

206. The persons who agree to insure cargo, hull or freight are called
   (a) Underwriters (b) Bookkeepers
   (c) Undertakers (d) Caretakers

207. Which bank has become the first foreign bank to open a branch in Israel's diamond exchange?
   (a) American Express Bank
   (b) State Bank of India
   (c) Citibank
   (d) Standard Chartered Bank

208. Under the guidelines of SEBI, pricing of first capital issues should be on par value only in the case of
   (a) a private company converting into a public company.
   (b) an existing company with no past reserves.
   (c) a new company with no connections with other companies.
   (d) a new company promoted by an existing company.

209. The main object of stock exchange is to
   (a) help in the capital formation in the country.
   (b) provide facilities for speculation.
   (c) provide a ready market for securities.
   (d) safeguard the interest of investors.

210. Exchange risk in case of foreign currency non resident (banks) scheme (FCNB) is borne by
   (a) Concerned Bank (b) RBI
   (c) Depositor (d) Govt. of India

211. Which one of the following stock exchange dealers buy shares in the expectation that the price will rise?
   (a) Stage (b) Brokers
   (c) Bears (d) Bulls

212. Insurance to cover risks arising out of professional negligence is known as
   (a) Professional insurance
   (b) Business insurance
   (c) Risk insurance
   (d) Liability insurance

213. Nayak committee recommendations are applicable for sanction of fund based working capital limit up to
   (a) ₹ 5 lacs (b) ₹ 5 crores
   (c) ₹ 3 crores (d) ₹ 1 crores

214. Risk of loss against strikes and riots is covered in which of the following fire insurance policies?
   (a) Average (b) Denary
   (c) Comprehensive (d) Floating

215. The definition of the term 'banker' can be found in
   (a) the Negotiable Instruments Act, 1881.
   (b) the Banking Companies (Acquisition and Transfer of Undertakings Act, 1971).
   (c) the Banking Regulation Act, 1949.
   (d) None of the above.

216. The definition of the word customer is contained in
   (a) Secton 34 of the Banking Regulation Act 1949.
   (b) Section 131 of the Negotiable Instrument Act, 1881.
   (c) Section 58 of the Bills of Exchanee Act 1882.
   (d) None of the above.

217. What is USGAAP?
   (a) Union State Generous Agreement & Accounting Principles
   (b) United States Generally Accepted Accounting Principles
   (c) Union State Generous Accounts & Affairs and Practices
   (d) United State General Allies & Army Practices

218. Who would you consider to be a customer of the bank?
(a) A person who has opened a savings account only two days ago.
(b) A person who has been visiting the branch for encashing cheques for quite some time.
(c) A person who has been retiring bills from the branch for last seven years.
(d) A person who has been coming to the bank for purchasing demand drafts, mail, transfers and telegraphic transfers for the last five years.

219. When a person maintains deposit account with the bank the principal relationship between the two is one of
(a) Trustee and beneficiary.
(b) Principal and creditor.
(c) Debtor and creditor.
(d) Bailor and bailee.

220. The fiscal deficit in 2001-2002 was ______ of GDP.
(a) 5.4% (b) 5.3%
(c) 5.2% (d) 5.1%

221. Upon the banker's allowing an overdraft to a customer in his current account, the realtionsship between the two will be that of
(a) Principal and agent
(b) Trustee and beneficiary
(c) Creditor and devtor
(d) None of the above

222. While collecting cheques/bills, etc., for a customer the bank acts as
(a) a debtor
(b) a pledgor
(c) an agent of the customer
(d) a trustee of the customer

223. The minimum capital adequacy ratio currently fixed by RBI for banks is
(a) 15% (b) 7%
(c) 9% (d) 12%

224. When a customer deposits a sealed box with bank for safe custody, the relationship between the two is that of
(a) bailor and bailee
(b) trustee and beneficiary
(c) principal and agent
(d) debtor and creditor

225. When a customer fakes a locker in the bank, the relationship between the bank and the customer is one of
(a) principal and agent
(b) lessor and lessee
(c) pledgor and pledgee
(d) None of the above

226. What should be the method of valuation for advances againstshares/debentures/ bonds?
(a) Book value (b) Average value
(c) Face value (d) Market price

227. When a customer gives standing instructions to the bank for remitting a specified sum of money every month towards payment to his rent to a person, the banks acts as
(a) an agent of the customer.
(b) a servant of the customer.
(c) a debtor of the customer's landlord.
(d) pledgor.

228. A banker is duty-bound to observer secrecy of a customer's account. However, disclosure would be justified when
(a) the banks replies to an status enquiry from a party who desires to supply some machinery on credit to the customer.
(b) it is under compulsion of law.
(c) the banker indicates the credit balance in the account at the time of returning a cheque for want of funds.
(d) None of the above.

229. The certificate to commence business is to be called for perusal andreturned for opening of an account of
   (a) Private limited company
   (b) Public limited company
   (c) Trust
   (d) Club and association

230. A banker is under statutory obligation to honour his customer's cheques provided that
   (a) there is no legal bar to such payment.
   (b) they are drawn in proper form and presented during banking hours.
   (c) there is sufficient balance in the account to meet the cheque or arrangements have been made for an overdraft.
   (d) All of the above.

231. A banker's obligation to honour his customers cheques is determined
   (a) on receipt of notice of customer's death.
   (b) when the customer is arrested for a criminal offence.
   (c) when the balance in the account comes to 'Nil'.
   (d) None of the above

232. The ceiling for Bank's daily borrowings in call money should not exceed ______ of owned funds.
   (a) 125% (b) 100%
   (c) 150% (d) 75%

233. When a customer owing two or more debts to the banker pays in money which is not sufficient to discharge all the debts without any specific direction for its appropriation
   (a) the amount will be appropriated in order of time the debts were incurred.
   (b) the bank has a right to use the payment at his discretion to wipe out any debt which is due including a time-barred debt.
   (c) the banker may appropriate the payment as per his choice against debts which are not time-barred.
   (d) None of the above

234. The Banking Regulation Act, 1949 was enacted with the objective of
   (a) stopping frauds in the banks.
   (b) consolidating and amending the law relating to banking companies.
   (c) checking banks failures.
   (d) ensuring adequate branch expansion in rural areas.

235. The Banking Regulation Act, 1949, does not at all apply to
   (a) Foreign Banks having their offices in India.
   (b) State Bank of India and its subsidiaries.
   (c) Primary agricultural credit societies and co-operative and mortagagee banks.
   (d) Nationalized banks.

236. Which one among the following has not started commercial banking?
   (a) ICICI (b) UTI
   (c) SIDBI (d) IDBI

237. No bank incorporated in India can open an office (place of business) outside India without obtaining prior permission of
   (a) ECGC
   (b) Reserve Bank of India
   (c) Controller of Imports and Exports
   (d) EXIM Bank

238. Section 16 of the Banking Regualtion Act, 1949 prohibits a person
   (a) to be appointed as director of a banking company if he is not of sound financial position.
   (b) to be appointed as director of more than one banking company.

(c) to be appointed as a director of a banking company if he is an undischarged insolvent.
(d) None of the above.

239. Endorsement is made by an authorised person on behalf of another is
(a) Perpro endorsement
(b) Authorised endorsement
(c) Qualified endorsement
(d) Recognised endorsement

240. A customer has a right to ask the bank to return him a paid instrument, before the expiry of period of preservation of such instrument, before the expiry of period of preservation of such instruments, under
(a) Section 45Z of the Banking Regulation Act, 1949.
(b) Section 131 of the Negotiable Instruments Act, 1881.
(c) Section 34 of Reserve Bank of India Act, 1934.
(d) None of the above.

241. As per Section 9 of the Banking Regulation Act, 1949, no banking company shall hold any immovable property how so ever acquired, except such as is required for its own use, for any period exceeding
(a) ten years (b) five years
(c) seven years (d) None of these

242. How many banks were in second phase of nationalisation?
(a) 6 (b) 7
(c) 8 (d) 10

243. Section 5(a) of the Banking Regulation Act, 1949 defines the term "approved securities" as
(a) the securities which are approved by IDBI.
(b) the securiteis so approved by the Central Government by notification in the official Gazette.
(c) the securities approved by the Indian Bank's Association.
(d) the securities in which a trustee may invest money under clause (a), clause (b), clause (bb), clause (c) or clause (d) of Section 20 of the Indian Trust Act, 1882.

244. In terms of Section 5 (n) of the Banking Regulation Act, 1949, "secured loan or advance" means
(a) the loans and advances made on the security of assets, the market value of which is not at any time less than the amount of such loan or advance.
(b) the loans and advances which are granted against third party guarantees.
(c) the advances which are backed up by mortgage of immovable property situated in India.
(d) the advances which are fully secured by fixed assets.

245. In accordance to [under Section 23(10) of the Banking Regualtion Act, 1949] a banking company is exempted from obtaining prior permission of Reserve Bank of India for
(a) opening a temporary branch on the occasion of an exhibition, a conference or a mela for a period not exceeding three months.
(b) change of premises within the same city town or village.
(c) opening a branch in a foreign country.
(d) opening an extension counter.

246. Section 14A(1) of the Banking Regulation Act, 1949 prohibits a banking company from
(a) creating floating charge on the undertaking or any property of the company or any part thereof.
(b) allowing advance against its own shares.

(c) opening a branch in foreign country.
(d) disclosing secret reserves created by it.

247. Which one of the following is a contract for the purchase or sale of securities for the performance of which no time is specified, and which is to be performed immediately or within a reasonable time?
(a) Ready delivery contract
(b) Spot delivery contract
(c) Option in securities
(d) Forward contract

248. In India, what is the term used to describe a company which actually deals with the corpus of the mutual fund?
(a) Mutual fund company
(b) Sponsor company
(c) Trustee company
(d) Asset management company

249. Which one of the following is not a feature of a confirmed letter of credit?
(a) The negotiating bank entails a definite commitment on its part to carry out the provisions of payment.
(b) The negotiating bank adds its own confirmation to the credit.
(c) The opening bank cannot modify the letter of credit once it is opened.
(d) The opening and negotiating banks carry confirmed guarantee for payment.

250. What does third party confirmation in auditing mean?
(a) Confirmation of bank balances.
(b) Confirmation of balances of sundry debtors or creditors.
(c) Confirmation of security deposits.
(d) Confirmation of contingent liabilities.

251. Principle of indemnity does not apply for
(a) Marine insurance.
(b) Fire insurance.
(c) Theft insurance.
(d) Life insurance.

252. When the shares of a company are listed on the stock exchange, it indicates
(a) company is financially sound.
(b) that the stock exchange guarantees the financial soundness of the company.
(c) the company is legally organised.
(d) All of the above.

253. In India, all insurance companies are
(a) privately owned but regulated but government.
(b) government owned.
(c) privately owned.
(d) All of the above.

254. EXIM bank can be described as a
(a) schedule bank.
(b) non-banking non-financial company.
(c) commercial bank.
(d) non-banking financial company.

255. Paid-up value is payable on a life insurance policy
(a) when the policy is surrendered.
(b) on maturity or death whichever is earlier.
(c) on the maturity of the policy.
(d) when the policy lapses.

256. Under which principle, all the rights of insured are transferred to insurance company after making payment of claim
(a) Average clause
(b) Contribution
(c) Utmost good faith
(d) Subrogation

257. In India, general insurance is
(a) privately owned under govt., regulation.
(b) government owned.
(c) privately owned.
(d) All of the above.

258. The biggest stock exchange of India is
(a) Calcutta (b) Bombay
(c) Madras (d) Delhi

259. Short sales in a stock exchange means
(a) signing transfer deed without filling in the name of the transferee.
(b) selling those shares which one does not have.
(c) selling shares and then buying the same shares.
(d) All of the above.

260. Principle of subrogation in insurance applies
(a) to all types of insurance.
(b) only to life insurance.
(c) only to fire and marine insurance.
(d) All of the above.

261. Average clause in a fire policy is to check the
(a) over-insurance (b) under insurance
(c) Both (a) and (b) (d) All of the above

262. Continuous forward selling to depress prices of securities in stock exchange is known as
(a) bear squeeze (b) short selling
(c) bear hammering (d) All of the above

263. Working of a stock exchange is governed by
(a) Governing board of that stock exchange.
(b) Govt. of India.
(c) Controller of capital issue.
(d) All of the above.

264. If a person buys shares at one market and sells at another at a higher price, it is called
(a) Bull liquidation
(b) Badla transaction
(c) Inside trading
(d) Arbitrage

264. Causa proxima implies that loss must arise form:
(a) cause insured against.
(b) act of God and not that of a person.
(c) any cause.
(d) more than one cause.

266. Principle of indemnity does not apply to
(a) theft insurance
(b) life insurance
(c) fire insurance
(d) marine insurance

267. In which type of life insurance policy, the insurance amounts payable only to the survivors of insured?
(a) Sinking fund policy
(b) Endowment policy
(c) Whole life policy
(d) All of the above

Directions: Questions 268 to 276 are of multiple statement type. Choose the correct answer from the codes given below.

268. The main functions of IFCI are
1. granting loans and advances for the establishment, expansion diversification and modernisation of industries in corporate and co-operative sectors.
2. guaranteeing loans raised by industrial concerns in the capital market, both in rupees and foreign currencies.
3. subscribing or underwriting the issue of shares and debentures by industries. Such investment can be held up to seven years.
4. guaranteeing credit purchase of capital goods imported as well as purchased within the country.

Codes:
(a) 1, 2, and 3 (b) 1, 2, 3 and 4
(c) 1 and 2 (d) 3, 4 and 2

269. Consider the following parties.
   1. Secured creditors
   2. Unsecured creditors
   3. Partners who have contributed loans
   4. Partners who have contributed over and above profit sharing ratio.

Codes:

(a) 1, 2, 4, 3 (b) 2, 1, 4, 3
(c) 2, 1, 3, 4 (d) 1, 2, 3, 4

270. Consider the following cases regarding doctrine of indoor management:
   1. Where the outsider had actual or constructive notice of the internal irregularity.
   2. Where the outsider had not made proper enquiries which would have revealed the irregularities, despite so suspicious circumstances as to invite further enquiries.
   3. Where the outsider is found to have relied upon a document which is forged one, for a forgery is a nullity.
   4. Where the outsider had relied on a resolution of a company meeting which was not properly passed.

Protection under the doctrine of indoor management cannot be claimed in which of the above circumstances?

Codes:

(a) 4 only (b) 1, 2 and 3
(c) 1 and 2 (d) 2 and 4

271. Who among the following is an insider/are insiders as per provisions of the SEBI (Insider Trading) Regulations, 1992?
   1. A broker who trades in the company's share.
   2. A leader who has provided term loans to the company.
   3. A person who is or was connected with the company and is expected to have access to unpublished price sensitive informtion with respect to the securities of the company.
   4. An underwriter who regularly underwrites the securities of the company.

Codes:

(a) 3 only (b) 1, 2, 3 and 4
(c) 1 and 2 (d) 1, 3 and 4

272. Identify sources of agricultural credit in India from the code given below:
   1. Commercial Banks
   2. Money Lender
   3. Regional Rural Bank
   4. Small Industries Development Bank of India

Codes:

(a) 1, 4 and 3 (b) 1, 2, 3 and 4
(c) 1, 2 and 3 (d) 2, 3 and 1

273. Consider the following statements regarding grey market in the context of security exchange.
   1. It is a market wherein trading in a security takes place before it is officially listed.
   2. It is legal and a form of private placement business.
   3. Securities are sold through prospectus.

Codes:

(a) 3 only (b) 1, 2 and 3
(c) 1 only (d) 2 and 3

274. In order to tackle with the grievances of the investors on priority basis, regulatory bodies of capital market have categorised the complaints of the investors in different types.
   1. Type I — Non-receipt of Annual Report, right forms/interest on delayed receipt of refund orders/dividend.
   2. Type II — Non-receipt of dividend.

3. Type III — Non-receipt of share certificates/bonus shares.
4. Type IV — Non-receipt of refund orders/ allotment letters/stock invest.

Codes:

(a) 2 only (b) 1 and 4
(c) 1 only (d) 2 and 3

275. Fiscal policy relates to the Government decision in respect of
1. Taxation
2. Government spending
3. Government borrowing
4. Public Debt

Codes:

(a) 3 and 4 are correct
(b) 2, 3 and 4 are correct.
(c) 1 and 2 are correct
(d) All the above are correct.

276. For the purposes of fire insurance, loss by fire means loss due to
1. ignition
2. accidental fire
3. causes arising from fire
4. damage caused during extinguishment of fire

Codes:

(a) 1 and 2 are correct
(b) 1, 2 and 3 are correct
(c) 3 and 4 are correct
(d) All are correct

Directions: Questions 277 to 279 are of matching type. Match List I with List II and select the correct answer using the codes given below the list.

277. **List I**

A. Principle of subrogation
B. Principle of ultra virus
C. Holding company
D. Contango

List II

1. Business combination
2. Insurance
3. Company Law
4. Stock Exchange

Codes:	A	B	C	D
(a)	4	2	1	3
(b)	3	1	2	4
(c)	1	2	3	4
(d)	1	3	2	4

278. **List I (Types of mutual fund)**

(a) Open-ended mutual fund
(b) Interval fund
(c) Close-ended mutual fund
(d) Balanced fund

List II (Explanation)

1. They are open for sale or redemption during pre-determind intervals at NAV related prices.
2. The fund is open for subscription only during a specified period.
3. Provides both growth and regular income.
4. One that is available for subscription all through out the year.

Codes:	A	B	C	D
(a)	3	2	1	4
(b)	4	1	2	3
(c)	3	1	2	4
(d)	4	2	1	3

279. **List I**

A. Screen trading
B. G.V. Ramakrishna Committee Report
C. BIFR
D. SEBI

List II

1. Capital market reforms
2. Industrial sickness
3. Disinvestment of PSU shares
4. Stock Exchange

Codes:	A	B	C	D
(a)	4	3	2	1
(b)	3	4	1	2
(c)	3	4	2	1
(d)	4	3	1	2

Directions: Questions 280 to 282 consist of two statements, one labelled as 'Assertion (A)' and the other as 'Reason (R)'. You have to examine these two statements carefuly and decide if the Assertion A and the Reason R are individually true and if so, whether the Reason is a correct explanation of the Assertion. Select your answer to these items using the codes given below.

(a) Both A and R are true and R is the correct explanation of A.
(b) Both A and R are true but R is not the correct explanaton of A.
(c) A is true but R is false.
(d) A is false but R is true.

280. **Assertion (A):** Shares must be listed on all the stock exchange.
Reason (R): Stock exchange listing provides liquidity of shares.

281. **Assertion (A):** Commercial banks in India are treated as social banks.
Reason (R): They provide finance for the upliftment of the downtrodden.

282. **Assertion (A):** EXIM Bank is mainly a supervising body for export finance.
Reason (R): Commercial banks cater to small needs of exporters.

283. Specialised financial institutions provide medium and long-term financial assistance to industry.
(a) False (b) True

284. Small-scale industries are not financed by any SFI.
(a) False (b) True

285. IFCI can underwrite issue of shares but cannot subscribe to share issues.
(a) False (b) True

286. Among other functions IFCI also guarantees foreign currency loans.
(a) False (b) True

287. The maximum limit of credit which IFCI can sanction to a single concern is ₹ 1 crore but it can be exceeded if permitted by government.
(a) False (b) True

288 IFCI can grant long-term loans to industries in the co-operative sector.
(a) False (b) True

289. To set up a transport undertaking a businessman can get financial assistance from the SFC of the concerned state.
(a) False (b) True

290 SFCs can guarantee loans of industrial concerns which are repayable within not more than 10 years.
(a) False (b) True

291. Loans granted by SFCs can be converted into shares of the industrial concern.
(a) False (b) True

292. Financial assistance cannot be granted by SFC to any proprietary concern.
(a) False (b) True

293. Fresh shares or units of the 'open-end' investment trust are continuously offered for sales at the face value
(a) False (b) True

294. A 'closed-end' investment trust does not buy back its shares or units.
(a) False (b) True

295. The UTI does not underwrite shares and debentures issued by companies.
(a) False (b) True

296. Investment through UTI results in lower risk of loss and higher return.
(a) False (b) True

297. The market value of shares of units of closed-end trusts depends of the market forces of demand and supply.
(a) False (b) True

298. ICICI is not a government controlled organisation.
(a) False (b) True

299. Industrial concerns can secure project consultancy services from the ICICI.
(a) False (b) True

300. Only industrial concerns in the private sector are eligible for grant of long-term finance by the ICICI.
(a) False (b) True

301. Loans under deferred payment agreements are guaranteed by the ICICI.
(a) False (b) True

302. One of the many objectives of ICICI is to expand employment opportunities in the rural areas.
(a) False (b) True

ANSWERS

1. (d)	2. (b)	3. (d)	4. (a)	5. (b)	6. (c)
7. (a)	8. (a)	9. (a)	10. (d)	11. (d)	12. (a)
13. (d)	14. (d)	15. (d)	16. (a)	17. (c)	18. (c)
19. (b)	20. (b)	21. (b)	22. (c)	23. (a)	24. (b)
25. (b)	26. (a)	27. (d)	28. (d)	29. (a)	30. (b)
31. (c)	32. (c)	33. (a)	34. (c)	35. (b)	36. (c)
37. (a)	38. (c)	39. (c)	40. (a)	41. (b)	42. (d)
43.. (c)	44. (d)	45. (b)	46. (d)	47. (d)	48. (d)
49. (b)	50. (b)	51. (c)	52. (b)	53. (b)	54. (c)
55. (a)	56. (c)	57. (a)	58. (a)	59. (c)	60. (c)
61. (a)	62. (b)	63. (a)	64. (a)	65. (d)	66. (d)
67. (b)	68. (b)	69. (a)	70. (c)	71. (a)	72. (d)
73. (b)	74. (c)	75. (a)	76. (d)	77. (a)	78. (b)
79. (a)	80. (a)	81. (c)	82. (a)	83. (d)	84. (d)
85. (c)	86. (b)	87. (d)	88. (a)	89. (d)	90. (c)
91. (c)	92. (b)	93. (a)	94. (b)	95. (b)	96. (b)
97. (d)	98. (c)	99. (d)	100. (a)	101. (a)	102. (d)
103. (b)	104. (d)	105. (b)	106. (c)	107. (a)	108. (a)
109. (d)	110. (d)	111. (a)	112. (a)	113. (b)	114. (a)
115. (a)	116. (b)	117. (d)	118. (c)	119. (a)	120. (d)
121. (d)	122. (d)	123. (c)	124. (a)	125. (d)	126. (c)

127. (a)	128. (c)	129. (a)	130. (d)	131. (a)	132. (b)
133. (b)	134. (a)	135. (b)	136. (d)	137. (a)	138. (d)
139. (d)	140. (a)	141. (b)	142. (c)	143. (b)	144. (b)
145. (d)	146. (d)	147. (c)	148. (a)	149. (d)	150. (a)
151. (a)	152. (b)	153. (a)	154. (a)	155. (b)	156. (c)
157. (a)	158. (d)	159. (b)	160. (c)	161. (b)	162. (a)
163. (a)	164. (c)	165. (d)	166. (a)	167. (a)	168. (c)
169. (b)	170. (a)	171. (a)	172. (a)	173. (d)	174. (a)
175. (a)	176. (d)	177. (b)	178. (a)	179. (c)	180. (b)
181. (b)	182. (a)	183. (c)	184. (d)	185. (d)	186. (a)
187. (a)	188. (b)	189. (c)	190. (a)	191. (c)	192. (b)
193. (c)	194. (d)	195. (d)	196. (c)	197. (a)	198. (c)
199. (d)	200. (d)	201. (d)	202. (d)	203. (a)	204. (b)
205. (c)	206. (a)	207. (b)	208. (c)	209. (c)	210. (a)
211. (d)	212. (b)	213. (b)	214. (c)	215. (c)	216. (d)
217. (b)	218. (a)	219. (c)	220. (a)	221. (c)	222. (c)
223. (c)	224. (a)	225. (b)	226. (d)	227. (a)	228. (b)
229. (a)	230. (d)	231. (a)	232. (b)	233. (b)	234. (b)
235. (c)	236. (c)	237. (b)	238. (b)	239. (a)	240. (a)
241. (c)	242. (a)	243. (d)	244. (a)	245. (c)	246. (a)
247. (b)	248. (d)	249. (c)	250. (b)	251. (d)	252. (c)
253. (b)	254. (d)	255. (b)	256. (d)	257. (b)	258. (b)
259. (b)	260. (c)	261. (a)	262. (a)	263. (a)	264. (d)
265. (a)	266. (b)	267. (c)	268. (b)	269. (d)	270. (b)
271. (a)	272. (c)	273. (c)	274. (b)	275. (d)	276. (a)
277. (b)	278. (b)	279. (a)	280. (c)	281. (c)	282. (a)
283. (b)	284. (a)	285. (b)	286. (b)	287. (b)	288. (a)
289. (b)	290. (a)	291. (b)	292. (a)	293. (a)	294. (b)
295. (a)	296. (b)	297. (b)	298. (b)	299. (b)	300. (a)
301. (b)	302. (a)				

10

International Business

1. Foreign trade helps each country to make ______ use of its natural resources.
   (a) loss (b) better
   (c) optimal (d) None of these
2. Purchase of goods from one country with the object of selling than to another country is called ______ trade.
   (a) export (b) indian
   (c) import (d) enterport
3. Traders have to face more difficulties in trade than trade
   (a) home, foreign (b) local, Indian
   (c) foreign, home (d) None of these
4. According to the theory of ______ each country should concentrate in production of these goods for which it is best suited.
   (a) average cost
   (b) comparative cost
   (c) fixed cost
   (d) variable cost
5. A clean letter of credit guarantees the acceptance and payment of bills without
   (a) Condition (b) Bank
   (c) Approval (d) None of these
6. An irrevocable letter of credit cannot be
   (a) Withdrawn (b) Shown
   (c) Duplicate (d) None of these
7. A bill of lading is a memorandum signed by ______ of ships.
   (a) clerk (b) owner
   (c) masters (d) None of these
8. A mate's receipt is issued on ______ at the ship
   (a) consignment (b) company
   (c) letter of credit (d) None of these
9. The number of copies to be prepared for a bill of lading is
   (a) Three (b) Five
   (c) Two (d) Four
10. In which year was the EXIM Bank established?
    (a) 1982 (b) 1985
    (c) 1986 (d) 1988
11. Which of the following organizations promotes trade?
    (a) MMTC (b) STC
    (c) ECGE (d) All of the above
12. The buyer bears all the expense in the following mode of price quotation
    (a) C and F (b) Franco
    (c) LOCO (d) CIF
13. The MMTC of India was established as a private limited company
    (a) under the Companies Act
    (b) as a result of amalgamation
    (c) under the Act of Parliament
    (d) as per of memorandum of association
14. Which one of the following is the subsidiary of the state trading corporation of India meant for increasing export?
    (a) Projects and equipment corporation of India.

(b) Minerals and metals trading corporation of India.
(c) Mica trading corporation of India.
(d) Manufactures' export agents and export commission house.

15. The term "duty-draw-back" means
(a) Refund of export duty for exporters.
(b) Handicap in the matter of export.
(c) Refund of import duty for the exporters.
(d) Higher rate of import duty.

16. A letter of credit is a
(a) letter containing conditions of a credit purchase of sale.
(b) letter from an exporter to importer sanctioning credit deal.
(c) letter sent by importer to exporter sanctioning credit deal.
(d) letter of importer's bank agreeing to accept and play on due date the exporter's bill.

17. The importer cannot take delivery of goods unless he produces the
(a) bill of leading
(b) certificate of origin
(c) bill of sight
(d) shipping bill

18. Which one of following items are not in vogue now?
(a) Advance licenses
(b) REP licenses
(c) Customs permit
(d) Special import licenses

19. Bill of lading is issued by
(a) Exporters
(b) Indian commercial banks
(c) Foreign banks
(d) Shipping company

20. Letter of credit is now becoming an increasingly popular method of financing
(a) Distribution of dividend
(b) Fixed capital needs
(c) Working capital needs
(d) Redemption of debentures

21. Import procedure begins with
(a) Marine insurance
(b) Mate's certificate
(c) Shipping order
(d) Indent

22. Which one of the following statements is correct?
(a) EXIM bank does not extend non-funded facility to Indian exporters.
(b) EXIM bank promotes Indian exports through a wise variety and range of landing programmes.
(c) EXIM bank was established to provide assistance in raising capital in international markets.
(d) Overseas investment finance facility is nota part of the functions of EXIM bank.

23. Which one of the following statements is true?
(a) EXIM bank generally deals with export transaction above ₹ 5 crore.
(b) Suppliers credit and buyer's credit are one and the same thing.
(c) ECGC provides no protection against hazards of nature.
(d) The main forces of EXIM bank is one export and import credit for short term.

24. EXIM bank can be described as a
(a) non-banking, non-financial company
(b) schedule bank
(c) commercial bank
(d) none-banking financial company

25. EXIM bank can be described as a
(a) Schedule bank
(b) Non-banking financial company

(c) Commercial bank
(d) Non-banking non financial company

26. LIBOR refers to
(a) Lowest rate of interest prescribed by the Reserve Bank of India.
(b) Liberalised system of foreign exchange transfer between banks.
(c) Inter-bank lending rate for Euro-dollars at London.
(d) Lowest rate of interest at which hauks in London lend sterling.

27. Which one of the following is not a commercial risk?
(a) Change in the exchange rate.
(b) Damage of goods in transit.
(c) Introducing of the buyer.
(d) New restrictions placed on import-export trade.

28. A red clause letter of credit authorizes the
(a) negotiating banker to provide advance credit to the beneficiary for purchase of materials.
(b) banker no transfer the L/C to some other person.
(c) banker to take recourse to the drawer in case of difficult.
(d) banker to fix the amount of credit.

29. Which one of following is not the primary cause of India's chronic balance of payment problem?
(a) Deficits in merchandise trade
(b) Value of imports not matched by value of exports
(c) POL imports
(d) Membership of W.T.O.

30. Globalization of financial services is being promoted by
(a) International Bank for Reconstruction and Development
(b) World Trade Organization
(c) International Monetary Fund
(d) International Finance Corporation

31. Which one of the following documents attests the fact that goods of specified quantity, value and description are entering the bounds of the country?
(a) Consular invoice
(b) Documentary bill
(c) Bill of entry
(d) Bill of lading

32. Export duty is borne by the importer in the mode
(a) FAS (b) CIF
(c) FOB (d) CIF

33. The export procedure begins with the
(a) Mate's receipts (b) Excise
(c) Indent (d) Shipping bills

34. Identify the document among the following that is a document of the file to the goods
(a) Bill of entry
(b) Bill of lading
(c) Letter of credit
(d) None of the above

35. The exporter bears the marine insurance premium in the following mode.
(a) Franco (b) FAS
(c) FCI (d) All of the above

36. How many copies are generally prepared of a bill to entry?
(a) One (b) Two
(c) Three (d) Four

37. What does the shipping company issue upon the entireship being hired?
(a) Bill of loading (b) Shipping bill
(c) L/C (d) Charter party

38. An importer wishing to re-export the goods is required to prepare
(a) Shipping bill (b) Bill of lading
(c) Shipping order (d) Charter party

39. Cashew corporation is a subsidiary wholly owned by
(a) STC (b) EXIM bank
(c) MMTC (d) RBI
40. Mercantilism originated in
(a) Britain (b) Span
(c) France (d) Germany
41. Mercantilism was based on the ideology of
(a) Nationalism (b) Regionalism
(c) Globalisation (d) None of these
42. Mercantilism supported
(a) Autarky
(b) Free trade
(c) Regulation of trade
(d) None of the above
43. Mercantilism advocated
(a) accumulation of industrial goods.
(b) increase in export of agricultural goods.
(c) metals.
(d) accumulation of gold and other precious metals.
44. Mercantilism favoured
(a) Soldiers (b) Civil servants
(c) Merchant class (d) Farmers
45. In France, mercantilism was known as
(a) Cameralism (b) Colbertism
(c) Physiocracy (d) None of these
46. German counterparts of mercantilists were
(a) Cameralists (b) Colbertism
(c) Physiocrates (d) None of these
47. Reaction against mercantilism in France manifested itself in the form of
(a) Camerslism (b) Colbertism
(c) Physiocracy (d) None of these
48. Mercantilism developed during the phase of transition for feudalism to
(a) Commercial capitalism
(b) Industrial capitalism
(c) Both (a) and (b)
(d) None of the above
49. Physiocrates were opposed to
(a) Cameralism (b) Colbertism
(c) Mercantilism (d) None of these
50. Physiocracy which developed as commercial capitalism was yielding place to
(a) Communism
(b) Socialism
(c) Industrial capitalism
(d) Feudalism
51. Absolute cost advantage theory was propounded by
(a) Malthus (b) Marshall
(c) Ricardo (d) Adam Smith
52. Comparative cost advantage theory was propounded oy
(a) Malthus (b) Marshall
(c) Adam Smith (d) Ricardo
53. Only factor of production which classical economist is considered for international trade was
(a) Labour (b) Land
(c) Capital (d) None of these
54. According to Heckscher-Ohlin theory, capital abundant country will export
(a) labour intensive goods
(b) capital intensive goods
(c) Both (a) and (b)
(d) None of the above
55. Cause of trade according to classical economists was
(a) differing labour productivity.
(b) difference in productivity of capital.
(c) Both (a) and (b).
(d) None of the above.
56. According to comparative advantage theory, international trade will not take place if

(a) one country is efficient in both the products.
(b) opportunity costs of the two products are same in both the countries.
(c) one country is efficient in both the products.
(d) None of the above.

57. Heckscher-Ohlin theory explains international trade in terms of
(a) differences in labour productivity.
(b) demand differences.
(c) differences in factor endowments.
(d) None of the above.

58. According to Heckscher-Ohlin theory, labour abundant country will import
(a) labour intensive goods
(b) capital intensive goods
(c) Both (a) and (b)
(d) None of the above

59. USA should import according to H-O theory
(a) labour intensive goods
(b) capital intensive goods
(c) Both (a) and (b)
(d) None of the above

60. India should export according to H-O theory
(a) labour intensive goods
(b) capital intensive goods
(c) Borh (a) and (b)
(d) None of the above

61. If a country enters international trade; the income of abundant factor
(a) Decreases (b) Constant
(c) Increases (d) None of these

62. If a country enters international trade, the income of scarce factor
(a) Decreases (b) Constant
(c) Increases (d) None of these

63. Autarky signifies
(a) Maximise imports
(b) Self-sufficiency
(c) Isolation
(d) Maximise exports

64. Factor price equalisation takes place when
(a) factor intensity in different countries is same.
(b) marginal productivity of factors of production in different countries is same.
(c) Both (a) and (b).
(d) None of the above.

65. Likelihood of complete specialisation increases if
(a) if technology used is two line of production is similar.
(b) factor endowment in two countries differ substantially.
(c) Both (a) and (b).
(d) None of the above.

66. Contradiction to Heckscher-Ohlin theory is
(a) Veblen paradox
(b) Smith paradox
(c) Leontief paradox
(d) Marshall paradox

67. Leontief paradox occurs because of
(a) complete specialisation.
(b) factor reversal.
(c) factor price equalization.
(d) None of the above.

68. Factor reversal matters when
(a) factors endowments differ significantly.
(b) factor price are same.
(c) factor endowments are similar.
(d) None of the above.

69. Leontief tested his paradox theory for the USA for the year

(a) 1950 (b) 1955
(c) 1940 (d) 1947

70. Leontief tested his hypothesis with the help of
(a) Input-output table
(b) Demand curve
(c) Cost curve
(d) None of the above

71. According to Leontief, USA exports
(a) capital intensive goods
(b) labour intensive goods
(c) Both (a) and (b)
(d) None of the above

72. Vent for surplus approaches is applicable to
(a) underdeveloped countries
(b) oil exporting countries
(c) rich countries
(d) None of the above

73. Availability theory was put forward by
(a) I.B. Kravis (b) M. Porter
(c) Marshall (d) Nurkse

74. Net barter terms of trade is
(a) $\frac{P_x}{P_m} \times 100$ (b) $P_x . P_m$
(c) $\frac{P_m}{P_x}$ (d) None of these

75. Income terms of trade is
(a) Pm̂/Px̂.Qx̂ (b) Pm̂/Px̂.1/Qx̂
(c) Px̂/Pm̂.Qx̂ (d) Pm̂/Px̂.Qx̂

76. Ricardo's laws of comparative advantage is based on the
(a) opportunity cost theory
(b) labour theory
(c) endowment of factors of production
(d) None of the above

77. In Heckscher-Ohlin mode, factor abundance is defined in terms of
(a) factor prices
(b) physical quantities of factors
(c) Both (a) and (b)
(d) None of the above

78. Assumption of Heckscher-Ohlin theory are
(a) perfect factor mobility within country.
(b) immobility of factors outside the country.
(c) perfect competition.
(d) All of the above.

79. According to Heckscher-Ohlin theory, production function of different countries for same product is
(a) Different
(b) Same
(c) Either (a) or (b)
(d) None of the above

80. Prebisch's argument is concerned with deterioration in terms of trade against
(a) oil producing countries
(b) developed countries
(c) undeveloped countries
(d) developing countries

81. According to Singer theory, increase in export will not help balance of payment if
(a) supply is inelastic.
(b) income elasticity of expert is low.
(c) demand is inelastic.
(d) All of the above.

82. Prebisch's argument is concerned with the effects of business cycle on
(a) Consumption
(b) Terms of trade
(c) Balance of payment
(d) Output

83. Export of agricultural products has
(a) low income elasticity
(b) low demand elasticity
(c) Both (a) and (b)
(d) high income elasticity

84. Adam Smith advocated
(a) Custom duty
(b) Quantitative restriction
(c) Free trade
(d) None of the above

85. Quantitative restriction will
(a) increase demand for imported products.
(b) decrease demand for imported products.
(c) decrease supply of imported products.
(d) increase supply of imported products.

86. Mercantilists objected to
(a) decrease imports
(b) free trade
(c) increase export
(d) None of the above

87. Imposition of tariff leads to
(a) decrease in prices of imports.
(b) decrease in prices of exports.
(c) increase in prices of imports.
(d) increase in prices of exports.

88. Imposition of tariff will lead to
(a) deterioration in terms of trade
(b) improvement in terms of trade
(c) Both (a) and (b)
(d) no effect on terms of trade

89. Selling a product in a foreign market at a lower price than in home market is called
(a) Dumping (b) Subsidy
(c) Cartel (d) None of these

90. Protection creates
(a) Corruption (b) Inefficiency
(c) Vested interest (d) All of the above

91. OPEC controls oil export through
(a) Dumping (b) Monopoly
(c) Cartel (d) None of these

92. Import substitution involves protection of
(a) consumer items.
(b) luxury items.
(c) products which are completing with imports.
(d) export products.

93. Export promotion involves encouragement of
(a) products which are completing with imports.
(b) export products.
(c) consumer items.
(d) luxury items.

94. Korea had followed
(a) export promotion policy.
(b) import substitution policy.
(c) Both (a) and (b).
(d) None of the above.

95. India has followed
(a) export promotion policy.
(b) import substitution policy.
(c) Both (a) and (b).
(d) None of the above.

96. Protection will benefit
(a) scarce factor of production.
(b) abundant factor of production.
(c) Both (a) and (b).
(d) None of the above.

97. In case of India, protection will benefit
(a) labour intensive industries.
(b) capital intensive industries.
(c) Both (a) and (b).
(d) None of the above.

98. Organisation, which is promoting free trade is

(a) World Bank
(b) World Trade Organisation
(c) United Nations Development Programme
(d) International Monetary Fund

99. India restrained the import of
(a) Petrol
(b) Capital goods
(c) Consumer goods
(d) Raw materials

100. Immersing growth refers to a situation where
(a) gains from trade is more than offset by deterioration in terms of trade.
(b) deterioration in terms of trade more than offset gains from trade.
(c) a country promotes exports.
(d) None of the above.

101. Misallocation of resource brought about by tariff is called
(a) import cost of protection.
(b) consumption cost of protection.
(c) production cost of protection.
(d) None of the above.

102. Distortion in consumption brought about by tarrif is called
(a) consumption cost of protection.
(b) production cost of protection.
(c) import cost of protection.
(d) None of the above.

103. Stapler-Samuelsion theorem is related to
(a) Tariff
(b) Balance of payment
(c) Both (a) and (b)
(d) Income distribution

104. According to Keneysian theory, tariff will lead to
(a) decrease in national income.
(b) increase in national income.
(c) unrelated to changes in national income.
(d) constant national income.

105. Government making purchase and distribution of imported products is called
(a) Gery marketing (b) Canalisation
(c) Cartel (d) None of these

106. Food grains in India are canalised by
(a) OIL (b) MMTC
(c) ONGC (d) FCI

107. Petrol in India is canalised by
(a) ICRA (b) OIL
(c) MMTC (d) FCI

108. Metals in India is canalised by
(a) FCI (b) MMTC
(c) OIL (d) ICRA

109. Effective rate of protection is the protection to the
(a) Cost (b) Value added
(c) Revenue (d) None of these

110. Nominal rate of protection is the protection to the
(a) Revenue (b) Cost
(c) Value added (d) None of these

111. Shift in production is determined by the size of
(a) effective rate of protection.
(b) nominal rate of protection.
(c) elasticity of demand.
(d) elasticity of supply.

112. Direction of resource flows induced by tariff is properly judged from
(a) nominal rate of protection.
(b) effective ra te of protection.
(c) elasticity of demand.
(d) elasticity of supply.

113. If final tariff on the good is 10% and inputs account for 50% of the value of production, then nominal rate of protection is
(a) 30% (b) 40%
(c) 10% (d) 20%

114. In the above question, effective rate of protection is
(a) 30% (b) 40%
(c) 10% (d) 20%

115. If there are no tariffs on final goods but there is tariff on intermediate goods, effective rate of protection will be
(a) Negative (b) Zero
(c) Positive (d) None of these

116. In the above question, nominal rate of above tariff will be
(a) Zero (b) Positive
(c) Negative (d) None of these

117. In case there is lower tariff in inputs than on outputs, which one will be higher?
(a) Nominal rate of protection
(b) Effective rate of protection
(c) Both (a) and (b) are equal
(d) None of the above

118. If rate of tariff is same on inputs and outputs, which one will be higher?
(a) Effective rate of protection
(b) Nominal rate of protection
(c) Both (a) and (b) are equal
(d) None of the above

119. Listing receipts and payments in international transaction for a country is called
(a) balance of payment
(b) balance of trade
(c) balance of capital amount
(d) balance of current account

120. Balance of payment is an application of
(a) Double entry book keeping
(b) Single entry book keeping
(c) Both (a) and (b)
(d) None of the above

121. In the balance of the payment, debit and credit entries will
(a) sometimes balance
(b) always balance
(c) always remain unequal
(d) None of the above

122. In the balance of the payment, balancing of debit and credit entries is a
(a) Axion (b) Model
(c) Equation (d) Identity

123. In the balance of payment, unrequired receipts are entered as
(a) Separate entry (b) Debit entry
(c) Credit entry (d) None of these

124. In the balance of payment, gifts from foreigners is
(a) Capital inflow
(b) Import of goods
(c) Unrequited payments
(d) Unrequited receipts

125. In the balance of payment, indemnities paid by foreigners is
(a) Unrequited receipts
(b) Unrequited payments
(c) Import of goods
(d) Capital inflow

126. Sale of fixed assets to foreigners is
(a) Capital receipts
(b) Export of goods
(c) Unrequited receipts
(d) None of the above

127. Borrowing from foreigners is
(a) Capital receipts
(b) Export of goods
(c) Unrequited receipts
(d) None of the above

128. Capital payment to foreigners is
(a) Capital payments
(b) Export of goods
(c) Capital receipts
(d) None of the above

129. Purchase of fixed assets from foreigners is
(a) Capital payments
(b) Imports of goods

(c) Unrequited payments
(d) None of the above

130. Who stated "The business of distribution is called commerce"?
(a) E.E. Clark
(b) Noel Branton
(c) G.M. Whitehead
(d) G.K. Bucknall

131. Indeminites to foreigners is
(a) Unrequited payments
(b) Capital payment
(c) Unrequited receipts
(d) None of the above

132. In the balance of payments, all the ways in which country can acquire foreign currency is entered out
(a) Debit side (b) Separately
(c) Credit side (d) None of these

133. In the balance of payments, all the ways in which country can acquire foreign currency is entered in
(a) Separately (b) Credit side
(c) Debit side (d) None of these

134. Balance of trade is a
(a) Stock concept
(b) Flow concept
(c) Both (a) and (b)
(d) None of the above

135. Balance of invisibles includes
(a) Export of services
(b) Import of service
(c) Both (a) and (b)
(d) None of the above

136. Balance of invisibles is a
(a) Stock concept
(b) Flow concepts
(c) Both (a) and (b)
(d) None of the above

137. Balance of unrequited transfer is a
(a) Flow concept
(b) Stock concept
(c) Both (a) and (b)
(d) None of the above

138. Balance of capital account is
(a) Change in stock concept
(b) Stock concept
(c) Flow concept
(d) None of the above

139. Difference in export and import of services is called
(a) Balance of current account
(b) Balance of invisible
(c) Balance of trade
(d) None of the above

140. If a country has exported more than its imports, balance of trade will be
(a) Positive (b) Negative
(c) Interminate (d) Zero

141. Balance of current account includes
(a) balance of unrequited transfers
(b) balance of trade
(c) balance of invisibles
(d) All of the above

142. All items of flow nature are included in
(a) balance of unrequited transfers
(b) balance of trade
(c) balance of current account
(d) balance of invisibles

143. All items of change in stock are included is
(a) balance of invisibles
(b) balance of trade
(c) balance of current account
(d) balance of capital account

144. If a country has deficit in balance of current account, balance of capital account will be

(a) Deficits (b) Zero
(c) Surplus (d) None of these

145. Autonomous capital flows are
(a) Planned
(b) Unplanned
(c) Both (a) and (b)
(d) Can be either (a) or (b)

146. Accommodating capitals flows are
(a) Planned
(b) Unplanned
(c) Both (a) and (b)
(d) Can be either (a) or (b)

147. Autonomous capital flows are because of
(a) difference in rate of return.
(b) balance of payment problem.
(c) Both (a) and (b).
(d) Either (a) or (b).

148. Accommodating capital flows are because of
(a) difference in rate of return.
(b) balance of payment problem.
(c) Both (a) and (b).
(d) Either (a) or (b).

149. Transport document representing movements of goods is called
(a) bill of ownership
(b) bill of lading
(c) bill of exchange
(d) None of the above

150. Expressions/abbreviations with their respective definitions and the obligations that each implies for the buyer and the seller is called
(a) Harmonised system
(b) Loading
(c) Incoterm
(d) None of the above

151. Export is usually valued at
(a) FOB (b) CFR
(c) CIF (d) FAS

152. Import is usually valued at
(a) CFR (b) FOB
(c) FAS (d) CIF

153. Commitment on the part of the bank to place an agreed sum at the seller's disposal on behalf of the buyer under precisely defined conditions is called
(a) Letter of credit
(b) Bill of exchange
(c) Bill of loading
(d) None of the above

154. All non-rupee exchange rates deals done in India are
(a) Dollar rates (b) Cross rate
(c) Exchange rates (d) Rupee rates

155. Accommodating capital flows are
(a) Planned
(b) Unplanned
(c) Both (a) and (b)
(d) Either (a) or (b)

156. Accommodating capital flows are
(a) Export
(b) Ex-ante
(c) Both (a) and (b)
(d) Either (a) or (b)

157. Autonomous capital flows are
(a) Export
(b) Ex-ante
(c) Both (a) and (b)
(d) Either (a) or (b)

158. Participants in autonomous capital flows are
(a) Individuals (b) Government
(c) Firms (d) All of the above

159. Participants in accommodating capital flows are
(a) Firms (b) Individuals
(c) Government (d) All of the above

160. Imbalance in the balance of payment can be corrected through policy changes in

(a) Current account
(b) Capital account
(c) Both (a) and (b)
(d) Either (a) or (b)

161. Balance of payment can be corrected by changes in current account through
(a) Canalisation
(b) Devaluation of currency
(c) Quantitative restriction
(d) All of the above

162. Balance of payment can be corrected by changes in capital account through
(a) Devaluation (b) Borrowing
(c) Canalisation (d) All of the above

163. In case of gold standard, equilibrium is maintained by
(a) Canalisation
(b) Capital flows
(c) Tariff
(d) None of the above

164. Canalisation is resorted to in case of
(a) Essential commodities
(b) Bulk commodities
(c) Both (a) and (b)
(d) Luxury goods

165. Gold standard is an example of
(a) floating exchange rate
(b) fixed exchange rate
(c) Both of the above
(d) None of the above

166. In case of fixed exchange rate regime, exchange rate is fixed by
(a) Individuals
(b) Government
(c) Companies
(d) None of the above

167. In case of fixed exchange rate regime, adjustment in balance of payment takes place through
(a) changes in interest rate
(b) changes in price level
(c) changes in exchange rate
(d) None of the above

168. Fixed exchange rate can survive in an economy if there is
(a) socialistic economy
(b) government intervention
(c) free market economy
(d) None of the above

169. Flexible exchange rate is based on concept of
(a) Demand theory
(b) Supply theory
(c) Both (a) and (b)
(d) None of the above

170. The Swan diagram explains
(a) both internal and external equilibrium.
(b) either internal or external equilibrium.
(c) internal equilibrium.
(d) external equilibriurn.

171. Under a system of flexible exchange rates, disequilibrium in balance of payment gets automatically corrected through
(a) decrease in tax
(b) increase in money supply
(c) devaluation
(d) None of the above

172. A change in the value of ₹ from ₹ 50 = 1$ to ₹ 55 = 1$ means
(a) Appreciation of Dollar
(b) Appreciation of Rupee
(c) Depreciation of Dollar
(d) None of the above

173. A balance of payment surplus can be corrected through
(a) increase in interest
(b) export promotion
(c) appreciation of currency
(d) exchange control

174. When a nation imposes an import tariff, the nation's offer curve will
(a) move closer to the axis measuring exports.
(b) no shift will take place.
(c) shift away from the axis measuring exports.
(d) None of the above.

175. Which one of the following items in the balance of payment is invisible
(a) Travel (b) Gifts
(c) Export of goods (d) Shipping

176. If automatic income adjustment mechanism operates in the real world, it will bring about (adjustment) in BOP
(a) Incompletely (b) Partially
(c) Completely (d) None of these

177. With one of the following is likely to help in remedying an adverse balance of payment?
(a) Reduction in custom duty
(b) Revaluation of currency
(c) Devaluation of currency
(d) Reduction in taxes

178. The imposition of custom duty improves nations welfare
(a) Always (b) Never
(c) Sometimes (d) None of these

179. The devaluation by a country which has some unemployed resources will have a positive effect on trade balances provided the propensity to absorb is
(a) Greater than one
(b) Infinity
(c) Less than one
(d) Zero

180. Which one of the following methods of protection depends for success on the elasticity of demand for imports being greater than unity?
(a) Quantitative restriction
(b) Restriction on capital inflow
(c) Canalisation
(d) Custom duty

181. If a nation facing a deficit in balance of payment uses expenditure increasing policies to correct the unemployment, the deficit is likely to
(a) Decrease
(b) Remain constant
(c) Increase
(d) None of the above

182. When no imported inputs are used in the production of a commodity, the effective rate of tariff on the commodity is
(a) equal to the nominal rate.
(b) greater than nominal rate.
(c) lower than nominal rate.
(d) None of the above.

183. For a country passing through depression, devaluation is an attractive policy provided propensity to absorb is less than unity, because it will have a positive effect on
(a) National income
(b) Balance of payment
(c) Both (a) and (b)
(d) None of the above

184. Vertical straight line portion of the offer curve depicts elasticity equal to
(a) Infinity
(b) Greater than unity
(c) Unity
(d) Less than unity

185. When an economy is fully employed, the main favourable effect of devaluation on the balance of payment is through
(a) increase in imports
(b) decrease in absorption
(c) change in real national income
(d) decrease in exports

186. Balance of payments under flexible exchange rates are corrected through
(a) Direct control (b) Canalisation
(c) Devaluation (d) Depreciation

187. In case of gold standard system, decrease in the value of currency with respect to gold is called
(a) Depreciation (b) Appreciation
(c) Devaluation (d) Revaluation

188. In case a country has unemployed resources, devaluation of its currency will lead to
(a) Increase in national income
(b) Increase in exports
(c) Increase in production
(d) All of the above

189. Devaluation will improve when elasticity of demand of country's exports and imports is
(a) Infinity
(b) Equal to one
(c) Greater than one
(d) Less than one

190. Expenditure switching policies used to correct deficits in balance of payments works mainly through changes in
(a) Exchange rates
(b) Interest rate
(c) Capital flows
(d) None of the above

191. Increase in budget deficit leads to
(a) deterioration in balance of payment
(b) improvement in balance of payment
(c) no effect on balance of payment
(d) Either (b) or (c)

192. Deficit in balance of payment can be solved by
(a) expenditure reducing policies
(b) expenditure switching policies
(c) Both (a) and (b)
(d) None of the above

193. The 'absorption approach' of analysing balance of payment was formulated by
(a) Sidney Alexander
(b) Marshall and Learners
(c) M. Freidman
(d) None of the above

194. Expenditure reducing policies can improve deficit balance of payment through
(a) increasing taxes.
(b) increase in rate of interest.
(c) reducing government expenditure.
(d) All of the above.

195. Exchange rate under flexible exchange system is determined by
(a) ministry of finance.
(b) forces of demand and supply of foreign exchange.
(c) central bank.
(d) None of the above.

196. Exchange rate in different geographical areas converge because of
(a) Insurance cover (b) Arbitrage
(c) Speculation (d) Hedging

197. Imbalance in balance of payment is corrected under gold standard through
(a) changes in interest rates
(b) changes in money supply
(c) Both (a) and (b)
(d) change in tariff

198. Foreign exchange is demanded by
(a) Importers
(b) Buyers of fixed assets abroad
(c) Both (a) and (b)
(d) Borrowing from abroad

199. Foreign exchange is supplied by
(a) Exporters
(b) Importers
(c) Borrowing from abroad
(d) Buyers of fixed assets abroad

200. The appropriate expenditure-switching policy to correct a deficit in the balance of payment is
(a) Monetary policy (b) Fiscal policy
(c) Revaluation (d) Devaluation

201. As a result of imposition of tariff, a nation's offer curve will
(a) shift towards axis measuring exports.
(b) shift towards axis measuring imports.
(c) remain unaffected.
(d) None of the above.

202. The purchasing power parity theory was formulated by
(a) Gustov Cassel
(b) Alfred Marshall
(c) Learner
(d) None of the above

203. Offer curves were developed by
(a) A. Pigou (b) David Ricardo
(c) Alfred Marshall (d) J.M. Keynes

204. The law of reciprocal demand is associated with
(a) J.S. Mill (b) David Ricardo
(c) Alfred Marshall (d) None of these

205. Mint parity theory is applicable only when countries are on
(a) different metallic standard.
(b) bimetallic standard.
(c) same metallic standard.
(d) None of the above.

206. In case of Mint parity theory, foreign exchange rate is determined on the basis of
(a) Demand for foreign exchange
(b) Purchasing of the countries
(c) Metallic contents of the two money units
(d) None of the above

207. Which theory states that equilibrium rate of foreign exchange between two inconvertible currencies is determined by the ratio of their respective purchasing powers?
(a) Balance of payment theory
(b) Mint parity theory
(c) Purchasing power parity theory
(d) None of the above

208. Country with higher rate of inflation will have to ______ in order to balance the balance of payment.
(a) revalue (b) devalue
(c) Both (a) and (b) (d) None of these

209. According to Balance of Payment theory, foreign exchange rate is determined by
(a) Autonomous factors
(b) Internal prices
(c) Money supply
(d) None of the above

210. Under balance of payment theory, foreign exchange rate is determined by
(a) Price of gold
(b) Demand and supply of foreign exchange
(c) Change in inflation
(d) None of the above

211. Physical delivery of foreign exchange has to take place in case of
(a) Future market
(b) Spot market
(c) Forward market
(d) Option market

212. Market at which transaction will be consummated at some specified time in future is called
(a) Forward market
(b) Spot market
(c) Current market
(d) Capital market

213. Exporters can reduce their risk by
(a) Arbitrage (b) Speculation
(c) Hedging (d) None of these

214. In case exporters enter forward market to sell foreign exchange at specified rate with choice to accept the contract or reject it, then it is called
(a) Futures (b) Spots
(c) Derivatives (d) Options

215. Shape of the offer curve are determined by
(a) Supply conditions
(b) Demand conditions
(c) Both (a) and (b)
(d) None of the above

216. Spot and forward market are intimately linked together by
(a) Hedging
(b) Speculation
(c) Interest arbitrage
(d) All of the above

217. Speculation in foreign exchange market is possible if market is operating under
(a) silver standard
(b) free exchange rate
(c) gold standard
(d) Both (a) and (b)

218. Devaluation takes place with respect to
(a) gold
(b) differential rate of monetary standards
(c) other currencies
(d) None of the above

219. Depreciation takes place with respect to
(a) gold
(b) differential rate of monetary standards
(c) other currencies
(d) None of the above

220. Expenditure switching policies primarily work by changing
(a) Investment
(b) Relative prices
(c) National income
(d) Consumption

221. Direct control includes
(a) expenditure switching policies.
(b) expenditure reducing policies.
(c) Both (a) and (b)
(d) Neither (a) nor (b)

222. Floating exchange rate became common 1950s
(a) 1960s (b) 1980s
(c) 1950s (d) 1960s

223. Most important of direct effects of absorption is
(a) Income distribution
(b) Money illusion
(c) Real balance effect
(d) None of the above

224. Exchange rates could diverge from their par values within a margin of 1% on either side of the exchange rate parity in the system of
(a) flexible exchange rate
(b) fixed exchange rate
(c) crawling peg
(d) adjustable peg

225. Exchange rates could diverge from their par values within a margin of 2.25% on either side of the exchange rate parity in the system of
(a) crawling peg
(b) adjustable peg
(c) flexible exchange rate
(d) fixed exchange rate

226. Britain adopted gold standard in
(a) 1810s (b) 1850s
(c) 1980s (d) 1890s

227. Gold standard was suspended at the time of
(a) Great Depression of 1930s
(b) First World War
(c) Second World War
(d) Oil Crisis of 1970s

228. Under gold standard equilibrium in Balance of payment takes place through
(a) flow of gold
(b) change in exchange rate
(c) tariff
(d) canalisation

229. Under gold standard, a country with deficit will have
(a) inflow of foreign exchange.
(b) outflow of foreign exchange.
(c) outflow of gold.
(d) inflow of gold.

230. After First World War, gold standard was restored in
(a) 1920s (b) 1930s
(c) 1940s (d) 1950s

231. In 1930s each country dealt with its external balance of payment by resorting to
(a) exchanging clearing arrangement
(b) blocked accounts
(c) Both (a) and (b)
(d) All of the above

232. In which year did the nations gathered at Bretton Woods?
(a) 1941 (b) 1942
(c) 1944 (d) 1943

233. Bretton Woods led to formation of
(a) IBRD (b) GATT
(c) IMF (d) All of the above

234. Bretton Woods system introduced
(a) adjustable peg system
(b) crawling peg system
(c) fixed exchange rate
(d) free exchange rate

235. Bretton Woods system introduced exchange rate which had characteristics of
(a) free exchange rate
(b) fixed exchange rate
(c) Both (a) and (b)
(d) Neither (a) nor (b)

236. Under Bretton Woods system, key currency was
(a) Yen (b) Mark
(c) Pound (d) Dollar

237. From 1945 to 1970, the world was on
(a) Pound standard
(b) Dollar standard
(c) Silver standard
(d) Gold standard

238. Bretton Woods system broke down in 1970's because of
(a) USA's trade deficit
(b) USA's budgetary deficit
(c) Both (a) and (b)
(d) Neither (a) nor (b)

239. In 1971, the dollar was delinked from
(a) SDR (b) Silver
(c) Gold (d) Pound

240. USA's deficit in balance of payment and surplus of Japan and Germany led to the problem of
(a) Devaluation (b) Depreciation
(c) Seignorange (d) None of these

241. Since 1971, world has been operating under
(a) Crawling peg
(b) Clean floating
(c) Dirty floating
(d) All of the above

242. Which institution provided finance to meet short-term balance of payment problems?
(a) GATT (b) WTO
(c) IMF (d) IBRD

243. Special drawing rights was created by
(a) ADB (b) IBRD
(c) WTO (d) IMF

244. Long-term financial assistance for development purpose is provided by
(a) ADB (b) WTO
(c) IMF (d) World Bank

245. International Bank for Reconstruction and Development was also called as
(a) World Bank
(b) African Bank
(c) Asian Development Bank
(d) None of the above

246. Asian Development Bank operates in regions of
(a) Asia (b) Pacific
(c) Atlantic (d) Both (a) and (b)

247. Asian Development Bank operates under the
(a) ECAFE (b) IMF
(c) IBRD (d) Both (a) and (b)

248. GATT was changed to
(a) WTO (b) ADB
(c) IBRD (d) IMF

249. International Trade Organisation came into existence in
(a) 1955 (b) 1965
(c) 1945 (d) None of these

250. Most favoured nation clause was introduced by
(a) ADB (b) IBRD
(c) WTO (d) GATT

251. Which of the agreement of GATT is related to textiles?
(a) MFA (b) TRIMs
(c) TRIPs (d) Both (a) and (b)

252. Which of the agreement of GATT is related to investment?
(a) TRIPs (b) TRIMs
(c) MFA (d) Both (a) and (b)

253. Which of the agreement of GATT is related to intellectual property?
(a) TRIPs (b) MFA
(c) TRIMs (d) Both (a) and (b)

254. Dunkel proposal was discussed in
(a) Uruguay round
(b) Tokyo round
(c) Kennedy round
(d) All of the above

255. Dunkel proposal was discussed in
(a) Asian Development Bank
(b) World Bank
(c) IMF
(d) WTO

256. Uruguay round of negotiations covered
(a) Tariff measures
(b) Non-tariff measures
(c) Neither (a) nor (b)
(d) Both (a) and (b)

257. Uruguay round of negotiations covered
(a) TRIMs (b) MFA
(c) TRIPs (d) All of the above

258. UNCTAD has main function of
(a) assuring free trade.
(b) managing internal liquidity.
(c) TRIMs.
(d) dealing with developing countries.

259. Cario declaration of developing countries called for convening of
(a) UNCTAD (b) ADB
(c) IMP (d) IBRD

260. GATT is a
(a) Binding contract (b) Organisation
(c) Corporate body (d) Institution

261. Structural adjustment facility is provided by
(a) WTO (b) IBRD
(c) IMF (d) ADB

262. Enhanced structural adjustment facility is
(a) WTO (b) IBRD
(c) IMF (d) ADB

263. If the IMF's holdings of member's currency are less than its quota, the difference is called
(a) Reserve tranche
(b) Paper tranche
(c) Credit tranche
(d) Both (a) and (b)

264. Each credit tranche consists of _____ of the member's quota.
(a) 30% (b) 35%
(c) 20% (d) 25%

265. Each member gets ______ credit branches.
(a) 1 (b) 2
(c) 3 (d) 4

266. IMF levies charge for using
(a) Credit tranche
(b) Reserve tranche
(c) Both (a) and (b)
(d) Neither (a) or (b)

267. Compensatory and contingency financial facility is provided by
(a) ADB (b) GATT
(c) IBRD (d) IMF

268. India is a member of
(a) ADB (b) IMF
(c) WTO (d) All of the above

269. Arthur Dunkel headed
(a) World Bank (b) ADB
(c) IMF (d) GATT

270. Uruguay round of multilateral trade negotiations was launched in
(a) 1985 (b) 1987
(c) 1984 (d) 1986

271. Special drawing rights scheme was initiated in
(a) 1970s (b) 1940s
(c) 1960s (d) 1980s

272. Major location of Euro currency market is
(a) London (b) Delhi
(c) Berlin (d) Paris

273. Currency of European Union is called
(a) Euro (b) Mark
(c) Pound (d) Bankcore

274. Finance for development of infrastructure is provided by
(a) UNCTAD (b) GATT
(c) World Bank (d) IMF

275. SDRs are allocated to member nation in proportion to their
(a) National income
(b) Population
(c) Subscription to the IMF
(d) Poverty

276. Non-regional members of the Asian Development Bank are
(a) UK (b) Canada
(c) USA (d) All of the above

277. International Development Association is administered by
(a) ADB (b) GATT
(c) IMF (d) IBRD

278. Group-24 is a specialised body of
(a) G-7 (b) UNO
(c) UNDP (d) G-77

279. UNDP is a part of
(a) UNO (b) ADB
(c) IMF (d) IBRD

280. Soft loans to underdeveloped countries is provided by
(a) ADB (b) GATT
(c) IBRD (d) IDA

281. Given that

l : literacy rate of the whole society

l_f : literacy rate for female population

l_m : literacy rate for male population, and

S : ratio between female and total population

Which one of the following is correct?

(a) $i = i_f + \left(\frac{S}{1+S}\right) i_m(1 + s)$

(b) $i = i_f S + i_m(1 - S)$

(c) $i = i_f S + i_m(1 + S)$

(d) None of the above

282. L.V. Charlier collected data on (i) the stork population in Oslo and (ii) the number of babies born in the city in 40 years. He found the correlation coefficient between (i) and (ii) to be 0.86.
From this it can be inferred that
(a) the correlation leads to a mysterious connection between the rate of stork and human populations in Norway
(b) the correlation is not very high
(c) the correlation is spurious
(d) the correlation is very high

283. The mercantilist theory of economic growth is primarily concerned with an increase in the
(a) size of population.
(b) volume of money in circulation through the import of gold.
(c) surplus in the balance of trade.
(d) state intervention for the creation of conditions for efficient entrepreneurial functions.

284. The country can improve its balance of payments by devaluation when the sum of elasticities of demand for exports and imports is
(a) less than unity
(b) greater than unity
(c) equal to unity
(d) zero

285. The Purchasing Power Parity (PPP) theory of the exchange rate implies that the currency of a country A would depreciate against that of country B if
(a) the normal interest rate in A exceeds that in B.
(b) the growth rate of GDP in B exceeds that in A.
(c) foreign direct investment moves from B to A.
(d) the inflation rate in A exceeds that in B.

286. In a freely floating exchange rate system
(a) exchange rate is determined by market forces.
(b) the current account and capital account add to zero.
(c) each account can individually be equal to zero.
(d) all the above statements are correct.

287. The balance of payment is an ____ system.
(a) tourist (b) social
(c) accounting (d) environmental

288. NABARD is
(a) A block (b) A department
(c) A bank (d) A board

289. Which of the following is not the items of current account?
(a) Investment income
(b) Private transfers
(c) Trade balance
(d) Amortisation

290. Which section is not of balance of payment?
(a) Loss account
(b) Capital account
(c) Official reserve account
(d) Current account

291. Which conference gives the birth to the "International Monetary Fund"?
(a) Bretownwoods (b) TIDA
(c) Congress (d) LIBOR

292. Which of the following bodies is not of IMF?

(a) Executive Board
(b) Board of Governor's
(c) UCO Bank
(d) Managing Director

293. Which is not part of the current account?
(a) Merchandise exports
(b) Merchandise imports
(c) Capital accounts
(d) Balance of current account

294. Which of the following is not the items of capital account?
(a) Disbursements
(b) External assistance
(c) NRI deposits
(d) Official transfers

295. Which of the following is not included under World Bank objective'?
(a) Reconstruction and Economic Development
(b) Encouragement to Capital Investment
(c) Delayed Implementation
(d) Balance Development

296. Which of the following is not included under the management of World Bank'?
(a) Chairman
(b) Executive Committee
(c) Board of Governor
(d) RBI's Governor

297. The International Finance Corporation came into force on
(a) August 1956
(b) January 1956
(c) December 1956
(d) July 1956

298. The World Bank formed on
(a) 1980 (b) 1966
(c) 1970 (d) 1944

299. The World Bank formed as a body of IMF?
(a) Legal body
(b) Holding body
(c) Competitive body
(d) Complementary body

300. What were the initial capital of World Bank?
(a) 2,000 million $
(b) 12,000 million $
(c) 10,000 million $
(d) 18,405 million $

301. Aid India club founded by the
(a) RBI
(b) India
(c) United Nations of State
(d) World Bank

302. Which of the following is not the objective of IMF?
(a) Reduction of International Payment
(b) Impose of Exchange Control
(c) Removal of Disparities in International Payment
(d) Removal of Exchange Control

303. Who is the successor of GATT?
(a) IFC (b) World Bank
(c) ABB (d) WTO

304. GATT is a
(a) Policy (b) Organisation
(c) Agreement (d) Method

305. Who proposed the proposal for formation of IDA first time in the America?
(a) E.S. Monrony (b) A. Linken
(c) D.S. Morya (d) B.L. Tandon

306. The functions of WTO has been start from
(a) 1 Jan. 1995 (b) 1 Jan. 1997
(c) 1 Jan. 1994 (d) 1 Feb. 1996

307. The minimum members of board of governance in World Bank may be
(a) 15 (b) 20
(c) 12 (d) 18

308. What are the authorised capital of the World Bank at this time'?

(a) 13,000 crore $
(b) 4,200 crore $
(c) 30,000 million $
(d) 18,405 crore $

309. Doha conference is related with
(a) World Bank (b) GATT
(c) USA (d) WTO

310. Eighth conference of GATT has been held at
(a) Madras (b) New Delhi
(c) Uruguay Round (d) Hempasayer

311. Inside trading is related to
(a) Horce racing
(b) Share market
(c) Public expenditure
(d) Taxation

312. The headquarter of Asian Development Bank (ADB) is at
(a) Hong Kong (b) Tokyo
(c) Singapore (d) Manila

313. GATT came into force in
(a) 1959 (b) 1956
(c) 1949 (d) 1947

314. A direct investment is one that gives the investor a controlling interest in a company.
(a) Multinational company
(b) Domestic company
(c) Foreign company
(d) Transnational company

315. A global company sometimes called
(a) A transnational company
(b) A globally integrated company
(c) A multidomestic company
(d) A joint stock company

316. The main security guard of International Trade is
(a) WTO (b) IFC
(c) IMF (d) World Bank

317. When India became the member of 'World Bank'?
(a) In 1950 (b) In 1975
(c) In 1945 (d) In 1947

318. "Foreign Trade has played a crucial role in India's economic development". Is this statement true?
(a) False (b) Can't say
(c) True (d) Sometimes

319. Export processing zones has been converted into
(a) Special Economic Zones
(b) Economic Export Zones
(c) Special Export Zones
(d) None of the above

320. The export-oriented units scheme introduced
(a) In 1985 (b) In 1984
(c) In 1981 (d) In 1980

321. The Government of India has issued notification on for conversion of the existing processing zones.
(a) 1 November 2001
(b) 1 December 2001
(c) 1 November 2000
(d) 1 December 2000

322. Which part of separated UTI is under SEBI's regulation?
(a) LM-II (b) UTI-I
(c) Both the above (d) None of these

323. A new scheme for setting up Special Economic Zones in the country to promote export was announced by the government in the Export and Import policy on
(a) 31 March 2003 (b) 31 March 2001
(c) 31 March 2002 (d) 31 March 2000

324. The balance of payment composed of two accounts, which are
(a) Current account
(b) Capital account

(c) Company account
(d) Both (a) and (b)

325. Induced capital movements have great significance from the point of view of formulation by a country.
(a) Fiscal policy
(b) Tax policy
(c) Monetary policy
(d) Economic policy

326. Each transaction is recorded as debits and credit side of balance of payment for amount.
(a) Loss (b) Reserve
(c) Large (d) Equal

327. The current account is made up of visibles and
(a) Expect (b) Invisibles
(c) Constraint (d) None

328. The account shows the inflow and outflow of capital commitments whose maturity is longer than
(a) Three year (b) One year
(c) Four year (d) Two year

329. The balance of payment is a funds statement (source and uses) that reflects changes in assets, liabilities and net worth during a period.
(a) Given (b) Financial
(c) Marketing (d) Specified

330. T.T. means in context of foreign exchange rates.
(a) Telegraphic transfer
(b) Transaction transfer
(c) Treasury and token
(d) Telephonic transfer

331. Premium implies that the foreign currency is expensive and has an high price than the
(a) Spot rate (b) Interest rate
(c) Forward rate (d) Both (a) and (b)

332. Cable rate known as
(a) Spot rate (b) Token rate
(c) Interest rate (d) Foreign rate

333. SDRs refer which term
(a) Special Drop Rotation
(b) Special Drawing Rights
(c) Special Deposits Receipts
(d) None of the above

334. LIBID means
(a) London Interbank Bought Rate
(b) London International Bank Rate
(c) London Interbank Bound Rate
(d) London Interbank Bid Rate

335. The market rate of exchange is a short-term rate of exchange that prevails in the
(a) Trade (b) Market
(c) Goods (d) All of the above

336. Which of the following objects is not objects of IMF?
(a) Issue of notes
(b) Short-term assistance
(c) Restrictions on business boundness
(d) Long-term capital investment

337. Which country is not permanent member of World Bank?
(a) America (b) France
(c) England (d) India

338. IMF indicates
(a) Indian Music Folio
(b) International Monetary Fund
(c) Indian Monetary Fund
(d) International Money Fund

339. International Monetary Fund was formed in
(a) 1947 (b) 1946
(c) 1950 (d) 1945

340. On _____, the Government of India indicated its decision to delink the rupee from dollar and to adopt a central rate for rupee.

(a) December 20, 1971
(b) December 19, 1960
(c) December 20, 1985
(d) December 20, 1980

341. Impage of products are affected by where they are
(a) Sold (b) Lost
(c) Bought (d) Made

342. An importer broker is an intermediary who helps an importer
(a) Clear customs
(b) According rules
(c) High force
(d) None of the above

343. The World Bank is an
(a) International agency
(b) International money fund
(c) International office
(d) International market

344. A company may enter a market gradually by limiting ______ coverage.
(a) economical (b) sociological
(c) political (d) geographic

345. The dollar crisis in resulted into an increased supply of the U.S. dollar and depreciation in its value in the international market.
(a) 1970 (b) 1974
(c) 1975 (d) 1971

346. The SDRs can be used by the participating countries.
(a) Freely
(b) Conditionally
(c) Warranties
(d) Unconditionally

347. If a brand name is used for a class of product, the company may lose the
(a) Goodwill (b) Profit
(c) Trademark (d) Ownership

348. Membership in IDA is open to all members of the
(a) Asian Development Bank
(b) Reserve Bank of India
(c) World Trade Organisation
(d) World Bank

349. The SDRs allocated by the
(a) America (b) RBI
(c) WTO (d) IMF

350. The International Development Association (IDA) was set up in
(a) 1960 (b) 1942
(c) 1970 (d) 1945

351. The IBRD known popularly as the
(a) IMF (b) World Bank
(c) IDA (d) WTO

352. Which of the following is not currency?
(a) Lira (b) Loko
(c) Mark (d) Pound

353. LIBOR means
(a) London Interbank Bid Rate
(b) London Interbank Offer Rate
(c) London Interbanking Original Rate
(d) London International Banking Rate

354. A US a dollar deposit with a bank in London is a
(a) Euro dollar deposit
(b) US dollar deposit
(c) Pound US dollar deposit
(d) Japani US dollar deposit

355. The World Bank is owned by
(a) Private firms
(b) RBI
(c) United States of America
(d) Member Countries

356. Rapid economic development or economic growth requires most efficient use of the
(a) Fixed assets
(b) Country's resources

(c) Foreign investment
(d) International trade

357. The IMF is governed by its
(a) Board of Governors
(b) A Managing Director
(c) A President
(d) An Executive Board

358. According to economic aspect, a typical MNC is a company with net sales of ____ or more.
(a) 100 crore dollars
(b) 50 crore dollars
(c) 1000 million dollars
(d) 100 million dollars

359. Countries with per capita incomes of less than $ 925 are eligible for
(a) IDA Credits (b) UBI Credits
(c) IMF Credits (d) RBI Credits

360. The Bank's Board of Executive Directors, which is resident at the World Bank's headquarter in
(a) Washington (b) Jaipur
(c) Germany (d) Hong Kong

361. Which one of the following is not the G-7 member/members?
(a) Itally (b) France
(c) India (d) Canada

362. Who has shown, how International Trade leads to equalisation of factor prices?
(a) Prof. I.M. Keynes
(b) Prof. Horst Kohaler
(c) Prof. P.U. Duglus
(d) Prof. Bertil Ohlin

363. How many per cent of the subscribed capital of World Bank has been called and paid by member countries?
(a) 15% (b) 12%
(c) 20% (d) 10%

364. The United States has the largest shareholding in
(a) IDA (b) World Bank
(c) IFC (d) RBI

365. Which country has the power to veto any changes in the World Bank's capital base Articles of Agreement?
(a) France
(b) India
(c) United Kingdom
(d) United States

366. For political co-operation which body came into existence?
(a) Reserve Bank of India
(b) World Bank
(c) International Monetary Fund
(d) United Nations Organisation

367. International trade brings developing countries in contact with
(a) Developing country
(b) Developed nations
(c) Sustainable growth
(d) Modern ideas

368. The World Bank is an open partnership between the Bank's 185
(a) Member countries
(b) Asian countries
(c) European countries
(d) Non-member countries

369. When the Indian rupee was developed on with September 1949. US par value come reduced to
(a) 2.16866 gram of gold
(b) 0.816621 gram of gold
(c) 0.186621 gram of gold
(d) 0.34667 gram of gold

370. SDR is
(a) An assets
(b) A liability
(c) An international unit of currency
(d) A paper gold

371. Total quarters of IMF is
(a) ₹ 340.4 billion
(b) ₹ 350.6 billion
(c) ₹ 360 crores
(d) SDR 212.4 billion

372. The International Monetary and Financial Committee consists of
(a) 30 (b) 24
(c) 7 (d) 15

373. The World Bank and the IDA are _____ International Financial Institutions.
(a) Different (b) Same
(c) Complementary (d) Private

374. When the IDA started its functioning?
(a) 8-11-1960 (b) 8-12-1960
(c) 13-6-1900 (d) 13-9-1906

375. The quotas of all the member countries with the IMF are valued in terms of
(a) Dollar (b) Swaps
(c) SDR (d) GDR

376. International Development Association administered by the
(a) RBI
(b) United States Organisation
(c) World Bank
(d) EURO Bank

377. The decision to establish the International Monetary Fund was made at conference held in Bretton woods in July
(a) 1945 (b) 1944
(c) 1950 (d) 1948

378. Who can become a member of the IDA?
(a) Any firm
(b) President of country
(c) Any company
(d) Any member country of the World Bank

379. New international plan of reserve known as
(a) US Treasury Bills
(b) US Dollar Deposits
(c) Global Depository Receipts (GDRs)
(d) Special Drawing Rights (SDRs)

380. The Multilateral Investment Guarantee Agency was created in
(a) 1995 (b) 1991
(c) 1988 (d) 1986

381. When International Financial Corporation came into existence?
(a) 20-6-1960 (b) 20-6-1963
(c) 20-6-1954 (d) 20-6-1957

382. 'SAPTA' is related to
(a) Security (b) Environment
(c) Education (d) Trade

383. Who is the Governor for India in ADB?
(a) RBI Governor
(b) Prime Minister
(c) Minister of Finance
(d) President of India

384. The European Coal and Steel Community formed in
(a) 1958 (b) 1960
(c) 1952 (d) 1955

385. First part of GATT consists of
(a) A code of fair trade
(b) Money
(c) Provision
(d) Staff

386. The organisation for European Economic Co-operation formed in
(a) 1945 (b) 1948
(c) 1950 (d) 1940

387. Which agreement was signed at Hawana conference?
(a) GATT (b) MIGA
(c) WTO (d) ECM

388. IDA is established by
(a) IMF (b) World Bank
(c) USO (d) ADB

389. The membership of the ADB (Asian Development Bank) is open to all countries in
(a) Erope (b) South Asia
(c) Africa (d) Asia

390. The World Bank gives financial assistance only to its
(a) Staff
(b) Member countries
(c) Governor
(d) Managing director

391. ECM means
(a) European common market
(b) Euro currency
(c) Euro market
(d) Euro money

392. The WTO covers
(a) Services
(b) Intellectual property
(c) Both (a) and (b)
(d) Goods

393. The UNCTAD is a permanent organisation of the
(a) GATT (b) IMF
(c) UNO (d) RBI

394. The GATT conference at Brussels in 1964 is known as the
(a) Kennedy Round
(b) Clinton
(c) Koolfs
(d) Prof. Holo Ports

395. The authorised capital of the IFC is
(a) ₹ 1000 lakh
(b) 5000 SDRs
(c) ₹ 50 crores
(d) 100 million US dollars

396. GATT was set up in
(a) 1948 (b) 1950
(c) 1947 (d) 1949

397. Who can become the member of MICA?
(a) A person
(b) Any member of World Bank
(c) A firm
(d) IMF

398. Which of the financial body promote Foreign Private Investment?
(a) IMF (b) IDA
(c) IFC (d) ADB

399. The first round of tariff negotiations was held at in April 1947.
(a) Geneva (b) Mexico
(c) New Delhi (d) Hong Kong

400. The IFC is affiliated to the
(a) ADB (b) RBI
(c) United States (d) World Bank

401. The Part IV of GATT consists of
(a) Code of conduct
(b) Money
(c) Code of trade
(d) Quotas

402. Which of the following body has been set up for promoting world trade and economic development?
(a) IFM (b) TTO
(c) IFC (d) ADB

403. EEC means
(a) Euro Currency
(b) Euro Cost
(c) European Economic Community
(d) Euro Economy

404. A change in exchange rate thus, brings about changes in the
(a) Foreign trade
(b) Export industries
(c) Balance of trade
(d) Exchange rate

405. The spot rate of exchange is quoted for the immediate delivery of

(a) Foreign rate
(b) Foreign treasury
(c) Foreign transaction
(d) Foreign exchange

406. The forward exchange rate may be quoted at a premium or at the spot rates.
(a) Proposed (b) Discount rate
(c) High price (d) All of the above

407. Governor and Executive Directors of the World Bank representing member countries of serve the corporation in similar capacities.
(a) RBI (b) IMF
(c) WTO (d) IFC

408. Which of the following is not example of foreign exchange rate?
(a) 1 US $ = ₹ 45
(b) 1 US $ = ₹ 00.07650
(c) 1 Iraqee Dinar = ₹ 30
(d) 1 Pound = ₹ = 78

409. A Euro currency deposit, is a deposit in III relevant currency with a bank outside the _______ of that currency.
(a) home country (b) foreign Ciwnll
(c) Business (d) UK country

410. GATT was the substitute of
(a) ECM (b) WTO
(c) ITO (d) IMF

411. MIGA is a member of the
(a) ADB (b) IDA
(c) World Bank (d) IMF

412. According to unit of IMF known as
(a) Special Depreciation Rate (SDR)
(b) Special Drawing Rate (SDR)
(c) Special Drawing Rights (SDR)
(d) Special Domestic Relation (SDR)

413. The Tokyo round held in
(a) 1970-76 (b) 1973-79
(c) 1964-66 (d) 1967-68

414. The organisation of the IDA is similar to that of the
(a) ICICI (b) IMF
(c) SBI (d) World Bank

415. SDR is the currency of IMF which is in the form of
(a) Silver and gold
(b) Book-keeping entry only
(c) Paper currency
(d) Gold

416. The main objective of the IDA is
(a) to promote fraud.
(b) to sell SDRs.
(c) to provide financial assistance to less developed countries on soft loan basis.
(d) to formulate policy.

417. The European common market was formed on
(a) 25-3-1960 (b) 25-3-1965
(c) 25-3-1957 (d) 25-3-1958

418. The IFC functions like a _____ investment firm.
(a) staff (b) government
(c) public (d) private

419. The headquaters of the UNCTAD is in
(a) Japan (b) Geneva
(c) Tokyo (d) Germany

420. GATT has
(a) Banks
(b) Contracting Parties
(c) Firms
(d) Members

421. The official exchange rate of Indian rupee is associated with
(a) A basket of selected companies
(b) Pound sterling
(c) Dollar
(d) SDR

422. "International Bank for Reconstruction and Development came into existence as

a consequence of IMF originated." Is this statement true?

(a) Can't say (b) Perhaps
(c) Yes (d) No

423. Which of the following is not types of disequilibrium in the balance of payment"?
(a) Cyclical disequilibrium
(b) Structural disequilibrium
(c) Secular disequilibrium
(d) Transactional disequilibrium

424. The IMF commenced operation in Washington on
(a) March 15, 1980
(b) March 15, 1960
(c) March 1, 1949
(d) March 1, 1947

425. Marketing decision covers
(a) Distribution strategies
(b) Pricing strategy
(c) Promotion strategty
(d) All of the above

426. India is not a member of
(a) UNO (b) G-15
(c) Commonwealth (d) ASEAN

427. Visible items relate to the merchandise account or the balance of trade covering the transactions relating to all goods exported and
(a) perishable nature
(b) goods
(c) general goods
(d) imported

428. "If all exchange rates fall, this evidence on appreciation in the value of the national currency". Is this statement true?
(a) Can't say (b) May be
(c) Yes (d) No

429. Which one of the following is the subsidiary of the State Trading Corporation of India meant for increasing exports?
(a) Manufacturers export agents and Export commission house.
(b) Minerals and Metals Trading Corporation of India.
(c) Mica Trading Corporation of India.
(d) Projects and Equipment Corporation of India.

430. A letter of credit is a
(a) letter containing conditions of a credit purchase or sale.
(b) letter of importer's bank agreeing to accept and pay on due date the exporter's bill.
(c) letter sent by importer to exporter sanctioning credit deal.
(d) letter from an exporter to importer sanctioning credit deal.

431. The importer cannot take delivery of goods unless he produces the
(a) certificate of origin
(b) bill of sight
(c) bill of lading
(d) shipping bill

432. Members of the WTO/GATT have not agreed even in principle on which one of the following issues?
(a) Protection of intellectual property rights.
(b) Observance of minimum labour standards.
(c) Export subsidies to agricultural produce.
(d) Dispute settlement mechanism.

433. Which one of the following best explains the term "Duty Draw Back"?
(a) Payment of duties in rupees and not in foreign currency.
(b) Refund of customs duty paid on imports and excise duty on customs purchases.

(c) Duty free import of raw materials and refund of excise duty on other indigenous purchases.
(d) Refund of excise duty for manufacture of goods exported out of the country.

434. A foreign company means
(a) a company incorporated outside India and having established place of business in India.
(b) a company incorporated in India and having a place of business outside India.
(c) Both of (a) and (b).
(d) All of the above.

435. When a full ship is hired, the shipping company issues
(a) Bill of entry (b) Shipping order
(c) R/R (d) Charter party

436. In the context of foreign trade, the CTF cost may be obtained by
(a) deducting freight and marine insurance premium for the FOB price.
(b) adding freight and marine insurance premium to the FOB price.
(c) deducting customs duties, freight and marine insurance premium from the price.
(d) adding customs duties, freight and marine insurance premium to the cost.

437. Letter of credit establishes
(a) bank account of the party.
(b) credit worthiness of the exporter.
(c) credit worthiness of the importer.
(d) None of the above.

438. In W.W. Rostow's 'Stages of Growth', the drive to maturity stage
(a) follows high mass consumption stage.
(b) completes development.
(c) follows take offstage.
(d) starts development.

439. Consider the following passage: "In a system of freely flexible exchange rates each country must be prepared to let the exchange rate fall or rise to whatever level is required to clear the foreign exchange market The authorities must not intervene. Only if these conditions are met will autonomous equilibrium in foreign exchange market and its equivalent (that is balance of payments equilibrium) be consistently achieved."
According to this passage, under freely flexible exchange rate
(a) foreign exchange market cannot bring about equilibrium.
(b) equilibrium of balance of payments is automatic.
(c) gold standard is required for equilibrium.
(d) Government's interference is necessary for equilibrium.

440. With commodity 'X' measured along the horizontal axis and commodity 'Y' measured along the vertical axis, if the production possibility curve is a straight line, then its slope would indicate
(a) the ratio of prices of X and Y.
(b) the marginal rate of transformation of X and Y.
(c) Neither of the situations indicated in (a) or (b).
(d) Both the situations indicated in (a) and (b).

441. Select True and False
1. Enterpot trade means sale of goods to a foreign country.
2. Foreign trade in subject to greater risk as compared to home trade.
3. Import trade boats home trade.
4. Foreign trade involutes the exchange of currencies.
5. Internal trade in known as foreign trade.

Codes:
(a) 1F, 2T, 3F, 4T, 5F
(b) 1F, 2T, 3T, 4F, 5F
(c) 1T, 2T, 3F, 4F, 5F
(d) 1F, 2T, 3F, 4F, 5T

Directions: Refer to the diagram given below questions 442 to 456

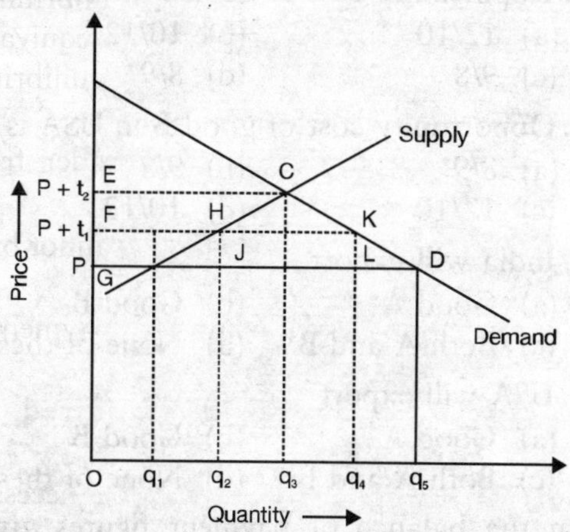

442. Loss of consumer surplus is equal to
(a) HKLG (b) IJH
(c) KLD (d) FKDG

443. Part of the consumer surplus going to government is
(a) IJH (b) GJFH
(c) JHKL (d) HKLJ

444. Part of the consumer surplus going to procedure is
(a) GIHF (b) IJH
(c) JHKL (d) FKDG

445. Production cost of protection is
(a) FKDG (b) KLD
(c) IJH (d) JHKL

446. Consumptions cost of protection is
(a) FKDG (b) KLD
(c) IJH (d) JHKL

447. Import will be zero when tariff will be
(a) t_1 (b) t_2
(c) Zero (d) None of these

448. At price P, import is equal to
(a) q_1q_4 (b) q_1q_5
(c) q_1q_2 (d) q_1q_3

449. At tarrif t_1 import is equal to
(a) q_2q_3 (b) q_2q_5
(c) q_1q_5 (d) q_2q_4

450. At tarrif t_2 import is equal to
(a) q_2q_4 (b) q_1q_5
(c) q_2q_3 (d) zero

451. Domestic production at price P is equal to
(a) Oq_2 (b) Oq_3
(c) Oq_4 (d) Oq_1

452. Domestic production at tarrif t_1 is equal to
(a) Oq_3 (b) Oq_4
(c) Oq_2 (d) Oq_1

453. Domestic production at tarrif t_2 is equal to
(a) Oq_3 (b) Oq_4
(c) Oq_1 (d) Oq_2

454. Domestic consumption at price P is equal to
(a) Oq_1 (b) Oq_2
(c) Oq_3 (d) None of these

455. Domestic consumption at tariff t_1 is equal to
(a) Oq_3 (b) Oq_4
(c) Oq_1 (d) Oq_2

456. Domestic consumption at tariff t_2 is equal to
(a) Oq_1 (b) Oq_2
(c) Oq_3 (d) Oq

Directions: If cost conditions of goods are as follows. Questions from 457 to 462

Labour cost of production (in hours)

	1 unit of good A	1 unit of good B
India	10	20
USA	20	10

457. India will export
(a) Good A (b) Good B
(c) Goods A and B (d) None of these

458. In the above question, USA will export
(a) Good A (b) Good B
(c) Both A and B (d) None of these

459. Opportunity cost of good A in India is
(a) 2 (b) 8
(c) 0.5 (d) 4

460. Opportunity cost of good A in USA is
(a) 2 (b) 0.5
(c) 8 (d) 4

461. Opportunity cost of good B in India is
(a) 2 (b) 8
(c) 0.5 (d) 1

462. Opportunity cost of good B in USA is
(a) 3 (b) 2
(c) 1 (d) 0.5

Directions: If cost conditions of goods are as follows. Questions 463 to 472

Labour cost of production (in hours)

	1 unit of good A	1 unit of good B
India	120	100
USA	80	90

463. USA is efficient in producing
(a) Good A (b) Good B
(c) Both A and B (d) None of these

464. India is efficient in producing
(a) Good A (b) Good B
(c) Both A and B (d) None of these

465. USA has comparative advantage in
(a) Good A (b) Good B
(c) Both A and B (d) None of these

466. India has a comparative advantage in
(a) Good A (b) Good B
(c) Both A and B (d) None of these

467. Opportunity cost of good A in India is
(a) 12/10 (b) 10/12
(c) 8/9 (d) 9/8

468. Opportunity cost of good A in USA is
(a) 10/12 (b) 12/10
(c) 9/8 (d) 8/9

469. Opportunity cost of good B in India is
(a) 12/10 (b) 10/12
(c) 9/8 (d) 8/9

470. Opportunity cost of good B in USA is
(a) 8/9 (b) 9/8
(c) 12/10 (d) 10/12

471. India will export
(a) Good A (b) Good B
(c) Both A and B (d) None of these

472. USA will export
(a) Good A (b) Good B
(c) Both A and B (d) None of these

From the balance of payment figures given below, answer the questions from (473-478)

'Balance of payment'

Credit

1. Export of goods	1100
2. Export services	300
3. Unrequited receipts	200
4. Capital receipts	400
	2000

Debit

1. Import of goods	1100
2. Import services	300
3. Unrequited payments	200
4. Capital payments	400
	2000

473. Balance of trade is equal to
(a) –1000 (b) –750
(c) –500 (d) –250

474. Balance of invisible is equal to
(a) 250 (b) 200
(c) 150 (d) 100

475. Balance of unrequited transfer is equal to
(a) 40 (b) 30
(c) 20 (d) 10

476. Balance of current account is equal to
(a) –260 (b) –200
(c) –350 (d) –320

477. Balance of capital account is equal to
(a) +320 (b) +350
(c) +200 (d) +260

478. Balance of payment is equal to
(a) –750 (b) Zero
(c) +500 (d) –500

Directions: Questions 479 to 486 are of multiple statement type. Choose the correct answer from the codes given below.

479. Consider.
1. Export duty
2. Export subsidy
3. Liberal import entitlement
4. Revaluation of currency

Codes:
(a) 3 and 4 (b) 2 and 3
(c) 1, 2 and 4 (d) 1 and 3

480. Steps to be taken in a selling system include
1. Receipt of order
2. Processing order
3. Shipment of merchandise
4. Accounting for sale

Codes:
(a) 1, 4, 2, 3 (b) 1, 4, 3, 2
(c) 1, 2, 3, 4 (d) 1, 2, 4, 3

481. The following steps are normally taken in an import trade
1. Indent and letter of credit
2. Ship's report
3. Delivery and customs formalities
4. Exchange and bill of exchange

Codes:
(a) 4, 1, 3, 2 (b) 1, 4, 3, 2
(c) 1, 4, 2, 3 (d) 4, 1, 2, 3

482. Which of the following pairs are correctly matched?
1. Cash compensatory scheme: It is allowed on a selective basis for compensation the exporter for the elements of undefined taxes and duties paid on the imports required for the manufacture of goods exported.
2. Inland container depots: Confer all the facilities of dry ports and facilitate the movement of exports.
3. Duty drawback scheme: The exporters are allowed reimbursement of customs and central excise duties paid on raw materials components and packaging.

Codes:
(a) 1 and 2 (b) 2 and 3
(c) 1 and 3 (d) 1, 2 and 3

483. Steps to be taken in a selling system include
1. receipt of order
2. processing order
3. shipment of merchandise
4. accounting for sale

Codes:
(a) 1, 2, 4, 3 (b) 1, 2, 3, 4
(c) 1, 4, 3, 2 (d) 1, 4, 2, 3

484. Consider.
1. Export duty
2. Export subsidy
3. Liberal import entitlement
4. Revaluation of currency

Which of the above policy measures would lead to an expansion of exports?

Codes:
(a) 3 and 4 (b) 2 and 4
(c) 1 and 3 (d) 1, 2, and 4

485. Which one of the following statements are correct?
1. Bills of lading is a document of file.
2. Green shipping bill is used for export of goods entitled to duty drawback.
3. An airway bills is not a document of title.
4. A consular invoice and a performa invoice are one and the same.

Codes:
(a) 1, 3 and 4 (b) 1, 2 and 3
(c) 2 and 4 (d) 1, 2 and 4

486. Which of the following items are not considered to be export promotion measures?
1. Quota certificate
2. Cash compensatory assistance
3. System of exchange control
4. Marketing development fund

Codes:
(a) 1 and 4 (b) 2 and 4
(c) 1 and 3 (d) 3 and 4

Directions: Questions 487 to 514 are of matching type. Match List I with List II and select the correct answer using the codes given below the list.

487.

List I	List II
A. Adam Smith	1. Availability
B. David Ricardo	2. Edowment
C. Ohlin	3. Absolute advantage
D. L.B. Kravis	4. Comparative advantage

Codes:	A	B	C	D
(a)	4	3	1	2
(b)	1	2	3	4
(c)	3	4	2	1
(d)	2	4	3	1

488.

List I	List II
A. Mercantilism	1. France
B. Cameralism	2. Spain
C. Physiocrats	3. England
	4. Germany

Codes:	A	B	C
(a)	3	4	1
(b)	1	2	3
(c)	4	2	3
(d)	2	3	4

489. **List I**
A. Shipping bill country
B. Bill of lading
C. Consular invoice
D. Packing slip

List II
1. To certify the origin of goods
2. For having loaded the cargo in the ship
3. To transport cargo by ship
4. To identify the cargo in transit

Codes:	A	B	C	D
(a)	3	2	1	4
(b)	3	2	4	1
(c)	2	3	4	1
(d)	2	3	1	4

490. **List I**
A. Shipping bill country
B. Bill of adding
C. Consular invoice
D. Packing slip

List II
1. To certify the origin of goods
2. For having loaded the cargo in the ship
3. To transport cargo by ship
4. To identify the cargo in transport

Codes:	A	B	C	D
(a)	3	2	1	4
(b)	2	3	4	1

(c)	3	2	4	1
(d)	2	3	1	4

491. **List I (Some usages in trade and marine insurance)**
A. Ex-workers contract
B. Freight paid
C. Force Majeure
D. Arbitration

List II (Practical implication or name)
1. C.I.F.
2. Method of settlement by importer of disputes.
3. Minimum obligation for the exporter.
4. Condition to be included in the contract if natural calamities are to be covered.
5. F.O.B. contract.

Codes:	A	B	C	D
(a)	1	2	3	4
(b)	3	5	2	1
(c)	3	5	4	2
(d)	1	2	4	3

492. **List I**
A. Free trade area
B. Customs union
C. Common market
D. Economic union

List II
1. No restrictions on trade and factor movement.
2. Trade is free and no custom duties.
3. No customs duties; duties on non-members.
4. Advanced stage of integration.

Codes:	A	B	C	D
(a)	1	3	4	2
(b)	2	1	3	4
(c)	3	2	4	1
(d)	2	3	1	4

493. **List I**
A. Hamilton-List
B. Marshall Lerner
C. F.Y. Edgeworth
D. Jacob Vuner

List II
1. Trade creation and trade diversion effects
2. Indian-industry argument
3. Elasticity approach
4. Impoverishing growth

Codes:	A	B	C	D
(a)	2	3	4	1
(b)	3	2	4	1
(c)	3	2	1	4
(d)	2	3	1	4

494.

List I	List II
A. LUT	1. DGFT
B. EPZ	2. Export promotion
C. EPCG	3. 100% exports
D. Valueaddition	4. 100% EOU

Codes:	A	B	C	D
(a)	2	4	1	3
(b)	1	3	2	4
(c)	3	2	1	4
(d)	1	4	3	2

495. **List I**
A. Net Barter terms of trade
B. Gross Barter terms of trade
C. Income terms of trade

List II
1. $P_x/P_m \times Q_x \times 100$
2. $Q_m/Q_x \times 100$
3. $P_x/P_m \times 100$
4. $P_x \cdot P_m/Q_x \times 100$

Codes:	A	B	C
(a)	1	3	2
(b)	1	3	4

(c)	3	2	1
(d)	4	1	2

496. **List I** / **List II**

A. Mercantilism — 1. Agricultural products
B. Physiocrats — 2. Labour
C. Comparative Advantage — 3. Capital
4. Precious metals

Codes:	A	B	C
(a)	1	2	4
(b)	4	1	2
(c)	3	2	4
(d)	4	2	3

497. **List I** / **List II**

A. India — 1. Oil
B. Brazil — 2. Textile
C. Chile — 3. Coffee
D. Iraq — 4. Copper

Codes:	A	B	C	D
(a)	2	1	4	3
(b)	1	2	3	4
(c)	3	2	4	1
(d)	2	3	4	1

498. **List I**

A. Oil India Corporation
B. Food Corporation of India
C. Metal and Metals trading corpo.

List II

1. Food grains
2. Gold
3. Petrol
4. Cars

Codes:	A	B	C
(a)	4	1	3
(b)	4	3	1
(c)	1	2	3
(d)	3	1	2

499. **List I** / **List II**

A. F. List — 1. Free trade
B. Singer — 2. Balance of Payment
C. Adam Smith — 3. Infant Industry
4. Terms of Trade

Codes:	A	B	C
(a)	3	4	1
(b)	1	4	3
(c)	2	4	1
(d)	4	2	1

500. **List I**

A. Canalisation
B. Effective rate
C. Nominal rate

List II

1. Take input into account
2. Govt. monopoly of protection on distribution
3. Tariff on final output
4. Tariff on raw materials

Codes:	A	B	C
(a)	3	4	1
(b)	4	2	3
(c)	2	1	3
(d)	2	4	1

501. **List I**

A. Balance of trade
B. Balance of invisibles
C. Balance of capital A/C

List II

1. Services
2. Capital
3. Goods
4. Unrequited transfers

Codes:	A	B	C
(a)	4	2	1
(b)	3	1	2
(c)	1	4	3
(d)	4	3	2

502. **List I**

A. Gifts
B. Sales of fixed
C. Sale of goods

List II
1. Unrequited receipts
2. Capital receipts assets
3. Capital payment
4. Export of goods

Codes:	A	B	C
(a)	2	3	4
(b)	1	2	3
(c)	4	1	2
(d)	3	4	2

503. List I
A. Indemnities to foreign govt.
B. Borrowing
C. Autonomous flow
D. Accommodating flow

List II
1. Ex-ante
2. Export
3. Flow concept
4. Change in stock concept

Codes:	A	B	C	D
(a)	3	4	1	2
(b)	1	2	3	4
(c)	2	1	4	3
(d)	4	3	2	1

504.

List I	List II
A. Devaluation	1. Direct control
B. Change in rate of interest	2. Current account policy
C. Canalisation	3. Capital account policy

Codes:	A	B	C
(a)	2	3	1
(b)	3	2	1
(c)	1	2	3
(d)	2	1	3

505.

List I	List II
A. Offer curve	1. Edge worth
B. Absorption approach	2. J.M. Keynes
C. Elasticity approach	3. Lemer
	4. Sidney Alexander

Codes:	A	B	C
(a)	3	1	2
(b)	4	3	1
(c)	2	4	1
(d)	3	4	1

506. List I
A. Mint parity theory
B. Purchasing power parity theory
C. Balance of payment theory

List II
1. Weight basis of the metallic contents
2. Differential purchasing powers
3. Demand and supply of foreign exchange

Codes:	A	B	C
(a)	3	1	2
(b)	2	3	1
(c)	1	2	3
(d)	2	1	3

507.

List I	List II
A. Mark	1. Japan
B. Yen	2. Mexico
C. Peso	3. Russia
D. Ruble	4. Germany

Codes:	A	B	C	D
(a)	4	2	3	1
(b)	3	4	1	2
(c)	4	1	2	3
(d)	2	1	3	4

508. List I
A. Before First
B. After First World War and till 1971
C. After 1971

List II
1. Crawling peg World War
2. Gold standard

3. Dollar standard
4. Silver standard

Codes:	A	B	C
(a)	2	3	1
(b)	2	1	3
(c)	4	1	3
(d)	4	3	1

509. List I

A. Adjustable peg
B. Crawling peg
C. Fixed exchange rate
D. Flexible exchange rate

List II

1. ± 4.5% fluctuation
2. ± 2% fluctuation
3. Infinite fluctuation
4. No fluctuation

Codes:	A	B	C	D
(a)	2	1	4	3
(b)	1	3	2	4
(c)	2	4	3	1
(d)	4	2	1	3

510. List I

A. GATT B. IMF
C. IBRD D. UNO

List II

1. Managing balance of payment
2. Developmental finance
3. Free trade
4. Maintain peace between nations

Codes:	A	B	C	D
(a)	4	1	3	2
(b)	2	1	4	3
(c)	3	1	2	4
(d)	2	3	1	4

511.

List I	List II
A. SDR	1. IBRD
B. Dunkel Proposal	2. GATT
C. Soft loans	3. IMF
	4. IDA

Codes:	A	B	C
(a)	2	3	4
(b)	4	3	2
(c)	1	4	2
(d)	3	2	4

512.

List I	List II
1. Kennedy Round	1. 1963
2. Tokyo Round	2. 1967
3. Uruguay Round	3. 1986
	4. 1990

Codes:	A	B	C
(a)	4	3	1
(b)	3	4	2
(c)	4	1	3
(d)	1	2	3

513. List I

A. Fiscal deficit
B. Revenue deficit
C. Budgetary
D. Capital deficit

List II

1. (Revenue and interest receipts) – (revenue expenditure)
2. (Revenue receipts + Recovery of loans and other receipts) – (Total expenditure)
3. Receipts – disbursements deficit in capital account
4. (Total receipts) – deficit (Total disbursement)

Codes:	A	B	C	D
(a)	2	1	3	4
(b)	1	2	4	3
(c)	1	2	3	4
(d)	2	1	4	3

514.

List I	List II
A. Alfred Marshall	1. Competition the Few
B. A.P. Lerner	2. Economics of Control

C. J.R. Hicks 3. Capital and Growth

D. William Fellner 4. The Principles of Economics

Codes:	A	B	C	D
(a)	3	2	1	4
(b)	4	2	3	1
(c)	2	3	1	4
(d)	4	1	3	2

Directions: Questions 515 to 544 consist of two statements one labelled as 'Assertion A' and the other labelled as 'Reason R'. You are to examine these two statements carefully and decide if the Assertion A and the Reason R are individually true and if so, whether the Reason is a correct explanation of the Assertion select your answers to these items using the codes given below and mark your answer sheet accordingly.

(A) Both A and R are true and R is the correct explanation of A.

(B) Both A and R are true but R is not a correct explanation of A.

(C) A is true but R is false.

(D) A is false but R is true.

515. **Assertion (A):** Formula for net barter terms of trade is $P_x/P_m \times 100$.

Reason (R): Formula for gross barter terms of trade is $Q_m/Q_x \times 100$.

516. **Assertion (A):** Vent for surplus theory is applicable to underdeveloped countries.

Reason (R): Availability theory is applicable to countries with natural resources.

517. **Assertion (A):** India exports garments.

Reason (R): India has abundant labour and garments is a labour intensive product.

518. **Assertion (A):** Germany exports engineering machinery.

Reason (R): Germany has abundant capital and engineering machineries is capital intensive.

519. **Assertion (A):** Leontief paradox contradicted Heckscher-Ohlin theory.

Reason (R): USA exported labour-intensive products.

520. **Assertion (A):** Tariff leads to decrease in imports.

Reason (R): Tariff leads to increase in prices.

521. **Assertion (A):** Effective rate of protection takes tariff on input into account.

Reason (R): Nominal rate of protection takes only tariff on output into account.

522. **Assertion (A):** Canalisation is resorted to in case of essential commodities.

Reason (R): Government has monopoly on purchase and distribution of imported commodities.

523. **Assertion (A):** Infant industry argument was supported by F. list.

Reason (R): Infant industry argument support free trade.

524. **Assertion (A):** Dumping means selling a product in a foreign market at a lower price than in the home market.

Reason (R): Dumping encourages domestic industry.

525. **Assertion (A):** Accommodating flows are unplanned.

Reason (R): Autonomous flows are planned.

526. **Assertion (A):** Balance of current account is a flow concept.

Reason (R): Balance of capital account is a change in stock concept.

527. **Assertion (A):** Devaluation improves balance of payment deficit.

Reason (R): Devaluation leads to decrease in prices of exports and increase in price of exports.

528. **Assertion (A):** Balance of trade is the difference between exports and imports of goods.

Reason (R): Balance of current accounts is the difference between exports and imports of services.

529. **Assertion (A):** Balance of capital account is the difference between foreign exchange earned and foreign exchange spent by the company.

Reason (R): Balance of invisibles is the difference between exports and imports of services.

530. **Assertion (A):** Adjustable peg allows fluctuation of 4.5%.

Reason (R): Crawling peg allows fluctuation of 2%.

531. **Assertion (A):** Gold standard broke down after First World War.

Reason (R): Countries had different rate of inflation.

532. **Assertion (A):** Free exchange rate in creases risk of exporters.

Reason (R): Speculation can reduce the risk of exporters.

533. **Assertion (A):** Hedging can increase the risk of exporters.

Reason (R): Arbitrage achieves equality of exchange rates at two places.

534. **Assertion (A):** In case of flexible exchange rate, government is free from the consideration about balance of payment and government can concentrate on domestic economic policy.

Reason (R): Automatic adjustment balance of payment is achieved in case of free exchange rate through changes in exchange rates.

535. **Assertion (A):** IMF introduced adjustable peg system.

Reason (R): IMF tried to prevent uncontrolled fluctuation of foreign exchange.

536. **Assertion (A):** IBRD was created to provide long-term finance.

Reason (R): IMF was created to solve short term balance of payment problem of member countries.

537. **Assertion (A):** Institutions created by Bretton Woods system could not solve LDC's problems.

Reason (R): UNCTAD had to be created.

538. **Assertion (A):** GATT was created to promote free trade.

Reason (R): Free trade always increases national welfare.

539. **Assertion (A):** IMF provides long-term loans for developmental purpose.

Reason (R): Long-term loans are important for development of LDCs.

540. **Assertion (A):** In the recent past, there has been a significant increase in the foreign exchange reserves of India.

Reason (R): The new economic policy has provided incentives for foreign direct investment.

541. **Assertion (A):** Special rules and procedures are followed in the import and export trade.

Reason (R): The need for import and export trade is explained by the principle of "Comparative Cost Theory".

542. **Assertion (A):** According to Schunpeter, development is a spontaneous and

discontinuous change in the channels of the circular flow.

Reason (R): The entrepreneur is the agent of this change.

543. **Assertion (A):** A monopolist enjoys considerable power to manipulate the price of his product.

Reason (R): The monopoly power of the monopolist is measured by the excess of price over marginal cost.

544. **Assertion (A):** Marshall-Lerner condition should be fulfilled if devaluation is to be successful.

Reason (R): Devaluation makes exports costly and imports cheaper.

ANSWERS

1. (c)	2. (a)	3. (c)	4. (b)	5. (a)	6. (a)
7. (c)	8. (a)	9. (a)	10. (a)	11. (d)	12. (c)
13. (a)	14. (c)	15. (c)	16. (d)	17. (a)	18. (d)
19. (d)	20. (c)	21. (d)	22. (b)	23. (d)	24. (d)
25. (a)	26. (d)	27. (d)	28. (a)	29. (b)	30. (c)
31. (d)	32. (a)	33. (c)	34. (b)	35. (a)	36. (c)
37. (d)	38. (a)	39. (a)	40. (a)	41. (a)	42. (c)
43. (d)	44. (c)	45. (b)	46. (a)	47. (c)	48. (a)
49. (c)	50. (c)	51. (d)	52. (d)	53. (a)	54. (b)
55. (a)	56. (b)	57. (c)	58. (d)	59. (a)	60. (a)
61. (c)	62. (a)	63. (c)	64. (c)	65. (c)	66. (c)
67. (b)	68. (a)	69. (d)	70. (a)	71. (b)	72. (a)
73. (a)	74. (a)	75. (c)	76. (a)	77. (c)	78. (d)
79. (b)	80. (d)	81. (d)	82. (b)	83. (c)	84. (c)
85. (c)	86. (b)	87. (d)	88. (b)	89. (a)	90. (d)
91. (c)	92. (c)	93. (b)	94. (a)	95. (b)	96. (a)
97. (b)	98. (b)	99. (c)	100. (a)	101. (c)	102. (a)
103. (c)	104. (b)	105. (b)	106. (d)	107. (b)	108. (c)
109. (b)	110. (a)	111. (a)	112. (b)	113. (c)	114. (d)
115. (a)	116. (a)	117. (b)	118. (c)	119. (a)	120. (a)
121. (b)	122. (b)	123. (c)	124. (d)	125. (a)	126. (a)
127. (a)	128. (a)	129. (a)	130. (d)	131. (a)	132. (c)
133. (c)	134. (b)	135. (c)	136. (b)	137. (a)	138. (a)
139. (b)	140. (a)	141. (d)	142. (c)	143. (d)	144. (c)
145. (a)	146. (b)	147. (a)	148. (b)	149. (b)	150. (c)

151. (a)	152. (d)	153. (a)	154. (b)	155. (b)	156. (a)
157. (b)	158. (d)	159. (c)	160. (c)	161. (d)	162. (b)
163. (b)	164. (c)	165. (b)	166. (b)	167. (b)	168. (c)
169. (c)	170. (a)	171. (c)	172. (a)	173. (c)	174. (a)
175. (a)	176. (a)	177. (c)	178. (c)	179. (c)	180. (d)
181. (c)	182. (a)	183. (c)	184. (c)	185. (b)	186. (d)
187. (c)	188. (d)	189. (c)	190. (a)	191. (a)	192. (c)
193. (a)	194. (d)	195. (b)	196. (b)	197. (c)	198. (c)
199. (a)	200. (d)	201. (b)	202. (a)	203. (c)	204. (a)
205. (c)	206. (c)	207. (c)	208. (b)	209. (a)	210. (b)
211. (b)	212. (a)	213. (c)	214. (d)	215. (c)	216. (d)
217. (b)	218. (a)	219. (c)	220. (b)	221. (a)	222. (a)
223. (c)	224. (d)	225. (a)	226. (a)	227. (b)	228. (a)
229. (c)	230. (a)	231. (d)	232. (c)	233. (d)	234. (a)
235. (c)	236. (d)	237. (b)	238. (c)	239. (c)	240. (c)
241. (d)	242. (c)	243. (d)	244. (d)	245. (a)	246. (d)
247. (a)	248. (a)	249. (d)	250. (d)	251. (a)	252. (b)
253. (a)	254. (a)	255. (d)	256. (d)	257. (d)	258. (d)
259. (a)	260. (a)	261. (c)	262. (c)	263. (a)	264. (d)
265. (d)	266. (a)	267. (d)	268. (d)	269. (d)	270. (d)
271. (a)	272. (a)	273. (a)	274. (c)	275. (c)	276. (d)
277. (a)	278. (d)	279. (a)	280. (d)	281. (b)	282. (c)
283. (c)	284. (d)	285. (d)	286. (a)	287. (c)	288. (c)
289. (d)	290. (a)	291. (a)	292. (b)	293. (c)	294. (d)
295. (c)	296. (d)	297. (d)	298. (d)	299. (d)	300. (c)
301. (d)	302. (b)	303. (d)	304. (b)	305. (a)	306. (a)
307. (c)	308. (d)	309. (d)	310. (c)	311. (b)	312. (d)
313. (d)	314. (c)	315. (b)	316. (a)	317. (c)	318. (c)
319. (a)	320. (c)	321. (c)	322. (a)	323. (d)	324. (d)
325. (d)	326. (c)	327. (b)	328. (b)	329. (d)	330. (a)
331. (a)	332. (a)	333. (b)	334. (d)	335. (b)	336. (a)
337. (d)	338. (b)	339. (d)	340. (a)	341. (d)	342. (a)
343. (a)	344. (d)	345. (a)	346. (d)	347. (c)	348. (d)
349. (d)	350. (a)	351. (b)	352. (b)	353. (b)	354. (a)

355. (a)	356. (b)	357. (a)	358. (a)	359. (a)	360. (a)
361. (c)	362. (d)	363. (d)	364. (b)	365. (d)	366. (d)
367. (b)	368. (a)	369. (c)	370. (a)	371. (d)	372. (b)
373. (c)	374. (a)	375. (c)	376. (c)	377. (b)	378. (d)
379. (d)	380. (c)	381. (c)	382. (d)	383. (c)	384. (c)
385. (a)	386. (b)	387. (a)	388. (b)	389. (d)	390. (b)
391. (a)	392. (c)	393. (c)	394. (a)	395. (d)	396. (c)
397. (b)	398. (c)	399. (a)	400. (d)	401. (d)	402. (b)
403. (c)	404. (c)	405. (d)	406. (b)	407. (d)	408. (b)
409. (a)	410. (c)	411. (c)	412. (c)	413. (b)	414. (d)
415. (b)	416. (c)	417. (c)	418. (d)	419. (b)	420. (b)
421. (a)	422. (d)	423. (d)	424. (d)	425. (d)	426. (d)
427. (d)	428. (c)	429. (d)	430. (b)	431. (c)	432. (c)
433. (d)	434. (a)	435. (d)	436. (d)	437. (c)	438. (a)
439. (b)	440. (b)	441. (a)	442. (d)	443. (c)	444. (a)
445. (b)	446. (b)	447. (b)	448. (b)	449. (d)	450. (d)
451. (d)	452. (c)	453. (a)	454. (c)	455. (b)	456. (c)
457. (a)	458. (b)	459. (c)	460. (a)	461. (a)	462. (d)
463. (c)	464. (d)	465. (a)	466. (b)	467. (a)	468. (d)
469. (b)	470. (b)	471. (b)	472. (a)	473. (c)	474. (b)
475. (a)	476. (a)	477. (d)	478. (b)	479. (b)	480. (c)
481. (d)	482. (d)	483. (b)	484. (b)	485. (a)	486. (c)
487. (c)	488. (a)	489. (d)	490. (d)	491. (c)	492. (d)
493. (a)	494. (d)	495. (c)	496. (b)	497. (d)	498. (d)
499. (a)	500. (c)	501. (b)	502. (b)	503. (a)	504. (a)
505. (d)	506. (c)	507. (c)	508. (a)	509. (c)	510. (c)
511. (d)	512. (d)	513. (d)	514. (b)	515. (b)	516. (b)
517. (a)	518. (a)	519. (a)	520. (a)	521. (b)	522. (b)
523. (c)	524. (b)	525. (b)	526. (b)	527. (a)	528. (c)
529. (d)	530. (b)	531. (a)	532. (c)	533. (d)	534. (a)
535. (a)	536. (b)	537. (a)	538. (c)	539. (d)	540. (a)
541. (b)	542. (d)	543. (b)	544. (b)		